T0399458

THE ROUTLEDGE HANDBOOK OF DIGITAL SPORT MANAGEMENT

The Routledge Handbook of Digital Sport Management provides students, researchers, and practitioners with a contemporary roadmap of the impact of digital technologies in sport management, at all levels and in all sectors, in a global context.

Divided into three sections addressing digital transformations, digital tools, and emerging digital issues, this book explores the impact of digital technology in the core functional areas of sport management, such as sponsorship, event management, and human resources. It introduces essential digital innovations such as esports, social media, VR, wearables, analytics, and artificial intelligence, and examines the debates and issues that are likely to shape and transform sport business over the next decade.

The only book to survey the full sweep of digital sport management, this book is an essential reference for all serious students of sport business and management, any researcher working in the nexus of sport business and digital, and all managers, policy-makers or associated professionals working in the sport industry.

Michael L. Naraine is an Associate Professor in the Department of Sport Management at Brock University, Canada. His research is in digital sport management and marketing, examining the strategy, fan engagement, and analytics related to new developments in the sport business landscape. He is a Research Fellow of the North American Society for Sport Management and a board member at Canada Snowboard.

Ted Hayduk III is an Assistant Professor at Tisch Institute for Global Sport at New York University, USA. His research explores entrepreneurship and consumer behavior in the sport and entertainment industry. In 2022, he was named a Research Fellow of the North American Society for Sport Management.

Jason P. Doyle is a Senior Lecturer within the Department of Tourism, Sport and Hotel Management at Griffith University, Australia. His research focuses on understanding sport consumer behavior, specifically determining how sport and event consumption impacts organizations, athletes, communities, and individuals.

The Routledge Handbook of Digital Sport Management

Edited by Michael L. Naraine, Ted Hayduk III, and Jason P. Doyle

LONDON AND NEW YORK

Cover image: © Getty Images/Pali Rao

First published 2023
by Routledge
4 Park Square, Milton Park, Abingdon, Oxon OX14 4RN

and by Routledge
605 Third Avenue, New York, NY 10158

Routledge is an imprint of the Taylor & Francis Group, an informa business

British Library Cataloguing-in-Publication Data
A catalogue record for this book is available from the British Library

Library of Congress Cataloging-in-Publication Data
Names: Naraine, Michael L., 1987- editor. | Hayduk, Ted, editor. |
Doyle, Jason P., editor.
Title: The Routledge handbook of digital sport management / edited by
Michael L. Naraine, Ted Hayduk III and Jason P. Doyle.
Other titles: Handbook of digital sport management
Description: Abingdon, Oxon ; New York City : Routledge, 2023. |
Series: Routledge international handbooks | Includes bibliographical references and index.
Identifiers: LCCN 2022025695 | ISBN 9780367543549 (hardback) |
ISBN 9780367543556 (paperback) | ISBN 9781003088899 (ebook)
Subjects: LCSH: Sports administration--Technological innovations. |
Sports--Marketing--Technological innovations. | Hosting of sporting
events--Technological innovations. | Sports--Technological innovations.
Classification: LCC GV713 .R658 2023 | DDC 796.06/9--dc23/eng/20220707
LC record available at https://lccn.loc.gov/2022025695

ISBN: 978-0-367-54354-9 (hbk)
ISBN: 978-0-367-54355-6 (pbk)
ISBN: 978-1-003-08889-9 (ebk)

DOI: 10.4324/9781003088899

Typeset in Bembo
by MPS Limited, Dehradun

Contents

List of Figures *viii*
List of Tables *ix*
Acknowledgments *x*
List of Contributors *xi*

Embracing the Digital Frontier: Introduction to The Routledge Handbook of Digital Sport Management 1
Michael L. Naraine, Ted Hayduk III, and Jason P. Doyle

PART I
Digital Transformations in Sport Management **5**

1 Organizational Behavior and Digital Transformation in Sport 7
Christopher R. Barnhill and Natalie L. Smith

2 Human Resource Management and Digital Technology 22
Shannon Kerwin

3 Virtual Volunteering 37
Erik L. Lachance and Graham Cuskelly

4 Digital Transformations in Youth Sport 52
Ryan Snelgrove and Vinu Selvaratnam

5 Digital Transformation in Not-for-Profit Sport Organizations 62
Ashley Thompson and Milena M. Parent

6 Virtual Participatory Sport Events 76
Millicent Kennelly and Kevin Filo

7 Digital Innovation in High-Performance Sport 91
Popi Sotiriadou

8 Corporate Social Responsibility and Digital Transformation in Professional Sport 100
Kathy Babiak, Adam Copeland, and Daniel Yang

9 Digital Transformation in Sport Sponsorship 116
T. Bettina Cornwell

10 Digital Sport Management and the Law 132
Thomas A. Baker III

11 Digital Technology and Sport for Development 148
Per G. Svensson and Mitchell McSweeney

PART II
Digital Tools in Sport Management 165

12 Fantasy Sport in the Digital Realm 167
Brody J. Ruihley

13 Podcasting and Sports Journalism 180
Galen Clavio and Brian P. Moritz

14 Evolution of Live Streaming 192
Sarah Wymer and Michael L. Naraine

15 Social Media and Sport Marketing in North America 206
Brandon Boatwright and Karen Freberg

16 Social Media and Athlete Branding 217
Caroline Riot and Michelle Hayes

17 Immersive Technology and the Virtual Sport Spectator Experience 232
Luke R. Potwarka, Peter A. Hall, Chad Goebert, and Hasan Ayaz

18 Business Analytics in Sport Organizations 245
Ted Hayduk III

PART III
Emerging Digital Issues in Sport Management 255

19 Collaborative Consumption in the Sport Industry 257
Brandon Brown, Eric C. Schwarz, and Michael M. Goldman

20 Data and the Sport Consumer 273
Adam Karg

21 Digital Fitness Ecosystem 285
Brianna Newland and Thomas J. Aicher

22 Convergence of Sport and Esports 293
Anthony D. Pizzo and Daniel C. Funk

23 Blockchain and the Sports Tech Dilemma 308
Brianna Newland and Martin Carlsson-Wall

24 Digitization of Sport Participation for Health 319
Ji Wu, Yuhei Inoue, and Mikihiro Sato

25 Artificial Intelligence 333
Heather Kennedy and Liz Wanless

26 Digital Technology and Sport Ecology 346
Maddy Orr and Walker J. Ross

27 Shifting Gender Power Relations in the Digitization of Sport 355
Simone Fullagar, Adele Pavlidis, and Millicent Kennelly

28 Sport Innovation 368
Benjamin Kinsky and Christopher Huth

29 Economics of Digital Sport Consumption 384
Ted Hayduk III

Index *395*

Figures

5.1	Levels of Strategy at the Olympic Movement	66
6.1	Establishing preconditions for social leveraging of virtual events	86
7.1	The Advancement of Technological and Digital Innovation in High-performance (Elite) Sport	93
7.2	Benefits and Risks of Technological and Digital Innovation in High-performance (Elite) Sport	96
8.1	Four Dimensions of Corporate Digital Responsibility	106
9.1	Sport Sponsorship Digital Framework	117
17.1	Panel (a) equipment montage for neural response imaging in the context of brain- as-predictor paradigms, using VR goggles for display of sport stimulus video. Panel (b) anatomical subregions of the prefrontal cortex and the temporoparietal junc-tion; region boundaries in some cases are approximated. Panel B image created with Biorender.com	239
18.1	Search history for statistics and analytics from 2004–2021	246
19.1	Modes of Collaborative Consumption	258
20.1	Systems Framework for Digital and Data Processes in the Sport Consumer Behavior Setting	277
21.1	The Digital Fitness Ecosystem	286
23.1	Pillars, Ownerships, and Objectives of Blockchain Technology	310
23.2	The Sports Tech Dilemma	314
24.1	A Social-Ecological Model for Digitalization in Sport Participation for Health	322
28.1	Barca Innovation Hub	369
28.2	TechTalents Model	370
29.1	Tradeoff of Technology Use and Adoption	391

Tables

2.1	Functions of e-HRM in Sport Practice	27
3.1	Examples of Investigated Topics in Virtual Volunteering Research	42
14.1	OTT Services	196
14.2	Leading SLSS Services in 2021	197
16.1	Overview of Theoretical Frameworks and Examples of Social Media Platforms Researched	219
20.1	Consumer Behavior: Key Manager Questions and Potential Outcomes	280
22.1	Key Chapter Terms and Definitions	295
22.2	Leading Esports Developers/Publishers and Titles	297
22.3	Primary Revenue Sources in Esports	298
25.1	AI Related Terminology	335
25.2	Statistics versus Machine Learning	339

Acknowledgments

We would like to take this opportunity to acknowledge and thank all the contributors to *The Routledge Handbook of Digital Sport Management* for their time and effort, especially in the midst of a global health pandemic. Your contributions are the cornerstone of this book and we are honored to be able to work with such talented contributors with a wealth of knowledge across the numerous aspects covered in this text. Thank you. A compilation of this scope would also be impossible without the support of our institutional affiliations, so thank you to Brock University, New York University, and Griffith University. We would also like to thank the team at Routledge, particularly Simon and Rebecca, for their understanding and guidance throughout this process. And, finally, a big thanks to our family and friends for putting up with us over these last 2.5 years as we took on this behemoth! We hope that this text elicits insightful and intellectual discussions and is helpful as both a teaching resource and catalyst for further research focused on elucidating further knowledge on digital sport management both now, and into the future.

Contributors

Thomas J. Aicher is an Associate Professor in the College of Business at the University of Colorado, Colorado Springs, USA. His research focuses on sport tourist behaviors with a particular focus on endurance sport event athletes. In addition, he focuses on the impact those events have on the host community and how to properly leverage the events to strengthen the positive impact on the community.

Hasan Ayaz is a Professor of biomedical engineering with teaching and research focusing on neuroengineering, neuroergonomics, and mobile neuroimaging across the lifespan and from healthy (typical to specialized groups) to diverse clinical conditions (mental health to neurological). His research aims to design, develop, and utilize next-generation brain imaging for neuroergonomic applications over a broad spectrum from aerospace to healthcare.

Kathy Babiak is a Professor of Sport Management and Director of the Michigan Center for Sport & Social Responsibility at the University of Michigan School of Kinesiology, USA. Her main line of research focuses on sport and social impact. In this area, she explores how organizations devise social responsibility strategies to maximize the value and benefit to both organizations and to society. Dr. Babiak's most recent research explores the corporate social responsibility (CSR)/philanthropy activities of professional sport organizations (NBA, NHL, MLB, and NFL) to better understand how teams and leagues benefit from these socially oriented activities, why sport organizations choose to ally themselves with particular causes, and what is the social impact/outcome of these efforts.

Thomas A. Baker is an Associate Professor and a former Commercial Litigator who researches the commercial regulation of sport and the influence of law on sport brand management. He conducts injury prevention research that focuses on the risk of sexual violence in sports. He is also the Editor of the *Journal of Legal Aspects of Sport* and a contributing author on sports law for Forbes.

Christopher R. Barnhill is an Associate Professor and Coordinator of the Georgia Southern Sport Management program, USA. His primary line of research explores relations between sport organizations and employees with a focus on the impact of leadership and communication on employee well-being. Outside of organizational behavior research, he engages in scholarship related to the education of undergraduate and graduate sport management students, as well as select issues in intercollegiate athletics.

Brandon Boatwright is an Assistant Professor of sports communication at Clemson University, USA. His research rests at the intersection of social media, strategic communication, and sport. He is particularly interested in sports organizations' use of social media to advance social advocacy initiatives. Dr. Boatwright teaches courses in Public Relations in Sport, Social Media and Sport, and Sport and Culture.

Brandon Brown is Professor at New York University, USA. In addition to serving as a marketing consultant for several professional sport entities such as Fox Sports and the NFL, Dr. Brown has spent his academic career researching sport consumption. In particular, Dr. Brown's research concentrates on minority sport consumption patterns.

Martin Carlsson-Wall is the Director of the Center for Sports and Business. His research interest lies in the intersection between sports, finance, and accounting. Theoretically, he is interested in how institutional complexity relates to hybrid organizations and emotions.

Galen Clavio is the Director of the Sports Media program at Indiana University, USA, teaching courses in sports broadcasting, social media, and sports media literacy. His research includes investigations into social media usage and trends within sports, as well as the broader impact of digital media technologies on the sports media landscape.

Adam Copeland is a Ph.D. student in Sport Management at the University of Michigan, USA. Prior to joining the University of Michigan, he completed his M.S. in Kinesiology at the Pennsylvania State University, focusing there on the philosophy and history of sport. He also joined Teach for America and spent four years founding a school in Springfield, Massachusetts. His research interests in sport management include institutional and organizational change from a variety of perspectives, in both long-term and acute timeframes.

T. Bettina Cornwell is a Professor of Marketing, Head of the Department of Marketing, and Academic Director of the Warsaw Sports Marketing Center at the University of Oregon's Lundquist College of Business, USA. She was also named Philip H. Knight Chair, one of the university's highest faculty honors. Her research focuses on marketing communications and consumer behavior and often includes international and public policy emphases.

Graham Cuskelly is a Professor Emeritus at Griffith University, Australia. His research interests are in community sport volunteerism, sports officiating, and sport organization and governance. He was Chief Investigator on four Australian Research Council grants and a Canadian Social Sciences and Humanities Research Council grant and is a foundation Editorial Board member and former Editor of *Sport Management Review*.

Kevin Filo is an Associate Professor in Sport Management. He is Deputy Head of Department in the Department of Tourism, Sport and Hotel Management in the Griffith Business School at Griffith University, Australia. Kevin's research examines the synergy between sport and philanthropy, with a particular focus on charity sport event participation. In addition, Kevin's research investigates the antecedents and outcomes of a meaningful sport event experience through the lens of positive psychology. Prior to his academic career, Kevin served as the Merchandising Coordinator for the Lance Armstrong Foundation (LAF), a nonprofit organization with the mission to inspire and empower individuals living with cancer.

Karen Freberg is a Professor in Strategic Communications at the University of Louisville, USA, where she teaches, researches, and consults in social media strategy, public relations, and crisis communication. She has written several award-winning books in PR and social media.

Simone Fullagar is a Professor of Sport Management and Chair of the Sport and Gender Equity research hub at Griffith University, Australia. Simone is an interdisciplinary sociologist who has published widely on gender equity in sport, mental health, active communities, and social well-being. With an interest in social and organizational change, her wide-ranging publications and funded research contribute to thinking differently about inequalities.

Daniel C. Funk is a Professor and Ed Rosen Senior Research Fellow in the School of Sport, Tourism and Hospitality Management and the Fox School of Business at Temple University, USA. His research examines sport consumer experiences to help organizations understand customer acquisition, retention, and expenditure. He teaches sport consumer behavior and marketing courses.

Chad Goebert is an Assistant Professor in the Sport Management program at Kennesaw State University, USA. His research focus is on the use of augmented reality in sport marketing and emerging technology use in sport. He currently teaches multiple courses including one on innovation and technology in sport.

Michael Goldman holds faculty roles with the University of San Francisco's Sport Management Program, USA, and the University of Pretoria's Gordon Institute of Business Science, South Africa. His research is in the fields of sport marketing, branding, sales, and sponsorship.

Peter Hall is a Full Professor in the School of Public Health Sciences at the University of Waterloo, Canada. He is primarily interested in translational neuroscience for the public health context. Within this framework, he examines the social neurobiology of disease prevention, rTMS-based cognitive assessment paradigms, and brain health impacts of COVID-19. He is a fellow of the Academy of Behavioral Medicine Research.

Michelle Hayes is a Senior Research Assistant at Griffith University and Victoria University, Australia. Her research predominately focuses on the implications and management of athletes of social media use, with specific interests in distraction and well-being. Michelle has published research in *Sport Management Review*, *Event Management*, and the *International Journal of Sport Communication*.

Christopher Huth is a Professor of Sports and Health Management at the Univeristät der Bundeswehr München, Germany. His research interests are sports governance, health management, and management-related topics in golf and team sports.

Yuhei Inoue is a Reader in Sport Management at Manchester Metropolitan University, UK, and leads the development of research-related initiatives for the Sport Policy Unit housed in the Department of Economics, Policy, and International Business. He is an expert on the management of sport organizations and events for positive social impacts.

Adam Karg is an Associate Professor of Marketing and a Director of the Sport Innovation Research Group at the Swinburne University of Technology in Melbourne, Australia. His research is focused on sport fan equity, consumer behavior, online engagement, media consumption, and innovation in sport. Adam has worked with over 80 research partners including state and local government, national, state, and local sport governing bodies, professional leagues and teams, agencies, and sport technology startups.

Heather Kennedy is an Assistant Professor of Sport Management at the University of Guelph's Gordon S. Lang School of Business and Economics, Canada. Her research interests relate to the intersections of technology and information systems, consumer behavior, and sport business, and often explore the use and impact of technology in the sport industry.

Millicent Kennelly is a Senior Lecturer in sport and event management in the Department of Tourism, Sport and Hotel Management, at Griffith University, Australia. Dr Kennelly's research examines sport events and sport tourism, with a particular emphasis on identifying and managing sport event stakeholders, understanding sport event experiences and examining sport event leveraging strategies and legacies.

Shannon Kerwin teaches and researches in the areas of organizational behavior and human resource management in the sport industry.

Benjamin Kinsky was a Research Associate in the Department of Sport Management at the Munich University of the Federal Armed Forces, Germany. His research interests focus on innovation ecosystems and entrepreneurship in sports. He is also Advisor for Innovation & Technology Transfer Strategies at the Fraunhofer Society.

Erik L. Lachance is a Ph.D. candidate at the University of Ottawa, Canada, interested in volunteers, governance, and strategic management in sport. Erik was awarded research grants via a Doctoral Fellowship (Social Sciences and Humanities Research Council of Canada) and Sport Participation Research Initiative (Sport Canada). He also holds the position of Board Chair for Event Management's Ph.D./ECR Editorial Board.

Mitchell McSweeney is an Assistant Professor of Sport Management in Innovation and Entrepreneurship at the University of Minnesota Twin Cities, USA. His research focuses on social entrepreneurship, innovation, sport for development and peace (SDP), and livelihoods, and he often utilizes postcolonial theory, institutional theory, and diaspora to critically investigate these areas. He has worked with various SDP organizations in Uganda, Canada, India, Eswatini, and a number of international organizations.

Brian Moritz is an internationally recognized sports media scholar and researcher whose work examines the societal, organizational, and economic models of digital journalism, with a particular focus on sports journalism.

Bri Newland is Academic Director of Undergraduate Programs and Associate Professor in the Tisch Institute for Global Sport at NYU, USA. Her research explores long-term sport participation via the sport development practices of organizations and events. She also examines sport events to leverage impacts. Dr. Newland is the Editor of *Sport Marketing Quarterly* and sits on several other editorial boards. She served as President for the North American Society for Sport Management, 2021–2022.

Madeleine Orr is a sport ecologist based at Loughborough University London, USA. She is also the Founder and Co-Director of The Sport Ecology Group, an international consortium of academics working in the sport sustainability space. Her research examines climate vulnerability and adaptation in sport.

Milena M. Parent is a Full Professor in sport (event) governance in the School of Human Kinetics, University of Ottawa, Canada, and tutor/lecturer in the MEMOS (Executive Masters in Sport Organizations Management) program. A North American Society for Sport Management Research Fellow, she has published in the leading management and sport management academic journals. She is also a governance and event consultant for governments and sport governing bodies around the world.

Adele Pavlidis is an interdisciplinary sociologist working at the intersection of sport, gender, and social change. She has published widely in this area with a particular focus on women in contact sport. She has received funding from the Australian Research Council and also consults for the sport industry body to improve gender equity and equality.

Anthony D. Pizzo is an Adjunct Professor at La Salle University's School of Business, USA, and Manager of Finance, for a large, urban school district. His research interests include strategic management, sport management, digitalization and esports, and cross-cultural business communication.

Luke Potwarka is the Director of the Spectator Experience and Technology (SEAT) Laboratory at the University of Waterloo, Canada. His research focuses on consumer behavior related to sport events. Using diverse methodologies (e.g., neuroscience, surveys, experimental designs) and theoretical approaches, Luke's research seeks to better understand the behaviors and experiences of elite sport spectators.

Caroline Riot is the Director and Senior Lecturer in Sport Management with Griffith Business School, Australia, and an expert in high-performance sport, elite athlete development, community engagement, and wellbeing. She is highly respected in the Olympic movement, with strong networks and a track record of achievement including being a two-time recipient of International Olympic Academy (IOA, Olympia Greece) nominations, and working with the International Olympic Committee across eight countries. Caroline is a strong advocate for student employability and leads the Business School's Work Integrated Learning program and is an engaging and pro-active leader of partnerships across universities, industry, government, community, and non-profit sectors. Caroline is currently working with the Committee for Brisbane to bring Queenslanders along the journey to the Brisbane 2032 Olympic and Paralympic Games to ensure enduring legacies for all people, in areas of employment and training, regional development, social justice, sport, and health.

Walker J. Ross is an Assistant Professor of sport business management at Florida Southern College, USA, and a member of the Sport Ecology Group. His research focuses on the relationship between sport and the natural environment with emphasis on the areas of the Olympic Games, FIFA World Cups, and venue management.

Brody J. Ruihley is an Associate Professor in the Department of Sport Leadership & Management at Miami University, Ohio, USA. Ruihley's primary research interests lie in the areas of fantasy sport, sport marketing, and public relations in sport.

Mikihiro Sato focuses on research that links sports and recreation services with the promotion of health and well-being. He has conducted research in the contexts of participatory sport events, spectator sport events, and Olympic Games. He has taught sport and recreation management courses, including strategic management, data analytics, and human resource management.

Eric C. Schwarz has been an academic and practitioner in sport business management for over 20 years. He currently serves as the Chair of the Postgraduate Courses in Sport Business and Integrity and a Senior Lecturer in Sport Management at Victoria University in Melbourne, Australia. Eric's research concentrates on sport marketing, and sport facility and event management.

Vinu Selvaratnam is a Ph.D. student interested in big data and technological change in recreation, leisure, and sport.

Natalie L. Smith researches organizational innovation and creativity in sport, currently focusing on engagement in the creative process and coopetition. Her primary teaching expertise is in esports, management, and organizational behavior.

Ryan Snelgrove's research develops the understanding of when, how, and why positive impacts and transformations are more likely to occur in the contexts of sport and events, including the circumstances that prevent them from happening. His research program draws on various theories, employs a diverse range of methodologies, and focuses on various levels of society.

Popi Sotiriadou's research interests are in the area of sport participant and athlete development from an organizational perspective (attracting-retaining-nurturing process), managing high-performance sport and athlete branding, managing sport development systems, sport policy, and gender equity and leadership. She has been invited to consult with the International Olympic Committee, Sports-Australia, Sarawak in Malaysia, and Queensland Academy of Sport. Popi is an Associate Editor of the *Journal of Sport Policy and Politics* and an editorial member for the *Journal of Sport Management*.

Per G. Svensson is an Associate Professor in Sport Management at Louisiana State University, USA. His research examines organizational capacity and innovation in the context of nonprofit sport organizations operating sport for development programs. His research is motivated by understanding how sport leaders can better mobilize the necessary resources and capabilities needed for addressing complex social issues and how they can do so in a sustainable manner. He is a Research Fellow with the North American Society for Sport Management.

Ashley Thompson is a Ph.D. candidate in the School of Human Kinetics at the University of Ottawa, Canada. Her research areas include organizational theory and change, nonprofit sport, governance, and qualitative research methods. She has published in leading sport management journals and has held two Ontario Graduate Scholarships (2017 and 2021). Over the years,

Ashley has worked in various sport industry capacities, including events, administration, and marketing and communications.

Ji Wu's primary research interest is to understand how sport and sport organizations can contribute to the movement of social change. This interest results in two research focuses: (1) examining determinants that can be leveraged for social impact through hosting sport events; and (2) understanding how social performances can be embedded into sport organizations' business activities as a means of creating shared value. Additionally, Wu teaches organizational behavior, sport marketing, and sport statistics

Liz Wanless is an Assistant Director of Analytics and Assistant Professor of Sports Administration at Ohio University, USA. She researches advanced analytics applications to various aspects of sport organization operations from customer relationship management to the use and diffusion of natural language processing (NLP) in the sport industry. She is the President of the Institute for Operations Research and Management Sciences (INFORMS) spORts track. In addition, she has conducted workshops explaining artificial intelligence applications and their impacts on sport (e.g., Sport Analytics Japan).

Sarah Wymer is an independent consultant, based on the Gold Coast, Australia. She currently teaches a variety of sport management courses across multiple universities in Australia. Her research interests are focused on sport marketing, digital media, live streaming & fan engagement.

Daniel Yang is a Lecturer of Sport Management in the School of Kinesiology at the University of Michigan, USA. His research uses institutional and organizational analyses to understand organizational change and strategy, with an emphasis on socially responsible behaviors of professional sport organizations. He is also interested in exploring how sports organizations can achieve business and social impact through socially-oriented activities. His work has appeared in the *Journal of Sport Management* and *European Sport Management Quarterly*.

Embracing the Digital Frontier

Introduction to *The Routledge Handbook of Digital Sport Management*

Michael L. Naraine, Ted Hayduk III, and Jason P. Doyle

In his 1995 Earle F. Zeigler Lecture Award address, the late Professor Trevor Slack discussed some of the great challenges impacting sport management as a discipline. At the time, the *North American Society for Sport Management* was merely a decade old, the *European Association for Sport Management* was in its infancy, and the *Sport Management Association of Australia and New Zealand* was not even in existence – though it would be formed later that year. Despite his acknowledgment of the need for the global proliferation of sport management, that sentiment only represented one-half of the lecture's foci; Professor Slack's call to the field was not just about *where* sport management research should be presented and housed, but *what* research should be disseminated altogether. In this spirit, Slack (1996) highlighted the field's narrow empirical focus on the delivery of physical education programs and intercollegiate athletics, overlooking numerous other sectors and research topics integral to the sport landscape. Given his organizational theory roots, it probably does not come as a surprise that strategy, culture, and interorganizational linkages were top of mind. However, Professor Slack also advanced an additional call, and that was to examine "the impact that technology has had on sport" (1996, p. 102).

With the advent of the World Wide Web and user-intuitive operating systems like Microsoft Windows 95, sport management was on the cusp of its foray into computerized technology. Instant messaging via "AIM," "MSN," and "ICQ" took off, e-mail communication became widespread, and sport entities were even getting involved with video games, licensing their marks to software developers. Then, of course, there was the Y2K computer glitch scare that plagued sport organizations' databases and records; the optimization of online searches with Yahoo and Google; the evolution of smartphones from BlackBerry to iPhone; and the boundary-shifting introduction of social networking sites like MySpace, Facebook, and Twitter. In the midst of this rapid change, sport management research has arguably lagged, lacking dedicated, thorough coverage across the impact of technology on sport management as a collective. That should not be misconstrued with an absence of research, as there were (and continue to remain) dedicated and insightful scholars seeking to highlight new tools or ways of doing. But, arguably, the field has been left without any intentional foundation or direction, specifically as it relates to the ever-evolving technological expanse.

However, as our world has become increasingly digitized, perhaps more so than ever as a result of the COVID-19 global health pandemic, there has been a shift toward embracing this new

DOI: 10.4324/9781003088899-1

frontier. Nearly a decade ago, Routledge published two handbooks related to sport and new media (Billings & Hardin, 2014) and sport technology (Fuss et al., 2014), testing the "intellectual waters" with emergent systems and processes. Today, many of those concepts and discussion threads once considered novel have now matured, and there exists a steadily growing influx of sport researchers uncovering developments within the digital sport frontier. Yet, there has yet to be a compilation that brings together the past, present, and future of sport management in the context of this digital expanse, a notable omission if the field is to truly heed Slack's (1996) call.

This leads us to the present text. A Handbook is a significant undertaking that, as Billings and Hardin (2014) so eloquently explained, "covers a great deal of intellectual terrain" (p. 1). But, that also means that there must be adequate terrain to discuss. Despite the many technological advancements that have taken place over the past three decades, in particular, what the short- and long-term impacts were, on sport management, remained unclear. It is our contention that this terrain not only exists but that those impacts are becoming clearer and more realized. Consequently, sharing these insights with a wider audience is an important step to embrace the nexus of sport management and digital technology. This is the impetus for *The Routledge Handbook of Digital Sport Management*, a diverse text dedicated to illuminating how technologies and digital tools have, and will continue to, impact the creation, consumption, management, and delivery of sport across a myriad of systems, contexts, and settings.

Specifically, the Handbook takes a three-pronged systematic approach to embracing digital sport management. Part One showcases some of the critical digital transformations that have occurred in the field by examining established subtopics (e.g., human resource management, sponsorship, youth sport) and sport stakeholders (e.g., volunteers, sport events, not-for-profits). This moment of reflection was an intentional choice; assessing where impact has already occurred is an important first step to knowing where our field is going. Following these contributions, Part Two of the Handbook highlights some of the powerful digital tools being used to facilitate intended outcomes in sport management. This sentiment spans multiple subdomains including – but not limited to – journalism (i.e., podcasting), broadcasting (i.e., live streaming), and sport marketing (i.e., fantasy sport). Subsequently, the Handbook takes a fresh, unique approach by discussing some of the emerging issues that the field needs to be aware of. Whether it is the pervasiveness of blockchain technology and artificial intelligence, the rise of big data, digital sport's impact on women in sport or the natural environment, or the behemoth that is the esports ecosystem, Part Three navigates through these emergent intellectual waters with key points of consideration and questions to digest. Ultimately, this conceptual progression of transformation to tools to emerging issues is meant to provide a holistic view of this space, with one key caveat being that many of the tools and issues that will profoundly shape sport management do not yet exist given the rapidly developing nature of digital tech.

Although this collection serves to inform and guide digital sport management scholarship, we would be remiss if we did not set boundaries and qualify what readers should, and should not, expect to see:

- First, contributors were strongly encouraged to explore their subject matter without making assumptions about knowledge competencies. This allowed authors to define terms and provide contextual case examples to emphasize or illustrate the focal process or paradigm. It also allowed authors to explore similar ideas through different digital lenses. Ultimately, we feel this reinforced the power and breadth of "digital" in sport management.
- Second, it is important to explain that this Handbook is not a "How-To" guide for digital products to enhance sport management research, such as using R, Python, Anaconda, or SQL. There is certainly a place for skill acquisition of these particular programs, but our

quest is knowledge acquisition, not technical instruction. Taking this approach allows the text to focus entirely on exploring the theoretical and methodological needs with respect to digital sport management. Such an approach also serves to move the needle in terms of encouraging authors to adopt external frameworks and apply them to sport settings – and vice versa (e.g., Chalip, 2006). Digital, entrepreneurial, and analytics-based scholarship provides numerous opportunities to do so, and we feel as though this text offers a strong review and analysis of these overarching theories and frameworks.
- Third, while this Handbook covers a range of topics at the intersection of sport and digital, we must also recognize there were topics that were not covered. For instance, the recent emergence of the metaverse and web3.0 will be highly relevant to digital sport management researchers in the near future to examine fan community, engagement, and the various discourse and interactions that will manifest in these virtual spaces. However, a Handbook of this magnitude cannot be exhaustive, and some discussion, such as that pertaining to the metaverse and web3.0 is omitted from this text.
- Last, but certainly not least, we must accept that in embracing the digital frontier, there is a real possibility that the contributions made will have a shortened shelf-life relative to other academic domains. For example – consider that during our first brainstorming session for this book, non-fungible tokens (NFTs) did not exist in the mainstream, collaborative telepresence (i.e., metaverse, Zoom meetings) were in their infancy, Peloton had just gone public, and Formula 1's Drive to Survive on Netflix was in its inaugural season. In the span of 2.5 years, these technologies and companies have become commonplace in our vernacular. Thus, the inherent nature of digital sport management requires that we accept this rapid change as inevitable and enduring. At the bleeding edge of technology and digital evolution, it's possible that there may be more research questions than there are answers. We see this as an immense opportunity for future research because, in many instances, this text serves as a catalog of those research questions. This Handbook is less about finding the "intellectual treasure" marked by an "X" on a map, and more about charting the path toward that treasure.

It is our sincere hope that scholars in our growing and evolving field will find value in this Handbook. We are humbled and thrilled that global contributions were made from over 50 authors, spanning early-career, mid-career, and influential researchers from the professoriate. Due to the breadth and depth of knowledge behind these contributions, we feel strongly that this text provides a wonderful resource for scholars seeking to embrace the digital frontier in sport management. Moreover, let this text serve as an important step toward uncovering the impact of technology in sport as Slack (1996) had called for those many years ago. Happy reading!

Michael L. Naraine, Brock University, Canada
Ted Hayduk III, New York University, USA
Jason P. Doyle, Griffith University, Australia

References

Billings, A. C., & Hardin, M. (2014). *Routledge handbook of sport and new media*. Routledge.

Chalip, L. (2006). Toward a distinctive sport management discipline. *Journal of Sport Management*, *20*, 1–21. 10.1123/jsm.20.1.1

Fuss, F. K., Subic, A., Strangwood, M., & Mehta, R. (2014). *Routledge handbook of sports technology and engineering*. Routledge.

Slack, T. (1996). From the locker room to the board room: Changing the domain of sport management. *Journal of Sport Management*, *10*, 97–105. 10.1123/jsm.10.1.97

Part I

Digital Transformations in Sport Management

1

Organizational Behavior and Digital Transformation in Sport

Christopher R. Barnhill and Natalie L. Smith

Introduction

Historically, sport organizations have been defined by a hierarchical structure (Hartnell et al., 2011), tradition-minded culture (Wolfe et al., 2006), and, depending on their size, lacking in key organizational capacities (Doherty & Cuskelly, 2019). With notable exceptions, these digital transformations were usually fan revenue-focused, such as dynamic ticket pricing, fan apps, or stadium self-service kiosks (Kang, 2017; Mondello & Kamke, 2014; Troilo et al., 2016; Yoshida et al., 2013), or on-field performance (Wolfe et al., 2006). Even in community sport organizations, many examples of digital tool adoption were participant-focused such as implementing WIFI, digital meet results, and streaming of the sport online (Hoeber et al., 2015). While these tend to be more consumer-focused digital transformations, more sport organizations have recently embraced innovative work behaviors and creative work environments (Barnhill & Smith, 2019; Smith & Green, 2020).

One such focus has been on intra-office communication and the introduction of digital tools to help organize and communicate. As Girginov et al. (2015) noted, many have argued the digitalization of knowledge is the most important change of the last 60 years. They highlighted how national sport federations in Australia, Belgium, and the United Kingdom have already used some digital technologies and the internet. However, digital transformation within sport organizations has varied quite a bit across the sports industry, depending on national origin, organizational structure (e.g., professional sport or voluntary sport club), and other factors, such as the external structure in which the sport organization is housed (Ehnold et al., 2020). For example, sport federations influenced clubs' adoption of digital tools for managing and reporting membership data (Ehnold et al., 2020). Additionally, Hoeber et al. (2015) found in Canada that administrative initiatives were adopted more frequently, whereas, in a ten European country study, technical initiatives were implemented more often (Corthouts et al., 2020).

Innovations in the area of digital transformation are particularly helpful for sport organizations that must cooperate and compete across large geographic areas. For example, the UEFA Women's Champions League competition coordinates clubs across all of Europe. Within sport organizations, there are often intense time constraints related to game schedules or event deadlines, which may impact the implementation of these tools (Smith & Green, 2020).

DOI: 10.4324/9781003088899-3

Organizational factors related to the adoption, usage, and implications of intra-office communication digital tools should be considered from a multi-level perspective, as with most holistic organizational behavior analyses (Hoeber & Hoeber, 2012; Smith & Green, 2020). Therefore, this chapter will review the elements of digital transformation for sport organizations from an individual employee, work group, organization, and environment levels. In addition, other potential influences and trends will be considered.

Individual Employee Level

At the individual employee level, internal aspects of the employees play a role in every stage of a digital transformation within a sport organization. These aspects include psychological capital, intrinsic motivation, domain-relevant skills, and engagement in the creative process. There are similarities within these concepts to other previously researched concepts of design-thinking, knowledge management, and the innovation process within the sports industry.

Psychological Capital

Psychological capital refers to an individual's positive organizational state of development, characterized by high levels of self-efficacy, optimism, resilience, and hope. Psychological capital enables employees to take on complex challenges and overcome setbacks. Sport management scholars have made calls for research on the psychological capital of sport organization employees as it seems especially applicable to the industry (Kim et al., 2019; Kim et al., 2017; Oja et al., 2019). Outcomes of psychological capital for employees include greater job satisfaction and better performance. Employees with high levels of psychological capital are also more likely to engage in extra-role behaviors beneficial to the organization (organizational citizenship behaviors; Kim et al., 2019; Kim et al., 2017).

Sport organization employees may be predisposed to psychological capital development because of what drew them to the industry. Sport industry employees are often highly identified with their work (Kim et al., 2017). These employees choose to work in the sports industry because they find it meaningful, and sport organizations can enhance their psychological capital through opportunities to express those feelings. In other words, providing employees with work that they find challenging and meaningful builds efficacy, hope, optimism, and resilience (Kim et al., 2017). Digital transformations provide opportunities for employees to acquire new skills and lead challenging projects. Further, by using technology for mundane tasks, employees can engage in other work that is more intrinsically rewarding. While sport employees may struggle with the initial adoption of digital tools, this high identification with sport may help them overcome potential obstacles. This concept is tied to the next concept of innovation adoption motivation.

Innovation Adoption Motivation

According to Amabile's (2013) componential theory of creativity, intrinsic motivation, domain-relevant skills, and engagement in the creative process for individuals are the antecedents to individual creativity in the workplace. Depending on an individual's experiences, motivation, and behaviors, their engagement with new digital tools can vary wildly. Having decision-makers who lack familiarity with digital tools, or resistance from individual employees, can hinder any digital transformation (Naraine & Parent, 2017; Caza, 2000). In sport, there is growing evidence that managerial attitudes impact the adoption decision-making process (Corthouts et al., 2020).

Intrinsic Motivation

One element of increasing the adoption of innovative ideas, such as digital tools, is the motivation of employees and important stakeholders. Aversion to risk may play a negative role within a sport organization for innovation adoptions (Wemmer et al., 2016), therefore, the likelihood of adoption of digital tools within a sport organization would increase based on their perceived risk by those managers. Something to consider for future research, Winand and Anagnostopolous (2017) suggested the reason non-profit sport organization managers and board members are more predisposed to innovativeness, despite its risks, is their background in the competitive pressure of elite sport. Attitudes of managers toward innovation or change significantly influenced any adoptions, including digital tools (Flanders et al., 2020; Hoeber & Hoeber, 2012; Winand et al., 2013). In opposition to the adoption of innovations within an organization, Nite and Washington (2017) noted NCAA President Byers' oppositional attitude toward television broadcasting was negatively impacting the adoption of that tool during his tenure.

Like psychological capital mentioned earlier in this chapter, recent research into employee creativity found emotionally intelligent sport employees were more likely to be creative through their increased engagement at work and the ability to regulate stress (Paek et al., 2022). For example, the adoption of rudimentary digital tools such as Microsoft Excel in organizing operations for sporting events, whereas creating and implementing an event management digital tool specifically to address the needs of the event organizers may feel too stressful for organizers. However, individual employee motivation is not enough for sport organizations to adopt or implement transformative digital tools; employees' knowledge and skills can also play a role.

Domain Relevant Skills

The domain-relevant skills of employees or other important stakeholders can play a role in discovering, adopting, or implementing new digital tools. Domain-relevant skills can be specific technical knowledge or experience in a diverse set of sectors (Amabile, 2013). Sport employees' "knowledge is an essential organizational process that leverages all value-creating activities such as innovativeness and organizational performance" (Delshab et al., 2020, p. 14). Having board members with technical knowledge related to digital tools available and appropriate as well as specific knowledge of that sport increases the likelihood of potential adoption and implementation (Wemmer et al., 2016). This knowledge can be beneficial during all stages of the creative process, as an increased amount of knowledge, specific to an area of sport or technology, can bring in new possibilities or increase the likelihood of discovering new knowledge during information searching.

Creativity Process Engagement

In creativity process engagement, Amabile (2013) theorized problem identification, information searching & encoding, and idea generation as the three stages of the creative process. The design thinking process also mirrors this general framework (Joachim et al., 2021; Smith & Green, 2020). While recent research did not find informal internal networks of advice impacting organizational creativity levels (Smith & Green, 2020), the increased use of digital tools may change how those advice-seeking actions take place. Smith and Green (2020) suggest an analysis of advice-seeking external to the professional sport organization may unveil mechanisms for increasing the generation of new and useful ideas for that organization. Electronic communications have made advice-seeking across a league or externally to a broader network more easily accessible. For example, if an online management platform is used within an organization, different geographic locations may be able to seek quick and informal advice from each other. Even the adoption of basic chat tools such as GroupMe, Slack, or group messaging could increase inter-team advice-seeking within a professional sport league. This influx of communication and pool of knowledge can only be useful to the sport organization if it is encoded efficiently and effectively to help generate new and useful ideas (Zhang & Bartol, 2010a, 2010b).

The information searching and encoding process also mirrors the knowledge acquisition and storage aspects of knowledge management. As recommended by Delshab et al. (2021), sport clubs would be more successful "if they create a network to share and discuss new ideas, and develop the spirit of cooperation through applying KM" (p. 14). Similarly, for a nonprofit sport organization, utilizing personal adoption of digital tools such as social media gave employees opportunities to share ideas from around the world related to a particular issue (Joachim et al., 2021). Networks of advice have also included lead users and user groups but have been more frequently seen in sporting good sport organizations (Hyysalo, 2009). Even the development of those user networks has benefited from the adoption of digital tools, such as social media and online data scrapping to understand user sentiment.

In idea generation, the utilization of digital tools can be helpful in improving capacities, as well as networks of relevant stakeholders. By seeking relevant knowledge through networks, sport organizations can improve capacities and better integrate this new knowledge into their organization (Delshab et al., 2021). Indeed, in the case study by Hoeber and Hoeber (2012), the adoption of technical innovation was partially the result of a pre-existing relationship between the community sport organization and an information technology company. Additionally, in some nonprofit sport clubs, adopting a new digital tool related to participation registration was motivated by communication with other comparable sport clubs and their adoption of the tool (Wemmer et al., 2016).

Work Group Level

The individual leaders or decision-makers within an organization are not enough to see a digital transformation within a sport organization (Caza, 2000), the dynamics within the organization or work team also play a role. Some concepts to consider when researching digital transformations within sport organizations from an organizational behavior perspective are resource dependency and innovative work climate. Resources include financial, human resources, knowledge, time, and access to technology. An innovative work climate includes clear vision and goals, participative safety, and support for innovation.

Resource Dependency

Resource dependency theory argues that for an organization to be successful, it must; (1) secure internal resources; (2) acquire critical resources from its environment; and (3) adapt to changing and challenging circumstances with which it is confronted (Pfeffer & Salancik, 2003). Failure to achieve in any one of these facets can put an organization's survival at risk. On the other hand, an organization's ability to acquire external resources and find innovative solutions to obstacles can set it apart from its peers. Resources can be any element that is critical to an organization's success. We often think of scarce resources related to an organization's finances and its ability to acquire needed funds, but that is just one of many scarce resources that a successful sport organization must secure.

Sport organizations, especially those that fit the definition of Small-Medium Enterprise (SMEs), often lack the internal resources required to undertake a digital transformation. When internal resources are insufficient, sport organizations should first determine whether a digital transformation is best for the organization. In many cases, the answer will be yes. External pressures from customers and partners are often a driving factor (Greenhalgh et al., 2014), but so are opportunities for the organization to be more efficient and innovative in its programs and processes. Thankfully, there are many external resources available to help sport organizations adopt technologies.

Financial Resources

Sport organizations often operate under constrained financial resources (Nowy et al., 2015; Wicker et al., 2014). Further, most sport organizations have a few clearly defined organizational missions to which a vast majority of generated funds are dedicated. Thus, sport organizations must not only be good stewards of their internally generated funding, but they must also be adept at acquiring capital from external sources for new initiatives or to cover financial shortfalls. There's evidence that in smaller sport organizations, a lack of financial resources impacts innovative behaviors within the organization (Barnhill & Smith, 2019), and this leads many of these organizations to seek funding from outside sources. For example, leagues are partnerships that allow clubs to portion money through revenue sharing, sponsorship, and media arrangements (Troilo et al., 2016). Many elite sport and community sport organizations receive funding through government allocations or grants, although this has been decreasing in recent years, further increasing the need for purposeful allocation (Hoeber et al., 2015). Others rely on fundraising or other types of partnerships. Sport organizations, that lack the financial resources to acquire hardware and software needed for a technological upgrade, often enter into partnerships with companies that can provide the needed resources (Hoeber & Hoeber, 2012). Value-in-kind partnerships with external technology-focused organizations can provide resources unable to be procured by the sport organization, such as IBM's partnership with Wimbledon. For small businesses, educational organizations and nonprofits, grants, and low-interest loan programs can ease hardware and software acquisition burdens.

Human Resources

Access to knowledgeable, skilled workers and volunteers is another scarce resource. Many sport organizations are located in regions that offer an abundance of skilled workers, but the nature of sport work and many sport organizations' inability to pay competitive wages pushes people to other industries. To retain employees, sport organizations must find ways to attract and retain employees that not only have options with other sport organizations but also in other industries. The modernization of sport organizations such as national governing bodies from volunteer-run to staff-run has had its challenges. High-performing sport organizations have focused on acquiring a diverse set of skills across their organization. Additionally, sport organizations, at all levels of sport, rely on volunteers. Most people are aware that local nonprofits like community soccer leagues rely upon volunteers to coach, officiate, and even govern offerings. Often, these volunteers are parents or highly engaged community members. However, even mega-events like the Olympics and Super Bowl rely on thousands of volunteers with critical roles that impact the event's success. Volunteers participate for many reasons that are often intrinsic to the individual. Sport organizations must find digital ways to engage and retain quality volunteers.

Knowledge

Knowledge management is a process through which organizations create, maintain, access, and share an organization's intellectual resources (Antunes & Pinheiro, 2020). Organizations often lack knowledge related to emerging technologies and, therefore, must acquire knowledge externally (Delshab et al., 2021; Troilo et al., 2016). Organizations seeking to gain knowledge can acquire it by hiring new employees with the desired expertise, paying for current employees to receive the desired information, or partnering with organizations willing to share information. Human capital and knowledge are often intertwined. Smaller organizations, organizations that are bound to traditional practices, and organizations that have yet to adopt technology generally lack employees who have the knowledge needed to make an informed digital transformation. That uncertainty or lack of resources can cause resistance or failure when adopting digital tools (Caza, 2000). In addition to hiring people with the expertise needed, sport organizations can offer support for current employees to receive training or partner with a growing number of contractors who specialize in technological solutions for sport and event organizations. Indeed, recent calls have been made to increase knowledge management and networks beyond the sport organization to increase capacity across sport clubs (Delshab et al., 2021).

Time

Time is an external resource of which sport organizations must be aware. Nearly all sport organizations function on seasonal cycles, with the timing of events generally outside of an organization's control. Sport organizations generally utilize off-seasons to implement new initiatives or adapt to changing environments (Joachim et al., 2021). However, there is a dearth of research as it relates to the specific challenges of time within a season and the implementation of innovative ideas (Smith et al., 2020). Even in those sports not based on a season format, time seems to be a scarce resource that sport leaders may use to focus on retaining current operations, rather than adopting new digital tools (Harris et al., 2020). When sport employees acknowledged the need to distribute tasks to maximize other resources such as knowledge or human resources, they often struggled with taking the time required to divvy up tasks (Wemmer & Koenigstorfer, 2016).

Access to Technology

Access to technology varies substantially from one community to the next. An organization's access to software, wireless technology, high-speed internet, and other digital platforms is dependent on its community and local infrastructure. Interestingly, Ehnold et al. (2020) found a reported deficiency in broadband infrastructure correlated with higher usage behavior. They suggested that many sport organizations are not aware of their own technological deficiencies and only those with the appropriate amount of knowledge identify issues in their current resources.

Innovative Work Climate

Beyond resources, the climate of the workgroup or organization may influence any digital transformations within any sport organization. Ehnold et al. (2020) argued in their analysis of voluntary sport organizations, that "their ability to innovate appears to be partially limited, which may also affect their use of new technologies" (p. 2). Thus, an innovative work climate and the capacities engendered by that climate may provide utility for any organization hoping to digitally transform its operations. Sport organizations designated into teams or workgroups can also be influenced by their work environment. Perhaps a sport-industry professional desires to introduce a new digital tool for intra-office communication; however, their work environment discourages such behavior. In contrast, workgroup environments with a clear vision, participative safety, and innovation support have been found to encourage the adoption of such innovations (Smith & Green, 2020; Winand et al., 2013). For example, Hong et al. (2015) argued the San Francisco Giants adopted many player-focused and fan-focused digital tools, due to their flexible organizational culture.

In professional sport, a sport organization's clear vision and goals provided a framework for understanding which problems to focus on, where to seek information, and whether the ideas that are generated are new and useful to the organization (Smith & Green, 2020). This is also reflected in a comparative examination of US national governing bodies, where high-performing organizations focused on maintaining consistency across the organization with their values and vision. These organizations even emphasized "drawing from 'changing technology and social media'" (Harris et al., 2020, p. 12).

Caza (2000) found that clarity and focused goals played a factor in improving the likelihood of positive outcomes for an adopted innovation. As the flood of possibilities for digital tools increases, sport organizations, who are maintaining a clear vision and goals, can analyze both problems and ideas more effectively within their context-specific vision framework. Beyond clear vision, the process of a creative work environment, such as participative safety and support for innovation, has also been shown to increase overall organizational creativity; this is the stepping stone to implementing innovations (Smith & Green, 2020). While the attitudes of a few leaders or change champions are a powerful mechanism (Hoeber & Hoeber, 2012), the overall innovative work environment within an organization also can play an important role (Winand & Anagnostopoulos, 2017).

Organizational and Environmental Level

Beyond the individual employee, or group/organization climate or resources, digital transformations within sport organizations are influenced by organizational and environmental level factors. Similar to the previous discussion on resources for workgroups and organizations, an escalation of commitment by the organization or league/association within which the organization is housed could influence digital transformations within the sport organization. Additionally, the structures of the league, association, or the simple act of competing in a game or match against another sport organization influenced the adoption of innovations or transformations within the sport organization.

Escalation of Commitment

An interesting theoretical application to the digital transformation of organizational behavior in sport is the escalation of commitment theory (Nite et al., 2019). While some of these digital transformations may have a low financial cost (i.e., Gmail usage), the time-cost of adopting new digital processes and communication tools could have two opposing reactions. Once a new tool is adopted, the sport organization or individuals within the organization may double down. However, in opposition, if the organizational identity is one of continual innovation and technology-focused, they may continually be adopting newer intra-office communication tools as they are developed. As Wemmer et al. (2016) highlighted in their study, stakeholders wanted innovation as long as it didn't take any additional effort or time. Similarly, Marquez et al., (2020) found the greater perception of complexity or difficulty, the lower likelihood of adoption of a digital tool for United States interscholastic athletic departments. Caza (2000) and Harris et al. (2020) showed how failures or successes in adopting digital tools could reinforce skepticism or encourage further innovativeness respectively in the technology space.

The commitment of resources such as time, capacity, and finances play a role in what extent sport organizations transform digitally. Competitive sport organizations that have fewer financial resources, yet feel they have more competition tend to implement more sport and general service initiatives than more traditional federations (Winand et al., 2013). When measuring actual organizational performance and innovative work behaviors, Smith et al. (2020) found no relationship between these for minor league baseball organizations. As mentioned earlier, they suggested that idea initiation before the season is much easier than implementation during the season, as smaller sport organizations may prioritize resources to "proven" methods. In the adoption failure of digital tools, in this case, a computer scoring system was partially the result of the vagueness of how it would be implemented (Caza, 2000). Particularly with digital tools, the technical details can be stumbling blocks without the necessary innovation implementation support within a sport organization. In contrast, having involved stakeholders with advanced technical knowledge or access to other sport organizations' experiences in adopting a digital tool increased the success of implementation (Wemmer et al., 2016).

Sport Structures and Coopetition

How the organizations in sport differ in their use and prevalence of digital tools may be influenced by the structure within which that sport organization is housed. For example, Seifried et al. (2017) indicated the level of environmental change surrounding US collegiate sport organizations impacted the level of adoption and implementation of innovations. That push from environmental shocks was the primary impetus for those organizations to adopt any innovation, including digital ones, such as television broadcasting or social media platforms. Institutions may see innovation as a positive opportunity to update practices, but it also may be seen as a threat to the maintenance of the institution. For example, many United States college athletic programs have been reluctant to allow college athletes to have social media accounts. As indicated by Nite and Washington in their analysis of the NCAA's history as it related to adopting the technology of television broadcasting, "primary challenges stemmed from disparate perceptions of impact of innovation and the institutions slowness to evolve (protracted regulatory pace)" (2017, p. 584). Similarly, in Germany and Austria, there seems to be an underestimation of the implications of digital transformation in their community sport organizations (Ehnold et al., 2020).

Rather than simply react to external forces, researchers have argued for more open innovation with increased co-creation between sport organizations and partners (Delshab et al., 2020; Wemmer et al., 2016). However, structures of cooperation and competition within sport organizations may hinder a digital tool's adoption if it is perceived to be unequally beneficial within a league or membership association (Turner & Shilbury, 2010). The power structure of a sport or sector within sport seems to influence the likelihood of digital transformation. For German non-profit sport organizations, clubs were more likely to adopt a digital tool if required by the sport federation (Ehnold et al., 2020). Similar to a professional sport where the power of the NFL league office proved the impetus for the adoption of a fan mobile app (Greenhalgh et al., 2014). This differs from looser league or association structures such as in professional football in Australia (Turner & Shilbury, 2010) or vote-based membership such as the NCAA (Nite & Washington, 2017). The decision-making process for any digital tool adoption is dependent on the structure of the organization. For example, Nite and Washington (2017) found the NCAA membership structure and power of exclusion from competition impacted how restrictively broadcasting of college football was adopted.

Sport organizations' willingness to use external expertise is becoming more common, as highlighted in the case study by Greenhalgh et al. (2014) on the adoption of a fan mobile app. The initiation stage for this digital tool adoption was a report commissioned by the NFL with the McKinsey Study (MS). What is interesting in this particular adoption of a digital tool is the league-led rather than team-led approach. This external focus on how an organization behaves includes elements of cooperation and coopetition. Wemmer et al. (2016) found a cooperative/competitive model improved organizational performance and innovation implementation through the use of outside knowledge. While not specifically analyzing digital tool adoption, Hong et al. (2019) found the adoption of new stadium construction was significantly impacted by external forces, particularly political elections and geographic proximity.

However, any call for increased adoption of digital tools within sport organizations may want to consider this key point from an institutional perspective. As indicated by Nite and Washington, "those who are either disadvantaged by the current institutional arrangement or who stand to benefit from altered arrangements tend to be the ones engaged in disruptive and creative institutional work" (2017, p. 576). The researchers found universities such as UPenn and Notre Dame saw the adoption of television broadcasting as a way to improve their university's national reputation. Another example, from US interscholastic sport, indicated that the need to enhance fan experience was an impetus for digital transformation (Marquez et al., 2020). Most likely, those institutions saw their disadvantage and desired to use communication innovations to improve their standing through increased resources or public relations.

Trends and Additional Considerations

Understanding digital transformations from an organizational behavior perspective provide utility, particularly when individual, group, organizational, and environmental factors are considered. Elements such as motivation, psychological capital, resources, work climate, and coopetition structures all play a role in the digital transformations of sport organizations. However, additional factors should be analyzed by researchers and practitioners. These include the important fact that many sport organizations are small enterprises and the increasingly important issue of turnover and burnout in the sport industry as a whole.

Sport Organizations as Small Enterprises

From an economic perspective, the sports industry adds approximately $1.5 trillion annually to the global economy (Plunkett Research, n.d.), making it approximately the tenth largest industry in the world (IBISWorld, n.d.). Major professional clubs such as Manchester United, the Los Angeles Lakers, and the New York Yankees spend millions to sign the most talented athletes. Colleges in the United States make headlines for the amount they spend hiring coaches and building facilities to attract amateur athletes to their campuses. It is easy to see why people believe that sport organizations have unlimited financial resources. Further, our views of the sports industry are biased by its outsized cultural and political impacts. Major events such as the FIFA World Cup captivate the globe, while local sport clubs improve the lives of local citizens and politicians use sport to further political agendas.

While some sport organizations are very large and have substantial financial resources, the industry as a whole is much more complicated. Nike, the largest sport organization globally, employs

75,000 people and generates annual revenues of nearly $40 billion (Nike, 2019). One of the most valuable sport clubs, Manchester United of the English Premier League, employs approximately 900 people and generates annual revenues of around £600 million (roughly $830 million USD; Manchester United, 2020). Manchester United is much smaller than Nike, but it is a behemoth compared to most other spectator sports franchises. For example, the Sacramento Kings of the National Basketball Association generate annual revenues of approximately $250 million and employ 200 workers (Statista, 2021).

The vast majority of sport organizations fit the definition of SMEs. Organizations employing less than 250 people can be considered medium-sized and employing less than 50 people can be considered small-sized. This is especially true in lower-division and minor league professional sport, amateur sport, and community sport. Take a look at most sport organizations' directories, and you will see only a small number of full-time employees. For example, the Savannah Sports Council employs just two full-time employees, yet hosts multiple events each year.

While SME size naturally lends itself to a "lean" organizational structure, in fact, many have a limited understanding of this concept (Yadav et al., 2019). However, by their nature, SMEs rely on employees carrying out multiple prescribed roles while also contributing to cross-functional projects (Nadin & Cassell, 2007). Due to the close proximity of employees and service focus in most SME sport organizations, many elements of a "lean" organization can be seen including identifying value for the consumer, continuous workflow, and facilitating improvement. Employees frequently communicate to find solutions to organizational challenges, and lower-level employees have much more interaction with upper managers compared to their counterparts in larger organizations (Eddleston et al., 2018). Employees of SMEs also develop tighter emotional bonds with their organizations (Nadin & Cassell, 2007). These factors would seemingly support innovative behaviors that would lead to the adoption of new technologies. Adoption of new technologies can allow sport-based SMEs to facilitate more efficient communication both internally and with customers, better identify revenue opportunities, enhance service offerings, and expand product offerings (Becker & Schmid, 2020; Ehnold, et al., 2020; Matarazzo et al., 2021). Whereas larger organizations often see digital transformation as a way to eliminate redundancy and possibly reduce staffing, SMEs adopt technology to enhance existing employees' output. In essence, larger organizations use technology to seek new competitive advantages while SMEs adopt technology to keep up with their peers. The level of external pressure faced by SMEs to adopt a digital transformation is different than those faced by larger organizations as is their level of risk tolerance. An ineffective digital transformation is likely to have greater consequences for organizations with substantial resource constraints. Unfortunately, this reflects how SMEs external pressure is often lower than larger corporations, which may have higher risk tolerance due to external pressure for competitive advantage. Therefore, SMEs' motivation for innovative digital transformations would also differ. However, SMEs are often ineffective in their digital transformations (Becker & Schmid, 2020).

More than half of SMEs enter a digital transformation without a clearly defined strategy (Becker & Scmid, 2020). This leads to confusion amongst employees regarding why the organization is transforming and how the new technology should be used to meet organizational objectives. Additionally, most SMEs lack the technical expertise needed to make informed decisions regarding technology adoption (Li et al., 2018); thus, they mimic other firms in their sectors instead of seeking a transformation that fits their own objectives (Garzoni et al., 2020). In sport, this mimicry may take the form of a club installing the same ticking software as others in their league, even if it does not fit the club's needs, and nobody on staff knows how to run the software properly.

In addition to lacking human resources and institutional knowledge of larger organizations, SMEs often have limited access to financial resources. Even the largest sport organizations function with small profit margins. A vast majority of revenues are redirected toward primary organizational goals. For a sport development organization like Soccer in the Streets, capital from donations and grants are pushed toward the construction of soccer fields and the organization's educational mission, leaving very little for other expenditures. NCAA athletic departments spend more than half of their revenue on scholarships and coaching salaries. Even Manchester United, one of the most financially successful sport organizations globally, spent 96% of its 2019 revenues on operating expenses (Manchester United, 2020). Sport-based SMEs often lack the financial resources needed to effectively implement innovations (Barnhill & Smith, 2019). Thus, sport organizations may develop a clearly defined digital strategy but lack the finances to implement it. Despite the challenges faced by SMEs in general, particularly sport-based SMEs, digital transformations can have many positive impacts when properly implemented. A "four-level approach" to digital transformation has been shown to improve SMEs' adoption of technology (Garzoni et al., 2020).

Level 1: Digital Awareness

This level is about education. Organizational members educate themselves on the needs of their organization and the potential value of digital transformation. Information collected during this level is general and focused on identifying organizational goals that could be achieved by adopting new technology.

Level 2: Digital Inquiry

At this level, organizations begin seeking information on technologies specific to the organizational needs outlined in Level 1. Organizational members meet with vendors, discuss organizational needs, and determine if specific technologies can be efficiently implemented in the organization.

Level 3: Digital Collaboration

Having chosen which technology or technologies can be adapted to meet organizational goals, the organization begins working closely with vendors to design an organization-specific system. Organizational members are highly involved in the system's design and are also educated on the technical knowledge needed for proper implementation.

Level 4: Digital Transformation

Software specifically designed for the organization's needs is implemented. Change agents within the organization are highly involved with the implementation and championing of the transformation to stakeholders.

The four-level approach forces organizations to focus on organizational goals throughout the process. It eliminates mimicry because organizations look for solutions in line with their objectives instead of competitor outcomes. The four-level approach also addresses technological ignorance issues as organizational members are required to acquire knowledge throughout the process. For sport organizations within the SME category, this four-level approach could be worth exploring by both researchers and practitioners.

Turnover and Burnout

Employee turnover and burnout have long been issues in the sports industry. Working in sports often requires employees to be present on nights and weekends in addition to regular business hours. Sport organizations work to foster feelings of commitment and engagement from employees. A massive study of athletic department employees found an epidemic of workaholism that increases burnout and turnover intentions (Taylor et al., 2019). Burnout decreases commitment and engagement while encouraging behaviors that are negative to organizational outcomes (Auh et al., 2016). Turnover is also costly. Recruiting new employees drains already scarce resources (McKinney et al., 2007). More damaging, departing employees take institutional knowledge when they exit, damaging organizational learning (Massingham, 2018). Adverse outcomes can be magnified in small organizations as departing employees may be the only organizational members with knowledge of vital systems (Durst & Wilhelm, 2012).

The COVID-19 pandemic accelerated technology-driven changes that encourage employees to be engaged when away from the office (Mastromartino et al., 2020). For example, the Atlanta Braves purchased workstations and software that allowed employees to access systems and make ticket and sponsorship sales from home. No longer are employees expected to just answer emails or phone calls when away from the office; most work tasks can now be completed without entering the organizational property. Although the ability to work from home can be freeing to employees, it also blurs the lines between when one is at work versus on personal time (Peeters et al., 2005; Rubenstein et al., 2020). Technology-driven work-life conflict can increase employees' stress and lead to burnout and intentions to leave the organization (Rubenstein et al., 2020). This does not mean that sport organizations should avoid digital transformations. A study of European sports clubs found that organizations adopted digitization to manage membership information, reporting procedures, accounting, and billing activities (Ehnold et al., 2020). For most sport organizations, particularly smaller organizations, digital processes can eliminate mundane tasks, freeing up employees to engage in more rewarding tasks or avoid unnecessary work hours.

Organizational culture and leader behavior are extremely important in avoiding employee burnout during digital transformations. Organizational cultures that prioritize work-life and work-family balance and employee health and well-being can avoid the pitfalls that come with digital transformations. Leaders can support healthy organizational culture through their own actions. For example, sending emails during off-hours can place pressure on employees to answer during off-hours. Telling workers to finish tasks as soon as possible creates anxiety over deadlines. Leaders can alleviate these issues by altering their behaviors. Simple behaviors like holding off on emails until the next day or assigning clear deadlines remove anxiety and pressures that blur work-life and home-life boundaries.

Conclusion and Future Directions

As seen in this review, there is a multitude of ways to understand digital transformation and organizational behavior in sport, from the individual, workgroup, organizational, and environmental levels. Researchers' future considerations are to understand the organizational behavior processes in regard to the differences between intra-office digital tool adoption and consumer or performance-facing digital tools. As well, how organizational culture impacts burnout rates as digitization of sport organizations may increase the work-life blur. An area of concern for the digital transformation of sport organizations is how the expansion of production may result in fragmentation and thus result in a loss of knowledge (Girginov et al., 2015). This fragmentation may favor certain powerful sport organizations or increase bias within the sports industry, not reduce it. Digital tools continue to be developed or considered by sport organizations. In understanding these tools for their roles in the sports industry, researchers may consider a multi-level perspective and understand through these frameworks and theories the potential impact on the sports industry as a whole. Very little has been written about related to intraoffice communication as it relates to these new digital innovations, a ripe opportunity for researchers to understand its role in sport organizations' behavior.

References

Amabile, T. M. (2013). Componential theory of creativity. In E. H. Kessler (Ed.), *Encyclopedia of management theory* (pp. 135–140). SAGE.

Antunes, H. J. G., & Pinheiro, P. G. (2020). Linking knowledge management and organizational learning. *Journal of Innovation & Knowledge, 5*, 140–149.

Auh, S., Menguc, B., Spyropoulou, S., & Wang, F. (2016). Service employee burnout and engagement: The moderating role of power distance orientation. *Journal of the Academy of Marketing Science, 44*(6), 726. 10.1007/s11747-015-0463-4

Barnhill, C. R., & Smith, N. L. (2019). Psychological contract fulfilment and innovative work behaviours of employees in sport-based SBEs: The mediating role of organisational citizenship. *International Journal of Sport Management and Marketing, 19*(1/2), 106–128.

Becker, W., & Schmid, O. (2020). The right digital strategy for your business: An empirical analysis of the design and implementation of digital strategies in SMEs and LSEs. *Business Research, 13*(3), 985–1005. 10.1007/s40685-020-00124-y

Caza, A. (2000). Context receptivity: Innovation in an amateur sport organization. *Journal of Sport Management, 14*(3), 227–242.

Corthouts, J., Thibaut, E., Breuer, C., Feiler, S., James, M., Llopis-Goig, R., ... & Scheerder, J. (2020). Social inclusion in sports clubs across Europe: Determinants of social innovation. *Innovation: The European Journal of Social Science Research, 33*(1), 21–51.

Delshab, V., Pyun, D. Y., Kerwin, S., & Cegarra-Navarro, J.-G. (2021). The impact of unlearning context on organizational performance through knowledge management: A case of community sport clubs in Iran. *Sport Management Review, 24*(1), 156–178.

Delshab, V., Winand, M., Boroujerdi, S. S., Hoeber, L., & Mahmoudian, A. (2020). The impact of knowledge management on performance in nonprofit sports clubs: The mediating role of attitude toward innovation, open innovation, and innovativeness. *European Sport Management Quarterly*, 1–22. 10.1080/16184742.2020.1768572

Doherty, A., & Cuskelly, G. (2019). Organizational capacity and performance of community sport clubs. *Journal of Sport Management, 34*(3), 240–259.

Durst, S., & Wilhelm, S. (2012). Knowledge management and succession planning in SMEs. *Journal of Knowledge Management, 16*(4), 637–649. 10.1108/13673271211246194

Eddleston, K. A., Kellermanns, F. W., & Kidwell, R. E. (2018). Managing family members: How monitoring and collaboration affect extra-role behavior in family firms. *Human Resource Management, 57*(5), 957–977. 10.1002/hrm.21825

Ehnold, P., Faß, E., Steinbach, D., & Schlesinger, T. (2020). Digitalization in organized sport – usage of digital instruments in voluntary sports clubs depending on club's goals and organizational capacity. *Sport, Business and Management: An International Journal.* 10.1108/SBM-10-2019-0081

Flanders, S., Smith, N., Jones, C., & Greene, A. (2020). Examining the innovation process of a graduate apprenticeship program for sport organizations. *Sports Innovation Journal, 1*, 106–119.

Garzoni, A., De Turi, I., Secundo, G., & Del Vecchio, P. (2020). Fostering digital transformation of SMEs: A four levels approach. *Management Decision, 58*(8), 1543–1562. 10.1108/MD-07-2019-0939

Girginov, V., Toohey, K., & Willem, A. (2015). Creating and leveraging knowledge to promote sport participation: The role of public governing bodies of sport. *European Sport Management Quarterly, 15*(5), 555–578.

Greenhalgh, G., Dwyer, B., & Biggio, B. (2014). There as an app for that: the development of an NFL team mobile application. *Journal of Applied Sport Management, 6*(4).

Harris, S. J., Metzger, M. L., & Duening, T. N. (2021). Innovation in national governing bodies of sport: Investigating dynamic capabilities that drive growth. *European Sport Management Quarterly, 21*(1), 94–115.

Hartnell, C. A., Ou, A. Y., & Kinicki, A. (2011). Organizational culture and organizational effectiveness: A meta-analytic investigation of the competing values framework's theoretical suppositions. *Journal of Applied Psychology, 96*(4), 677.

Hoeber, L., & Hoeber, O. (2012). Determinants of an innovation process: A case study of technological innovation in a community sport organization. *Journal of Sport Management, 26*(3), 213–223.

Hoeber, L., Doherty, A., Hoeber, O., & Wolfe, R. (2015). The nature of innovation in community sport organizations. *European Sport Management Quarterly, 15*(5), 518–534.
Hong, S., Magnusen, M., & Coates, D. (2019). Collaborative innovation in professional sport stadium construction: An event history analysis. *Journal of Applied Sport Management, 11*(4), 7.
Hong, S., Magnusen, M., & Mondello, M. (2015). Collaborative innovation in sport: Conceptualizing the adoption of new stadium construction from professional sport team and government perspectives. *Journal of Physical Education and Sport Management, 6*, 70–81.
Hyysalo, S. (2009). User innovation and everyday practices: Micro-innovation in sports industry development. *R&D Management, 39*(3), 247–258.
IBISWorld (n.d.). *The 10 global biggest industries by revenue.* IBISWorld. Accessed February 22, 2021 from https://www.ibisworld.com/global/industry-trends/biggest-industries-by-revenue/
Joachim, G., Schulenkorf, N., Schlenker, K., Frawley, S., & Cohen, A. (2021). "No idea is a bad idea": Exploring the nature of design thinking alignment in an Australian sport organization. *Journal of Sport Management, 35*(5), 381–394.
Kang, S. (2017). Mobile communication and pro sports: Motivation and fan loyalty. *International Journal of Mobile Communications, 15*(6), 604–627.
Kim, M., Kim, A. C. H., Newman, J. I., Ferris, G. R., & Perrewé, P. L. (2019). The antecedents and consequences of positive organizational behavior: The role of psychological capital for promoting employee well-being in sport organizations. *Sport Management Review, 22*(1), 108–125.
Kim, M., Perrewé, P. L., Kim, Y. K., & Kim, A. C. H. (2017). Psychological capital in sport organizations: Hope, efficacy, resilience, and optimism among employees in sport (HEROES). *European Sport Management Quarterly, 17*(5), 659–680. 10.1080/16184742.2017.1344284
Li, L., Su, F., Zhang, W., & Mao, J. Y. (2018). Digital transformation by SME entrepreneurs: A capability perspective. *Information Systems Journal, 28*(6), 1129–1157. 10.1111/isj.12153
Manchester United. (2020). 2020 Annual Report. *Manchester United football club 2020 annual report.* Retrieved from https://ir.manutd.com/~/media/Files/M/Manutd-IR/documents/2020-mu-plc-form-20-f.pdf
Marquez, A., Cianfrone, B., & Kellison, T. (2020). Factors affecting leaders' adoption of innovation: An analysis of high school athletic directors and digital ticketing. *Sports Innovation Journal, 1*, 152–171.
Massingham, P. R. (2018). Measuring the impact of knowledge loss: A longitudinal study. *Journal of Knowledge Management, 22*(4), 721–758. 10.1108/JKM-08-2016-0338
Mastromartino, B., Ross, W. J., Wear, H., & Naraine, M. L. (2020). Thinking outside the 'box': A discussion of sports fans, teams, and the environment in the context of COVID-19. *Sport in Society, 23*(11), 1707–1723.
Matarazzo, M., Penco, L., Profumo, G., & Quaglia, R. (2021). Digital transformation and customer value creation in 'Made in Italy' SMEs: A dynamic capabilities perspective. *Journal of Business Research, 123*(2020), 642–656. 10.1016/j.jbusres.2020.10.033
McKinney, W. R., Bartlett, K. R., & Mulvaney, M. A. (2007). Measuring the costs of employee turnover in Illinois public park and recreation agencies: An exploratory study. *Journal of Park & Recreation Administration, 25*(1), 50–74.
Mondello, M., & Kamke, C. (2014). The introduction and application of sports analytics in professional sport organizations. *Journal of Applied Sport Management, 6*(2), 11.
Naraine, M. L., & Parent, M. M. (2017). Examining social media adoption and change to the stakeholder communication paradigm in not-for-profit sport organizations. *Journal of Amateur Sport, 3*(2), 55–81.
Nadin, S., & Cassell, C. (2007). New deal for old? Exploring the psychological contract in a small firm environment. *International Small Business Journal, 25*(4), 417–443. 10.1177/0266242607078587
Nike (2019, July). *2019 Annual report and notice of annual meeting.* Retrieved from https://s1.q4cdn.com/806093406/files/doc_financials/2019/ar/354352(1)_76_Nike-Inc_COMBO_WR_R1.pdf
Nite, C., & Washington, M. (2017). Institutional adaptation to technological innovation: Lessons from the NCAA's regulation of football television broadcasts (1938–1984). *Journal of Sport Management, 31*(6), 575–590.
Nite, C., Hutchinson, M., & Bouchet, A. (2019). Toward an institutional theory of escalation of commitment within sport management: A review and future directions. *Sport Management Review, 22*(5), 571–583.
Nowy, T., Wicker, P., Feiler, S., & Breuer, C. (2015) Organizational performance of nonprofit and for-profit sport organizations. *European Sport Management Quarterly, 15*(2), 155–175.
Oja, B. D., Kim, M., Perrewé, P. L., & Anagnostopoulos, C. (2019). Conceptualizing A-HERO for sport employees' well-being. *Sport, Business and Management: An International Journal, 9*(4), 363–380. 10.1108/SBM-10-2018-0084

Paek, B., Martyn, J., Oja, B. D., Kim, M., & Larkins, R. J. (2022). Searching for sport employee creativity: A mixed-methods exploration. *European Sport Management Quarterly, 22*(4), 483–505.

Parent, M. M., Naraine, M. L., & Hoye, R. (2018). A new era for governance structures and processes in Canadian national sport organizations. *Journal of Sport Management, 32*(6), 555–566.

Peeters, M. C. W., Montgomery, A. J., Bakker, A. B., & Schaufeli, W. B. (2005). Balancing work and home: How job and home demands are related to burnout. *International Journal of Stress Management, 12*(1), 43–61. 10.1037/1072-5245.12.1.43

Pfeffer, J., & Salancik, G. R. (2003). *The external control of organizations: A resource dependence perspective.* Stanford University Press.

Plunkett Research (n.d.). *Sports & recreation business statistics analysis, business and industry statistics.* Plunkett Research. Accessed February 22, 2021 from https://www.plunkettresearch.com/statistics/sports-industry/

Rubenstein, A. L., Peltokorpi, V., & Allen, D. G. (2020). Work-home and home-work conflict and voluntary turnover: A conservation of resources explanation for contrasting moderation effects of on- and off-the-job embeddedness. *Journal of Vocational Behavior, 119*, 103413. 10.1016/j.jvb.2020.103413

Seifried, C., Katz, M., & Tutka, P. (2017). A conceptual model on the process of innovation diffusion through a historical review of the United States Armed Forces and their bowl games. *Sport Management Review, 20*(4), 379–394.

Smith, N. L., & Green, B. C. (2020). Examining the factors influencing organizational creativity in professional sport organizations. *Sport Management Review, 23*(5), 992–1004.

Statista (2021, February 17). *Revenue of the Sacramento Kings from 2001/02 to 2019/20.* Statista. Accessed March 12, 2021 from https://www.statista.com/statistics/196768/revenue-of-the-sacramento-kings-since-2006/

Taylor, E. A., Huml, M. R., & Dixon, M. A. (2019). Workaholism in sport: A mediated model of work–family conflict and burnout. *Journal of Sport Management, 33*(4), 249–260. 10.1123/jsm.2018-0248

Troilo, M., Bouchet, A., Urban, T. L., & Sutton, W. A. (2016). Perception, reality, and the adoption of business analytics: Evidence from North American professional sport organizations. *Omega, 59*, 72–83.

Turner, P., & Shilbury, D. (2010). The impact of emerging technology in sport broadcasting on the preconditions for interorganizational relationship (IOR) formation in professional football. *Journal of Sport Management, 24*(1), 10–44.

Wemmer, F., Emrich, E., & Koenigstorfer, J. (2016). The impact of coopetition-based open innovation on performance in nonprofit sports clubs. *European Sport Management Quarterly, 16*(3), 341–363.

Wemmer, F., & Koenigstorfer, J. (2016). Open innovation in nonprofit sports clubs. *VOLUNTAS: International Journal of Voluntary and Nonprofit Organizations, 27*(4), 1923–1949.

Wicker, P., Breuer, C., Lamprecht, M., & Fischer, A. (2014). Does club size matter: An examination of economies of scale, economies of scope, and organizational problems. *Journal of Sport Management, 28*, 266–280.

Winand, M., & Anagnostopoulos, C. (2017). Get ready to innovate! Staff's disposition to implement service innovation in nonprofit sport organisations. *International Journal of Sport Policy and Politics, 9*(4), 579–595. 10.1080/19406940.2017.1308418

Winand, M., Vos, S., Zintz, T., & Scheerder, J. (2013). Determinants of service innovation: A typology of sports federations. *International Journal of Sport Management and Marketing, 13*(1–2), 55–73.

Wolfe, R., Wright, P. M., & Smart, D. L. (2006). Radical HRM innovation and competitive advantage: The Moneyball story. *Human Resource Management, 45*(1), 111–145.

Yadav, V., Jain, R., Mittal, M. L., Panwar, A., & Lyons, A. C. (2019). The propagation of lean thinking in SMEs. *Production Planning & Control, 30*(10–12), 854–865.

Yoshida, M., James, J. D., & Cronin, J. J. (2013). Sport event innovativeness: Conceptualization, measurement, and its impact on consumer behavior. *Sport Management Review, 16*(1), 68–84.

Zhang, X., & Bartol, K. M. (2010a). Linking Empowering Leadership and Employee Creativity: The Influence of Psychological Empowerment, Intrinsic Motivation, and Creative Process Engagement. *Academy of Management Journal, 53*(1), 107–128.

Zhang, X., & Bartol, K. M. (2010b). The influence of creative process engagement on employee creative performance and overall job performance: A curvilinear assessment. *Journal of Applied Psychology, 95*(5), 862–873.

2

Human Resource Management and Digital Technology

Shannon Kerwin

HRM and Digital Technology in the Sport Industry

Human resource management (HRM) is traditionally defined as "all management decisions related to policies and practices that together shape the employment relationship and are aimed at achieving individual, organizational, and societal goals" (Bach & Edwards, 2013, p. 19). This definition highlights the strategic and complex elements that define, influence, and result from the management of human resources. Sport organizations are functioning in a global context that is rapidly changing and mobilizing toward efficiency. Specifically, the development of integrative technologies and social media has pushed sport managers to consider how they can leverage social media and embrace emergent trends to stay relevant (functional) (Naraine & Parent, 2017; Parent et al., 2018). This is particularly relevant in post-pandemic spaces where sport organizations must streamline processes to recover or maintain an audience. Given these vital and uncertain times, there is a greater need to dissect HRM policies and practices in relation to contextualized individual (micro), organizational (meso), and societal (macro) factors (MacLean, 2016; Parent et al., 2018; Taylor, 2016). Effectively managing personnel requires a comprehensive understanding of internal and external factors that help or hinder the creation of competitive advantage for sport organizations (Kerwin, 2015).

Sport managers view human resources as the capital where managers must spend time enhancing individual development to contribute to performance and productivity (Chelladurai & Kerwin, 2017). Development within HRM has typically been viewed from a micro and meso level where human resources (e.g., volunteers, professionals, interns, clients) and individual differences (e.g., personality, values) contribute to management practices (e.g., staffing, training, orientation, performance appraisals) that are adopted, and subsequently impact attitudinal outcomes (e.g., satisfaction, commitment, productivity) of human resources (e.g., Kerwin, 2015; MacLean, 2016). As outlined by Taylor (2016), many sport managers now focus on strategic human resource management (SHRM) that bridges traditional HRM policies and practices with a planned strategy for an organization. Within SHRM, the strategic objectives of sport organizations should be implemented into HRM decisions made by managers (Taylor, 2016). These strategic objectives, set by sport managers, must include a reflection on the agency of society where the social, political, legal, and technical world around them are considered (Kerwin, 2015).

DOI: 10.4324/9781003088899-4

Unfortunately, sport managers have historically been found to adopt HRM policies and practices that omit strategic foresight (e.g., Moore & Levermore, 2012; Taylor, 2016; Taylor & McGraw, 2006), thus leaving organizations vulnerable to becoming irrelevant in changing and turbulent times. Moore and Levermore (2012) emphasized that a large proportion of the sport industry can be characterized as small- and medium-sized enterprises (SME) that require unique management and strategy compared to other larger industry sectors. In particular, Taylor and McGaw's (2006) exploration of 43 non-profit sport organizations found that only one-quarter of their sample adopted formalized human resource practices within the SME framework. Therefore, despite the emphasis on formalization in larger businesses and corporations, sport managers have room to grow regarding strategically adopting HRM practices to suit their context. Further, Taylor and McGaw highlighted that reasons for adopting more formalized human resource practices were to respond to (1) new skill requirements for employees and volunteers (i.e., technological requirements), and (2) the needs of a diverse membership or client base. It is, therefore, important for sport managers to scan their micro-, meso-, and macro-level contexts to become strategic, contemporary, and forward-thinking regarding formalized HRM.

The Emergence of e-HRM

One way for sport managers to adopt SHRM is to consider the presence and adoption of electronic human resource management (e-HRM). e-HRM is a meso-level application that provides the information required to manage micro-HR practices and processes while considering macro-level (i.e., societal) adaptions (Welbourne, 2010). Applications or resources linked to e-HRM typically include employee databases and payroll systems, but can also extend to include systems such as e-recruitment, e-learning, performance management, and reward systems. The most sophisticated systems allow each HRM practice to amalgamate into one platform. Welbourne (2010) suggests the main goals of implementing and adopting e-HRM are cost reduction, improving HR services, and improving strategic orientation, thus meeting the call for SHRM in sport (Taylor, 2016).

The push for enhanced technologies connected to the management of personnel in sport is in its infancy. Large sport enterprises like Adidas and Under Armour have embraced big data and artificial intelligence in the move toward digital technology to improve HRM practices; however, many are still far behind. The term digital transformation is now used in contemporary management practices where human resource processes are altered by the use of technology to become more effective in connecting HRM to broader employment processes (Vardarlier, 2020). Moreover, the process by which positive outcomes arise is linked to digital ecosystems where management must be strategically (and thoughtfully) implemented to complement organizational strategy (Dossena & Mochi, 2020).

Given the variable context, lack of strategy, and resourcing typically associated with HRM in sport (Moore & Levermore, 2012; Taylor & McGraw, 2006), not all sport managers have moved toward adopting e-HRM in their organizations. Specifically, sport organizations typically function with relatively few human resources (therefore lacking a robust HR department) and, consequently, often do not operate in a strategic manner (Taylor, 2016; Taylor & McGraw, 2006). Moreover, Hoeber et al. (2015) outlined that community sport organizations focus on innovation and changes that are process-related, administrative, and incremental in nature, which may make a shift from traditional HRM to e-HRM feel overwhelming to sport managers. Therefore, it is important to break down the strategic elements of e-HRM in a way that addresses the efficient use of such functions in the sports domain.

This chapter outlines relevant theory regarding e-HRM and digital ecosystems, functions of e-HRM in organizations, the factors that have been shown to influence the implementation of e-HRM within digital ecosystems in organizations, and directions ahead for understanding the theoretical relevance of e-HRM in sport.

Theory and Movement Forward

The presence of an HR department and HRM strategy in an organization will significantly influence if e-HRM is adopted (Rahman et al., 2018). To unpack the strategy related to e-HRM and to explore the adoption (or lack thereof) of e-HRM in sport, the technology-organization-environment (TOE) theory is adopted here within. TOE maintains that the adoption and implementation of any innovation system are underpinned by three contextual factors: technology, organization, and environment (Tornatzky & Fleischer, 1990).

The *technological context* outlines the features of the technologies existing for adoption by the organization, and the existing technology within an organization that could be utilized within an innovation process (DePietro et al., 1990; Tornatzky & Fleischer, 1990). In sport, this would be a review of the current technology that is available to sport organizations in the management of human resources. For example, something as simple as strategically using an organization's Twitter account to recruit participants from a larger pool of individuals may fall under this factor of technological context. Moreover, an informed HR manager will start to navigate the utility of software platforms such as ADP©, UKG©, and SAP ©, to name a few. By reviewing the technological context, change toward e-HRM may be less overwhelming as the use of existing resources is emphasized and efficient interfaces are presented.

Organizational context highlights the structure of the organization and the availability of processes to apply the technology. For example, in sport, the nature and frequency of communication internally and externally, types of human resources (e.g., volunteers, employees, interns), size of the organization, financial capital, and organizational capital (Taylor, 2016) frame the organizational context that would impact the adoption and maintenance of e-HRM practices (DePietro et al., 1990; Tornatzky & Fleischer, 1990). Moore and Levermore (2012) emphasize the need to critically review the size of the organization (through its human resources and financial resources) when exploring the capacity to engage in new and strategic practices. Further, Taylor's (2016) assessment of the lack of SHRM in sport underscores the notion that the organizational context may be the most challenging in a move toward e-HRM.

Finally, *environmental context* clarifies the ecological conditions that are available for a sport organization to innovate and be strategic within e-HRM. As an example, the structure of the sport system, government regulations, and government funding are all environmental context factors that would influence e-HRM within TOE theory (DePietro et al., 1990). With this wholistic TOE theoretical frame in mind, a discussion of e-HRM in organizations is presented to outline the benefits and strategies linked to this process of seeing technology, the organization, and the environment as an interrelated system.

e-HRM in Organizations

The Positive Influence of e-HRM

Given the reluctance to change (Taylor, 2016), sport managers may be asking why they need to adopt e-HRM practices in a context where traditional HRM practices have worked well. The first response to such a question revolves around the need to be strategic. Within HRM, no matter the context, human resources can be leveraged to create a competitive advantage (Kerwin, 2015). Given TOE theory, understanding the environment around an organization is essential to creating this competitive advantage. As noted by Armstrong (2006), there are many benefits of e-HRM that connect the external environment to internal goals. Specifically, the implementation of e-HRM enables the improvement of activities and processes from the HRM domain by achieving the following goals (from Armstrong, 2006):

- Improving the quality of information available to make decisions,
- Reducing the administrative burden on the HR department by keeping systems within databases,
- Improving the speed at which information is available,
- Improving the flexibility of information to support business planning,
- Improving services to employees,
- Producing HR metrics such as performance indicators,
- Aiding human capital reporting,
- Improving productivity,
- Reducing operational costs, and
- Managing people's working time more effectively.

Regarding *improvement of services to employees* listed above, in sport, this is particularly relevant to nonprofit organizations or small for-profit entities that operate on limited budgets. The use of e-HRM could reduce operational costs around onboarding and provide a systemic process that ensures each new paid-staff member or volunteer board member receives the same information entering their position. The lead time to set up videos and information pieces can be put into place in the front end, while most time can then be spent to ensure new individuals feel adequately resourced and welcomed. This would improve the quality of information available and the speed at which individuals can receive information (e.g., they don't have to wait for an appropriate time to meet with current volunteer board members or administrative staff for knowledge translation and transfer). Instead, the technological capability is available to record information and send it to staff and volunteers, and the organization has the knowledge pieces on hand (e.g., board member handbook) that can easily be shared online. The application of TOE emphasizes how e-HRM can be contextually relevant for sport managers.

Each factor in the above list emphasizes the utility of e-HRM, however, *aiding in the reporting of human capital* has become increasingly important. Specifically, there has been a push for sport managers to be more socially aware of the decisions they are making. As an example, the #MeToo and Black Lives Matter movements have made managers more aware of how their decisions are impacting marginalized groups (e.g., Agyemang & Singer, 2014; Hindman & Walker, 2020). In particular, the recruiting, hiring, and treatment processes of marginalized individuals have come under the microscope. For sport managers who think strategically and thoughtfully, the environment can prompt this look toward which technologies and current organizational resources can be used to increase the information available regarding those they recruit and hire, as well as aid in the effective reporting of their human capital context. These new e-processes may cause managers who are forward-thinking and strategic to pause and either enhance current HRM practices or change less inclusive practices.

The outcomes associated with e-HRM are strategic and link to the goals of an organization. Within TOE, a sport manager would look to leverage their current resources in a way to harness technology that is most effective for their organization. The change associated with these processes certainly requires thought but may not be as daunting as some may think.

What Does e-HRM Look Like?

Given the positive outcomes and link to TOE theory, sport managers may be convinced that e-HRM is the best strategy for their sport organization; however, the next step is operationalizing e-HRM into current policy and practice. As such, sport managers may be asking, what does e-HRM look like? As an example, within the sport industry, many organizations are striving to move forward with plans for gender equity and inclusion (Cooper et al., 2020; Jeanes et al., 2021). In order to recruit more females and underrepresented individuals into positions, it is important to have a thoughtful and comprehensive recruitment plan; e-HRM can help with process planning regarding linking recruitment to overall organizational strategy. Online tools such as ADP©, UKG©, and InitLive© can help support classic recruitment strategies and supplement the use of online recruitment through websites and social networks. Implementing search tool parameters around target groups that may help facilitate a wider network of candidates (e.g., Canadian Women & Sport, Indigenous social networks), and software platforms such as UKG© allow managers to track language used within recruiting and selection practices.

The complexity of these processes relates to a new sport world where employees, customers, and suppliers are working side-by-side (virtually) in a digital ecosystem. Within this new space, concepts such as radio frequency identification (RFID), cloud computing, artificial intelligence, decision-making/supporting systems, and big data mining are used to outline the interconnectivity of e-HRM processes (Wang et al., 2017). These advanced ecosystems connect stakeholders and allow for shared value, but they must be managed effectively to ensure that practices match organizational objectives.

The following section details the elements of HRM that have been linked to e-HRM processes. Specifically, the section starts with Table 2.1 which provides a description of common HRM practices, the function of e-HRM, and a description of what the practice would look like in sport. It is important to recognize that each of these practices should be considered within the larger digital ecosystem as a way of connecting the technology to the organization and the environment (TOE theory).

As described by Rahman et al. (2018), there are many factors that influence the implementation of e-HRM. Therefore, the functions of e-HRM listed in Table 2.1 must be thoughtfully considered before adopted within a sport organization. As an example, e-Recruitment is defined as using online technology to recruit, assess, interview, and hire personnel (Dhamija, 2012). From the TOE perspective, the organization must have the human capacity to understand the various online (e.g., Indeed, Monster) and social media channels (e.g., LinkedIn, Twitter) that may appropriately target individuals from wider pools of applicants. Second, the software (i.e., technology) used to store and organize the information garnered from an online search must be accessible to sport managers. When looking through the various options (e.g., ADP©, SAP©, UKG©), a sport manager must under which capabilities matter most to the organization (e.g., interface between departments, data input points, tracking, monitoring, etc.). And, finally, the environment around the sport organization must be attuned to the platforms that the sport manger(s) are using to recruit individuals. For instance, if a sport organization is recruiting employees from rural or Indigenous communities, the type of social networking site used to target members of the community must be thoughtfully chosen as relevant to those communities. The factors of the technology available, the organizational capacity, and the environment for which the e-HRM process is serving must always be considered.

Further, within e-Recruitment is e-Selection, which outlines that online selection systems are important because the system can link job description requirements to an individual's personal qualifications (Parry, 2011). This allows a sport manager to assess an incumbent's

Table 2.1 Functions of e-HRM in Sport Practice

HRM	e-HRM	Sport Example
Administrative support	• Basic record of employees including presence, absence, earnings, etc. • Database management, attendance systems, workday, etc.	When managing a large-scale sport event with thousands of volunteers, e-HRM allows sport managers to adopt an online system to schedule, track, and record volunteer hours and absences. This makes it efficient when schedule changes inevitably occur.
HR planning	• Statistical analysis of fluctuations in labor force • Trend analysis software and simulation models.	A professional sport organization may use a program like SAS to track performance of coaches when looking to hire the most effective coach for their team.
Job analysis	• Management of business job descriptions and analysis of organizational structure • Documentation of results of job analysis, and visualization of existing and planned organizational structures	Nonprofit sport organizations may use job analysis software to collect data that identifies all tasks performed by individuals as well as desired performance. This information is then stored and matched against the organizational mission and values, policies, and systems to then be flagged for update as needed.
Recruitment	• Process planning, documentation of recruitment implementation • Creating, registering, and managing data from advertisements, application forms, support for classical and online recruitment, use of social networks	All sport managers looking to diversify their workplace can use e-recruitment software to manage larger databases of potential employees. This data can be matched to pair candidates with mission and values, as well as assess fit with specific organizational parameters.

(*Continued*)

Table 2.1 (Continued)

HRM	e-HRM	Sport Example
Training and development	• Research in the educational and developmental needs of employees, planning of training programs, organization of training, and storage of teaching materials • Online questionnaires, analysis of development trends, data management, implementation of e-learning programs	Post COVID-19 pandemic, the training, and development of employees around the health and safety of members and consumers will be at the forefront of activities. E-training and development will allow these programs to be planned in line with organizational goals, and information to be stored to enhance organizational memory.
Individual performance management	• Performance Management • Documentation, analysis, feedback, trend analysis	As metrics and analytics become a key pillar of grant funding, for profit and nonprofit sport organizations must find efficient ways to monitor performance of key stakeholders. E-performance management provides databases for sport managers to document performance, analyze trends, provide feedback to individuals, and then summarize trend analyses that will be useful for grant funding reports.
Compensation	• Creation of salary structure, salary modeling, level of compensation analysis • Analysis, calculation based on internal and external information.	National sport organizations are nonprofit entities that work with limited budgets. Their mandates require paid staff, but they must be strategic in terms of budget for salaries. A compensation software would allow for salary modeling and long-term planning with regard to tenured positions versus contracts.

Source: From Gupta & Saxena (2013) and Berber et al. (2018).

ability to meet role requirements, elements which can be assessed through tests such as online, audio and video conferencing (Parry, 2011; Sanjeev & Makkar, 2014). Further, a software program link SAP© allows managers to track and review inclusive language within materials used for hiring and selection. The process of e-Recruitment and e-Selection becomes strategically relevant as an individual who enters an organization through these systems can then be tracked to determine performance metrics – as they relate to job descriptions – as well as contribute to the trend analysis of the company's strategic plan. e-Compensation plans can then be embedded into the performance management system that links each of these processes in a thoughtful and analytic manner. Further, for sport organizations that are at the SME level and do not have a formal human resource manager, e-Compensation management provides a system to administer and track employee participation in benefits programs and reimbursement plans (Hendrickson, 2003). By adopting e-Compensation structures, managers within SMEs can track performance metrics and compare standards more efficiently for an individual and across individuals in an enterprise. Having performance statistics and comparable indices at a manager's fingertips enhances efficiency and ensures accuracy when determining the compensation that is allocated to individuals. Data-based, accurate decisions are directly linked to perceptions of fairness for employees and increased perceptions of fairness reduce negative forms of conflict (Kerwin et al., 2015). Therefore, sport managers can track participation in vital employee services such as health, dental, and life insurance, compensation, profit sharing, and retirement (if applicable) that can be monitored by managers or the volunteer board of directors (Hendrickson, 2003). This monitoring can lead to more efficient and effective decisions and workflow, which influence individual attitudes and behaviors. The ability to adopt these strategies is based on how sport managers strategically view their context and capacity.

Sport Industry Trends

As indicated by Naraine and Parent (2017), organizational sustainability and strategic planning must be linked to advances in technology. Sport organizations must stay connected to industry trends to maintain a competitive advantage and strategically align with progressive visions. Further, the global COVID-19 pandemic has emphasized the need to maintain technologically relevant platforms, where the in-person connection is not available or safe. Given the need to embrace technology to stay relevant and viable, there are many ways sport managers can use TOE theory to consider (1) the technology available, (2) their organization and its capacity for e-HRM, and (3) the environmental factors around them to influence the strategy, goal setting, and focus of e-HRM. The next section outlines four contexts that represent the benefit of e-HRM within the TOE framework in sport.

Recruitment of Diverse Populations – The Context

It is widely recognized that sport organizations possess a relatively homogenous group of human resources (Chelladurai & Kerwin, 2017; Fink, 2008; Melton & Bryant, 2017). While organizations like the NBA and NASCAR have recently taken steps to improve inclusive policy, there are still large gaps to be filled in executive, leadership, coaching, and official positions within the industry. This lack of diversity suggests that the recruitment of employees, volunteers, and interns would benefit from a more strategic and thoughtful approach. Within each sport organization, there are resources that could be placed toward the recruitment of a wider population of individuals. From a human resource management perspective, something as simple as the wording of job postings can be inherently limiting and therefore could ultimately cut off perspective candidates before they even apply (Whisenant et al., 2005). Therefore, it becomes increasingly relevant to monitor the nature of job recruitment within an organization to ensure that each piece of the recruitment puzzle is inclusive. The very nature of e-Recruitment enhances inclusivity by casting a wider net. As we move toward a policy that requires sport organizations to enhance diversity, it is important to consider the technology that would be available to reach more individuals from diverse populations.

The e-HRM Case: Strategically Targeting Diversity, Equity, and Inclusion

The issue (environment and organization): The government of Canada, and Sport Canada specifically, has made a call to sport organizations to be more diverse in terms of those who comprise their staff and volunteer boards of directors. Many executive directors and CEOs of nonprofit sport organizations have critically reviewed their employee and volunteer databases to find that their current HRM policy and practice for recruiting are done without the use of technology. Further, the postings typically involve word of mouth solicitation and dated modes of posting jobs on job boards. These leaders need to recognize that the traditional methods of recruitment may be limiting the number of individuals the job postings are reaching and may be missing large groups of individuals.

The solution (technology): Boards of directors should consider the use of software platforms (e.g., ADP©, SAP©, UKG©, Workday©) that help automate time-consuming tasks and provide tailored guidance that connects protocols from recruitment to selection, hiring and onboarding. This includes the strategic implementation of policy that specifies diversity management protocol through these software systems. As an example, ADP© provides the opportunity to connect to stakeholders within their digital ecosystem to link recruitment to strategic goals and priorities outlined by members, the board of directors, and others. This way leaders can have metrics and information about recruits at their fingertips when making decisions about recruitment and selection.

The result: Sport organizations can increase their recruitment pools of candidates using unique demographic touchpoints that reflect broader strategic goals.

Training and Scheduling Volunteers and Staff – The Context

The impact of the COVID-19 pandemic has shown sport managers they must be nimble in how they deliver HRM practices. In particular, when training and scheduling volunteers and part-time staff, it is important to recognize what organizational aspects are most crucial to the process (policy, resources, individuals) and which technologies will best suit the outcome that is desired (i.e., effective training of volunteers to engage in program development; scheduling volunteers and part-time staff to set up and deliver an event). With a crisis in the ability to interact face-to-face, it becomes increasingly important that sport managers understand the organization and available technologies (Doherty et al., 2020). As noted by Doherty et al. (2020), nonprofit sport organizations that rely on volunteers and part-time staff must embrace new technology in order to manage HRM processes through shutdowns. This is especially important in a post-pandemic landscape where nonprofit sport managers are struggling to stay relevant and connect with stakeholders. With technology in place, a sport organization can create systems that link training and scheduling to HR development. This link allows for system tracking of where gaps exist in expertise/skill and provides opportunities for gaps to be filled immediately to ensure that services are not stalled for sport members.

The e-HRM case: Sport organizations must manage personnel in virtual spaces

The issue (environment and organization): Following the global pandemic associated with COVID-19, there has been a reduction of the number of individuals who can safely engage in onsite live events. Therefore, sport organizations that host large events or manage large groups of part time staff must be flexible in how they train and manage individuals to be involved in the operations (course/arena/stadium set up and take down) of events and championships. Therefore, online training and scheduling becomes an essential element in effective management of volunteers.

The solution (technology): Leaders within the sport space can use a combination of InitLive© and ADP© or consider SAP© to first onboard and train volunteers or part time staff through InitLive©, and then strategically manage scheduling (e.g., ADP©, SAP©). The use of online software platforms such as InitLive© allows managers to attach performance metrics to job descriptions and track when and how well personnel perform within the training protocol. Videos and training manuals can be added to the system and shared on various platforms to ensure accessibility to all individuals. Big data analytics can also be used to track and model the use of time to ensure that efficient scheduling is linked to championship operations. Furthermore, software such as ADP© and SAP© tracks part time staff and volunteer time and attendance. Online hours tracking is particularly helpful when volunteers or part time staff need to post shift change requests and request movements from shift to shift.

The result: Part time staff and volunteers are trained and prepared for their roles without face-to-face content, therefore reducing any health risks that may come with large groups for orientation and/or training protocol. In addition, managers can track and maintain hours and scheduling data that can be used to create efficiency within HRM models within future event planning.

Living in an Evidence-Based Sport Industry – The Context

Sport organizations are functioning in a world that is performance-based and reliant on the ability of sport managers to track and report a variety of performance indices. From a business analytics standpoint, the ability to forecast and strategically manage human resources is a skill that will separate thriving organizations from those who simply fall behind (Wang & Cotton, 2018). It is important for sport managers to consider how they are tracking the performance of their human resources both on and off the field. On the field of play, there are scouts and statisticians who track any and all data points of play (cf. Fried & Mumcu, 2016); however, new information is being used to track the performance of our sport employees in the boardroom (e.g., Trolio et al., 2016). Therefore, in order to gain a competitive advantage, tracking performance has become an essential element to SHRM and e-HRM practices.

The e-HRM case: Evidence-based compensation and performance management

The issue (environment and organization): Sport leaders and managers are expecting performance management systems that allow for the communication of goals from the strategic plan to individual, frontline employees. Leaders recognize that the alignment of organizational and individual goals is essential in ensuring employees understand their roles within an organization and are engaged in shared responsibility toward meeting these goals to deliver superior service to their fans. Progressive leaders must understand that performance management will start with selection and training of high-quality employees and needs to be a part of an overall e-HRM system. As an example, within UKG software©, corporate, department and individual goals are explicitly tied to metrics that can be tracked through online portals. In real time, employees can input their indicators and managers can track performance standards on a variety of criteria. Moreover, SAP© and other software platforms allow managers to engage in 360-degree feedback where cross communication can occur with various departments and reports can be generated that link specific outcome indicators. These metrics are posted in historical data where performance appraisal meetings are directly linked to accurate, up to date, and comprehensive data points (e.g., UKG©, SAP©).

The solution (technology): Efficiency and customer service are organizational goals that represent the values of most sport organizations. The use of performance management systems associated with software like ADP©, UKG©, SAP©, and otherwise, interface to incorporate organizational goals into performance appraisals (PA) processes for employees. Implementing these goals into the PA e-HRM system ensures evaluations that measure employees consistently on items related to organizational strategy. Relatedly, by using e-performance management systems, strategic goals are communicated across the organization, employees understand business objectives, and everyone is committed to their own specific and measurable goals associated with larger organizational objectives.

The result: Upper management and employees see the performance measures and the link to organizational strategy when they log into the e-HRM system. Performance metrics can be tracked daily and are linked to training requirements and compensation packages.

Working on the Road: Reimbursement Systems – The Context

Sport employees often find themselves on the road or working from home offices (Chelladurai & Kerwin, 2017). When working with events or sport programs, sport managers may have to travel to be onsite or work from physical spaces that do not always have the equipment or supplies of the main office space (e.g., working from the operations trailer at the US Open tennis championship). Within this job design, employees may encounter business expenses that by policy must be reimbursed. As such, the compensation and reimbursement system of sport organizations becomes extremely important to ensuring that employees are not "out of pocket" for business-related expenses (e.g., printer paper, internet connection, office supplies). Traditional systems that rely on tracking expenses through pencil and paper reporting take time and are less efficient in the management of employee compensation. Thus, it is important for sport managers to scan their environment to uncover technology that may help their reimbursement and compensation system.

The e-HRM case: Efficient and effective reimbursement systems

The issue (environment and organization): Employees in sport and event management are constantly on the road or working from home office spaces. These work from home spaces are increasingly more common in our post-pandemic context. The need to be agile and available requires that workspaces are fluent and the ability to travel is always a priority. In this context, online expense tracking systems need to be adopted that provide a virtual place for employees to upload and record their expense transactions in real time. The expenses need to be simultaneously cross-listed and verified by their accounting department back at the head office, no matter where globally they reside.

The solution (technology): Leaders can use e-HRM software like MetaViewer© that offers expense tracking systems that can be linked to employee-based credit cards. Further, from a SHRM perspective, the employee compensation system could also be linked to a performance appraisal and monitoring system that are tied to organizational goals.

The result: Sport organizations can link workflow within one department (finance) to other departments (e.g., operations) that require efficiency in their budgeting and reimbursement policy. Specifically, adopting a program like MetaViewer© allows for seamless movement on the payment of reimbursement to employees and the documentation of expenses within organizational balance sheets.

e-HRM in Sport: The Move Forward

As e-HRM practices are adopted within sport organizations, it is important to be mindful of evaluating their effectiveness within HRM systems. For example, sport managers must start to see the role of e-HRM from micro-, meso-, and macro-level perspectives. This intuitively creates a broader understanding of the digital ecosystem that should be managed. First, from a micro perspective, the influence of e-HRM on the performance, motivation, satisfaction, and commitment of employees, volunteers, and interns should be a topic of interest moving forward. In the example cases above, volunteers are now tasked with running through e-training modules. From an empirical perspective, it is important to ask if e-training is relevant to the individual volunteer. Was the platform accessible? Did the training meet the needs of the managers who monitored the volunteers? Further, it is important to explore if the components of a digital platform are contributing to a larger and more effective digital ecosystem. The benefit of TOE theory is that it provides a framework to determine the effectiveness of an ecosystem through the principles of technology-organization-environment.

Evaluating the effectiveness of e-HRM will be an essential element of understanding the theoretical relevance of these processes in our sport organizations. These are valuable questions that should target an assessment of the role of e-HRM within sport and contexts where human resource management may include unique strategic outcomes (e.g., for profit versus nonprofit, recreational sport versus elite sport, rural versus urban committees) and unique populations of human resources (e.g., more volunteers than paid staff, homogenous groups versus heterogeneous groups).

From the meso-level, for organizations in small, medium, and large enterprises, it is important to dissect which technologies are best suited for varying levels of human and financial capacity. It is also relevant to ask; which technologies require more "know-how"? Does financial cost of an e-HRM platform impact the effectiveness of its implementation? Alternatively, we may ask how the e-HRM system(s) that are adopted coordinate with an organization's mission, vision, and values? In the context examples above, sport organizations must adopt new recruiting systems to ensure they are reaching out to a more diverse pool of applicants. Does this e-HRM strategy align with the organization's strategic plan? How are policy statements connected with the e-Recruitment strategy? There are claims that e-HRM allows managers more time to think of strategy and strategic functioning. It is, therefore, relevant to explore if strategic outcomes are realized in contexts where e-HRM is put into practice.

From the macro-level, within the TOE framework, the environment around an organization will influence if and how technology is adopted. Therefore, as we move forward, we must ask, what environmental factors impact technology and the organization when adopting e-HRM systems? How do external pressures to be nimble dictate the e-HRM practices that are put into place? Are there political influences on how and when e-HRM practices are adopted? What are the legal and privacy issues attached to creating online databases and tracking systems? How has the COVID-19 pandemic influenced the presence of e-HRM in sport? When considering the external environment related to e-HRM, the social, political, economic, and legal landscape must contribute to an understanding of the agency of society that is an imperative within SHRM practice (Chelladurai & Kerwin, 2017). The digital ecosystem relies on the interface of e-HRM practices to be effective in serving larger organizational goals.

Conclusion

As sport managers navigate a complex and evolving sport industry, e-HRM technologies that are adopted must be meaningful within the environment and to the organization. Therefore, we must explore the organizational and technology aspects of e-HRM that are relevant for SME and large sport enterprises. In particular, we understand that organizational capacity is an issue within SMEs within sport and that human resources are a vital component of the organizational capacity process (e.g., Doherty et al., 2014; Doherty & Cuskelly, 2019; Millar & Doherty, 2016). However, researchers must engage in the sport context to determine how e-HRM and digital technology can contribute to the development of capacity in our SMEs. The use of digital technology in our larger sport enterprises (e.g., San Jose Sharks, San Antonio Spurs, the Canadian Football League) points to contexts where the use of e-HRM platforms and tools has enabled more efficient HRM practices. Applying the theoretical lens of TOE, researchers can investigate the digital technology used in large enterprises, to then explore the organization and environment characteristics of SMEs to determine which technologies would be most influential when considering the capacity in these enterprises. It is clear there are numerous software platforms that can assist sport managers in making their HRM processes more efficient and contribute to effective workflow. When exploring the adoption of a specific platform, organizational goals and needs must be assessed. It is important that the micro-level processes are connected to meso- (organizational) level needs. For example, which functions need to be accounted for in the platform? As an example, if a sport manager works with a large group of part-time staff who require flexibility in scheduling, UKG© or SAP© may be the most effective platforms to engage in because of their functionality related to swapping shifts, requesting shifts, and creating wait lists for shifts within the part-time workers' schedules.

From a research perspective, we must answer the call to engage in a critical review of human resource management practice. Wicker (2017) outlined the need to explore multi-level factors that influence volunteer management in sport. Future research application of TOE, as outlined in this chapter, provides a transformational perspective of the management of volunteers in sport in that technology could be used to track, capture, and manage the recruitment, training, and retention of this vital pool of human resources. For SMEs who must manage large groups of volunteers to run effective programs and events, the adoption of digital technology must be explored and evaluated to ensure strategic priorities around training. Specifically, Cuskelly et al. (2020) outlined that traditional modes of training in the event context prioritized a short-term goal of filling volunteer positions rather than addressing long-term strategic goals. Therefore, the exploration of digital technology in these contexts can provide a valuable framework to address the call for more strategic HRM processes (Taylor, 2016). Future research must respect the varying capacity issues that occur within sport enterprises and apply a TOE framework to determine the most effective digital technologies, in context.

It is also important to examine training that occurs when online software platforms are adopted. This is vital in sport organizations where human resource capacity for such innovations is low. Therefore, intersecting research that relates e-HRM with capacity becomes increasingly relevant. And finally, contemporary sport management research must explore the role of e-HRM in creating processes that contribute to our strategic human resource management functioning. E-HRM must be deemed essential (not optional) as we move through and into a post-pandemic sport system.

Acknowledgment

I would like to acknowledge Tracey Villeneuve HR Business Partner, Ottawa Sports and Entertainment Group. Her knowledge and expertise in this space helped shape the practical examples provided here.

References

Agyemang, K. J., & Singer, J. N. (2014). Race in the present day: NBA employees sound off on race and racism. *Journal of African American Studies, 18*(1), 11–32.

Armstrong, M. (2006). *A handbook of human resource management practice.* Kogan Page.

Bach, S., & Edwards, M. R. (2013). *Managing human resources* (5th ed.). Wiley.

Berber, N., Đorđević, B., & Milanović, S. (2018). Electronic human resource management (e-HRM): A new concept for digital age. Strategic Management. *23*(2), 22–23.

Chelladurai, P., & Kerwin, S. (2017). *Human resource management in sport and recreation.* (3rd ed.). Human Kinetics.

Cooper, J. N., Newton, A. C., Klein, M., & Jolly, S. (2020). A call for culturally responsive transformational leadership in college sport: An anti-ism approach for achieving equity and inclusion. *Frontiers in Sociology, 5*, 65.

Cuskelly, G., Fredline, L., Kim, E., Barry, S., & Kappelides, P. (2020). Volunteer selection at a major sport event: A strategic human resource management approach. *Sport Management Review*, ahead of press. 10.1016/j.smr.2020.02.002

Dhamija, P. (2012). E-recruitment: a roadmap towards e-human resource management. *Researchers World, 3*, 33–39.

DePietro, R., Wiarda, E., & Fleischer, M. (1990). The context for change: organization, technology and environment. In L. G. Tornatzky and M. Fleischer (Eds.), *The process of technological innovation* (pp. 151–175). Lexington Books.

Doherty, A., & Cuskelly, G. (2019). Organizational capacity and performance of community sport clubs. *Journal of Sport Management, 34*(3), 240–259.

Doherty, A., Millar, P., & Misener, K. (2020). Return to community sport: leaning on evidence in turbulent times. *Managing Sport and Leisure*, ahead of press. 10.1080/23750472.2020.1794940

Doherty, A., Misener, K., & Cuskelly, G. (2014). Toward a multidimensional framework of capacity in community sport clubs. *Nonprofit and voluntary sector quarterly, 43*(2_suppl), 124S–142S.

Dossena, C., & Mochi, F. (2020). Organizational capabilities for social media management: How restaurant managers approach to the digital ecosystem. In R. Agrifoglio, R. Lamboglia, D. Mancini, & F. Ricciardi, *Digital Business Transformation* (pp. 269–284). Springer.

Fink, J. S. (2008). Gender and sex diversity in sport organizations: Concluding comments. *Sex Roles, 58*(1-2), 146–147.

Fried, G., & Mumcu, C. (Eds.). (2016). *Sport analytics: A data-driven approach to sport business and management*. Routledge.

Gupta, A., & Saxena, S. (2013). Electronic human resource management (e-HRM): Growing role in organisations. *Management Insight, 8*, 60–66.

Hendrickson, A. (2003). Human resource information systems: Backbone technology for contemporary human resources. *Journal of Labor Research, 24*, 381–394.

Hindman, L. C., & Walker, N. A. (2020). Sexism in professional sports: How women managers experience and survive sport organizational culture. *Journal of Sport Management, 34*(1), 64–76.

Hoeber, L., Doherty, A., Hoeber, O., & Wolfe, R. (2015). The nature of innovation in community sport organizations. *European Sport Management Quarterly, 15*, 518–534.

Jeanes, R., Spaaij, R., Farquharson, K., McGrath, G., Magee, J., Lusher, D., & Gorman, S. (2021). Gender relations, gender equity, and community sports spaces. *Journal of Sport and Social Issues, 45*(6), 545–567.

Kerwin, S. (2015). Human resource management in sport. In T. Byers (ed.). *Contemporary issues in sport: An introduction* (pp. 135–148). Sage.

Kerwin, S., Jordan, J. S., & Turner, B. A. (2015). Organizational justice and conflict: Do perceptions of fairness influence disagreement? *Sport Management Review, 18*(3), 384–395.

MacLean, J. (2016). Performance management. In R. Hoye & M. Parent (Eds.), *The SAGE handbook of sport management* (pp. 160–180). SAGE.

Melton, E. N., & Bryant, M. J. (2017). Intersectionality: The impact of negotiating multiple identities for women in sport leadership. *Women in Sport Leadership: Research and Practice for Change*, 62–82.

Millar, P., & Doherty, A. (2016). Capacity building in nonprofit sport organizations: Development of a process model. *Sport Management Review, 19*(4), 365–377.

Moore, N., & Levermore, R. (2012). English professional football clubs: Can business parameters of small and medium-sized enterprises be applied? *Sport, Business and Management: An International Journal, 2*, 196–209.

Naraine, M. L., & Parent, M. M. (2017). This is how we do it: A qualitative approach to national sport organizations' social-media implementation. *International Journal of Sport Communication, 10*(2), 196–217.

Parent, M. M., Naraine, M. L., & Hoye, R. (2018). A new era for governance structures and processes in Canadian national sport organizations. *Journal of sport management, 32*(6), 555–566.

Parry, E. (2011). An examination of e-HRM as a means to increase the value of the HR function. *The International Journal of Human Resource Management, 22*, 1146–1162.

Rahman, M., Mordi, C., & Nwagbara, U. (2018). Factors influencing E-HRM implementation in government organisations. *Journal of Enterprise Information Management, 47*, 247–275.

Sanjeev, R., & Makkar, D. (2014). Determining employees' perception through effective HRIS: An empirical study. *Journal of Strategic Human Resource Management, 3*, 135–147.

Taylor, T. (2016). Human resource management. In R. Hoye and M. Parent (Eds.), *The SAGE handbook of sport management* (pp. 62–79). SAGE.

Taylor, T., & McGraw, P. (2006). Exploring human resource management practices in nonprofit sport organisations. *Sport Management Review, 9*, 229–251.

Tornatzky, L. G., & Fleischer, M. (1990). *The process of technology innovation*. Lexington Books.

Troilo, M., Bouchet, A., Urban, T. L., & Sutton, W. A. (2016). Perception, reality, and the adoption of business analytics: Evidence from North American professional sport organizations. *Omega, 59*, 72–83.

Vardarlier, P. (2020). Digital transformation of human resource management: Digital applications and strategic tools in HRM. In U. Hacioglu (Ed.). *Digital Business Strategies in Blockchain Ecosystems* (pp. 239–264). Springer.

Wang, L., & Cotton, R. (2018). Beyond *Moneyball* to social capital inside and out: The value of differentiated workforce experience ties to performance. *Human Resource Management, 57*, 761– 780.

Wang, Y., Ma, H. S., Yang, J. H., & Wang, K. S. (2017). Industry 4.0: A way from mass customization to mass personalization production. *Advanced Manufacturing, 5*, 311–320.

Welbourne, T. M. (2010). New media: Opportunity or curse for HR? *Human Resource Management, 49*, 1–3.

Whisenant, W., Miller, J., & Pedersen, P. M. (2005). Systemic barriers in athletic administration: An analysis of job descriptions for interscholastic athletic directors. *Sex Roles, 53*, 911–918.

Wicker, P. (2017). Volunteerism and volunteer management in sport. *Sport Management Review, 20*(4), 325–337.

3
Virtual Volunteering

Erik L. Lachance and Graham Cuskelly

Introduction

Digital technology, refers to the use of electronic means such as systems, devices, platforms, and/or resources for the creating, processing, or storing of data and completion of tasks (Price et al., 2013; Strader, 2011), is omnipresent in contemporary society and institutions. Whether it is completing work from a personal computer using various software application suites (e.g., Microsoft Office, Adobe Creative Cloud) at the office, the unprecedented changes in the workplace and organizational operations due to the COVID-19 pandemic (e.g., restricted to virtual meetings through various internet-based platforms such as Zoom, Cisco Webex, and Microsoft Teams), or human's evolution toward the need for engagement and communication through technological means (e.g., social media platforms like Twitter and Instagram), digital technology's prominence is ever-present and in constant development in contemporary times. Such prominence and trends in the external environment of organizations (e.g., usage of internet and/or internet-based applications or platforms by stakeholders) have created an influence and pressure to harness digital technology as they operate in the so-called digital age (e.g., Fitzgerald et al., 2013; Price et al., 2013). Whether small or large, public, non-profit, or for-profit, organizations have been unable to ignore the rise of digital technology (Cravens & Ellis, 2014; Daft, 2021; Fitzgerald et al., 2013). For instance, Starbucks, the multi-national coffeehouse conglomerate, added Wi-Fi and a digital landing page that contained free subscriptions to magazines in all stores in an effort to re-engage with customers after a poor performance in 2009 (Fitzgerald et al., 2013). Social media applications (e.g., Twitter, Facebook) have also been used by organizations to engage with, or improve relations with, customers or key stakeholders (Fitzgerald et al., 2013; Daft, 2021; Naraine, 2019; Naraine & Karg, 2019; Parent et al., 2020). As such, the importance of digital technology for organizations resides in its ability to enhance processes (e.g., information, data, communication), performance, and innovation (Fitzgerald et al., 2013; Daft, 2021).

While digital technology is well-discussed by practitioners and researchers in the broader management field (e.g., Fitzgerald et al., 2013; Isensee et al., 2020; Johnston, 2019; Kane et al., 2015; Li et al., 2020; Price et al., 2013; Strader, 2011; Saarikko et al., 2020), such discussions in the context of sport organizations and events have not been as fruitful. Despite less evidence,

DOI: 10.4324/9781003088899-5

organizations (e.g., Canada Soccer, 2020; Sport Information Resource Centre, 2019) and researchers (e.g., Diacin & VanSickle, 2014; Koronios et al., 2020; Naraine et al., 2020; Naraine et al., 2019a; Ratten, 2019, 2020a) have demonstrated the use of digital technology in sport organizations and events (e.g., Twitter; Naraine & Parent, 2016a, 2016b, 2017a, 2017b). To date, such digital technology has been researched among sport entrepreneurs (e.g., Ratten, 2019, 2020a; Ratten & Jones, 2020; Ratten & Thompson, 2020), sport consumers (e.g., Naraine et al., 2020; Naraine & Karg, 2019; Stadder & Naraine, 2020), social media platforms (e.g., Twitter, Instagram; Naraine, 2019; Pegoraro, 2010; Smith et al., 2019; Toffoletti et al., 2019), and from the perspective of human resources, namely lower-level paid-employees (e.g., Diacin & VanSickle, 2014).

Despite the importance of this research to identify the usage of various digital technology programs and platforms in sport, a crucial resource for the operations and survival of organizations and events has been overlooked in this regard: volunteers. Notably, compared to research from the broader literature on volunteering through virtual spaces and digital technology (e.g., Ackermann, 2019; Ackermann & Manatschal, 2018; Cox et al., 2018; Cox et al., 2019; Cravens, 2000, 2003, 2006; Cravens & Ellis, 2014; Ellis & Cravens, 2000; Harrison et al., 2004; Ihm, 2017; Mukherjee, 2010, 2011; Murray & Harrison, 2002, 2005; Liu et al., 2016; Silva et al., 2018), the sport and event volunteer literature has yet to empirically examine virtual volunteering in the context of sport organizations and events (cf. Lachance, 2020) despite two issues.

First, there has been a shift in the adoption and utilization of digital technology in sport organizations and events (e.g., data analytics software, information and communication technology, information processing software; Diacin & VanSickle, 2014; Hutchins & Rowe, 2013; Liebermann et al., 2002; Ratten, 2019, 2020a, 2020b). For instance, sport organizations have reported using digital technology programs to complete various tasks (Diacin & VanSickle, 2014). Further, many professional sport organizations have embraced the recent data analytics movement in Major League Baseball (otherwise known as Sabermetrics), which was pioneered by the Oakland Athletics at the beginning of this century and required complex quantitative calculations and analyses using computer technology to predict team and player performance (Lewis, 2004). Such application of digital technology has led to its basic principles being implemented by other professional sport teams inside and outside of baseball (Lewis, 2004; Gerrard, 2004). Despite these discussions on digital technology in sport organizations and events, its impact on volunteers – a vital source for operations and program delivery – is absent. Notably, this lack of research on the impact of digital technology in sport organizations and events on volunteers is somewhat surprising and troublesome considering that this human resource is ubiquitous and central to the survival of organizations and events (Chelladurai & Kerwin, 2018; Hallmann & Fairley, 2018; Hoye et al., 2020).

Second, a more recent discussion has focused on volunteering and the COVID-19 pandemic (e.g., Lachance, 2020), a circumstance that forced the temporary or permanent transitions of sport organization and event operations to virtual spaces due to government regulations or social distancing restrictions (e.g., Doherty et al., 2020; Ludvigsen & Hayton, 2020; Mastromartino et al., 2020; Sheptak & Menaker, 2020). Considering government regulations and social distancing regulations, COVID-19 has arguably forced sport organizations and events to become virtual, such as offering more programs and services online or holding meetings via video conferencing platforms for internal and external stakeholders. With this in mind, the rise in volunteering through virtual spaces is perhaps more relevant than ever for sport organizations and events because of the COVID-19 pandemic. For instance, considering that "[s]ocial distancing is the recommended course for containing virus spread. This may mean looking for volunteer opportunities that can be done virtually or remotely from your home" (Volunteer Canada, 2020, p. 1). Given the ability for individuals to partake in their chosen leisure activity away from others, the relevancy and benefit of virtual volunteering are becoming increasingly important as the majority of organizational and event operations continue to be confined to virtual spaces. More precisely, virtual volunteering may be the only viable option for civic participation and individuals to contribute to their communities, organizations, and events considering the unpredictability and uncertainty regarding the restrictions, the impact, and the length of the COVID-19 pandemic (Lachance, 2020). Despite these above claims and the relevancy of digital technology during the COVID-19 pandemic, however, empirical research on virtual volunteering in sport organizations and events is absent. Such an absence in empirical research is problematic considering the dependence on digital technology in sport organizations and events because of the COVID-19 pandemic in which their most central and vital resource – volunteers – ability to function in a traditional in-person manner has been inhibited; thus, illustrating an opportunity for a rise in virtual volunteering for sport organizations and events to continually operate (e.g., delivery programs and services) and survive (Lachance, 2020).

In an effort to advance the sport and event volunteer literature, the purpose of this chapter is to present and discuss past virtual volunteering research to suggest future research directions in the context of sport and event organizations. To do so, previous virtual volunteering research is presented and discussed according to conceptualization and trends in participation along with contexts, topics investigated, and main findings. Next, future research directions in the context of sport and event organizations based on the reviewed virtual volunteering research are suggested. Finally, a conclusion discusses the future of virtual volunteering in sport.

Virtual Volunteering Research: Processes and Trends

Since the inception of the World Wide Web, virtual volunteering has emerged as a popular variation to the traditional in-person activity (Cravens & Ellis, 2014; Liu et al., 2016). Specific to volunteering through virtual spaces, virtual volunteering is synonymous with other terms used in reference to this volunteer-type including online volunteering, cyber volunteers, e-volunteers, tele-volunteers, micro-volunteering, digital volunteers, remote volunteering, cyber service, internet-mediated service, tele-mentoring, e-mentoring, crowdsourcing, crowd casting, smart mob, distributed development, distributed thinking, micro-tasking, virtual teams, or virtual workforce (Cravens & Ellis, 2014; Hoye et al., 2020; Liu et al., 2016). Given the variety of terms associated with virtual volunteering, its definition has varied among scholars and practitioners. For instance, Volunteer Canada (2020, p. 2) defined virtual volunteering as "volunteering done online, via computers, tablets, or smartphones, usually off-site," while the United Nations Volunteer (2004) discussed it as "tasks completed, in whole or in part, by a person via the internet from a home, work, university, cybercafé or telecenter computer." Scholars have also provided varying definitions, such as Cravens' (2000, p. 121) conceptualization of virtual volunteering as "volunteers conduct their activities for agencies and clients over the internet, in whole or in part" or an activity that "involves completion of long- or short-term volunteer assignments off-site through the use of an internet-connected device" (Medina, 2018, p. 1). Others have associated virtual volunteering with activities completed through smartphones or social media applications (e.g., Paylor, 2012). A more recent definition, which encompasses many of the fundamental features iterated in the aforementioned definitions, was offered by Cravens and Ellis (2014, p. 1) where virtual volunteering is defined as "volunteering activities completed, in whole, or in part, using the internet and a home, school, telecenter, or work computer or other internet-connected devices."

Despite variations in definitions of virtual volunteering, unlike traditional in-person volunteering which occurs in formal settings (e.g., major sport events, community sport organizations), virtual volunteering is generally understood as a freely chosen activity in which (in)formal volunteer-related tasks are completed away from the organization or event through virtual spaces (e.g., internet, internet-connected devices, social media applications) without renumeration (Cravens, 2000; Cravens & Ellis, 2014; Liu et al., 2016; Murray & Harrison, 2005; Paylor, 2012; Volunteer Canada, 2020). While this fundamental distinction exists between these two types of volunteering, both are recognized as being a freely chosen activity occurring in a formal setting (i.e., organization or event) without financial renumeration (cf. Cnaan et al., 1996).

Given the variations in its definition, virtual volunteering is discussed according to different typologies (e.g., Ihm, 2017; Liu et al., 2016; Peña-Lopez, 2007). For instance, different types of virtual volunteering were attributed to four types (i.e., complete, traditional/virtual, virtual/traditional, fully traditional) based on two dimensions: how volunteers are recruited (i.e., online or traditional) and how volunteers completed tasks (i.e., online or traditional; Murray & Harrison, 2005). More precisely, complete virtual volunteers are those who are recruited through virtual means and completed their tasks virtually, while those who are recruited through traditional means but completed tasks virtually are traditional/virtual volunteers (Murray & Harrison, 2005). In contrast, virtual/traditional volunteers use virtual means to be recruited and performed their tasks in-person in comparison to fully traditional volunteers who do not use any virtual means to be recruited or perform tasks (Murray & Harrison, 2005).

Beyond the above examples, Ihm (2017) also developed a typology of virtual volunteering according to the organizations (i.e., number involved with), frequency (i.e., times per month), and longevity (i.e., number of years). This typology yielded three types of virtual volunteers: (a) low-level (i.e., participates in the smallest number of organizations, the fewest times per month, and for the shortest period of time), (b) medium-level (i.e., "individuals whose degree of online volunteering is at the middle level of the three types," p. 411), and (c) high-level (i.e., "active participants whose degree of online volunteering is the highest among the three types"; Ihm, 2017, p. 411). While these three types were empirically developed through a cluster analysis from data derived from a questionnaire of 816 volunteers from the United States, the highest number of virtual volunteers were found to be associated with the lower-level type, while the high-level type was found to have the smallest number of participants (Ihm, 2017).

More recently, Liu et al. (2016) discussed virtual volunteering according to four types: (a) online advocacy (i.e., campaigns to promote political change or human rights), (b) online assessment and consultancy (i.e., providing specific knowledge or expertise), (c) online-offline volunteers (i.e., combination of completing volunteer tasks in-person and through virtual spaces), and (d) pure online volunteering (i.e., completing volunteer tasks entirely through virtual spaces; Liu et al., 2016; Peña-Lopez, 2007).

Given the focus of this chapter on volunteering uniquely through virtual spaces, the pure online volunteering type is used to present previous research as it better reflects the intended nature and fundamental basis of virtual volunteering. However, it is important to note that previous research has indicated that volunteers combine both traditional in-person volunteering and virtual volunteering to complete tasks (e.g., Ackermann, 2019; Cravens & Ellis, 2014; Ellis & Cravens, 2000; Ihm, 2017; Liu et al., 2016; Murray & Harrison, 2002, 2005; United Nations Volunteer, 2004).

Virtual Volunteering: Participation Trends, Demographics, and Roles

In general, it is challenging to find research and information on the global or country-specific participation rates of virtual volunteering in comparison to the amount of data available for traditional in-person volunteering (cf. Australian Bureau of Statistics, 2015; McGregor-Lowndes et al., 2017; National Council for Voluntary Organisations, 2018; UK Office for National Statistics, 2017; UN Volunteers, 2011, 2018; Statistics Canada, 2015; Vezina & Crompton, 2012;

Volunteer Canada, 2015; Volunteering Australia, 2016). However, data from Volunteering Australia (2016) has indicated that 44% of the general volunteer population participated in some form of virtual volunteering in the past year (i.e., pre-COVID-19 pandemic), while an additional 19% showed interest in pursuing virtual volunteering opportunities. Nevertheless, virtual volunteering began more than 30 years ago with the inception of the World Wide Web (Cravens & Ellis, 2014; Liu et al., 2016) in comparison to traditional in-person volunteering, which has been arguably practiced for centuries (e.g., Ellis & Campbell, 2005; Sills, 1957; Smith & Freedman, 1972; Warburton & Oppenheimer, 2000). Virtual volunteering is practiced more by males and individuals aged between 20 and 30 years (Liu et al., 2016). Further, virtual volunteers have been found to spend more time on their tasks, but have limited experiences before participating in comparison to traditional in-person volunteers (Liu et al., 2016). The majority of virtual volunteers have been found in developed countries given their reliance on completing tasks through virtual spaces, which requires access to the internet and/or internet-based devices or applications (Cravens, 2003; Liu et al., 2016; UN Online Volunteering Service, 2004).

While these are general trends, other scholars have demonstrated that virtual volunteering is practiced among other groups, such as individuals with time issues (e.g., parents), older adults, or individuals with disabilities (e.g., Cravens & Ellis, 2014; Ellis & Cravens, 2000; Liu et al., 2016; Mukherjee, 2010, 2011; Murray & Harrison, 2002, 2005). Despite assumptions that older adults are less knowledgeable about technology and prefer traditional in-person volunteering, various physical, physiological, or personal constraints, such as family, transportation, or mobility, are not present in virtual volunteering (Cravens & Ellis, 2014; Ellis & Cravens, 2000; Hoye et al., 2020; Murray & Harrison, 2002, 2005; Liu et al., 2016). For instance, individuals are not required to travel to a specific location to volunteer considering they can complete their assigned tasks remotely from home. As such, individuals with transportation or physical constraints can more easily partake in an activity like virtual volunteering. Such features within virtual volunteering make it "suitable for those who may be restricted from participating in traditional volunteering activities due to mobility issues" (Hoye et al., 2020, p. 13). Virtual volunteering also allows for individuals to partake in their freely chosen activity with greater flexibility in terms of time and location (Cravens & Ellis, 2014; Ellis & Cravens, 2000; Hoye et al., 2020; Murray & Harrison, 2002, 2005; Liu et al., 2016). For instance, assigned tasks can be completed at a variety of locations (e.g., from an individual's home, on public transit) and at any time (Cravens & Ellis, 2014; Murray & Harrison, 2002, 2005; Liu et al., 2016), rather than being completed at an assigned location (e.g., organization headquarters, event location) at a specified time period. Thus, considering "the ubiquitous nature of the internet, combined with increasingly time-poor lifestyles, it is little wonder that individuals choose to contribute" as volunteers through virtual spaces (Hoye et al., 2020, p. 12).

Despite the above trends, scholars have advocated that virtual volunteering is practiced by a diverse array of individuals in terms of gender, age, skills, and experiences (Cravens & Ellis, 2014). Such variety in the demographics amongst virtual volunteers is also highlighted in the plethora of roles that can be completed through virtual spaces. Examples of such roles include translating documents, creating and reviewing documents, research and data gathering, software design and coding, transcribing, graphic design, mentoring, consulting, tutoring, volunteer management, board or committee work or meetings, website design, and database development (Cravens & Ellis, 2014; Murray & Harrison, 2002, 2005). While these aforementioned roles are discussed, there are additional roles that can be practiced in various types of organizations where virtual volunteering "[utilizes] technology in order to advance public agency goals by providing a new means for volunteers to provide service" (Medina, 2018, p. 4).

Virtual Volunteering Research

Research on virtual volunteering has occurred in organizations, such as non-profit organizations, non-governmental organizations, government agencies and/or initiatives, and charitable organizations and/or initiatives (Cravens & Ellis, 2014; Liu et al., 2016). For instance, Cravens (2003) found more than 40 different online mentoring programs in Canada and the United States where virtual volunteers were present. While these data are quite dated, there is an absence of recent research providing a landscape of virtual volunteering in different countries involving a large sample of organizations (e.g., Volunteering Australia, 2016).

However, in comparison to the majority of research on volunteers in sport which is conducted in events (Kim & Cuskelly, 2017; Wicker, 2017), there appears to be an absence of virtual volunteering research in this context. This is despite the plethora of events (e.g., festivals, concerts, political rallies) where volunteers are relied upon (Getz, 2005; Hoye et al., 2020), but might be completing tasks off-site through virtual spaces. For example, volunteers involved in the planning mode of an event, such as members of the organizing committee, may be completing tasks off-site, such as at home, through virtual spaces (e.g., creating policies for the roles and responsibilities of volunteers during the event). However, this remains to be investigated to understand the potential presence and value of virtual volunteering in event-related contexts.

To date, virtual volunteering research has investigated a variety of topics such as participation rates and demographics (e.g., Murray & Harrison, 2005), personality traits (e.g., Ackermann, 2019), motivations (e.g., Silva et al., 2018), engagement (e.g., Mukherjee, 2011), differences with traditional in-person volunteering (e.g., Cox et al., 2019), and management practices (e.g., Cravens, 2003). An overview of these investigated topics in virtual volunteering research is depicted in Table 3.1.

Table 3.1 Examples of investigated topics in virtual volunteering research

Author(s):	*Topic(s) investigated:*
• Ihm (2017) • Liu et al. (2016)	• Classification of virtual volunteer types
• Ackermann (2019)	• Psychological basis (i.e., Big Five Personality Traits)
• Ackermann & Manatschal (2018)	• Inequalities according to socio-demographics, resources, networks, and engagement
• Cox et al. (2019)	• Relationship between motivation, activity, and retention
• Filsinger & Freitag (2019)	• Relationship between internet use and civic life
• Mukherjee (2011) • Silva et al. (2018)	• Motivations
• Mukherjee (2010)	• Engagement
• Amichai-Hamburger (2008) • Butgereit (2011) • Cravens (2003) • Lachance (2020) • Medina (2018) • Murray & Harrison (2002, 2005) • Rajan (2013)	• Management practices (e.g., participation rates, demographics, successful management practices, advantages and/or disadvantages of virtual volunteers)

Note. Some of these aforementioned studies have also discussed differences between virtual volunteers and traditional in-person volunteers (e.g., Ackermann, 2019; Ackermann & Manatschal, 2018; Cox et al., 2019; Ihm, 2017; Murray & Harrison, 2005).

The examination of these topics on virtual volunteers from the broader volunteer literature has uncovered a number of findings. Notably, virtual volunteers' personality traits have been found to be positively related to openness to experience, but negatively associated with agreeableness (Ackermann, 2019). Research on the motivations of virtual volunteers has demonstrated a positive relationship between altruistic and learning/career motives (Silva et al., 2018), while others have found the importance of understanding and value motivations to positively impact activity and retention (Cox et al., 2018). Relatedness also has a positive relationship with the motivations of virtual volunteers (Naqshbandi et al., 2020). A smaller number of studies have also been conducted on older adults partaking in virtual volunteering. Findings have demonstrated a positive impact on social engagement (Mukherjee, 2010) and the development of social connections in relation to social capital (Mukherjee, 2011). Further, older adults were found to be more likely to volunteer the more they used the internet, while a negative relationship between internet use and volunteering among youth was reported (Filsinger & Freitag, 2019).

Another line of research pertains to the management of virtual volunteers. Several authors have discussed the successful characteristics of managers when managing virtual volunteers (e.g., Amichai-Hamburger, 2008; Butgereit, 2011; Dhebar & Stokes, 2008; Murray & Harrison, 2005; Rajan, 2013). Such characteristics include having adequate technology, ethics/security/legalities, the structure of responsibility/authority, easy online registration, easy scheduling, a sense of community, and recognition (Butgereit, 2011). Other researchers have suggested different characteristics for virtual volunteer management such as planning with clarity, communicating, and monitoring and learning from results (Dhebar & Stokes, 2008). Murray and Harrison (2005) suggested a number of recommendations for the management of virtual volunteers including having a positive attitude toward virtual volunteering, developing the benefits and costs of virtual volunteering, establishing a pilot program, defining descriptions for virtual volunteering postings, creating a recruitment plan, providing orientation and training, establishing frequent communication to virtual volunteers, evaluating the work of virtual volunteers, and offering technical assistance.

Scholars have also highlighted additional advantages for those participating in virtual volunteering such as enhancing information and communication at the personal (e.g., overcoming disabilities, easy of accessing information), interpersonal (e.g., high-level of self-discourse, social compensation), and group levels (e.g., various information exchange channels, group identity; Amichai-Hamburger, 2008), the minimal monetary burden, schedule flexibility to work around other commitments (e.g., work, family), and ability to be done on a long-term basis (Rajan, 2013). However, disadvantages of virtual volunteering include lack of bilateral communication, lack of recognition, lack of engagement to become familiar with the organization and/or community, and capacity and time for the recruitment, orientation, and support of this volunteer-type (Liu et al., 2016). With these disadvantages in mind, virtual volunteering is argued to be less rich and engaging than traditional in-person volunteering. This is because individuals do not benefit from face-to-face contact or socializing with other volunteers, communication is limited to technological means (e.g., emails and video conference meetings), and the level of engagement can be inhibited by the remoteness of virtual volunteering where individuals complete their tasks alone and away from a formal organizational setting. Despite these listed disadvantages, other scholars have argued that such disadvantages are not unique to virtual volunteers and can be found among traditional in-person volunteers (Cravens, 2006).

While the findings from previous research are necessary and important to gather empirical data on trends and topics in virtual volunteering, there is an absence of empirical studies on virtual volunteering in sport and events organizations. A lack of research on virtual volunteering contrasts with the variety of traditional in-person volunteer types that have been examined in sport and event organizations, such as pioneer volunteers (e.g., Fairley et al., 2007; Fairley et al., 2014), planning and on-site volunteers (e.g., Doherty, 2009), marginal and career volunteers (e.g., Cuskelly et al., 2002), episodic and continuous volunteers (e.g., Holmes & Smith, 2009; Lockstone-Binney et al., 2010), or core and peripheral volunteers (e.g., Ringuet-Riot et al., 2014). To date, only a single academic commentary regarding virtual volunteering in sport organizations and events (e.g., Lachance, 2020) appears to have been published.

In the sport and event sector, virtual volunteering has been discussed in relation to the COVID-19 pandemic as allowing individuals to partake in leisure activities while respecting government guidelines (e.g., social distancing), as well as contributing to the operations and survival of sport organizations and events (Lachance, 2020). Both opportunities, such as creating accessibility for new and current volunteers to have access to leisure activities and management challenges related to virtual volunteering were discussed (Lachance, 2020). For instance, current volunteers had the ability to continue their volunteer activities through virtual spaces, such as holding Board meetings virtually despite restrictions due to the COVID-19 pandemic (Lachance, 2020). Sport organizations and events also had the ability to engage groups, such as older adults, youth, and individuals with disabilities, in volunteering during the pandemic as this leisure activity occurs through virtual spaces. Further, virtual volunteering, for the most part, does not discriminate on the basis of physical, physiological, or personal constraints (e.g., mobility, disabilities, family, work) that are often present in traditional in-person volunteering (Lachance, 2020). Specific to management challenges, the majority of the recruitment of virtual volunteers has not occurred through the medium that is fundamental to these types of volunteers; the internet (Lachance, 2020; Murray & Harrison, 2005). To combat the inability to harness digital technology to recruit virtual volunteers, Lachance (2020) suggested that practitioners use the pandemic as an opportunity to conduct internal analyses to identify needs (e.g., absent roles, missing skills from the organization) and partner with volunteer-related agencies (e.g., Volunteer Canada, Volunteering Australia) to promote positions through the internet. These challenges were not uniquely attributed to recruitment as engagement of virtual volunteers can also be a daunting task for practitioners. For example, engagement of virtual volunteers is not face-to-face, and communication occurs through virtual spaces. Such challenges highlight the importance of frequent bilateral communication with virtual volunteers to ensure their engagement is maintained (Lachance, 2020). Finally, virtual volunteers have been found to be more involved in short-term roles – creating a challenge for retention. Overall, this commentary has highlighted the relevancy of virtual volunteering given imposed restrictions during the COVID-19 pandemic, while considering that with "the current digital age, [digital] technology is not something we can escape, but instead, a tool [practitioners] should seek to leverage through its most indispensable resource; volunteers" (Lachance, 2020, p. 6).

Despite this recent commentary, there is a dearth of empirical research as it pertains to virtual volunteering in the context sport organizations and events (Lachance, 2020). This absence remains despite the prominence and ubiquity of technology in contemporary society and institutions (Price et al., 2013; Ratten, 2019, 2020a, 2020b) and discussions regarding the potential for virtual volunteering to be present in sport organizations and events (e.g., Lachance, 2020).

Future Research Directions

Given the absence of empirical research on virtual volunteering in the sport and event volunteer literature, four future research directions are suggested. These future research directions are based on previous virtual volunteering research in the broader volunteer literature and seek to advance the sport and even volunteer body of knowledge by providing recommendations for various topics, contexts, and approaches worthy of inquiry.

First, future research should explore the presence, participation rates, and demographics of virtual volunteers in sport organizations and events. While empirical data exists on the participation rates and demographics of virtual volunteers from the mainstream management field (e.g., Cravens 2003; Murray & Harrison, 2002, 2005), such data is absent in the sport and events sector. This absence remains despite the increasing importance of digital technology and assumptions that virtual volunteering is occurring in sport organizations and events (e.g., Lachance, 2020). Thus, empirical data should be gathered to determine if virtual volunteers are present in sport organizations and events, and, if so, describe the participation rates and demographic information. To accomplish this, future research should employ an online survey research methodology and questionnaires as the primary data collection method. Such an approach would allow for the participation rates and demographic information of virtual volunteers to be generated from a representative sample of both sport organizations and events, while frequency-based analyses could be applied to derive conclusions (e.g., number of virtual volunteers, hours contributed).

Second, assuming that virtual volunteers remain in sport organizations and events in a post-COVID-19 environment, future research should determine the transferability of findings from previous virtual volunteer research in the context of sport organizations and events. Despite empirical research from the broader volunteer literature (e.g., Ackermann, 2019; Ackermann & Manatschal, 2018; Cox et al., 2018; Cox et al., 2019; Ihm, 2017; Mukherjee, 2010, 2011; Silva et al., 2018), few studies have examined the transferability of such findings in other contexts beyond non-profit organizations, non-governmental organizations, government agencies or initiatives, and charitable organizations or initiatives. Such research is worthy of inquiry to confirm or challenge previous findings in relation to virtual volunteering research. To accomplish this, researchers should attempt to replicate the chosen topics and approaches from previous virtual volunteering research. For instance, the motivation of virtual volunteers in sport organizations and events could be examined through a survey research methodology and an online self-administered questionnaire. Such empirical examination could use previously applied scales (e.g., Volunteer Functions Inventory) to further determine the transferability of previous findings, such as the relationship found between motivation (i.e., understanding and values) and retention (e.g., Cox et al., 2018), to virtual volunteers in sport organizations and events. Additional research could also explore the ability of virtual volunteers in sport organizations and events to achieve strategic outcomes like competitive advantage (cf. Lachance & Parent, 2021).

Third, future research should explore virtual volunteers in sport events in an attempt to advance research from the broader volunteer literature conducted in organizations (e.g., Ackermann, 2019; Ackermann & Manatschal, 2018; Cox et al., 2018; Cox et al., 2019; Cravens, 2000, 2003, 2006; Harrison et al., 2004; Ihm, 2017; Mukherjee, 2010, 2011; Murray & Harrison, 2002, 2005; Silva et al., 2018). Given the temporary nature of sport events (Parent & Ruetsch, 2021) relative to sport organizations, the latter which seeks to endure and survive over time, this context could be used to challenge previous research conducted in the broader volunteer literature on virtual volunteers. For instance, sport event volunteers are typically episodic in nature and are often required to assume multiple informal and formal roles that are temporary given that their duties end following the completion of an event. Such characteristics would potentially challenge previous findings conducted on virtual volunteers given their fundamental differences with events. To explore virtual volunteers in events, researchers could use both quantitative and qualitative methodologies and methods. For example, survey research and questionnaires (e.g., Bakhsh et al., 2021; Lachance et al., 2021) could be used to measure relationships between constructs (e.g., motivations and experiences of virtual volunteers, experiences and future volunteer intentions of virtual volunteers) whereas autoethnographies using overt participation observations, informal interviews, and documents, which have recently been applied in sport volunteer research (e.g., Kodama et al., 2013; Lachance & Parent, 2020, 2021; Sadd, 2018), could provide rich insight on the experiences of virtual volunteers in events.

Fourth, future research should explore the impact of COVID-19 on traditional in-person volunteers to understand if the pandemic has created opportunities for virtual volunteering to occur. For instance, did traditional in-person volunteers transition some of their tasks to virtual spaces due to restrictions and health guidelines limiting or temporarily suspending organizational or event operations? If so, what was the experience of these individuals transitioning their volunteer roles to virtual spaces? Was this experience positive or negative and what factors contributed to this perception? In contrast, why didn't individuals partake in virtual volunteering? What barriers were present, such as personal (e.g., access to the internet from rural areas, employment situation) or organizational (e.g., limited operations during the pandemic, impact of restrictions and health guidelines)? Such questions could be answered through a case study methodology featuring a single in-depth case or multiple cases (e.g., sport organizations or events) combining semi-structured interviews and documents (cf. Yin, 2018) or conducting semi-structured interviews using an interpretative phenomenological analysis to interpret the experience of virtual volunteers. This research would be important to further examine the impact of the COVID-19 pandemic on traditional in-person volunteers, and if the circumstances of the pandemic led to the development of virtual volunteering opportunities in sport organizations and/or events (cf. Lachance, 2020).

Conclusion

This chapter sought to provide definitions, benefits and disadvantages, and future research directions on virtual volunteering in the context of both sport organizations and events by presenting and discussing previous research from the wider volunteer literature. Beyond the aforementioned future research directions, the future of virtual volunteering is worthy of discussion considering that previous deliberations on this topic have critiqued the demand for this type of volunteer in organizations (e.g., Murray & Harrison, 2005; Liu et al., 2016). However, recent changes in the external environment of organizations and events due to increased digitization and the COVID-19 pandemic may well provide the needed spark in interest and, ultimately, demand for virtual volunteers. For instance, as "the use of the internet and mobile technology expands worldwide, virtual volunteering management practices will become highly sought-after skills for success" (Medina, 2018, p. 6) of organizations as virtual volunteering becomes a more popular volunteer type since first emerging the early 2000s (Liu et al., 2016). With this statement in mind and recent environmental challenges, empirical inquiries on virtual volunteers are arguably needed more than ever to provide an understanding of the scope (e.g., participation rates), experiences, and management (e.g., practices, advantages, challenges) of this valuable, yet overlooked, resource in the context of sport organizations and events.

References

Ackermann, K. (2019). Predisposed to volunteer? Personality traits and different forms of volunteering. *Nonprofit and Voluntary Sector Quarterly, 48*, 1119–1142. 10.1177/0899764019848484

Ackermann, K., & Manatschal, A. (2018). Online volunteering as a means to overcome unequal participation? The profiles of online and offline volunteers compared. *New media & Society, 20*, 4453–4472. 10.1177/1461444818775698

Amichai-Hamburger, Y. (2008). Potential and promise of online volunteering. *Computers in Human Behavior, 24*, 544–562. 10.1016/j.chb.2007.02.004

Australian Bureau of Statistics. (2015). *General social survey: Summary results, 2014*. www.abs.gov.au/ausstats/abs@.nsf/mf/4159.0

Bakhsh, J. T., Lachance, E. L., Thompson, A., & Parent, M. M. (2021). Outcomes of the sport event volunteer experience: examining demonstration effects on first-time and returning volunteers. *International Journal of Event and Festival Management*. Advance online publication. 10.1108/IJEFM-09-2020-0057

Butgereit, L. (2011). Seven characteristics of a successful virtual volunteering platform. In P. Cunningham & M. Cunningham (Eds.), *IST-Africa 2011 conference proceedings* (pp. 1–8). IIMC International Information Management Corporation. http://www.IST-Africa.org/Conference2011

Canada Soccer. (2020, August 12). *Canada Soccer launches new digital platform at* www.canadasoccer.com. https://sirc.ca/news/canada-soccer-launches-new-digital-platform-at-www-canadasoccer-com/

Chelladurai, P., & Kerwin, S. (2018). *Human resource management in sport and recreation* (3rd ed.). Human Kinetics.

Cnaan, R. A., Handy, F., & Wadsworth, M. (1996). Defining who is a volunteer: Conceptual and empirical considerations. *Nonprofit and Voluntary Sector Quarterly, 25*, 364–383. 10.1177/0899764096253006

Cox, J., Oh, E. Y., Simmons, B., Graham, G., Greenhill, A., Lintott, C., Masters, K., & Woodcock, J. (2018). Doing good online: The changing relationships between motivations, activity, and retention among online volunteers. *Nonprofit and Voluntary Sector Quarterly, 47*, 1031–1056. 10.1177/0899764018783066

Cox, J., Oh, E. Y., Simmons, B., Graham, G., Greenhill, A., Lintott, C., Masters, K., & Meriton, R. (2019). Getting connected: An empirical investigation of the relationship between social capital and philanthropy among online volunteers. *Nonprofit and Voluntary Sector Quarterly, 48*, 151–173. 10.1177/0899764018794905

Cravens, J. (2000). Virtual volunteering: Online volunteers providing assistance to human service agencies. *Journal of Technology in Human Services, 17*, 119–136. 10.1300/J017v17n02_02

Cravens, J. (2003). Online mentoring: Programs and suggested practices as of February 2001. *Journal of Technology in Human Services, 21*, 85–109. 10.1300/J017v21n01_05

Cravens, J. (2006). Involving international online volunteers: Factors for success, organizational benefits, and new views of community. *The International Journal of Volunteer Administration, 24*, 15–23.

Cravens, J., & Ellis, S. J. (2014). *The last virtual volunteering guidebook: Fully integrated online service into volunteer involvement*. Energize.

Cuskelly, G., Harrington, M., & Stebbins, R. A. (2002). Changing levels of organizational commitment amongst sport volunteers: A serious leisure approach. *Leisure/Loisir, 27*, 191–212. 10.1080/14927713.2002.9651303

Daft, R. L. (2021). *Organization theory & design* (13th ed.). Cengage.

Diacin, M. J., & VanSickle, J. L. (2014). Computer program usage in sport organizations and computer competencies desired by sport organization personnel. *International Journal of Applied Sports Sciences, 26*, 124–137.

Dhebar, B. B., & Stokes, B. (2008). A nonprofit manager's guide to online volunteering. *Nonprofit Management and Leadership, 18*, 497–506. 10.1002/nml.200

Doherty, A. (2009). The volunteer legacy of a major sport event. *Journal of Policy Research in Tourism, Leisure and Events, 1*, 185–207. 10.1080/19407960903204356

Doherty, A., Millar, P., & Misener, K. (2020). Return to community sport: Leaning on evidence in turbulent times. *Managing Sport and Leisure*. Advanced online publication. 10.1080/23750472.2020.1794940

Ellis, S. J., & Campbell, K. H. (2005). *By the people: A history of Americans as volunteers*. Energize.

Ellis, S. J., & Cravens, J. (2000). *Virtual volunteer guidebook*. United Nations Volunteer Program.

Fairley, S., Kellett, P., & Green, B. C. (2007). Volunteering abroad: Motives for travel to volunteer at the Athens Olympic Games. *Journal of Sport Management, 21*, 41–57. 10.1123/jsm.21.1.41

Fairley, S., Green, B. C., O'Brien, D., & Chalip, L. (2014). Pioneer volunteers: The role identity of continuous volunteers at sport events. *Journal of Sport & Tourism, 19*, 233–255. 10.1080/14775085.2015.1111774

Filsinger, M., & Freitag, M. (2019). Internet use and volunteering: Relationships and differences across age and applications. *VOLUNTAS: International Journal of Voluntary and Nonprofit Organizations, 30*, 87–97. 10.1007/s11266-018-0045-4

Fitzgerald, M., Kruschwitz, N., Bonnet, D., & Welch, M. (2013). *Embracing technology: A new strategic imperative*. MIT Sloan Management Review.

Gerrard, B. (2004). Why does Manchester United keep winning on and off the field? A case study of sustainable competitive advantage in professional team sports. In D. L. Andrews (Ed.), *Manchester United: A thematic study* (pp. 65–86). Routledge.

Getz, D. (2005). *Event management and event tourism* (2nd ed.). Cognizant Communication Corporation.

Hallmann, K., & Fairley, S. (2018). *Sports volunteers around the globe*. Springer International Publishing.

Harrison, Y., Murray, V., & MacGregor, J. (2004). *The impact of ICT on the management of Canadian volunteer programs*. Canadian Centre for Philanthropy. http://sectorsource.ca/sites/default/files/resources/files/harrison_report_eng.pdf

Holmes, K., & Smith, K. A. (2009). *Managing volunteers in tourism: Attractions destinations and events*. Elsevier.

Hoye, R., Cuskelly, G., Auld, C., Kappelides, P., & Misener, K. (2020). *Sport volunteering*. Routledge.

Hutchins, B., & Rowe, D. (2013). *Digital media sport: Technology, power and culture in the network society*. Routledge.

Ihm, J. (2017). Classifying and relating different types of online and offline volunteering. *VOLUNTAS: International Journal of Voluntary and Nonprofit Organizations, 28*, 400–419. 10.1007/s11266-016-9826-9

Isensee, C., Teuteberg, F., Griese, K-M, & Topi, C. (2020). The relationship between organizational culture, sustainability, and digitalization in SMEs: A systematic review. *Journal of Cleaner Production, 275*, 1–19. 10.1016/j.bushor.2020.07.005

Johnston, N. (2019, September 18). *Are your files safe? Reflections from Ringette Canada on a ransomware attack*. https://sirc.ca/blog/are-your-files-safe-reflections-from-ringette-canada-on-a-ransomware-attack/

Kane, G. C., Palmer, D., Phillips, A. N., Kiron, D., & Buckley, N. (2015). *Strategy, not technology, drives digital transformation: Becoming a digitally mature enterprise*. https://sloanreview.mit.edu/projects/strategy-drives-digital-transformation/

Kim, E., & Cuskelly, G. (2017). A systematic quantitative review of volunteer management in events. *Event Management, 21*(1), 83–100. 10.3727/152599517X14809630271195

Kodama, E., Doherty, A., & Popovic, M. (2013). Front line insight: An autoethnography of the Vancouver 2010 volunteer experience. *European Sport Management Quarterly, 13*, 76–93. 10.1080/16184742.2012.742123

Koronios, K., Dimitropoulos, P., Travlos, A., Douvis, I., & Ratten, V. (2020). Online technologies and sports: A new era for sponsorship. *The Journal of High Technology Management Research*. Advanced online publication. 10.1016/j.hitech.2020.100373

Lachance, E. L. (2020). COVID-19 and its impact on volunteering: Moving towards virtual volunteering. *Leisure Sciences, 43*, 104–110. 10.1080/01490400.2020.1773990

Lachance, E. L., & Parent, M. M. (2020). The volunteer experience in a para-sport event: An autoethnography. *Journal of Sport Management, 34*, 93–102. 10.1123/jsm.2019-0132

Lachance, E. L., & Parent, M. M. (2021). Understanding the sport event volunteer experience in the implementation mode of a para-sport event: An autoethnography. *Event Management*. Advanced online publication. 10.3727/152599520X15894679115 56

Lachance, E. L., & Parent, M. M. (2021). Volunteers in sport organizations and events: A source of competitive advantage? *International Journal of Sport Management, 22*(3), 1–24.

Lachance, E. L., Bakhsh, J. T., Thompson, A., & Parent, M. M. (2021). What predicts the sport event volunteer experience? Examining motivation, satisfaction, commitment, and sense of community. *Event Management*. Advanced online publication. 10.3727/152599521X16106577965107

Lewis, M. (2004). *Moneyball: The art of winning an unfair game* (1st ed.). WW Norton.

Liebermann, D. G., Katz, L., Hughes, M. D., Bartlett, R. M., McClements, J., & Franks, I. M. (2002). Advances in the application of information technology to sport performance. *Journal of Sports Sciences, 20*, 755–769. 10.1080/026404102320675611

Li, Y., Dai, J., & Cui, L. (2020). The impact of digital technologies on economic and environmental performance in the context of industry 4.0: A moderated mediation model. *International Journal of Production Economics, 229*, 1–13. 10.1016/j.ijpe.2020.107777

Liu, H. K., Harrison, Y. D., Lai, J. J. K., Chikoto, G. L., & Jones-Lungo, K. (2016). Online and virtual volunteering. In D. H. Horton, R. A. Stebbins, & J. Grotz (Eds.), *Palgrave handbook of volunteering, civic participation, and nonprofit associations* (pp. 290–310). Palgrave Macmillan.

Lockstone-Binney, L., Holmes, K., Smith, K., & Baum, T. (2010). Volunteers and volunteering in leisure: Social science perspectives. *Leisure Studies, 29*(4), 435–455. 10.1080/02614367.2010.527357

Ludvigsen, J. A. L., & Hayton, J. W. (2020). Toward COVID-19 secure events: considerations for organizing the safe resumption of major sporting events. *Managing Sport and Leisure*. Advanced online publication. 10.1080/23750472.2020.1782252

Mastromartino, B., Ross, W. J., Wear, H., & Naraine, M. L. (2020). Thinking outside the 'box': A discussion of sports fans, teams, and the environment in the context of COVID- 19. *Sport in Society*. Advanced online publication. 10.1080/17430437.2020.1804108

McGregor-Lowndes, M., Crittall, M., Conroy, D., & Keast, R. (2017). *Individual giving and volunteering: Giving Australia 2016*. Australian Government Department of Social Services.

Medina, P. (2018) Virtual volunteering and nonprofit organizations. In A. Farazmand (Ed.) *Global encyclopedia of public administration, public policy, and governance* (pp. 1–6). Springer.

Mukherjee, D. (2010). An exploratory study of older adults' engagement with virtual volunteerism. *Journal of Technology in Human Services, 28*, 188–196. 10.1080/15228835.2010.508368

Mukherjee, D. (2011). Participation of older adults in virtual volunteering: A qualitative analysis. *Ageing International, 36*, 253–266. 10.1007/s12126-010-9088-6

Murray, V., & Harrison, Y. (2002). *The impact of information and communications technology on volunteer management*. Canada Centre for Philanthropy.

Murray, V., & Harrison, Y. (2005). Virtual volunteering. In J. L. Brudney (Ed.), *Emerging areas of volunteering* (pp. 33–50). Association for Research on Nonprofit Organizations and Voluntary Action.

Naqshbandi, K. Z., Liu, C., Taylor, S., Lim, R., Ahmadpour, N., & Calvo, R. (2020). "I am most grateful." Using gratitude to improve the sense of relatedness and motivation for online volunteerism. *International Journal of Human–Computer Interaction*. Advanced online publication: 10.1080/10447318.2020.1746061

Naraine, M. L. (2019). Follower segments within and across the social media networks of major professional sport organizations. *Sport Marketing Quarterly, 28*, 222–233. 10.32731/SMQ.284.122019.04

Naraine, M. L., & Karg, A. J. (2019). Digital media in international sport: Engaging fans via social media and fantasy sports. In E. MacIntosh, G. Bravo, & M. Li (Eds.), *International sport management* (pp. 315–331). Human Kinetics.

Naraine, M. L., & Parent, M. M. (2016a). "Birds of a feather:" An institutional approach to Canadian national sport organizations' social media usage. *International Journal of Sport Communication, 9*, 140–162. 10.1123/IJSC.2016-0010

Naraine, M. L., &Parent, M. M. (2016b). Illuminating centralized users in the social media ego network of two national sport organizations. *Journal of Sport Management, 30*, 689–701. 10.1123/jsm.2016-0067

Naraine, M. L., & Parent, M. M. (2017a). This is how we do it: A qualitative approach to national sport organizations' social-media implementation. *International Journal of Sport Communication, 10*, 196–217. 10.1123/IJSC.2017-0006

Naraine, M. L., & Parent, M. M. (2017b). Examining social media adoption and change to the stakeholder communication paradigm in not-for-profit sport organizations. *Journal of Amateur Sport, 3*, 55–81. 10.17161/jas.v3i2.6492

Naraine, M. L., O'Reilly, N., Levallet, N., & Wanless, L. (2020). If you build it, will they log on? Wi–Fi usage and behavior while attending National Basketball Association games. *Sport, Business and Management: An International Journal, 10*, 207–226. 10.1108/SBM-02-2019-0016

Naraine, M. L., Pegoraro, A., & Wear, H. (2019a). #WeTheNorth: Examining an online brand community through a professional sport organization's hashtag marketing campaign. *Communication & Sport*. 1–21. 10.1177/2167479519878676

National Council for Voluntary Organisations. (2018). *UK civil society almanac 2018*. https://data.ncvo.org.uk/a/almanac18/

Parent, M. M., & Ruetsch, A. (2021). *Managing major sports events: Theory and practice* (2nd ed.). Routledge.

Parent, M. M., Taks, M., Séguin, B., Naraine, M. L., Hoye, R., Thompson, A., & Lachance, E. L. (2020). *Governance, branding, and social media in Canadian national sport organizations*. The University of Ottawa. https://health.uottawa.ca/human-kinetics/sites/health.uottawa.ca.human-kinetics/files/workshop-report.pdf

Paylor, J. (2012). *Micro-volunteering: Doing some good through smartphones?* http://www.ivr.org.uk/images/stories/Micro-volunteering_bulletin_final_version_June.pdf

Pegoraro, A. (2010). Look who's talking—Athletes on Twitter: A case study. *International Journal of Sport Communication, 3*, 501–514. 10.1123/ijsc.3.4.501

Peña-López, I. (2007). Online volunteers: Knowledge managers in nonprofits. *The Journal of Information Technology in Social Change, 1*, 136–152.

Price, S., Jewitt, C., & Brown, B. (2013). *The Sage handbook of digital technology research*. SAGE.

Rajan, P. (2013). Virtual Volunteerism and its impact on international community development. *Disability, CBR & Inclusive Development, 24*, 111–112.

Ratten, V. (2019). *Sports technology and innovation: Assessing cultural and social factors*. Springer.

Ratten, V. (2020a). Sport technology: A commentary. *The Journal of High Technology Management Research*. Advanced online publication. 10.1016/j.hitech.2020.100383

Ratten, V. (2020). Coronavirus disease (COVID-19) and sport entrepreneurship. *International Journal of Entrepreneurial Behavior & Research, 26*(6), 1379–1388.

Ratten, V., & Jones, P. (2020). New challenges in sport entrepreneurship for value creation. *International Entrepreneurship and Management Journal, 16*, 961–980. 10.1007/s11365-020-00664-z

Ratten, V., & Thompson, A. J. (2020). Digital sport entrepreneurial ecosystems. *Thunderbird International Business Review, 62*, 565–578. 10.1002/tie.22160

Ringuet-Riot, C., Cuskelly, G., Auld, C., & Zakus, D. H. (2014). Volunteer roles, involvement and commitment in voluntary sport organizations: Evidence of core and peripheral volunteers. *Sport in Society, 17*, 116–133. 10.1080/17430437.2013.828902

Saarikko, T., Westergren, U., & Blomquist, T. (2020). Digital transformation: Five recommendations for the digitally conscious firm. *Business Horizons, 63*, 825–839. 10.1016/j.bushor.2020.07.005

Sadd, D. (2018). Proud to be British: An autoethnographic study of working as a Games Maker at London 2012. *Event Management, 22*, 317–332. 10.3727/152599518X15239930463136

Sheptak, R. D., & Menaker, B. E. (2020). When sport event work stopped: Exposure of sport event labor precarity by the COVID-19 pandemic. *International Journal of Sport Communication, 13*(3), 427–435. 10.1123/ijsc.2020-0229

Sills, D. L. (1957). *The volunteers: Means and ends in a national organization*. The Free Press.

Silva, F., Proença, T., & Ferreira, M. R. (2018). Volunteers' perspective on online volunteering: A qualitative approach. *International Review on Public and Nonprofit Marketing, 15*, 531–552. 10.1007/s12208-018-0212-8

Smith, C., & Freedman, A. (1972). *Voluntary associations: Perspectives on the literature*. Harvard University Press.

Smith, L. R., Pegoraro, A., & Cruikshank, S. A. (2019). Tweet, retweet, favorite: The impact of Twitter use on enjoyment and sports viewing. *Journal of Broadcasting & Electronic Media, 63*, 94–110. 10.1080/08838151.2019.1568805

Sport Information Resource Centre. (2019, May 13). *Technology*. https://sirc.ca/knowledge_nuggets/show-me-the-money-report/

Stadder, E., & Naraine, M. L. (2020). Place your bets: An exploratory study of sports- gambling operators' use of twitter for relationship marketing. *International Journal of Sport Communication, 13*, 157–180. 10.1123/ijsc.2019-0114

Statistics Canada. (2015). *Volunteering in Canada, 2004 to 2013*. http://volunteeralberta.ab.ca/wp-content/uploads/2015/11/Volunteering-in-Canada-2004-2013.pdf

Strader, T. J. (2011). *Digital technology in the 21st century*. IGI Global.

Toffoletti, K., Pegoraro, A., & Comeau, G. S. (2019). Self-representations of women's sport fandom on Instagram at the 2015 FIFA Women's World Cup. *Communication & Sport*. 1–23. 10.1177/2167479519893332

United Nations Volunteer. (2004). *Online volunteering: Nothing virtual about it!* United Nations Volunteers.

UN Online Volunteering Service. (2004). *Who is using the OV service?* United Nations Volunteers (UNV) Programme.

UN Volunteers. (2011). *State of the world's volunteerism report, 2011: Universal values for global well-being*. United Nations Volunteers (UNV) Programme. www.unv.org/publications/2011-state-world's-volunteerismreport-universal-values-global-well-being

UN Volunteers. (2018). *2018 State of the world's volunteerism report: The thread that binds*. United Nations Volunteers (UNV) Programme. www.volunteering.com.au/uns-state-of-the-worlds-volunteerism-report-2018-thethread- that-binds/

UK Office for National Statistics. (2017). *Changes in the value and division of unpaid volunteering in the UK: 2000 to 2015*. www.ons.gov.uk/economy/nationalaccounts/satelliteaccounts/articles/changesinthevalueanddivisionofunpaidcareworkintheuk/2015

Vezina, M., & Crompton, S. (2012). *Volunteering in Canada*. Statistics Canada.
Volunteering Australia. (2016). *State of volunteering in Australia*. www.volunteeringaustralia.org/research/stateofvolunteering/
Volunteer Canada. (2015). *The Canadian volunteer landscape*. https://volunteer.ca/vdemo/IssuesAndPublicPolicy_DOCS/Canadian%20volunteer%20landscape%20EN.pdf
Volunteer Canada. (2020). *Virtual volunteering*. https://volunteer.ca/vdemo/ResearchAndResources_DOCS/Virtual%20Volunteering%20Mar2020.pdf
Warburton, J., & Oppenheimer, M. (2000). *Volunteers and volunteering*. The Federation Press.
Wicker, P. (2017). Volunteerism and volunteer management in sport. *Sport Management Review*, *20*(4), 325–337. 10.1016/j.smr.2017.01.001
Yin, R. K. (2018). *Case study research and applications: Design and methods* (6th ed.). SAGE.

4

Digital Transformations in Youth Sport

Ryan Snelgrove and Vinu Selvaratnam

Introduction

Sport continues to be an important part of many young people's lives. For decades, children and adolescents have flocked to sport because it provides an ability to engage in physical activity, compete, have fun, build friendships, and shape identities due to its cultural status (Bowers & Green, 2013; Hyman, 2012). These motivations have remained stable over time, yet the youth sport experience now differs drastically from past decades (Hyman, 2009). Indeed, youth sport is no longer "kids play" as it is packaged and sold in a way that mimics the professional sport ranks. To date, scholars have dutifully identified the influence of changes to the cultural, social, economic, and political environments on youth sport policy, system structure, program delivery, athletic performance, and experiences (Legg et al., 2016). However, the rise of digital technology as a specific mechanism of influence on changes in youth sport has been overlooked (Naraine & Parent, 2017). This oversight is significant as the current landscape of youth sport was heavily shaped by the rise of digitality.

Photoshoots, individualized coaching using digital tools, virtual-reality-based training, live streaming of games, and the online promotion of athletes have created an environment that is a far cry from pick-up baseball games on the sandlot (Holmes, 2018; Hyman, 2012; Thorpe & Dumont, 2019). An occurrence that was once confined to local fields, courts, and arenas viewed by a small collection of family members, youth sport is now everywhere thanks to the utilization of new digital media (Hyman, 2012; Thorpe & Dumont, 2019).

This trend shows no signs of slowing down as it has played a significant role in enabling the media industry to reach an estimated $24.9 billion USD worldwide in 2019 and is expected to reach $77.6 billion USD by 2026 (GlobeNewswire, 2019). Elite youth sport, in particular, has been the recipient of massive capital injections from media companies such as Entertainment and Sports Programming Network (ESPN) and Creative Artists Agency (CAA). For example, The Little League Baseball World Series (LLBWS) has received significant attention from ESPN due to its ability to generate robust audience share and advertising revenue (Southall et al., 2012). In 2018, LLBWS averaged 1.02 million viewers in the United States across ESPN, ESPN2, and ABC, up 13% from the previous year (Lewis, 2018). This viewership earned it the third-largest baseball audience in 2018, just behind the MLB all-star game and MLB home run

DOI: 10.4324/9781003088899-6

derby (Lewis, 2018). Furthermore, the existence of social media has allowed athletes and their families to capitalize on lower-cost forms of media (e.g., YouTube) to drive attention and interest. It is not uncommon for videos of young action sport athletes to reach over a million views (Thorpe & Dumont, 2019).

The ways in which community sport organizations (CSOs) operate have also changed. In the absence of the digital milieu, CSOs had a more difficult time increasing participation levels without a multitude of digital marketing strategies, and relied on the "paper and pencil" method for registration and to document match scores and results. However, with the adoption of computers and information technology, youth sport organizations generally experienced improvements in terms of efficiency in the documentation of fees and organizing team rosters, and helping parents access schedules and keep up with the action amidst busy schedules – enhancing the value proposition offered by clubs.

Youth sport organizations have responded to the availability of digital technology by also implementing new digital technology to bolster their overall performance. For example, Hoeber et al. (2015) found that CSOs invested in websites to target new youth and immigrants, added wireless internet in sport facilities, provided live updates and streaming of match/game results, and executed new modes of program delivery for tournaments and leagues by drawing on digital technologies. Moreover, the Football Association's (FA) digital strategy called "The FA Matchday" allows youth soccer clubs to gather up-to-date information on players, clubs, fixtures, and leagues via an app. Similarly, Groundwork, a company that organizes, tracks, and accepts team payments online, directly makes it easier for parents to pay registration fees.

The question begs, why and how did this all happen? The remainder of this chapter explores the contexts and processes that have supported digital transformations in youth sport. This exploration is presented in three stages, including a description of precipitating jolts, challenges to the status quo, and widespread adoption. This approach mirrors a staged-based approach similar to that of institutional change (cf. Tolbert & Zucker, 1996; Greenwood et al., 2002). Within this framework, change starts with a jolt and response by an actor(s) (e.g., community sport club, governing association, entrepreneur) and builds toward widespread adoption at the institutional field level (e.g., youth sport). Therefore, in addition to describing the nature of digital transformations, we focus on "*how* elements of the broader social environment become manifest and elaborated inside organizations" (Suddaby et al., 2010, p. 1234). A focus on field-level change is important because the majority of studies on innovation and change within CSOs do not address how changes are connected to what is happening in society or how and why new approaches achieve widespread adoption (see Dowling et al., 2014; Washington & Patterson, 2011). As such, this chapter also provides a framework for the development of future research that seeks to understand the widespread adoption or resistance of digital transformations.

Precipitating Jolts in Youth Sport

Significant change within any context typically occurs as a result of a major pressure or "jolt" to an institutional field, a community of organizations, or an individual organization (Greenwood et al., 2002). Meyer et al. (1990) characterized change, inducing jolts, as being social, technological, or regulatory in nature. Similarly, other influential scholars have also categorized destabilizing pressures as functional, normative, and political (DiMaggio & Powell, 1983; Oliver, 1992). These jolts can destabilize (but not always change) established practices (Greenwood et al., 2002). From the internet becoming faster and widely accessible with mobile and WiFi networks to the development of smartphones, tablets, social media, and artificial intelligence, the 21st century undoubtedly encompasses a remarkable evolution of digital technology. These developments represent a technological jolt. A major cultural shift toward digitality (Negroponte, 1995) opened an entirely new set of possibilities for organizations to change the ways in which sport is managed and experienced (Hoeber & Hoeber, 2012; Hoeber et al., 2015; Thorpe & Dumont, 2019). Importantly, for jolts to change a field a number of processes must occur. First, there must be a challenge to the status quo.

Challenges to the Status Quo in Youth Sport

The deinstitutionalization of widespread established practices occurs as a result of efforts by actors who are new to the field, existing players who gain prominence or take control, or entrepreneurs (Greenwood et al., 2002). For jolts to translate into deinstitutionalization, an actor needs to perceive these jolts as worthy of their attention, and the motivation to do so may be different (see George et al., 2006; Oliver, 1991). The effect of the actions taken by these actors is "to disturb the socially constructed field-level consensus by introducing new ideas and thus the possibility of change" (Greenwood et al., 2002, p. 60). Essentially, these institutional actors are potential trendsetters or influencers who start by questioning the status quo. They ask, "why do we do things this way?" or "why do we not do things this other way?" Several main actors are influential in the disruption of the status quo in youth sport through the introduction of possible alternatives, such as sport governing bodies, club staff and volunteers, and entrepreneurs. Therefore, deinstitutionalization can start with actors within or external to an institution.

The role that governing bodies play in initiating a change process across a sport system has received the most attention in the sport management literature (Dowling et al., 2014; Legg et al., 2016; Parent et al., 2018). This occurrence is not surprising given the significant role they play in all forms of sport, including youth sport. Governing bodies typically challenge existing ways of doing things or introduce new ideas as a precursor to change that furthers their own agenda (e.g., athlete development, enhanced elite performance). Put another way, early disruption by governing bodies of institutionalized practices occurs as a way of maintaining control, legitimacy, and/or survival of the institution (Trank & Washington 2009). These governing bodies may be driven to explore the adoption of digital technologies because of the potential opportunity it presents to achieve an objective or because it presents a way for them to adhere to the pressures in the social environment, such as professionalization (Naraine & Parent, 2017; Thorpe & Dumont, 2019).

Another source of deinstitutionalization (and the introduction of new ideas) derives from the local club level. Research on CSOs has identified individual instances of digital transformations at the local level (e.g., Hoeber & Hoeber, 2012; Hoeber et al., 2015), yet the likelihood of this occurring in a youth sport context may depend on a number of factors. More specifically, the adoption of change depends on the nature of the change (e.g., controversial, incremental), the power of the individual club relative to its institutional field (Wigfield & Snelgrove, 2019), the existence of a tightly controlled governance structure (Legg et al., 2016), the strength of institutional norms (Riehl et al., 2019), assessments of threats to resources and control (George et al., 2006), and the leadership and pro-innovation characteristics of the club (Hoeber & Hoeber, 2012).

The third type of actor who has destabilized ways of doing things in youth sport is entrepreneurs. Driven by the motive for profit, entrepreneurs have played a significant role in introducing digital innovations in youth sport, among other innovations. For example, families have been directly sold opportunities to watch live streams of their athletes' games made possible by companies such as BallerTV or MVPCast. These companies whose names consist of strategic messaging, also offer opportunities for families to create highlight videos to share with recruiters. CSOs are also encouraged to promote the services to club members and earn a percentage of the sales (Hyman, 2012). Entrepreneurs have also offered digital business tools directly to governing associations and CSOs, such as the early adoption of a handheld device and software program to record and share information (Hoeber & Hoeber, 2012). Young athletes themselves (with the help of their parents) have also become entrepreneurs by leveraging the latest digital technologies, such as YouTube and Instagram, to promote themselves as a brand. As Thorpe and Dumont (2019) described it, "social media is playing an important role in raising the awareness of very young action sports participants and corporate awareness of their talent" and that "by the time these athletes reach their early and mid-teens some are deeply entrenched in the action sports economy" (p. 1645). The digital nature of these entrepreneurial activities can make this influencer particularly disruptive of the status quo as children and parents widely consume media and wish to emulate what they see (Thorpe & Dumont, 2019).

Following a period of deinstitutionalization in which existing practices are questioned, a stage described as pre-institutionalization occurs. In this stage, early innovation occurs independently by organizations, and the viability of potential new practices is considered (Greenwood et al., 2002). Although independent innovation can occur at any point in time, it is more likely to occur within an institutional field when a period of deinstitutionalization occurs first because it creates an opportunity for institutional members to maintain legitimacy (Scott, 2014). As potential solutions or innovations are developed, a key consideration is a technical viability. In other words, will the new practice work and achieve a purpose.

The development of solutions can be developed for problems perceived as being local (e.g., by a community sport club) or explored by governing or professional associations for specific issues or potential widespread use (Greenwood et al., 2002). For example, one study found that a CSO changed the way it tracked members, recorded game statistics, and shared results by using digital technologies instead of a paper and pencil method (Hoeber & Hoeber, 2012). The benefits of this switch were an increase in capacity to focus on value-added services as several hours were saved using the new approach and an enhancement to the participant experience (Hoeber & Hoeber, 2012).

At a governing body level, many national sport organizations (NSOs) have adopted the use of new social media platforms as a way of connecting with members as well as adhering to the pressures of appearing legitimate through modern business practices (Naraine & Parent, 2017). Therefore, a new practice can be developed at various levels of a sport system hierarchy, but, in either case, it can entail development in the early stages that may not reach widespread use. Furthermore, as the focus of these studies was at the organizational and not systemic or field level (Dowling et al., 2014), it is unclear whether these changes were linked to widespread adoption. For example, does the NSO's adoption of a new social media platform influence CSOs' subsequent adoption (i.e., top-down influence), or conversely does early adoption by CSO influence other CSOs (i.e., lateral influence) or NSOs (i.e., bottom-up influence).

Widespread Adoption of Digital Transformations in Youth Sport

Local practices become more widely adopted when *theorized* (Greenwood et al., 2002; Strang & Meyer, 1993). Theorization is particularly important in contexts that are highly institutionalized; that is, when practices (i.e., ways of doing things) are well established and structured (Greenwood et al., 2002). The youth sport system and associated practices and experiences in many countries fit this description.

The process of theorization begins with a *specification* of a problem. Typically, this specification involves the framing of a general organizational failing (Greenwood et al., 2002; Purdy et al., 2019). For example, an organization may not be achieving functional goals or acting in accordance with societal trends or norms. This type of approach was used by the Ontario Soccer Association, the governing body for the sport in Ontario, Canada to frame the need for a shift in its programming by arguing that elite performance was falling behind other nations and youth at the local levels were dropping out of soccer because they were not enjoying the sport as designed at the time (Legg et al., 2016).

When framing problems, disassociation of the moral foundations of the practice, as well as the assumptions and beliefs associated with it must be undertaken (Lawrence & Suddaby, 2006). When practices are highly institutionalized, which is often the case in sport, they become accepted as the only way of doing things (Riehl et al., 2019). Although disrupting the regulative foundations of a practice can be accomplished through policy change by actors with authority, a disruption of a practice's normative and cultural cognitive practices can be challenging (Scott, 2014). The framing of a problem need not dismantle the moral foundations of a practice to be successful. Instead, it may be more successful if it challenges the consistency of the existing practice with its institutional foundations (Purdy et al., 2019). In doing so, framing makes moral judgments about an existing practice (Entman, 1993), thereby leaving room for an alternative approach.

The framing of the problem can also draw on precipitating jolts and the greater environmental context when identifying a problem, such as an organizational field not keeping up with shifts in business practices or technological advances (e.g., a shift in the governance structure of amateur sport in Canada from an outdated kitchen-table type archetype to either a boardroom or executive office approach; Hoye et al., 2020; Kikulis et al., 1992; Parent et al., 2018). Within a federated sports model, such as the ones utilized in countries like Canada and Australia, these changes can be pushed down to CSOs through coercive or normative means. The role that governing bodies play in deinstitutionalizing change in youth sport outside of federated models has not been well documented by researchers, presenting an opportunity to understand the mechanisms they have employed to facilitate widespread adoption.

Next, theorization involves a *justification* of an innovation that is a viable solution (Tolbert & Zucker, 1996). Greenwood et al. (2002) argued that "diffusion occurs only if new ideas are compellingly presented as more appropriate than existing practices" (p. 60). Therefore, although the specification of a problem may be presented well, the justification of the specific solution is also important for diffusion. The importance of this distinction is illustrated by the example of a change to soccer programming in Ontario, Canada. Although stakeholders generally accepted the specified problem, there was much more resistance by stakeholders to the justification of a solution (Legg et al., 2016). Specifically, many stakeholders did not believe that the removal of scorekeeping, standings, and travel for kids would result in greater athlete development, elite performance, or athlete enjoyment (Snelgrove & Wigfield, 2019). The idea that it was not "real soccer" was expressed widely, meaning that the solution lacked moral legitimacy. This phenomenon has also been reported in other youth sport research (Green, 1997; Riehl et al., 2019).

For theorization to be effective, a new practice needs to be perceived as having pragmatic legitimacy (i.e., functionally useful) and formulated so other actors perceive it to have moral legitimacy (i.e., new ideas aligned with prevailing institutional norms; Greenwood et al., 2002). For example, the adoption of new digital technology such as virtual reality has to be perceived as being one that solves a problem effectively (e.g., skill training for young athletes to provide competitive advantage) and is perceived as being suitable for a context such as youth sport (Neumann et al., 2018). Therefore, messaging must be tailored with these two elements in mind.

Furthermore, another important issue related to theorization that is particularly relevant in the context of youth sport is determining how the innovation will be viable in various contexts, including the capacity of local clubs to implement a solution. Organizational members, consumers, and/or partners need to be ready and willing to adopt new technology. For example, in contrast to the past, roughly 76% of adults own a smartphone, 90% use the internet, and 67% use social media in advanced economies (Pew Research Centre, 2019). From a youth sport club perspective, technology has the potential to enhance operational capacity and member experiences, but it must have the organizational capacity (e.g., staff or volunteer expertise, infrastructure, finances) to invest in, implement, and/or utilize a new digital technology effectively. A lack of human and financial resources to implement an innovation has been found to be a key constraint to adoption by sport organizations (Hoeber & Hoeber, 2012; Hoeber et al., 2015; Legg et al., 2016; Naraine & Parent, 2017). Addressing this issue in the theorization stage increases the likelihood of adoption and reduced resistance (Legg et al., 2016). One way of doing so is through the use of local success stories which can be used as proof of concept and examples of the benefits of a change (e.g., adoption of new digital technology).

Innovations diffuse as they achieve pragmatic legitimacy (Greenwood et al., 2002). In the case of youth sport, we suggest that digital technology achieved pragmatic legitimacy because it was *perceived* to enhance club management and improve the development, recognition, and experience of young athletes. To date, sport management researchers have focused on digital transformations from the organizational side of youth sport; however, the consumer side is also worthy of attention as young athletes and their parents exert significant influence over the delivery of sport. Therefore, receptivity to digital technology should be discussed in terms of CSOs as well as athletes and their families.

Widespread changes at the CSO level can be attributed to a number of mechanisms. First, CSOs have had to diversify their revenue streams due to rising costs and limited revenue streams. The commercialism movement has provided a convenient backdrop to acquiesce to this environmental pressure and further commodify youth sport (Hyman, 2012); digital technology has served as one way of doing so. Second, as widespread use grows among clubs, threats related to legitimacy can lessen which makes adoption less risky. At this point, adoption is reliant on a CSO's leadership, capacity, and culture if it is to welcome and implement a digital innovation (Hoeber & Hoeber, 2012; Naraine & Parent, 2017). Third, CSOs have been pressured to change (either normatively or coercively) via a club certification process put forth by governing bodies (Schlesinger & Doherty, 2021). Although not specifically about embracing digitality, the implementation of specific processes, measures, and structures – all part of a certification process driven by the professionalization movement – is made possible in part through the use of digital technology.

Fourth, increased media coverage of certain youth sport clubs or leagues that are using it (e.g., live streaming) or featured in it (e.g., television) can create mimetic pressures for other clubs to adopt a similar approach to not appear to be behind. Additionally, as digital media coverage increases, parents and youth can pressure their own clubs to adopt a similar approach because they see personal benefits from being similarly featured. Elite youth soccer clubs, for example, understand many athletes aspire to play in the club's premier teams, and for this reason, youth soccer clubs make it a priority of developing players who can compete at an elite level (Bidaurrazaga-Letona et al., 2019). In order to achieve this vision, clubs invest in digital media and online communication for talent identification and development programs in pursuit of maximizing the effectiveness and efficiency of resources and avoid losing out on high-caliber prospects (Deprez et al., 2015; Hyman, 2012; Huijgen et al., 2014; Huijgen et al., 2010). As such, the adoption of digital technology can help CSOs remain relevant and competitive.

Future Directions

In addition to the mechanisms discussed, the future management and diffusion of digital technology also depend on an ability to tackle the potential negative effects of digitality on the youth sport experience. Pining for the days of old where technology was not pervasive aside, a critical perspective is still needed to avoid myopia. For example, parents' desire to leverage sport as a career option for their children and pay for college via sport scholarships increases early specialization among youth athletes (Meân & Kassing, 2007). The pressure for parents to do so is not simply the result of their personal fantasies of stardom (Hyman, 2012), it is also reflective of the increasing professionalization and commercialization of the sport industry as a whole (Thorpe & Dumont, 2019). Central to the problematic nature of early specialization is an overemphasis on competition and a suspension of enjoyment, central bi-products of a professionalized youth sport environment which are critical factors in dropout from sport (Duncan, 1997). Additionally, digitality enables other negative effects such as abuse (Sanderson & Weathers, 2020), and experience mission creep, where sport organizations move farther away from their core mission of delivering sport programming.

Although digital technology needs to continually undergo an evaluation to assess its usefulness in enhancing the governance and design of the youth sport landscape, digital advancements continue nevertheless and have yet to reach a peak. More and more companies are integrating artificial intelligence capabilities in human-experience platforms, developing new technological processes for budgeting and planning, and deploying disruptive technologies such as virtual reality, blockchain technology, and artificial intelligence (Deloitte, 2020; Naraine, 2019; Naraine & Wanless, 2020). How these technologies will be taken up to improve the management of youth sport clubs and alter the experiences of young athletes and their families remain to be seen. Several possibilities likely exist, such as the use of blockchain technology to enhance the management of CSOs (e.g., nonfungible tokens for ticketing, the secure storage of private information, selling collectible highlights). Other digital opportunities will inevitably develop, and it will be a matter of the degree to which they are perceived as providing an opportunity for sport organizations, taken up by a champion internal or external to the field of youth sport, and if the digital opportunity achieves pragmatic and moral legitimacy to diffuse across organizations.

Several questions remain underexplored as it relates to digital transformations in youth sport representing opportunities for future research. First, who engages in theorization initiatives is unclear. In the context of other types of transformations in youth sport, governing associations have been the focus of much attention; however, the role that governing associations or any other actors play in the process of theorization for digital transformations has not been addressed in the academic literature. Second, an investigation of successful and unsuccessful theorization of digital change in sport has not been the focus of much research. The integration of framing theory with institutional theory holds promise in this regard (George et al., 2006). Third, as digital technology continues to advance, and its adoption is widespread among CSOs and parents, it remains unclear to what extent the cost of adoption results in decreased participation or dropout (cf. Hyman, 2012). Increased costs continue to be identified as a significant constraint to participation for many families (Cohen, 2019) and any increases as a result of digital technology adoption may further serve to disadvantage youth from low and middle-income families. Future research might explore the decision process among leaders of sport at all levels in relation to these undesirable outcomes.

Last, there are few empirical examples in the sport management literature of failed attempts at the widespread implementation of digital transformations or acts of resistance (e.g., Hill et al., 2021). This lack of focus mirrors the general change literature in sport management (Riehl et al., 2019). Importantly, though, the professionalization of youth sport is not universal around the world. For example, many of New Zealand's community sport organizations (CSOs) have continued to use kitchen table archetype as an organizational and operational structure (Hill et al., 2021). Hill et al. attributed the continued usage of this approach to the valuation of symbolic and social capital over cultural and economic capital, as well as a lack of incentives and resources for CSOs to professionalize. Although the adoption of the kitchen table archetype over a more modern approach does not preclude the adoption of digital technologies, adoption and diffusion can be slowed as the infrastructure, processes, and policies in place are inadequate to support its implementation. These variations in professionalization provide a window into why some youth sport in some countries do not move to the next phase of change (e.g., differences in values and resources); however, further research is needed to deepen understanding.

In all of these aforementioned gaps, there is an opportunity to explore the role of the underlying logic that permeates the management and experience of youth sport, including how they are challenged or transformed by the rise of digitality. We have argued that logic related to professionalization and commercialization can be linked to digital transformations and their impact on changes in youth sport, but much empirical work is needed to explicate these relationships in detail.

References

Bidaurrazaga-Letona, I., Lekue, J. A., Amado, M., & Gil, S. M. (2019). Progression in youth Soccer: Selection and identification in youth soccer players aged 13–15 years. *The Journal of Strength and Conditioning Research*, *33*, 2548–2558. 10.1519/JSC.0000000000001924

Bowers, M., & Green, B. C. (2013). Reconstructing the community-based youth sport experience: How children derive meaning from unstructured and organized settings. *Journal of Sport Management*, *27*, 422–438. 10.1123/jsm.27.6.422

Cohen, K. (2019, August). Kids aren't playing enough sports. The culprit? Cost. *ESPN*. Retrieved from https://www.espn.com/espn/story/_/id/27356477/kids-playing-enough-sports-culprit-cost

Cuskelly, G., Taylor, T., Hoye, R., & Darcy, S. (2006). Volunteer management practices and volunteer retention: A human resource management approach. *Sport Management Review*, *9*, 141–163. 10.1016/S1441-3523(06)70023-7

Deloitte. (2020). Deloitte insights. *Deloitte*. Retrieved from https://www2.deloitte.com/content/dam/Deloitte/pt/Documents/tech-trends/TechTrends2020.pdf

Deprez, D. N., Fransen, J., Lenoir, M., Philippaerts, R. M., & Vaeyens, R. (2015). A retrospective study on anthropometrical, physical fitness, and motor coordination characteristics that influence dropout, contract status, and first-team playing time in high-level soccer players aged eight to eighteen years. *The Journal of Strength and Conditioning Research*, *29*, 1692–1704. 10.1519/JSC.0000000000000806

DiMaggio, P. J. & Powell, W. W. (1983). The iron cage revisited: Institutional isomorphism and collective rationality in organizational fields. *American Sociological Review*, *48*, 147–160.

Doherty, A., Misener, K., & Cuskelly, G. (2013). Toward a multidimensional framework of capacity in community sport clubs. *Nonprofit and Voluntary Sector Quarterly*, *43*, 124S–142S. 10.1177/0899764013509892

Duncan, J. (1997). Focus group interviews with elite young athletes, coaches and parents. In S. Ogle, J. Kremer, & K. Trew (Eds.), *Young people's involvement in sport* (pp. 153–175). Psychology Press.

Dowling, M., Edwards, J., & Washington, M. (2014). Understanding the concept of professionalisation in sport management research. *Sport Management Review*, *17*, 520–529. 10.1016/j.smr.2014.02.003

Entman, R. M. (1993). Framing: Toward clarification of a fractured paradigm. *Journal of Communication*, *43*, 51–58.

Friedman, H. (2013, September 20). When did competitive sports take over American childhood? *The Atlantic*. Retrieved from https://www.theatlantic.com/education/archive/2013/09/when-did-competitive-sports-take-over-american-childhood/279868/

George, E., Chattopadhyay, P., Sitkin, S. B., & Barden, J. (2006). Cognitive underpinnings of institutional persistence and change: A framing perspective. *Academy of Management*, *31*, 347–365. 10.5465/amr.2006.20208685

GlobeNewswire. (2019, December 26). *Youth sports market projected to reach $77.6 Billion by 2026 – comprehensive industry analysis & insights. Global NewsWire.* Retrieved from https://www.globenewswire.com/news-release/2019/12/26/1964575/0/en/Youth-Sports-Market-Projected-to-Reach-77-6-Billion-by-2026-Comprehensive-Industry-Analysis-Insights.html

Green, B. C. (1997). Action research in youth soccer: Assessing the acceptability of an alternative program. *Journal of Sport Management, 11*, 29–44. 10.1123/jsm.11.1.29

Greenwood, R., Suddaby, R., & Hinings, C. R. (2002). Theorizing change: The role of professional associations in the transformation of institutionalized fields. *Academy of Management Journal, 45*, 58–80. 10.5465/3069285

Hill, S., Kerr, R., & Kobayashi, K. (2021). Around the kitchen table with Bourdieu: Understanding the lack of formalization or professionalization of community sports clubs in New Zealand. *Sport in Society, 24*, 115–130. 10.1080/17430437.2019.1615893

Hoeber, L., & Hoeber, O. (2012). Determinants of an innovation process: A case study of technological innovation in a community sport organization. *Journal of Sport Management, 26*, 213–223. 10.1123/jsm.26.3.213

Hoeber, L., Doherty, A., Hoeber, O., & Wolfe, R. (2015). The nature of innovation in community sport organizations. *European Sport Management Quarterly, 15*, 518–534. 10.1080/16184742.2015.1085070

Holmes, E. (2018, February 16). DFB agrees Beyond Sport VR training deal. *SportsPro Media.* Retrieved from https://www.sportspromedia.com/news/dfb-agrees-beyond-sport-vr-training-deal/

Hoye, R., Parent, M. M., Taks, M., Naraine, M. L., Seguin, B., & Thompson, A. (2020). Design archetype utility for understanding and analyzing the governance of contemporary national sport organizations. *Sport Management Review, 23*, 576–587. 10.1016/j.smr.2019.10.002

Huijgen, B. C., Elferink-Gemser, M. T., Lemmink, K. A., & Visscher, C. (2014). Multidimensional performance characteristics in selected and deselected talented soccer players. *European Journal of Sport Science, 14*, 2–10. 10.1080/17461391.2012.725102

Huijgen, B. C., Elferink-Gemser, M. T., Post, W. J., & Visscher, C. (2010). Development of dribbling in talented youth soccer players aged 12–19 years: A longitudinal study. *Journal of Sports Sciences, 28*, 689–698. 10.1080/02640411003645679

Hyman, M. (2009). *Until it hurts: America's obsession with youth sports and how it harms our kids.* Beacon Press.

Hyman, M. (2012). *The most expensive game in town.* Beacon Press.

Kikulis, L. M., Slack., T., & Hinings, B. (1992). Institutionally specific design archetypes: A framework for understanding national sport organizations. *International Review for the Sociology of Sport, 27*, 343–368. 10.1177/101269029202700405

Lawrence, T., & Suddaby, R. (2006). Institutions and institutional work. In S., Clegg, C., Hardy, T., Lawrence, and W. Nord (Eds.), *Handbook of organisation studies* (pp. 215–254). SAGE.

Legg, J., Snelgrove, R., & Wood, L. (2016). Modifying tradition: Understanding organizational change in youth sport. *Journal of Sport Management, 30*, 369–381. 10.1123/jsm.2015-0075

Lewis, J. (2018). LLWS title game hits high, tournament up double-digits. *Sports Media Watch.* Retrieved from: https://www.sportsmediawatch.com/2018/08/little-league-ratings-highest-years/

Meân, L. J., & Kassing, J. W. (2007). Identities at youth sporting events: A critical discourse analysis. *International Journal of Sport Communication, 1*, 42–66. 10.1123/ijsc.1.1.42

Meyer, A. D., Brooks, G. R., & Goes, J. B. (1990). Environmental jolts and industry revolutions: Organizational responses to discontinuous change. *Strategic Management Journal, 11*, 93–110. http://www.jstor.org/stable/2486672

Naraine, M. (2019). The blockchain phenomenon: Conceptualizing decentralized networks and the value proposition to the sports industry. *International Journal of Sport Communication, 12*, 313–335.

Naraine, M., & Parent, M. (2017). Examining social media adoption and change to the stakeholder communication paradigm in not-for-profit sport organizations. *Journal of Amateur Sport, 3*, 55–81. 10.1123/ijsc.2019-0051

Naraine, M., & Wanless, L. (2020). Going all in on AI: Examining the value proposition of and integration challenges with one branch of artificial intelligence in sport management. *Sports Innovation Journal, 1*, 49–61. 10.18060/23898

Negroponte, N. (1995). *Being digital.* Knopf.

Neumann, D. L., Moffitt, R. L., Thomas, P. R., Loveday, K., Watling, D. P., Lombard, C. L., Antonova, S., & Tremeer, M. A. (2018). A systematic review of the application of interactive virtual reality to sport. *Virtual Reality, 22*, 183–198. 10.1007/s10055-017-0320-5

Oliver, C. (1991). Strategic responses to institutional processes. *Academy of Management Review, 16*, 145–179.

Oliver, C. (1992). The antecedents of deinstitutionalization. *Organizational Studies, 13*, 565–588. 10.5465/amr.1991.4279002

Parent, M. M., Naraine, M. L., & Hoye, R. (2018). A new era for governance structures and processes in Canadian national sport organizations. *Journal of Sport Management, 32*, 555–566. 10.1123/jsm.2018-0037

Pettigrew, A. M. (1990). Longitudinal field research on change: Theory and practice. *Organization Science, 1*, 267–292. 10.1287/orsc.1.3.267

Pew Research. (2019, March 7). Mobile connectivity in emerging economies. *Pew Research Center*. Retrieved from https://www.pewresearch.org/internet/2019/03/07/use-of-smartphones-and-social-media-is-common-across-most-emerging-economies/

Purdy, J., Ansari, S., & Gray, B. (2019). Are logics enough? Framing as an alternative tool for understanding institutional meaning making. *Journal of Management Inquiry, 28*, 409–419. 10.1177/1056492617724233

Riehl, S., Snelgrove, R., & Edwards, J. (2019). Mechanisms of institutional maintenance in minor hockey. *Journal of Sport Management, 33*, 93–105. https://doi.org/10.1123/jsm.2018-0041

Schlesinger, T., & Doherty, A. (2021). The utility of certification for managing the state-voluntary sport club relationship: An agency theory perspective. *Managing Sport & Leisure, 26*, 116–132. 10.1080/23750472.2020.1804438

Scott, W. R. (2014). *Institutions and organizations* (4th ed.). SAGE.

Southall, R. M., Hancock, K. L., Cooper, C. C., & Nagel, M. S. (2012). College World Series broadcasts: "They are what they are." *Journal of Sports Media, 7*, 41–60.

Snelgrove, R., & Wigfield, D. (2019, July 15). Making youth soccer less competitive: Better skills or a sign of coddled kids? *The Conversation*. Retrieved from https://theconversation.com/making-youth-soccer-less-competitive-better-skills-or-a-sign-of-coddled-kids-119061

Strang, D., & Meyer, J. W. (1993). Institutional conditions for diffusion. *Theory & Society, 22*, 487–511. https://www.jstor.org/stable/658008

Suddaby, R., Elsbach, K. D., Greenwood, R., Meyer, J. W., & Zilber, T. B. (2010). Organizations and their institutional environments – bringing meaning, values, and culture back in: Introduction to the special research forum. *Academy of Management Journal, 53*, 1234–1240. 10.5465/amj.2010.57317486

Thorpe, H., & Dumont, G. (2019). The professionalization of action sports: Mapping trends and future directions. *Sport in Society, 22*, 1639–1654. 10.1080/17430437.2018.1440715

Tolbert, P. S., & Zucker, L. G. (1996). Institutionalization of institutional theory. In S. Clegg, C. Hardy, & W. Nord (Eds.), *The handbook of organization studies* (pp. 175–190). SAGE.

Trank, C. Q., & Washington, M. (2009). Maintaining an institution in a contested organizational field. In T. B. Lawrence, R. Suddaby, and B. Leca (Eds.), *Institutional work* (pp. 236–261). Cambridge University Press.

Washington, M., & Patterson, K. D. W. (2011). Hostile takeover or joint venture: Connections between institutional theory and sport management research. *Sport Management Review, 14*, 1–12. 10.1016/j.smr.2010.06.003

Wigfield, D., & Snelgrove, R. (2019). Managing conflict and resistance to change in a minor hockey system. Case Studies in Sport Management, *8*(S1), S15–S20.

5

Digital Transformation in Not-for-Profit Sport Organizations

Ashley Thompson and Milena M. Parent

Introduction

Over the last 30 years, there have been dramatic shifts in organizations' economic, geopolitical, and sociocultural environments (Amis & Aïssaoui, 2013; Thompson & Parent, 2021). One such dramatic shift, globalization, has fostered connectivity among organizations worldwide while also simultaneously bringing challenges such as dealing with a variety of regulations and stakeholders (Daft, 2021; Hoye et al., 2020; Parent et al., 2018). Alongside this period of globalization, there has also been severe turbulence, like the 2008 economic recession that resulted in many organizations failing to survive (Burnes, 2017). There is also increased importance and focus on climate change and sustainability, stemming from the 2015 Paris UN Conference on Climate Change, which has pressured organizations to change from a strictly "profit" focus to one that also accounts for the public interest (Burnes, 2017; Daft, 2021). In addition, organizations are subject to increasing competitiveness, with mergers, acquisitions, and strategic alliances intensifying the business landscape (Burnes, 2017). Then, of course, there has been the COVID-19 pandemic, impacting organizations and practitioners all over the world (e.g., Byers et al., 2021; Doherty et al., 2020; Lachance, 2020; Mastromartino et al., 2020; Nauright et al., 2020).

Beyond these changes, the growth of digital technology has impacted organizations and their stakeholders. Digital technologies such as cloud computing, mobile connectivity, and social media (Moreira et al., 2018) have affected nearly every facet of human life, leading scholars to suggest we live in a "digital revolution" (Neugebauer, 2018) or a "digital age" (Ready et al., 2020). The exponential growth of digital technology has occurred in a relatively short period of time (Burnes, 2017). Much of the taken-for-granted technologies we rely on today did not exist prior to the late 1990s (Burnes, 2017). The internet, while still in its formative years in 1992, was seen as ineffective until Google emerged in 1998. Additionally, the launch of the iPhone in 2007 significantly impacted the course of human interaction as "smartphones and ubiquitous mobile access to the internet … have changed the way we communicate, work, access information, teach and learn, and – very importantly – how, what, and where we consume" (Neugebauer, 2018, p. 313).

DOI: 10.4324/9781003088899-7

These external environmental disruptions have forced organizations to adapt and engage in greater and faster changes (Burnes, 2017; Daft, 2021). Failing to recognize the prevalence and impact of digital technologies on today's organizations threaten their survival (Fenton et al., 2019). Organizations that recognize the disruption caused by digital technology have engaged in what is referred to as digital transformation (also called digitization, digitalization, or digital change; El Sawy et al., 2016). As we will see later in this chapter, digital transformation is the use of digital technologies to engage in major organizational change (Fitzgerald et al., 2013).

Despite the need for all types of organizations to respond to these environmental shifts and engage in organizational change in general – and digital transformation in particular – most research examining digital transformation has focused on for-profit organizations. For example, scholars have explored digital transformation in single organizations like LEGO (El Sawy et al., 2016) and in multiple organizations across various industries such as forestry and energy management (Fitzgerald et al., 2013; Imran et al., 2021). This research on the for-profit context has occurred at the expense of understanding digital transformation in not-for-profit organizations. This is problematic in a sport context because, in many parts of the world, not-for-profit sport organizations (NFPSOs) deliver sport-related services to millions of people (cf. Doherty et al., 2020; Thompson & Parent, 2021). How NFPSOs respond to these environmental changes will impact their organizations, their stakeholders, and thus society overall (Parent et al., 2018). NFPSOs are not immune to the environmental disruptions presented above, especially digital technology (Hoye et al., 2020; Parent et al., 2018). They must also adapt or risk losing critical funding as well as potentially face dissolution altogether while dealing with limited capacity issues, regulatory changes, and increasing demands from external funders (Parent et al., 2018).

As such, the purpose of this chapter is to examine digital transformation in NFPSOs. To do so, we start by examining the concept of organizational change. Then, we move to digital technology in organizations before combining the two ideas when we examine digital transformation in organizations. We present emerging trends before offering concluding remarks and potential future directions.

Organizational Change

As Tabrizi et al. (2019) and El Sawy et al. (2016) asserted, digital transformation is not about digital technology per se; it is primarily concerned with organizational change and change management practices. As such, to understand digital transformation, it becomes important to first understand organizational change.

Organizational change is an organization's response to external or internal pressures that cause it to move from its current form, quality, or state toward a future one (Fox-Wolfgramm et al., 1998; Poole & Van de Ven, 2004; Welty Peachey & Bruening, 2011). Changes can occur in areas such as the organization's structures, systems, processes, culture, people, products, services, and digital technology (Daft, 2021; Slack & Parent, 2006; Thompson & Parent, 2021). Change in these areas can be large-scale or small-scale. Large-scale changes – or radical changes – are fundamental changes that alter an organization's core components such as its orientation and structure (Thompson & Parent, 2021). On the other hand, small-scale changes – or convergent changes – are changes that occur within an existing orientation or structure (Legg et al., 2016).

As Tabrizi et al. (2019) argued, digital transformation is considered a large-scale/radical change. The distinctions between the sizes of change will become important as we discuss digital transformation later in this chapter. However, before discussing digital transformation in organizations, it is important to first define and understand digital technology.

Digital Technology in Organizations

The term *digital technology* can be interpreted in different ways by different individuals (Stone, 2019). In other words, managers and executives may have different understandings of what digital technology in organizations necessitates (El Sawy et al., 2016). Despite this ambiguity, organizations use digital technology in some form, either directly or indirectly (Fenton et al., 2019). Digital technology can be what Stone (2019) refers to as small "d" digital, which focuses on convergent changes in organizations such as changes in communication and information technology (IT) processes, while big "D" Digital focuses on radical changes and leveraging digital technologies to transform core organizational aspects such as structures, strategy, and culture. In the case of NFPSOs, previous research (e.g., Naraine & Parent, 2017a; Thompson & Parent, 2021) indicates these organizations have remained at the small "d" digital level as opposed to the big "D" Digital – a point we will return to later in this chapter.

Daft (2021, p. 12) asserted that "the digital revolution has changed everything – not just how we communicate with one another, find information, and share ideas, but also how organizations are designed and managed, how businesses operate, and how employees do their jobs." Digital technology has the potential to impact every aspect of organizations including their relationships with stakeholders (e.g., clients, partners, and employees), their use of data, and their structure (e.g., the nature of the roles and responsibilities within these organizations). Digital technology allows organizations to collaborate more effectively with key stakeholders (Bobsin et al., 2019), such as members in the case of NFPSOs. As we alluded to in our discussion of small "d" digital versus big "D" Digital, during change processes, digital technology can hold a dual role: it can be an area in which an organization chooses to change while also acting as a tool to leverage other changes such as strategy, structure, culture, or products and services. This latter situation is what digital transformation means.

Digital Transformation in Organizations

Digital transformation is "the use of new digital technologies ... to enable *major business improvements*" (Fitzgerald et al., 2013, p. 2). Major business improvements – or large-scale/radical changes – can include enhancing customer experiences, increasing organizational efficiencies, and changing existing business structures (Fitzgerald et al., 2013). Digital technologies like social media, mobile applications (Apps), analytics, and cloud computing – referred to by the acronym SMAC – are four primary technologies which drive digital transformation in organizations (El Sawy et al., 2016; Fitzgerald et al., 2013). Digital transformation helps organizations become more flexible, nimble, and adapt to the changing environmental conditions we discussed at the beginning of this chapter (Stone, 2019). It focuses on altering the organization to allow for faster changes to be made on a continuous basis.

Beyond the SMAC digital technologies mentioned above, there are six additional drivers of digital transformation in organizations. The first driver is the ability for certain products and services to be delivered using digital technology (Andal-Ancion et al., 2003). For many NFPSOs like national sport organizations (NSOs), multi-sport organizations (MSOs), and community sport organizations, the process of selling and delivering products and services to consumers is transferable to digital delivery, like the use of online systems to manage reservations and distribute tickets digitally to customers for sport events. In the same vein, many NSOs and MSOs have transitioned to online national membership registration systems. For example, in 2016, U SPORTS – the national governing body for university sport in Canada (Government of Canada, 2021) – transitioned its paper-based registration system to an online portal where student-athlete registration information was tracked from their entrance into university sport until their graduation. This portal allowed the organization to be more effective and efficient in tracking student-athlete eligibility, medical information, and participation rates (Thompson & Parent, 2021).

A second driver of digital transformation is the ability of organizations to use digital technology like the internet to share information with consumers (Andal-Ancion et al., 2003). For example, many NFPSOs use their websites as a space to share information with stakeholders such as athletes and coaches (Hoeber & Hoeber, 2012). This information can be placed in a members-only area on the website or be publicly available for all to access (Parent et al., 2019).

The third driver is the customizability of certain products as a result of digital technology (Andal-Ancion et al., 2003). For the Tokyo 2020 Olympic Games, the International Olympic Committee's (IOC) Olympic App allowed the organization to customize its offering to millions of consumers around the world. Through the App, users could personalize their experience and content by selecting their favorite team and sports.

A fourth driver of digital transformation is the ability of organizations to interact in real-time with consumers (Andal-Ancion et al., 2003). We are seeing NFPSOs increasingly opt for Apps like WhatsApp for both internal (i.e., between staff members) and external communication (i.e., between staff members and athletes and coaches) instead of using more traditional communication tools such as emails. For example, during sport events, NSOs can tap into the increasingly free Wi-Fi and communicate quickly with coaches and athletes about changes in event schedules using WhatsApp, as it is not device-specific (e.g., not specific to iPhones).

A fifth driver of digital transformation is how digital technology has enabled organizations to standardize processes (Andal-Ancion et al., 2003). For NSOs and MSOs, the implementation of national registration systems previously mentioned exemplifies the organizational standardizing processes across a sport operating in a federated network (i.e., "the delegation of power and authority from a central (national) authority to various regions usually within a bounded geographical context"; O'Boyle & Shilbury, 2020, p. 94). In this case, standardizing the membership registration practice is beneficial for the NSO but also for its provincial and local partners, as it removes the duplication of administrative tasks in the sport and increases efficiency between the organizations in the federated model (cf. Thompson & Parent, 2021). In addition, Hoeber and Hoeber (2012) examined technological innovation in a community sport organization that organized adult soccer leagues for 175 teams and 2,500 athletes. The organization moved away from using paper-based game sheets to electronic game sheets, which were used to register players at the beginning of games using their ID cards, keep track of their playing stats, and register game scores. This information could then be instantly uploaded to the organization's website for all to see. The electronic game sheets also allowed the organization to standardize these processes across its various leagues.

The sixth driver of digital transformation is how digital technology can facilitate relationships with external partners or create alliances when organizations lack knowledge or competencies in IT (Andal-Ancion et al., 2003). In the case of NFPSOs, many NSOs and MSOs have used expert consultants to engage in various digitally-related activities such as rebranding initiatives, website developments, creating national registration systems, and IT (e.g., Taks et al., 2020; Thompson, 2018; Thompson & Parent, 2021).

Digital transformation is therefore not only about implementing new technologies; rather, it involves changing the core fabric of organizations (Stone, 2019), including their (a) strategy, (b) structure and design, and (c) leadership and human resources. As we alluded to previously, the concept of digital transformation originated from the for-profit management literature and thus remains a relatively new concept in NFPSOs. Although we are seeing some momentum toward big "D" Digital transformations in NFPSOs, these organizations are still predominantly leveraging digital technology at a small "d" level (see Naraine & Parent, 2017a; Parent et al., 2020). Therefore, we discuss digital transformation and each organizational aspect (i.e., strategy, structure and design, and leadership and human resources) in the context this concept originated – for-profit organizations – and end each section discussing NFPSOs given the focus of this chapter. Finally, though each aspect is presented separately in this chapter, digital transformation issues regarding strategy, structure and design, and leadership and human resources are not mutually exclusive. As we illustrate below, changes in one area (e.g., strategy) can result in changes in another area (e.g., structure or leadership).

Organizational Strategy

Strategy is defined as "the determination of the basic long-term goals and objectives of an enterprise and the adoption of courses of action and the allocation of resources necessary for carrying out these goals" (Chandler, 1962, p. 13). There are three levels of strategy: corporate-level, business-level, and functional-level strategy (O'Brien et al., 2019). Corporate-level strategy is used in organizations that compete in multiple industries (Shank & Lyberger, 2015), whereas business-level strategy is concerned with how organizations position themselves to gain a competitive advantage over competitors within a given industry (O'Brien et al., 2019; Shank & Lyberger, 2015). Conversely, functional-level strategy is specific to each functional area in the organization such as marketing, operations, finance, and human resources (O'Brien et al., 2019; Shank & Lyberger, 2015). Using the Olympic Movement as an example, Figure 5.1 illustrates these different levels of strategy. As Figure 5.1 shows, the IOC is situated at the corporate level, the individual national Olympic committees are situated at the business level, and each has its own functional-level strategies. The distinction between these levels of strategy is important as we discuss the impact of digital technology on strategy next.

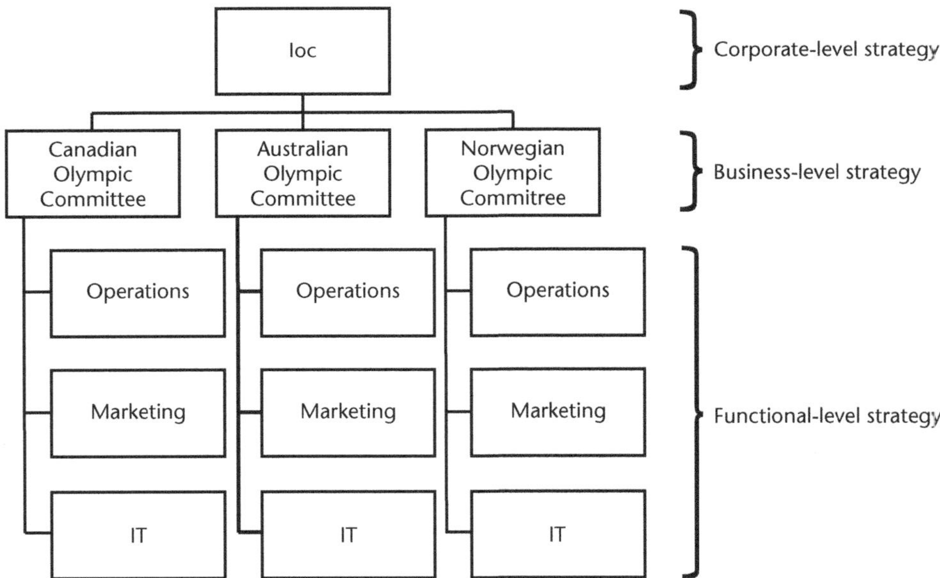

Figure 5.1 Levels of Strategy at the Olympic Movement

Digital transformation requires organizations to reflect on their *raison d'être* – who they are, why they do what they do, what services they provide, and how they measure their success (Stone, 2019). In for-profit and not-for-profit organizations, digital technology has traditionally been part of an organization's IT strategy, that is, the organization's functional-level strategy. However, with the prevalence of digital technology today, for-profit organizations, in particular, are adapting their existing business-level strategies to integrate digital technology by "rethink[ing] the role of IT strategy, from that of a functional-level strategy—aligned but essentially always subordinate to business strategy—to a fusion between IT strategy and business strategy into an overarching phenomenon" (Bharadwaj et al., 2013, p. 472).

This fusion or integration between IT strategy and business strategy has been named *digital business strategy* (Bharadwaj et al., 2013). Digital business strategy is trans-functional (Bharadwaj et al., 2013); in other words, it transcends organizations' functional areas. In the traditional organizational structure, digital technology is housed under the IT function of the organization as its own siloed functional area (see Figure 5.1). But in an organization that follows a digital business strategy, IT becomes part of every other function in the organization by having IT-specific or digitally-savvy employees dispersed across all functional areas in the organization (see below).

Bharadwaj et al. (2013) argued the increasingly pervasive digitalization of industries and organizations means digital business strategy will become a standard business strategy. There are several key benefits to incorporating digital business strategy for organizations. First, through digital technologies such as cloud computing, organizations become nimbler and can more readily adapt to changing circumstances through digital business strategies. Cloud computing is important for IT functions, but it is also becoming essential support for other organizational functions, including operations, marketing, human resources, and services (Bharadwaj et al., 2013). Second, organizations can scale their business up or down more quickly and easily. For example, a digital business strategy increases the speed at which organizations can and should launch their products (Bharadwaj et al., 2013; Bongiorno et al., 2018). In addition, a digital business strategy increases the speed at which organizations and their managers need to make decisions and respond to stakeholders in a timely manner (Bharadwaj et al., 2013; Bongiorno et al., 2018).

Compared to for-profit organizations, NFPSOs have historically lagged behind, especially in terms of professionalizing their organizations (cf. Amis et al., 2004; Kikulis et al., 1992; Thompson & Parent, 2021). This is no different when it comes to digital technology. It was only a few years ago that Canadian NSO leaders and staff members began to use digital technologies like social media as tools to engage with their key stakeholders (e.g., Naraine & Parent, 2016, 2017a, 2017b). Beyond social media, other forms of digital technology remain largely absent from NFPSOs' strategies (e.g., Nordiq Canada, n.d.-b; U SPORTS, n.d.-b; Water Ski and Wakeboard Canada, n.d.-b). So, the question becomes, what could digital business strategy look like in NFPSOs?

One organization, U SPORTS, is at the forefront of what digital business strategy could look like for NFPSOs. As previously mentioned, the organization underwent large-scale/radical changes in the past few years and leveraged digital technology to achieve its professionalization goal by developing a new website, increasing its social media engagement, and developing an online portal (Thompson, 2018; Thompson & Parent, 2021). Although digital technology is not explicitly stated in its strategy (see U SPORTS, n.d.-b) and these changes are still not quite to the scale of digital transformation or digital business strategy we see in for-profit organizations, there has been a visible increase in U SPORTS' digital technology use to achieve its desired changes, particularly as it relates to promoting its brand and student-athletes through digital channels.

Organizational Structure and Design

Along with strategy, digital transformation impacts organizations' structures and designs. Organizational structure can be defined as "the relatively stable arrangement and division of responsibilities, tasks, and people within an organization" (Carpenter & Sanders, 2009, p. 367) while organizational design can be defined as "the patterning of the structural elements of an organization" (Slack & Parent, 2006, p. 6). The digital revolution has propelled organizations to adapt to these changes by redesigning their structures, in other words, redesigning how organizations' tasks, responsibilities, and reporting structures are divided between IT and other functional areas (Bongiorno et al., 2018).

Digital technology impacts organizations' structures in several ways. First, like strategy, the digital revolution has resulted in organizations engaging in digital transformation to move IT from its siloed functional area to one integrated into each of the organization's functional areas such as marketing, operations, and finance. For example, in its digital transformation effort, LEGO restructured by moving its IT employees to other functional areas of the organization. This ensured IT employees were spread out in all its offices across the world so they could interact with their colleagues in other departments and understand their work challenges. It also ensured the IT staff understood they were, first and foremost, employees of LEGO as a whole rather than IT employees. In other words, although IT staff's work centered on the digital platforms, LEGO executives wanted to ensure all employees in the organization remained focused on their core product: the LEGO brick (El Sawy et al., 2016). LEGO's strategy could also work in the context of NFPSOs. Although NFPSOs like NSOs are traditionally smaller organizations with few staff members (see Parent et al., 2019) and are thus unlikely to have the capacity to hire IT staff for each functional area, these organizations could focus on hiring employees not only for their specific role or function (e.g., marketing, finance) but also who are digitally savvy. This would allow these organizations to better integrate IT with the other functional areas as these employees would be knowledgeable in using digital technology in their respective functions (see the discussion on digital transformation and leadership and human resource later in this section).

Second, employees are expected to be more flexible and have a positive attitude towards learning and adapting on the job (Neugebauer, 2018). For example, as part of its digital transformation process, LEGO changed its hiring practices by focusing on hiring digital generalists who fit its new flexible and adaptive culture instead of hiring people with highly specialized roles related to digital technology and IT. This allowed LEGO to move its employees around from different business and IT areas, which resulted in employees having a greater understanding of the overall organization. In other words, LEGO hired employees for *careers* at the organization rather than specific jobs (El Sawy et al., 2016). In the case of NFPSOs, hiring employees for careers rather than specific jobs is already common practice: in NSOs, employees can be hired for one role but often end up changing roles during the course of their career in the same NSO (Parent et al., 2019) or a new NSO. This is also the case in sport events where we see the job description is often more of a suggestion than a reality; organizing committee members reshape their job descriptions the moment they onboard to "get the job done" (Parent & Ruetsch, 2021, p. 146). Thus, continuing this inherent flexibility in NFPSO hiring practices combined with the practice of hiring digitally-savvy people highlights how digital technology can impact organizational structure and design in NFPSOs.

Third, with the number of digital technologies available to organizations, there has been an increase in "virtual" organizations. Virtual organizations are those which do not work in or own physical office space but collaborate via digital technologies to achieve their goals (cf. Cascio & Shurygailo, 2003; Zigurs, 2003). As a result of the COVID-19 pandemic and some workplace closures, an increasing number of organizations are now (at least temporarily if not permanently) virtual. Advancements in digital technology facilitated this process, and NFPSOs can leverage software and programs such as Zoom, Samepage, and Trello to conduct their day-to-day business (cf. Parent et al., 2020). "Going virtual" is beneficial for organizations as it reduces the (overhead) costs associated with traditional brick-and-mortar infrastructures. This is especially important for NFPSOs that constantly deal with limited financial resources (Parent et al., 2018) and are therefore incurring major cost savings by going virtual. For example, one early adopter of the virtual organization was Water Ski and Wakeboard Canada which fully transitioned to a virtual model in 2015 (Water Ski and Wakeboard Canada, n.d.-a). We are also seeing other NSOs either partly virtual, meaning some of their staff work in a physical office while others work from home (sometimes in another part of the country), or intending to become fully virtual in the near future as most of their staff already work from home. These organizations have recognized the cost savings associated with virtual models as well as the opportunity to hire the best employees, regardless of geography.

Fourth, one of the newer forms of organizing that began as a result of the digital revolution is the platform-based organization (Daft, 2021). Daft (2021) describes how traditional organizations follow a linear "pipe" model – similar to a systems-based approach – where resources are obtained by an organization (i.e., inputs), the organization then undergoes a process of converting the resources into products and/or services (i.e., throughputs) followed by pushing the products and/or services through the end of the pipe to their consumers (i.e., outputs). However, thanks to digital technology, new organizational forms are taking shape, including platform-based organizations, which "connect and enable users to both create and consumer something of value" (Daft, 2021). Platform-based organizations connect producers and consumers through digital technology and allow users to create something of value via the platform for other users to consume. These organizations create value by linking producers and consumers in one space. In the for-profit context, companies such as YouTube, Uber, and Airbnb would fall under a platform-based design (Daft, 2021; Moazed, 2016). Within NFPSOs, one example of a platform-like model is the Sport Information Resource Centre (SIRC; see www.SIRC.ca) which, through its website, facilitates the connection between producers of knowledge (e.g., researchers) to consumers of knowledge (e.g., practitioners). Its SIRC Forum is a platform that facilitates discussion among members of the sport community. SIRC is more of a platform-*like* model because they also produce content themselves, not just facilitate the experience for producers and consumers as is the case for organizations such as Uber and Airbnb.

Leadership and Human Resources

Given the prevalence of digital technology and digital transformation, El Sawy et al. (2016) discussed the importance of digital leadership, defined as "doing the right things for the strategic success of digitalization for the enterprise and its business ecosystem" (p. 142). Digital transformation has impacted leadership and human resources in organizations in three main ways.

First, while executives recognize the criticality of engaging in digital transformation, they may not always have the skills or competencies to lead organizations through this process (El Sawy et al., 2016; Fitzgerald et al., 2013; Ready et al., 2020; Stone, 2019). Senior organizational leaders often fail to understand how to lead and be successful in the digital economy (Ready et al., 2020). Thus, digital transformation starts with personal transformation. In other words, digital transformation requires leaders leading these changes to first and foremost transform themselves and then their teams (Ready et al., 2020). According to Ready et al. (2020), few employees feel their current leaders have the right mindset to lead their organization forward in this digital age. Moving forward in this digital age means leaders will need to be digitally savvy (Ready et al., 2020). Some of the skillsets and behaviors leaders needed in the last few decades are no longer relevant to the digital age while others may still be relevant. Ready et al. (2020) discuss some behaviors which are eroding, enduring, or emerging as a result of digital technology:

- *Eroding behaviors* – or behaviors that are no longer applicable in the digital age – include micromanaging, managing from the top-down, creating rigid and inflexible long-term plans, and taking a one-size-fits-all approach to managing organizations and teams.
- *Enduring behaviors* include demonstrating ethical conduct and integrity, building trust among stakeholders, leading by example, being customer-focused, and creating a clear vision.
- *Emerging leadership* behaviors as a result of digital technology include being digitally savvy, increasing collaboration among stakeholders to solve problems collectively, and making data-driven decisions.

To address this issue, we are seeing some NFPSOs hire senior staff members who understand and can use digital technology. For example, when Water Ski and Wakeboard Canada went virtual, they hired a CEO who had previous experience working in virtual organizations. Thus, hiring digitally-savvy leaders will be especially important for NFPSOs looking to transition to virtual models.

Second, digital technology has changed the nature of staff roles at all levels of the organization: leadership roles, middle-management roles, and lower-level employee roles. Digital transformation has brought new leadership roles to organizations, such as Chief Information Officers (CIOs) and Chief Digital Officers (CDOs) (Bongiorno et al., 2018; Fitzgerald et al., 2013; Neugebauer, 2018). Furthermore, digital technology and digital transformation have also increased the need for "data scientists" or people who specialize in data and digital technology at all levels of the organization (Davenport & Patil, 2012). This is especially the case as an increasing number of organizations use big data to help them in their decision-making processes (Dorner & Edelman, 2015). Digital transformation will also result in organizations needing more IT-related support through increased IT staff numbers given the overall greater use of digital technology (El Sawy et al., 2016). For example, as LEGO engaged in its digital transformation and integrated more digital technology, the organization's IT workforce grew by 20% yearly (El Sawy et al., 2016). Likewise, NFPSOs will sooner or later need to restructure to have one or more staff hired specifically for "digital" aspects, individuals who can leverage digital technologies to allow the organization to be more efficient and adaptable to the changing environmental circumstances discussed above. We are starting to see this already occurring in NSOs which have added roles specific to digital and social media (e.g., Alpine Canada, n.d.; Nordiq Canada, n.d.-a; Sport Information Resource Centre, n.d.; U SPORTS, n.d.-a). Despite this early progress, these roles remain at the lower organizational level, as opposed to senior leadership roles, which could mitigate the effect of digital transformations related to integrating digital technology in these organizations' business-level strategies.

Third, the impacts of digital technology and the need for digital transformation will require organizations and their employees to adopt new and different ways of thinking. Although we have already discussed the importance of digitally-savvy senior leadership, digital transformation will require members at *all levels* of the organization to also be digitally savvy (Ready et al., 2020). For NFPSOs, this means hiring more "digitally-minded" people (El Sawy et al., 2016; Ready et al., 2020). Millennials, Generation Z, and future generations will form NFPSOs' core workforce in the near future. These generations have grown up, to various extents, with digital technology and will come into organizations with their own expectations regarding the use of technology in their everyday work (El Sawy et al., 2016). They will enter the workforce with greater expectations regarding flexible working hours and locations, as well as expectations regarding their workplaces' use and quality of digital technologies (El Sawy et al., 2016). These expectations have, in fact, already emerged due to the COVID-19 pandemic. Thus, organizations will have to be prepared to continue to account for and adapt to these changes in the workplace environment.

In summary, digital transformation does not come without challenges. Like all major change initiatives, digital transformation is a long-term process. All organizations, including NFPSOs, will succeed in some aspects of their digitalization while failing in others. However, the important piece is to learn from the failures and adjust strategies as needed until they become successful (El Sawy et al., 2016).

Emerging Trends

We see three emerging trends related to digital transformation which will impact NFPSOs. The first is the increase in virtual-based models. A key driver of this trend has been the COVID-19 pandemic: NFPSO staff have been required to work from home. As discussed above, there are many benefits to working in virtual models including greater flexibility for employees, significant overhead cost savings for the organization, and the ability and flexibility to hire the best person regardless of geographical restrictions (cf. Cascio & Shurygailo, 2003; Fenton et al., 2019; Zigurs, 2003).

A second emerging trend for organizations in general – and NFPSOs in particular – is the development of a stronger digital infrastructure (Dimension Data, 2019); integrating new programs, software, and applications to help organizational operations and efficiencies is becoming the norm. We are already seeing these trends in some NFPSOs that have adopted digital technologies like new digital registration systems, communication tools, and digital file storage systems.

Third, the increasingly rapid pace of digital transformation occurring in organizations and society also brings increased importance on risk and security issues surrounding digital technologies (Neugebauer, 2018). Cybersecurity in organizations has and will become an even more important trend for organizations engaging in digital transformation moving forward (Dimension Data, 2019). This trend has become especially important for NFPSOs given their limited financial and human resources capacity (Parent et al., 2018), as well as their lack of IT-specific roles. Natasha Johnston, Executive Director of Ringette Canada, illustrated this vulnerability when she explained how Ringette Canada had experienced a cyber-attack (see Johnston, 2019). The organization's server was hit by ransomware, a type of malware that blocked access to all of the organization's files stored on a server. In exchange for the software needed to decrypt the malware, the organization was required to pay money to the cybercriminals. Ultimately, Ringette Canada did not pay the ransom and opted to recreate its files anew. After this experience, the organization chose a cloud-based solution as an added layer of security against future attacks (Johnston, 2019). This example highlights the criticality of cybersecurity for organizations as digital technology – particularly those used by cybercriminals – becomes more sophisticated (Neugebauer, 2018).

Conclusions and Future Research Directions

Digital transformation has arrived and is here to stay. Some NFPSOs have already started adapting but the remainder will need to follow suit if they want to survive and thrive. Properly undertaking digital transformation will require NFPSOs to make changes to their strategy, their structure and design, and their leadership and human resources, which, as we previously noted, are not mutually exclusive.

Considering the information presented in this chapter, there are several areas for future research we believe would deepen researchers' and managers' understanding of digital transformation in NFPSOs. In particular, there is a need to empirically explore the use of digital technology and digital transformation in NFPSOs. In terms of digital technology, research should explore what digital technologies NFPSO staff and Board members are using in NFPSOs' management and governance, respectively, and which digital technologies are more important in gaining and sustaining a competitive advantage in light of limited capacity. Researchers should also examine the benefits, challenges, and best practices associated with implementing digital technology.

Building off these initial research questions, scholars should then further explore how NFPSO leaders conceptualize and understand digital transformation and how NFPSOs are engaging in digital transformation, if at all. Research should also focus on the barriers, facilitators, and best practices related to digital transformation.

There are also several research questions that can be developed related to the three core organizational aspects discussed above. First, in terms of strategy, potential questions include:

- What does digital business strategy look like in NFPSOs?
- How can NFPSOs integrate digital technology into their business strategies?

Second, in relation to structure and design, potential research questions include:

- How are NFPSOs changing their organizational structures to integrate digital technologies (if at all)?
- At what organizational level are NFPSOs hiring digital-specific roles (e.g., senior-level, middle-management, and/or lower-level roles)?

Third, regarding leadership and human resources, research questions could include:

- What does digital leadership look like during digital transformation in NFPSOs?
- In a federated model, to what extent can digital transformation and digital leadership affect sport system alignment?
- Can efficiencies be garnered through digital transformation that could not otherwise have occurred?

In conclusion, given the dramatic technological shifts brought on by the digital revolution, we cannot stress enough how imperative it is for NFPSOs to leverage digital technologies and engage in transformative change to ensure the continued success of their organizations and sports for generations to come.

References

Alpine Canada. (n.d.). *Alpine Canada: Staff and board*. Retrieved December 12, 2020, from https://alpinecanada.org/about/staff

Amis, J., & Aïssaoui, R. (2013). Readiness for change: An institutional perspective. *Journal of Change Management*, *13*(1), 69–95. 10.1080/14697017.2013.768435

Amis, J., Slack, T., & Hinings, C. R. (2004). Strategic change and the role of interests, power, and organizational capacity. *Journal of Sport Management*, *18*(2), 158–198. 10.1123/jsm.18.2.158

Andal-Ancion, A., Cartwright, P. A., & Yip, G. S. (2003). The digital transformation of traditional business. *MIT Sloan Management Review*, *44*(4), 34–41.

Bharadwaj, A., El Sawy, O. A., Pavlou, P. A., & Venkatraman, N. (2013). Digital business strategy: Toward a next generation of insights. *MIS Quarterly*, *37*(2), 471–482. 10.25300/MISQ/2013/37:2.3

Bobsin, D., Petrini, M., & Pozzebon, M. (2019). The value of technology affordances to improve the management of nonprofit organizations. *RAUSP Management Journal*, *54*(1), 14–37. 10.1108/RAUSP-07-2018-0045

Bongiorno, G., Rizzo, D., & Vaia, G. (Eds.). (2018). *CIOs and the digital transformation*. Springer International Publishing. 10.1007/978-3-319-31026-8

Burnes, B. (2017). *Managing change* (7th ed.). Pearson Education Limited.

Byers, T., Gormley, K.-L., Winand, M., Anagnostopoulos, C., Richard, R., & Digennaro, S. (2021). COVID-19 impacts on sport governance and management: A global, critical realist perspective. *Managing Sport and Leisure*. Advance online publication. 10.1080/23750472.2020.1867002

Carpenter, M. A., & Sanders, W. G. (2009). *Strategic management: A dynamic perspective: Concepts and cases* (2nd ed.). Pearson Prentice Hall.

Cascio, W. F., & Shurygailo, S. (2003). E-leadership and virtual teams. *Organizational Dynamics*, *31*(4), 362–376. 10.1016/S0090-2616(02)00130-4

Chandler, A. D. (1962). *Strategy and structure: Chapters in the history of the industrial enterprise*. Martino Fine Books.

Daft, R. (2021). *Organization theory & design* (13th ed.). Cengage.

Davenport, T. H., & Patil, D. J. (2012). Data scientist: The sexiest job of the 21st century. *Harvard Business Review*, *90*(10). https://hbr.org/2012/10/data-scientist-the-sexiest-job-of-the-21st-century

Dimension Data. (2019). *Turn disruption into opportunity* [E-Book]. NTT Ltd.

Doherty, A., Millar, P., & Misener, K. (2020). Return to community sport: Leaning on evidence in turbulent times. *Managing Sport and Leisure*. Advance online publication. 10.1080/23750472.2020.1794940

Dorner, K., & Edelman, D. (2015). *What 'digital' really means*. McKinsey Digital. https://www.mckinsey.com/industries/technology-media-and-telecommunications/our-insights/what-digital-really-means

El Sawy, O. A., Amsinck, H., Kræmmergaard, P., & Vinther, A. L. (2016). How LEGO built the foundations and enterprise capabilities for digital leadership. *MIS Quarterly Executive*, *15*(2), 141–166.

Fenton, A., Fletcher, G., Griffiths, M., Fletcher, G., & Griffiths, M. (2019). *Strategic digital transformation: A results-driven approach*. Routledge. 10.4324/9780429020469

Fitzgerald, M., Kruschwitz, N., Bonnet, D., & Welch, M. (2013). Embracing digital technology: A new strategic imperative. *MIT Sloan Management Review*, *55*(2), 1–12.

Fox-Wolfgramm, S. J., Boal, K. B., & Hunt, J. G. (1998). Organizational adaptation to institutional change: A comparative study of first-order change in prospector and defender banks. *Administrative Science Quarterly*, *43*(1), 87–126. 10.2307/2393592

Government of Canada. (2021, July 5). *National multisport service organizations*. https://www.canada.ca/en/canadian-heritage/services/sport-organizations/national-multisport-service.html

Hoeber, L., & Hoeber, O. (2012). Determinants of an innovation process: A case study of technological innovation in a community sport organization. *Journal of Sport Management*, *26*(3), 213–223.

Hoye, R., Parent, M. M., Taks, M., Naraine, M. L., Seguin, B., & Thompson, A. (2020). Design archetype utility for understanding and analyzing the governance of contemporary national sport organizations. *Sport Management Review*, *23*(4), 576–587. 10.1016/j.smr.2019.10.002

Imran, F., Shahzad, K., Butt, A., & Kantola, J. (2021). Digital transformation of industrial organizations: Toward an integrated framework. *Journal of Change Management*. Advance online publication. 10.1080/14697017.2021.1929406

Johnston, N. (2019, September 18). Are your files safe? Reflections from Ringette Canada on a ransomware attack. *The Sport Information Resource Centre*. https://sirc.ca/blog/are-your-files-safe-reflections-from-ringette-canada-on-a-ransomware-attack/

Kikulis, L. M., Slack, T., & Hinings, C. R. (1992). Institutionally specific design archetypes: A framework for understanding change in national sport organizations. *International Review for the Sociology of Sport*, *27*(4), 343–368. 10.1177/101269029202700405

Lachance, E. L. (2020). COVID-19 and its impact on volunteering: Moving towards virtual volunteering. *Leisure Sciences*, 1–7. 10.1080/01490400.2020.1773990

Legg, J., Snelgrove, R., & Wood, L. (2016). Modifying tradition: Examining organizational change in youth sport. *Journal of Sport Management*, *30*(4), 369–381. 10.1123/jsm.2015-0075

Mastromartino, B., Ross, W. J., Wear, H., & Naraine, M. L. (2020). Thinking outside the 'box': A discussion of sports fans, teams, and the environment in the context of COVID-19. *Sport in Society, 23*(11), 1707–1723. 10.1080/17430437.2020.1804108

Moazed, A. (2016, May 1). *Platform business model—Definition: What is it?* Applico. https://www.applicoinc.com/blog/what-is-a-platform-business-model/

Moreira, F., Ferreira, M. J., & Seruca, I. (2018). Enterprise 4.0 – the emerging digital transformed enterprise? *Procedia Computer Science, 138*(1), 525–532. 10.1016/j.procs.2018.10.072

Naraine, M. L., & Parent, M. M. (2016). "Birds of a feather": An institutional approach to Canadian National Sport Organizations' social-media use. *International Journal of Sport Communication, 9*(2), 140–162. 10.1123/ijsc.2016-0010

Naraine, M. L., & Parent, M. M. (2017a). This is how we do it: A qualitative approach to National Sport Organizations' social-media implementation. *International Journal of Sport Communication, 10*(2), 196–217. 10.1123/IJSC.2017-0006

Naraine, M. L., & Parent, M. M. (2017b). Examining social media adoption and change to the stakeholder communication paradigm in not-for-profit sport organizations. *Journal of Amateur Sport, 3*(2), 55. 10.17161/jas.v3i2.6492

Nauright, J., Zipp, S., & Kim, Y. H. (2020). The sports world in the era of COVID-19. *Sport in Society, 23*(11), 1703–1706. 10.1080/17430437.2020.1834196

Neugebauer, R. (Ed.). (2018). *Digital transformation.* Springer International Publishing.

Nordiq Canada. (n.d.-a). *Our people.* Nordiq Canada. Retrieved December 12, 2020, from https://nordiqcanada.ca/about/our-people/

Nordiq Canada. (n.d.-b). *Strategic ends.* Nordiq Canada. https://nordiqcanada.ca/wp-content/uploads/Strategic-Ends.pdf

O'Boyle, I., & Shilbury, D. (2020). Sport systems, national sport organisations and the governance of sport codes. In D. Shilbury & L. Ferkins (Eds.), *Routledge handbook of sport governance* (1st ed.). Routledge. 10.4324/9780429440250

O'Brien, D., Parent, M. M., Ferkins, L., & Gowthorp, L. (2019). *Strategic management in sport.* Routledge.

Parent, M. M., Naraine, M. L., & Hoye, R. (2018). A new era for governance structures and processes in Canadian national sport organizations. *Journal of Sport Management, 32*(6), 555–566. 10.1123/jsm.2018-0037

Parent, M. M., & Ruetsch, A. (2021). *Managing major sports events: Theory and practice.* Routledge.

Parent, M. M., Taks, M., Naraine, M. L., Hoye, R., Seguin, B., & Thompson, A. (2019). *Canadian national sport organizations' governance landscape study—Survey results* [Research Report]. The University of Ottawa.

Parent, M. M., Taks, M., Seguin, B., Naraine, M. L., Hoye, R., Thompson, A., & Lachance, E. L. (2020). *Governance, branding, and social media in Canadian national sport organizations: 2020 workshop report* [Research Report]. The University of Ottawa.

Poole, M. S., & Van de Ven, A. H. (Eds.). (2004). *Handbook of organizational change and innovation.* Oxford University Press.

Ready, D. A., Cohen, C., Kiron, D., & Pring, B. (2020). The new leadership playbook for the digital age. *MIT Sloan Management Review, 97*(1), 1–19.

Shank, M. D., & Lyberger, M. R. (2015). *Sports marketing: A strategic perspective* (5th ed.). Routledge.

Slack, T., & Parent, M. M. (2006). *Understanding sport organizations: The application of organization theory* (2nd ed.). Human Kinetics.

Sport Information Resource Centre. (n.d.). *Contact SIRC.* The Sport Information Resource Centre. Retrieved December 12, 2020, from https://sirc.ca/contact-sirc/

Stone, S. M. (2019). *Digitally deaf: Why organizations struggle with digital transformation.* Springer International Publishing. 10.1007/978-3-030-01833-7

Tabrizi, B., Lam, E., Girard, K., & Irvin, V. (2019). Digital transformation is not about technology. *Harvard Business Review.* https://hbr.org/2019/03/digital-transformation-is-not-about-technology

Taks, M., Seguin, B., Naraine, M. L., Thompson, A., Parent, M. M., & Hoye, R. (2020). Brand governance practices in Canadian national sport organizations: An exploratory study. *European Sport Management Quarterly, 20*(1), 10–29. 10.1080/16184742.2019.1690538

Thompson, A. (2018). *Understanding the impact of radical change on the effectiveness of national-level sport organizations* [Master's thesis, University of Ottawa]. 10.20381/ruor-22340

Thompson, A., & Parent, M. M. (2021). Understanding the impact of radical change on the effectiveness of national-level sport organizations: A multi-stakeholder perspective. *Sport Management Review, 24*(1), 1–23. 10.1016/j.smr.2020.04.005

U SPORTS. (n.d.-a). *Contact Us*. U SPORTS. Retrieved December 12, 2020, from https://usports.ca/en/about/contact

U SPORTS. (n.d.-b). *U SPORTS strategic plan 2019-2024*. U SPORTS. https://usports.ca/uploads/hq/By_Laws-Policies-Procedures/Strategic_Plan/2019-2024/USports_StrategicPlan19_digital_EN.pdf

Water Ski and Wakeboard Canada. (n.d.-a). *Our structure*. Water Ski and Wakeboard Canada. Retrieved December 14, 2020, from https://wswc.ca/about-us/our-committees/

Water Ski and Wakeboard Canada. (n.d.-b). *Strategic plan*. Water Ski and Wakeboard Canada. https://wswc.ca/policies/strategic-plan/

Welty Peachey, J., & Bruening, J. (2011). An examination of environmental forces driving change and stakeholder responses in a football championship subdivision athletic department. *Sport Management Review*, *14*(2), 202–219. 10.1016/j.smr.2010.09.002

Zigurs, I. (2003). Leadership in virtual teams: Oxymoron or opportunity? *Organizational Dynamics*, *31*(4), 339–351. 10.1016/S0090-2616(02)00132-8

6

Virtual Participatory Sport Events

Millicent Kennelly and Kevin Filo

Introduction

This chapter will examine the emergence of virtual participatory sport events, with a specific focus on running events. It will start by considering the growth in participatory sport events over the past decade. It will touch on the gradual emergence of virtual running event options and the upsurge in these events during the COVID-19 pandemic. This chapter will consider how digital advancements (i.e., wearable physical activity trackers, fitness apps, and social media) have facilitated the disruption of the participatory sport event landscape and what it means for the management of the sector moving forward. Finally, this chapter will discuss social leveraging (Chalip, 2006) in the context of participatory sport events and will examine (if) how the *communitas* commonly associated with participating in-person can translate to the world of virtual events. An adaptation of Chalip's (2006) work on social leveraging is proposed, and scholarly and applied implications are discussed.

Participatory Sport Events

There has been immense growth and commercialization of events in recent decades (Lundberg et al., 2019), denoting the significant role that events of differing types play in entertaining, socially connecting, and contributing economically and culturally to communities. Internationally, events play a variety of critical roles for sport organizations at all levels (Kennelly, 2011). For example, sport events provide revenue through participation fees, tickets sales, sponsorships, the sale of media rights, merchandise, and corporate hospitality. Sport events also provide a "shop front" for sports and athletes to gain exposure and build relationships with prospective members, supporters, and other community stakeholders. Further, sport events provide opportunities for athletes and technical officials to advance their fitness, performance, skills, and knowledge (Kennelly, 2011).

In recent decades, participatory sport events such as fun runs, triathlons, obstacle-endurance races, open water swims, and cycling challenges, have grown in popularity. For example, the inaugural Gold Coast Marathon in Australia was held in 1979 and comprised a marathon, half-marathon, and fun run with a combined field of 691 runners. By 2019, the Gold Coast

DOI: 10.4324/9781003088899-8

Marathon had grown into an eight-race weekend attracting 26,287 runners, 3678 of whom traveled from overseas (Gold Coast Marathon, n.d.).

The Gold Coast Marathon is owned and run by a government agency, and illustrates how traditional sport organizations are no longer the only entities delivering sport events (Kennelly, 2017; Phillips & Newland, 2014). Many participatory sport events are organized by third-party providers who operate "outside ... recognized traditional and institutionalized sport development pathways" (Phillips & Newland, 2014, p. 107). These third-party providers include professional event management companies, charities, and a range of other entities (i.e., universities, media companies, travel companies, community groups, and government agencies) that are based outside the sport industry. For such entities, participatory sport events provide a vehicle to raise money (i.e., for profit or community causes and charities), promote awareness (i.e., of a business, cause, or community issue), encourage community health and wellbeing outcomes, and/or may be held with sport-for-development objectives in mind (Kennelly, 2017; Schulenkorf et al., 2019).

While Armrecht and Andersson (2020) described the rapid growth of participatory sport events as somewhat "baffling" (p. 457), other authors have attributed their popularity to their challenging yet fun and achievable nature, alignment with charity fundraising objectives, use of accessible locations, and openness to people of all ages, and varying levels of physical fitness and skill (Filo et al., 2009; Kennelly, 2017; Zhou & Kaplanidou, 2018). In a study mapping global running participation, Jakob Andersen (2019) surveyed the race results of international running events and concluded that contemporary runners are on average older and slower than in the past and that in recent years female runners had outstripped male participation. These findings suggest that participatory sport events such as marathons, previously viewed as the "great suburban Everest" (Shipway & Jones, 2008) and a preserve of serious, competitive, and largely male athletes, are now more accessible to runners of varying skill and fitness levels (Hillman et al., 2021; Lamont & Kennelly, 2019). Further, such participatory sport events represent a flexible way for people to engage in physical activity in an era characterized by time fragmentation, individualism, and an aversion to committing to more traditional forms of sport (Hajkowicz et al., 2013).

For the above reasons, participatory sport events have been conceptualized as disruptors of traditional models of sport participation, as well as catalysts for entrepreneurialism (Lamont & Kennelly, 2019). As discussed below, this entrepreneurialism is evident in relation to participatory running events, which are the focus of this chapter. Running events range from short fun runs (i.e., 5–10 km), through to half (21.1 km), full (42.2 km), or ultra-marathons (over 42.2 km), which have traditionally been staged in a variety of repurposed outdoor spaces including on footpaths, roads, parks, and off-road trails. As discussed below, technological advancements during the 2010s saw the emergence of virtual running events and while the uptake of such events was initially gradual, the COVID-19 pandemic saw a rapid increase in the number and range of virtual running events on offer.

Digital Disruption of the Participatory Sport Event Market

Digital disruption refers to the transformation of modes of doing business caused by emerging digital technologies and innovations. The 2010s saw progressive digital disruption of the participatory sport event space with the introduction of virtual running events, which Race Roster (2020) predicted would become a "powerful industry trend" (p. 2). In the same decade, wearable physical activity trackers exploded in popularity (particularly between 2016 and 2017), with an ever-expanding range of devices hitting the market (Bunn et al., 2018). Wearable GPS-enabled devices (i.e., smartwatches produced by brands such as Fitbit, Garmin, Polar, and Suunto) track and map an individual's performance and fitness through a collection of real-time data (i.e., distance traversed, heart rate, step count, and calorie expenditure). Individuals can use this data to monitor and improve their training and event performance. Wearable devices also provide a foundation for virtual events. They offer a means for individuals to track, measure, and prove their participation in a remotely organized virtual event.

The widespread adoption of such wearable technology has been accompanied by gamification of physical activity, whereby statistics collected on an individual's smartwatch can be synced to a range of fitness applications which can then be used to score or compare performance to others over the same distances or on the same routes, and which enable individuals to share their physical activity on social media (Bitrián et al., 2020; Tu et al., 2019). While some virtual races have used an honor system (i.e., individuals sign up, pay their registration fees and the organizers trust they will accomplish the event requirements), most virtual events require participants to prove their participation by uploading data collected by wearable activity trackers to commercial fitness tracking apps such as Strava or ASICS RunKeeper.

The organizers of virtual running events were starting to embrace these technological advancements in the 2010s; however, at that time such events were uncommon relative to the thriving provision of in-person event options (Miller, 2019). The COVID-19 pandemic turned the participatory sport event sector on its head, with many events being postponed or canceled. In response, an increasing number of event organizers sought to innovate through the introduction of various permutations of virtual events (i.e., synchronous or asynchronous races, races over modified distances, innovative challenges, and/or races with atypical approaches to recording performance). For example, the Gold Coast Marathon was canceled in both 2020 and 2021, with organizers instead offering virtual event options to those who had signed up. During the COVID-19 pandemic, virtual events thrived: in many instances, they were the only option for runners who wished to participate in an event (Miller, 2020; Race Roster, 2020). Under pandemic conditions, virtual events enabled individuals to participate flexibly – to choose a convenient time and route which accommodated local circumstances (i.e., lockdowns and/or regulations related to outdoor exercise). Stories and images of individuals running marathons inside apartments, on balconies, or in tiny backyards emerged (Associated Press, 2020).

While the COVID-19 pandemic rapidly propelled the market for virtual running events, anecdotally, other contemporary trends and features of such events have also contributed to their success. In an article discussing the rise of virtual events pre-COVID-19, Miller (2019) suggested that virtual event options make running events accessible to new markets. Miller advanced the idea that virtual events could serve as stepping-stones for novice runners who are initially too intimidated to try in-person events. The flexibility of virtual events could also suit parents with dependent children, particularly single parents, who may find it challenging to arrange childcare in order to complete in-person events (Miller, 2019). From this perspective, virtual events provide a way for individuals to overcome cost and geographical constraints associated with in-person event participation. A runner without local access to in-person events could sign up for a virtual race in any part of the world. Finally, Miller (2019) suggested that virtual races could serve as an avenue for returning to running competition after injury.

While empirical evidence is yet to elucidate why participants register for virtual running events, it appears virtual events have effectively tapped into ongoing trends in contemporary sport and physical activity participation, specifically the growing concern for individual health and wellbeing, and individuals' increasing preference for flexibility in participation options (Hajkowicz et al., 2013). In addition, virtual events have the added advantage of enabling event organizers to rapidly (and relatively cheaply) innovate their products in response to market demand. Sehl (2020) pointed out that in addition to reducing costs, virtual options can also be a way to reduce the carbon footprint of events. For these reasons, it is worth considering if and how virtual events may co-exist with traditional in-person events in the future. In research on the virtualization of cycling, Westmattelmann et al. (2021) questioned whether "sport transferred into the virtual sphere … has the potential to actually complement traditional sport events" (p. 120). Alternatively, could the upsurge in virtual running events precipitated by COVID-19 represent competition to the previously thriving market for in-person running events?

In 2020 in Australia, the lobbying group called the Australian Mass Participation Sporting Events Alliance (AMPSEA) (n.d.) was inaugurated to help participatory sport event organizers survive the COVID-19 pandemic and pave the way toward the sector's recovery. AMPSEA (n.d.) predicted that due to COVID-19 over 8500 mass participation events in Australia were canceled or postponed and that 45% of the industry would not survive COVID-19 without financial support. AMPSEA's calculations underpin a stunning opportunity for the organizers of virtual running events to grow and maintain their market share, perhaps representing a viable threat to the resumption of full in-person event calendars. This situation is not isolated to Australia. Cohen (2020) noted that by mid-March of 2020, around 7500 running events in the United States had been canceled, with thousands more subsequently canceled or postponed.

The recent widespread adoption of virtual running events challenges academic understandings of how events may be managed and capitalized upon (and by whom). In particular, the opportunity for social interaction with like-minded others is central to the value proposition of in-person events (Green, 2001). Past research has highlighted the importance of the social, interactive aspects of event participation in endurance sports: sport events represent junctures where geographically-dispersed, like-minded individuals can congregate, display their subcultural identities (as runners, triathletes, and cyclists) and celebrate their involvement in the unique social world of their sport (Green, 2001; Lamont & Kennelly, 2012). Do virtual events offer these same opportunities? Miller (2020) argued, "Runners [in virtual events] may be running alone, but can still feel as if they're part of a larger group," while Race Roster (2020) suggested, "virtual events are a great way to continue offering value and engagement opportunities" to participants (p. 1). Hence, it is worth examining social interaction and social leveraging in the context of virtual sport events in a bid to understand how such virtual offerings could create social value and complement or disrupt the traditional sport event landscape.

Social Leveraging of Participatory Sport Events

Event leveraging involves proactively designing and implementing strategies that optimize the benefits of an event (or portfolio of events) for the hosting community and other key stakeholders (Chalip, 2004; Misener, 2015). The likelihood of long-term, positive event outcomes is greatly increased if such outcomes are proactively planned for prior to an event (Chalip, 2004; O'Brien & Chalip, 2008). In 2006, Chalip proposed that sport events may be leveraged to produce social outcomes. Specifically, Chalip (2006) described how events can be liminoid spaces, wherein strategically encouraging socializing and festivity can produce a sense of community or *communitas*. The significance of this communal atmosphere may be "*felt* more than understood" by event participants (emphasis added, Chalip, 2006, p. 110), as in liminoid event spaces, normal social rules and distinctions may be temporarily suspended and it may be safe to explore contentious social issues. These aspects of events underpin the opportunity for social leveraging and, Chalip (2006) argued, can be strategically achieved by fostering social interaction and prompting a feeling of celebration.

Fostering Social Interaction

Chalip (2006) advocated that events could foster social interaction by (1) encouraging participants to mingle at or around an event venue (thereby enabling sociability); (2) running social events for participants; (3) encouraging other informal opportunities for social engagement (i.e., through fan zones, or other event activations). Chalip (2006) referred to each of these options as "means" for fostering social interaction (p. 114). The first of these means (i.e., enabling sociability) focuses on creating opportunities for event attendees to "share time, space and activities with one another" in and around the event venue (p. 113). For example, Chalip (2006) pointed to the way food vendors and spaces for consuming food within and around event sites can be arranged to encourage people to congregate and interact. The second means (i.e., creating event-related social events), relates to the organization of social events around a sport competition program. For example, the social program attached to the Australian Masters Games is considered a key drawcard for participants and includes an opening parade and party for athletes, as well as a closing ceremony (2021 Australian Masters Games, n.d.).

The final means to foster interaction proposed by Chalip (2006) involves facilitating informal social opportunities for event participants through the creation of celebratory spaces beyond sport venues or the event's competition or social program. An example of celebratory social spaces in the context of large-scale sport events is the establishment of LiveSites or FanFests remote from the event venue, where fans can congregate to watch the event broadcast live on a big screen (Kolyperas & Sparks, 2018).

Prompting a Sense of Celebration

Chalip (2006) suggested facilitating informal social opportunities can also double as a means to create a sense of celebration. In addition, a sense of celebration could be developed through ancillary events (i.e., complementary cultural festivals or arts events) that use "event symbols, colors, and decorations" to theme widely and provide a "visual statement that something special is happening" (Chalip, 2006, p. 118).

Overall, Chalip (2006) suggested that in combination, strategically enabling sociability, creating event-related social events, facilitating informal social opportunities, producing ancillary events, and theming widely create the preconditions (i.e., a liminal space in which *communitas* can emerge) for the social leveraging of an event. Specifically, Chalip (2006) argued that the "liminal character of sport events can bring together groups that might otherwise never confer" (p. 121) and "creates a safe space for otherwise sensitive [social] matters" to be considered (p. 120). These ideas were subsequently developed by O'Brien and Chalip (2008) who advanced a social leveraging framework underpinned by the assumption that events can create a liminal space.

O'Brien and Chalip's (2008) model recognized that, within this liminal space, *communitas* and event media provide opportunities to encourage collective effort around targeted social issues. They proposed that event stakeholders can be engaged in identifying and acting upon prescient social issues in the host community that may be positively influenced by the sport event. Meanwhile, event advertising and reporting can be used to showcase social issues to a wider audience. The notion that events can be strategically leveraged to produce beneficial social outcomes has received widespread support (i.e., Misener, 2015; Schulenkorf et al., 2019; Ziakas, 2010, 2016; Zhou & Kaplanidou, 2018).

Yet Chalip's (2006) and O'Brien and Chalip's (2008) works are built on the assumption that people are physically present at an event: that is, a physical presence is necessary to create and capitalize on liminality through the development of *communitas* among participants. Hence, many of the ways Chalip (2006) suggested to strategically connect people require participants' physical attendance (i.e., through ancillary events such as opening ceremonies, pre- or post-event dinners and parties, a hospitality tent, kid-zone, exposition, or an entertainment hub at the event site (Zhou & Kaplanidou, 2018)). Further, an intended recipient of social leveraging efforts is the host community, which may use events to build social capital, and as a safe space to address challenging local issues (O'Brien & Chalip, 2008; Ziakas, 2016; Zhou & Kaplanidou, 2018). Both premises need revision in light of the growth in virtual events – events that may be delivered remotely, synchronously, or asynchronously, and where people do not congregate in a set location (or traditional host community) to participate, volunteer, support or do business.

Consequently, the next section of this chapter will discuss approaches to establishing the preconditions for social leveraging (per Chalip, 2006) of virtual participatory sport events. This involves examining questions such as: What can event organizers do to build a sense of community among participants when physical attendance is not part of a sport event product? Can (and how can) digital advancements be embraced to complement (or, in the case of pandemics, create a substitute for) in-person events? To whom may the benefits of virtual events flow? Through considering these questions we will propose adaptations to Chalip's (2006) work on social leveraging to suit virtual events.

Social Leveraging and Virtual Running Events

This section considers how virtual running events may be designed to create the preconditions for social leverage (per Chalip, 2006) despite the lack of physical contact between participants. Embracing the opportunities provided by digital advancements is central to this discussion and a range of virtual events will be drawn on to illustrate what event organizers can do/have done to foster social interaction and build a sense of community among participants when physical attendance is not part of their sport event. As highlighted below, some, but perhaps not all of Chalip's (2006) suggestions on how to create *communitas* are possible/practicable in the context of virtual running events.

Social Leveraging Through Participants' Experiences of Virtual Running Events

In a study on the virtualization of cycling races, Westmattelmann et al. (2021) argued that "virtual races can serve as complements for real-world interactions" (p. 129). A similar finding may apply to virtual running events. For example, the Personal Peak Quarantine Backyard Ultra, held in April 2020, used digital technology to enable sociability by creating opportunities for event attendees to "share time, space and activities with one another" (Chalip, 2006, p. 113), albeit digitally, rather than in and around a physical event venue. The event challenged runners to run 4.167 miles (~6.7 km) every hour, on the hour (in their backyard, living room, local streets, on a treadmill, etc.), until they could no longer run (Personal Peak, n.d.). The event attracted 2413 runners from 65 countries and utilized Zoom, YouTube, Facebook Live, and other social media platforms to keep participants accountable, motivated, and connected for the duration of the event (Dawson, 2020). The event ran for 63 hours before all contestants stopped. The event's organizers described how they were motivated to produce a virtual event in order to fill the void arising from the cancellation of all physical events due to COVID-19 and to create a community where people could do something together despite not being able to leave their homes or neighborhoods due to lockdowns and social distancing requirements (Maese, 2020). The live streaming of the event meant that between laps, participants and (online) spectators could converse and offer encouragement (Maese, 2020). In this example, the organizers of the event utilized digital technology to design and manage a unique event experience that established a sense of community among international participants and fostered social interaction in a way that transcends geographical boundaries.

Chalip's (2006) work on social leveraging also advocated that fostering social interaction could occur through creating event-related social events and facilitating informal social opportunities. While there are numerous platforms available for meeting online, there are challenges to designing effective online social events (i.e., large events that enable actual interaction). Here, inspiration can be drawn from other parts of the event industry. For example, the online group Daybreaker (n.d.) describes itself as a "morning dance community," which hosts "surprise" gatherings for registered members to come together to dance or do yoga before work. In 2020, Daybreaker hosted virtual dance events which featured performers and participants on Zoom dancing synchronously from their own locations. Participants were encouraged to interact by posting comments, with the first online session achieving over 17,000 posts (Daybreaker, 2020). In the context of sport events, Race Roster (2020) suggested live streaming warm-ups, medal ceremonies, or event-related entertainment. Similar approaches could be used to offer ancillary events, which Chalip (2006) positioned as a means for promoting a feeling of celebration.

Alternatively, the organizers of the Boston Marathon encouraged participants to stay connected by joining their online Athlete's Village. The Athlete's Village gives registered members access to challenges and training programs and is promoted as "a community to connect with fellow runners" (Boston Athletic Association, n.d.). Similarly, Ironman (n.d.) introduced the Ironman Virtual Club during the COVID-19 pandemic to enable individuals to "train, compete and celebrate" with a "global community of fellow athletes." Race Roster (2020) promoted the idea of challenges and incentives to engage participants and build social interaction around a virtual event. While such options may facilitate some social interaction among participants, future research is needed to examine whether in practice virtual events capture the spontaneity, richness, excitement, and energy required to truly develop a sense of *communitas*.

To date, there is limited empirical research on this issue, although recent work by Lizzo and Liechty (2020) may be instructive. Lizzo and Liechty (2020) conducted a netnography of the Facebook feed of a virtual running club, the Hogwarts Running Club. They found that the virtual group exhibited the four factors underpinning the Sense of Community theory, that is, membership, influence, integration/fulfillment of needs, and shared emotional connection. The group convened around their collective love of Harry Potter and running. In posts on the group's Facebook page, members exhibited a sense of belonging, pride, and personal investment, all of which underpin membership per the Sense of Community theory (Lizzo & Liechty, 2020). Shared symbols, emotional safety, and established boundaries are also critical components of membership. Lizzo and Liechty (2020) described the running club's site as a source of moral support, encouragement, and advice for group members and noted limited evidence of negativity or troll-like behavior. The authors suggested this may have been because of the individuals attracted to the group, emergent group behavioral norms, and/or the actions of the of group's administrator (in removing offensive posts).

Sense of Community theory also posits that people are more likely to join and stay part of groups when they feel they can contribute and be influential. Social media sites, including the Hogwarts Running Club page, have become important locations for drawing attention to issues, promoting discussion, and agitating for change (Lizzo & Liechty, 2020). Lizzo and Liechty (2020) also found evidence that group membership helped fulfill the needs of its members, and that members had established a shared emotional connection through their collective history and group identity. Overall, they noted the importance of a sense of community to the sustainability and survival of virtual communities (Lizzo & Liechty, 2020), signifying that social interaction is also both a central and possible aspect of participation in the digital realm.

Finally, Chalip's (2006) work on social leveraging promoted the idea of theming widely to create a visual statement that "something special is happening" (p. 117), through physical decorations and artifacts, symbols, and colors. The purpose of theming widely is to enhance the celebratory nature of events and to foster a sense of meaningfulness among those who participate (Chalip, 2006). While the hanging of physical decorations in public spaces does not apply to virtual events, event organizers can still theme through the consistent use of symbols and colors. For example, many virtual running events offer medals, t-shirts, or other paraphernalia for finishers. Virtual Running Events (n.d.), a UK company that claims to be "virtually giving medals away" produces and promotes attractive medals for each of its virtual running challenges.

Race Roster (2020) suggested event organizers consider an event mascot to stimulate "social sharing and engagement opportunities" (p. 6), or the creation of shareable "digital assets" (p. 13) such as badges, Instagram frames or downloadable certificates. These items may feature extensively in the social media posts of participants – either through formal event channels, or posts on the pages of other online running groups. For example, the community Facebook page attached to Running Mums Australia regularly features posts from women sharing their running event achievements using the visual imagery of medals and finisher t-shirts and supported by commentary explaining their race experience or motivation, and signifying the overall meaningfulness to them of participating in the event. Encouraging (or incentivizing) participants to share their experiences of virtual events online, complete with images featuring finishers' paraphernalia, whilst using the event's formal social media channels or a common hashtag can help event managers to substitute for physical theming around an event site by enhancing the sense of meaning and achievement/celebration among participants.

The above event examples illustrate that some of Chalip's (2006) "means" of fostering social interaction and promoting a feeling of celebration can be recreated in the digital realm. For example, wearable technologies, live streaming and social media can be used to enable interaction and sociability between participants: to give participants the opportunity to feel part of a community either in real-time (synchronously through live streaming options) or asynchronously (through post-event statistics-sharing and social media posts). These examples suggest ways in which virtual events may become leverageable resources: they can be designed to promote a sense of community where normal social distinctions are suspended, by connecting participants around the world, supporting their mental and physical wellbeing, and empowering them to celebrate their achievements.

Extending the Benefits of Virtual Running Events

It is worth considering how virtual events may be leveraged to benefit stakeholders beyond direct participants. Conventionally, much of the event leveraging literature has focused on how social and economic benefits can accrue to host communities (i.e., businesses, tourism operators, and local institutions) (Chalip, 2004, 2006; O'Brien & Chalip, 2008). In the absence of a conventional host community, can virtual events produce social value for anyone beyond participants?

Numerous authors have examined the tendency of event organizers to combine their events with charitable programs (i.e., Filo et al., 2009; Kennelly, 2017; Zhou & Kaplanidou, 2018), with Palmer and Dwyer (2019) describing how charity-linked participatory sport events have unleashed the phenomenon of "fitness philanthropy" (p. 609). Following this vein, many virtual events have connected with charitable causes, as well as focusing on raising awareness of challenging social issues. For example, the Run Against Violence is a 1300 km virtual team challenge held over 19 days. The event focuses on family and domestic violence and aims to precipitate conversation around this challenging social issue (Run Against Violence, n.d.). Online searches reveal virtual events aiming to start discussions/ raise awareness on a range of social issues, including community mental health, the impacts of climate change, racism, and homophobia. Zhou and Kaplanidou (2018) commented that social media outlets can be used to engage diverse groups of people around events and can also be useful in drawing public attention to social issues. Hence, in combination, virtual events and social media may be powerful vehicles to raise money and awareness for a range of charitable causes and challenging/pressing social issues.

In summary, in this section, we have drawn on a range of virtual running event examples to illustrate ways in which Chalip's (2006) work on social leveraging can be applied to virtual events. This section illustrates that some, but perhaps not all, of Chalip's suggested "means" for producing liminality and *communitas* may apply in the case of virtual events. In the next section, we focus on potential management implications and opportunities for future research.

Implications for Future Sport Event Design and Research

This section concludes this chapter by discussing theoretical and applied implications arising from the digital disruption of the participatory sport event landscape. We propose modifications to Chalip's (2006) work on social leveraging which are aimed at creating the preconditions for social leveraging (i.e., liminality and *communitas*) in the emergent virtual event market. We then consider the potential management implications of virtual participatory sport events moving forward.

Virtual participatory sport events may be considered the product of two entrepreneurial disruptions to traditional modes of delivering and managing sport. First, most contemporary participatory sport events are run by third-party providers or entities that may not traditionally be considered part of the sport industry (i.e., for-profit event management companies and charities) (Kennelly, 2017; Phillips & Newland, 2014). These entities have capitalized on trends in sport participation, such as increased community awareness of the importance of physical and mental wellbeing, and a desire for more flexible ways to engage in physical activity (Hajkowicz et al., 2013). Second, in the 2010s the uptake of emergent wearable fitness tracking technologies and fitness apps led to the creation of virtual events, representing another wave of disruption to the delivery and management of sport events. While virtual events were gaining traction through the 2010s, the COVID-19 pandemic precipitated an explosion in such events in 2020.

It remains to be seen if virtual events will retain their popularity as countries around the world move to manage COVID-19 (Westmattelmann et al., 2021). Some predict that virtual events represent a powerful industry trend (Race Roster, 2020), as they cost less, produce less carbon footprint, and eliminate some of the logistic and risk management concerns of in-person events (Sehl, 2020). Yet the sustainability of events, including virtual events also derives from their value proposition – or the ability of event organizers and marketers to entice participants, fans, sponsors, and authorities to support their event option over potential competition (i.e., other events, other forms of entertainment, other projects vying for the same funding or resources) (Race Roster, 2020). This chapter has focused on the way events can be designed to create social value for individuals and other event stakeholders, with reference to Chalip's (2006) work on social leveraging.

Chalip (2006) argued that event organizers can strategically design events to create the preconditions for social leverage, specifically *communitas* or a sense of connection and community wherein normal social rules may be suspended and there are opportunities to broach challenging social issues. Chalip (2006) proposed five means via which event organizers could foster social interaction or prompt a feeling of celebration, but all five means were contingent upon physical attendance at an event or associated social activities. Hence, this chapter considered how virtual participatory sport events, specifically running events, may be designed to achieve *communitas*, despite participants and stakeholders being geographically dispersed.

Enhancing Meaningfulness Through Event Design

Examples from practice discussed in this chapter illustrate that Chalip's (2006) means for creating *communitas* can be recreated in the digital realm, albeit to varying degrees and with challenges. Literature considering the creation of virtual running events and communities is scant. However, Lizzo and Liechty (2020) used the Sense of Community theory to suggest that in order to thrive, virtual communities need to build group cohesion, and fulfill the needs of and empower their members. Chalip (2006) also noted the importance of imbuing an event with a sense of meaningfulness through theming and event symbols. Finally, Race Roster (2020) suggested event organizers make participation in their virtual events meaningful by giving runners a "sense of purpose" (p. 10) through fundraising for charity or other acts of support. Current events and initiatives in the field exemplify how participatory sport events, and particularly virtual events, have been mobilized by event organizers and participants alike to raise awareness or funds for various charities or community causes/issues. This may be a significant consideration for the value proposition of virtual events which otherwise lack the potential to deliver traditional tourism/financial and social outcomes to a physical host destination.

For these reasons, it is suggested that Chalip's (2006) work be modified for the context of virtual events by giving a more prominent place to activities that enhance the sense of personal meaning or social purpose underpinning an event. These activities may contribute to the development of *communitas* among disparate people within a virtual event community by uniting them around a common cause or shared experience of perseverance, transformation, challenge, and accomplishment in preparing for and completing the virtual event. As depicted in Figure 6.1, an enhanced sense of meaning could be achieved by giving virtual event participants an opportunity to connect to a charity or cause fixed by the event organizer or self-selected. Research has illustrated that in the in-person charity sport event realm, the connection shared among participants based upon the charitable cause supported, along with having the challenge inherent to the event contextualized within the charity, increases the sense of meaning derived by participants (Filo et al., 2008). Hence, connecting events to important social causes, and providing opportunities for participants to share their virtual running event preparation and participation journeys online could increase the meaningfulness of the virtual event experience and concomitantly participants' investment in the social world and community attached to the event. Once *communitas,* as a pre-condition for social leveraging, is achieved (Chalip, 2006), virtual events could work with the media and cause-based organizations to educate participants, start conversations, raise funds, and initiate social change, as proposed by O'Brien and Chalip (2008).

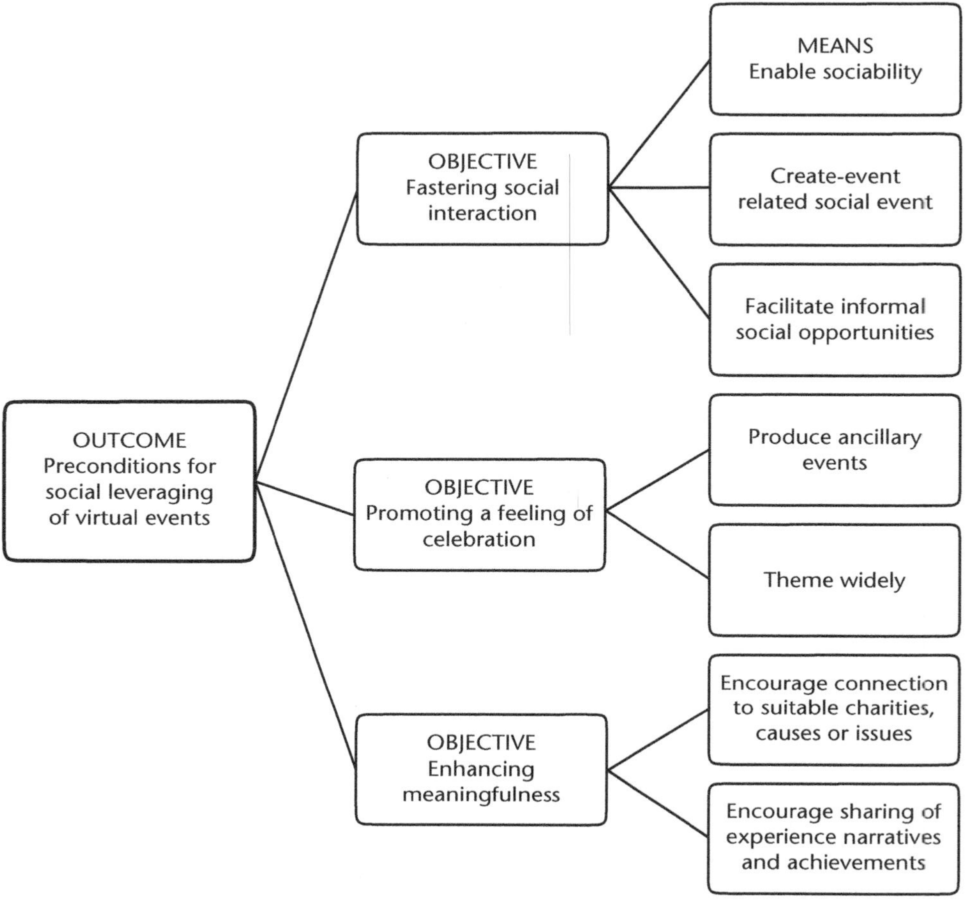

Figure 6.1 Establishing preconditions for social leveraging of virtual events
Source: Adapted from Chalip (2006), p. 114.

Management Implications of Virtual Events

There are also applied implications associated with the emergence of virtual events and the social leveraging activities suggested in Figure 6.1. The management and social leveraging of virtual events relate largely to the provision and promotion of digital platforms that enable people to connect to a virtual community and share their achievements via apps, imagery, and narratives. As participants chose their own running routes and times, some of the key logistic and risk management elements of staging events are eliminated. Race Roster (2020, p. 5) stated, "Without physical limitations, a virtual event lets you lean into ideas that might be harder to execute for an in-person event." Hence, significant management considerations for virtual sport event organizers include delivering a creative and enticing event product, providing clear instruction on event expectations, and facilitating the creation of an accessible virtual community around their event. Those involved in managing sport and events may find themselves needing to upskill in order to utilize a range of digital technologies. There is an ever-expanding range of options available for online meetings, seminars, conferences, informal gatherings and sharing (i.e., Twitter, Instagram, Facebook, TikTok, Snapchat, and various live streaming platforms), and the challenge for virtual event organizers is creating online spaces that are accessible, inclusive, intuitive, free of technical problems, safe (from trolling and offensive comments) and supportive, engaging/interactive and capable (where relevant) of supporting fundraising or awareness-raising efforts. Designing and managing virtual events, therefore, requires a skill set that may previously have been peripheral in event management and which also opens up new avenues for the education and/or professional development of future event managers.

While the rapid emergence of virtual sport events precipitated by COVID-19 produced immediate opportunities and challenges for event organizers, questions remain regarding the long-term future of the participatory sport event market. Will runners opt to return to in-person events when possible and abandon virtual options, or will virtual events remain a viable alternative due to their flexible and affordable nature? Can the market sustain both options? Could these two products complement each other, or will they be in competition? Pundits (i.e., Steigman, 2020) predict that in the future, virtual and in-person events will co-exist as they did pre-COVID-19, while some (i.e., Race Roster, 2020) forecast that the uptake of virtual events represents a vigorous industry trend.

In the 2010s, some event organizers introduced virtual event options to complement their in-person races, as a means of remaining connected to their customers between major in-person events which were often held only once per annum (Miller, 2019). In these cases, virtual events were designed to complement in-person events. In contrast, in Australia (pre-COVID-19), Running Heroes started to offer a range of in-person runs and events to complement their online/virtual offerings. Running Heroes (n.d.) is an online community (application and website) for runners, which sets running-related challenges for its registered members. Those who complete challenges win prizes and access discounts on a range of commercial partner brands. Running Heroes is part of the French startup Sport Heroes, established in 2014, which creates, manages, and capitalizes on a range of predominately virtual, international communities built around different sports (Sport Heroes, n.d.). Sport Heroes were early in recognizing the opportunities provided by (and leveraging the digital disruption created by) the exponential uptake of wearable fitness trackers and the gamification of physical activity. Yet, by introducing in-person running events for members, Running Heroes acknowledged the importance of (and market for) in-person social engagement within its running community. Despite the success of its virtual offerings, Running Heroes still saw a need/opportunity to physically bring runners together to connect socially. These examples suggest that in the pre-COVID-19 period, virtual running events were perceived to complement (rather than compete with) in-person event offerings and were perhaps not considered to pose a viable threat to in-person event participation.

A related consideration is that digital disruption of the participatory sport event sector, which started pre-COVID-19, ultimately became a life saver in the height of the pandemic (i.e., by providing capacity for some sport event organizers to make a rapid transition to virtual events which enabled ongoing product delivery). Considering the situation from this perspective, virtual events may have helped some sport event organizations survive and remain connected to their clients and sponsors during the pandemic. The above scenarios position virtual events as a product that may co-exist and even supplement the provision of in-person event offerings in the future. However, the present virtualization of events, and the available wearable and mixed-reality technology will no doubt evolve in the future. As discussed, the managerial implications of this development see sport event organizers requiring enhanced knowledge of existing and evolving digital technologies in order to choose and effectively manage apps, social media platforms, live streaming, and other options to support virtual events and to accommodate for the creation of safe, supportive, and engaging virtual communities around those events.

To conclude, this chapter has focused on the emergence and management implications of virtual participatory sport events, particularly running events. This chapter commenced by considering the burgeoning popularity of in-person participatory sport events over recent decades. Then this chapter discussed digital disruption of the sector in the 2010s caused by the introduction of wearable physical activity trackers, apps that gamify physical exercise, social media platforms that enable runners to share their experiences and achievements, and virtual events that afford individuals opportunities to engage flexibly and affordably in running events. Next, this chapter turned to the value proposition of virtual running events, specifically focusing on how the organizers of such events can generate *communitas,* an important pre-condition for social leveraging. Chalip's (2006) work on social leveraging was introduced and then used to underpin discussion of how virtual events may be designed and managed to create a sense of community among disparate and geographically dispersed runners. A range of event examples was drawn on to illustrate that Chalip's (2006) leveraging work could largely be translated into the virtual world, albeit with attendant challenges. However, it was suggested that "enhancing meaningfulness" should be added to Chalip's (2006) suggestions to ensure that virtual events are designed to connect participants through meaningful and socially valuable experiences.

Finally, the managerial implications of the upsurge in virtual running events were considered, particularly the need for future sport event organizers to be competent in the digital realm. As virtual events are a relatively recent phenomenon, they are largely under-researched and avenues for future investigation abound. Suggested lines of inquiry include studies examining both demand and supply-side perspectives of the benefits of virtual events, and how virtual event experiences compare with in-person event attendance. In addition, as foregrounded in this chapter, understanding how virtual events can be leveraged to maximize their social value, and overall value proposition also warrants further empirical consideration.

References

2021 Australian Masters Games. (n.d.). Social program. Retrieved 20 June 2021, from https://australianmastersgames.com/games/social-program/

Armbrecht, J., & Andersson, T. (2020). The event experience, hedonic and eudaimonic satisfaction and subjective well-being among sport event participants. *Journal of Policy Research in Tourism, Leisure and Events, 12*(3), 457–477. 10.1080/19407963.2019.1695346

Associated Press. (2020, March 22). Man runs marathon on 7-metre balcony during French lockdown. *The Guardian.* https://www.theguardian.com/world/2020/mar/21/man-runs-marathon-on-7-metre-balcony-during-french-lockdown

Australian Mass Participation Sporting Events Alliance (AMPSEA). (n.d.). Providing leadership and representation to inspire a world class events industry. Retrieved 21 March 2021, from https://www.ampsea.com.au/

Bitrián, P., Buil, I., & Catalán, S. (2020). Gamification in sport apps: The determinants of users' motivation. *European Journal of Management and Business Economics, 29*(3), 365–381. 10.1108/EJMBE-09-2019-0163

Boston Athletic Association. (n.d.). Boston marathon race information. Retrieved 17 June 2021, from https://www.baa.org/races/boston-marathon/enter

Bunn, J., Navalta, J., Fountaine, C., & Reece, J. (2018). Current state of commercial wearable technology in physical activity monitoring 2015–2017. *International Journal of Exercise Science, 11*(7), 503–515.

Chalip, L. (2004). Beyond impact: A general model for host community event leverage. In B. W. Ritchie & D. Adair (Eds.), *Sport tourism: Interrelationships, impacts and issues,* (pp. 236–262). Channel View.

Chalip, L. (2006). Towards social leverage of sport events. *Journal of Sport and Tourism, 11*(2), 109–127. 10.1080/14775080601155126

Cohen, K. (2020, May 7). Running on empty: Coronavirus has changed the course for races big and small. *ESPN.* https://www.espn.com/olympics/story/_/id/29137444/coronavirus-changed-course-races-big-small

Dawson, A. (2020, April 10). The craziest things you might have missed in the quarantine backyard ultra. *Runner's World.* https://www.runnersworld.com/races-places/a32073652/quarantine-backyard-ultra-best-moments/?fbclid=IwAR0gZcDxzdZzOHF74y3WJ_d0mlME6xIcqc2OeSYuoDTDi4sSJYS-JMojpKE

Daybreaker. (2020, July 8). *Daybreaker live- episode #1.* https://vimeo.com/436475870

Daybreaker. (n.d.). *We are daybreaker.* Retrieved 30 June 2021, from https://www.daybreaker.com/about/

Filo, K. R., Funk, D., & O'Brien, D. (2008). It's really not about the bike: Exploring attraction and attachment to the events of the Lance Armstrong Foundation. *Journal of Sport Management, 22*(5), 501–525. 10.1123/jsm.22.5.501

Filo, K., Funk, D., & O'Brien, D. (2009). The meaning behind attachment: Exploring camaraderie, cause, and competency at a charity sport event. *Journal of Sport Management, 23*(3), 361–387. 10.1123/jsm.23.3.361

Gold Coast Marathon. (n.d.). *History.* Retrieved 1 October 2021 from https://goldcoastmarathon.com.au/about/history/

Green, B. C. (2001). Leveraging subculture and identity to promote sport events. *Sport Management Review, 4*(1), 1–19. 10.1016/S1441-3523(01)70067-8

Hajkowicz, S., Cook, H., Wilhelmseder, L., & Boughen, N. (2013). The future of Australian sport: Megatrends shaping the sports sector over coming decades. *A consultancy report for the Australian Sports Commission.* CSIRO: Belconnen, Australia.

Hillman, P., Lamont, M., Scherrer, P., & Kennelly, M. (2021). Reframing mass participation events as active leisure: Implications for tourism and leisure research. *Tourism Management Perspectives,* 39. 10.1016/j.tmp.2021.100865

Ironman. (n.d.). Ironman virtual club. Retrieved 10 August 2021, from https://ironman-virtual-club.webflow.io/

Jakob Andersen, J. (2019, June 15). The state of running 2019. *RunRepeat.* https://runrepeat.com/state-of-running

Kennelly, M. (2011). *Developing sport tourism: A multiple-case study of interaction between Australian national sport organisations and a sport tour operator.* [Doctoral dissertation, Griffith University]. https://research-repository.griffith.edu.au/handle/10072/366210

Kennelly, M. (2017). "We've never measured it, but it brings in a lot of business": Participatory sport events and tourism. *International Journal of Contemporary Hospitality Management, 29*(3), 883–899. 10.1108/IJCHM-10-2015-0541

Kolyperas, D., & Sparks, L. (2018). Exploring value co-creation in Fan Fests: The role of fans. *Journal of Strategic Marketing, 26*(1), 71–84. 10.1080/0965254X.2017.1374298

Lamont, M., & Kennelly, M. (2012). A qualitative exploration of participant motives among committed amateur triathletes. *Leisure Sciences, 34*(3), 236–255. 10.1080/01490400.2012.669685

Lamont, M., & Kennelly, M. (2019). Sporting hyperchallenges: Health, social and fiscal implications. *Sport Management Review, 22*(1), 68–79. 10.1016/j.smr.2018.02.003

Lizzo, R., & Liechty, T. (2020). The Hogwarts running club and sense of community: A netnography of a virtual community. *Leisure Sciences,* 10.1080/01490400.2020.1755751

Lundberg, E., Andersson, T., & Armbrecht J. (2019). Introduction. In J. Armbrecht, E. Lundberg, & T. Andersson, (Eds.). *A research agenda for event management* (pp. 1–6). Edward Elgar Publishing.

Maese, R. (2020, April 8). Michael Wardian set out for a virtual ultra marathon. He kept running for 2½ days. *The Washington Post* (online). https://www.washingtonpost.com/sports/2020/04/07/michael-wardian-set-out-virtual-ultra-marathon-he-kept-running-2-days/?fbclid=IwAR1wWQkprHech0M5SwzMLoEzHNxhRQQFOPYnxye17UASz3-J2VpARWJrzS4

Miller, J. A. (2019, March 29). The races are virtual but the running is real. *The New York Times.* https://www.nytimes.com/2019/03/29/well/move/the-races-are-virtual-but-the-running-is-real.html

Miller, J. A. (2020, April 4). The rise of virtual races. *The New York Times.* https://www.nytimes.com/2020/04/04/well/move/the-rise-of-virtual-races.html

Misener, L. (2015). Leveraging parasport events for community participation: Development of a theoretical framework. *European Sport Management Quarterly, 15*(1), 132–153. 10.1080/16184742.2014.997773

O'Brien, D., & Chalip, L. (2008). Sport events and strategic leveraging: Pushing towards the triple bottom line. In A. G. Woodside & D. Martin (Eds.). *Tourism management: Analysis, behaviour, and strategy* (pp. 318–338). CABI.

Palmer, C., & Dwyer, Z. (2019). Good running?: The rise of fitness philanthropy and sports-based charity events. *Leisure Sciences*, *42*(5-6), 609–623. 10.1080/01490400.2019.1656122

Personal Peak. (n.d.). *Quarantine Backyard Ultra*. Retrieved 10 August 2021, from https://personalpeak.ca/quarantinebackyardultra/#1594262041374-048f3fc3-74d0

Phillips, P., & Newland, B. (2014). Emergent models of sport development and delivery: The case of triathlon in Australia and the US. *Sport Management Review*, *17*(2), 107–120. 10.1016/j.smr.2013.07.001

Race Roster. (2020). *A guide to helping your virtual event stand out*. https://raceroster.com/wp-content/uploads/2020/04/RR_Ebook_A_Guide_to_Helping_Your_Virtual_Events_Stand_Out.pdf

Run Against Violence (n.d.). *Run against violence*. Retrieved 10 August 2021, from https://www.runagainstviolence.com/

Running Heroes. (n.d.). *Running heroes*. Retrieved 10 August 2021, from https://au.runningheroes.com/en/

Schulenkorf, N., Giannoulakis, C., & Blom, L. (2019). Sustaining commercial viability and community benefits: Management and leverage of a sport-for-development event. *European Sport Management Quarterly*, *19*(4), 502–519. 10.1080/16184742.2018.1546755

Sehl, K. (2020, March 26). How to host a successful virtual event: Tips and best practices. *Hootsuite*. https://blog.hootsuite.com/virtual-events/

Shipway, R., & Jones, I. (2008). The great suburban Everest: An "insiders" perspective on experiences at the 2007 Flora London Marathon. *Journal of Sport and Tourism*, *13*(1), 61–77. 10.1080/14775080801972213

Sport Heroes. (n.d.). *Sport Heroes*. Retrieved 10 August 2021, from https://www.sportheroes.com/en/home

Steigman, P. (2020). A dedicated runner's perspective on virtual events. *Running USA*. https://runningusa.org/RUSA/News/2020/A-Dedicated-Runner-s-Perspective-on-Virtual-Events.aspx

Tu, R., Hsieh, P., & Feng, W. (2019). Walking for fun or for "likes"? The impacts of different gamification orientations of fitness apps on consumers' physical activities. *Sport Management Review*, *22*(5), 682–693. 10.1016/j.smr.2018.10.005

Virtual Running Events. (n.d.). Welcome to virtual running events. Retrieved from 10 August 2021, from https://www.virtualrunningevents.co.uk/

Westmattelmann, D., Grotenherman, J., Sprenger, M., & Schewe, G. (2021). The show must go on; virtualisation of sport events during the COVID-19 pandemic. *European Journal of Information Systems*, *30*(2), 119–136. 10.1080/0960085X.2020.1850186

Ziakas, V. (2010). Understanding an event portfolio: The uncovering of interrelationships, synergies, and leveraging opportunities. *Journal of Policy Research in Tourism, Leisure and Events*, *2*(2), 144–164. 10.1080/19407963.2010.482274

Ziakas, V. (2016). Fostering the social utility of events: An integrative framework for the strategic use of events in community development. *Current Issues in Tourism*, *19*(11), 1136–1157. 10.1080/13683500.2013.849664

Zhou, R., & Kaplanidou, K. (2018). Building social capital from sport event participation: An exploration of the social impacts of participatory sport events on the community. *Sport Management Review*, *21*(5), 491–503. 10.1016/j.smr.2017.11.001

7

Digital Innovation in High-Performance Sport

Popi Sotiriadou

Introduction

Technology affects many aspects of sport ranging from performance on and off the field to sports venues and spectator experiences. Increasingly, advances in technology influence mass participation as well as an elite sport. The focus of this chapter is on the influence and impact of digital innovation-based technologies used in high-performance sport and how sports, teams, and athletes can benefit from these advancements. Before analyzing digital innovation in high-performance sport, it is important to contextualize these technologies starting with the fundamental questions of "what is digital innovation and why is it important?."

Digital innovation is the use of digital technology and applications to create novel products and services that improve existing business processes and workforce efficiencies, enhance customer experience, and replace or complement existing rules of the game within organizations and fields (Hinings et al., 2018). The importance of digital transformation rests on its pervasive nature and ubiquity that affects all sectors of society as it opens new networking possibilities and enables cooperation between different stakeholders who can exchange data and initiate novel processes.

Digital technology plays an instrumental part in just about every facet of human activity, be it for work-related or personal consumption. Some of the latest technological innovations include wearable devices such as head-mounted displays for virtual or augmented reality experiences, chatbots used for customer engagement, internet of things devices used to connect to the internet to send and receive data such as smartwatches and fitness trackers, artificial intelligence (AI) and big data to mention a few. Business application of these technologies includes, for example, a healthcare company implementing AI to help better diagnose patients' ailments or a bank using a chatbot app to engagement is customer feedback on a service. Similar applications can be transferrable into a sporting context to, for instance, diagnose athlete training fatigue through motion sensors mounted on computers and other advanced software (e.g., fusionsport), or promote fan engagement at a sporting venue during a game using advanced technologies like holograms, AI, and drones to create an even more immersive experience for sports fans (e.g., Digital horse racing platform Zed Run).

DOI: 10.4324/9781003088899-9

These digital innovations are commonly referred to as "disruptive technologies"; innovations that significantly alter the way that consumers, industries, or businesses operate. A disruptive technology eradicates the systems or habits it replaces because it has attributes that are vastly superior (e.g., e-commerce, online news sites, ride-sharing apps, and GPS systems) (Smith, 2020). Subsequently, unless businesses evolve to embrace and apply such technologies, they become irrelevant. To stay relevant, organizations digitally innovate or adapt to evolving consumer and business habits (Majumdar et al., 2018).

The section that follows examines how the world of high-performance sport and elite athletes has managed to not only remain relevant but rapidly adjusted and adopted technologies in a contemporary, fast-paced, and evolving technological environment.

The Role of Technological and Digital Innovation in High-Performance (Elite) Sport

In an era where the world's largest taxi company has no taxi, the largest accommodation provider has no real estate and mobile applications no longer require months of writing lengthy complex codes – it's a simple case of disruption or be disrupted (Kennedy, 2015). This is a cliché statement that holds truth in all aspects of society and economies globally. The sport sector has been far from immune to technological adaptations within sport businesses and entire sport systems venturing into digitizing internal operations to "do things" better, faster, and cheaper; to advance athlete performance, and to stay at the forefront of applied scientific innovations; find new ways to engage participants and spectators or users; bring new products and services to the sport industry.

Digital technologies in sport are about the application of digital innovations to existing sports-related business problems. In high-performance sport, athlete competitiveness and success are and have been for decades at the forefront of the most fiercely contested battles to be won by many nations globally (Brouwers et al., 2015). Combining this drive for performance superiority with the application of digital technologies was a natural affinity driven by global competition to stay abreast of advancements in elite sport.

In the arms race project, Sotiriadou and De Bosscher (2013) argued that in the fast-changing conditions that elite sport operates in, high-performance sport is like planning around a moving target, and with disruptive startups popping up all over, competition is mounting. Hence, doing nothing is certain to help you move backward and become reductant and obsolete. Elite sports need a fast path to transform innovative new ideas into winning applications (Sotiriadou & De Bosscher, 2018). This is where digital transformation and innovative platforms come in; to create value and competitive advantage through new offerings, new business models, and new relationships. For instance, there are now advanced research centers around the world, such as Sheffield Hallam University's *Sports Engineering Research Group* which develops technological innovations to support the performance of Team GB athletes at Olympic competitions, and the *Sport Intelligence Research Partnership* project which is dedicated to collecting data on elite sports to ensure Olympic success.[1]

Individual athletes, sports teams or leagues, coaches, high-performance managers, and nations across the globe seek to continuously improve performance, invest efficiently in sports, and accomplish elite success (Sotiriadou & De Bosscher, 2013, 2018). New techniques of performance analysis are a significant part of the drive for athletic perfection (Evans et al., 2017). The rise of performance analysis in sports dates back to Roman times and the Ancient Olympic Games. Simple things to us now, like consistency in the length of an Olympic pool to ensure Olympic records are accurate, have resulted in sports becoming legitimized entities with organizational structures and processes characterized by specialization and standardization. However, today's digital innovations and technological advancements such as cutting-edge uses of augmented reality and virtual reality, have resulted in interventions that alter substantially coaching and training systems and processes that result in knowledge augmentation in coaching and training as well as ultimately athletes' performances and results.

Following a systematic analysis of the role of technologies and digital innovations in high-performance (elite) sport, Sotiriadou (2021) proposed an Entity-Relationship $(ER)^2$ model (see Figure 7.1) that shows the combined fields of biomedicine, sports engineering, and nanotechnology (e.g., Nanobiosensors) enable real-time biological data to be collected from athletes (Evans et al., 2017). This information forms what is commonly referred to as big data; a term used to describe large volumes of data – both structured and unstructured – that can be analyzed (i.e., data analytics) to inform training, performance, competition, as well as fan engagement decisions. Big data is far from a new concept, nor a new application within sport. The movie *Moneyball*, released in 2011, tells the real story of the Oakland Athletics baseball team and its general manager Billy Beane, who in order to address budgetary issues, used algorithms based on statistical procedures to hire players that took the team to the top of the playoffs.

However, as technologies in the combined fields of biomedicine, sports engineering, and nanotechnology advance, big data is entering a new era of influence on managing high-performance sport as it can be used directly by athletes, players and teams, their coaches, and a great suite of other technicians and scientists as a useful tool to study and improve performance (see Figure 7.1). For instance, many football/soccer clubs use data in their decision-making processes. The way they do that and the extent to which they use big data varies from club to club. Arsenal FC has a team of around 15 people working on performance, analysis, and data science, while Liverpool, Barcelona, and Manchester City are more recently seen as the frontrunners in the area of data (Scott, 2021). Furthermore, not only can data analytics help teams win games, but also prevent player injuries and encourage fans to attend games, and enhance their engagement.

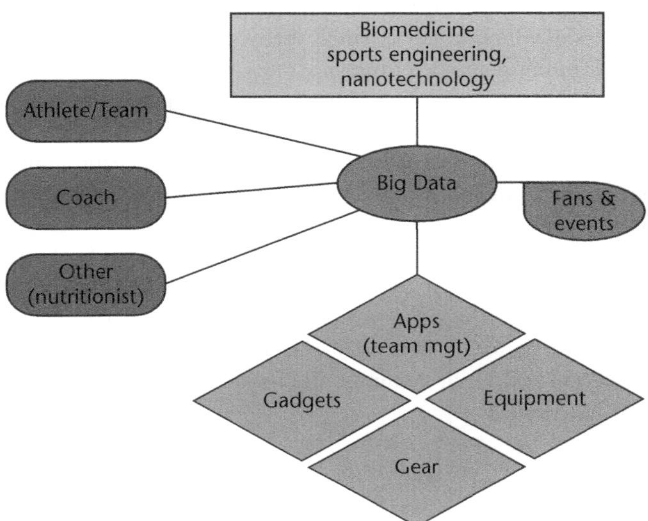

Figure 7.1 The Advancement of Technological and Digital Innovation in High-performance (Elite) Sport

The development of advanced feedback systems utilizing sensors and image processing techniques enables instant data transfer to computers or smart devices for analysis (Haake, 2013). This has allowed for a sophisticated feedback system through high levels of data generated instantly (Baca & Kornfeind, 2006). Consequently, big data has revolutionized several aspects of high-performance sport which have resulted in a non-exhaustive list of technological innovations. For the purposes of this chapter, as Figure 7.1 shows, these innovations form predominantly advances in four key areas: applications, gadgets, gear, and equipment.

Applications

An example of an application is a "Team management app" which can help coaches, trainers, or instructors to manage their players or team, decide their training time, and keep a record of their performance during different games, training sessions, or matches. Functionalities also facilitate adding in-app messengers so that the coaches can connect and communicate with the team members of a sport. Many athletes, such as gymnasts, have happily embraced such technologies, utilizing sensors and chips to aid them in evaluating their performance. These advanced stats are then used by teams to inform scouting, personnel decisions, and much more within the front office. Arguably the greatest of all sport technology advancements has been the development of devices that can measure different metrics during a game or race. The Zepp is an impressive example of sports technology that provides metrics. It is a small sensor that athletes attach to their golf glove, or baseball or softball bat to measure metrics such as speed, swing, angles, and backswing (Kingsley, 2020).

Gear

Cutting-edge sport gear, equipment, and gadgets can help athletes directly gather information that helps them understand their bodies, training, and performance better, avoid overtraining or undertrain, track their movement and technique, progress and advance their performance, and increase their chances of winning. For instance, many sports use the Global Positioning System (GPS) technology to monitor and determine distances, speeds, and workload of athletes and the team to inform game strategy or tailor coaching and training programs. Innovation also extends to areas like athlete sleep. Seshadri et al. (2019) found that wearable sleep trackers (e.g., wristbands, armbands, smartwatches, headbands) enable the "detection and subsequent application of metrics pertinent to and indicative of the physical performance, physiological status, biochemical composition, and mental alertness of the athlete" (p. 1) ranging from sleep patterns to other biological data which have been shown to reduce the risk of injuries and improve performance have "enabled the development of athlete-centered protocols and treatment plans by team physicians and trainers" (p. 1). As technology improves, so do the devices powered by technology. The latest iteration of the Apple Watch is certified as a class II medical device by the United States Food and Drug Administration due to its improved heart monitoring and electrocardiogram functionalities.

Gadgets and Equipment

Another well-applied data tracking is Gadget used in UK Rugby since 2016 and it involves sensors placed under the players' jerseys to track heart rate, field position, fatigue, rehabilitation, and injury prevention. Examples of "smart" equipment technologies comprise devices to measure reaction time and frequency of movements. Computer-Aided Design, more commonly known as CAD, has played an integral part in designing enhanced sporting equipment. These technologies employ motion capture to identify problems with techniques so they can be corrected. For instance, researchers at Birmingham City University have developed a wearable device the MotivePro; a vibrating suit that contains a modular system including sensors for keeping track of all movements of the athlete's body. British gymnast Mimi Cesar uses MotivePro during performing her routine and the sensors provide her real-time responses on her position in space. The sensors vibrate when parts of her body go beyond the desired range of motion. As this reaction is immediate, Mimi can refine her position during her routine. Further to this, the whole performance can be played back to further analyze her moves (Kingsley, 2020). Most sports technologies focus on the physical aspect of athlete performance and as the mind plays just as large a role in performance, groundbreaking solutions (e.g., Reflexion) emerge that help athletes improve their mental cognition and peak both mentally and physically. Virtual reality headsets too can be used to create simulated scenarios such as rugby line-ups and attacks to improve players' mental learning, visualizations, and decision making. Technologies are also continually advancing in modern protective equipment, such as helmets, pads, and gloves. Helmet manufacturers, for instance, combine years of impact data with technologically advanced materials to produce safer and more comfortable helmets to protect players from skull fractures or developing chronic traumatic encephalopathy.

The list of technologies and their uses, such as photo finish equipment, clothes designed to evaporate sweat, Halo headbands, video assistance refereeing, and Hawk-Eye systems, is quite exhaustive. These technologies have wider applications that go beyond athlete performance to enhance spectator and fan experiences. For instance, from line calls in tennis to goal-line technology in football, Hawk-Eye is now an integral part of the spectator experience when watching sport live. Hawk-Eye is now being used to officiate NASCAR, horse racing, and even hurling. But, arguably its biggest contribution is making sport more exciting through its now-iconic graphics. Any soccer fan can tell you that the referees on the field are far from perfect. While the human element of refereeing is a necessary and exciting part of sports, as fans, we want to see the best team (or athlete) win. VAR helps ensure that referees make the correct calls, so the game is fair and equitable. In addition, advances in digital streaming also allow fans to watch live games and exclusive content from anywhere in the world. Undoubtedly, from athletes to coaches and managers, to the fans in the stands, and spectators at home, sports technologies make it easier for everyone to enjoy the sports they love or optimize their physical output (Roda, 2019). Nevertheless, VAR technology remains controversial, labeled as killing sport, as it can take the joy out of spectators waiting for the outcome before they can celebrate.

The Benefits and Risks of Technological and Digital Innovation in High-Performance (Elite) Sport

Technology brings benefits to elite athletes, coaches, umpires, spectators and fans, and sports overall as a sector. However, technologies also come with risks. Figure 7.2 highlights some of the advantages and risks of technology in sport that the current literature points toward.

As the previous examples of the different types of technological innovations and the ways they can be applied show, there is indisputable evidence of the benefits of technologies in improving athlete performance. The use or application of those technologies to gain a *competitive advantage* is an increasingly important feature of elite sports as marginal gains can make all the difference (Giblin et al., 2016). Another beneficial feature of accessing big data on athletes and the use of innovative technologies to *store and analyze* these data is improvements in athlete medical care which can result in fewer injuries or faster recovery from injury (Osborne, 2017).

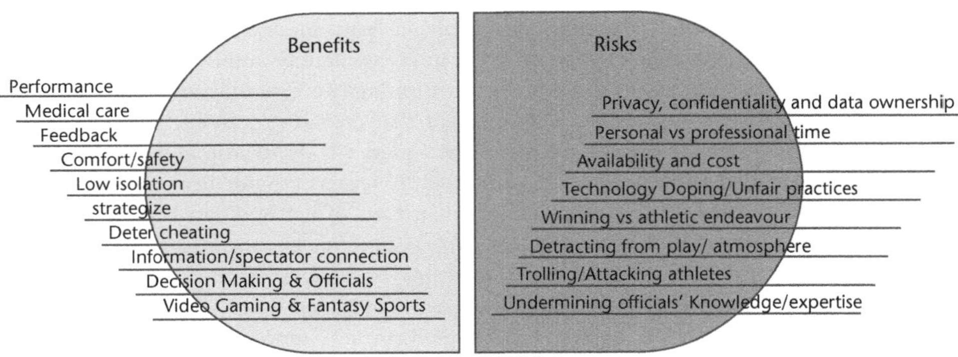

Figure 7.2 Benefits and Risks of Technological and Digital Innovation in High-performance (Elite) Sport

Advances in big data approaches to assessing athlete health and performance suggest that using technology with biochemical and hematological data "can be powerful in identifying the balance between training and recovery in each unique individual" (Lee et al., 2017, p. 2920).

Pickering and Kiely (2019) refer to this phenomenon as *individualization* of athlete training, and it includes the use of genetic information, alongside data on workload and wellness and analysis of technique. All this information along with other details offered from gadgets, recordings, and equipment that athletes use to coaches enables them to offer *feedback* that is more focused, objective, and helpful, even from *distance.* This ability to operate from a distance, and for athletes to share their training and progress with their coaches, followers, and other team members, offers the ability to stay "in touch" with the sporting world during very testing times of isolation including the COVID-19 pandemic during 2020–2021. Another benefit of technological innovation in elite sport is the comfort and safety that novel equipment (from clothing to protective equipment and technological equipment) advances in high-performance sports.

Furthermore, technological and digital innovation may benefit sport teams. Apps and big data for instance offer a "health check" for teams to compare where they are against the opposition or understand the opposition better. This allows sports or teams to *benchmark* and make informed decisions when they strategize. The *sport system* benefits overall as invariably these technologies and the data help increase safety and deter cheating in sport.

In saying all that, there is also evidence that there are risks associated with performance analytics and data collection from athletes. These issues revolve mainly around confidentiality and data ownership. For fans, these technologies offer information and statistics that allow them to measure player performance which in some cases results in trolling or attacking athletes through social media platforms or privacy invasion. In the sport system at large, there are concerns regarding "technology doping"; a term used to express unfair access to technologies (due to cost or availability) from well-off countries and competition in sport that present a risk to undermine the integrity and the spirit of fair play. At the same time, technologies such as video refereeing have also helped to even out the playing field advancing transparency in decision making and results, making decisions and scoring more reliable and accurate. However, such technologies have been criticized for slowing down the game, and more importantly, undermining respect for officials' knowledge and expertise and athletes or crowds no longer trusting people's decisions.

Clearly, the world of technological advancements is divided between the good and the evil. Hence, it is deep awareness of both sides of the argument that offers an informed and ethical decision on what technologies to use, when and to what extent. It is no surprise that whilst in yachting we exhibit boats racing at America's Cup using technologies that propel them at speeds three times faster than the wind, in Formula 1 manufacturers are restricted by exact design regulations to protect the integrity of the car and the safety of the drivers.

The Case of Australia: "We've Done it Before ... and We Will Do It Again"

In 1981, in response to Australia's poor performances at the Montreal Olympics 1976, the Australian Institute of Sport was created to provide resources, services, and facilities to enable Australians to pursue and achieve sporting excellence (Sotiriadou & Brouwers, 2012). This reform and support resulted in Australia becoming a sports "powerhouse," with many countries choosing to emulate its systems and processes (Sotiriadou, 2009). Almost four decades later, Australia launched a Technology in Sport project to revisit its systems and processes to ensure it achieves world leadership across its objectives in physical health and high-performance outcomes (Australian Sports Commission, 2016). Specifically, in 2016, the statutory authority responsible for sport in Australia, the Australian Sports Commission (ASC), now Sport Australia, published the findings of the Technology in Sport project. The project was set out to better understand how technology was impacting the Australian sport industry and how the industry needed to respond. The aim was to lead and sustain the world's best national sport system in the use of digital and technology, and to support sports to develop digital and technology leadership and capability (Australian Sports Commission, 2016).

To adapt and adjust to new technologies, it is common for industries to assess their business model against emerging trends and opportunities (Westermann et al., 2014). This phenomenon is referred to in recent literature as the concept of "digital maturity." Key findings in assessing Australian sport's digital maturity showed that, outside a handful of professional sports, it is low and as an industry, Australia's response to digital disruption "is slow, fragmented and lacks innovation" (p. 15). It was concluded that, even though Australia is globally competitive in the high-performance sport technology race, there is a need to increase investment. The overall findings raised concerns about the low maturity status of major professional and Olympic sport organizations in Australia including the ASC, golf, and basketball that are meant to be at the forefront of technological advancements compared to other countries. This is in stark contrast to reports suggesting that Australian athletes and sports teams "have traditionally been early adopters of technology as they strive for competitive advantages over their opponents" (Tibco-SVB, 2020). Australia's relatively low levels of investment or under-investment in sport technology compared to other industries and competitor countries, represents a threat and a cause for concern that this lack of investment will inhibit Australian athletes' ability to stay competitive. The report recommended that the ASC develop and leverage tailored programs such as a Sport Research Network, a Sport Accelerator, and a Sport Data Hub; develop the Sport Cloud, Sport Collective, and Sport Marketplace and work with sports, academia, government, industry, Australians and the global community "to build the dynamic ecosystem required to create the foundations for a sustainable Aussie 'Sport Valley'" (p. 27).

Conclusion and Future Directions

Technologies and technological innovations have advanced the world of high-performance sport. These technologies make it easier than ever for athletes to optimize their performance, for coaches to monitor training and for fans to get into the game. These exciting new technologies in sports are revolutionizing sports training, offering a competitive advantage, perfecting athlete movements, enhancing communication and eliminating injuries, and transforming the way that we play and watch the games we love. Technologies in sport have gradually become part of athlete life and it is normal for professional sports, teams, and athletes to exploit its possibilities. At the same time, these technologies raise concerns about the impact they may have long-term on the credibility of sport, the people that deliver it, and the people to follow it.

There is no doubt that performance analysis, the use of big data, and other newly found technologies are and will increasingly be essential training and competitive tool for elite athletes. However, the sport industry does not appear to be fully prepared to embrace the technology at its full throttle and a lot of coaches and high-performance managers do not fully comprehend how it all manifests itself in sports, teams, athletes, and the sport system. Research is needed to understand how these technologies manifest in all aspects of high-performance sport and how different countries embrace, address, and adopt these and up-and-coming technologies.

As countries around the world are constantly seeking a competitive advantage and as athletes feel pressured to improve their performance it is likely that technologies hold the key to addressing these pressures and future success. Despite the existence of regulatory frameworks presently available to protect athlete or teams' data and confidentiality, Evans et al. (2017) argued that concerns over privacy and consent remain unresolved. Therefore, whilst sport systems are encouraged to support new technologies, it is important that the integrity of sports and the safety of the athlete are a priority and measures are developed to "ethically integrate this technology into sport and consider the development of a robust governance framework" (Evans et al., 2017, p. 1503). Future directions in digital innovation in high-performance sport should assess the adaptations that various countries have achieved to technologies in sport, as well as countries' relative capacity to invest in these technologies and the impact these levels of investment have in comparison to countries less adapted.

Notes

1 See more at https://www.shu.ac.uk/sport-physical-activity-research-centre/sports-engineering/projects/performance-innovation-research-partnership.
2 An entity-relationship model (or ER model) describes interrelated things of interest in a specific domain of knowledge.

References

Australian Sports Commission (2016). *Connecting digital and technology with Australia's competitive sport obsession*. Author: Canberra. Retrieved from https://www.sportaus.gov.au/__data/assets/pdf_file/0010/665857/34871_Connecting_Digital_with_Sport_Final_V3.pdf

Baca, A., & Kornfeind, P. (2006). Rapid feedback systems for elite sports training. *IEEE Pervasive Computing*, *5*(4), 70–76.

Baca, A., & Kornfeind, P. (2012). Stability analysis of motion patterns in biathlon shooting. *Human Movement Science*, *31*(2), 295–302.

Brouwers, J., Sotiriadou, P., & De Bosscher, V. (2015). Sport-specific policies and factors that influence international success: The case of tennis. *Sport Management Review*, *18*(3), 343–358.

Evans, R., McNamee, M., & Guy, O. (2017). Ethics, nanobiosensors and elite sport: The need for a new governance framework. *Science and Engineering Ethics*, *23*(6), 1487–1505.

Giblin, G., Tor, E., & Parrington, L. (2016). The impact of technology on elite sports performance. *Sensoria: A Journal of Mind, Brain & Culture*, *12*(2), 3–9.

Haake, S. (2013). Olympic success: It's a numbers game. Retrieved from https://engineeringsport.co.uk/2013/01/04/olympic-success-its-a-numbers-game/

Hinings, B., Gegenhuber, T., & Greenwood, R. (2018). Digital innovation and transformation: An institutional perspective. *Information and Organization*, *28*(1), 52–61.

Kennedy, J. (2015). How digital disruption changed 8 industries forever. *Silicon Republic*. Retrieved from https://www.siliconrepublic.com/business/digital-disruption-changed-8-industries-forever

Kingsley, D. (2020). How have new technologies improved athletic performances? Retrieved from https://channels.theinnovationenterprise.com/

Lee, E. C., Fragala, M. S., Kavouras, S. A., Queen, R. M., Pryor, J. L., & Casa, D. J. (2017). Biomarkers in sports and exercise: Tracking health, performance, and recovery in athletes. *Journal of Strength and Conditioning Research*, *31*(10), 2920–2937.

Majumdar, D., Banerji, P. K., & Chakrabarti, S. (2018). Disruptive technology and disruptive innovation: Ignore at your peril!. *Technology Analysis & Strategic Management*, *30*(11), 1247–1255.

Osborne, B. (2017). Legal and ethical implications of athletes' biometric data collection in professional sport. *Marquette Sports Law Review*, *28*, 37–46.

Pickering, C., & Kiely, J. (2019). The development of a personalised training framework: Implementation of emerging technologies for performance. *Journal of Functional Morphology and Kinesiology*, *4*(2), 25–36.

Roda, M. (2019). New examples of sports technology that's changing the game. *Reflexion*. Retrieved from https://www.reflexion.co/blog/sports-technology

Scott, Z. (2021). Data experts become high-profile football signings as new trend emerges. *Ministry of Sport*. Australia. Retrieved from https://ministryofsport.com.au/data-experts-become-high-profile-football-signings-as-new-trend-emerges/

Seshadri, D. R., Li, R. T., Voos, J. E., Rowbottom, J. R., Alfes, C. M., Zorman, C. A., & Drummond, C. K. (2019). Wearable sensors for monitoring the internal and external workload of the athlete. *NPJ digital medicine*, *2*(1), 1–18.

Smith, T. (2020). What is disruptive technology? Retrieved from https://www.investopedia.com/terms/d/disruptive-technology.asp

Sotiriadou, P. (2021). Digital innovation in high performance sport: The State of Play. FISU World Conference: Challenges and Opportunities in Sport in modern society, Lucerne, Switzerland.

Sotiriadou, K. (2009). The Australian sport system and its stakeholders: Development of cooperative relationships. *Sport in Society*, *12*, 842–860.

Sotiriadou, P., & Brouwers, J. (2012). A critical analysis of the impact of the Beijing Olympic Games on Australia's sport policy direction. *International Journal of Sport Policy and Politics*, *4*(3), 321–341.

Sotiriadou, P., & De Bosscher, V. (Eds.). (2013). *Managing high performance sport*. Routledge: NY.

Sotiriadou, P., & De Bosscher, V. (2018). Managing high-performance sport: introduction to past, present and future considerations. *European Sport Management Quarterly*, *18*, 1–7.

Tibco-SVB (2020). The high performance project – talking sports technology, sports science, elite sport & MoreTeam Tibco-SVB – pandemic learnings for pro cyclists. https://luminsports.com/media/32-how-has-covid-19-impacted-sports-technology-for-athletes

Westermann, G., Bonner, D., & McAfee, A. (2014). *Leading digital*. Harvard Business Review Press.

8

Corporate Social Responsibility and Digital Transformation in Professional Sport

Kathy Babiak, Adam Copeland, and Daniel Yang

Introduction

Corporate social responsibility (CSR) has evolved to become a core business function over the past 20 years in the sport industry (Babiak & Wolfe, 2009, 2013; Cobourn & Frawley, 2017; Francois et al., 2019; Walzel et al., 2018). In accordance, the research focus has aligned with shifts in practice and informed a deeper understanding of the key drivers motivating businesses to engage in CSR (Bason & Anagnostopoulos, 2015; Godfrey, 2009; Yang & Babiak, 2021) and has uncovered insights into customer/fan responses to socially responsible actions, the impact of CSR on brand loyalty of sport businesses, and the sponsorship dynamic linked to CSR (Habitzreuter & Koenigstorfer, 2018; Kim et al., 2018; Plewa et al., 2016; Yu, 2020). CSR efforts have significantly benefited from digital transformations that have been supported by advances in communication, analytics, and data management. This has contributed to shifting practices in domains including framing and messaging CSR, engaging with organizational stakeholders around CSR, enhancing CSR program implementation and management, as well as evaluating and measuring CSR programs and initiatives. It has now "… become easier to collect and share [CSR] information worldwide, to receive feedback from stakeholders rapidly and easily, and to turn CSR into an [digitally] interactive process" (Kıymalıoğlu, 2020, p. 15).

This chapter will highlight the nature of the digital role in CSR in the professional sport industry and discuss how digital technology has helped to refocus, enhance, and improve the CSR efforts of professional sport organizations – including leagues, teams, athletes, and other key stakeholders. In the following sections, we discuss the focus of digital transformation in research on CSR and highlight several examples of how these changes have impacted CSR practice in sport organizations. This chapter will spotlight the following emerging areas of digital transformation in CSR in sport: digital fundraising, digital philanthropy, and communication of CSR efforts through social media and other digital channels. We also discuss the emerging concept of "corporate digital responsibility" in sport itself – that is, being a responsible "digital" citizen in the management and organization of a sport business. We conclude this chapter by identifying opportunities for further academic scholarship in this burgeoning area.

 DOI: 10.4324/9781003088899-10

Concept Grounding: CSR and Digital Transformation – What Does it Mean?

CSR is defined as an intentional business activity that considers a company's accountability to society broadly. McWilliams and Siegel (2001) defined CSR as the "… actions that appear to further some social good, beyond the interests of the firm and that which is required by law" (p. 117). Carroll (1991) framed CSR as four domains of a firm's responsibilities: (a) economic (creating a profit as economic agent); (b) legal (obeying laws and regulations); (c) ethical (operating in an ethical manner aligned with social norms and expectations); (d) discretionary (embracing philanthropic behaviors beyond those expected of business). The concept of CSR also considers dimensions of social, environmental, and economic impact on key stakeholders and constituents (Dahlsrud, 2008). Given the broad scope of the definition, this organizational practice spans a range of functional areas in its implementation and execution and takes into account the varied stakeholders and constituents a firm may affect in its actions.

There has been a close connection between digital advances and the role and position of businesses in society, and this evolution of the digital landscape has changed the nature of CSR work in organizations (Spanos, 2018). Over time, the evolution of technology and the digital landscape may have also contributed to some of the social problems that firms today are trying to remedy. For example, issues such as environmental damage caused by advances in production and technological innovation have been detrimental to society and have caused lasting environmental issues (Orbik & Zozul'aková, 2019). However, digital transformation has also helped in streamlining efforts at designing, implementing, managing, and evaluating CSR itself. Some research has begun to explore the connection between CSR and digital transformation, including ethics and responsibilities around smart devices and wearables, Big Data, mobility, computing cloud, social platforms, bio and nanotechnologies, Internet of Things, renewable energy, or the sharing economy (Okazaki et al., 2020; Schultz & Seele, 2020). In fact, Orbik and Zozul'aková (2019) noted that "Corporate social responsibility and digital transformation are one of the most important factors of global competitiveness in the modern world" (p. 70). The significance of the scope of digital transformation across industries has impacted business models, systems, and strategies. While digital transformation has impacted all business practices, it is also being used by companies to solve social problems and pressing issues, as well as making the process of CSR more efficient and effective.

Sport firms such as professional teams and leagues may engage in CSR through a number of distinct areas including philanthropy, community relations, labor/HR relations, good governance, responsible and ethical community engagement, and leadership, or by ensuring environmentally friendly business practices (Babiak & Wolfe, 2013; Yang & Babiak, 2021). Many authors have highlighted the unique nature of CSR in sport (such as youth appeal, visibility, unique stakeholder relationships (c.f., Babiak & Wolfe, 2009; Smith & Westerbeek, 2007)) – and the transformation of the digital landscape has magnified the visibility, outcomes, and impact of these efforts. Today, CSR practices have evolved to serve important strategic objectives for sport organizations. CSR in professional sport has been integrated into community programming and incorporated into branding and marketing activities, reflecting organizational values, impacting human resources, and helping to foster and maintain partnerships (Walker & Kent, 2009, 2013). The internet has become a critical tool for CSR communications in the digital age. While research on CSR and digital transformation in sport is only beginning to develop, we believe that significant areas of opportunity exist in this domain for scholars to pursue. Below, we offer an overview of two key areas of CSR practice that have been significantly affected by digital transformation and disruption – fundraising and communication – and identify opportunities for scholarship and investigation.

Sport Philanthropy and Digital Fundraising

The establishment of charity and philanthropy as a CSR practice has evolved in the realm of professional sport over the past three decades (Anagnostopoulos et al., 2014; Babiak & Wolfe, 2009; Inoue et al., 2013; Walker & Kent, 2013; Yang & Babiak, 2021). Through the development of charitable foundations/corporate-linked nonprofit organizations, professional sport entities (from athletes to teams, and even leagues) use their platforms to positively impact social change. Acquiring and disseminating financial resources is a key dimension of CSR practice for sport entities (Yang & Babiak, 2021). The changing digital landscape has impacted these practices across numerous dimensions. In this section, we focus primarily on the changes that digital platforms have offered in the realm of fundraising and donor engagement and the opportunities for scholarly knowledge development in this area.

Crowdfunding has emerged as an alternative form of charitable financing that raises funds from the "crowd" typically via a digital platform and channels them into various social causes or business projects. This approach provides opportunities that can significantly change the traditional landscape of CSR and corporate philanthropy (Spanos, 2018). Crowdfunding is an increasingly popular platform that has connections to charity, especially considering how most companies today have social causes embedded in their CSR strategies, practices, or products. There are emerging linkages, interconnections, and complementarities between crowdfunding and CSR. "Companies can use crowdfunding when designing and implementing their CSR strategies in various ways, such as increasing available funding, raising awareness and engagement, building communication channels with stakeholders and increasing marketing" (Spanos, 2018, p. 1). Crowdfunding has the potential to impact the way donors engage with sport teams and athletes. "Using sports-oriented crowdfunding websites allow fans to donate directly, but also offer features like 'pledging for performance' - allowing fans to donate for each goal, point, strikeout … Thus, aligning the team's charitable cause and the fan's desire for performance" (Yellen, 2017). These platforms have led to increases in giving with the Major League Baseball (MLB) teams doubling their fundraising for charitable causes using such tools (Podder, 2017). The peer-to-peer fundraising model occurs through digital/online platforms, which facilitates the donation process. There are a growing number of platforms that athletes, teams, and leagues can use to raise money for causes they care about such as PledgeIt, Classy, Sportfunder, Rallyme, Makeachamp, and GoFundMe. In 2017, after the successful crowdfunded campaigns for Hurricane Harvey (started by JJ Watt of the Houston Texans) and victims of a warehouse fire that killed 16 people (started by the Oakland Athletics franchise) (Phillips Erb, 2017), MLB formed an official partnership with YouCaring, a crowdfunding platform, to offer its players and teams the ability to create online, peer-to-peer fundraising campaigns for the charities they support (Newman, 2017).

The COVID-19 pandemic has accelerated virtual fundraising in professional sport. By leveraging the internet and social media, athletes and teams have been able to generate philanthropic funds to support communities and individuals. Online auctions (e.g., the National Football League (NFL)'s online auction initiative where fans can bid online or via text for authentic game used items or experiences), social media influencers on emerging platforms such as Snapchat, TikTok, and Twitch (e.g., NFL's 'Draft-a-Thon' for Covid relief) have also been facilitated by changes in the digital landscape and have allowed teams and leagues to increase philanthropic revenues – thus allowing for greater social impact in charitable giving (Denton, 2020; National Basketball Association, 2020; Thomas, 2020).

The academic exploration of crowdfunding as a socially responsible/philanthropic revenue generation strategy in the professional sport realm is still in its infancy. Studies focused on issues related to revenues and corporate charitable giving in professional sport are starting to emerge (Inoue & Kent, 2014; Sparvero & Kent, 2014; Yang & Babiak, 2021). However, many gaps and questions remain about how the changing digital landscape has affected this practice in professional sport. We believe this is an area that has the potential for scholars to develop a deeper understanding. Issues exploring the power of sport and professional athletes and their social networks to leverage and encourage online giving can potentially shed light on how digital innovations facilitate generosity by fans, partners, and other constituents. Further, given that crowdfunding can be used to micro-fund many social activities in line with a team's CSR goals, understanding the prosocial behaviors and motivations of actors involved in these efforts and exploring the context in which they occur (e.g., urgent/imminent needs emerging from a crisis or disaster, to fund an ongoing CSR platform or effort) can shed light on the effectiveness of this practice.

CSR Digital Communication and Engagement

Changes in the digital environment have also aligned with advances in CSR communication, messaging, and engagement (Cortado & Chalmeta, 2016; Wang & Huang, 2018), with some scholars suggesting that the intersection of CSR and social media is a marriage made in heaven (cf., Etter, 2013; Kent & Taylor, 2016). In the evolving digital context, Tench and Jones (2015) noted that "… increasingly businesses of all sizes and types are expected to communicate, explain and justify their CSR credentials" (p. 4). Communicating CSR activity and outcomes to stakeholders has become a significant and continual challenge for firms – and social media has served as a viable pathway to overcome some of these issues (Ogilvy Public Relations Worldwide, 2010) – but has also introduced new challenging aspects to messaging around CSR. The benefits of social media to communicate CSR efforts include its relational nature, and the immediate and real-time feedback potential these platforms offer which lead to greater engagement, input, and even co-creation of social efforts. Academic research has begun to explore questions around effective strategies and approaches to using digital communication tools such as websites, social media platforms, blogs, and other digital outlets (e.g., YouTube, Twitch, etc.) (Cortado & Chalmeta, 2016; Korschun & Du, 2013, Wang & Huang, 2018). Research in this area has investigated topics such as how message source and type (content) of CSR communication impact the consumer–brand relationship, loyalty, or positive word of mouth (Sreejesh et al., 2020; Wang & Huang, 2018); how social media has elevated CSR from a one-way information sharing practice to an activity where stakeholders can engage, influence, and interact with firms' CSR initiatives (Kent & Taylor, 2016); how CSR social media messages can lead to behavior change or knowledge acquisition (Tench & Jones, 2015); or how activists (hacktivists) may challenge corporate CSR messaging on social media by highlighting corporate irresponsibility (Tench & Jones, 2015). In regard to the broad research in the area of CSR communication and digital transformation (social media), Kent and Taylor (2016) stated that they "… believe that current research has not reached its potential for explaining how to create ethical, empowering, and long-lasting, public relations relationships" (p. 60). They acknowledge that this is an emerging field with much potential for scholarly investigation.

In the sport context, social media and web-based communication to connect with potential beneficiaries as well as the use of these platforms to highlight and promote team CSR efforts have become a critical activity for sport organizations (Formentin & Babiak, 2014). Social media and CSR research in sport is also evolving as a topic of academic investigation. Kim et al., (2018) and Kim and Hull (2017) found that MLB teams have a dual approach to the use of Instagram focused on either sport action (e.g., photos of game and player action) or social impact (e.g., photos of charitable activities). Teams and leagues are increasingly communicating their CSR efforts through social media – either through generic team/league accounts or hashtags (e.g., #hockeytowncares (Detroit Red Wings), #hockeyfightscancer (NHL), @MavsOffCourt (Dallas Mavericks)), or via dedicated CSR oriented accounts like @Tigerscommunity (Detroit Tigers), @NBACares, or @NFLFoundation.

We believe that for sport scholars, the area of communicating CSR through digital media has tremendous potential as an area of inquiry – particularly given the media focus on professional teams, leagues, and athletes (Babiak & Wolfe, 2009). Understanding successful models of relationship building and co-creation of social impact initiatives using social media are one area that has potential for academic investigation in sport management. For instance, using a stakeholder involvement strategy, Morsing and Schultz (2006) explored organization-stakeholder dialogic relationships – both internal and external. We currently know little about how sports organizations manage these relationships and messaging. A recent relevant example demonstrates how stakeholders use social media to influence and advocate for league (or team) change. In 2020 at the height of the social justice movement, the NFL (Commissioner Roger Goodell) tweeted a statement about the league's stance on racial justice. Both internal stakeholders (players Kenny Stills and Eric Reid) – criticized Goodell's statement as being inauthentic and disingenuous (Schad, 2020). Similarly, external stakeholders – fans, followers, and customers, also voiced their critiques in response to Goodell's tweet on racial injustice (Gatto, 2020). Emerging issues and problems around this dynamic include how sport businesses and communication professionals manage CSR messages in a fractious, largely unregulated social media environment. Other pertinent questions include decision-making around CSR messaging (which messaging resonates, which social causes to communicate about, frequency of communication, how to frame CSR activities, which platforms to use); how do sport organizations best respond and engage with stakeholders and critics; the role of social media influencers in driving social change; and understanding how values-driven vs. strategic driven messaging is perceived by stakeholders and impacts consumer behaviors.

In terms of direct CSR practice, both philanthropy/fundraising and communication activities are two of the most prominent functions affected by digital transformation. Other areas including environmental sustainability and sport data, analytics, and measurement and evaluation have also been impacted by the evolution of digital technology. These will be discussed next in the context of the emerging concept of Corporate Digital Responsibility.

Corporate Digital Responsibility and Sport Organizations

Over the last decades, digitalization has dramatically changed individuals' daily lives as well as business operations and strategies (Herden et al., 2021). Nowadays, nearly all forms of business have embraced some type of digital transformation, such as automation, online (mobile) commerce, artificial intelligence (AI), machine learning, and data analytics (Lobschat et al., 2021; Wirtz et al., 2018). While these digital technologies have created new opportunities for corporations to enhance efficiency in their business models and increase competitiveness, digital advances have also raised new ethical issues and risks around the uses of digital technology (Lobschat et al., 2021; Martin et al., 2017; Richter & Riemer, 2013). For example, the development of online commerce systems has increased the risks related to privacy, data vulnerability, data breaches, and cyber-attacks (Arachchilage & Love, 2014; Vial, 2019). The use of malleable AI systems may lead corporations to wrong decision-making and unintended consequences (Nambisan et al., 2017). Given the opportunities and threats of digital transformation, there has been an increasing debate over norms, codes, and responsibilities in the digital age for corporations with respect to the development and deployment of digital technology and related data (Lobschat et al., 2021).

Digital advances have transformed the sport industry as well. Many professional sport teams and leagues have adopted new digital technologies to improve their operations and competitiveness including player and team performance, in-stadium experiences, and fan engagement. For example, the National Basketball Association (NBA) announced a multi-year partnership with Microsoft to create a direct-to-consumer platform for fan engagement based on AI and machine learning, which delivers more customized and localized content to global fans (Microsoft, 2020). Partnering with Intel True View, Manchester City FC, the English Premier League football club, has provided their fans with multi-angle camera replays and player-eye views of the action from games at their stadium within the official club mobile application, which offers an immersive experience to the fans (Carp, 2020).

While professional sport teams are leveraging digital technologies in myriad ways, a growing number of incidents related to cybercrime or data breaches have been reported across leagues. For example, in MLB, a former scouting director of the Saint Louis Cardinals was charged and punished for hacking the Houston Astros' database and email system over the course of two years (Graczyk & Tucker, 2016). In 2018, Pacers Sports and Entertainment, the legal entity of the Indiana Pacers (NBA) and Fever (WNBA), was the target of an email phishing campaign that resulted in unauthorized access to employee personal information (Indiana Pacers, 2019). Moreover, in 2020, it was reported that the NFL and at least 15 football teams were compromised by a hacking group, which gained unauthorized access to multiple social media accounts of the organizations (e.g., Twitter, Instagram, and Facebook) (Cohen, 2020).

Notably, the global pandemic in 2020 has accelerated the adoption of the digital transformation within the professional sport industry as sport teams had to expand their business model beyond traditional stadium-based revenue generation (Neureiter, 2021). In terms of alternative revenue sources, data monetization, the process of using data to increase revenue, will be more important than ever as data-driven platforms and data analytics can help teams to better understand fan behavior and elevate fan experience, and ultimately, increase revenues. Despite the growing importance of digital transformation and its impact on sport organizations, there is relatively little scholarly work on ethical challenges and responsibilities arising from digital technology and data in sport management. In the next section, we will introduce the concept of corporate digital responsibility (CDR), discuss how it can be applied to the context of sport, and present emerging questions of scholarly interest to sport management researchers.

Dimensions of Corporate Digital Responsibility

While the concept of CSR may encompass corporate responsibilities at a multidimensional and broader level (Carroll, 1991), CDR is a more specific area of corporate responsibility that focuses on ethical principles in the digital age. CDR can be defined as "the set of values and specific norms that govern an organization's judgments and choices in matters that relate specifically to digital issues" (Lobschat et al., 2021, p. 876). Lobschat and colleagues elaborate on the distinctions between CDR and CSR and suggest these two areas of focus differ in notable ways. First, the exponential growth of technologies creates a rapidly changing milieu that organizations and actors have to navigate. In addition to exponential growth, technologies are continually being recombined to generate new capacities that outstrip the collective understanding of how to manage those capacities responsibly. The second distinction between CDR and CSR is due to the malleability of new technologies. In other words, technologies can be co-opted to serve unforeseen and undesired purposes. The final distinction between CDR

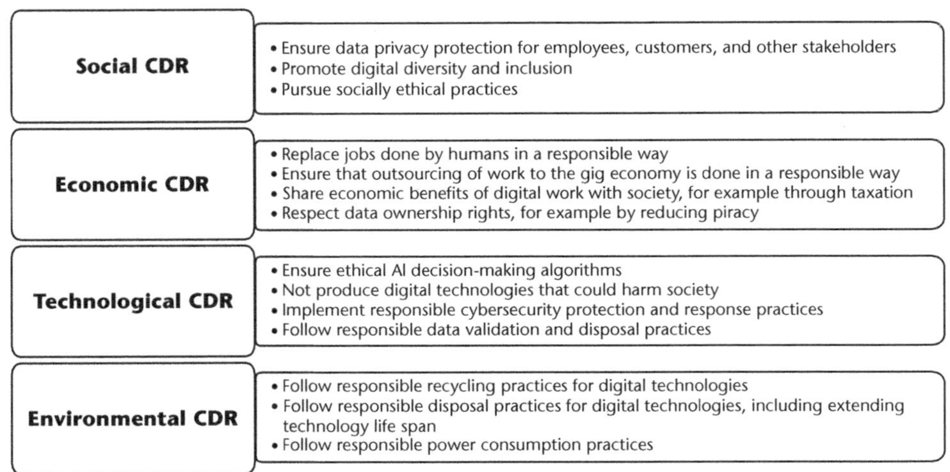

Figure 8.1 Four Dimensions of Corporate Digital Responsibility

Source: Adapted from Wade (2020).

and CSR is brought about by the inescapable digital presence in all elements of society. Given the omnipresence of digital technologies, organizations and stakeholders have no choice but to confront the best practices around the use of technology. The triumvirate of digital distinctions makes CDR a separate and salient issue to consider in management research and practice.

A conceptual framework developed by Wade (2020) depicts pertinent domains of CDR for companies. The author focused on the concept of organizational CDR along four specified dimensions including practices and behaviors related to social, economic, technological, and environmental responsibility. Within those four categories of CDR, Wade elaborated on considerations that organizations need to make in adopting CDR-focused practices (Figure 8.1). We discuss these domains and their relevance to sport organizations next.

Social CDR concerns an organization's responsibilities in digital practices within the context of the relationship with organizational stakeholders (e.g., employees and customers) and society at large. Digital transformation has increased the vulnerability of individuals and businesses to cybercrimes, and data privacy issues have been a core aspect of digital ethics (Eißfeller, 2020). Corporations are responsible for communicating with employees and customers to create a shared understanding of data privacy and developing policies and guidelines related to cybersecurity. Moreover, the ethical and transparent data collection and processing of customer data would be a vital corporate obligation in the new era of big data (Liyanaarachchi et al., 2020). In addition, corporations should endeavor to promote digital inclusion by ensuring the availability and accessibility of digital technologies to individuals and communities as a whole (Herden et al., 2021).

Social CDR and Sport

With increasing focus on performance analytics, athlete "data is of huge interest to the public and the media, and it has huge commercial value to teams, as well as their opponents" (Hampshire, 2015). Ensuring this information is protected and private should be a critical responsibility for sport teams and leagues. Additionally, protecting the information of sport fans, consumers, and partners should also be of paramount importance to sport teams and leagues as they collect and store a substantial volume of sensitive personal and corporate data. Hampshire (2015) noted the value of this information to outside parties "Hackers value information regarding business strategy; insight into large deals such as sponsorships and partnerships; and large volumes of personal and payment card data from online retail, ticketing sales and supporter programs, all of which can be leveraged and monetized." Furthermore, given the unique context of professional sport, prominent athletes often operate highly followed and visible accounts on various digital platforms (Twitter, Facebook, Instagram). Many of those athletes have decided to leverage their visible prominence on social media to further social causes. This has not come without debate about how to do so responsibly (Boren, 2021) and what the role of teams and leagues in monitoring and controlling messaging should be.

Sport organizations must continue to explore optimal ways to allow their internal stakeholders to express themselves while doing so in a way that moves society in a productive, unifying direction. Future research should support this goal by both describing current practices as well as proposing practical goals for sport organizations to best manage player data and digital presence. How are sport organizations managing player data acquired through wearable technology? How do sport organizations currently manage the digital presence of their athletes, if at all? Connected to those previous two questions, how and if do sport organizations create governance around data acquisition and digital presence? What are the effects on sport organizations of athletes making explicit social statements through digital platforms?

Economic CDR refers to the responsible management of the economic impacts of digital technologies (Wade, 2020). With the increased scope for automatization and AI, many jobs may disappear, leading to the unemployment of people responsible for these tasks (United Nations Conference on Trade and Development, 2019). Moreover, the emergence of a new business model based on digital technologies has increased the demand for a workforce with new skills and knowledge (Arntz et al., 2017). From a corporate perspective, the transition to digitalization may increase productivity and create new opportunities to expand business activities. However, these changes should be socially compatible and thoughtful rather than antagonistic and cut-throat (Herden et al., 2021). Bean (2017) noted that organizations should support and retrain their employees to be prepared for such technological changes in advance. Furthermore, economic CDR also relates to ethical behaviors of organizations in sharing economic benefits from digitalization, such as protecting data ownership and the compensation of monetized data (Wade, 2020).

Economic CDR and Sport

The progression of digital advancement raises economic concerns relevant to society and to sport. As new technologies are developed, the economic landscape will change. Of great interest to society is the impact of automation on the job market, and thereby, the economic well-being of many sport stakeholders. This is especially salient given the current context of a world increasingly divided between the wealthy and the less so (Zucman, 2019). McKinsey Global Institute estimates that a quarter of the American workforce will lose their jobs to automation by the year 2030 (McKinsey Global Institute, 2021). There are debates though about the degree of disruption to be caused by automation, as well as hope that new technologies will subsequently create the need for new jobs (Carey, 2021). How automation will specifically impact sport is yet to be fully understood. Given the increasing acceptance and use of technologies such as instant replays, and data analytics that can partially or fully replace human capital, sport organizations would be wise to responsibly develop and adopt emerging digital transformations. As jobs capable of being replaced by technology are emerging, sport organizations should ensure that new jobs provide accessible opportunities for a diversity of talent to assume and fulfill. Doing so will reduce the likelihood that sport's adoption of automation will exacerbate the wealth inequality already present in the economic landscape.

In addition to changing what economic opportunities are available to sport stakeholders, digital transformation will likely change the economic extraction abilities of sport organizations. With the rise of big data comes the ability of organizations to understand their stakeholders more intimately, most relevant of which are fans and customers. The utility of customer data provides a double-edged sword of potential for sport organizations. The data can allow for increased customization, engagement, and relevance of marketing campaigns (Columbus, 2016). With that increased effectiveness of marketing and sales initiatives, comes an ethical question about how far should sport organizations go in leveraging data and digital technologies in generating lucrative economic opportunities? Given the public's reaction to the data usage for political purposes by Cambridge Analytica discovered in 2018, sport organizations should be wary of demonstrably instrumental data usage (Confessore, 2018). Instead, sport organizations should align their data usage with organizational values and institutional values. For example, one of the NFL's stated values is that of integrity (National Football League, 2021). According to the league, "We do the right thing when no one is looking, and even if it's unpopular when they are looking." Aligning data collection and usage with the value of integrity might reduce the chance of malevolent or instrumental data usage by league entities.

Future research should consider the ethics surrounding the use of data as it pertains to economic issues. What jobs in sport are most susceptible to the progression of artificial intelligence and digital technologies, and how can sport organizations proactively create new economic opportunities for a diverse pool of possible candidates? How can sport organizations use data to ensure that economic transactions with external stakeholders create maximal value for all parties involved?

Technological CDR is related to the responsible use and creation of technologies by organizations. Due to the proliferation of data-driven business platforms and data analytics, data security would be key CDR practice within corporations. The practices include the establishment of secure technical infrastructure, internal data security regulations and monitoring systems, and employee cybersecurity training. Corporations also should be aware of the potential risk of digital technologies. For example, machine learning and AI enables businesses to offer personalized product/service/content recommendations by collecting and analyzing customers' data (from previous purchases, search activities, and demographic information) (Moreno, 2019). However, corporations should constantly monitor any misinterpretations or fallacies by the AI systems (e.g., biased algorithms leading to discriminative customer treatment) and ensure the whole process accords with ethical principles (Herden et al., 2021).

Technological CDR and Sport

Considering the rate at which digital technologies are evolving, and the ever-increasing capabilities of those technologies, forming concrete standards and practices for their use is imperative (Bryson & Winfield, 2017). Emerging technologies such as AI and virtual reality (VR) are considered to improve sport fan experiences related to information seeking and sports service consumption (Rynarzewska, 2018). An example of such new technology is synthetic media, which allows for the generation of media content (images, video, audio) using only previously aggregated data and artificial intelligence (Jaiman, 2020). The Washington Wizards have adopted synthetic media, developing a virtual influencer to connect with a diverse and international audience (Williams, 2020). Such synthetic media usage raises important ethical questions regarding the organizational use of the media, and the deployment of virtual actors like the Wizards' virtual influencer, Liam Nikuro.

Sport organizations leverage the likenesses of their athletes in order to connect with stakeholders in a myriad of ways. Given the use of athlete physical and vocal representation, sport organizations have access to large quantities of data that they could hypothetically use in creating synthetic media. That technological potential raises questions about what sport organizations can and cannot have synthetic versions of what their athletes say and do? How should sport organizations and their athletes come to agreements on how their likenesses and voices can be used in developing synthetic media? Similar questions can be extended to entirely virtual influencers such as the Wizards' Liam Nikuro. How should sport organizations use the influential capabilities of a completely malleable entity such as a virtual influencer? The CDR framework proposed by Wade (2020) offers some guidance in that he suggests firms create AI that is ethical and does not harm human society. While those overarching guidelines are useful, establishing more nuanced standards and best practices in response to those questions will be of paramount importance for researchers and sport organizations going forward.

Some other critical technological considerations for sport organizations revolve around the use, transfer, and disposal of acquired player data (Torre & Haberstoh, 2014). As players are exposed to more wearable technologies such as NFL players and the WHOOP strap (Pickett, 2020), how that data is used in managing and making decisions around that player will be under increased scrutiny. Can or should that data be used to make inter-game or intra-game decisions regarding playing time? Such decisions could impact the ability of players to earn contractually embedded bonuses or not. Can or should the data be transferred from team to team in the event of the possibility of an acquisition or trade? What about when a player retires? Who is responsible for storing athlete performance data? Does the player have rights to it or does the organization have a responsibility to dispose of it? How do organizations such as league governing bodies and players' associations navigate the thorny power and ethical issues related to player health and performance data? Exploring and researching extant and best practices around those questions can help assure that data use, transfer, and disposal do not negatively impact internal or external stakeholders.

Finally, *environmental CDR* addresses the environmental impact of technology choices, such as responsible recycling or the disposal of old computer equipment. Digital technologies are evolving continuously driven by the development of new products and equipment (Malmodin et al., 2014). Thus, responsible replenishment and recycling of digital equipment would be one CDR practice that corporations can implement to contribute to environmental sustainability.

Environmental CDR and Sport

Professional sport involves the creation/use of extensive technologies and the implementation of new ones (Costa, 2020). The continual evolution of sports-involved technology introduces the challenge of sustainable practices. The overlap between digital transformation and environmental responsibility has two primary elements. First, the evolution of certain technologies has the potential to improve environmental outcomes. It has been found that an attendee of a major sporting event increases their carbon footprint by seven times (Collins, et al., 2007). As a response, there is a growing number of Major League Baseball teams incorporating technological solutions such as solar panels in their physical infrastructure in order to reduce their organizations' environmental impact (Chetwynd, 2019; Independent Power Systems, 2020). In addition to the actual use of environmentally responsible technology, sports organizations have the ability to leverage their brand capital in order to reinforce responsible environmentally responsible technology use. For example, the NBA has used their web platform to put forward information on how to manage digital technology use in order to reduce power consumption (National Environmental Education Foundation, 2021). Second, as organizations continually adopt new audiovisual, communication, and computing technologies, obsolete devices need to be disposed of in environmentally responsible ways. The lifecycle of technology offers a variety of possible sustainable solutions, including the dissemination of unneeded technology to external groups that could benefit and learn from its use. Future research should investigate the ways in which sport organizations do or do not have an impact on their own environmental outcomes, as well as the outcomes of external stakeholders exposed to their environmentally concerned messaging. In addition, research should investigate what practices, if any, sport organizations have in place to responsibly dispose of or repurpose obsolete technology. Both lines of inquiry could yield practically relevant outcomes for sport organizations as they and society strive to take care of the environment.

Conclusions, Implications, and Future Research

Given that sport organizations are increasingly adopting digitalized practices and systems, CDR may shed light on a new direction for sport organizations in terms of fusing ethical considerations into the way they create, deliver, and capture the value of digital transformation. For sport management scholars and practitioners, it is imperative to explore the ways in which CDR might take on even more distinctiveness in the domain of sport. What about corporate digital responsibility, if anything, might need to be updated for the institution of sport, sport organizations, and sport stakeholder interactions (both internal and external)?

To understand how CDR might take on a unique manifestation within sport, the relevant stakeholders should be explored. Lobschat et al. (2021) highlight four important stakeholder groups to consider: organizations, individual actors, artificial technological actors, and institutional actors. Seeing that CDR is an emerging body of norms and practices, the adoption is likely mediated significantly by organizations (Edleman, 1992), something that Lobschat et al. (2021) recognize. Beyond organizations, the group of individual actors centers around internal and external users interfacing with technologies that organizations either create or adopt. This includes managers and agents within organizations making decisions about technological implementation, those using or intersecting with digital technology (such as employees and athletes), as well as consumers interacting with technologies to establish connections with those organizations.

Institutional actors account for the various entities to which organizations are accountable, which include, but are not limited to, governmental authorities and legal regulatory agencies, and, while not explicitly mentioned by Lobschat et al. (2021), social institutions could bring to bear relevant pressures on organizational practice around corporate digital responsibility. The single most distinct stakeholder in the concept of CDR is that of artificial actors. By this, Lobschat et al. raise the ethical considerations that apply to the creation, regulation, and autonomy of artificial actors. To what degree are the human creators of artificial actors responsible for the actions of their algorithmic and technological creations? Also, what kinds of ethical protections should artificial actors receive? Given the recent adoption of technological advancements such as virtual influencers by a variety of organizations in the sport landscape, those questions become increasingly relevant and urgent (Dodt, 2020). Taking into consideration the four categories of CDR proposed by Wade (2020) (social, economic, environmental, technological) along with some of the nuancing from Lobschat et al. some possible distinctive overlaps between CDR and sport (specifically professional sport) exist.

Lobschat et al. (2021) noted that "the ethical design and uses of digital technologies and related data is not solely a technological challenge (e.g., developing algorithms for ethical reasoning). Rather, it requires organizations to develop a comprehensive, coherent set of norms, embedded in their organizational culture, to govern the development and deployment of digital technology and data" (p. 876). Understanding emerging risks created in a digital era and how CDR can be applied to sport organizations would be a fruitful focus of investigation in sport management. This is an emerging area with a small but growing focus in scholarly work to date in the management literature. As of yet, there has been little substantive research exploring this concept in the sport management field. However, as we have noted in this chapter, the topic has seen increasing significance for sport organizations. Scholarly investigation into this area can uncover a deeper understanding of the ethical, moral, strategic, economic, environmental, policy, and social dimensions of CDR in sport. Thus, given this emerging area of organizational focus, we propose several more generalized research questions based on our prior discussion that relate to capacity, structure, governance, leadership, and the unique context of sport.

- What new capacities and organizational capabilities need to be developed and fostered by sport organizations to ensure high levels of CDR?
- How do sport organizations manage and govern the potential risks emerging from cybercrime/data privacy/AI techniques?
- What are the new roles of leadership in sport organizations in cultivating an organizational culture around transparency, security, and privacy in the use of digital technologies?
- What are the unique conditions/environments/stakeholders that sport organizations should consider related to the ethical and responsible use of digital technologies?
- What leads to variation in how professional sport leagues and teams respond to shifting norms and expectations around the adoption of CDR?
- How can sport organizations address the issue of digital inclusion/digital divide?
- How do ethics around the development of artificial intelligence overlap with sport? Do virtual sport influencers have different rights and/or duties than virtual influencers outside of sport?

In closing, this chapter has explored how digital transformation has revolutionized the landscape of CSR in professional sport organizations. We also introduced the concept of CDR as an essential function of CSR for sport businesses. We argue that this emerging area is poised for increased scholarly attention. There are also numerous practical implications of these changes that sport leaders must entertain. We leave our readers with the final words of Herden et al. (2021) who comment on the practical considerations of this burgeoning space: "With technology accelerating at a lightning speed and new innovations continuously evolving in the digital space, companies should take an agile approach to CDR implementation and regularly revisit and update their current structures and CDR policies to ensure an optimum level of digital responsibility" (p. 3).

References

Anagnostopoulos, C., Byers, T., & Shilbury, D. (2014). CSR in professional team sport organisations: Towards a theory of decision-making. *European Sport Management Quarterly*, *14*(3), 259–281.

Arachchilage, N., & Love, S. (2014). Security awareness of computer users: A phishing threat avoidance perspective. *Computers in Human Behavior*, *38*, 304–312.

Arntz, M., Gregory, T., & Zierahn, U. (2017). Revisiting the risk of automation. *Economics Letters*, *159*, 157–160.

Babiak, K., & Wolfe, R. (2009). Determinants of CSR in professional sport: Internal and externalf. *Journal of Sport Management*, *23*(6), 717–742.

Babiak, K., & Wolfe, R. (2013). Perspectives on social responsibility in sport. In J. Paramio-Salcines, K. Babiak, & G. Walters (Eds.), *Routledge handbook of corporate responsibility in sport* (pp. 17–34). Routledge: New York, NY.

Bason, T., & Anagnostopoulos, C. (2015). CSR through sport: A longitudinal study of the FTSE100 companies. *Sport, Business and Management, 5*(3), 218–241.

Bean, S. (2017, July 13). *Employers must prepare for emerging technologies that will reshape work by 2030.* https://workplaceinsight.net/employers-must-prepare-for-emerging-technologies-that-reshape-working-lives-by-2030/

Boren, C. (2021, April 22). *LeBron James says his deleted tweet about police shooting was 'being used to create more hate'.* The Washington Post. https://www.washingtonpost.com/sports/2021/04/22/lebron-james-deleted-tweet-police/

Bryson, J., & Winfield, A. (2017). *Standardizing ethical design for artificial intelligence and autonomous systems.* Computer.org. https://ieeexplore.ieee.org/stamp/stamp.jsp?arnumber=7924235

Carey, K. (2021). *Do not be alarmed by wild predictions of robots taking everyone's jobs.* Slate. https://slate.com/technology/2021/03/job-loss-automation-robots-predictions.html

Carroll, A. B. (1991). The pyramid of corporate social responsibility: Toward the moral management of organizational stakeholders. *Business Horizons, 34*(4), 39–48.

Carp, S. (2020, June 25). *Man City retain Intel's immersive viewing tech in multi-year extension.* https://www.sportspromedia.com/news/man-city-intel-true-view-highlights-multi-angle-replays-immersive-viewing

Chetwynd, J. (2019, May 5). *Major League Baseball's environmental pitch.* https://medium.com/environment-america/major-league-baseballs-environmental-pitch-392183ddb257

Cobourn, S., & Frawley, S. (2017). CSR in professional sport: An examination of community models. *Managing Sport and Leisure, 22*(2), 113–126.

Cohen, A. (2020, January 29). *Investigation opened after hackers target NFL league and team social accounts.* https://www.sporttechie.com/nfl-super-bowl-liv-social-media-accounts-hacked/

Collins, A., Flynn, A., Munday, M., & Roberts, A. (2007). Assessing the environmental consequences of major sporting events: The 2003/04 FA Cup Final. Urban studies, 44(3), 457–476.

Collins, A., Jones, C., & Munday, M. (2009). Assessing the environmental impacts of mega sporting events: Two options? *Tourism Management, 30*(6), 828–837.

Columbus, L. (2016). *Ten ways big data is revolutionizing marketing and sales.* Forbes. https://www.forbes.com/sites/louiscolumbus/2016/05/09/ten-ways-big-data-is-revolutionizing-marketing-and-sales/?sh=1857af4821cf

Confessore, N. (2018). *Cambridge analytica and Facebook: The scandal and the fallout so far.* The New York Times. https://www.nytimes.com/2018/04/04/us/politics/cambridge-analytica-scandal-fallout.html

Cortado, F. J. & Chalmeta, R. (2016) Use of social networks as a CSR communication tool. *Cogent Business & Management,* 3(1). DOI: 10.1080/23311975.2016.1187783.

Costa, B. (2020, December 22). *Fox Sports worked a live mirrorless camera into an NFL broadcast — and it caught viewers' attention.* https://www.sportsvideo.org/2020/12/22/fox-sports-worked-a-live-mirrorless-camera-into-an-nfl-broadcast-and-it-caught-viewers-attention/

Dahlsrud, A. (2008). How CSR is defined: An analysis of 37 definitions. *Corporate Social Responsibility and Environmental Management, 15*(1), 1–13.

Deloitte. (2018). *A whole new ball game: Navigating digital change in the sports industry.* https://www2.deloitte.com/content/dam/Deloitte/global/Documents/Technology-Media-Telecommunications/gx-digital-transformation-sports.pdf

Denton, J. (2020, April 9). *Orlando Magic broadcasters to host virtual fundraiser to assist food insecure families in Central Florida.* https://www.nba.com/magic/orlando-magic-broadcasters-host-virtual-fundraiser-assist-food-insecure-families-central-florida

Dodt, D. (2020, January 27). *How virtual influencers are taking off in digital marketing.* https://dmexco.com/stories/how-virtual-influencers-are-gaining-a-foothold-in-digital-marketing/

Edleman, L. (1992). Legal ambiguity and symbolic structures: Organizational mediation of civil rights law. *American Journal of Sociology, 97*(6), 1531–1576.

Eißfeller, C. (2020, April 20). *Corporate digital responsibility: Why digital ethics are essential.* https://dmexco.com/stories/corporate-digital-responsibility-why-digital-ethics-are-essential/

Erb, K. (2017, August 31). *J.J. Watt raises millions for flood relief, making charitable crowdfunding history.* Forbes. https://www.forbes.com/sites/kellyphillipserb/2017/08/31/j-j-watt-raises-millions-for-flood-relief-making-charitable-crowdfunding-history/?sh=11a0c9325cbb

Etter, M. (2013). Reasons for low levels of interactivity: (Non-) Interactive CSR communication in Twitter. *Public relations review, 39*(5), 606–608.

François, A., Bayle, E., & Gond, J. P. (2019). A multilevel analysis of implicit and explicit CSR in French and UK professional sport. *European Sport Management Quarterly, 19*(1), 15–37.

Formentin, M., & Babiak, K. (2014). Communicating CSR in sport organizations. In M. Hardin & A. Billings (Eds.), *Handbook of Sport and New Media*. Routledge.

Gatto, T. (2020, May 20). *Roger Goodell issues statement on police brutality, racial injustice; Twitter blinks in Colin Kaepernick*. https://www.sportingnews.com/us/nfl/news/nfl-kaepernick-george-floyd-death-protests/6cx19a4hdgkz1kyh1r1gchnb2

Godfrey, P. C. (2009). Corporate social responsibility in sport: An overview and key issues. *Journal of Sport Management, 23*(6), 698–716.

Graczyk, M. & Tucker, E. (2016, January 8). *Former cardinals official pleads guilty to hacking Astros*. AP News. https://apnews.com/article/063d4e8493614626a3943a71fc1db3f4

Habitzreuter, A. M., & Koenigstorfer, J. (2018). The impact of environmental CSR-linked sport sponsorship on attitude toward the sponsor depending on regulatory fit. *Journal of Business Research, 124*, 720–730.

Hampshire, J. (2015). Professional sports teams are risking a cybersecurity own goal. *Infosecurity Magazine*. https://www.infosecurity-magazine.com/opinions/professional-sports-teams/

Herden, C., Alliu, E., Cakici, A., Cormier, T., Deguelle, C., Gambhir, S., Griffiths, C., Gupta, S., Kamani, S., Kiratli, Y., Kispataki, M., Lange, G., de Matos, L., Moreno, L., Betancourt Nunez, L., Pilla, V., Raj, B., Roe, J., Skoda, M., & Edinger-Schons, L. (2021). Corporate digital responsibility. *Nachhaltigkeits Management Forum*.

Independent Power Systems. (2020, August 16). *Power hitters: MLB stadiums and solar*. https://www.solarips.com/about/blog/2020/august/power-hitters-mlb-stadiums-and-solar/

Indiana Pacers. (2019, May 10). *Notice of data incident*. https://www.nba.com/pacers/notice-data-privacy-event

Inoue, Y., & Kent, A. (2014). A conceptual framework for understanding the effects of corporate social marketing on consumer behavior. *Journal of Business Ethics, 121*(4), 621–633.

Inoue, Y., Mahan III, J. E., & Kent, A. (2013). Enhancing the benefits of professional sport philanthropy: The roles of corporate ability and communication strategies. *Sport Management Review, 16*(3), 314–325.

Jaiman, A. (2020). *AI generated synthetic media, aka deepfakes*. Towards Data Science. https://towardsdatascience.com/ai-generated-synthetic-media-aka-deepfakes-7c021dea40e1

Kent, M. L., & Taylor, M. (2016). From homo economicus to homo dialogicus: rethinking social media use in CSR communication. *Public Relations Review, 42*(1), 60–67.

Kim, J. K., & Hull, K. (2017). How fans are engaging with baseball teams demonstrating multiple objectives on Instagram. *Sport, Business and Management*, 7(2), 216–232. 10.1108/SBM-01-2017-0002

Kim, J. K., Overton, H., Hull, K., & Choi, M. (2018). Examining public perceptions of CSR in sport. *Corporate Communications: An International Journal, 23*(4), 629–647.

Kıymalıoğlu, A. (2020). Impact of digital transformations on CSR practices in Turkey: A study of the current environment. In K. Sandhu (Eds.), *Digital transformation and innovative services for business and learning* (pp. 102–118). IGI Global.

Korschun, D., & Du, S. (2013). How virtual CSR dialogs generate value: A framework and propositions. *Journal of Business Research, 66*(9), 1494–1504. 10.1016/j.jbusres.2012.09.011

Liyanaarachchi, G., Deshpande, S., & Weaven, S. (2020). Market-oriented corporate digital responsibility to manage data vulnerability in online banking. *International Journal of Bank Marketing*. Advance online publication.

Lobschat, L., Mueller, B., Eggers, F., Brandimarte, L., Diefenbach, S., Kroschke, M., & Wirtz, J. (2021). Corporate digital responsibility. *Journal of Business Research, 122*, 875–888.

Malmodin, J., Lundén, D., Moberg, Å, Andersson, G., & Nilsson, M. (2014). Life cycle assessment of ICT. *Journal of Industrial Ecology, 18*(6), 829–845.

Martin, K. D., Borah, A., & Palmatier, R. W. (2017). Data privacy: Effects on customer and firm performance. *Journal of Marketing, 81*(1), 36–58.

McKinsey Global Institute. (2021). *The future of work after COVID-19*. https://www.mckinsey.com/featured-insights/future-of-work/the-future-of-work-after-covid-19#

McWilliams, A. & Siegel, D. (2001). Corporate social responsibility: A theory of the firm perspective. *Academy of Management Review, 26*(1),117–127.

Microsoft. (2020, April 16). *NBA announces new multiyear partnership with Microsoft to redefine and personalize the fan experience*. https://news.microsoft.com/2020/04/16/nba-announces-new-multiyear-partnership-with-microsoft-to-redefine-and-personalize-the-fan-experience/

Moreno, L. (2019, August 28). *10 impressive examples of AI in marketing*. https://blog.socialmediastrategiessummit.com/10-examples-of-ai-in-marketing/

Morsing, M., & Schultz, M. (2006). Corporate social responsibility communication: Stakeholder information, response and involvement strategies. *Business Ethics: A European Review*, *15*(4), 323–338.

Nambisan, S., Lyytinen, K., Majchrzak, A., & Song, M. (2017). Digital innovation management: Reinventing innovation management research in a digital world. *MIS Quarterly*, *41*(1), 223–238.

National Basketball Association. (2020, March 19). *Devin Booker tips off Twitch fundraising campaign with $100,000 donation in support of COVID-19 relief efforts*. https://www.nba.com/news/devin-booker-twitch-covid-19-donation

National Football League (2021). *Mission and values*. https://www.nfl.com/news/mission-and-values

National Environmental Education Foundation (2021). *NBA+NEEF*. Retrieved from https://www.neefusa.org/nba#sleepmode

Neureiter, J. (2021, February 10). *How technology could help sports survive the pandemic*. https://www.sportspromedia.com/opinion/sports-technology-covid-social-media-digital-content-revenue-strategy

Newman, M. (2017, July 26). *MLB, YouCaring team up for crowdfunding*. https://www.mlb.com/news/mlb-youcaring-form-crowdfunding-partnership-c244523112

Ogilvy Public Relations Worldwide (2010). Communicating corporate responsibility. available at http://www.ogilvypr.com/en/content/communicating-corporate-responsibility.

Okazaki, S., Plangger, K., West, D., & Menéndez, H. D. (2020). Exploring digital corporate social responsibility communications on Twitter. *Journal of Business Research*, *117*, 675–682.

Orbik, Z. & Zozul'aková, V. (2019). Corporate social and digital responsibility. *Management Systems in Production Engineering*, *2*(27), 79–83.

Phillips Erb, K. (2017). *J.J. Watt Raises Millions For Flood Relief, Making Charitable Crowdfunding History*. Forbes. https://www.forbes.com/sites/kellyphillipserb/2017/08/31/j-j-watt-raises-millions-for-flood-relief-making-charitable-crowdfunding-history/?sh=11a0c9325cbb

Pickett, Z. (2020, September 8). *An interview with WHOOP CEO will Ahmed about its NFL players association deal*. Forbes. https://www.forbes.com/sites/moorinsights/2020/09/08/an-interview-with-whoop-ceo-will-ahmed-about-its-nfl-players-association-deal/?sh=39790bc374eb

Plewa, C., Carrillat, F. A., Mazodier, M., & Quester, P. G. (2016). Which sport sponsorships most impact sponsor CSR image? *European Journal of Marketing*, *50*(5/6), 796–815.

Podder, A. (2017, May 23). *"Pledge it" teams with 150+ professional athletes on unique crowdfunding charitable campaigns; on record pace with 15 MLB campaigns*. https://goodcrowd.info/pledge-teams-150-professional-athletes-unique-crowdfunding-charitable-campaigns-record-pace-15-mlb-campaigns/

Richter, A., & Riemer, K. (2013). Malleable end-user software. *Business & Information Systems Engineering*, *5*(3), 195–197.

Rynarzewska, A. I. (2018). Virtual reality: a new channel in sport consumption. *Journal of Research in Interactive Marketing*, *12*(4), 472–488. 10.1108/JRIM-02-2018-0028

Schad, T. (2020, Jun 1). *Kenny Stills, Eric Reid criticize NFL Commissioner Roger Goodell's statement on George Floyd's death*. USA Today. https://www.usatoday.com/story/sports/nfl/2020/06/01/kenny-stills-eric-reid-criticize-roger-goodells-statement/5306788002/

Schultz, M. D., & Seele, P. (2020). Conceptualizing data-deliberation: The starry sky beetle, environmental system risk, and Habermasian CSR in the digital age. *Business Ethics: A European Review*, *29*(2), 303–313.

Smith, A. C., & Westerbeek, H. M. (2007). Sport as a vehicle for deploying corporate social responsibility. *Journal of corporate citizenship*, *25*(1), 43–54.

Spanos, L. (2018). Complementarity and interconnection between CSR and crowdfunding: A case study in Greece. In G. Grigore, A. Stancu, & D. McQueen (Eds.), *Corporate responsibility and digital communities* (pp. 29–49). Palgrave Macmillan: Cham.

Sparvero, E., & Kent, A. (2014). Sport team nonprofit organizations. *Journal of Applied Sport Management*, *6*(4), 98–116.

Sreejesh S., Sarkar, J. G., & Sarkar, A. (2020). CSR through social media: Examining the intervening factors. *Marketing Intelligence & Planning*, *38*(1), 103–120.

Tench, R. & Jones, B. (2015). Social media: The wild west of CSR communications. *Social Responsibility Journal*, *11*(2), 1747–1117. DOI: 10.1108/SRJ-12-2012-0157

Thomas, I. (2020, April 23). *NFL leans on influencer network to boost fundraising effort*. https://frontofficesports.com/nfl-draft-influencer-network/

Torre, P. & Haberstoh, T. (2014, October 2). *New biometric tests invade the NBA*. ESPN. https://www.espn.com/nba/story/_/id/11629773/new-nba-biometric-testing-less-michael-lewis-more-george-orwell

United Nations Conference on Trade and Development. (2019). *Digital development: Opportunities and challenges*. https://unctad.org/system/files/official-document/tdb66_d5_en.pdf

Vial, G. (2019). Understanding digital transformation: A review and a research agenda. *The Journal of Strategic Information Systems, 28*(2), 118–144.

Wade, M. (2020, April 28). *Corporate responsibility in the digital era*. https://sloanreview.mit.edu/article/corporate-responsibility-in-the-digital-era/

Walker, M., & Kent, A. (2009). Do fans care? Assessing the influence of corporate social responsibility on consumer attitudes in the sport industry. *Journal of Sport Management, 23*(6), 743–769.

Walker, M., & Kent, A. (2013). The roles of credibility and social consciousness in the corporate philanthropy-consumer behavior relationship. *Journal of Business Ethics, 116*(2), 341–353.

Walzel, S., Robertson, J., & Anagnostopoulos, C. (2018). CSR in professional team sports organizations: An integrative review. *Journal of Sport Management, 32*(6), 511–530.

Wang, R. & Huang, Y. (2018). Communicating CSR on social media. *Corporate Communications: An International Journal*, 23(3), 326–341.

Williams, B. (2020). *Wizards extend Japanese outreach by partnering with CGI influencer*. Sport Business. https://www.sportbusiness.com/news/wizards-extend-japanese-outreach-by-partnering-with-cgi-influencer/?logged_in=1

Wirtz, J., Patterson, P. G., Kunz, W. H., Gruber, T., Lu, V. N., Paluch, S., & Martins, A. (2018). Brave new world: Service robots in the frontline. *Journal of Service Management, 29*(5), 1757–5818.

Yang, D., & Babiak, K. (2021). How league and community affect corporate philanthropy in professional sport: A multiple field embeddedness perspective. *Journal of Sport Management*. Advance online publication. 10.1123/jsm.2020-0084.

Yellen, E. (2017, February 3). *Crowdfunding: A perfect partner for pro sports teams to engage fans while raising money*. https://pages.fanangel.com/blog?author=57b8840fff7c50e4a7f0022b

Yu, C. L. (2020). The role of CSR in sport consumption decision-making. *Marketing Intelligence & Planning, 39*(1), 17–32.

Zucman, G. (2019). Global wealth inequality. *Annual Review of Economics*, 11, 109–138.

9

Digital Transformation in Sport Sponsorship

T. Bettina Cornwell

Introduction

Any given sport property may be, at the same time, a laggard and a leader in digital technology transformation. They may be struggling with a legacy customer management system where they cannot clean up duplicate and triplicate contacts, while at the same time launching an augmented reality app for fans and sponsors. The attraction, even the pressure, to offer a fun, minimum viable app product (e.g., US$10,000) for a single sponsor can result in many one-off projects. To develop something like the IKEA PLACE app that allows customers to view virtual furniture in their home takes technological savvy and development and US$60,000 (Kovach n.d.). At the same time, brands sponsoring sport may vary in their digital sophistication and also their strategic willingness to outsource any digital marketing. Thus, partnerships may exhibit a wide range of digital skills on either side of the contract.

There are many descriptions of the digital transformation of business. Following is one from Salesforce.com (n.d.): "Digital transformation is the process of using digital technologies to create new—or modify existing—business processes, culture, and customer experiences to meet changing business and market requirements." The digital transformation of sport sponsorship is no less far-reaching, but we tend to focus overly on the fan-facing aspects (Cornwell & Kwon, 2020). With this in mind, there is a need for a process model that encompasses sport, sponsors, media, and fans/consumers. Therefore, the Sport Sponsorship Digital Framework is introduced and then followed by a discussion of particular types of digital marketing employed or potentially employed in sponsorship. The final sections offer conclusions about the challenges to digital sponsorship and future directions in research.

Sport Sponsorship Digital Framework

Figure 9.1 presents a Sport Sponsorship Digital Framework. The goal of the framework is to map process and structure in a rudimentary but contextually specific way. The centerpiece is the digital sponsorship process which captures the essence of digital sponsorship activities. This process model is responsive to the business models (Bonakdar et al., 2013), and ultimately strategies, of both the sport property and the sponsor. All of these activities reside within a

DOI: 10.4324/9781003088899-11

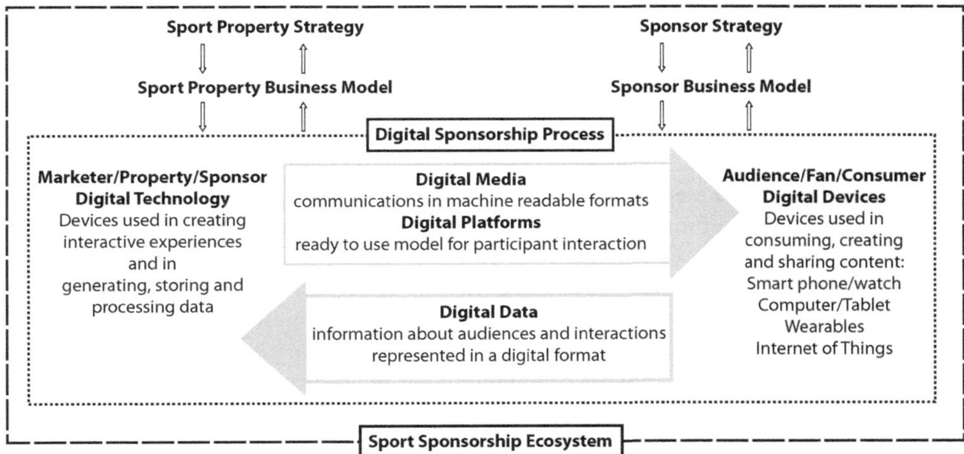

Figure 9.1 Sport Sponsorship Digital Framework

bounded sport sponsorship ecosystem. The following sections detail the framework, and this begins with the components of the digital sponsorship process. Importantly, this sport sponsorship framework refers to business models but is nonetheless relevant to nonprofits because, even without profits, they have revenues and must manage a viable business model.

Digital Sponsorship Process

In the center of Figure 9.1 is the digital sponsorship process. Here, the two-way flow of information between the Marketer/Property/Sponsor and the Audience/Fan/Consumer is detailed. Each aspect of the digital sponsorship process is described in the following sections.

Marketer/Property/Sponsor Digital Technology

Firstly, it is important to note that the creation of digital sponsorship leverage and activation is undertaken by sport properties and sponsors but is often under the purview of some marketing intermediary (Cornwell, 2020). Sport marketing agencies (e.g., GMR Marketing, IMG), integrated marketing communications firms, and talent management groups (e.g., Wasserman Media Group) utilize digital technologies to reach audiences on behalf of sponsors and properties. Technological capabilities that form the potential to create interactive experiences for consumers are wide-ranging (Naraine & Karg, 2018).

The basic devices like a powerful computer with a high-resolution monitor, good lighting, and a quality camera and microphone are only as essential as the many software tools (e.g., Adobe Spark, Canva, iMovie, Photoshop, Pixlr, and Giphy) that support digital creativity. Advancing to a digital media lab adds hardware and software and going out of the lab might add drones or a GoPro digital action camera, but with equipment so rapidly changing, no list would be meaningful for long.

In terms of management of the returning digital data, and in terms of integrating marketing data with other organizational data, again, the software is as important as the hardware. Comprehensive platforms from major players such as SAP Data Management and the Oracle Suite may address needs broadly. Those managing digital content related to sponsorship might focus on tools such as Tableau that are more accessible for non-technical users.

Digital Media

Essentially digital media are images, video, and audio that are encoded in a machine-readable format. They are the paid, earned, owned communications channels (Fulgoni, 2015) that marketers, properties, and sponsors think of when planning digital sponsorships. Just a short list of digital media would include blogs, digital radio, publications, television, email, social media and networks, podcasts, text messages, and webcasts. Strategic choices about the use of digital media include considerations of search optimization, permanence, access, and of course, audiences.

What is the nature of communications in digital media? In terms of marketer-generated content, posts from brands have been categorized as informative (factual knowledge about a brand, products, or related subjects), entertaining (arousing and positive in tone), or persuasive (functioning as sales promotion) (Weiger et al., 2019). In terms of a sport brand communicating about themselves or a sponsor brand communicatin4g about themselves, these three categories seem adequate; however, when considering sponsorship, there may need to be an additional category. For example, the National Women's Hockey League (NWHL) posted a photo of the sponsor's Discover card in their arena and in the ice. The March 28, 2021 post read:

> As we reflect on this weekend, we want to extend a heartfelt thank you to @Discover. The moment we suspended the season, they were committed to helping us provide the platform our athletes deserve. Support from sponsors like @Discover is the key to growth of women's pro sports.

This communication on Twitter could be categorized as informative (telling the team's sponsor is Discover) or promotional (the logo of the brand is featured) or possibly even entertaining (there is positive emotion in the thank you). The communication is, however, more representative of the effort to pair or to communicate the relationship. For the moment, this might be called a "bridging" communication, one that connects the sport property and the sponsor. Sponsorship is replete with communications of this type because bridging communications build a mental association between the brand and the sport and both partners benefit from strong associations.

Digital Platforms

A digital platform is a business model or housing that allows participants to interact and exchange. The success of a digital platform is in large part determined by the size and activity of the community. Social media platforms like TikTok or Instagram spring to mind, but there are other platforms important to digital sponsorship. Just a few examples include media sharing platforms such as YouTube, live streaming platforms such as Twitch, and service platforms such as Ticketmaster. All of these platforms produce and support the capture of digital data and may be a channel for sponsor-related information. Importantly, digital platforms play a role in developing community, and feeling a sense of community can support sport and event engagement and patronage (Cornwell et al., 2018, Jahn et al., 2018).

Audience/Fan/Consumer Digital Devices

In short, digital devices are computers or equipment that contains a computer or a pre-programmed micro-controller (as found in an office printer, a car engine, or a drone). The desktop, laptop, tablet, and smartphone are ubiquitous digital devices. Smartwatches and a range of wearable technologies are also examples of digital devices. It is on these devices that audience members, fans and consumers either ignore or engage with communications (Ha et al., 2017). Consumer engagement with content can be categorized as productive (e.g., active sharing with others) or consumptive (e.g., passive decisions to follow) (Weiger et al., 2019). Importantly, productive and consumptive engagement, as well as a seemingly endless host of other data are generated when individuals use their digital devices.

Creative activations that reach digital devices (as they should be experienced without degradation from device or software limitations) hold the potential to allow sponsors to build a link from the sport event to the fan. For example, in the 2018 PyeongChang Winter Olympic Games, Intel, a US-based computer chip maker, developed a drone light show that mesmerized attendees and viewers at home. It resulted in 12 billion media impressions in 12 hours (Huggity, 2018). While the company's microprocessors may have been working behind the scenes to bring a sky lit with the Olympic rings, it was the emotion of the visual that remade the company's image at the moment.

Digital Data

Technically, digital data are digital representations of analog data found in the physical world. Digital data arise in myriad ways, and it is the bringing together of varied data sources that leads to the big data rubric. Bridgewater (2018), in enumerating various types of data, offers the following quote:

> "While definitions of 'big data' may differ slightly, at the root of each are very large, diverse data sets that include structured, semi-structured and unstructured data, from different sources and in different volumes, from terabytes to zettabytes. It's about data sets so large and diverse that it's difficult, if not impossible, for traditional relational databases to capture, manage, and process them with low-latency," said Rob Thomas, general manager for IBM Analytics.

In measurement and evaluation, sponsorship-linked marketing is typically interested in data compiled from multiple sources (Cornwell & Kwon, 2020). For example, combining the information about fan status from customer relationship management data (local fan versus out-of-market fan) and response to past team social media posts tagging sponsors, to image response to a digital coupon that could only be redeemed at local restaurants.

Business Models and Strategies

Whatever is agreed-upon as the digital strategy in sponsorship should meld with the sport property business model, the sponsor business model, and their respective strategies. Sport property business models vary but revenue streams are rather similar: media rights, partnerships, ticket sales, merchandising, and to some extent, activities such as talent trading for large enterprises and donations for small organizations. Not all sport organizations will utilize all resource forms.

According to Matos (2020), three basic sport property models are the Relational model (utilized by grassroots sports and potentially supported through donation), the Reputational model (typical with mega-events and reliant on media rights), and the Fan Relationship Management model (common with teams reliant on media and non-media revenues). Team-based models can be further detailed as, for example, the rent-seeking model characterize by elite ownership structures, stock market models where shares are publicly traded, and public-private partnerships (Pittz et al., 2020). Different business models suggest different digital strategies in sponsorship. For example, community-based sport may prefer a digital focus on online social networking with local personalities whereas reputational business models may employ celebrity athletes in online sponsorship-linked advertising (Kelly et al., 2012).

Sponsor business models vary more widely than sport business models due to their natural business diversity. Perhaps the best know business model is the franchise model that is popular with quick-service restaurants. Another popular business model is the subscription model as utilized by Netflix and Amazon Prime. There are dozens more such as the e-commerce model, brokerage business models such as those found in real estate, or consulting business models such as Deloitte auditing and advisory services. As with sport property business models, sponsor strategies and the type of digital assets employed to accomplish them will depend on the nature of their business model. A consulting business model may value in-person events over digital assets whereas an e-commerce model may only value digital assets with live links to electronic storefronts.

The reason that business models are important in the discussion of digital sponsorship, in particular, is that they have direct implications for the digital sponsorship process possible, and the technology architecture, integration, and quality of systems needed to enact strategies. Consider a sports betting sponsor interested in team sports. If the team sport has live streaming in the media distribution strategy, how will this influence in-game betting? High latency in streaming, or lag, results in delay. Bad enough that friends on social media might know the outcome before you, even worse if you placed a bet after the outcome was known.

Sport Sponsorship Ecosystem

Despite the fact that digital communications can be worldwide in many instances, digital leveraging and activation are often bounded in systematic and idiosyncratic ways. As Cornwell and Kwon (2020) discuss, there are sponsorship ecosystems that, while permeable, can clearly be seen as geographically oriented. For example, truly grassroots sports will perhaps stream on an available platform but in terms of sport audience and sponsorship, remain local.

Consumers/Fans – The Ways They Interact Digitally

The myriad of ways in which digital sport sponsorship might unfold is, at the same time, inspiring and numbing. With the technology potential, there is something like the "feature fatigue" that consumers have experienced in the last decade where there is just too much of a good thing in technology-based products (Thompson et al., 2005). On the other hand, as sport sponsorship moves from "advertising-like" to sponsorship-linked marketing as authentic engagement (Cornwell, 2019), digital has a front-row seat. Importantly, behind the technology, there needs to be a strategy for sponsors so that fun tactics do not hijack the communication potential. Following are some of the main areas in digital sport sponsorship. There is overlap in these groupings where technologies have merged.

Online Following

Perhaps the most pervasive channel for digital sponsorship engagement is the online following of a sport, a league, a team, or a player. As an example, researchers studying the points of contact for professional mixed martial arts (MMA) league Ultimate Fighting Championship (UFC) found that individuals contacted through MMA news websites typically spent 15 hours per week following UFC (Reams et al., 2015). Importantly, this was in addition to attending fights.

Naturally, online following in sport presents an opportunity for digital sponsorship engagement. A sponsor may choose to advertise to fans and potential consumers in one-way passive communication, but the opportunity lies in engaging with content. Research considering if event website visitors clicking through and reaching a sponsor's "activational" (interaction encouraging) landing page, versus a non-activational page, found the activational landing resulted in more positive sponsor attitudes (Weeks et al., 2008). Understandably to move from an area of personal interest to an online storefront could be jolting and perceived as commercially oriented.

Across nine contexts including sport, Tonietto and Barasch (2020) found that individuals increase feelings of enjoyment when they are generating content during ongoing experiences. Fans, at Super Bowl football, felt more immersed and their perception of time accelerated when they were also creating and sharing content (i.e., time flies when you are having fun). Focused examples, such as survey work on the pro-Kabaddi league in India found social media communications boosted fans' online community engagement, game attendance, and sponsor product purchase intention (Trivedi et al., 2020).

In sum, the online following tends to be a measure of engagement potential for sport properties and athletes as influencers (Cornwell & Katz, 2021). Even if a large following is difficult to manage and segment (Naraine, 2019), having followers is viewed as a communication strength. That potential is highly correlated with sponsorship investment. For example, Barcelona and Real Madrid Football Clubs have the highest number of followers (Statistica, 2021) and the highest revenues (Deloitte, 2021).

Digital Assets

Digital assets, old and new, are likely stored by the sport property and the sponsor in one of the dozens of digital asset management software systems on the market. These digital assets may be recovered from the original print, analog video, or audio, and they may be purposefully made for marketing or sponsorship. They may be held as a historical file of the sport team or the sponsoring company but, importantly, they can be repurposed by the rights holder in new ways. Take, for example, the Baltimore Ravens' #ThrowbackThursday campaign on Instagram that featured players pictured from past events with the Miller Lite tag and logo.

Creating new digital assets made for sharing is another way to support fan and consumer engagement with a sponsor. For example, the Portland Thorns Football Club develops GIFs for use on Twitter that feature players and, often, sponsors. One Thorns GIF featured player, Meghan Klingenberg, and sponsor, Jersey Mike's Subs. A series of GIFs with different athletes expressing different emotions and moments provides a catalog for fans to utilize.

The topic of digital assets cannot be complete without a discussion of non-fungible tokens (NFTs) back by cryptocurrencies and the tokens related to digital assets verify the authenticity of the asset. NBA top shots offer collectible moments in basketball and have since October 2020 made over $400 million in sales. After name, image, and likeness legislation began to expand across the United States allowing colligate athletes to benefit financially from sponsorship, NFT deals were early corporate investments. For example, University of Oregon defensive end, Kayvon Thibodeaux struck a NIL deal for non-fungible tokes with Nike founder Phil Knight and designer Tinker Hatfield (Schlabach, 2021).

Virtual Reality

One definition of virtual reality is an environment created by a computer or other media in which the user feels present (Biocca, 1992). In turn, presence refers to the subjective feeling of existence in an experienced environment in the natural, social, or virtual worlds (Heeter, 1992). Research on sport consumption suggests that virtual reality is positively perceived particularly by those positively disposed to the technology and to what improvements it might bring (Rynarzewska, 2018).

Virtual reality has been a part of sport sponsorship for many years now. Over time, the executions have evolved and expanded. In 2016, digital potential allowed MasterCard to offer a virtual tour of the iconic 17th hole at the Sawgrass Stadium course, and the San Francisco 49ers to offer players in action as if one were a quarterback in a game (IEG Sponsorship Report, 2016). More recently, Adidas used mixed reality (a combination of virtual and augmented reality) in their "Climb a Mountain with Adidas" campaign to offer a "very solid mountain climbing experience for the user" (Tandem, 2019).

Virtual and augmented reality, in a gamification context, has been identified as a possible income stream for sports and a new path for sponsor interaction. For example, researchers have argued that the steep financial requirements of Formula 1 racing might be offset by a virtual reality gaming approach where fans globally might engage with digital cars owned and driven by anyone at any time (Markopoulos et al., 2019). The game would then have a portfolio of virtual sponsors.

Augmented Reality

According to Allan Cook, head of Deloitte's digital reality business, "The next generation of AR can bring the yellow first-down line in football, live stats, and player identification to the stadium" (Santana, 2019). We know that men and women experience presence in augmented reality differently, with men orienting to interaction and women orienting to watching the environment (Nicovich et al. 2005). There is still a great deal to be learned about optimal augmented reality experience for varied audiences. Goebert (2020) argues that the way we begin to think of AR is as a group of technologies that should complement the sport product, focus on visual appeal, and strive for immersion. All of these recommendations apply to sponsorship activation as well.

Augmented reality clearly can make sports clips, highlights, and live events more interesting and informative. For example, adding identifiers and statistics or special effects is commonplace in short-form content. Incremental monetization found through selling sponsorship in sport holds potential but could be challenged by coordinating the rights held by broadcasters, teams, and leagues. Yet another hurdle is to make the experience positive for the viewer and not a distraction in the game. Research has shown that color and animation can impact the sport viewer's attention (Breuer & Rumpf, 2015).

Fantasy Sports

Early in the expansion of fantasy sports, it was identified that fantasy sports players also increased their viewership of televised games (Nesbit & King, 2010). As well, the attachment formed with the sport fantasy experience holds the potential to influence sponsorship response (Reams et al., 2015). For sponsors, this was a sort of "double-dip" in terms of potential exposure. It is important, however, to distinguish between season-long fantasy sports and daily fantasy sports. The former has been a part of the sports landscape for several decades, whereas the latter is a more recent development. Daily fantasy sports are more akin to gambling and have been for this reason, banned in some states (Dwyer et al., 2019). Indeed, research on problem gambling behaviors associated with this form of fantasy sport finds it is associated with behaviors seen in other forms of gambling (Dwyer et al., 2018).

Researchers in public policy cautioned that fantasy sport with its combination of a resemblance to gambling and exemption from regulation creates concern (Houghton et al., 2019). This observation may have been prescient in that the fantasy sport conditioned the embrace of subsequent legalization of gambling in the United States (Purdum, 2018). Goldsmith and Walker (2015) found when studying NASCAR auto racing, that fantasy sport was a way to convert self-identified sport non-fans into involved fans. It seems that it may also convert fantasy sports players into sports bettors.

Video Games

Brands placed in computer games get the most attention and recall when they are high in special prominence or when they are related to the action of the game (Schneider & Cornwell, 2005). Other work has found only a limited effect of billboards within the gaming environment on product purchase intentions (Chaney et al., 2004). Different findings are perhaps understood by the collateral activations now commonplace in social media.

In 2018, Burger King, the quick-service restaurant, decided to sponsor Stevenage FC, a team at the bottom of England's fourth football division. The sponsorship of the little-known team "succeeded beyond all expectations" (Thomas, 2020). This is because Burger King sponsored the team knowing that they were included in the popular EA Sports FIFA video game. As jersey sponsors of the real team, they would be included in the game. With this component of the strategy in place, they created the Stevenage Challenge that asked gamers to play with the team, pick popular players, and share their experiences on social media. The result was 25,000 goals posted on social media, and Stevenage jerseys selling out for the first time in the history of the team. They subsequently sponsored the Stevenage FC Women's team on the same terms as the men's team and they wear "Burger Queen" on their jersey.

Sports Betting

Globally, sports betting has been an aspect of digital sponsor engagement for decades. Taking a sociology view of the last few decades, Lopez-Gonzalez and Griffiths (2018a) view digital betting as a consumer product that converges with (1) digital integration of data, social gaming, eSports, and immersive reality; (2) sporting integration of sport journalism, influencers, sponsorship, endorsement, virtual and fantasy sports; and (3) gambling integration of in-venue and in-stadium wagering, poker, and transactions akin to trading exchanges. Lopez-Gonzalez and Griffiths conclude that the convergence related to sports betting extend beyond it by substituting sport events for a simulacrum that is beneficial to gaming industries but potentially detrimental to some in society.

Gambling, betting and gaming industries held 50% of shirt sponsorships in the English Premier League in 2020, though that number has dropped to 40% in 2021 (Score & Change, 2020). Even without a shirt sponsor, all league teams have some level of partnership with gaming companies. In fact, a small qualitative study of 71 families in the UK found that nearly half of young people (aged 8–16), and two-thirds of adults, were able to name at least one gambling brand (Djohari et al., 2019). Researchers have studied the "gamblification" of English football and found newer gambling forms (mostly digital) are a public health issue affecting vulnerable groups such as minorities and problem gamblers (Lopez-Gonzalez & Griffiths, 2018b).

In 2018, the US Supreme Court struck down the Professional and Amateur Sports Protection Act that had been in place since 1992. This decision allowed states to establish their own regulated sports betting. Expansion of sports betting followed quickly. The rule change brought about the transformation of firms like DraftKings and Fanduel that had focused on digital sports entertainment and fantasy sports to legalized betting. The shift also brought about the transformation of gambling casino powerhouses such as MGM Resorts and Caesars Entertainment to offer BetMGM and Caesars Sportbook respectively. As well, the US decision attracted the attention of international players such as Australian PointsBet.

Novel betting products such as "custom sports bets" that allow gamblers to create their own unique bets can arguably increase fan engagement. Research on custom sports bets suggests however that they are used more frequently by problem gamblers (Newall et al., 2020). This research further identified that the illusion of control was significantly positively correlated with using a custom sports betting product.

Clearly, sports betting has many sides. Advantages for the gambling industries stem from expanded sport engagement. Leagues and teams (but less so individual athletes) find in sports betting an outsized revenue stream, outsized in the sense that betting sponsors pay well. A body of research shows that individual fans and consumers, especially problem gamers, suffer from the everywhere, all-the-time nature of online betting (for a review see Winters & Derevensky, 2019). The intersection of betting, sports, and sponsorship is complex, and not straightforwardly altered by legislative changes. As discussed by Cornwell and Kwon (2000), and investigated by Yang and Goldfarb (2015), changing the sponsorship landscape away from gambling or alcohol sponsor revenues through legislation or bans would negatively impact lower-level teams that would have their current sponsors poached by higher-level teams.

In addition to being an aspect of digital engagement in and of itself, sports gambling operators and their third-party promotional affiliates also post content to attract customers to betting. Researchers (i.e., Houghton et al., 2019) studied British gambling operators and found their content on the platform Twitter to be of several types: direct advertising, betting assistance, sports content, customer engagement, humor, update of current bet status, promotional content, and safer gambling. Unfortunately, there were very few posts regarding safe gambling. While engagement via betting was not the goal of recent research from Germany, evidence suggests that sponsors may benefit from understanding betting odds during the consumer experience as an indicator of attention and emotion (Breuer et al., 2021). These researchers predict sponsors will be able to manage message placement by understanding moment-by-moment betting odds as a proxy of outcome uncertainty.

Conclusions about the Current Context Digital Transition for Sport

In discussing the digital transformation of sport, Lopez-Gonzalez et al. (2017) described it as follows:

> From the death of "appointment" television to the explosion of modularised, mobile content, the future of sport broadcasting is uniquely positioned between the analogue paradigm of long-standing television broadcast networks and the digital prototype of agile new entrants. (p. 176–177)

These authors follow to describe an inevitable digital disruption in sport. This disruption is here with major players such as Amazon Prime Video and Disney/ESPN announcing new broadcasting with the NFL and NHL respectively.

It is expected that single professional broadcasts will give way to distributed and customized models that would allow for new types of user-generated content (Akhavan, 2021). This opens the door for new forms of sponsor interaction and provides an expanded role for Influencer marketing as sport content live-streamed may be accompanied by steamed live commentary. The digital transformation of sport means an even more profound digital transformation of sponsorship-linked and influencer marketing.

Esports, "Born Digital"

Esports is, at the same time, a sport to be sponsored and a digital activation channel. All evidence finds that esports is one component of brands seeking to rethink their sponsorship portfolio (Allenstein et al., 2020). The increasing comfort of nonendemic brands in entering esports partnerships is due to the attractive youth demographic as well as the born-digital nature of esports. Currently, esports is growing dramatically, the question is what all will they replace?

The Skills Gap

At this point in the digital transformation of sport management, it would be remiss not to identify talent as a major obstacle to the process. An international study conducted with SAP (a multinational software corporation) user groups found a disturbing skills gap in organizations engaged in a digital transformation (Hoberg et al., 2017). Only 15% of respondents believed they had "enough personnel with the skills necessary for the digital transformation of our company" (p. 6). This is a challenge that is also faced by sport organization and some sponsoring companies, especially at the sponsorship interface. Sport organizations may be particularly challenged when skilled individuals are in demand because salaries for those individuals are elevated.

McKinsey & Company (2018), a global consultancy company, surveyed managers on successful digital transformations and they found five key factors:

1 Having digitally savvy leaders – their research found that 70% of organizations had changes to their leadership teams to guide the digital transformation.
2 Building talent and skills – this may require training, hiring, and redefining roles.
3 Empower employees to embrace the changes sought – this may mean establishing new ways of working and allowing employees to contribute ideas about where digitization will support organizational goals.
4 Make use of digital tools the new organizational norm – by providing information and implementing digital self-service and modifying procedures to include new technologies.
5 Communicate regularly via traditional and digital methods – and begin with a change story that helps individuals see where the organization is headed.

Interestingly, but perhaps not surprising, digital transformation is easier for small organizations than for large, with organizations with under 100 employees nearly three times more successful than those over 50,000 (McKinsey & Company, 2018). It is difficult to imagine if this rule of thumb would hold in sport management since the competition for talent may favor larger organizations.

Future Directions

Marketing managers have been oriented for decades to understanding how different marketing mix models (product, price, place, promotion) decisions and business drivers influence financial outcomes for their brands. Digital marketing ushered in the possibility of measurement models that are oriented to multi-touch attributions that follow a consumer's journey. In digital advertising, these models are valued for allowing the brand manager to attribute conversion credit to the various media channels that have contributed to purchase conversion (Nisar & Yeung, 2018).

Many multi-touch models capture online impressions or exposure leading to purchase; or recency or frequency of online behavior leading to a conversion metric but lack an understanding of offline behavior. Sponsorship-linked marketing matches well to models that combine offline and online touchpoints to understand behavior, especially when focused and time-bound activations surround an event or activity.

Devices Used

Returning to the Sport Sponsorship Digital Framework, new digital devices are coming online (and becoming obsolete) at an ever-increasing pace. Those technologies that more seamlessly support the digital sponsorship process through format and platforms to reach audiences, will have the most impact on marketers and the most staying power. For example, brands utilizing GoPro video in extended reality sponsorship activations were found to offer tangible benefits to consumers (Burton & Schlieman, 2021), thus moving from marketer to audience and creating value in the process. What aspects of both creation and consumption smooth the digital sponsorship process?

Data Visualization

No doubt many managers feel the glut of data in their industry is overwhelming and sport marketers surely deserve a seat at that table. When one considers the history of data management in sport and the nexus of demands for insights it is only logical to seek to streamline communications. Data visualization is "a set of methods for graphically displaying information in a way that is understandable and straightforward, ideally while also incorporating aesthetic considerations to drive engagement and interest to in turn capture the attention of the intended audience" (Sinar, 2015, p. 161). Data visualization summarizes the glut of data to make insights possible. In Figure 9.1, digital communications are commonly data visualizations and are often supported by digital platforms and software utilized by properties and sponsors.

Data visualization is becoming a content product for sports and their sponsors as individuals, teams, leagues, and events produce "infographics" for dissemination. Students are learning how to use data analytics to create digital strategies that drive engagement and social media views (e.g., Pierce & Sherman, 2020). The consumerism side of data analytics and visualization is well underway, however, there is still more to learn about this type of digital communication. From research on the decision to critically evaluate pro-environmental messages, we have learned that infographics, as compared with text or illustrations, are more engaging (Lazard & Atkinson, 2015). What type of infographic in sport marketing and sponsorship produces engagement?

Data visualization is the connective tissue between the business models and business strategies in Figure 9.1. Data visualization also has a back story in executive decision-making that is not widely discussed. Data visualization is paramount in manufacturing (e.g., Sackett & Williams, 2003), accounting services (Dilla et al., 2010), and healthcare (Stadler, 2016). Data visualization (or the potentially interactive data visualization dashboard) as decision support has not really been examined in sport marketing and sponsorship, although currently employed. In the main, data visualization in decision-making is heralded as positive in its ability to make vast quantities of data digestible by non-specialists. It is worth asking, how do data visualization decisions such as parameters included, ranges of those parameters, and the nature of their representation influence decision making?

The Nature of New Research

A review of social media in marketing covering 144 research articles found that most research has been conducted with university students and from a limited number of countries. (Alawan et al., 2017). The actual audiences, fans, and consumers in Figure 9.1 are often not the study participants in research that informs practice. Further, these researchers specifically called for research in different contexts such as tourism, sport, and government. Each of these areas has obvious connections to sport marketing and sponsorship, such as in sport tourism, or programs, such as the United Nations Sport for Development and Peace division.

Digital marketing has shortened the time horizon in research in part because adjustments to communications can be made in near real-time. Traditional advertising historically took months to prepare, weeks in media planning, and weeks if not months in the distribution before being assessed. Timeframes were quarterly at best and annually for most. Consider this discussion of the Major League Soccer team, Los Angeles Football Club, and their new research partner, Zoomph (Bassam, 2020):

> "The data that we are provided now from Zoomph allows us to have better clarity on why things work or don't work," he explains. "For example, being able to look at and categorize every single post and piece of content that we create into categories of different types of content, or analyze it photo versus video, or looking at it by subject matter, or look at it sponsored/non-sponsored, or look at it by different timing related to matchdays. All those different things combined - you're smarter."

The data provided by Zoomph analytics allows LAFC to service the 50 sponsor contracts of the team. We have very little research on servicing sport sponsors (for an exception see O'Reilly & Huybers, 2015). While practice is focused on digital sponsorship servicing, academic research has lagged, perhaps because this partner-based servicing is not the norm in marketing. In sum, the sport sponsorship ecosystem depicted in Figure 9.1 is fast-paced and evolutionary but at the same time lacks fundamentals in areas such as sponsorship service.

Artificial Intelligence

Sport is already utilizing artificial intelligence and machine learning techniques in areas such as match outcome prediction, tactical decision making, player investments, fantasy sports, and injury prediction (Beal et al., 2019). When looking at products like "Trading Players" where the concept of a fantasy sports league is combined with the concept of a stock market, the potential for artificial intelligence is already obvious. When buying and selling shares of athletes, one would want to know as much as possible about the investment. Conceptual understanding of these evolving product offerings is important from both a brand and a policy perspective.

There are other, behind-the-scenes aspects of AI that are part of the future of sport management and sponsorship. For example, Naraine and Wanless (2020) find that sports management could increase their use of natural language processing to support listening to the public narrative, automating the sales process, customizing content, and the development of self-operating services (such as in responding to issues in social media). These computer-trained algorithms could be useful to sponsors directly in use or indirectly through the sport organization and the consumer understanding they can afford. The future of digital sport sponsorship will address the massive amounts of digital data returning from individuals, as shown in Figure 9.1, in part through AI.

The Digital Divide

The topic of the digital divide was ushered in with the widespread adoption of computers. The focus is on those having or not having access to digital devices and the internet. The conversation, now more nuanced, focuses on types of access, namely motivation, physical, skills, and usage (Van Dijk, 2006). A digital divide persists (see Campbell & Kwak, 2012) and has been documented in sport (e.g., Kang, 2017) in terms of mobile competence that is associated with attitudinal loyalty and sport fandom.

New topics in the digital divide continue to arise. For example, the understanding of algorithms, recommendation agents based on one's interaction history, is an evolving concern in digital communications. Research conducted in Norway found demographic differences in algorithm awareness with six groups of users identified: the unaware, the uncertain, the affirmative, the neutral, the skeptic, and the critical (Gran et al., 2020).

As new technologies are utilized in sport sponsorship leveraging and activation, more digital differences will be discovered. Researchers and practitioners interested in inclusivity might work to identify any differences in advance of social concern, especially when artificial intelligence is being used to develop algorithms. Both the sport property and the sponsor strategies and business models featured in Figure 9.1 must be vigilant in developing a digital sponsorship process that is as inclusive as possible.

References

Akhavan, A. (2021). The future of watching sports. *The National Law Review*, *11*(87), March 26, 2021. https://www.natlawreview.com/article/future-watching-sports

Allenstein, U., Gediehn, O., Lehmann, S., & Singer, D. (2020). *Esports and the next frontier of brand sponsorship*. https://www.mckinsey.com/business-functions/marketing-and-sales/our-insights/e-sports-and-the-next-frontier-of-brand-sponsorships

Alalwan, A. A., Rana, N. P., Dwivedi, Y. K., & Algharabat, R. (2017). Social media in marketing: A review and analysis of the existing literature. *Telematics and Informatics*, *34*, 1177–1190. 10.1016/j.tele.2017.05.008

Bassam, T. (2020, September 15). *How LAFC's pursuit of better data helped create a major league soccer powerhouse*. SportsPro. https://www.sportspromedia.com/analysis/lafc-zoomph-mls-data-social-media-marketing-strategy

Beal, R., Norman, T. J., & Ramchurn, S. D. (2019). Artificial intelligence for team sports: a survey. *The Knowledge Engineering Review*, *34*(28), 1–37. 10.1017/S0269888919000225

Biocca, F. (1992). Communication within virtual reality: Creating a space for research. *Journal of Communication*, *42*, 5–22. 10.1111/j.1460-2466.1992.tb00810.x

Breuer, C., Boronczyk, F., & Rumpf, C. (2021). Message personalization and real-time adaptation as next innovations in sport sponsorship management? How run-of-play and team affiliation affect viewer response. *Journal of Business Research*, *133*, 309–316. 10.1016/j.jbusres.2021.05.003

Burton, N., & Schlieman, T. (2021). User response to extended reality sponsorship activations on social media: Exploring impressions of GoPro's use of 360° video in marketing. *Journal of Interactive Advertising*, 1–15. 10.1080/15252019.2021.1944405

Bridgewater, A. (2018). *The 13 types of data*. Forbes. https://www.forbes.com/sites/adrianbridgwater/2018/07/05/the-13-types-of-data/?sh=67ff62743362

Bonakdar, A., Weiblen, T., Di Valentin, C., Zeißner, T., Pussep, A., & Schief, M. (2013, January). Transformative influence of business processes on the business model: Classifying the state of the practice in the software industry. In *2013 46th Hawaii International Conference on System Sciences* (pp. 3920–3929). IEEE. 10.1109/HICSS.2013.573

Breuer, C., & Rumpf, C. (2015). The impact of color and animation on sports viewers' attention to televised sponsorship signage. *Journal of Sport Management*, *29*(2), 170–183. 10.1123/JSM.2013-0280

Campbell, S. W., & Kwak, N. (2012). Mobile communication and strong network ties: shrinking or expanding spheres of public discourse? *New Media and Society*, *14*(2), 262–280. 10.1177/1461444811411676

Chaney, I. M., Lin, K. H., & Chaney, J. (2004). The effect of billboards within the gaming environment. *Journal of Interactive Advertising*, *5*(1), 37–45. 10.1080/15252019.2004.10722092

Cornwell, T. B. (2019). Less "sponsorship as advertising" and more sponsorship-linked marketing as authentic engagement. *Journal of Advertising*, *48*(1), 49–60. 10.1080/00913367.2019.1588809

Cornwell, T. B. (2020). *Sponsorship in marketing: Effective partnerships in sports, arts and events*. Routledge. 10.4324/9780429325106

Cornwell, T. B., & Katz, H. (2021). *Influencer: The science behind swaying others*. Routledge. 10.4324/9781003037767

Cornwell, T. B., Jahn, S., Xie, H., & Suh, W. S. (2018). Feeling that in-group feeling at a sponsored sporting event: Links to memory and future attendance. *Journal of Sport Management*, *32*(5), 426–437. 10.1123/jsm.2017-0248

Cornwell, T. B., & Kwon, Y. (2020). Sponsorship-linked marketing: Research surpluses and shortages. *Journal of the Academy of Marketing Science*, *48*(4), 607–629. 10.1007/s11747-019-00654-w

Deloitte (2021). *Deloitte football money league 2021: Testing times*. https://www2.deloitte.com/uk/en/pages/sports-business-group/articles/deloitte-football-money-league.html#

Dilla, W., Janvrin, D. J., & Raschke, R. (2010). Interactive data visualization: New directions for accounting information systems research. *Journal of Information Systems*, *24*(2), 1–37. 10.2308/jis.2010.24.2.1

Djohari, N., Weston, G., Cassidy, R., Wemyss, M., & Thomas, S. (2019). Recall and awareness of gambling advertising and sponsorship in sport in the UK: A study of young people and adults. *Harm reduction journal*, *16*(24), 1–12. 10.1186/s12954-019-0291-9

Dwyer, B., Drayer, J., & Shapiro, S. L. (2019). To play or not to play? An analysis of dispositions, gambling, and daily fantasy sport. *Journal of Sport Management*, *33*(3), 174–188. 10.1123/jsm.2018-0115

Dwyer, B., Shapiro, S. L., & Drayer, J. (2018). Daily fantasy football and self-reported problem behavior in the United States. *Journal of Gambling Studies*, *34*(3), 689–707. 10.1007/s10899-017-9720-4

Fulgoni, G. M. (2015). How brands using social media ignite marketing and drive growth: Measurement of paid social media appears solid but are the metrics for organic social overstated? *Journal of Advertising Research*, *55*(3), 232–236. 10.2501/JAR-2015-004

Goebert, C. (2020). Augmented reality in sport marketing: Uses and directions. *Sports Innovation Journal*, *1*, 134–151. 10.18060/24227

Goldsmith, A. L., & Walker, M. (2015). The NASCAR experience: Examining the influence of fantasy sport participation on 'non-fans'. *Sport Management Review*, *18*(2), 231–243. 10.1016/j.smr.2014.06.001

Gran, A. B., Booth, P., & Bucher, T. (2020). To be or not to be algorithm aware: A question of a new digital divide?. *Information, Communication & Society*, 1–18. 10.1080/1369118X.2020.1736124

Ha, J. P., Kang, S. J., & Kim, Y. (2017). Sport fans in a "smart sport" (SS) age: Drivers of smartphone use for sport consumption. *International Journal of Sports Marketing and Sponsorship*, *18*(3), 281–297. 10.1108/IJSMS-08-2017-093

Heeter, C. (1992). Being there: The subjective experience of presence. *Presence: Teleoperators & Virtual Environments*, *1*(2), 262–271. http://www.mitpressjournals.org/doi/10.1162/pres.1992.1.2.262

Hoberg, P., Krcmar, H., & Welz, B. (2017). Skills for digital transformation. *IDT survey*. http://www.corporate-leaders.com/sitescene/custom/userfiles/file/Research/sapskillsfordigitaltransformation.pdf

Houghton, D. M., Nowlin, E. L., & Walker, D. (2019). From fantasy to reality: The role of fantasy sports in sports betting and online gambling. *Journal of Public Policy & Marketing*, *38*(3), 332–353. 10.1177/0743915619841365

Houghton, S., McNeil, A., Hogg, M., & Moss, M. (2019). Comparing the Twitter posting of British gambling operators and gambling affiliates: A summative content analysis. *International Gambling Studies*, *19*(2), 312–326. 10.1080/14459795.2018.1561923

Huggity (2018). *8 best sponsorship activation ideas humanizing the brand*. http://huggity.com/8-best-sponsorship-activation-ideas-humanizing-brand/

Hutchins, B., Li, B., & Rowe, D. (2019). Over-the-top sport: Live streaming services, changing coverage rights markets and the growth of media sport portals. *Media, Culture & Society*, *41*(7), 975–994. 10.1177/0163443719857623

IEG Sponsorship Report (2016). *Three examples of virtual reality activation*. https://www.sponsorship.com/iegsr/2016/03/28/2016--The-Year-Of-Virtual-Reality/Three-Examples-Of-Virtual-Reality-Activation.aspx.

Jahn, S., Cornwell, T. B., Drengner, J., & Gaus, H. (2018). Temporary communitas and willingness to return to events. *Journal of Business Research*, *92*, 329–338. 10.1016/j.jbusres.2018.08.005

Kang, S. (2017). Mobile communication and pro sports: motivation and fan loyalty. *International Journal of Mobile Communications*, *15*(6), 604–627.

Kovach, N. (n.d.) *How much does it cost to create an app like IKEA?* https://thinkmobiles.com/blog/how-much-cost-make-app-like-ikea/

Kelly, S. J., Bettina Cornwell, T., Coote, L. V., & McAlister, A. R. (2012). Event-related advertising and the special case of sponsorship-linked advertising. *International Journal of Advertising, 31*(1), 15–37. 10.2501/IJA-31-1-15-37

Lazard, A., & Atkinson, L. (2015). Putting environmental infographics center stage: The role of visuals at the elaboration likelihood model's critical point of persuasion. *Science Communication, 37*(1), 6–33. 10.1177/1075547014555997

Lopez-Gonzalez, H., & Griffiths, M. D. (2018a). Understanding the convergence of markets in online sports betting. *International Review for the Sociology of Sport, 53*(7), 807–823. 10.1177/1012690216680602

Lopez-Gonzalez, H., & Griffiths, M. D. (2018b). Betting, forex trading, and fantasy gaming sponsorships—a responsible marketing inquiry into the 'gamblification' of English football. *International Journal of Mental Health and Addiction, 16*(2), 404–419. 10.1007/s11469-017-9788-1

Lopez-Gonzalez, H., Stavros, C., & Smith, A. C. (2017). Broadcasting sport: Analogue markets and digital rights. *International Communication Gazette, 79*(2), 175–189. 10.1177/1748048517694969

Markopoulos, E., Markopoulos, P., Liumila, M., Chang, Y. C., Aggarwal, V., & Ademola, J. (2019, July). Virtual and augmented reality gamification technology on reinventing the F1 sponsorship model not purely focused on the team's and car's performance. In *International Conference on Applied Human Factors and Ergonomics* (pp. 364–376). 10.1007/978-3-030-20476-1_37

Matos, G. (2020). *The business models of sport organizations.* https://gabrielaamatos.medium.com/the-business-models-of-sports-organizations-6d63f357f511

McKinsey & Company (2018). *Unlocking success in digital transformations.* https://www.mckinsey.com/business-functions/organization/our-insights/unlocking-success-in-digital-transformations.

Naraine, M. L. (2019). Follower segments within and across the social media networks of major professional sport organizations. *Sport Marketing Quarterly, 28*(4), 222–233. 10.32731/SMQ.284.122019.04

Naraine, M. L., & Karg, A. J. (2018). Digital media in international sport: Engaging fans via social media and fantasy sports. In E. MacIntosh, G. Bravo and M. Li (Eds.), *International Sport Management* (2nd ed.), Chapter 21. http://hdl.handle.net/1959.3/441626

Naraine, M. L., & Wanless, L. (2020). Going all in on AI: Examining the value proposition of and integration challenges with one branch of artificial intelligence in sport management. *Sports Innovation Journal, 1*, 49–61. 10.18060/23898

NWHL. [@NWHL] (2021, March 28). As we reflect on this weekend, we want to extend a heartfelt thank you to @Discover. [Image attached] [Tweet]. *Twitter.* https://twitter.com/NWHL/status/1376352476618747904

Nesbit, T. M., & King, K. A. (2010). The impact of fantasy sports on television viewership. *Journal of Media Economics, 23*(1), 24–41. 10.1080/08997761003590721

Newall, P. W., Cassidy, R., Walasek, L., Ludvig, E. A., & Meyer, C. (2020). Who uses custom sports betting products?. *Addiction Research & Theory*, 1–7. 10.1080/16066359.2020.1792887

Nicovich, S. G., Boller, G. W., & Cornwell, T. B. (2005). Experienced presence within computer-mediated communications: Initial explorations on the effects of gender with respect to empathy and immersion. *Journal of Computer-Mediated Communication, 10*(2), JCMC1023. 10.1111/j.1083-6101.2005.tb00243.x

Nisar, T. M., & Yeung, M. (2018). Attribution modeling in digital advertising: An empirical investigation of the impact of digital sales channels. *Journal of Advertising Research, 58*(4), 399–413. 10.2501/JAR-2017-055

O'Reilly, N., & Huybers, T. (2015). Servicing in sponsorship: A best-worst scaling empirical analysis. *Journal of Sport Management, 29*(2), 155–169. 10.1123/JSM.2013-0292

Pierce, D., & Sherman, G. (2020). Using data analytics to create a digital strategy that drives engagement and views on social media. *Case Studies in Sport Management, 9*(S1), S9–S12. 10.1123/cssm.2019-0028

Pittz, T., Bendickson, J. S., Cowden, B. J., & Davis, P. E. (2020). Sport business models: A stakeholder optimization approach. *Journal of Small Business and Enterprise Development, 28*(1), 134–147. 10.1108/JSBED-12-2019-0409

Purdum, D. (2018). *Inside how sports betting went mainstream.* ESPN, https://www.espn.com/chalk/story/_/id/24310393/gambling-how-media-daily-fantasy-new-thinking-us-pro-sports-commissioners-helped-sports-betting-become-accepted

Rynarzewska, A. I. (2018). Virtual reality: A new channel in sport consumption. *Journal of Research in Interactive Marketing, 12*(4), 472–488. 10.1108/JRIM-02-2018-0028

Reams, L., Eddy, T., & Cork, B. C. (2015). Points of attachment and sponsorship outcomes in an individual sport. *Sport Marketing Quarterly, 24*(3), 159.

Sackett, P. J., & Williams, D. K. (2003). Data visualization in manufacturing decision making. *Journal of Advanced Manufacturing Systems, 2*(02), 163–185. 10.1142/S0219686703000307

Salesforce.com. (n.d.) https://www.salesforce.com/eu/products/platform/what-is-digital-transformation/.

Santana, D. (2019, December 6). *Augmented reality activations offer teams a source of revenue.* Front Office Sports. https://frontofficesports.com/augmented-reality-sports-advertising/

Schlabach, M. (2021, July 7). *Star Oregon Ducks DE Kayvon Thibodeaux has NFT deal with Phil Knight, Thinker Hatfield.* ESPN. https://www.espn.com/college-football/story/_/id/31776772/star-oregon-ducks-de-kayvon-thibodeaux-nft-deal-phil-knight-tinker-hatfield

Schneider, L. P. & Cornwell, T. B. (2005). Cashing in on crashes via brand placement in computer games: The effects of experience and flow on memory. *International Journal of Advertising, 24*(3), 321–343. 10.1080/02650487.2005.11072928

Score and Change (2020, September 15). *Overview of the 2020/21 Premier League Sponsors.* https://www.scoreandchange.com/overview-of-the-2020-2021-premier-league-sponsors/

Sevilla, J., Lu, J., & Kahn, B. E. (2019). Variety seeking, satiation, and maximizing enjoyment over time. *Journal of Consumer Psychology, 29*(1), 89–103.

Sinar, E. F. (2015). Data visualization. *Big data at work: The data science revolution and organizational psychology*, 115–157.

Stadler, J. G., Donlon, K., Siewert, J. D., Franken, T., & Lewis, N. E. (2016). Improving the efficiency and ease of healthcare analysis through use of data visualization dashboards. *Big Data, 4*(2), 129–135.

Statistica (2021). Leading football clubs in the world by size of digital following on social media in 2019, by platform. https://www.statista.com/statistics/827759/largest-soccer-clubs-worldwide-digital-community-size/

Tandem. (2019, April 11). The most exciting virtual and augmented reality activations we've seen. https://tandempartnerships.com/most-exciting-vr-and-ar-activations/

Thomas, J. (2020) *Burger King reveals the FIFA ploy behind decision to sponsor League Two side Stevenage.* https://www.goal.com/en-us/news/burger-king-reveals-the-fifa-ploy-behind-decision-to-sponsor/1b2ijd2vv00mw1r90rzsalko2y.

Thompson, D. V., Hamilton, R. W., & Rust, R. T. (2005). Feature fatigue: When product capabilities become too much of a good thing. *Journal of Marketing Research, 42*(4), 431–442.

Thorpe, H. (2017). Action sports, social media, and new technologies: Towards a research agenda. *Communication & Sport, 5*(5), 554–578. 10.1177/2167479516638125

Tonietto, G. N., & Barasch, A. (2020). Generating content increases enjoyment by immersing consumers and accelerating perceived time. *Journal of Marketing*, 1–18. 10.1177/0022242920944388

Trivedi, J., Soni, S., & Kishore, A. (2020). Exploring the role of social media communications in the success of professional sports leagues: An emerging market perspective. *Journal of Promotion Management, 27*(2), 306–331. 10.1080/10496491.2020.1829774

Van Dijk, J. A. (2006). Digital divide research, achievements and shortcomings. *Poetics, 34*(4–5), 221–235. 10.1016/j.poetic.2006.05.004

Weeks, C. S., Cornwell, T. B., & Drennan, J. C. (2008). Leveraging sponsorships on the Internet: Activation, congruence, and articulation. *Psychology & Marketing, 25*(7), 637–654. 10.1002/mar.20229

Weiger, W. H., Hammerschmidt, M., & Scholdra, T. P. (2019). Giving or receiving in social media: Can content marketing simultaneously drive productive and consumptive engagement? In L. D. Hollebeek & D. E. Sprott, (Eds.). *Handbook of research on customer engagement* (pp. 186–203), Edward Elgar Publishing. 10.4337/9781788114899.00015

Winters, K. C., & Derevensky, J. L. (2019). A review of sports wagering: Prevalence, characteristics of sports bettors, and association with problem gambling. *Journal of Gambling Issues, 43.* DOI: 10.4309/jgi.2019.43.7

Yang, Y., & Goldfarb, A. (2015). Banning controversial sponsors: Understanding equilibrium outcomes when sports sponsorships are viewed as two-sided matches. *Journal of Marketing Research, 52*(5), 593–615. 10.1509/jmr.14.0225

10

Digital Sport Management and the Law

Thomas A. Baker III

Introduction

For decades, the term "media rights" almost exclusively applied to rights to broadcast content (e.g., a baseball game) on radio or television networks. The advent of the internet and social media platforms have significantly influenced the way sport is consumed, and these changes create the demand for the development of new strategies for managing and regulating sport media rights. Before delving into a discussion on that demand, it is first necessary to recognize that this is not the first time the sport industry has had to adapt to disruptive technologies that changed the way sport is consumed. In particular, the development of radio led to the first radio broadcast of a baseball game in 1921 (Walker & Hughes, 2015). Before radio, the only way to consume baseball was to either attend games as a spectator or read about the results of matches in the newspaper. The first World Series radio broadcast in 1922 was free for broadcast without the need for a license and without advertisements. However, it didn't take long for the sport industry to realize that it was leaving money on the table by not charging for advertisement space, and by not selling the rights to broadcast games (Jensen, 2013). The sport industry had to adapt again less than 20 years later on August 26, 1939, with the first telecast of a baseball game. Radio and television brought professional sports to the masses, to cities across the United States of America in which teams were not based. Furthermore, the widespread adoption of these technologies resulted in a demand for higher broadcast fees and advertising rights for popular sport events. For these reasons, it could be argued that the distribution of sport via these new media technologies is what transformed sport, making it both a professionalized and commercially-successful industry (Jensen, 2013).

Similarly, the advent of the internet and social media has fundamentally changed the way sport is consumed. First and foremost, the rise of live streaming services has resulted in the creation of worldwide distribution infrastructure for audio-visual content (Evens & Donders, 2018). As a result, the multi-billion-dollar broadcast rights model that the sport industry has been dependent on for so long is eroding as more consumers turn to cheaper online services for the same content (Strangelove, 2015). It remains unresolved as to how new media will influence the amounts that sport event operators can charge for media and advertising rights, nor which avenues of consumption may emerge in the future. These new technologies have

DOI: 10.4324/9781003088899-12

resulted in new ways to reach more consumers. However, just as the sport industry had to learn to maximize profits from radio and television (old media), it will now have to do the same with these new forms of digital media. The following chapter discusses regulatory measures for digital sport with a focus on social media and esport regulation.

Social Media Regulation

In addition to major sport organizations and events, individuals are also capable of leveraging social media for commercial success. Athletes, coaches, and other sport personnel regularly use social media platforms (e.g., Twitter) to expand social connections and thereby increase their influence (Torphy et al., 2020). Whilst the potential benefits of social media use are well documented, problems may arise, however, when individuals within the sport industry make controversial statements on social media that result in some form of negative public image of the sport organization or league with which the athlete is involved.

For example, in 2019, Houston Rockets general manager Daryl Morey retweeted the phrase, "Fight for Freedom, Stand with Hong Kong" – a phrase that the Chinese government viewed as supportive of a Hong Kong separatist movement (Greer, 2019). Four years prior to Morey's retweet, the National Basketball Association (NBA) entered into a five-year contractual relationship with a Chinese company (Tencent) for the media rights to NBA games in China. Despite that relationship, following the tweet, Chinese television stations stated that they would not broadcast NBA games and Chinese agencies canceled NBA-related events within China. It did not matter to Chinese authorities that Morey had already deleted the controversial retweet and issued two follow-up tweets stating that he "did not intend … to cause any offense to Rockets fans and friends of mine in China," and that his tweets are his own and "in no way represent the Rockets or the NBA" (Greer, 2019).

Fortunately for the NBA, China Central Television, China's state broadcaster, resumed live streaming of NBA games on March 8, 2021 (Global Times, 2021). Yet the Morey situation demonstrates the way in which employee statements on social media can create financially-difficult situations for their employers (Baker et al., 2020). In Morey's case, his attempt at social activism could have cost the NBA, its players, and its teams hundreds of millions, if not billions, of dollars had the broadcast ban been made permanent. This begs the question, what policies could sport organizations implement to better protect their brand image and business operations from social media-related harm?

Social Media Policies Governing Sport Professionals

In examining the legality of a social media policy, it is first important to determine whether the sport organization seeks to restrict employee speech. Employment status matters because some legal jurisdictions have laws in place to protect employee speech, although even in the case of employment-related speech, most existing legal protections for speech are limited in scope by the employer's right to protect their business interests (Baker et al., 2020). The United States is perceived as affording the most supportive environment for free speech and internet freedom (Wike, 2016); and thus provides the perfect subject for testing the legal limits on athlete speech.

In the United States, employee speech is protected under both the First Amendment of the United States Constitution and the National Labor Relations Act (NLRA). The First Amendment protects freedom of expression by guaranteeing that Congress and the government cannot act to prohibit people from speaking freely (U.S. Const. amend. 1). However, the First Amendment is limited in its reach because it first requires the existence of state (meaning government) action on the part of the party who is restricting speech. Most professional sport organizations are private entities in that they do not act in furtherance of governmental interests and as such are likely under no obligation to uphold First Amendment standards for protecting the speech of those who they employ (McKinny, 2002). Even for those employees of state actors within the US sport industry, the protections afforded to their speech are not absolute under the First Amendment.

Take, for example, a case involving a college basketball coach at a state institution who was caught using a racial slur as part of his player training (Dambrot v. Central Michigan, 1995). The coach in this instance asserted First Amendment protection for his speech given that his employer was a public institution. The standard, however, for resolving First Amendment cases involving employee speech requires courts to balance the interests of the speaker to comment on matters of public concern against the interests of the State, as an employer, in promoting workplace efficiency (Pickering v. Board of Ed. of Township High School Dist., 1968). The problem for Dambrot, the coach, was that the court found that his use of the racial slur did not touch on a matter of public concern. This case is very instructional to the extent that it illustrates the importance of public interest or concern in evaluating whether the employee speaker deserves First Amendment protection for their employment-related conduct. Had Dambrot, instead, engaged his athletes in actual instruction and debate over the use of the controversial word, then that might have risen to the level of public concern, given the public debate over racial slurs. Even then, however, Dambrot's interest in engaging in controversial speech would still need to be balanced against the school's (as employer) interest in promoting workplace efficiency. Disruptive speech that impairs workplace cohesion will likely not be protected if the resulting harm from the speech outweighs the public's interest in what was communicated.

In addition to the First Amendment, federal labor law in the United States also provides limited protection for employee speech. Specifically, Section 7 of the NLRA states that:

> Employees shall have the right to self-organization, to form, join, or assist labor organizations, to bargain collectively through representatives of their own choosing, and to engage in other concerted activities for the purpose of collective bargaining or other mutual aid or protection.
>
> *(29 U.S.C. § 157)*

Section 7 has been interpreted by the courts in the United States as providing protection for employee speech that is concerted and made for either the purpose of collective bargaining or for the mutual aid and protection of employees, even if they are nonunionized (NLRB v. City Disposal Systems, Inc, 1984). What this means is that Section 7 only protects employee speech that is made for the purpose of establishing a union, for collective negotiation, or that concerns problematic working conditions. In Morey's situation, the NLRA would not have provided him with protection had the NBA or the Rockets decided to take action for his controversial retweet by either sanctioning or firing him. Thus, in cases involving applications of the NLRA, there exists very little protection for social media activism from employees that are disconnected from their employment or working conditions (Baker et al., 2020).

If, however, social media activism touches on what is happening in the workplace, then there may be some legal protection afforded to the employee by the NLRA. For example, in May of 2019, approximately 150 employees at Riot Games engaged in what could be called concerted activity by walking out of their jobs in protest of the way the gaming and esports company handled claims of sexual harassment from female employees (Grayson & D'Anastasio, 2019). That protest could be identified as concerted speech because it was performed for the mutual aid and protection of the female employees who were sexually harassed at Riot Games. While that protest did not happen on social media, any social media use in its organization or development likely would have also qualified for protection under the NLRA had Riot Games taken punitive action against any of the protest organizers.

In fact, employee speech on social media that involves collective bargaining or workplace conditions likely will be protected even if the communication was not made directly to management and even if there was no expressed intent to eventually bring the complaint to management (*Hispanics United of Buffalo, Inc.*, 2012). Accordingly, sport employees complaining about their employer on social media may warrant protection from retaliation by the employer. Protection is available even if the language used by the employees was offensive, because "concerted activity is not always courteous" (*Karl Knauz Motors, Inc.*, 2012, p. 174).

The substantial influence of social media has led some to criticize the current legal standard for protecting employee speech as not affording enough protection to employers in defending against public statements that can substantially harm their business (Jaremus, 2014–2015). Some protection, however, for employers exists in that the law does not prevent employees from being fired for "indefensible disloyalty" (*NLRB v. Local Union No. 1229, International Brotherhood of Electrical Workers*, 1953). If employees engage in tactics designed to cause significant reputational harm to their employers, then that speech will not warrant protection under the law (*Miklin Enterprises, Inc. v. NLRB*, 2016). Similarly, if an employee makes use of social media platforms that have an extensive reach, that fact may provide evidence of disloyalty based on the magnitude or impact of the speech (*Endicott Interconnect Technologies v. NLRB*, 2006).

Social media use by athletes is common, often employed for criticism and for raising awareness of issues of concern (MacPherson & Kerr, 2021). The use of social media is even more pronounced within esports since social media has served as the "catalyst for the growth of e[s]ports" (Nino De Guzman, 2014). Additionally, professional athletes within both traditional and esports sometimes have large numbers of followers across multiple social media platforms. When high-profile athletes post, they have the potential to influence a large segment of the public; this is the basis for most paid social endorsements. Yet, the factors that make athletes great brand endorsers can also be used against them if their employers retaliate for any sharp, public, disparaging attacks made at their expense and that result in substantial reputational harm.

The nature of esports may make professional players particularly vulnerable to crossing the line into disloyal speech. The reason for this is found in the fact that, presently, there exist serious concerns regarding workplace conditions for esports professionals (Holden & Baker, 2019). As more within esports begin to address labor-related problems with their profession, the potential for both protectable speech and for disloyal commentary intensifies. Furthermore, the interactive structure of streaming sites and the substantial use thereof by esports professionals create both the opportunity for disloyal commentary and the public reach needed to magnify the potential for any speech to be deemed disloyal (Baker et al., 2020).

Social Media Policies Governing Olympic Athletes

Leading up to the London Olympics in 2012, the hashtag #wedemandchange trended from tweets made by US track and field athletes. The use of this hashtag stemmed from athlete resistance to changes the International Olympic Committee (IOC) made to its controversial Rule 40, which then created a "blackout" period during the Games during which athletes were not permitted to market sponsors who were not also official Olympic sponsors (Grady, 2017). Rule 40 stated:

> Except as permitted by the IOC Executive Board, no competitor, coach, trainer or official who participates in the Olympic Games may allow his person, name, picture or sports performances to be used for advertising purposes during the Olympic Games.
>
> *(London Organizing Committee of the Olympic Games and Paralympic Games Limited, 2011)*

The rule's purpose was to protect official sponsors from ambush marketing. Ambush marketing is a term that applies whenever a brand that is not an official sponsor for an event engages in marketing or other promotional activities in order to build an association with an event in the minds of consumers, which then allows the brand to capitalize on the event's goodwill at the expense of rival brands that paid for an association with that event (McKelvey & Grady, 2008). The IOC's argument for restricting athlete sponsorship rested on its desire to prevent ambushing brands from using Olympic athletes for the purpose of building false associations with the event (Grady, 2017).

The athletes, however, utilized Twitter to fight back against what they felt was an unjust restriction of their commercial speech rights as well as their right to publicity in making use of their name, image, and likeness (NIL). As a result, commentators began to identify the London Olympics as the "Twitter Games." Race walker Maria Mitcha reflected the athlete's position with her comment that

> [B]ecause of rules like Rule 40 and others I could not use the image of myself at Olympic Trials or the title U.S. Olympian in any pictures, posts or Tweets to fundraise money to help pay for my travel expenses … .
>
> *(Rogers, 2012)*

Mitcha's reference to social media pictures, posts, or tweets was particularly connected to athlete concerns because Rule 40 required athletes to receive a waiver prior to engaging in promotional activities for non-sponsors (Grady, 2017). This scripted, highly structured approach does not apply well to social media use, which tends to be relatively organic and spontaneous, making it difficult to provide pictures, posts, and tweets to the IOC for approval of a waiver in advance.

Public pressure produced by the #wedemandchange Twitter campaign led the IOC to issue new guidelines for Rule 40 prior to the 2016 Rio Olympics so as to allow "generic advertising" by non-official sponsors (Jung, 2021). Even with that change, however, athletes and IOC critics were not appeased, with some identifying Rule 40 as an "afront to athlete rights" (Morgan & Bartley, 2016). Criticism in the wake of the Rio Games led athletes to draft the Athletes' Rights and Responsibilities Declaration for submission to the IOC. The Declaration was created to promote athlete rights to leverage opportunities so as to generate income related to their sports careers (IOC Athletes' Commission, 2018). In response, the IOC published an amended version of Rule 40 in June of 2019 that included five principles for permitting athletes to represent non-Olympic partners during the Olympics, so long as the promotions are generic and comply with a fairly long list of requirements and restrictions to which the non-Olympic partner brand has to adhere. The amended Rule 40 also permitted athletes to thank/congratulate their personal sponsors on social media, even during the two-week period of the Olympic Games. However, athlete sponsors that were not Olympic partners would have to wait until after the Olympics to thank/congratulate their athletes for participation or success in the Olympics (Allgood, 2021).

Athlete commercial speech is not the only form of expression that is restricted by the IOC. Leading up to the Tokyo Games, the IOC amended its Rule 50, a controversial policy that restricts political speech during the Olympics. The summer of 2020 included substantial numbers of protests and rallies held around the world in the name of social, and racial, justice. The IOC was proactive in addressing public protests by issuing new rules restricting the ways in which athletes were permitted to express their political views (IOC, 2021). Based on the new Rule 50, athletes are permitted to share their viewpoints on the field of play before the competition starts, or during the introduction of the athlete or team, but religious or racial propaganda are prohibited (e.g., Black Lives Matter shirts are not allowed). Political statements are to be tolerated so long as they are consistent with Olympic principles, are not disruptive, and do not target any group of people or country and their dignity (IOC, 2021). Unlike Rule 40, the new Rule 50 does not restrict athletes from expressing their political views electronically via social media, or when speaking to the press (IOC, 2021).

Digital Media and Regulation Moving Forward

The age of new media brings with it new and exciting opportunities, but also raises novel and interesting challenges that demand regulatory attention. For example, one challenge to monitor concerns the rights that professional athletes have in their names, images, and likeness (NILs). There are many ways in which these concerns manifest within the sport industry, but some of the more high-profile problems involve athlete branding, both at the professional and collegiate levels. On the professional stage, athletes need to be careful to protect the commercial value that they have built into their professional reputations by securing the rights to their names and any images or symbols that represent their personal brands. One such problem that requires attention is trademark squatting.

The digitization and subsequent communication or transition of popular professional sports competitions have made it possible for fans to monitor their favorite international teams. The globalization of professional sports has even facilitated the growth of fan communities for foreign sports teams. While the market expansion of sport via the internet or through commercial broadcasts is generally a good thing, it brings with it problems in the form of international trademark protection. Trademark squatting is a process by which a company or person registers names or marks that belong to another person or entity, who is usually not from the jurisdiction in which the marks were registered by the squatter (Fink et al., 2014). Trademark squatting takes place around the world, but there exists a phenomenon involving transliterated words and trademark squatting of athlete names. Baker et al. (2017) identified the existence of what they conceptualized as a "transliteration loophole," through which trademark squatters in countries with character-based languages (e.g., China, Korea, and Japan) are able to hide behind multiple meanings for character-based words that actually represent real athletes or sport brands. The transliteration loophole relates to the digitization of sport in that the stream or broadcast of live, foreign sports directly enables the creation of transliterated names by domestic media or the consumers. For example, Michael Jordan became known as "Qiaodan" by Chinese media when he made his Olympic debut in 1984. The Chinese broadcasters transliterated Jordan to 乔丹 (which sounds like qiáodān).

Accordingly, the digitization and communication of popular sports leagues such as the NBA and the English Premier League have made foreign athletes vulnerable to international trademark squatting. In fact, a study conducted by Liu et al. (2021) examined the extent of trademark squatting of NBA player names in China and found examples of trademark squatting for the names of 57% of the players who made up their sample. As for regulatory answers, most governments already have anti-trademark squatting provisions within their intellectual property regimes (see below for a description of IP regimes). Additionally, there are protections against squatting that are enforced by the World Trade Organization. Still, the fact that it took Michael Jordan more than 10 years and a significant amount of money to win back the right to his NIL should serve as a warning for those who rely on remedial responses to this growing concern (Baker et al., 2017). Accordingly, Liu et al. (2021) advised foreign athletes within any league (e.g., La Liga) or international sport organization (e.g., the Olympics or Ladies Professional Golf Association) that has games or events streamed or telecast in China to take steps necessary to secure the rights to their names in China in advance of the broadcast of their performances there.

Esports and Intellectual Property Law

Electronic sports (or esports) is an umbrella term that applies to electronic sport activities involving competitive video game play that takes place either on online platforms or with the aid of electronic gaming consoles (Baker & Holden, 2018). What makes esports unique from traditional sports is the fact that the sports themselves are video games, which are played by electronically manipulating images created from computer code. Accordingly, the video games that comprise esports are also intellectual property and the rights thereto are enforceable via intellectual property law. Intellectual property is a term that refers to the products of human intellect (e.g., artistic, literary, or inventive); video games definitely fall within the type of creative works that qualify as property (WIPO, n.d.). Intellectual property law exists to serve the important purpose of incentivizing invention and creativity through the provision of (limited) monopolistic protections that permit creators to control reproduction of their work. Intellectual property law is enforced via legal systems (often called "regimes") that are designed to balance the creator's interests against the competing interests of those who want to access or replicate technological advancements and creative expressions that are otherwise under the exclusive control of that creator. Internationally, intellectual property rights are afforded by the World Intellectual Property Organization (WIPO) and the World Trade Organization.

Esports & Copyright Control

Similar to the term "esports," intellectual property law is also an umbrella term for a collection of laws that include patent, trademark, and copyright. While all three areas of intellectual property law are relevant to the management of esports, it is copyright that has the most influence. Whereas patent law controls invention and trademark law brand identifiers (e.g., logos and trade names), copyright governs rights flowing from the origination of creative expressions. Copyright law affords creators of original works the right to control all reproductions, distributions, and derivative versions of their original creations. The copyright law for most jurisdictions around the world allows for the copyright to exist for the author's life plus 70 years (Patry, 2003). The international standard set by the Berne Conventions calls for an author's copyright to survive them by only 50 years.

While each nation likely has its own copyright regime (set of copyright law), transnational protection is provided by the World Intellectual Property Organization (WIPO) the WIPO Copyright Treaty (WCT), and the Digital Millennium Copyright Act (DMCA). The copyright regime within each legal jurisdiction sets the conditions that must be met in order for copyright protection to be afforded to a creative work; but for the most part, copyright laws have been standardized across legal jurisdictions. The US Copyright Act will provide the model source material for the proceeding discussion on the three basic copyright requirements.

First and foremost, for copyright protection to be extended, the creation must qualify as the type of work that warrants copyright protection. The types of works of authorship deserving of protection include literary works, dramatic works, music, poetry, novels, movies, songs, computer software, and architecture (Copyright Act of 1976, 2021). Video games qualify as computer software, but the storylines and characters built into video games are also expressions that deserve protection, including free expression protection under the First Amendment to the Constitution within the United States (*Brown v. Entertainment Merchants Association*, 2011). In fact, the Supreme Court of the United States in *Brown* described video games as a "new form of storytelling" (*Brown v. Entertainment Merchants Association*, 2011, p. 2738).

Second, the work must be original (Copyright Act of 1976, 2021). While originality has been described as "[t]he *sine qua non* of copyright" (meaning that it is central to copyright), the degree of creativity required for copyright protection is surprisingly low (Feist Publications, Inc. vs. Rural Tel. Ser. Co, 1991, p. 345). Generally, all that is required is for the author to establish that they independently made the work, with some *minimal degree* of creativity. There is a good reason why only minimal amounts of creativity are required and it is found in the fact that judges and other reviewing authorities should not be expected to hold expertise in whatever medium of expression the author chose for the work for which copyright is sought. In the case of video games, it would be misguided to require judges to discern how creative one video game is in comparison to another. After all, judges are not video game critics. However, judges are capable of identifying the existence of (objectively) creative elements (*Feist Publications, Inc. vs. Rufal Tel. Ser. Co.*, 1991). For a video game, the inclusion of any creative component (e.g., a unique character or story arc) would satisfy the originality requirement.

The third and final requirement for copyright protection demands that the work take some tangible form (Copyright Act of 1976, 2021). A tangible medium for expression can take almost any form. For the purpose of esports, tangible mediums are found in the computer discs that store the data for use with console video games and/or with the monitors and other screens used to communicate online games for play (Atari, Inc. v. Amusement World, Inc., 1981).

The fact that the sports (the video games) qualify for copyright protection is what makes the regulation of esports so distinct from traditional sports. After all, nobody owns football, baseball, basketball, hockey, or any of the other non-digital professional sports. Accordingly, participants do not have to agree to any terms or conditions prior to playing a recreational game of basketball with friends. Conversely, video game producers have the right to – and do – control gameplay for their titles by requiring gamers to agree to the express terms of an End User Licensing Agreement (EULA) prior to playing (Holden et al., 2020). This degree of control over reproductions of their creations also affords video game producers the ability to restrict, or even block, their commercial products (the video games) from being used for competitive play (esports). For example, at one time Nintendo objected to the use of their game titles for esports and even went so far as to attempt blocking their use in the 2013 EVO Tournament (Pitcher, 2013). Ultimately, Nintendo acquiesced to the use of their titles for the tournament, but it took significant consumer backlash for Nintendo to make that decision. While the Nintendo example best demonstrates how video game producers can exercise their copyright controls to restrict or regulate the use of their titles for competitive play, it also reveals the power that consumers possess, which provides them with a market-generated check on the game producer's power.

In addition to the producer's ability to restrict the use of its game titles, it also can control the way the games are played through modifications made to existing titles, and through the incorporation of new styles of play and characters for use in subsequent and derivative games (Holden et al., 2020). By making substantive changes to their video games, the producers can actually control constitutive components for the sports built around their titles. Thus, competitive play may need to adjust based on changes made to games. Typically, sport product manufacturers craft their products in a way that is tailored to meet the rules and restrictions imposed by the governing bodies for traditional sports. Thus, the dynamic between esports and video game producers is very different from the relationships that exist between traditional sports and the manufacturers who produce equipment for those sports (Holden et al., 2020).

Compounding the problem, for now, is the reality that the game producers are primarily focused on the commercial use of their game titles, rather than the esports built around them. Presently, esports are still perceived as a means to an end by game producers who primarily invest in esports for the promotional purpose of stimulating consumer involvement in the games more so than spectatorship of esports (Taylor, 2018). Therefore, the possibility exists that a game producer could alter a video game in a way to meet consumer interests, but that works against continuity or functionality in competitive tournaments or league play. In practice, however, the majority of popular esports tournaments and leagues are operated by, in whole or in part, the producers of the games used for esports (Holden et al., 2020). Game producer involvement in conducting esports should, eventually, mitigate the threat of game-related changes on competition if and when revenues from esports draw closer to the revenues generated from consumer video game play.

Copyright Defenses

Those accused of copyright infringement are not without recourse, and this is true also in the use of video games. The copyright defenses that best apply to esports include: (a) fair use, (b) the merger doctrine, (c) scènes à faire ("scenes to be made"), and (d) joint authorship. Starting with the fair use doctrine, third parties may legally use (without prior authorization) copyright-protected work for criticism, comment, news reporting, teaching, scholarship, or research (Copyright Act of 1976, 2021). Even if the use does not fit one of the aforementioned types of fair use, the doctrine may also apply if the new work that is created includes sufficient transformative elements so as to make it an entirely new expression. Fair use is a commonly-asserted defense by influencers (called streamers) on YouTube and Twitch who stream their gameplay on the popular social media platforms for profit, and rarely with authorization to do so from the game producer. Whether or not the streaming of gameplay qualifies as fair use remains to be tested by courts, but some experts on the subject matter have likened the practice to copyright piracy (Brusa, 2015). To date, video game producers have had no problem exerting their copyright interests against third parties who have sold streaming rights of tournament play without producer authorization, but have yet to flex their rights against those who stream their own gameplay (Holden et al.,2020). The reason for inaction may be found in the fact that streamers provide the game producers with countless hours of free promotion from people who influence large numbers of consumers.

Another copyright defense is the merger doctrine, which prevents copyright owners from gaining monopolistic control over an idea or concept that could only be expressed in very limited ways (Baker, June 5, 2018). For example, a game producer could assert the merger doctrine as a defense against their use of a video game element that should be common to all within the genre (e.g., the use of Health Points to signify the health of an in-game character). The scènes à faire doctrine is similar to the merger doctrine in that it also blocks the monopolization of ideas; the difference is that this defense applies to the ability to limit cultural settings that are important for society (Baker, June 5, 2018). For example, the sub-genre of gameplay called "battle royal," which requires players to kill off each other until only one remains, should not be the exclusive property of PUBG, the game title that is often credited with being the first within the battle royal genre. Society not only has an interest in the production of other games within that growing sub-genre (e.g., Fortnite) but the term "battle royal" also has significance in literature and film, including *Battle Royal*, the novel by Koushun Takami and the film based on that novel directed by Kinji Fukasaku (Baker, June 5, 2018).

The joint authorship defense simply recognizes that there could be more than one creator of copyright-protected work. The interests of all authors are recognized under the joint authorship doctrine; thus, one author is not able to sustain a copyright claim against a co-author (Copyright Act of 1976, 2021). A possible application to esports might arise if a streamer asserts the defense against a game producer with the argument that the streamed gameplay amounts to a new creation, for which the streamer is a co-author alongside the producer of the game played (Brusa, 2015).

Sexual Harassment and Electronic Gaming

Thus far, the conversation on regulating esports has primarily focused on the applicability of copyright law to restrain the ways in which video games may be used for esports and esports-related commercial activity (e.g., streaming). However, there is a need to also focus on ways to regulate gameplay, specifically gameplay that involves harassment directed at other players during online play. Unfortunately, girls, women, and the LGBTQ+ community are often targeted for unwanted harassment in online gaming communities and during online play. In fact, reports reflect a culture of harassment that permeates all aspects of electronic gaming (Holden et al., 2019).

Perhaps no other example reflects the "toxicity" within esports better than the Gamergate controversy. Gamergate began as a series of blog posts by the ex-boyfriend of video game developer Zoe Quinn alleging infidelity by Quinn as means of advancing her career (Edelman et al., 2021). The blog posts inspired gamers to join in the harassment by posting their own anonymous online attacks against other women in electronic gaming. In fact, the online attacks led to video game journalist Jenn Frank and game designer Mattie Brice leaving esports (Rott, 2014). On June 23, 2020, *The New York Times* ran an expose of sexual toxicity within esports with a report from 70 people within the gaming industry, most of whom were women, each of whom had experienced either gender-based discrimination, harassment or were sexually assaulted while working, playing, or competing within esports (Lorenz & Browning, 2020).

The Effect of Harassment on Esports

As a result of harassment, girls and women are limited in terms of professional opportunities within esports (Darvin et al., 2020). In fact, professional gaming is dominated by men, with only 5% of professional gamers identifying as women (Hilbert, 2019). Furthermore, the highest-paid woman in esports is Sasha Hostyn ("Scarlette") who in 2019 had amassed a total of \$335,551, whereas her male equivalent had already earned more than \$7 million (Romanek, 2019). The gender pay gap in esports is not reflective of a lack of interest on the part of girls and women in electronic gaming. In fact, 57% of women between the ages of 18–29 self-identify as participating in electronic gaming. Despite this interest, participation rates for girls and women for the game titles that have the most commercially-successful tournaments are very low, with rates ranging from 20% (Dota2) to 26% (Heathstone) (Interpret, 2019). In total, only 35% of those who play the game titles that compromise professional esports identify as women (Interpret, 2019). In effect, sexual harassment in electronic gaming results in sex-based segregation within esports in which girls and women are forced out of the most-relevant spaces through a phenomenon identified as "gender-zoning" (Darvin et al., 2021).

In a 2021 study, Darvin et al. found a need for girls and women to break through a "glass monitor" (borrowing from the glass ceiling concept) in order to advance in esports. They reached that determination based on an examination of the career experiences of women esports competitors, content creators, and executives. Unlike most traditional sports, esports has the potential to transcend the perceived or real social and physical boundaries that result in gender-segregated sports (Holden et al., 2020). Unfortunately, sexism within electronic gaming and esports prevent the actualization of esports' potential for gender neutrality by effectively pushing girls and women out of gaming and esports. More and more parents are concerned about exposing their young children, especially girls, to the online harassment that takes place within electronic gaming (Holden et al., 2020). As a result, girls are not growing up playing the same games as boys and developing the same skill sets needed to advance in their play at the same rate and to the same levels as the boys. Thus, the girls who are kept out of electronic gaming never grow into women who are elite professional players for the most commercially-successful video game titles (Darvin et al., 2021).

Anti-Harassment Regulation and Esports

To fight sexual harassment within esports, we first need to recognize that problems exist in both professional and recreational settings, which matters in regards to the availability of extant regulations to compensate for and stamp out harmful conduct. In regards to workplace harassment, most legal jurisdictions around the world have laws that attempt to regulate sexual harassment in employment settings (Earle & Madek, 1994). The problem is that laws vary among jurisdictions. Similarly, the definitions for what conduct constitutes harassment may be very different from culture to culture (Fiedler & Blanco, 2006). In the United States, Congress enacted Title VII of the Civil Rights Act in 1964 with the purpose of making workplace discrimination based on sex or gender unlawful (42 U.S.C. § 20003-2(a)(1)). Under Title VII, harassment can take the form of a single event that is severe and extreme in nature, or through a series of events or pervasive workplace conduct that a reasonable person would consider to render the work environment hostile (Moorman & Masteralexis, 2008). Hostile work environments are those in which intimidation and ridicule permeate the workspace in ways that are severe and pervasive to the point that the conditions for the victim's employment are altered.

Accordingly, professionals within the esports industry have the option of relying on the law where they live to fight against both extreme cases of sexual violence or discrimination and repeated gender-based harassment that creates a hostile environment for the professional. Granted, victims of sexual harassment or sexual assault will face challenges in bringing complaints against their employers, and those challenges will vary based on local laws. However, a path for recourse exists and there are examples already within esports of plaintiffs successfully navigating the legal challenges needed to hold wrongdoers accountable. For example, League of Legends publisher Riot Games announced on December 27, 2021, that it had reached a $100 million settlement with a class of plaintiffs consisting of current and former women employees (Liao, 2021). The settlement resolved a lawsuit brought on behalf of women employees at Riot and based on alleged gender discrimination and sexual harassment. The lawsuit followed an expose by online media outlet Kotaku, which published an article that exposed a culture of sexism at Riot Games (Liao, 2021).

The course for fighting sexual harassment in recreational spaces within online electronic gaming has, unfortunately, not yet been sufficiently charted, much less cleared (Holden et al., 2019). To better understand the problems, we must first identify the online recreational spaces in which harassment typically takes place. First, it is important to address the abuse that is common during online play within games. As mentioned earlier in this Chapter, game producers possess the power under copyright law to control the terms of use for their video games, which are commercial products. The problems for producers are twofold: (1) developing the technology or system of management for policing online abuse, and (2) their resistance to adopt measures that turn off consumers (Holden et al., 2019). The first problem requires both technical expertise, and perhaps, consumer buy-in. Until game producers are able to build protections into their online systems for play that control abusive conduct, the need for moderation will persist. Unfortunately, moderation as of now requires consumers to report each other when that abuse takes place. In other words, whistleblowers are necessary, which places a burden on consumers to self-regulate (Holden et al., 2019). As for the second limitation, perhaps the best way to address game producer concerns is to stress how ridding abuse from esports and electronic gaming is needed in order to expand the markets for both electronic gaming and esports. In terms of electronic gaming, game producers are leaving money on the table by failing to tap into the growing interest of girls and women in electronic gaming. The percentages of girl and woman involvement for the major game titles do not match the self-reported interest that girls and women have in participating in electronic gaming. Furthermore, the appeal of electronic gaming for girls is real, but informed parents have and will continue to push their daughters away from the keyboards and consoles so as to insulate them from toxicity and harassment (Holden et al., 2019). Similarly, for esports to expand further within mainstream or even traditional sport markets, there will be a need to rid the sports of the negative perceptions of toxicity that turn off corporate investors and consumers alike. For example, Mark Emmert, President of the National Collegiate Athletic Association (NCAA) in the United States, identified misogyny within esports in his public statement explaining the organization's decision not to recognize and sponsor competitions for collegiate esports.

The third and final types of spaces for abuse within esports that require treatment are the online streaming services and message board communities built around game titles. Specifically, abuse is common in the comments sections on YouTube channels, Twitch channels, and Reddit forums (Holden et al., 2019). To the credit of streaming services such as YouTube and Twitch, there have been intensified efforts to address abusive content, although the reporting processes could still stand some improvement. For example, YouTube took aggressive steps to stamp out sexual situations, fetishes, obscenity, drugs, alcohol, and inappropriate toilet humor from channels listed as "child friendly" in what has been dubbed Elsagate (Brandon, 2017). In addition to removing offensive content, the streaming services could consider placing more responsibilities on content creators to control what happens in the chats on their channels, which may also be a potential answer for developing better policing practices. The content creators have an economic incentive to prevent their channels from being removed or demonetized, and that motivation provides services with the power to impose more police powers on their creators. Still, much more needs to be done to address abuse in real-time and no magic answer has yet to be found for doing so.

The actual use of copyright-protected content on streaming services also opens the door for game producers to leverage both the streaming services and content creators to better manage the abuse. Unfortunately, game producers have far less authority to control what happens in online chat forums found on services such as Reddit (Holden et al., 2019). One possible approach to this concern involves game producers creating official online communities for their game titles that afford them the control needed to police against sexual abuse and harassment from those who engage in their online communities.

This chapter details the problems related to sex/gender abuse, harassment, and misogyny within electronic gaming and esports. While there are no quick fixes to these problems, the esports industry needs to be more responsive to these serious concerns. As mentioned, expanding girl and woman involvement within both electronic gaming and esports will also lead to more consumption and spending on esports-related properties (Holden et al., 2019). Accordingly, ridding esports of gender and sex-related toxicity is not only the right thing to do from an ethical and moral position, but it also makes good business sense.

Esports Moving Forward

In addition to what has been discussed already, there are other developing trends that require attention in the months and years to come. One such issue involves unionization and the possibility of collective bargaining in esports. There have been some initial efforts within some specific esports and competitions, but to date, the type of collective bargaining that transpires in traditional sports leagues such as the National Basketball Association in the United States has not yet been established (Holden et al., 2020). Stronger player representation is needed within esports to address other player concerns like compensation, as most esports players earn very little wages from their team involvement. Working conditions are another serious concern within esports, where it is common for players to train for more than 12 hours a day; these rigorous playing demands often necessitate unhealthy eating and sleeping patterns as well as substance abuse (Holden et al., 2020). Another issue to monitor involves the growth and development of collegiate esports, which involve tournaments in which college students compete for education-related prize money (Baker & Holden, 2018). While most collegiate tournaments are primarily composed of club or privately-formed teams that don't officially represent the schools the students attend, varsity esports are growing in interest in the United States with more schools officially sponsoring teams and offering scholarships to students on those teams. In this sense, what is forming within the United States is a model for intercollegiate esports that in many ways resembles traditional intercollegiate sports that are sponsored by the NCAA (Baker & Holden, 2018). The growing popularity of collegiate sports will necessitate the construction of additional regulatory structures for managing this emerging phenomenon.

References

45B Am. Jur. 2d *Job Discrimination* § 844 (1993).

Allgood, K. (2021). *Updates to Olympic Charter Rule 40: Impact of name, image, likeness changes for Tokyo Games*. IPWatchdog. https://www.ipwatchdog.com/2021/07/27/updates-olympic-charter-rule-40-impact-name-image-likeness-changes-tokyo-games/id=135955/

Atari, Inc. v. Amusement World, Inc., 547 F. Supp. 222 (D. Md. 1981).

Brusa, E. (2015). Professional video gaming: Piracy that pays. *The John Marshall Law Review*, *49*(1), 217–270.

Baker III, T. A., Liu, X., Brison, N. T., & Pifer, N. D. (2017). Air Qiaodan: An examination of transliteration and trademark squatting in China based on *Jordan* vs *Qiaodan Sports*. *International Journal of Sports Marketing and Sponsorship*, *18*(1), 95–105. 10.1108/IJSMS-05-2016-0009

Baker III, T. A., & Holden, J. T. (2018). College eSports: A model for NCAA reform. *South Carolina Law Review*, *70*, 55.

Baker III, T. A. (June 5, 2018). What we know and what we don't about PUBG's legal fight with 'Fortnite' in Korea. *Forbes*, https://www.forbes.com/sites/thomasbaker/2018/06/05/what-we-know-and-what-we-dont-about-pubgs-legal-fight-with-fortnite-in-korea/#3310e6293901

Baker III, T. A., Edelman, M., & Holden, J. T. (2020). Global sports leagues and China's free speech problem. *Tulane Law Review*, *95*(4), 821.

Brandon, R. (2017). *Inside Elsagate, the conspiracy-fueled war on creepy YouTube kids videos*. The Verge. https://www.theverge.com/2017/12/8/16751206/elsagate-youtube-kids-creepy-conspiracy-theory

Brown v. Entertainment Merchants Association, 131 S.Ct. 2729, 2738 (2011).

Copyright Act of 1976, 17 U.S.C. §101–122 (2021).

Dambrot v. Central Michigan Univ., 55 F.3d 1177 (1995).

Darvin, L. (2020). Voluntary occupational turnover and the experiences of former intercollegiate women assistant coaches. *Journal of Vocational Behavior, 116*, 1–17. 10.1016/j.jvb.2019.103349

Darvin, L., Holden, J., Wells, J., & Baker, T. (2021). Breaking the glass monitor: Examining the underrepresentation of women in esports environments. *Sport Management Review, 24*(3), 475–499. 10.1080/14413523.2021.1891746

Darvin, L., Vooris, R., & Mahoney, T. (2020). The playing experiences of esport participants: An analysis of treatment discrimination and hostility in esport environments. *Journal of Athlete Development and Experience, 2*(1). 10.25035/jade.02.01.03

Edelman, M., Baker, T. A., Holden, J., & Rosenthal, R. (2021). *Esports and the law: A game plan for business and legal trends*. American Bar Association Publishing.

Earle, B. H., & Madek, G. A. (1994). An international perspective on sexual harassment law. *Minnesota Journal of Law & Inequality, 12*(1), 43–91. https://scholarship.law.umn.edu/cgi/viewcontent.cgi?article=1528&context=lawineq

Endicott Interconnect Technologies v. NLRB, 453 F.3d 532 (2006). https://www.leagle.com/decision/2006985453f3d5321978

Evens, T., & Donders, K. (2018). *Platform power and policy in transforming television markets*. Palgrave Macmillan.

Feist Publications, Inc. v. Rural Telephone Service Co., 499 U.S. 340, 111 S. Ct. 128 2, 113 L. Ed. 2d 358 (1991).

Fink, C., Helmers, C., & Ponce, C. (2014). Trademarks Squatters: Evidence from Chle. *WIPO*, Vol. 22.

Fink, C., Helmers, C., & Ponce, C. (2018). Trademark squatters: Theory and evidence from Chile. *International Journal of Industrial Organization, 59*, 340–371. 10.1016/j.ijindorg.2018.04.004

Fiedler, A. M., & Blanco, R. I. (2006). The challenge of varying perceptions of sexual harassment: An international study. *Journal of Behavioral and Applied Management*, 7(3), 274–291. 10.21818/001c.16671

Gin, E. B. (2004). International copyright law: Beyond the WIPO & TRIPS debate. *Journal of Patent & Trademark Office Society, 86*, 763.

Ginsburg, J. C. (2020). Minimum and maximum protection under international copyright treaties. *The Columbia Journal of Law & The Arts, 44*(1), 1–19. 10.52214/jla.v44i1.7308

Global Times (2021, February 21). CCTV to officially resume NBA broadcasts in early March. *Global Times*. https://www.globaltimes.cn/page/202102/1216084.shtml

Grady, J. (2017). Analyzing Rule 40's restrictions on using athletes in Olympic sponsorship at Rio 2016. *Entertainment and Sports Law Journal, 15*(1), 1. doi: 10.16997/eslj.205

Grayson, N., & D'Anastasio, C. (2019, May 6). Over 150 Riot employees walk out to protest forced arbitration and sexist culture [Updated]. *Kotaku*. https://kotaku.com/over-150-riot-employees-walk-out-to-protest-forced-arbi-1834566198 [https://perma.cc/4UJX-X9BA].

Greer, J. (2019, October 23). The Daryl Morey controversy, explained: How a tweet created a costly rift between the NBA and China. *Sporting News*. https://www.sportingnews.com/us/nba/news/daryl-morey-tweet-controversy-nba-China-explained/togzszxh37fi1mpw177p9bqwi

Hilbert, J. (2019). *Gaming & gender: How inclusive are eSports?* The Sports Integrity Initiative. https://www.sportsintegrityinitiative.com/gaming-gender-how-inclusive-are-esports/

Hispanics United of Buffalo, Inc., 359 N.L.R.B. 368, 368-70 (2012). https://www.laborrelationsupdate.com/wp-content/uploads/sites/20/2012/12/Hispanics-United-of-Buffalo-359-NLRB-No.-37-December-14-2012.pdf

Holden, J. T., & Baker III, T. A. (2019). The econtractor? Defining the esports employment relationship. *American Business Law Journal, 56*(2), 391–440.

Holden, J., Baker, T. A., & Edelman, M. (2019). The #E-Too movement: Fighting back against sexual harassment in electronic sports. *Arizona State Law Journal, 52*(1), 1–47.

Holden, J. T., Edelman, M., & Baker III, T. A. (2020). A short treatise on esports and the law: How America regulates its next national pastime. *University of Illinois Law Review], 2020*(2), 509–582.

International Olympic Committee (2021). *IOC extends opportunities for athlete expression during the Olympic Games Tokyo 2020*. https://olympics.com/ioc/news/ioc-extends-opportunities-for-athlete-expression-during-the-olympic-games-tokyo-2020

Interpret. (2019, March). *Female esports watchers gain 6% in gender viewership share in last two years*. https://interpret.la/female-esports-watchers-gain-6-in-gender-viewership-share-in-last-two-years/

IOC Athletes' Commission. (2018). *Athletes' rights and responsibilities declaration*. International Olympic Committee. https://olympics.com/athlete365/who-we-are/athletes-declaration/

Jaremus, C. (2014-2015). #FiredForFacebook: The case for greater management discretion in discipline or discharge for social media activity. *Rutgers Law Record*, *42*(1), 1–41. http://lawrecord.com/files/42_Rutgers_L_Rec_1.pdf

Jensen, R. (2013). Holy cow! How the advent of early sports broadcasting dramatically changed how professional sports teams in the United States are marketed. In D. S. Coombs & R. Batchelor (Eds.), *American history through American sports: From colonial lacrosse to extreme sports* (pp. 19–38). Praeger.

Jung, J. H. (2021, May 24). A relaced Rule 40 will allow athletes greater endorsement opportunities at the Olympic Games. *Swimming World*. https://www.swimmingworldmagazine.com/news/a-relaxed-rule-40-will-allow-athletes-greater-endorsement-opportunities-at-tokyo-games/

Karl Knauz Motors, Inc, d/b/a Knauz BMW *and* Robert Becker 358 NLRB 1754 (2012).

Liu, X., Baker III, T. A., & Leopkey, R. (2021). Examining the extent of trademark squatting of NBA athlete names in China. *European Sport Management Quarterly*, 1–17. 10.1080/16184742.2021.1902366

Liao, S. (2021, December 27). Riot Games agrees to pay $100 million in settlement of class-action gender discrimination lawsuit. *The Washington Post*. https://www.washingtonpost.com/video-games/2021/12/27/riot-discrimination-100-million-settlement/

London Organizing Committee of the Olympic Games and Paralympic Games Limited. (2011). *Rule 40 guidelines*. London: LOCOG. https://library.olympics.com/Default/doc/SYRACUSE/72307/rule-40-guidelines-july-2011-london-organizing-committee-of-the-olympic-games-and-paralympic-games-l?_lg=en-GB

Lorenz, T., & Browning K. (2020, June 23). Dozens of women in gaming speak out about sexism and harassment. *The New York Times*. https://www.nytimes.com/2020/06/23/style/women-gaming-streaming-harassment-sexism-twitch.html

MacPherson, E., & Kerr, G. (2021). Sport fans' responses on social media to professional athletes' norm violations. *International Journal of Sport and Exercise Psychology*, *19*(1), 102–119.

Miklin Enterprises, Inc. v. NLRB, 818 F.3d 397 (2016).

Moorman, A. M., & Masteralexis, L. P. (2008). An examination of the legal framework between Title VII and Title IX sexual harassment claims in athletics and sport settings: Emerging challenges for athletics personnel and sport managers. *Journal of Legal Aspects Sport*, *18*(1), 1–37.

McKelvey, S., & Grady, J. (2008). Sponsorship program protection strategies for special sport events: Are event organizers outmaneuvering ambush marketers? *Journal of Sport Management*, *22*(5), 550–586. 10.1123/jsm.22.5.550

McKinny, C. J. (2002). Professional sports leagues and the First Amendment: A closed marketplace. *Marquette Sports Law Review*, *13*(2), 223–256. https://scholarship.law.marquette.edu/sportslaw/vol13/iss2/5

Morgan, M., & Bartley, D. (2016). Rule 40 – An affront to athlete rights. *Morgan Sports Law*. https://www.morgansl.com/en/latest/rule-40#:~:text=4%20Rule%2040%20was%20first,not%20official%20sponsors%20but%20that

Mulvenney, N. (2012, July 31). *No regrets over 'Twitter Games' for IOC*. Reuters. http://www.reuters.com/article/2012/07/31/us-oly-twitter-dayidUSBRE86U0PA20120731

NLRB v. City Disposal Systems, Inc., 465 U.S. 822 (1984).

NLRB v. Local Union No. 1229, Internationall Brotherhood of Electrical Workers, 346 U.S. 464 (1953). https://supreme.justia.com/cases/federal/us/346/464/

Nino De Guzman, J. (2014, April 30). *How social media changed esports forever*. Red Bull. https://www.redbull.com/gb-en/how-social-media-has-changed-esports

Patry, W. (2003). The United States and international copyright law: From Berne to Eldred. *Houston Law Review*, *40*, 749–762.

Pickering v. Board of Ed. of Township High School Dist. 205, Will Cty., 391 U.S. 563, 568 (1968).

Pitcher, J. (2013, July 11). *Nintendo wanted to shut down Super Smash Bros. Melee Evo event, not just stream*. Polygon. http://www.polygon.com/2013/7/11/4513294/nintendo-were-trying-to-shut-down-evo-not-just-super-smash-brosmelee

Romanek, N. (2019, October 4). *Where are the women warriors?* Feed. https://feedmagazine.tv/features/women-in-esports/

Rott, N. (2014, Sep. 24). *#Gamergate controversy fuels debate on women and video games*. NPR. https://www.npr.org/sections/alltechconsidered/2014/09/24/349835297/-gamergate-controversy-fuels-debate-on-women-and-video-games

Rogers, M. (2012, July 30). *American athletes lead revolt against IOC ban on social media ue to promote sponsors*. Yahoo! Sports. http://sports.yahoo.com/news/olympics--u-s--leads-revolt-against-ioc-banagainst-social-media-use-to-promote-sponsors.html

Strangelove, M. (2015). *Post-TV: Piracy, cord-cutting, and the future of television*. University of Toronto Press.
Taylor, H. (2018, December 14). *The state of esports: Radical growth and inevitable failure*. Gameindustrybiz. https://www.gamesindustry.biz/articles/2018-12-14-the-state-of-esports-radical-growth-and-inevitable-failure
Torphy, K. T., Brandon, D. L., Daly, A. J., Frank, K. A., Greenhow, C., Hua, S., & Rehm, M. (2020). Social media, education, and digital democratization. *Teachers College Record, 122*(6), 1–7. 10.1177/016146812012200601
U.S. Const. amend.I
Walker, J. R., & Hughes, P. (2015). *Crack of the bat: A history of baseball on the radio*. University of Nebraska Press.
Wike, R. (2016, October 12). *Americans more tolerant of offensive speech than others in the world*. Pew Research Center. https://www.pewresearch.org/fact-tank/2016/10/12/americans-more-tolerant-of-offensive-speech-than-others-in-the-world/
World Intellectual Property Organization. *What is intellectual property?* WIPO. Int., retrieved on August 6, 2021. https://www.wipo.int/about-ip/en/

11

Digital Technology and Sport for Development

Per G. Svensson and Mitchell McSweeney

Introduction

Sport for Development (SFD) organizations are sport organizations whose primary focus is on *intentionally* leveraging sport to achieve various non-sport outcomes (e.g., conflict resolution, gender equality, peacekeeping) (Svensson & Woods, 2017). Historically, the community-based organizations implementing SFD programs in societies around the world have aligned their work with the United Nations Sustainable Development Goals (and previously with the Millennium Development Goals), which refer to 17 broad goals agreed upon by member states as imperative for addressing critical global challenges. In 2019, world leaders gathering at the Sustainable Development Goals Summit recognized a lack of sufficient progress toward the 2030 goals and issued an urgent call to action for transformative new practices for accelerating progress toward achieving the SDGs. The report from that summit, UN Resolution 74/4, emphasized the importance of leveraging technology as a potential pathway to accelerate sustainable development. On July 13, 2020, members of the United Nations General Assembly adopted Resolution 75/155, entitled "Sport: A global accelerator of peace and sustainable development for all." Although the United Nations have adopted numerous SFD-focused resolutions during the past two decades (e.g., 58/5, 69/6, 73/24), Resolution 75/155 explicitly highlights the pivotal role of digital technology in advancing the SFD field by overcoming existing resource constraints, allowing for more inclusive access through remote program delivery, and for sharing the work of SFD organizations with stakeholders around the world. Therefore, it is essential to consider the role of technology in the field of SFD.

Although research on information and communication technology for development (ICT4D) dates back to the 1980s and 1990s (Walsham, 2017), the literature on technology in SFD remains scarce compared to other segments of the sport management field. One possible explanation is the common (yet incorrect) assumption that technology is not readily available in many of the contexts where SFD organizations operate. The purpose of this chapter is to synthesize relevant scholarship on the digital transformation of the sport for development (SFD) field. Specifically, we aim to: (a) introduce the field of SFD and why new technologies are of relevance to this field of study; (b) synthesize prior literature on the use of digital tools in SFD; (c) discuss current trends in the broader field of information and communication technology for

DOI: 10.4324/9781003088899-13

development (ICT4D); (d) outline an agenda for future directions on the role of technology as a potential means for transforming the SFD field.

A number of cases from the field will be outlined in this chapter to highlight specific examples of how SFD practitioners are actively and creatively utilizing different technologies to help them better serve their social missions. The unforeseen challenges of COVID-19 have further stimulated the use of new digital tools, as many SFD organizations have had to pivot their operations accordingly. Additionally, up-to-date reports and industry statistics will be presented to challenge existing assumptions of access to technologies across the diverse geographical locations where SFD organizations operate. Current trends within the broader ICT4D field will also be identified along with how that body of literature can inform future SFD research. Finally, a future research agenda will also be presented around several different digital tools used in SFD including SMS-based technology, social media, organizational websites, communication applications, community-based technology centers, and specialized mobile applications designed for SFD contexts.

Prior SFD Literature

The idea of leveraging technology in SFD is far from a new concept. Wilson (2007) argued for the importance of considering the implications of web-based technologies for sport-related social movements groups and sport-related activism to better achieve their desired goals. In a subsequent study, Wilson and Hayhurst (2009) explored how four SFD organizations used different forms of new technologies and found that web-based technology enabled SFD organizations to better connect with new potential staff members, partners, funders, and broader audiences while acknowledging the importance of aligning online and offline activities to ensure their social mission drives organizational practices. Thorpe and Rinehart (2013) reported similar reasons for why Skateistan and Surf Aid International, two established SFD organizations, leveraged social media and that the organizations found the platforms particularly important as they operated in remote locations with limited resources for supporting the organizations.

New technologies have become critical for SFD nonprofits to raise awareness of their programs, which subsequently can serve as pathways for fundraising as well as to forge new relationships with external partners. The research in the broader nonprofit field clearly suggests it is much more likely that people do not donate to a particular organization due to a lack of awareness of its existence and its programs rather than people not liking the organization's work (Bekkers & Wiepking, 2011). Local ownership and involvement have often been emphasized as important areas for improvement in prior literature if the SFD field is to result in meaningful, relevant, and sustainable outcomes (Darnell & Dao, 2017; Spaaij et al., 2016; Svensson & Levine, 2017). At the same time, prior studies on the lived experiences of SFD managers have indicated that local funding, particularly in low- and middle-income countries, remains limited and practitioners often end up relying on existing external funders despite intentions to remain locally supported (Svensson & Hambrick, 2016).

Several researchers have since examined the role of different technologies in how SFD organizations interact with various stakeholder groups. For example, Svensson and colleagues (2015) examined how hundreds of SFD organizations utilized Twitter as a communication tool to disseminate information, interact with followers, and facilitate action and found that such practices varied noticeably among organizations, yet no significant differences were found based on organizational size, age, or thematic area of focus within the SFD domain. Nevertheless, messages communicated were overwhelmingly one-way communication from the nonprofits to their external audiences while action-oriented requests and two-way dialog were significantly less common. At first glance, such results seemingly suggest that SFD practitioners need to shift their focus since an established body of literature has emphasized the importance of two-way communications if the full potential of social media is to be realized (Lovejoy et al., 2012). Yet, other studies have revealed that several SFD practitioners recognize and intend to leverage the dialogic value, but have largely been unable to do so in light of the restricted resource profiles of SFD agencies (Hambrick & Svensson, 2015).

A significant shift during recent years in the SFD field is the recognition of improved inter-organizational collaborations to secure shared funding and support for like-minded organizations (Svensson & Loat, 2019). As an example, there are now many different organizational collaboratives, which leverage different technologies for members to interact while also prompting and disseminating information about the collective impact of these groups of organizations. Examples include streetfootballworld, Nike's Sport for Social Change Network, Laureus Sport for Good Network, the Alliance of Sport in Criminal Justice, and the Sport for Development Coalition in the United Kingdom. Over a decade ago, Hayhurst et al. (2011) studied one of the oldest online networks in SFD, the International Platform on Sport and Development, by exploring how practitioners of a Canadian SFD agency and a Swiss SFD organization viewed such a platform. Their findings indicated the potential for communication technologies to play a critical role in advancing the field, yet that unequal power structures were limiting the true potential of such digital tools. Surprisingly, no similar studies have been conducted on a larger scale despite the increased significance of these inter-organizational networks (Svensson & Loat, 2019; Svensson & Hambrick, 2019; Welty Peachey et al., 2018).

Technology has also been studied in terms of the resourcefulness and organizational capacity of SFD agencies to leverage existing digital tools. For example, Svensson & Hambrick (2016) case study of an SFD organization operating in Eastern Africa indicated the direct influence of limited resources on the organization's ability to leverage the full capabilities of social media. Similarly, Svensson et al.'s (2017) study identified technology infrastructure as one of the critical dimensions of infrastructure capacity in the SFD field. Technology can also serve a critical role in the delivery of SFD programs. For example, prior studies have reported the use of Facebook to coordinate among program implementers in Eastern Africa (Hambrick & Svensson, 2015), the use of WhatsApp for communications among participants outside of program hours (Açıkgöz et al., 2022), and the significant role of mobile phones to help improve participants' family livelihood (Stewart-Withers et al., 2017). More recently, Herasimovich and Alzua-Sorzabal (2021) leveraged digital tools to map the complexity of the global SFD field in their analysis of over 500 SFD agencies, which revealed a number of important findings for advancing the existing knowledge base around power relations, leadership, and organizational cohesion in SFD.

Information and Communication Technology for Development

Information and communication technologies for development (ICT4D) is concerned with people's accessibility to digital tools, particularly members of low- to middle-income countries, individuals and groups who are socioeconomically disadvantaged, and the possibilities that technology holds for development (Heeks, 2014). ICT4D research has grown from being mostly conducted in the field of information systems to becoming an interdisciplinary field concerned not only with issues of technology (e.g., internet access) but also with the social, cultural, economic, and political context in which ICT is given meaning, utilized, and distributed (Walsham, 2017). The continuously evolving nature of ICT and availability of the internet, search engines, digital applications, and mobile phones at lower costs around the world have contributed to increasing research on varied technologies in disparate geographical locations and their uses for development. In the following sections, we outline various digital tools and trends that have been discussed in the ITC4D literature and their relevance in SFD.

Communication Platforms

One of the most significant roles of ICT4D is in transforming how people communicate in more effective and efficient ways. Mobile phones are increasingly used even in remote regions across low- and middle-income countries and provide the most inclusive technology since almost all phones can send and receive basic text messages. A number of solutions have been developed to leverage such technological advancements for social change. The most common and well-known is a service known as FrontlineSMS, which was founded in 2005 by Ken Banks to leverage the power of technology for social change. For example, over a decade ago, Bardgett et al. (2009) identified FrontlineSMS as a critical technological solution for addressing existing communication issues experienced within the Kenya Sport for Social Change Network. The use of such SMS communication technologies enables SFD leaders to transform how local programs are operated since it supports multiple languages and two-way communication.

Likewise, the Beyond Unity Cup, a sport-based conservation initiative run by the Zeitz Foundation, Mathare Youth Sports Association, Laikipia Wildlife Forum, and several other local agencies, has leveraged the FrontlineSMS platform to transform their communication with internal and external stakeholders (Banks, 2013). In addition to the Beyond Unity Cup, an ongoing league is also operated where half of the points are allocated based on participants' conservation and community-based projects. The FrontlineSMS tool has helped the organization organize conservation activities and environmental education initiatives.

However, the use of SMS for communication purposes should not be viewed as a technology limited to low-income and rural areas. Rather, SMS technology can be a valuable mechanism for any SFD organization to communicate with different stakeholder groups considering industry reports suggests text messages (i.e., SMS) are associated with up to a 98% open rate, which is significantly higher than other forms of communication. Moreover, people on average respond to SMS much faster than via email or other forms of communication.

Other digital communication platforms such as Facebook Messenger and WhatsApp have also transformed SFD practice. For example, local leaders utilize these technologies to communicate with coaches, program participants, and other community leaders to coordinate local programming (Svensson & Hambrick, 2016). These communication tools can be particularly useful and transformative in rural contexts and are frequently used in the geographical locations where a lot of SFD organizations operate programming such as in India (Singh, 2019).

Monitoring and Evaluation

The digital transformation of the SFD field is perhaps no more evident than in how organizations monitor and evaluate how their programs contribute to achieve desired goals and objectives. Historically, staff members in SFD had to travel to program locations to gather data, which was associated with significant travel and opportunity costs. The magnitude of such costs was often prohibitive due to the diverse geographical locations and challenging terrain where a lot of organizations operate. However, technological advances have transformed how SFD collates data in a more systematic way as staff members increasingly leverage digital tools to collect and analyze data on existing programs.

A lot of SFD organizations utilize online database platforms such as Salesforce to manage their operations, particularly in regard to data collection for monitoring and evaluation of existing SFD programs in local communities. For example, Kaufman and colleagues (2013) reported that A Ganar and Deportes para la Vida, two SFD agencies operating programs in the Caribbean and South America, were already utilizing the Salesforce software almost a decade ago. Many more organizations have adopted such digital tools since then to better manage data collection across other locations such as India and Kenya (Macklin, 2019; Ndeche & Chama, 2016; Veen, 2015). For example, Grassroots Soccer – an organization that implements soccer programs for adolescents in Global South nations to live healthier and be change agents in their communities – has local community coaches record attendance and similar participant data from programs at a field level, which are then compiled and uploaded to a Salesforce database by Grassroots Soccer staff (Hershow et al., 2015). This digital repository of data allows the organization's staff to easily monitor their initiatives and to identify and address issues as they emerge. SFD agencies have also used Salesforce to conduct pre- and post-surveys among program participants, which automatically populate an online database where staff is able to examine participant experiences (Mashale, 2012).

Open-Source and User-Driven Solutions

A growing trend within the ICT4D field is an emphasis on open-source solutions, which means that solutions are freely available and continuously co-created by users and the original founders. In fact, more than 8 out of 10 such technologies (e.g., FrontlineSMS) incorporate open-source elements (Vota, 2019). One explanation for the common emphasis on open-source solutions is that it enables continuous innovation to ensure solutions remain relevant and driven by user experiences and needs. The importance of open-source solutions has also been reported in prior studies on the intra-organizational conditions necessary for social innovation (Svensson & Mahoney, 2020).

For example, SAP, which is a company founded in Germany focused on developing systems, application software, and products in data processing, provides a perfect example of the role that local stakeholders play in the ongoing digital transformation of the SFD space. SAP partnered with streetfootballworld, which is a global network organization of around 100 football-based SFD agencies, to conduct a series of hackathons, known as the KickApp Cup. A hackathon is an event often hosted by a technology organization or company that brings program and software developers together for a short period of time to work collaboratively on creating solutions for existing issues using technology and is sometimes organized as a contest (Briscoe & Mulligan, 2014).

Specifically, SAP engaged local participants and staff members of streetfootballworld member organizations in the mobile application development process to create a locally relevant mobile application. Local youth worked with SAP developers to create mobile applications integrating football, development, and social engagement (Machmeier, 2016).

Supporting Livelihood

Another important area where ICT4D increasingly serves a critical role is in terms of the digital transformation of agriculture in low- and middle-income countries (Gurin, 2014; Misaki et al., 2018). Although seldom discussed, many participants in SFD programs and their families depend on agriculture for their livelihood. As a result, some organizations have integrated agriculture-focused initiatives and support programs within their broader programs in local communities. For example, Society Empowerment Project, a local SFD organization in the former Nyanza Province in western Kenya, combines global football (i.e., soccer) and agriculture programs to support the livelihood of program participants. Their program is intentionally focused on engaging youth in learning about agribusiness management in response to new technologies which are transforming what farming looks like (Senyo, 2018). There is some evidence in prior SFD literature that participation in SFD programs have enabled participants and their families to not only gain access to new technology, which helped them significantly improve their own agriculture practices through immediate access to weather reports and current market prices for their crops (Stewart-Withers et al., 2017).

Digital Program Delivery

The COVID-19 pandemic has rapidly intensified the digital transformation of the SFD field as organizations in communities around the world have had to pivot their operations in response to the global health pandemic. Unfortunately, a lot of the community-based nonprofits operating SFD initiatives lacked the resource endowments and the technological infrastructure needed to operate digital programs (Svensson et al., 2017). Nevertheless, there were exceptions as some organizations have been able to succeed in implementing digital programs. For example, based on our own experiences, we know that the Horn of Africa Initiative in Kenya have operated a technology center for years as part of their program offerings, while others such as YALLA, which operates in San Diego, used Google Chromebook laptops and similar technology to engage refugee and immigrant participants in educational program components. Some organizations have also developed their own mobile applications and digital solutions to engage participants and their families outside of regular program hours. For example, Chicago Run has leveraged digital tools to deliver education on healthy eating habits to participants while also providing interactive ways to engage with physical activity programs such as finding safe, local running paths. Yet, no studies have been conducted to explore these types of technological tools from either the organization's perspective or the participants' perspective.

Another way that some SFD organizations are transforming their program delivery is through the adoption of esports into their existing program methodologies, supporting calls for leveraging esports during the pandemic (Mastromartino et al., 2020). For example, Kids in the Game, which operates SFD programming in New York City, have implemented a new program for middle-school-aged youth in Harlem which combines esports and traditional sport programs (Newcomb, 2019). Similarly, the UEFA Foundation has leveraged esports for their refugee-focused programming by organizing an eSports program and tournament in a refugee camp in Zaatari, Jordan, which helped engage 200 youth (Beyond Sport, 2020).

Future Directions

Next, we now turn our attention to discussing current trends in the broader field of ICT4D and identify a number of pathways for future research on the role of technology as a potential means for transforming the SFD field. This section includes the identification of suitable theories as well as types of technologies warranting scholarly attention in the context of SFD.

Capability Approach

Future research on the role of technology in SFD needs to go beyond studying whether people and organizations have access to various technologies and, instead, seek to engage deeper in the contexts where SFD organizations operate to alleviate broader social challenges. The "Capability Approach" provides a potentially useful framework for a deeper analysis of technology in this domain since there is a "need for enhanced information capabilities for the poor, including communication capabilities, information literacy, and knowledge sharing abilities" (Walsham, 2017, p. 25). The value in the Capability Approach is that it provides a more holistic framework for analyzing *how* technology may contribute to development outcomes across different geographical contexts such as Nepal, Kenya, and Indonesia (Sein et al., 2019). In fact, a growing number of researchers have begun to explore the utility of Sein's Capability Approach and Nussbaum's Capabilities Approach to better understand the role of SFD in local communities (Darnell & Dao, 2017; Svensson & Levine, 2017; Suzuki, 2017; Zipp et al., 2019; Zipp & Nauright, 2018). Researchers could explore how technology can support the development of capabilities and how certain capabilities influence the use of new technologies.

Critical Pedagogy

The growing role of technology in program implementation also warrants attention to the relationship between technologies and pedagogy in SFD. A number of scholars have previously explored SFD initiatives through the lens of critical pedagogy (e.g., Nols et al., 2019; Oxford & Spaaij, 2017; Spaaij & Jeanes, 2013; Spaaij et al., 2016). Although this line of research has yet to engage with emerging digital tools, scholars in the broader ICT4D field have found Freire's critical pedagogy framework to be a powerful lens for exploring critical agency and new technologies in low- and middle-income countries (Poveda & Roberts, 2017). Future studies on technology in SFD could explore the use of eSports in SFD programming, how mobile phones and applications influence staff and program participants, or the role of WhatsApp or Facebook Groups in promoting local agencies outside of regular program hours.

Innovation Diffusion Theory

In our experience, a common critique of the SFD field among funders and industry is that many organizations continue to often operate in isolation from one another and with little understanding of current trends in this space. At the same time, there is a growing recognition that SFD organizations need to be more innovative if desired social change outcomes are to be achieved (Svensson et al., 2020). When it comes to digital technology, a common misconception is that such tools are uncommon or not applicable in the contexts where many SFD organizations operate. As emphasized in this chapter, there are indeed several SFD agencies that have successfully leveraged digital tools for many years to better serve their missions. The apparent disconnect between the many different organizations operating in the global SFD space suggests the Diffusion of Innovation Theory could be a useful theory for generating new insight into how new technological innovations spread through the global SFD sector. The diffusion of innovation theory has previously been applied by sport management scholars to study the management processes of bowl games (Seifried et al., 2017) to environmental sustainability in sport (McCullough et al., 2016).

Technology Acceptance Model

Whereas innovation diffusion theory is centered around how an innovation is disseminated or spread within a particular field, it is equally important to generate new knowledge on how, why, and when SFD practitioners utilize certain technologies. With the exception of a few studies where researchers interviewed practitioners about their intended use of organizational websites and social media platforms (e.g., Hambrick & Svensson, 2015; Thorpe & Rinehart, 2013; Wilson & Hayhurst, 2009), little remains known about how and why SFD stakeholders have adopted certain technologies. The technology acceptance model (TAM) provides a relevant theoretical framework for addressing this knowledge gap by emphasizing both perceptions and behavioral intentions as well as external factors (King & He, 2006). TAM has previously been applied by prior sport management scholars to explore how sport consumers accept new technologies (e.g., virtual reality; Kunz & Santomier, 2019).

Digital Literacy

Future research in SFD should be conducted on the digital literacy of program participants, families, and staff members. Digital literacy generally refers to the ability to comprehend and utilize information from a range of digital sources and technologies (Gilster, 1997). With the rise of access to digital technologies in low- to middle-income countries, there are increased opportunities for individuals, particularly young people who are often enthusiastic to adopt technology, to gain abilities to use digital tools (UNICEF, 2020). This is encouraging for Global South nations (e.g., Uganda) as younger individuals (up to 25 years old), especially in Africa, make up a majority of the population (ITU, 2020).

Digital literacy is also important given the pervasiveness of technology around the world and its central role in sport (e.g., Naraine et al., 2020). Approximately 93% of the world's population has access to a mobile-broadband network (ITU, 2020), while about 4.66 billion people, or 60% of the world's population, use the internet; around 91% of users access the internet using mobile phones (DataReportal, 2020). Furthermore, social media use has also increased in usage with approximately 4.14 billion people using social media in October 2020 (DataReportal, 2020). This supports the previously mentioned point that the use of mobile phones within SFD may be able to include more participants than other technologies (e.g., desktop computers, laptops) utilizing the internet, specifically in Africa where a large portion of SFD organizations operate (Svensson & Woods, 2017). However, there is sometimes limited access within low- and middle-income countries to the internet using computer devices in both urban households (28% have access) and rural households (in which a limited 6.8% have access; ITU, 2020). In most rural areas, there remain challenges in providing technologies such as the internet due to limited infrastructure, as an estimated 17% of people living in rural areas have no mobile coverage, whereas almost all urban areas are covered by a mobile-broadband network (ITU, 2020).

In addition, while most high-income countries in both rural and urban areas have access to technologies such as the internet and mobile coverage, there are wide-ranging disparities for access in different geographical locations (e.g., South Asia, West, and Central Africa) as well as in relation to urban and rural residence and household income levels in low- to middle-income countries (UNICEF, 2020). Thus, based on such industry reports of the many factors pertaining to digital literacy and technological access, SFD research should seek to examine the different digital tools, methods, and geographical locations in which technologies are integrated into SFD programs.

Additionally, scholars in the broader ICT4D field have suggested that future research ought to explore the role of women as users of new digital technologies since they play critical roles (Walsham, 2017). Industry reports have shown evidence that although 70% of the world's youth are using the internet, gender disparities remain both in internet usage and mobile phone ownership by women in low- to middle-income countries (ITU, 2020). For example, 55% of men in developing countries use the internet and, in many low- to middle-income nations, mobile phone ownership of men is higher than women (ITU, 2020). These statistics are important to recognize given that mobile phones have been recognized as an important tool for women's empowerment (ITU, 2020). Furthermore, a Pew Research Center report revealed that many families, young people, and adults, while acknowledging social media may be problematic given the exposure to harmful or sensitive content, benefit from having mobile phones and social media for both personal and societal life, especially in developing nations (Silver et al., 2019).

Considering the benefits of digital technologies in low- to middle-income countries, as well as gender disparities in access to technologies, more research in SFD is needed to understand how programs seek to reduce barriers to digital literacy, particularly for women and girls, and how SFD programs contribute to enhancing access to and participation in a digital society (Sherry & Rowe, 2020). During times of COVID-19, anecdotal evidence has also shown some increases in the use of digital tools (e.g., searching for health information, shopping) and their usefulness during lockdown periods and physical distancing (ITU, 2020). Future research in SFD should examine how the use of mobile phones and digital technologies has impacted organizational operations and programs during the global pandemic as well as the use of digital tools in a "post"-pandemic world.

Ecological Theories/Models

Another potentially useful approach for future research on technology in SFD is to explore digital transformation through different types of ecological theories. For example, Bronfenbrenner's ecological framework for human development could provide a useful foundation for investigating the role of technology in the environments where SFD organizations are located and how popular local technologies impact the human development of participants. Likewise, the Social-Ecological Model (Kolff et al., 2018; Wold & Mittelmark, 2018) provides a well-established theoretical framework for exploring the relationship between health promotion and technology.

Virtual and Augmented Reality

UNICEF began using virtual reality as a training tool for people to experience life in refugee camps in order to develop improved understanding and empathy (Popovic, 2015). Likewise, the United Nations have its own virtual reality unit, United Nations Virtual Reality (UNVR), which has utilized virtual reality technology to engage youth from places such as South Africa, Argentina, Spain, and other locations in educational programs as well as advocacy for policy changes and fundraising efforts (United Nations, n.d.). While no prior studies have been conducted on these types of technologies in SFD, scholars in other disciplines have begun to examine the ethical components of using VR in similar contexts (Nash, 2018). Future studies could explore the potential role of augmented and virtual reality for organizational training purposes, particularly in programs where external staff and volunteers are involved in program delivery.

Actor-Network Theory

Actor-Network Theory (ANT) is another potential theoretical framework presented in recent ICT4D literature as a useful lens for overcoming existing shortcomings in the theoretical foundations of research on the role of technology in social change (Sein et al., 2019). The use of ANT remains limited in the current SFD literature, but there are a few exceptions (Darnell et al., 2018; McSweeney et al., 2021). For example, Webb and colleagues (2019) used Latour's ANT framework in their recent investigation of social innovation pertaining to the fact-building processes within SFD organizations. As far as digital technologies and SFD, ANT could serve as a fruitful framework for exploring the processes of how technologies are used in SFD organizations. Future research should investigate the role of technologies and humans in program operations and the nuances of how technologies play a role in the development aspirations (and challenges) of SFD organizations and practitioners.

Technology for Peacebuilding and Conflict Resolution

Several SFD organizations operate conflict resolution and peacebuilding initiatives in communities with a history of violent conflict. Prior SFD literature have highlighted the complexities associated with peacebuilding and the potential role of sport in such efforts (Schulenkorf & Sherry, 2021). What has not been examined, however, is the potential use of technology to achieve such goals. Yet there is an established body of literature spanning over two decades on the use of ICT4D in divided societies. The types of technologies used for such purposes include wikis, blogs, video-sharing platforms, social media, video conferencing solutions, and games (Firchow et al., 2017; Ioannou & Antoniou, 2016; Veletsianos & Eliadou, 2009).

Technologies have the potential to bring people together and improve learning among diverse groups if strategically incorporated into peacebuilding and conflict resolution approaches (Vrasidas et al., 2007). Specifically, technologies provide tools and platforms that can promote contact between members of different groups (Yablon, 2007). In SFD, Schulenkorf and Sherry (2021) identified intergroup contact theory as an important framework well suited for advancing our understanding of the design, implementation, management, and evaluation of sport for peace programs. Nevertheless, facilitating contact between groups of people in divided communities is a difficult task, which puts significant pressure on SFD staff members (Schulenkorf & Edwards, 2012). Technology has the potential to complement existing practices and could transform how SFD organizations extend intergroup contact outside of regular program hours and events. Future research is needed to identify potential technologies currently used in the field for peacebuilding and conflict resolution, as well as the perceptions and experiences of technology for such purposes among staff and program participants.

Technology and Institutional Work

Institutional work may also be a viable theoretical framework to explore the use of technology in SFD and how organizations introduce new digital technologies within institutional contexts. Institutional work is concerned with the work of actors in creating, maintaining, and disrupting institutions (Lawrence & Suddaby, 2006). In the context of SFD, institutional work has been applied to understand how organizational actors engage in intentional, purposeful work to contest institutional structures of global North hegemony/global South dependence (McSweeney et al., 2019). Yet, there has been no research to our knowledge that investigates how SFD actors adopt and implement technologies for program operation through the lens of institutional work, despite there being several studies in relation to institutional theory and ICT4D (e.g., Bass et al., 2013; Binz et al., 2016; Madon et al., 2009).

For example, Rajão and Hayes (2009) explored how the control of a rainforest monitoring system in Brazil was changed over time through the work of institutional actors to be utilized for ecological means (e.g., detection of deforestation) rather than for military and economic concerns (e.g., protecting the Amazonian region for economic and political sovereignty) by introducing a new monitoring system that aligned with growing climate concerns within the institutional context. Institutional work would serve as an important framework to analyze how SFD actors succeed or fail in introducing digital technologies for organizational goal attainment, and how their intentional and purposeful work contributes to creating, maintaining, or disrupting the institutional contexts in which organizations carry out social change programs. Future research is needed to understand how organizational actors, including both practitioners and program participants, utilize ICT4D in SFD settings and the associated practices and strategies that they adopt for the purposes of institutional work, as well as the ways that ICT4D may enable or constrain SFD programs effectiveness, sustainability, and innovation.

Mobile Applications

Another area needing additional empirical studies is the use of mobile applications in SFD. As mentioned earlier in this chapter, some organizations have already developed their own mobile apps. However, the existing knowledge of the role of such technology remains limited in SFD. Yet, numerous examples of potential mobile applications are used for development in the broader ICT4D field. Poverty Stoplight, for example, combines mobile technology and social innovation to engage local community members in addressing social challenges with an intuitive system resembling a traffic stoplight (Burt, 2013).

With the rise in bicycling for development programs within the SFD space (Ardizzi et al., 2020; Marchesseault, 2016; McSweeney et al., 2021), exploring the intersection of mobile technology, social enterprise, and bicycles could be a fruitful endeavor. For example, the potential role of a web-based second-hand marketplace for bicycles such as BikeFair. Another creative example is WeCycle, a social enterprise founded by Bilikiss Adebiyi-Abiol in Nigeria. WeCycle utilizes mobile technology to incentive people in low-income communities in Lagos to practice recycling. WeCycle staff collects waste for recycling on their bicycles and provides credits to people's mobile devices in exchange for their recycled plastics (Schmidt, 2018).

A lot of prior ICT4D literature has also focused on the use of mobile solutions for health promotion, and provision of services, better known as "m-health" (e.g., Bervell & Al-Samarraie, 2019; Brown & Skelly, 2019; Curioso & Mechael, 2010). The prevalent focus on health in SFD programming warrants future inquiries into the possible role of mobile applications in transforming how SFD organizations work toward their health-related goals, particularly in rural or isolated communities. The dependence on agriculture for livelihood in many communities where SFD programs are operated also warrants future studies on the role of mobile technology in agriculture. For example, Farmerline – a social enterprise focused on leveraging digital technologies to help low-income farmers across Africa to improve their livelihoods (Gurin, 2014; Misaki et al., 2018) – provides one example of a potential mobile solution that could help SFD organizations better support the livelihood of program participants. Livelihood remains one of the most pressing knowledge gaps in the current SFD literature (Schulenkorf et al., 2016). Mobile technology provides a potential avenue for researchers to begin to address this gap.

Concluding Thoughts

In this chapter, we have (a) discussed the relevance of technologies to the SFD field; (b) provided an overview of existing literature in relation to the use of digital tools in the SFD field; (c) highlighted current trends in the ICT4D field which are relevant for SFD; and (d) offered future directions for the role of digital technologies in the SFD sector. Overall, there is much more work needed in the SFD field on the use of digital technologies, particularly given the worldwide impact of the COVID-19 global pandemic and the need to adapt SFD programming to online forms and/or digital ways of implementation during periods of lockdown and physical distancing. This chapter offers a number of ways to investigate the use of new technologies in SFD, as well as outlines various digital tools that have been used or are currently adopted in SFD programs and the broader ICT4D field. The relevance of digital technologies in SFD, based on the continuous innovation and growth of technology around the world, will necessitate future emphasis on the role of mobile phones, the internet, digital applications, virtual reality, digital literacy, and existing and new forms of technology within the SFD sector. The importance of technology to SFD organizations, practitioners, and researchers is thus an area requiring significant attention in the SFD field.

References

Açıkgöz, S., Haudenhuyse, R., & Hacısoftaoğlu, İ. (2022). 'There is nothing else to do!': The impact of football-based sport for development programs in under-resourced areas. *Sport in Society*, *25*, 281–298. 10.1080/17430437.2020.1778670

Ardizzi, M., Wilson, B., Hayhurst, L., & Otte, J. (2020). "People still believe a bicycle is for a poor person": Features of "bicycles for development" organizations in Uganda and perspectives of practitioners. *Sociology of Sport Journal*, *38*, 36–49. 10.1123/ssj.2019-0167

Bardgett, M., Bowers, J., Sokoloff, D., & Wells, J. (2009). *Playing for the future*. George Washington University.

Banks, K. (2013, August 15). Kicking conflict into touch; How sport and technology unity community and conservation in Kenya. *National Geographic*. Retrieved from https://blog.nationalgeographic.org/2013/08/15/kicking-conflict-into-touch-how-sport-and-technology-unite-community-and-conservation-in-kenya-3/

Bass, J. M., Nicholson, B., & Subhramanian, E. (2013). A framework using institutional analysis and the capability approach in ICT4D. *Information Technologies & International Development*, *9*, 1–19.

Bekkers, R., & Wiepking, P. (2011). A literature review of empirical studies of phil anthropy: Eight mechanismsthat drive charitable giving. *Nonprofit and Voluntary Sector Quarterly*, *40*(5), 924–973.

Bervell, B., & Al-Samarraie, H. (2019). A comparative review of mobile health and electronic health utilization in sub-Saharan African countries. *Social Science & Medicine*, *232*, 1–16.

Beyond Sport (2020). http://beyondsport.org/articles/uefa-foundation-refugee-esports-cup/

Binz, C., Harris-Lovett, S., Kiparsky, M., Sedlak, D. L., & Truffer, B. (2016). The thorny road to technology legitimation—Institutional work for potable water reuse in California. *Technological Forecasting and Social Change*, *103*, 249–263. 10.1016/j.techfore.2015.10.005

Briscoe, G., & Mulligan, C. (2014). Digital innovation: The hackathon phenomenon. *Creativeworks London Working Paper*, *6*, 1–13. http://www.creativeworkslondon.org.uk/wp-content/uploads/2013/11/Digital-Innovation-The-Hackathon-Phenomenon1.pdf

Brown, A. N., & Skelly, H. J. (2019). How much evidence is there really? Mapping t he evidence base for ICT4D interventions. *Information Technologies & International Development*, *15*, 18.

Burt, M. (2013). The "Poverty Stoplight" approach to eliminating multidimensional poverty: Business, civil society, and government working together in Paraguay. *Innovations: Technology, Governance, Globalization*, *8*, 47–67.

Curioso, W. H., & Mechael, P. N. (2010). Enhancing 'M-health'with south-to-south collaborations. *Health Affairs*, *29*, 264–267.

Darnell, S. C., & Dao, M. (2017). Considering sport for development and peace through the capabilities approach. *Third World Thematics: A TWQ Journal*, *2*, 23–36. 10.1080/23802014.2017.1314772

Darnell, S. C., Giulianotti, R., Howe, P. D., & Collison, H. (2018). Re-assembling sport for development and peace through actor network theory: Insights from Kingston, Jamaica. *Sociology of Sport Journal, 35*, 89–97. 10.1123/ssj.2016-0159

DataReportal (2020). Digital around the world. *DataReportal*. Retrieved from https://datareportal.com/global-digital-overview

Dìaz-Andrade, A. D., & Urquhart, C. (2010). The affordances of actor network theory in ICT for development research. *Information Technology & People, 23*, 352–374. 10.1108/09593841011087806

Firchow, P., Martin-Shields, C., Omer, A., & Ginty, R. M. (2017). PeaceTech: The liminal spaces of digital technology in peacebuilding. *International Studies Perspectives, 18*, 4–42. 10.1093/isp/ekw007

Gilster, P. (1997). *Digital literacy*. Wiley.

Gurin, J. (2014). Open governments, open data: A new lever for transparency, citizen engagement, and economic growth. *SAIS Review of International Affairs, 34*, 71–82.

Hambrick, M. E., & Svensson, P. G. (2015). Gainline Africa: A case study of sport-for-development organizations and the role of organizational relationship building via social media. *International Journal of Sport Communication, 8*, 233–254. 10.1123/ijsc.2014-0087

Hayhurst, L. M., Wilson, B., & Frisby, W. (2011). Navigating neoliberal networks: Transnational internet platforms in sport for development and peace. *International Review for the Sociology of Sport, 46*, 315–329. 10.1177/1012690210380575

Heeks, R. (2014). *Future priorities for development informatics research from the post-2015 development agenda* (Working Paper No. 57). Institute for Development Policy and Management, University of Manchester: Manchester.

Herasimovich, V., & Alzua-Sorzabal, A. (2021). Communication network analysis to advance mapping 'sport for development and peace' complexity: Cohesion and leadership. *International Review for the Sociology of Sport, 56*(2), 170–193. DOI: 1012690220909748

Hershow, R. B., Gannett, K., Merrill, J., Kaufman, E. B., Barkley, C., DeCelles, J., & Harrison, A. (2015). Using soccer to build confidence and increase HCT uptake among adolescent girls: A mixed-methods study of an HIV prevention programme in South Africa. *Sport in Society, 18*, 1009–1022. 10.1080/17430437.2014.997586

International Telecommunication Union (ITU). (2020). Measuring digital development: Facts and figures 2020. *International Telecommunication Union*. Retrieved from https://www.itu.int/en/ITU-D/Statistics/Documents/facts/FactsFigures2020.pdf

Ioannou, A., & Antoniou, C. (2016). Tabletops for peace: Technology enhanced peacemaking in school contexts. *Journal of Educational Technology & Society, 19*, 164–176.

Kaufman, Z., Rosenbauer, B. P., & Moore, G. (2013). Lessons learned from monitoring and evaluating sport-for-development programs in the Caribbean. In N. Schulenkorf & D. Adair (Eds.), *Global sport-for-development: Critical perspectives* (pp. 173–193). Palgrave Macmillan.

King, W. R., & He, J. (2006). A meta-analysis of the technology acceptance model. *Information & Management, 43*, 740–755. 10.1016/j.im.2006.05.003

Kolff, C. A., Scott, V. P., & Stockwell, M. S. (2018). The use of technology to promote vaccination: A social ecological model based framework. *Human Vaccines & Immunotherapeutics, 14*, 1636–1646. 10.1080/21645515.2018.1477458

Kunz, R. E., & Santomier, J. P. (2019). Sport content and virtual reality technology acceptance. *Sport, Business and Management: An International Journal, 10*, 83–103. 10.1108/SBM-11-2018-0095

Lawrence, T. B., & Suddaby, R. (2006). Institutions and institutional work. In S. R. Clegg, C. Hardy, T. B. Lawrence, & W. R. Nord (Eds.), Sage *handbook of organization studies* (2nd ed.) (pp. 215–254). Sage.

Lovejoy, K., Waters, R. D., & Saxton, G. D. (2012). Engaging stakeholders through Twitter: How nonprofit organizations are getting more out of 140 characters or less. *Public Relations Review, 38*, 313–318. 10.1016/j.pubrev.2012.01.005

Macklin, K. M. (2019). *The Goal Programme: A critical feminist analysis. To what extent do girl-centred sport for development programmes impact participants awareness of gender-based violence?* (Master's Thesis, Utrecht University). Utrecht University Repository. https://dspace.library.uu.nl/handle/1874/383939

Machmeier, C. (2016, March 30). Kickapp cup: A new code for football. *SAP*. Retrieved from: https://news.sap.com/2016/03/a-new-code-for-football/

Madon, S., Reinhard, N., Roode, D., & Walsham, G. (2009). Digital inclusion projects in developing countries: Processes of institutionalization. *Information Technology for Development, 15*, 95–107. 10.1002/itdj.20108

Marchesseault, D. J. J. (2016). *The everyday breakaway: Participant perspectives of everyday life within a Sport for Development and Peace program* [Doctoral Dissertation, University of Toronto]. University of Toronto Repository. https://tspace.library.utoronto.ca/handle/1807/76481

Mashale, T. R. (2012). *Fit for life: an exploration of the approaches used by sport-for-development NGOs to monitor and evaluate programmes offered in schools* [Doctoral dissertation, University of Cape Town]. https://open.uct.ac.za/bitstream/item/11825

Mastromartino, B., Ross, W. J., Wear, H., & Naraine, M. L. (2020). Thinking outside the 'box': A discussion of sports fans, teams, and the environment in the context of COVID-19. *Sport in Society, 23*, 1707–1723. 10.1080/17430437.2020.1804108

McCullough, B. P., Pfahl, M. E., & Nguyen, S. N. (2016). The green waves of environmental sustainability in sport. *Sport in Society, 19*, 1040–1065. 10.1080/17430437.2015.1096251

McSweeney, M., Kikulis, L., Thibault, L., Hayhurst, L., & van Ingen, C. (2019). Maintaining and disrupting global-North hegemony/global-South dependence in a local African sport for development organisation: The role of institutional work. *International Journal of Sport Policy and Politics, 11*, 521–537. 10.1080/19406940.2018.1550797

McSweeney, M., Millington, B., Hayhurst, L., Wilson, B., Ardizzi, M., & Otte, J. (2021). 'The bike breaks down. What are they going to do?' Actor-networks and the Bicycles for Development movement. *International Review for the Sociology of Sport, 56*, 194–211. 10.1177%2F1012690220904921

Misaki, E., Apiola, M., Gaiani, S., & Tedre, M. (2018). Challenges facing sub-Saharan small-scale farmers in accessing farming information through mobile phones: A systematic literature review. *The Electronic Journal of Information Systems in Developing Countries, 84*, e12034. 10.1002/isd2.12034

Naraine, M. L., O'Reilly, N., Levallet, N., & Wanless, L. (2020). If you build it, will they log on? Wi-Fi usage and behavior while attending National Basketball Association games. *Sport, Business and Management: An International Journal, 10*, 207–226. 10.1108/SBM-02-2019-0016

Nash, K. (2018). Virtual reality witness: Exploring the ethics of mediated presence. *Studies in Documentary Film, 12*, 119–131. 10.1080/17503280.2017.1340796

Ndeche, E., & Chama, S. (2016). Skillz Kenya: An HIV/AIDS youth prevention initiative. In D. Conrad & A. White (Eds.), *Sports-based health interventions* (pp. 161–171). Springer.

Newcomb, A. (2019, January 31). The world's first-ever middle school e-sports league mixes physical and virtual play. *Fortune.* Retrieved from https://fortune.com/2019/01/31/middle-school-e-sports-league

Nols, Z., Haudenhuyse, R., Spaaij, R., & Theeboom, M. (2019). Social change through an urban sport for development initiative? Investigating critical pedagogy through the voices of young people. *Sport, Education and Society, 24*, 727–741. 10.1080/13573322.2018.1459536

Oxford, S., & Spaaij, R. (2017). Critical pedagogy and power relations in sport for development and peace: Lessons from Colombia. *Third World Thematics: A TWQ Journal, 2*, 102–116. 10.1080/23802014.2017.1297687

Popovic, A. (2015). Unicef uses virtual reality to bring donors into Syrian refugee camp. Retrieved from https://childhub.org/en/child-protection-news/unicef-uses-virtual-reality-bring-donors-syrian-refugee-camp?language=hu

Poveda, S., & Roberts, T. (2017). Critical agency and development: Applying Freire and Sen to ICT4D in Zambia and Brazil. *Information Technology for Development, 24*(1), 119–137. 10.1080/02681102.2017.1328656

Rajão, R. G. L., & Hayes, N. (2009). Conceptions of control and IT artefacts: An institutional account of the Amazon rainforest monitoring system. *Journal of Information Technology, 24*, 320–331. 10.1057/jit.2009.12

Schmidt, J. (2018, August 28). Wecycle: Bicycle-powered recycling in Africa's second biggest city. *Reset.* Retrieved from https://en.reset.org/blog/wecycle-bicycle-powered-recycling-africas-second-biggest-city-08272018

Schulenkorf, N., & Edwards, D. (2012). Maximizing positive social impacts: Strategies for sustaining and leveraging the benefits of intercommunity sport events in divided societies. *Journal of Sport Management, 26*(5), 379–390. 10.1123/jsm.26.5.379

Schulenkorf, N., & Sherry, E. (2021). Applying intergroup contact theory to sport-for-development. *Sport Management Review, 24*(2), 250–270. 10.1016/j.smr.2020.08.004

Schulenkorf, N., Sherry, E., & Rowe, K. (2016). Sport for development: An integrated literature review. *Journal of Sport Management, 30*, 22–39.

Seifried, C., Katz, M., & Tutka, P. (2017). A conceptual model on the process of innovation diffusion through a historical review of the United States Armed Forces and their bowl games. *Sport Management Review, 20*(4), 379–394. 10.1016/j.smr.2016.10.009

Sein, M. K., Thapa, D., Hatakka, M., & Sæbø, Ø. (2019). A holistic perspective on the theoretical foundations for ICT4D research. *Information Technology for Development, 25*, 7–25. 10.1080/02681102.2018.1503589

Senyo, W. (2018). Farmerline: A for-profit agtech company with a social mission. In R. Duncome (Ed.), *Digital Technologies for Agricultural and Rural Development in the Global South*, (pp. 123–133).

Sherry, E., & Rowe, K. (Eds.). (2020). *Developing sport for women and girls*. Routledge: Abingdon.

Silver, L., Smith, A., Johnson, C., Jiang, J., Anderson, M., & Rainie, L. (2019, March 7). Mobile connectivity in emerging economies. *Pew Research Center*. Retrieved from https://www.pewresearch.org/internet/2019/03/07/mobile-connectivity-in-emerging-economies/

Singh, M. (2019, July 26). WhatsApp reaches 400 million users in India, its biggest market. *Tech Crunch*. Retrieved from https://techcrunch.com/2019/07/26/whatsapp-india-users-400-million/

Spaaij, R., & Jeanes, R. (2013). Education for social change? A Freirean critique of sport for development and peace. *Physical Education and Sport Pedagogy, 18*(4), 442–457.

Spaaij, R., Oxford, S., & Jeanes, R. (2016). Transforming communities through sport? Critical pedagogy and sport for development. *Sport, Education and Society, 21*, 570–587. 10.1080/13573322.2015.1082127

Stewart-Withers, R., Sewabu, K., & Richardson, S. (2017). Rugby union driven migration as a means for sustainable livelihoods creation: A case study of iTaukei, indigenous Fijians. *Journal of Sport for Development, 5*, 1–20.

Svensson, P. G., & Hambrick, M. E. (2016). "Pick and choose our battles"–Understanding organizational capacity in a sport for development and peace organization. *Sport Management Review, 19*, 120–132. 10.1016/j.smr.2015.02.003

Svensson, P. G., & Mahoney, T. Q. (2020). Intraorganizational conditions for social innovation in sport for development and peace. *Managing Sport and Leisure, 25*(3), 220–238.

Svensson, P. G., Mahoney, T. Q., & Hambrick, M. E. (2015). Twitter as a communication tool for nonprofits: A study of sport-for-development organizations. *Nonprofit and Voluntary Sector Quarterly, 44*, 1086–1106. 10.1177/0899764014553639

Svensson, P. G., Hancock, M. G., & Hums, M. A. (2017). Elements of capacity in youth development nonprofits: An exploratory study of urban sport for development and peace organizations. *VOLUNTAS: International Journal of Voluntary and Nonprofit Organizations, 28*, 2053–2080. 10.1007/s11266-017-9876-7

Svensson, P. G., & Levine, J. (2017). Rethinking sport for development and peace: The capability approach. *Sport in Society, 20*, 905–923. 10.1080/17430437.2016.1269083

Svensson, P. G., & Woods, H. (2017). A systematic overview of sport for development and peace organisations. *Journal of Sport for Development, 5*, 36–48.

Svensson, P. G., & Loat, R. (2019). Bridge-building for social transformation in sport for development and peace. *Journal of Sport Management, 33*, 426–439. 10.1123/jsm.2018-0258

Svensson, P. G., & Hambrick, M. E. (2019). Exploring how external stakeholders shape social innovation in sport for development and peace. *Sport Management Review, 22*, 540–552. 10.1016/j.smr.2018.07.002

Svensson, P. G., Mahoney, T. Q., & Hambrick, M. E. (2020). What does innovation mean to nonprofit practitioners? International insights from development and peace-building nonprofits. *Nonprofit and Voluntary Sector Quarterly, 49*, 380–398. 10.1177/0899764019872009

Suzuki, N. (2017). A capability approach to understanding sport for social inclusion: Agency, structure and organisations. *Social Inclusion, 5*, 150–158. 10.17645/si.v5i2.905

Thorpe, H., & Rinehart, R. (2013). Action sport NGOs in a neo-liberal context: The cases of Skateistan and Surf Aid International. *Journal of Sport and Social Issues, 37*, 115–141. 10.1177%2F0193723512455923

United Nations. (n.d.). United nations virtual reality. *United Nations*. Retrieved from http://unvr.sdgactioncampaign.org/home/about/

United Nations International Children's Emergency Fund (UNICEF). (2020). *How many children and young people have internet access at home? Estimating digital connectivity during the COVID-19 pandemic*. https://www.itu.int/en/ITU-D/Statistics/Documents/publications/UNICEF/How-many-children-and-young-people-have-internet-access-at-home-2020_v2final.pdf

Veen, K. L. (2015). *They bloom like flowers ...: Indian girls' leadership development through sports* [Master's Thesis, Utrecht University]. Utrecht University Repository. https://dspace.library.uu.nl/handle/1874/311811

Veletsianos, G., & Eliadou, A. (2009). Conceptualizing the use of technology to foster peace via adventure learning. *Internet and Higher Education, 12*, 63–70. 10.1016/j.iheduc.2009.06.003

Welty Peachey, J., Cohen, A., Shin, N., & Fusaro, B. (2018). Challenges and strategies of building and sustaining inter-organizational partnerships in sport for development and peace. *Sport Management Review, 21*, 160–175. 10.1016/j.smr.2017.06.002

Wilson, B. (2007). New media, social movements, and global sport studies: A revolutionary moment and the sociology of sport. *Sociology of Sport Journal, 24*, 457–477. 10.1123/ssj.24.4.457

Wilson, B., & Hayhurst, L. (2009). Digital activism: Neoliberalism, the Internet, and sport for youth development. *Sociology of Sport Journal, 26*, 155–181. 10.1123/ssj.26.1.155

Vota, W. (2019). For better or worse: ICT4D is open source software. *ICT Works*. Retrieved from https://www.ictworks.org/ict4d-open-source/#.X71lOC2ZODV

Walsham, G. (2017). ICT4D research: reflections on history and future agenda. *Information Technology for Development, 23*(1), 18–41.

Webb, A., Richelieu, A., & Cloutier, A. (2019). From clipboards to annual reports: I nnovationsin sport for development fact management. *Managing Sport and Leisure, 24*(6), 400–423.

Wold, B., & Mittelmark, M. B. (2018). Health-promotion research over three decades: The social-ecological model and challenges in implementation of interventions. *Scandinavian Journal of Public Health, 46*(20), 20–26. 10.1177/1403494817743893

Vrasidas, C., Zembylas, M., Evagorou, M., Avraamidou, L., & Aravi, C. (2007). ICT as a tool for environmental education, peace, and reconciliation. *Educational Media International, 44*, 129–140.

Yablon, Y. (2007). Feeling close from a distance: Peace encounters via internet technology. *New Directions for Youth Development, 116*, 99–107. 10.1002/yd.237

Zipp, S., & Nauright, J. (2018). Levelling the playing field: Human capability approach and lived realities for sport and gender in the West Indies. *Journal of Sport for Development, 6*, 38–50.

Zipp, S., Smith, T., & Darnell, S. (2019). Development, gender and sport: Theorizing a feminist practice of the capabilities approach in sport for development. *Journal of Sport Management, 33*, 440–449. 10.1123/jsm.2019-0126

Part II

Digital Tools in Sport Management

12

Fantasy Sport in the Digital Realm

Brody J. Ruihley

The Role of Fantasy Sport in the Digital Realm

Fantasy sport is an interactive team-management game involving statistics and real-life performances of athletes (Ruihley & Hardin, 2011a). Participants in fantasy sport (hereinafter referred to as "fantasy" when discussing the activity) take part in the activity by selecting athletes from a sport to represent one's fantasy team. Points are assigned to statistical categories of an athletic contest and a participant's fantasy team points are tallied and compared against other teams to determine league standing. Fantasy competition can range from daily and weekly contests, where new teams are selected frequently, to season-long competition, where one's team is formed, retained, and modified throughout an entire sport season. The industry surrounding this activity has seen many changes throughout the early part of the 21st century, in large part due to technological advancements, expansion of communicative reach, battling for the right to statistical information, fighting for the legitimacy and lawfulness of the activity, mass expansion into daily/weekly fantasy sports (hereinafter referred to as DFS), and navigating the expanding sport betting landscape. Digital advancements have taken this, once pen-and-paper activity, to a thriving communicative sport entertainment enterprise. Before widespread internet access, fantasy participation was estimated at 500,000 North American participants in 1988 and one to three million participants between 1991–1994 (Fantasy Sports & Gaming Association, 2020). The creation and widespread use of the internet changed the fantasy sport industry in myriad ways. From that time in the mid-1990s, when communication expansion and digital advancements changed the world forever, the fantasy landscape has remarkably transformed into a formidable industry of nearly 60 million North American participants (Fantasy Sports & Gaming Association, 2020).

Stating fantasy participants as a pen-to-paper activity is not dramatizing the archaic nature of the early stages of this game. The reality is that scores were tallied by hand, statistics were obtained from printed box scores, team selection and drafts *had* to happen in person, roster changes were literally mailed or phoned in, and magazines and newspapers were consistently used for information and analysis. Paper notebooks (or primitive computer data programs) would house rosters, point totals, league results, and standings. Manual bookkeeping was the primary way of league organization. With the internet creating an environment for web pages

DOI: 10.4324/9781003088899-15

and data storage, fantasy leagues quickly conformed to their new online homes. Record-keeping activities and league information were able to be accurate, automated, and accessible. The delivery of information is another aspect of how fantasy has been altered by digital advancements. The internet did and continues to provide a platform for information to be shared without any real concern over length, word count, illustrations, pictures, size, or space. Player profiles, statistical breakdowns, and analyses are at the fingertips of fantasy participants as they prepare for a draft, analyze a trade, or consider a roster move. Digital advancements in audio, video, and social media have magnified the reach of information sharing and have allowed fantasy-specific voices and programs to connect with their audience in a multitude of ways.

In contemporary times, the industry is heavily reliant on digital technology to create, host, and share the fantasy sport experience and products. This chapter focuses on how fantasy sport is uniquely tied to the digital realm in sport management, as the two are intertwined in the growth, accelerated popularity, and industry stronghold of fantasy play. This chapter will continue to discuss the relationship between fantasy sport and digital sport communication, how fantasy consumption and motivation depends on digital features, how current trends utilize digital technology, and how digital communication will play a role in the future of the fantasy sport industry.

Understanding Fantasy Sport Participation

Exploring how digital technology has influenced and shaped the fantasy sport environment starts with understanding those that participate in the activity. A young, but growing collection of research has explored the prosperous growth of fantasy participation. Many of these explorations of the fantasy participant lean on the conceptual and theoretical backing of the Uses and Gratifications theory. Introduced by Katz et al. (1973), this theory proposes that media consumers select outlets based on satisfying a particular need. In their work, Katz et al. state that this approach "represents an attempt to explain something of the way in which individuals use communications, among other resources in their environment, to satisfy their needs and to achieve their goals" (p. 510). Ruggiero (2000) argues for the application of Uses and Gratifications when investigating cutting-edge technology. While some may not consider the act of fantasy cutting edge, the exponential growth over 25 years has moved the needle and gained the attention of participants and sport media in many ways. Although fantasy sport is over two decades removed from the mid-1990s internet boom, it is easy to see, feel, and experience an upward trend in fantasy sport participation and with that, deserving of scholarly attention (Dwyer & Drayer, 2010; Lomax, 2006).

Katz et al. (1973) introduced five elements guiding the development of Uses and Gratifications. Revisited on several occasions, a modernized five elements provide context for further understanding of this framework over a several-decade time frame (Rubin, 2002). One element is that an audience actively consumes with goal direction, with a purpose, and guided by motives (McQuail et al., 1972; Rubin, 2002). A second element states that the audience initiates "linking need gratification and media choice," placing the control on the audience member and not the outlet (Katz et al., 1973, p. 511). Additionally, Rubin (2002) adds that people select and use media "instead of being used by the media" (p. 578). A third element is that the individual is aware of their usage choices. Katz et al. (1973) indicate that "people are sufficiently self-aware to be able to report their interests and motives in particular cases, or at least to recognize them when confronted with them in an intelligible and familiar verbal formulation" (p. 511). This notion dismisses the idea that consumers *unknowingly* or *unwillingly* select a media outlet to fulfill a need. Rubin (2002) states this as the acknowledgment that "a host of social and psychological factors guide, filter, or mediate communication behavior" (p. 578). A bit of an understatement in contemporary media times, a fourth element indicates that communication outlets compete with "other forms of communication [or] alternatives" in order to fulfill audience needs (p. 578). In contemporary times, there are a host of personal and communicative outlets vying to be the resolution in satisfying our informational or media needs. A final element suggests that people can be more influential than the media. Rubin states that "our own initiative mediates the patterns and consequences of media use. Through this process, media may affect individual characteristics or social, political, cultural, or economic structures of society and how people may come to rely on certain communication media" (p. 578; Rosengren, 1974; Rubin & Windahl, 1986).

The intersection of digital technology and fantasy participation is an appropriate environment for explorations viewing this phenomenon through a Uses and Gratifications' lens. Simply, people seek out fantasy game providers, analysts, information suppliers, and real game contests to scratch a particular fantasy-related itch they may have. As it relates to the activity and relationship to the aforementioned five elements, there are many parallels with fantasy consumption. Associated with the first element of Uses and Gratifications, consumption of fantasy products, information, or game material begins with a goal in mind. From expert advice, statistics, and matchup data, to watching fantasy sport-related content or real games, the consumption has a purpose and is guided by many different fantasy motives (as discussed later in this chapter). The second element relates to the fantasy sport environment due to the many outlets one has to choose from (e.g., host-provided information, social media, television programming, satellite radio, or web media). Consumers seek out a fantasy-oriented outlet based on a need they possess. For example, if one is preparing for a fantasy draft, experts have their own draft rankings online, magazines have their draft kits, websites have analysis and statistical breakdowns, and ESPN has even been in the habit of hosting an annual 24-hour (or more) draft marathon program to recruit and prepare people for their fantasy football drafts.

Related to the third element, fantasy participants are aware of their usage when partaking in the fantasy experience. Fantasy participants knowingly have particular places they visit for draft information, player updates, injury reports, or matchup data. Thanks to social media and web-based information providers, all kinds of data can be obtained from general inquiries (how many points did a player earn in their last contest) to the most specific (how does this kicker perform on the road at night in frigid temperatures). Additionally, there are dedicated television shows, streaming programs, and radio (terrestrial and satellite) outlets to enhance the experience of fantasy play. Stumbling upon and staying on these avenues does not occur by accident. The fourth element fits with fantasy participation in a major way. Competition for fantasy consumers is highly prevalent amongst providers, writers, and analysts in an effort to gain the, oh so important, *attention* of sport fans and fantasy participants alike. Whether it is a start/sit column, a fantasy football draft show, a website complete with player information, or a game provider recruiting consumers, communication outlets are seeking to be read, seen, or heard. ESPN's John Diver told Billings and Ruihley (2014) about how season-long fantasy sport providers don't necessarily try to poach participants from one another due to the loyalty consumers have with a provider, but rather, they compete for newcomers to the activity. He states, "We've focused more in the last few years on trying to get that 18-year-old who is going to college. He's got nine buddies. We get them to sign up and play fantasy football with us, and we have them for the next 40 years" (p. 77). This seems to hold true for season-long play where there is history and year-to-year carryover and statistics, but the sentiment could be evolving with DFS providers, like DraftKings and FanDuel introducing new games and frequently recruiting new consumers.

The final element describing the Uses and Gratifications framework has over-arching societal and cultural meaning. Scaling this idea down to the fantasy sport industry and experience allows one to consider the impact fantasy play can have on the structure and experience of consuming sport and change how people rely on communication activities. In one example, those participating in fantasy activity begin to value player productivity and success differently from wins and losses, batting average, or efficiency. Fantasy relies on point-producing activities within a *real* contest regardless of the *real* outcome for that player. It's not enough for a quarterback to secure a divisional win or for a shortstop to go 3-4 in the game and drive in the winning run. The quarterback needs 300 yards, three touchdowns, and little to no turnovers and the shortstop needs a walk, two doubles, four runs batted in, and perhaps a stolen base or two (not to mention some of the advanced statistics many are using). This mindset is changing what a successful performance looks like. In another example, communication media outlets are having to alter the way statistics are presented or framed. Fantasy participants, along with sport bettors, are looking for key results to help them determine their own ancillary success. In a discussion with Billings and Ruihley (2014) about fantasy play and mainstream sport media, Fox Sports' Jim Bernard recalled a time around 2005 when a discussion was had with a television production team about this very topic. He recalls:

> I remember eight years ago, they were just going to put just scores [on the television screen graphics]. [We said], "No, you can't. These guys care. You've got to say who scored that touchdown." Certain times the graphics do have it, certain times they don't. We like to keep pushing it forward. You'll see in the halftime shows, they definitely have bullet points that are directed to the fantasy guy. (p. 79)

In the same way that the bottom-line scroll, halftime graphics, or in-game updates are changing to include more individual achievement and statistics, so too are the formats in box scores, fantasy totals, and player news updates. Fantasy participants are requiring information outlets to change their culture and provide a different angle on the information in order to better assist them in their lineup formation, creation, alterations, and discovery of results.

Examining fantasy participation with an understanding of the Uses and Gratifications' framework has allowed researchers to uncover much about the activity. For example, many have studied the types of people that participate in the activity (Farquhar & Meeds, 2007) and the motives behind the play (Dwyer & Kim, 2011; Brown et al., 2012; Ruihley & Hardin, 2011a; Spinda & Haridakis, 2008; Suh et al., 2010). In addition, Ruihley and Hardin (2013) examined message-board use in the fantasy experience, Nesbit and King (2010) researched how fantasy impacts television viewership, and Weiner and Dwyer (2017) along with Billings et al. (2017) both studied the evolving DFS consumer. Regardless of focus, researchers have been able to employ the uses and gratifications framework in an effort to understand more about this evolving sport and gaming phenomenon.

An additional theory that has been used to help explain fantasy usage and acceptance of advancements in the Diffusion of Innovation theory. Diffusion has been defined as "a process by which an innovation is communicated through certain channels over time among members of a social system" (Rogers, 2003, p. 5). The diffusion of innovation process includes many types of adopters, with Rogers (2003) identifying five types identified as innovators, early adopters, early majority, late majority, and laggards. In research focused on fantasy and alternative forms of sport gambling and gaming, Ruihley et al. (2021) describe diffusion of innovations as a media theory that explains the expansion of newer forms of technology and media and "how an audience is tacitly invited to embrace or repel the evolution" (p. 683).

Understanding consumer acceptance in the fantasy realm has come in the forms of (a) initial acceptance of the activity as a complement to a real game, (b) the shift to an online environment, (c) the introduction of mobile applications and programs, (d) new forms of play (e.g., DFS, dynasty leagues, etc.), and (e) current movements and convergence with organizations with interests in legalized sports betting within the United States.

Fantasy sport has been examined in many other ways when examining specific facets of play. Social Identity Theory, Team Identification, and Entertainment Theory have all been used to examine participation motivation, commitment to one's favorite team versus a fantasy team, and aspects of the fantasy experience. Additionally, with North American fantasy sport primarily consumed by white men (Billings & Ruihley, 2014; Fantasy Sports & Gaming Association, 2020), frameworks and concepts of hegemonic masculinity, Social Role Theory, media framing, and gender role constraints have been utilized in research focused on the gender imbalance within the demographic makeup of participants.

Motivations for play

Understanding the intersection of fantasy activity and digital technology is not too difficult on the surface because in contemporary play, the fantasy sport industry is entrenched with internet technology and its offerings are abundant, due to access provided with digital technology. A deeper dive into the motives of fantasy participation and how each one of those is impacted by or impacts digital technology offers further insight into this intertwined relationship. A growing number of scholars have examined why people are interested in this phenomenon of fantasy sport and what makes up their participation (see Billings & Ruihley, 2014; Davis & Duncan, 2006; Dwyer & Drayer, 2010; Dwyer & Weiner, 2018; Farquhar & Meeds, 2007; Roy & Goss, 2007; Ruihley et al., 2017; Ruihley & Hardin, 2011a; Spinda & Haridakis, 2008). This section will outline the key motives for fantasy participation and discuss the relationship with digital technology for each.

Arousal & Self-Esteem

Arousal and self-esteem in the fantasy context refer to the emotion stirred as a result of participating in the activity. In one of the earliest examinations of fantasy play, Farquhar and Meeds (2007) defined arousal in terms of the thrill of victory or "the thought that next victory is just around the corner" (p. 1212). Of course, in season-long or DFS play where money is part of the emotional attachment to a victory, arousal can take on a more economical meaning (Dwyer & Weiner, 2018). As previously mentioned, fantasy sport is an activity where a participant is competing against others. This activity pits one manager's strategy and team against another single team, an entire league, or in a DFS contest with up to hundreds of entries. It is understandable how one would try to "achieve success and outperform" in this domain (Roy & Goss, 2007, p. 101) The personalized aspects of the activity (ability to create a team and compete against people within one's circle) can cause positive and negative fluctuations in a participant's fantasy self-worth (Ruihley et al., in press; Spinda & Haridakis, 2008).

Digital technology has provided so many opportunities for fantasy participants to engage with sport, specifically one's fantasy team. One way is through the consumption of live contests. Once confined to a local broadcast, sport fans now can follow any game with the advancement of television contracts, league or team offerings, expanded radio coverage, and live updates on numerous sport information websites and social media. This gives the fantasy participant the ability to chase that thrill of victory through many different digital avenues. Another way digital technology has aided the fantasy sport experience, as it relates to arousal, is through a live fantasy scoreboard. For any fantasy sport matchup, participants can follow along with the live statistics and point totals to measure their team's results against the competition. This feature is present within the fantasy sport experience through the web, phone, watch, and television applications. These advancements, along with social media, texting, and other communicative avenues allow for the emotional side of fantasy play to take hold within a fantasy sport experience.

Camaraderie & Social Sport

Fantasy sport is a social activity. For season-long play, leagues are formed (usually) with 10-12 people, drafts take place, and competition ensues for the entirety of a sport season. Discussion of results, trades, sport, and even some banter or trash talk takes place within the normal flow of a season. For DFS play, similar conversations take place if participating with the same group of people or the social circle can be expanded as new contests are more frequent and include variable and ever-changing competitors. Ruihley and Hardin (2011a) examined the social side of fantasy play and split a broad social factor into two: camaraderie and social sport. Camaraderie focuses on the relationship side of socializing that comes through sport or fantasy participation. Fantasy provides an environment where socializing, bonding, and areas of commonality are part of the foundation of the activity (Billings & Ruihley, 2014; Ruihley et al., in press; Ruihley & Hardin, 2011a). Within this context, the act of fantasy play brings people together in many contexts (friendships, family relationships, work colleagues, neighbors, etc.) and creates a connection to others. Social sport within the fantasy sport environment involves interaction about the sport. This factor was measured with items involving chatting about sports, sharing opinions about sport teams and players, and debating sport-related issues (Hur et al., 2007; Ruihley & Hardin, 2011a). This is simply thought of as the actual conversations fantasy participants have involving sport and fantasy play, whereas camaraderie focuses on the relational aspects of socialization.

Digital technology assists greatly with both of these social-based motives. The ability to communicate via mobile device, social media, or email are the over-arching general contributions, but there are also specific fantasy applications. One such fantasy advancement is a message board visible only to fantasy sport participants within a certain league. These boards are designed to host league-wide chat and most offer the ability to have individual conversation as well. This keeps the *social sport* conversation moving within a particular fantasy community and the connection people have throughout the contest or season contributes to the *camaraderie* built within an experience. Ruihley and Hardin (2011b) examined message board use and found those engaged with message boards did so for four main reasons consisting of logistical conversation, socializing, surveillance, and seeking advice or opinion. Further, those that utilized this communicative feature were involved in more leagues, consumed more fantasy-sport-specific content (measured in hours per week), were more satisfied with their fantasy experience, and had a higher intention to return to the activity in the subsequent season than non-using fantasy participants. Ruihley and Huber (2018) discovered that as more personalized elements (league name, live drafts, custom scoring, group messaging, etc.) were included in league play, the more fantasy participants' motivational scores, satisfaction, intent to return to the activity and consumption of fantasy and sport content also increased. Their argument was that personalized elements added to the experience, the socialization, and the camaraderie amongst league participants.

Control

For fantasy play, controlling one's roster is the primary obligation in creating a team to compete with others. In early examinations on motivation for play, Roy and Goss (2007) identified this type of managerial decision-making motive as a "strong psychological influence" of fantasy consumption (p. 99). Additionally, Spinda and Haridakis (2008) explained this aspect as an ability for one to own his or her team and make decisions like that of a coach or general manager. The ease at which fantasy participants can control their team is largely credited to digital advancements and the engineers behind the scenes and screens. As mentioned in the introduction, this activity used to be one where phone calls, paper mail, or in-person requests had to be made for roster changes. Websites and mobile applications in contemporary play have been created to be extremely user-friendly when attempting to draft players, start/sit players at any time, and offer/evaluate trades. This type of control allows participants to make decisions as often as they like, when they like, and grants people the ability to change their mind.

Escape & Pass Time

Stemming from work on sport fan motivation and online sport consumption (Hur et al., 2007; Seo & Green, 2008; Wann, 1995), escape has been used as a measurement for fantasy motivation in order to gauge how the activity allows participants to forget or compartmentalize daily routines, worries, or concerns while participating. Also, from the work on online sport consumption, the motivation of pass time is defined in its name. Fantasy activity can be seen as a way to assist in occupying time, as something to do when bored, or as an activity to participate in during one's free time (Ruihley & Hardin, 2011a).

These two motives can be perceived as opposites when examining the activity through a lens that shows fantasy participation as a prevalent part of everyday life. In much of the work of Ruihley, Billings, and Hardin, the motivating factor of escape resides near, if not at, the bottom of measured motivations for play. Reasons given for these constant findings revolve around the idea that fantasy is *a part* of daily life and not an *escape* from it. Billings and Ruihley (2014) state that this factor can be seen as "disengaging from daily issues" (p. 23). For many, sport news, fantasy activity with coworkers or family, checking player news, and making lineup changes is all part of life. Fantasy sport conversations happen with league mates and sporting contests take place nearly every day of the week. This is all made possible by the incredible access granted by digital technologies like social media, mobile access, website content, and fantasy applications. These advancements have allowed for fantasy sport to be integrated seamlessly into our daily lives. Passing time, as a motive for play, is possible for all the aforementioned advancements and reasons. It's easy to check a lineup quickly while on the subway, in the bathroom, on a lunch break, or during commercial breaks. Fantasy becomes a major ancillary sport activity and hobby for many and allows people to pass and occupy the time to alleviate boredom.

Surveillance

To be successful in fantasy play, a participant will make many decisions about their team when drafting, trading, or making roster decisions. These decisions are influenced by the "gathering of sport-related information across the sport media landscape," all in an effort to make better decisions and find answers to questions or concerns about their fantasy play (Ruihley & Hardin, 2011a, p. 236). This surveillance of the media environment for information is critical not only to success in competition, but this is a major factor in the clout of the fantasy sport industry. Information providers, game hosts, broadcasters, and analysts all know the importance of having information to provide the fantasy participant. From weather, injuries, and matchups to start/sit advice, free-agent pickups, and game analysis, participants are seeking information to learn more about their team or validate a move they have already decided upon.

Fantasy participants consume content at exponential rates when compared to non-fantasy sport participants. In a 2010 report, ESPN's Department of Integrated Media Research indicated non-fantasy participant consumption at around seven hours of ESPN media each week, while fantasy participant consumption was tripled at 22 hours and 40 minutes per week (Billings and Ruihley, 2014; ESPN Department of Integrated Media Research, 2010). Subsequent work from Ruihley, Billings, and Hardin has found a near doubling of sport consumption per week to support these findings. Digital technology and the advancement of internet-based platforms have created environments and avenues for niche fantasy information and statistics to become mainstream. Fantasy participants can easily locate the type of information they need, from an assortment of analysts and information providers, and through myriad of media outlets. Major media providers like ESPN, Yahoo!, NBC Sports have recognized this demand for information and have dedicated resources to the fantasy space. Professional leagues have even created their own fantasy presence with games, analysts, and platforms to promote their sport and their athletes. Additionally, there are many fantasy-sport-specific companies, like Rotoworld, Rotowire, and FantasyPros that are able to create, manage and deliver time-sensitive content to millions of users because of the ease and accessible nature digital advancements provide.

Competition

The act of pitting one's team or strategy against another is the core of fantasy activity. Competition is simply the desire to defeat a rival and each day, week, or season brings about competition amongst people. The previously discussed motives and their relationship to digital technology and advancements, culminate in an experience that allows for fantasy competition amongst many different people through many different means.

Contemporary Trends

RedZone

The creation of ESPN in 1979 put sport highlights on full display with a 24-hour cable sports network. Highlights are important to fantasy participants, but not particularly a trend specific to fantasy play. One contemporary trend takes the idea of National Football League (NFL) highlights of completed plays or events and offers that viewing experience live. In 2009, the NFL created *RedZone*; a visual medium offered through television providers and mobile applications. This channel offers an opportunity fans to see "every touchdown from every game Sunday afternoon" (NFL RedZone, 2020, para. 3). While only a decade old, this product continues to capture the attention of fantasy participants and sport bettors, as they try to follow the action and keep up with their fantasy or gambling interests. Whitaker and Lovett (2011) of *The New York Times* states the following about this incredible advancement of the ancillary activities aligned with sport:

> RedZone, reacting to a new kind of demand, seems a kind of naked acknowledgment that a viewer's interest in his or her fantasy leagues may actually trump loyalty to a single team. Pro football is, as well, a magnet for gamblers, and no one much pretends they are not among the most avid fans of RedZone. (para. 11)

A fantasy roster consists of players from all over a given sport league. With territorial restrictions and access to only a few nationally broadcasted games, visually following a fantasy team live is next to impossible. Even a feature like NFL Game Pass or MLB.TV, where you purchase access to all out-of-market games or viewing rights to one team, is difficult to navigate when following a dozen or more athletes on a fantasy roster. A channel, like RedZone, allows precise access to all scoring plays during a typically crowded day of games. As Greene (2017) states, "While [RedZone] started as a sort-of gimmick for fantasy football enthusiasts with short attention spans, it has become the only way to watch the league without losing your mind" (para. 6). After consuming *RedZone* with fantasy or gambling interests, a single game broadcast appears slow and lacking action. This advancement might be hard to come back from with those with ancillary activity attention spans.

Mobile Advancements

Pew Research (2019) reports that 96% of US adults own a cellphone, with 81% of those owning a smartphone. This has created incredible advancement for the delivery of communication activity, information gathering, entertainment, games, and sport. On the fantasy sport front in 2016, ESPN's John Diver stated that beyond a fantasy draft, nearly 80% of ESPN's fantasy consumption was through mobile means, with 20% coming via desktop/laptop use (Business of Fantasy Sport–Guest Interview, 2016). Ruihley and Billings (2019) explored ESPN's fantasy presence and place within the market and inquired about the lopsided nature of ESPN's fantasy consumption. Not only was the imbalance confirmed, but the number had also actually increased to an 88% share of fantasy consumption for mobile devices (K. Ota, personal communication, 2018). Ruihley and Billings followed up with ESPN Director of Communications, Kevin Ota, and asked if this figure seemed surprising (K. Ota, personal communication, 2018). Ota responded,

> Not surprising at all. This trend began with NFL Sundays skewing higher for mobile usage. With the exception of a fantasy league draft, where a larger screen lends itself to doing more in-depth player research, setting a lineup, monitoring a team, following live scores, etc. are all activities that are easily done on a mobile device.
>
> *(Ruihley & Billings, 2019, p. 62)*

The reliance on mobile technology has opened a floodgate of sport and fantasy sport-based apps all designed to meet the consumer where they are with up-to-date news, scores, highlights, and personalized notifications. Echoing the discussion regarding fantasy activity becoming part of daily life and not an escape, this type of digital advancement has made it possible to engage with fantasy activity at any time and with just the tap of a finger.

Web & Social Media

The global importance of digital advancements like the web and social media is abundantly obvious when considering speed, access, and storage that includes an incredible amount of information. The introduction of this chapter outlined many of the ways this has impacted the fantasy sport industry. In an effort to understand the importance of and selection of communication avenues strictly for fantasy participation, Ruihley partnered with representatives from the Fantasy Sport Writers Association and administered a survey to 751 fantasy sport participants. One of the key findings from this research was determining what communicative outlets were utilized for fantasy-specific information. Results indicated top outlets as web-based articles, stories, or features (98.1% of participants indicated use), social media (88.0%), and podcasts (51.4%). Respondents were asked to choose only one outlet as their primary outlet for information and web articles, stories, or features ranked first (60.2%) followed by social media (26.5%). Other important findings from this research show fantasy participants seeking out fantasy-relevant information in a myriad of ways including 37.2% for weekly lineup changes, 30.0% for daily fantasy sport league information, and 25.8% for daily lineup changes. When prompted to identify what constitutes high-quality fantasy-relevant information, survey participants responded with top markers being that the information is timely (90.4%) and opinions, projections, or predictions are explained (82.4%). These two findings appropriately support the need and appreciation of digital advancements. In pre-internet days, where fantasy information may be confined to generic newspaper box scores or specialized magazines, neither of the high-quality markers would be perfectly met. Space is limited in a printed outlet and niche magazines were better than general sport coverage, but the process of creating and distributing took weeks or months to complete. For fantasy participants, timeliness is important as injuries, weather, and matchups are fluid in the time leading up to a contest and having space for writers and analysts to explain their prognostications is key when trying to decipher reasoning.

FNTSY Sports Network

Advancements in communication delivery in the fantasy sport community advanced even further in 2014 with the creation of the FNTSY Sports Network. FNTSY Sports Network became available on 30+ North American cable providers including DISH Network and streaming providers like Apple TV, Xbox, Roku, Amazon Fire TV, Klowd TV, Pluto TV, Fubo TV, and Twitch (FNTSY, 2021). This concept blended video, audio, and social media into a streaming and web-based platform solely dedicated to covering fantasy sport activity. The specificity of this outlet to a burgeoning industry was made entirely possible by the digital and technological advancements of streaming video, audio, and platforms. With the touch of a button, a click of the mouse, and all the features that computers, phones, and cameras offer, people were and are able to deliver and receive broadcasts instantly and direct the message to a perfectly segmented consumer base. Time will tell if this type of "all-in" strategy cuts through the litany of media offerings in the sport environment. Even as of late 2020, FNTSY acquired SportsGrid to become an all-encompassing sport media offering, but it appears the fantasy offerings have been pushed aside for sport gambling and betting information as the name and mission of SportsGrid is taking center stage. As a part of that mission, in January 2021, SportsGrid announced the launch of a dedicated channel on SiriusXM satellite radio (SportsGrid, 2021) to expand its overall reach.

Future Directions

The future of the fantasy industry is difficult to predict due to major advancements in gaming, sport technology, legal understandings of sport wagering. Gaming advancements, particularly in North American esport, have accelerated and gained popularity and attention from media, sponsors, and spectators. This bleeds into the world of fantasy in several ways. One way is that sport leagues are taking notice and embracing esport teams and competition. For example, the NBA 2K League is gaining viewership, television partners, and sponsors (Murray, 2020). This then opens the door for fantasy esport. Truly a game within a game, participants are able to "build a fantasy team of your favorite pro players, score based on their in-game performance, compete against your friends and the community" (E1 Fantasy, 2021, para. 1). A second way esport is merging with the world of fantasy is that companies originally aligned with fantasy activity are now incorporating sport and non-sport options into their own offerings.

DraftKings, for example, is now offering fantasy play for games like Call of Duty, Counter-Strike: Global Offensive, League of Legends, Rocket League, and ENASCAR (DraftKings Fantasy Esports, 2021). These advancements could just be the tip of the iceberg as it relates to the future of esport, fantasy sport, and sport gambling and how each interacts with one another.

Technological advancements are allowing more access than ever to spectators and consumers of sport. The future of fantasy could look and feel a lot different as ways to view a game, experiences in a fantasy contest, and interaction with technology all continue to expand and grow. For example, similar to in-game sports wagering, fantasy roster substitutions could become instantaneous as a real game is in progress. This would truly mimic decisions a coach or manager makes in the reality of a sporting contest. This would need a reliable and fast connection to the consumer, a compatible platform, and enhanced technology to accommodate such actions for thousands, if not millions, of participants at one time. Additionally, as video advancements continue, fantasy participants may have the option to only view their players in a personalized live video broadcast (in a traditional view or even a first-person view of the action). Imagine a split-screen filled with players from only one fantasy team. The fantasy participant would never miss a single play from their team. Lastly, with data and analytics so prevalent in the sport environment and the ability to measure just about anything, the scoring systems for fantasy play could expand to include aspects like running speed, missed opportunities, distance covered, kicking height, golf shot distances, or even calories burned!

The fantasy environment has the potential to morph in many different ways over the next several decades. Advancements in DFS, esport, and legalized sport betting have changed the way ancillary sport activities will operate and conduct business. Along with states voting on DFS activity, in 2018, the United States Supreme Court struck down the 1992 Professional and Amateur Sports Protection Act to now allow each state to create and pass its own sports gambling legislation. These major paradigm shifts opened the door for the Fantasy Sports Trade Association, the voice of the fantasy industry, to change its mission and its name to the Fantasy Sports & Gaming Association in 2019 (Fisher, 2019). The association, much like most of the sport industry, understood the culture shift and saw a future in the financial side interests in sporting contests through online, digital, and mobile delivery (Ruihley et al., 2021). In addition to understanding more about the sports-wagering impact on fantasy sport, other areas of exploration can include topics of race, media, and motivations. Future research should seek to understand why fantasy tends to be operated, hosted, discussed, and played by mostly white men. While advancements have been made to include more women in the field, there is still a major lack of racial diversity. With a plethora of sport media outlets, streaming platforms, and mobile applications, fantasy voices are finding space to express their analysis, opinion, and fantasy expertise. Research could explore how and in what ways fantasy is utilizing new and traditional media sources. Lastly, as time progresses and generations take on new roles, it is important to consistently monitor why people participate in the activity and constantly gauge satisfaction and return intentions. Fantasy sport has had consistent growth and participation since the mid-1990s (Fantasy Sports & Gaming Association, 2020), but with more ways for sport fans to engage in ancillary activities, fantasy providers must actively observe their environment.

Conclusions

The popularity and growth of fantasy participation, consumption, and the industry surrounding the activity would not be possible without the digital and technological intervention that has been taking place since the mid-1990s. Advancements in statistical gathering, video, audio, streaming, traditional and social media, and web-based communication outlets have transformed this ancillary sport activity into a thriving industry full of entrepreneurs, writers, developers, and media members. This chapter has outlined the ways that research, consumption, motivation, play, current industry trends, and future considerations all have embraced digital, media, and communicative platforms allowing for the development of better processes, decisions, and products. These platforms have changed the way vital information can be collected, sorted, and analyzed all in an effort to help a niche pastime become a gaming phenomenon. In an ever-changing sporting environment full of technological advancements, legal updates, and information-seeking consumers, the future of the fantasy sport industry may not be defined, but it will be strong.

References

Billings, A. C., & Ruihley, B. J. (2014). *The fantasy sport industry: Games within games*. London: Routledge.

Billings, A. C., Ruihley, B. J., & Yang, Y. (2017). Fantasy gaming on steroids?: Contrasting perceptions of traditional and daily fantasy sport participants. *Communication & Sport*, *5*(6), 732–750.

Brown, N., Billings, A. C., & Ruihley, B. J. (2012). Exploring the change in motivations for fantasy sport participation during the life cycle of a sports fan. *Communication Research Reports*, *29*(4), 333–342.

Business of Fantasy Sport–Guest Interview. (2016). J. Diver, personal communication, March, 15, 2016.

Davis, N. W., & Duncan, M. C. (2006). Sports knowledge is power reinforcing masculine privilege through fantasy sport league participation. *Journal of Sport & Social Issues*, *30*, 244–264.

DraftKings Fantasy Esports. (2021). Fantasy esports. Retrieved from https://www.draftkings.com/esports

Dwyer, B., & Drayer, J. (2010). Fantasy sport consumer segmentation: An investigation into the differing consumption modes of fantasy football participants. *Sport Marketing Quarterly*, *19*(4), 207–216.

Dwyer, B., & Kim, Y. (2011). For love or money: Developing and validating a motivational scale for fantasy sport participation. *Journal of Sport Management*, *25*(1), 70–85.

Dwyer, B., & Weiner, J. (2018). Daily grind: A comparison of causality orientations, emotions, and fantasy sport participation. *Journal of Gambling Studies*, *34*(1), 1–20.

E1 Fantasy. (2021). Fantasy esports is here. Retrieved from https://fantasy.esportsone.com/

ESPN Department of Integrated Media Research (2010, April 15). ESPN top ten list for sport research. Broadcast Education Association Research Symposium, Las Vegas, NV.

Fantasy Sports & Gaming Association (2020). Industry demographics. Retrieved from: https://thefsga.org/industry-demographics

Farquhar, L. K., & Meeds, R. (2007). Types of fantasy sport users and their motivations. *Journal of Computer-Mediated Communication*, *12*, 1208–1228.

Fisher, E. (2019). Fantasy Sports Trade Association rebranding to include gambling. *Sports Business Journal*. Retrieved at: https://www.sportsbusinessdaily.com/Daily/Issues/2019/01/22/Gambling/Fantasy.aspx

FNTSY (2021). Fantasy Sports Network (FNTSY). Retrieved from https://fantasysportsnetwork.com/about_us/

Greene, N. (2017). RedZone is the cause of and solution to all of the NFL's problems. https://slate.com/news-and-politics/2017/09/redzone-is-the-cause-of-and-solution-to-all-of-the-nfl-s-problems.html.

Hur, Y., Ko, Y. J., & Valacich, J. (2007). Motivation and concerns for online sport consumption. *Journal of Sport Management*, *21*(4), 521–539.

Katz, E., Blumler, J. G., & Gurevitch, M. (1973). Uses and gratifications research. *The Public Opinion Quarterly*, *37*(4), 509–523.

Lomax, R. G. (2006). Fantasy sport: History, game types, and research. In A. Raney and J. Bryant (Eds.), *Handbook of Sport and Media* (pp. 383–392), LEA: Mahwah, NJ.

McQuail, D., Blumler, J. G., & Brown, J. R. (1972). The television audience: A revised perspective. In P. Marris and S. Thornham (Eds.) *Sociology of Mass Communications*. Harmondsworth: England.

Murray, P. (2020). With the growth of esports, NBA 2K League is taking off. Retrieved from https://www.forbes.com/sites/patrickmurray/2020/10/11/with-the-growth-of-esports-nba-2k-league-is-taking-off/?sh=59cc106d23b6

Nesbit, T. M., & King, K. A. (2010). The impact of fantasy sports on television viewership. *Journal of Media Economics*, *23*(1), 24–41.

NFL RedZone. (2020). RedZone from NFL Network. Retrieved from https://www.nfl.com/redzone/

Ota, K. (2018, April 9). Personal communication.

Pew Research. (2019). Mobile fact sheet. Retrieved from https://www.pewresearch.org/internet/fact-sheet/mobile/

Rogers, E. M. (2003). *Diffusion of innovations.* Free Press: New York, NY.

Rosengren, K. E. (1974). Uses and gratifications: A paradigm outlined. In J. G. Blumler & E. Katz (Eds.), *The uses of mass communications: Current perspectives on gratifications research* (pp. 269–286). Sage: Beverly Hills, CA.

Roy, D. P., & Goss, B. D. (2007). A conceptual framework of influences on fantasy sports consumption. *Marketing Management Journal, 17*(2), 96–108.

Rubin, A. M. (2002). The uses-and-gratifications perspective of media effects. In J. Bryant & D. Zillmann (Eds.), *Media effects: Advances in theory and research* (2nd ed., pp. 525–548). Erlbaum: Mahwah, NJ.

Rubin, A. M., & Windahl, S. (1986). The uses and dependency model of mass communication. *Critical Studies in Mass Communication, 3*, 184–199.

Ruggiero, T. E. (2000). Uses and gratifications theory in the 21st Century. *Mass Communication & Society, 3*(1), 3–37.

Ruihley, B. J., & Billings, A. C. (2019). Ascending as the fantasy giant: ESPN fantasy, mainstreaming fantasy gaming, and the role of Goliath. In G. Armfield, J. McGuire, & A. Earnheardt (Eds.) *ESPN and the changing sports media landscape.* Peter Lang.

Ruihley, B. J., Billings, A. C., & Rae, C. (2017). Not sport, yet defining sport: The mainstreaming of fantasy sport participation. In Klein, S., (Ed.) *Defining Sport.* Lexington Books: London.

Ruihley, B. J., Billings, A. C., & Buzzelli, N. (2021). A swiftly changing tide: Fantasy sport, gambling, and alternative forms of participation. *Games & Culture, 16*(6), 681–701.

Ruihley, B. J., Buzzelli, N. R., & Billings, A. C. (in press). The fantasy sport context: Altering the uses and gratifications of sport fandom. *Journal of Sports Media.*

Ruihley, B. J., & Hardin, R. L. (2011a). Beyond touchdowns, homeruns, and 3-pointers: An examination of fantasy sport participation motivation. *International Journal of Sport Management and Marketing, 10*(3/4), 232–256.

Ruihley, B. J., & Hardin, R. (2011b). Message board use and the fantasy sport experience. *International Journal of Sport Communication, 4*(2), 233–252.

Ruihley, B. J., & Hardin, R. (2013). Meeting the informational needs of the fantasy sport user. *Journal of Sports Media, 8*(2), 53–80.

Ruihley, B. J., & Huber, S. (2018, April). *Personalizing the fantasy sport experience.* International Association for Communication and Sport: Bloomington, Indiana.

Seo, W. J., & Green, B. C. (2008). Development of the motivation scale for sport online consumption. *Journal of Sport Management, 22*(1), 82–109.

Spinda, J. S. W., & Haridakis, P. M. (2008). Exploring the motives of fantasy sports: A uses and gratifications approach. In L. W. Hugenberg, P. M. Haridakis, & A. C. Earnheardt (Eds.), *Sports mania: Essays on fandom and the media in the 21st Century* (pp. 187–199). McFarland & Company: Jefferson, NC.

SportsGrid. (2021). SportsGrid Radio launches on SiriusXM Channel 204. Retrieved from https://www.sportsgrid.com/press/sportsgrid-radio-launches-on-siriusxm-channel-204/

Suh, Y. I., Lim, C., Kwak, D. H., & Pedersen, P. M. (2010). Examining the psychological factors associated with involvement in fantasy sports: An analysis of participants' motivations and constraints. *International Journal of Sport Management, Recreation and Tourism, 5*, 1–28.

Wann, D. L. (1995). Preliminary validation of the sport fan motivation scale. *Journal of Sport and Social Issues, 19*(4), 377–396.

Weiner, J., & Dwyer, B. (2017). A new player in the game: Examining differences in motives and consumption between traditional, hybrid, and daily fantasy sport users. *Sport Marketing Quarterly, 26*(3), 140–152.

Whitaker, L., & Lovett, I. (2011). Red meat for N.F.L. fans: Football channel sees all. Retrieved from https://www.nytimes.com/2011/09/21/sports/football/red-meat-for-nfl-fans-redzone-channel-sees-all.html

13

Podcasting and Sports Journalism

Galen Clavio and Brian P. Moritz

Podcasting History and Industry

In the first two decades of the 2000s, podcasting grew from a niche media platform used by a few early adopters into one of the fastest-growing and most popular media platforms in the digital and social media world. The following section will detail the history, growth, and state of the podcast industry in the early 2020s, followed by a specific look at podcasting in the sports media world.

A podcast is an episodic online audio program that is downloadable or streamable by users and listened to primarily on a mobile phone or other internet-connected devices. Two key elements of that definition are that podcasts are downloadable or streamable (meaning they can be listened to by individual episodes or binged in the way that a Netflix show is) and that they are episodic by nature. Podcasts can be serialized or standalone episodes. They can mimic the structure of TV shows with seasons, or they can be a continuous run.

The word podcasting itself is an amalgamation of a piece of technology (the iPod) and a media type (broadcasting). The earliest credited use of it was by Ben Hammersley in a 2004 article in the *Guardian* (Radio 4 in Four – *The Man Who Accidentally Invented the Word "podcast"* – BBC Sounds, n.d.):

> I was writing about this new phenomenon of automatically downloading audio programs in about 2004, and it was one of those sort-of last-minute articles that I was writing very very close to the press deadline, and I emailed it over, and with about 10 minutes to go before the presses ran, I get an email back very very quickly from the sub-editor saying, "Brilliant piece, but it's about 20 words to short. Can you just pad it out a little bit?" And so I sort of re-read the piece that I had written and realized that the phenomenon that I was talking about didn't have a name. And I sort of made up this sentence which said something like "But what do we call this new phenomenon?" And I made up some words, and one of them was "audioblogging," and then there was "guerilla media" and then the last one was "podcasting." And I sort of sent that off and everything was fine. And then six or seven months later, I get an email from the Oxford English Dictionary saying "Hey, this podcasting word, where did you get that? Because you're the earliest citation we can find."

DOI: 10.4324/9781003088899-16

> And I said "Well, basically, I made it up. I was really close to a deadline. Sorry." And they said. "Great, it's the Word of the Year."

From Hammersley's deadline inspiration, podcasting has become one of the most important and fastest-growing media platforms of the 21st century. The popularity of podcasts grew steadily throughout the 2000s. In 2006, the first year their audience was measured by Pew, only 11 percent of Americans had ever listened to a podcast. By 2019, that number had grown to 51 percent, and in the same year, 22 percent of Americans had listened to a podcast in the past week (Pew, 2021). In 2018, podcasts produced by National Public Radio were downloaded 7.1 million times (Pew, 2021).

Audience Growth and Revenue

The growth of podcasting as an industry has been one of the constants in media throughout the 2010s and into the 2020s, growing at an annual rate of 16 percent (Edison, 2020). Nielsen (2020) predicted that the audience for podcasting would grow at the rate of 30 percent per year, and the overall podcast audio size could double by 2023. In 2020, more than one-third of all Americans over the age of 12 listened to podcasts weekly (Edison, 2020), an increase of five percent over the previous year. The podcast audience is split nearly 50–50 along gender lines and is majority white (Edison, 2020). Nearly half of Americans between the ages of 12–34 had listened to a podcast in the past month, and 40 percent of Americans between the ages of 35–55 had done so as well. That number drops significantly for users 55 and older (Edison, 2020). In all, Edison's research found that the average podcast user listens to six podcasts a week for an average of 6 hours, 39 minutes.

Podcast listeners are an audience coveted by advertisers because they are local and economically advantaged. According to Nielsen (2020), the average age of a podcast listener is 39 years of age with an average household income of $96,500. The Interactive Advertising Bureau reported that in 2020, US podcasting ad revenues are near $1 billion, and ad rates were predicted to rise by 15 percent in 2020 despite the COVID-19 pandemic that slowed many sectors of the media economy.

Apple officially added a podcasting category to iTunes in 2005, adding 3,000 shows to its online directory and allowing for users to upload their own podcasts, pending editorial and copyright review. That update also added a podcasting label on the main menu of the iPod. Apple introduced a standalone iPhone app for podcasts in 2012.

Podcasts as a Media Product

An important thing to understand about podcasting is that it is a media product, not a media type. There is no one platonic ideal of what a podcast is. In the same way that the term "broadcasting" includes TV game shows, live sporting events, news programs, cartoons, call-in radio, and a hundred other types of programs, the word "podcasting" is an umbrella term that includes multitudes of shows. "Podcasting emerged from a collection of other practices rather than an invented medium" (Berry, 2015, p. 172).

Some of the earliest podcasts, and some of the most popular to this day, are pre-existing radio shows that are published as podcasts. Examples of this include *This American Life* (a co-production of WBEZ radio in Chicago and the Public Radio Exchange and heard on public radio stations), *Radiolab* (a production of WNYC radio in New York), and National Public Radio shows like *Fresh Air* and *Wait, Wait, Don't Tell Me.* As podcasts, these programs are fundamentally the same program that is broadcast on over-the-air radio. For these shows, the podcast is a different distribution platform (Berry, 2015).

As of 2020, there were more than 1.5 million different podcast series and 34 million individual episodes (Winn, 2021). Podcast metrics are notoriously difficult to come by, as podcasts are ranked not by subscribers but by individual episode downloads. In the November 2020 rankings from Podtrac, *The Daily* from *The New York Times* was the most-downloaded podcast, with *NPR News Now* and *Up First* from *NPR* coming in second and third, respectively. *The Ben Shapiro Show* from the *Daily Wire* was fourth, and *This American Life* rounded out the top five. Given that a US presidential election was held that month, it is perhaps no surprise that the top-four podcasts were politically focused.

Serial and The Long Tail of Podcasts

Podcasting has been around since the mid-00s and was initially popular in the tech community and among comedians, with well-known entertainers Marc Maron and Kevin Smith serving as popular early adopters of podcasting as a creative form. However, it was the 2014 release of the *Serial* podcast that "helped jumpstart the podcast craze of the 2010s" (Dockterman, 2017). Serial, a production of This American Life, tracked host Sarah Koenig's reporting into the 1999 murder of Baltimore teenager Ha Mihn Lee, the arrest and conviction of Adnan Syed for the crime, and the investigation into whether or not Syed actually committed the crime. The podcast was downloaded 80 million times and became a legitimate pop-culture phenomenon, to the point that it was parodied on Saturday Night Live. Serial's success is widely credited with making podcasts popular on a larger scale (Mallenbaum, 2015). "Serial represented a key moment for podcasting, moving it from a niche activity to a mainstream media platform" (Berry, 2015, p. 171). Berry reported that nearly a third of Serial's listeners discovered the series after it was released in its entirety, which researchers have interpreted as evidence of podcasts' long-term viability:

> The slow-burning success of these programs reflects the belief by many that podcasts have a "long tail," referring to the idea that a larger proportion of the population exists in the tail of a probability distribution than what is normally seen in a distribution. … After an initial wave of popularity, a podcast maintains its high monthly download numbers as new listeners discover the podcast, spurred by favorable reviews from friends or influencers on social media and/or an increase in available time to give the podcast a listen.
>
> *(Crider, 2019, p. 3)*

In addition to the popularity of Serial, technological improvements led to the podcast boom. Apple introduced a standalone Podcasts app in 2012 (breaking it out of iTunes) and created automatic wireless downloading of new podcast episodes. In addition, improvements to car stereo systems made it easier to connect smartphones and Bluetooth audio players, and it's no surprise that 22 percent of all podcast listening happens in cars (Winn, 2021). In short, podcasts became a thing in the culture at the same time as it became easier for people to find, subscribe and listen to them.

> Podcasting has been shown to be successful not only because of the intimate properties of audio media, but also because their on-demand nature feeds perfectly into the binge-consuming habits of listeners accustomed to video services like Netflix and Hulu. Podcasts add subscription and mobility to audio content, creating an audience that has committed to

receiving consistently updated content that they can enjoy at their leisure through a variety of different devices.

(Crider, 2019, p. 2)

While podcasting has long been associated with Apple, iPhones, and the Mac (the name, after all, came from an Apple product), music streaming giant Spotify has emerged as a major player in the podcasting world. (more on that later in this chapter). The continued popularity of podcasts in the late 2010s led to international music streaming giant Spotify fully integrating podcasts into their platform. Spotify added a podcast search function and encouraged podcasts to distribute their shows to the platform. The company announced plans to invest $500 million in its podcasting business (Kafka, 2019) and purchased major podcast publishers Gimlet Media and Parcast. In 2020, Spotify completed a surprise purchase of The Ringer, perhaps best known for former ESPN personality Bill Simmons' popular podcasting series. This served as a harbinger for Spotify's larger leap into podcasting as a whole, which included purchasing and distributing comedian Joe Rogan's highly successful podcast in 2020 (Carman, 2020; Steele, 2020) for a reported $100 million, acquiring app-based podcast producing company Anchor, and ultimately rolling out an ability to have audiences monetarily subscribe to podcasts that are created and distributed within the Spotify ecosystem (Carman, 2021).

The Sports Podcasting Landscape

According to iTunes ratings, in 2018 the most popular category of podcasts was comedy, a genre that included early adopters like Maron, as well as popular shows like Rogan. Following this category were educational podcasts and news podcasts. The fourth most popular podcast topic was sports.

With its rabid collective fan bases and a media environment built on the discussion/argument genre of sports talk radio and debate shows on ESPN, sports are a natural fit for podcasting. The 2018 ratings show that Pardon my Take, Fantasy Focus Football, and 30-for-30 accounted for 27 percent of the podcasting total audience (Desjardins, 2018).

In the November 2020 ratings from Podtrac (2020), two sports shows were among the top-20 overall – Call Her Daddy and Pardon My Take, both published by Barstool Sports. ESPN/ABC produce 102 podcasts and ranked fifth among podcast publishers with nearly 8.4 million unique downloads. Barstool Sports ranked seventh overall with 7.3 million downloads in the United States with half as many shows as ESPN and ABC. The Bill Simmons Podcast on The Ringer has consistently ranked in the Top 50 in audience size among all podcasts (Edison Research, 2021).

Similar to the rest of the podcasting genres, many early sports podcasts were essentially re-broadcasts of previously aired shows, either from TV or radio. Examples of this include an audio version of ESPN's Pardon The Interruption television program hosted by Tony Kornheiser and Michael Wilbon, an audio version of ESPN's First Take hosted by Stephen A. Smith and Max Kellerman, The Dan LeBatard Show with Stugotz, the Paul Finebaum show. In some cases, such as with The Dan Patrick Show, the podcast versions of the show include smaller segments that are released as independent pieces, while in other cases the full two or three hours of the show is released as one file.

In talking about sports podcasting, two names stand above all others in the development of the platform – Bill Simmons and Barstool Sports. ESPN has had success in podcasting, including its numerous radio and TV shows described above and bringing its 30-for-30 documentary series to the platform, but the success of ESPN's podcasts is built on decades of institutional success and aggressive cross-platform marketing and utilization of existing media stars and personalities. Simmons' success with The Ringer and Barstool Sports' success has been built largely on their own.

Simmons, whose career rise from blogger in Boston to a true media mogul is the stuff of internet sports legend, was an early adopter in the podcasting world. When Simmons was still serving primarily as a writer and columnist for ESPN's Page 2 in the mid-00s, he began hosting a new podcast called The BS Report. The show gained a significant amount of independent momentum thanks to its personal style, broad array of guests from both inside and outside the sports industry, and integration of non-sports elements of pop culture. A key element of the show's success was that it was conceived and executed as a podcast first and foremost, rather than simply being a downloadable audio version of a television program or radio show.

Simmons' ESPN podcast gained notoriety when he used the platform to call NFL commissioner Roger Goodell a liar, a move that led to his being fired from ESPN (Sandomir, 2015) and the creation of The Ringer, a website that featured a podcast network at the core of its business model. The BS Report name stayed with ESPN, but the rebranded show, titled The Bill Simmons Podcast, served as The Ringer Podcast Network's flagship show. In 2017, Time Magazine listed the show as one of its 50 essential podcasts, which was notable as it was the only sports podcast on that list. By 2020, The Ringer Podcast network was producing more than 30 regular podcasts (Spangler, 2020). As mentioned in the previous section of this chapter, Spotify bought The Ringer in 2020 as part of its buying spree of podcast networks, paying $196 million (US) for the company (Spangler, 2020).

Barstool Sports, the controversial sports site founded by Dave Portnoy in 2003 as a free gambling tip sheet, rode the waves of a devoted fan base and increasing interest in podcasting to a $450 million purchase by Penn National Gaming in early 2020 (Kafka, 2020). Barstool Sports produces more than 30 unique shows, and in 2019 was the No. 6 rated podcast producer in the world, ranked higher than ESPN in the same category. Thanks in large part to the Pardon My Take podcast, which often exceeds two million downloads per episode (Weber, 2017), more than a third of Barstool Sports' revenue in 2019 came directly from podcasts (Spangler, 2019). Call Her Daddy, which Variety called "a raunchy sex talk show" (Spangler 2019), was the platform's highest-rated podcast in November 2020 and the ninth-highest-rated overall podcast (Podtrac, 2020).

> For Barstool, podcasting is a very high-margin business and far more cost-effective than TV production … "In television, you're working toward someone else's definition of what's funny or what's allowed. With podcasts, you're getting graded on by the fans … We control our own destiny."
>
> *(Spangler, 2019)*

Podcasts and Sports Entities

One interesting aspect of the sports podcast world is how sports organizations have chosen to use the platform. Throughout the 2000s, team websites and social media feeds became sources of news, videos, GIFS, highlights, and other content for fans. However, podcasting has yet to become as deeply rooted within the sports industry as other forms of content.

A search of official team websites shows that a majority of the teams in the four major North American sports leagues have a podcast, though it varies greatly by sport. All 32 NFL teams have at least one official podcast, and the NFL itself produces seven podcasts. Major League Baseball's media arm, MLB Advanced Media, produces nine podcasts league-wide, and all 30 MLB teams have at least one official podcast. But things are very different in the NBA and NHL. The NBA produces two league-wide podcasts, and only nine of the 30 franchises have podcasts that are actively produced. In the NHL, 14 of the 31 teams in 2020 had active podcasts, while the league produced eight podcasts. It is interesting to note that there are many NBA and NHL teams that produced podcasts in the past (dating back as far as 2009) but stopped producing them somewhere along the line.

It is also noteworthy that although there are at least 85 official team podcasts (as of 2020), they rarely (if ever) come up in a search on Apple podcasts. On its sports page, Apple has created podcast collections by sport and by league, and the podcasts listed on these pages are overwhelming independent podcasts from ESPN, Barstool, The Ringer, SB Nation, and other networks not affiliated with leagues or teams. The easiest way to find sports teams' podcasts is by looking on their official websites, rather than a podcast platform. When one of the authors of this chapter searched for Los Angeles Kings podcasts on Apple, the first six results were podcasts about the Los Angeles Lakers. While this is clearly anecdotal evidence and nothing more, it does at least suggest that teams and leagues have yielded the podcasting space to independent media outlets as of the time of writing.

In contrast, athletes and coaches have started utilizing the podcasting space to develop their own brands and extend their media reach. Both Yahoo Sports and The Ringer Podcast Network served as a host for NBA guard J.J. Redick's podcast, which he eventually moved to his own company in late 2020 (Contes, 2020). Redick's podcast, though relatively small in audience size, demonstrated the power that the medium can have for sports figures who are interested in moderating their image. Listener comments on episodes of Redick's podcast have indicated that people grew to like Redick as a person after hearing him speak, despite not having liked him previously as a player (Cacciola, 2020). Redick has utilized the podcast to provide a platform for both himself and his guests to be themselves, and a *New York Times* profile on Redick as a podcaster noted that "He wants his guests to open up. In the process, he has done the same" (Cacciola, 2020). Kevin Durant, the highly successful but somewhat mercurial NBA superstar, has appeared on Bill Simmons' podcast numerous times and given unusually wide-ranging and deep interviews when compared to what he has provided traditional media outlets and figures during the latter stages of his career.

Former NFL punter Pat McAfee started eyeing a career in sports media while still playing football and parlayed some successful media content forays into a full-time position with Barstool Sports upon his retirement from the league. The centerpiece of McAfee's position with Barstool was a combination of podcasting and video appearances, and McAfee has continued to utilize podcasting as his primary avenue for developing his brand, even after leaving Barstool (Hussey & Keefer, 2018) and forming his own podcasting entity.

Steve Kerr, head coach of the NBA's Golden State Warriors, and Pete Carroll, head coach of the NFL's Seattle Seahawks, joined forces and worked with The Ringer to record a podcast series called Flying Coach. This show, which was launched during the 2020 COVID pandemic, existed in a 10-episode arc and featured a combination of the two coaches discussing their thoughts on leadership in coaching and sports, their respective careers, and interacting with guests from both inside and outside the sports world. These guests included fellow active coaches such as Doc Rivers and Gregg Popovich, as well as political figures like the United States Senator Cory Booker and popular authors such as Michal Lewis.

The Modern Podcasting Environment

The popularity of podcasting lies in part with the ease by which podcasts can be created, produced, and distributed. Hobbyists and part-time podcasters are able to execute their creative visions and build direct connections with audiences, operating side-by-side with professional media organizations in the same digital spaces. Digital technology has continued to make the process of podcasting easier for people to engage in, and that has led to the huge roster of podcasts that currently exist across most sports marketplaces.

Many sports podcasts start off with an idea for a show and at least one person enthusiastic enough to transform that idea into something tangible. The list of sports media podcast concepts is vast and covers a spectrum of ideas that includes fan commentary on specific team performances, interview-based podcasts, shows that maintain a broader focus on a whole sports league, highly technical shows that focus on niche areas like sports betting or sports analytics, and many more.

Starting Out in Sports Podcasting

Once a podcaster has an idea for a show, the next step is recording and producing that show. Hobbyists and other non-professional podcasters have a remarkable array of tools at their command for creating podcasts, and at a relatively low level of expense.

Most beginning podcasters start with acquiring a microphone, headset, and audio interface, which are used in combination with computer software to execute the recording process. Many major retailers offer starter podcasting bundles that contain all of these items, allowing the aspiring podcaster to simply plug things in and get started for a reasonable amount of money. As podcasters continue in the field, they have a myriad of different equipment options to choose from, and as with most hobbies, the costs can range from quite affordable to thousands of dollars.

Podcast Planning and Podcast Typographies

Proper podcasting requires a good amount of planning and evaluation ahead of time. Prior to the launch of any podcast, it is advisable that the creator of the show think of the following items:

- What is the podcast about? Choosing a topic for the podcast is very important because all podcasts operate in an episodic manner, with multiple shows focused on a particular area. The creator of the podcast needs to conceive of the podcast's topic, its limitations, and how many episodes it will run for. In some cases, such as a show that focuses on a particular sports team, the number of episodes may be indefinite. For other shows, such as those that are focusing on a particular story or event, it may be better to have a set number of shows for the whole run of the podcast.
- Who is the primary audience? Launching a podcast without thinking about the audience is inadvisable, especially with the podcasting field becoming consistently more crowded. Having a clearly identified target audience in mind helps with the creation of the podcast's content, while also assisting with the decision-making process of marketing the podcast.
- What elements will the podcast include? Should the show be focused on one or two people providing commentary and analysis on an area of expertise? Do you want to focus it to be on interviews with professionals? Can you create show segments that are consistent across episodes and provide the audience with something to look forward to?

Podcasts vary quite a bit in the personnel required to properly record one. Some podcasts work perfectly well with a single host, while others work best with two, three, or more individuals talking. There is no one proper way to approach creating a podcast, but it is important that the methodology used be appropriate for the subject matter and the capacities of those creating it.

There is no consensus list of the types or categories of podcasts, as the medium continues to change with the introduction of new approaches and ideas. However, within sports podcasting it is generally found that most podcasts fit into one of the following five typologies:

- *Conversational Podcasts*: These podcasts involve two or more regular hosts and panelists engaging in an extended conversation about the show topic. The bulk of these types of shows are generally not scripted, although they may contain some pre-written elements. While similar in nature to Interview Podcasts, this typology differs because the voices heard tend to be consistent from episode to episode.
- *Interview Podcasts*: The central focus of these podcasts is on interviewing a notable figure within the industry or area that the podcast's topic focuses on. In sports, this often means interviewing an athlete, coach, traditional media member, or another notable podcaster that has insights into the area. These podcasts tend to start with some expository dialog from the host(s), before transitioning to the interview proper, often consisting of a back-and-forth between the host and the interviewee on a variety of topics.
- *Repurposed Content Podcasts*: As discussed earlier, repurposed content is still very popular in the podcasting world, as it requires minimal production time and allows for the ephemeral nature of radio or television shows to be turned into something that can be consumed by a wider audience. Repurposed content shows are generally audio tracks taken directly from live shows, often with commercials and in-the-moment items taken out.
- *Scripted Podcasts*: These shows are almost entirely pre-written, with the host(s) reading off of a script and focusing on particular topics. The ESPN Daily podcast is a good example of this type of show, with a 20–30 minute array of stories scripted and delivered by the host, accompanied by a very professional-sounding mix of music and sound bytes.
- *Storytelling Podcasts*: These are generally multi-episode arcs of podcasts that focus on a particular theme or topic, feature a small number of reporters and producers working specifically on the topic at hand, and have a finite number of episodes. These podcasts are sometimes referred to as episodic podcasts, but the term *storytelling podcasts* does a better job of capturing their place within the podcasting landscape. In some cases, such as ESPN's 30-for-30 podcasts, the show will take a deep dive into a particular topic, then move on to a different topic in the next episode. Others have more finite arcs as a series, such as *American Fiasco*, the 11-episode podcast on the failure of the US Men's National Soccer team in the 1998 World Cup which was reported and voiced by *Men In Blazers* co-host Roger Bennett. Much like the scripted podcast typology, these podcasts tend to be very heavily produced, with music, quotations, sound effects, and other items woven into the soundscape.

Of course, even with these typologies, many podcasts will mix and match what they do, depending on what is needed for a given day. Sports podcasts will often alternate between multiple typologies over the arc of a few months, such as switching between conversational and interview podcast types as needed.

Distributing Podcasts

Once the topic of the show is settled and the episodes are being recorded, the next step is figuring out how to get the show out to the audience. This is a process that has become significantly easier over the lifespan of the podcasting genre.

The early days of podcasting required a good amount of technical know-how from the podcaster, as syndication feeds and hosting often had to be arranged manually due to a lack of existing infrastructure. This process eventually got slightly easier as open-source platforms like WordPress offered hosting and distribution of podcasts through third-party applications, and companies like Libsyn offered paid hosting of podcasts without having to maintain a separate website.

Since the dawn of the 2020s, podcast hosting and distribution has become far more automated and the difficulty curve for distribution has been eased. Companies such as Spreaker offer reasonably priced annual hosting plans for podcasts, including free storage and automatic distribution to popular distribution services such as Apple Podcasts, Spotify, and Amazon Music. Spotify's integration with Anchor allows podcasters to record and distribute directly through an app and allows audiences the ability to subscribe to those podcasts directly (Carman, 2021). These and other features have made the business and logistics sides of podcasting much more achievable for the aspiring podcaster.

Building a Podcast Audience

While it is much easier now for people to create and distribute podcasts, it is arguably much harder to build an audience. This is largely due to the huge number of existent podcasts that are out there, a number that has been said to exceed 2 million individual shows and over 48 million episodes as of 2021 (Winn, 2021). Additionally, existing media giants use their market power and brand recognition to attract audiences to their podcasts (Bassam, 2020). This leaves the aspiring podcaster with a difficult set of circumstances, as attracting an audience requires some degree of marketability and recognition.

For many sports podcasters, the answer comes in leveraging the power of social networks to reach audiences interested in the sports topics they cover. Organically building audiences on social media can take a long time and only yield incremental progress in the early stages, but it is still the most reliable way for a non-corporate podcasting entity to turn audiences on to the existence of their shows.

Each social network has some aspect of its architecture that can positively contribute to audience growth and show awareness. Twitter's open network design, ability to embed media, and utilization of topically-focused hashtags make it among the most effective venues for publicizing podcasts to larger audiences. A podcast publisher can promote a podcast episode on a sports team via a tweet, using the hashtag(s) popular among fans and media, and that makes the show potentially visible to all users who are monitoring that hashtag. Likes and retweets of the original promotional tweet can lead to increased reach and broader engagement with audiences, including the ability of audiences to respond with feedback or questions about the show.

Facebook's network design is not as open as Twitter's, but Facebook does contain groups and communities which are built around areas of topical focus, including sports teams and leagues. Podcasters can use their own open Facebook groups to publish podcasts, then share those published episodes to Facebook groups for fans of the team or sport that the show is about. These Facebook groups are often full of highly identified fans who are actively seeking additional content about their interests.

Instagram has become a popular network for promoting podcasts since the start of the 2020s. Companies like The Ringer or ESPN will include short snippets of podcasts on Instagram, serving as previews of the content of a particular episode or show. These snippets are used as an enticement for audiences to access the whole episode and can be used by smaller media entities or independent podcasters as well. YouTube can be used for a similar purpose, which provides the podcaster access to a completely new algorithm and potentially new listeners.

The Future of Sports Podcasting

The continued growth of sports podcasting in both popularity and revenue means that the 2020s and beyond could be an exciting and curious time for podcasters and sports media companies. Although podcasts have been around for a while, the format is still relatively nascent, which means that podcasting as a form of communication is likely to undergo continuous change.

Podcasting maintains several advantages over sports radio as a consumer product. It is comparatively unrestricted in terms of format compared to radio, with most terrestrial radio stations having to adhere to a broadcast clock that requires breaks every few minutes for commercials or non-sports content. As such, the conversation tends to be more free-flowing on podcasts, and guests who might not be able to appear during a narrow three-hour window of a radio program are often able to engage with a podcast host because of the flexibility that podcasting provides.

Podcasts also allow for a different type of targeted advertising, one backed by direct consumer metrics and able to cover large geographic areas without the constraints of having to syndicate programming to radio stations across a variety of markets. The primary downside of podcasting compared to traditional radio is that consumers have to make active choices in their listening. Unlike the traditional radio program that can be "stumbled upon" by someone flipping through the channels in their car, sports podcasts have to be actively searched for by the consumer.

The continued growth of podcasting as a business seems to indicate that podcasts are going to be commercially viable as the industry moves forward. The level of commercial viability is still yet to be fully understood. Podcast revenues grow on average every year, and by 2024 are projected to have global revenues of over $3 billion and an estimated global audience of over 1.5 billion listeners (InsideRadio, 2020). It is important to note that the projected number is still dwarfed by the amount of revenue generated by traditional radio, which is projected to be approximately $18 billion in 2024 (InsideRadio, 2020). So while podcasting represents a rapidly growing piece of the media revenue pie, it is still quite small compared to its more traditional content cousins. Will media companies choose to throw more resources at podcasting due to its potential growth, or will we see that growth start to tail off?

The integration of social networks and other media forms into audio podcasting is another area to consider. As mentioned earlier, some podcast producers have started to utilize video on Instagram and other social networks to promote podcasts, and in some cases, podcasts have a live video stream built in to the show presentation. With the converged digital nature of media and the short distance between doing a podcast and doing a live video on social media, it would not be surprising for many podcasts to include a built-in video element, a "live show" feel akin to traditional radio, or both.

Conclusion

Podcasting has become an accepted and celebrated part of the sports media ecosystem over the past 15 years. The freedom of expression within the podcast format, combined with the flexibility of digital publishing, has allowed individuals to create shows that capture the imagination of sports fans and audiences, and filling gaps in media content that traditional media offered.

The development of sports podcasts as a content type and a format has been slow, and the commercial prospects of podcasting only started to hit their stride at the end of the 2010s.

Traditional sports media companies have utilized podcasts to extend their brands and capitalize more fully on their talent, while new companies have used podcasting as a primary content source to develop their business models and attract audiences.

The future of podcasting in sports is intriguing, as technological advancements make the recording and delivery of shows easier, audiences grow more technically adept, and young consumers used to podcasting and digital delivery replace older consumers used to traditional broadcast delivery. If sports podcasting were an episodic series, we would find ourselves on episode three or four as of the time of this writing, with many more to come.

References

Bassam, T. (2020, November 12). Casting a wide net: The business of sports podcasting. *SportsPro Media*. Retrieved from https://www.sportspromedia.com/from-the-magazine/spotify-podcast-blue-wire-kleiman-anfield-wrap-totally-football-show

Berry, R. (2015). A golden age of podcasting? Evaluating serial in the context of podcast histories. *Journal of Radio & Audio Media, 22*(2), 170–178. Communication & Mass Media Complete.

Cacciola, S. (2020, August 3). After 100 Podcasts, JJ Redick Widens His Range. *The New York Times*. Retrieved from https://www.nytimes.com/2020/08/03/sports/jj-redick-podcast.html

Carman, A. (2020, May 21). The podcasting world is now Spotify versus anybody else. *The Verge*. Retrieved from https://www.theverge.com/21265005/spotify-joe-rogan-experience-podcast-deal-apple-gimlet-media-ringer

Carman, A. (2021, April 27). Spotify launches podcast subscriptions, but you can't subscribe in-app. *The Verge*. Retrieved from https://www.theverge.com/2021/4/27/22404273/spotify-podcast-subscriptions-monetize-subscriber-shows

Contes, B. (2020, August 6). JJ Redick leaves The Ringer, launching new podcast company. *Barrett Sports Media*. Retrieved from https://barrettsportsmedia.com/2020/08/06/jj-redick-leaves-the-ringer-launching-new-podcast-company/

Crider, D. (2019). Community voices on demand: An assessment of local podcasting. Paper presented at the Broadcast Education Association Convention in Las Vegas.

Desjardins, J. (2018, February 3). The podcasting Boom explained. *Visual Capitalist*. https://www.visualcapitalist.com/podcasting-boom-explained-infographic/

Dockterman, E. (2017, March 30). The 50 best podcasts right now. *Time*. https://time.com/4709592/best-podcasts-2017/

Edison. (2017, July 6). 2020 Podcast stats & facts (New Research From Oct 2020). *Podcast Insights®*. https://www.podcastinsights.com/podcast-statistics/

Edison. (2020, March 19). The infinite dial 2020. *Edison Research*. https://www.edisonresearch.com/the-infinite-dial-2020/

Edison. (2021, February 9). The Top 50 most listened to U.S. podcasts of 2020. *Edison Research*. Retrieved from https://www.edisonresearch.com/the-top-50-most-listened-to-u-s-podcasts-of-2020/

Edison Research (2021, November 16). The top 50 most listened to podcasts in the U.S. https://www.edisonresearch.com/the-top-50-most-listened-to-podcasts-in-the-u-s-q3-2021/?utm_source=podnews.net&utm_mediu m=web&utm_campaign=podnews.net:2021-11-17

Goldberg, K. (2018, February 14). The serial effect: How True crime came to dominate podcasts. *Discover the Best Podcasts | Discover Pods*. https://discoverpods.com/serial-effect-true-crime-dominate-podcasts/

Hussey, A. & Keefer, Z. (2018, August 31). *Indy Star*. Retrieved from https://www.indystar.com/story/sports/2018/08/31/former-colts-punter-pat-mcafee-leaving-barstool-sports/1159521002/

Inside Radio (2020, October 12). PwC: Podcast ad revenue of $800 million in 2020 with a doubling by 2024. *Inside Radio*. Retrieved from http://www.insideradio.com/free/pwc-podcast-ad-revenue-of-800-million-in-2020-with-a-doubling-by-2024/article_2ffd4f2a-0c51-11eb-8daa-1317a1c8f84b.html

Kafka, P. (2019, February 6). Spotify has bought two podcast startups and it wants to buy more. *Vox*. https://www.vox.com/2019/2/6/18213456/spotify-podcast-gimlet-anchor-q4-results

Kafka, P. (2020, January 29). A casino company is buying Barstool Sports in a $450 million deal. *Vox*. https://www.vox.com/recode/2020/1/29/21113130/barstool-sports-penn-national-deal-dave-portnoy-chernin

Mallenbaum, C. (2015). The "Serial effect" hasn't worn off. *USA TODAY*. https://www.usatoday.com/story/life/2015/04/13/serial-podcast-undisclosed/25501075/

Nielsen. (n.d.). Nielsen at podcast movement 2020: Opportunities in a skyrocketing industry. Retrieved December 17, 2020, from https://www.nielsen.com/us/en/news-center/2020/nielsen-at-podcast-movement-2020-opportunities-in-a-skyrocketing-industry

Nielsen (2020). Podcast Content is Growing Audio Engagement. The Neilsen Company. https://www.nielsen.com/insights/20 20/podcast-content-is-growing-audio-engagement/

Pew Research Center (2021, June 29). Audio and Podcasting Fact Sheet. Pew Research Center. https://www.pewresearch.or g/journalism/fact-sheet/audio-and-podcasting/

Podtrac. (2020). Top podcasts. *Podtrac*. http://analytics.podtrac.com/podcast-rankings

Sandomir, R. (2015). ESPN is splitting with Bill Simmons, who offers an uncharacteristic word count: Zero—The New York Times. *New York Times*. https://www.nytimes.com/2015/05/09/sports/bill-simmons-and-espn-are-parting-ways.html

Spangler, T. (2020, February 12). Spotify paying up to $196 million in cash for Bill Simmons' The Ringer—Variety. *Variety*. https://variety.com/2020/digital/news/spotify-acquires-the-ringer-196-million-cash-bill-simmons-1203502471/

Spangler, T., & Spangler, T. (2019, August 20). For barstool sports, podcasts are now around one-third of revenue. *Variety*. https://variety.com/2019/digital/news/barstool-sports-podcast-revenue-1203305912/

Steele, A. (2020, May 19). WSJ News Exclusive | Spotify strikes podcast deal with Joe Rogan worth more than $100 million. *Wall Street Journal*. https://www.wsj.com/articles/spotify-strikes-exclusive-podcast-deal-with-joe-rogan-11589913814

Weber, J. (2017, June 12). How "Pardon My Take" took over sports podcasting. *Awful Announcing*. https://awfulannouncing.com/online-outlets/pardon-take-took-sports-podcasting.html

Winn, R. (2021, April 10). 2021 podcast stats & facts (new research from Jan 2021). *Podcast Insights®*. https://www.podcastinsights.com/podcast-statistics/

14

Evolution of Live Streaming

Sarah Wymer and Michael L. Naraine

Introduction

The development of digital media has provided the opportunity to cultivate and strengthen fan relationships by providing real-time access to sport team and athletes' personal and professional lives, and as such has reshaped the communication and interaction process (Williams & Chinn, 2010). Most recently, the emergence of live streaming has provided sport organizations and athletes with a new tool to connect with fans. Live streaming contains two sub-categories: Social Live Streaming Services (SLSS) and Over-the-top (OTT) services. Although both are characterized by their ability to transmit online visual media by simultaneously recording and broadcasting in real-time, there are differences in their capabilities, transmission, and engagement. Notably, SLSS is integrated within an existing social media platform and free access, whereas OTT is typically integrated through subscription service and broadcast via a standalone digital application.

For instance, professional sport leagues such as the National Football League (NFL) and Major League Baseball (MLB) have partnered with OTT technology companies such as Amazon and Twitch to leverage the power of live streaming. Likewise, professional athletes such as Stephen Curry, Carmelo Anthony, Odell Beckham Jr., and Serena Williams and have turned to SLSS to broadcast their own content, often featuring interviews with other notable figures or providing a higher level of intimate personal access to fans. Of note, in Australia, Rugby Australia (RA), Queensland Rugby League (QRL), and New South Wales Rugby League (NSWRL) have all recently announced digital strategies that embrace a live streaming focus. For example, NSWRL revealed the launch of NSWRL TV, which will be hosted on Facebook Live, providing global audiences real-time access to 100 junior and senior games, across all competitions in 2021 (Antoniadis, 2021).

We have seen a recent emergence and emphasis on live streaming disrupting traditional television broadcast agreements (Hutchins et al., 2019; Kim & Kim, 2020), such as Rugby Australia's partnership with Stan Sport (Hytner, 2020) worth over $100 million AUD, by-passing diminishing subscription models and instead offering a higher level of accessibility and coverage for a shifting audience that demand lower fees and commitments. However, we have also witnessed the use of live streaming for the purpose of fan engagement outside of the "main game" through supplementary content in pre- and post-game periods (Naraine et al., 2019).

DOI: 10.4324/9781003088899-17

The potential of live streaming imposes a strategic change in digital marketing, as sport organizations seek to stay relevant with the distribution, transmission, and consumption of sport (Hutchins et al., 2019). Yet, stakeholders are potentially hesitant to include live streaming within their digital strategy due to uncertainty and the concept of "real-time." The inclusion of live streaming disrupts what was previously a highly curated, cultivated, and edited digital strategy that may provide a heightened level of risk or ethical and legal concerns. Further, live streaming frequently receives the focus of negative media attention due to the raw and immediate characteristics showcasing frightening unmoderated content such as a terrorist attack in Christchurch, New Zealand, and sexual abuse or self-harm incidents.

Although the previously highlighted concerns are crucial to consider, the advancement of SLSS and OTT is an exciting prospect for the sport industry, and as such, leveraging live streaming requires attentive consideration of a digital strategy that carefully understands fans' needs, delivery purpose, and resource management. The evolution of live streaming (SLSS and OTT) within sport has an appealing potential to reach and engage new and existing audiences. Though researchers have determined SM to be an effective tool for fan engagement (Mastromartino & Naraine, 2021; Naraine et al., 2019; Vale & Fernandes, 2018; Yoshida et al., 2014), we suggest live streaming has altered the fan engagement process that has been theorized through traditional digital media tools (i.e., Wymer et al., 2021), and as such, we argue that the inclusion of live streaming within digital strategies provide a unique consideration in comparison to other types of content such as a photo or native video. In contrast to other purposefully considered content, live streaming may provide unique challenges and unique engagement through prospective sense of personal interactivity and sociality to build digital communities which is an important regard for sport organizations and athletes (Popp & Woratschek, 2016).

As such, this chapter aims to provide theoretical understanding toward defining and theorizing live streaming in sport management for the purpose of connecting fans with athletes and sport teams and how content may influence levels of engagement.

In the first section, we provide an overview of the key components and characteristics of live streaming for the purpose of fan engagement including the presentation and comparison of two distinct tools. In the second section, building on the overview of characteristics and dimensions, we examine the incorporation of athlete and organizational-driven live streaming fan engagement opportunities, focusing on the implementation, delivery, and management of this specific content. We also provide a case example of the Sydney Swans of the Australian Football League (AFL) and their partnership with a mental health organization, the Black Dog Institute, to explore this application from an athlete and sport organization perspective. In the third section, we examine the changing shift and consideration of existing fan-engagement models that have been influenced by the implementation of live streaming, considering key challenges and opportunities. We conclude this chapter with a consideration of future direction which may have an influence on the management and delivery of live streaming for sport organizations and athletes.

The Growth of Live Streaming

Live streaming has the potential to become a driver and disruptor in sports consumption with 99% growth between April 2019 and April 2020 and an expected value of 184.27 billion USD by 2027 (Yanev, 2020). The COVID-19 pandemic has accelerated consumer behaviors that are defining a new era of sport consumption. In the United States, streaming consumption accounts for 68% of television viewing, compared to 28% of traditional television (Zurich, 2021). Consequently, the Trade Desk (2021) reported by the end of 2021, 27% of US cable television subscriptions will be canceled. This trend is not unique to North American markets, with Australia declining by 15% in

2020 (Myer, 2020). While we acknowledge that live streaming is not the exclusive reason behind shifting consumption of television, we have seen a steady increase of major sport events available via streaming services that provide more convenient, affordable, and accessible opportunities for sport fans (e.g., Super Rugby, ATP Tennis, NFL, MLB).

In addition, the personalization capabilities of live streaming tools are driving its growth. Rather than replicating television coverage of the "main game," there are now additional opportunities to reach new markets and focus on fan engagement by generating immersive and interactive experiences for fans to engage with other fans, their favorite athletes and teams. One notable example is *Thursday Night Football* (NFL) partnership with Amazon Prime. Through their Twitch channel, fans can no longer just simply watch the game, but now have access to live chat, custom extensions with statistics, polls and custom emoticons.

At the forefront of live streaming, capabilities are the consideration for athletes and sport teams to consider unique opportunities to become broadcasters outside of game coverage rather than relying on league-dominated and controlled traditional television exposure. Digital TV Europe (2019) found that live streaming is fueled by fans' demand for complimentary content over and beyond what is traditionally supplied by traditional television broadcasters. The opportunities for this type of content are an important consideration to enhance access for fans alongside traditional sport coverage and provide innovative consideration for both sport teams and athletes to create, develop and maintain fan relationships (Kim & Kim, 2020). The remainder of this section will aim to define and conceptualize the differences in strategy and content delivery for the purpose of fan engagement from two unique live streaming tools (1) SLSS and (2) OTT.

Characterizing Live Streaming

The overarching capabilities of live streaming encompass the digital technologies that allow anyone the ability to transmit online media by simultaneously recording and broadcasting in real-time. The concept of "real-time" is the defining feature of live streaming, in comparison to "Video-on-Demand" (VOD) which allows viewers the opportunity to watch at any suitable time (such as YouTube or Facebook Watch). It can be argued that VOD can provide a higher level of production, a sense of professionalism, lower levels of risk due to the ability to record, edit, and preview videos before distribution (reference). Compared to VOD, the inherent live nature, the need for available and online viewers, and a more complex data collection pipeline can make the implementation of live streaming daunting for many potential broadcasters.

Before defining the unique characteristics of live streaming, the distinctive differences in live streaming tools facilitate a need for categorization to understand the disparities in strategic direction, delivery, and interaction that vary between the technologies.

Over the Top Services (OTT)

OTT services are generally incorporated into a subscription service through digital applications (such as Stan, Kayo, or Amazon Prime) and provide viewers the ability to watch live sport and related content from their mobile devices. In 2020, Convivia (2021) suggests that this type of content is commonly viewed through a connected television device (such as Roku, Chromecast) and viewed for longer periods of time than mobile devices but may encourage lower levels of commitment or engagement as commonly paired with a second-screen device. The proliferation of OTT services is commonly controlled by sport leagues or service providers, rather than individual teams or athletes. Alternatively, rather than being dictated by social media capabilities,

OTT can be commonly customized and built for specific purposes such as statistical analysis, variable camera views, gambling, and alternative commentary (Hutchins et al., 2019). From an organizational perspective, OTT services provide new potential to reach fans beyond their primary market and gain a deeper understanding of viewer demographics, viewing patterns, habits, and preferences, in turn, providing enhanced personalization opportunities.

In Australia, OTT services have a 51% market penetration, with Kayo and Stan the leading subscription sport services (Carney 2019). Most recently, Amazon Prime has announced they will live stream the Australian Olympic Swimming trials which aims to reach a new global audience that was previously not accessible through traditional broadcasting ecosystems. Whilst access to live sport was previously limited by geography, OTT may create significant ramifications for the sport industry and broadcast rights negotiations. Accessibility and opportunities to reach larger global audiences are attractive for sport organizations to consider with Amazon Prime also securing global rights to NFL, ATP Tennis, US Open, and the English Premier League.

The characteristics of OTT are important to consider when comparing to other live streaming tools. MTM Analysis (2019) proposes OTT can be delivered as either (a) rights holder or (b) distributor and can be split into six categories of OTT providers (Table 14.1).

A key characteristic of OTT services is the ability to monetize content through either ad-supported video on demand (AVOD), subscription video on demand (SVOD), and transactional video on demand (TVOD). However, to reap the commercial benefits of OTT services, there needs to be a focus on strategic management toward developing platform capabilities and content that focus on gathering specific fan insights to drive engagement to personalize the fan experience. OTT data provides unique opportunities to understand fan audiences in comparison to other broadcasting models and therefore provides the ability to continuously analyze and optimize various OTT revenue streams, benefiting content owners, fans, and associated sponsors.

However, we argue that OTT is resource-heavy, and often is used for the purpose of the "main game" mirroring the expectations of a professional television broadcast production. This may provide challenges for sport managers to implement within digital strategies, and consequently, to prepare for the rise in demand for OTT services, Sportsradar (2019) suggest that sport organizations are expected to invest $6.6 billion USD by 2021, an increase from $5.6 billion USD in 2018. This investment suggests that coverage of the "main game" may become increasingly fragmented.

Social Live Streaming Services

Social Live Streaming Services (SLSS) provides synchronized distribution of real-time broadcast video with an overlay of comments via text-based chat and engagement functions on the same screen (Scheibe et al., 2016). SLSS content is distinct from OTT as they are integrated within social media (such as Facebook or Instagram) and allow synchronous communication through a live broadcast. Through the integration of social media, there is a pre-established and connected audience and content is focused on personal live streaming of video content (Bründl et al., 2017), without the involvement of a third-party organization. Further, there is a heightened sense of accessibility with no ongoing subscription or payment walls inhibiting broadcast access. The ease of accessibility is further heightened through the authorization and ability for any social media user to broadcast live at any time from their mobile device (which inherently can present a risk for athletes).

Table 14.2 provides an overview of social media platforms, their monthly active users, and the year SLSS was launched on the platform. As highlighted, these tools are relatively new in

Table 14.1 OTT Services

Delivery type	*Provider*	*Description*	*Example broadcast*	*Example sport*
Rights Owner	Sport Leagues (Rights Owner)	Provides access to games for fans that do not have market access (such as an international audience).	WatchNRL, NFL League Pass, NBA League Pass	The International NBA League Pass offers live and on-demand coverage of every NBA game of the regular and postseason for out-of-market fans.
	Sport Clubs	Supplementary content created specifically for fans.	Manchester United TV	MUTV offers fans on-demand and live content including interviews with players and staff, full matches, reserve and academy games, footballing news, and shows.
Distributer	PayTV or Freeview	Aggregated bundles of content for a specific interest.	Stan Sport, (Foxtel), 7Now, 10 Play	In 2021, Stan launched a new sub-service "Stan Sport" which acquired the broadcast rights to all Super Rugby Australia, Super Rugby Aotearoa, and the Trans-Tasman tournament matches.
	Broadcaster	Existing broadcasters that leverage their brand name and audience to create additional programs for an engaged audience.	ESPN+	The US Soccer League has a three-year agreement with ESPN+ to broadcast the USL Championship and League One matches up until the 2022 season.
	Emerging Sport	Combining sports rights that were previously not available in a market or sport that received limited traditional television broadcast attention.	FloSport, DAZN	DAZN has exclusive broadcasting rights for Italy's Serie A football for the 2021–2024 season.
	Major Digital Organisation	A variety of models, leveraging global scale and technical capabilities.	Amazon Prime	Amazon has had an agreement with the National Football League (NFL) to exclusively broadcast games (Thursday night rights from Twitter). Exclusive ATP tour tennis rights in the UK (including the US Open). Exclusive right to broadcast 20 Premier League games in the UK.

Source: Adapted from MTM Analysis (2019).

Table 14.2 Leading SLSS Services in 2021

Social platform	*Monthly active users*	*Year social platform launched*	*Year live streaming tools available*
Facebook	2.7 b	2004	2016
YouTube	2b	2005	2008
Instagram	1b	2010	2016
TikTok	1b	2016	2020
Twitter	330 m	2006	2020 (previously Periscope, launched 2015)
LinkedIn	303 m	2003	2019

comparison to the platform; however, the "ready-made" audience has taken up these tools with great encouragement. Notably, the largest audience share, Facebook Live generates over 8 million daily streams and receives three times the amount of viewership compared to VOD, and ten times the amount of comments compared to VOD (Saas Scout, 2020).

As previously discussed in Table 14.1, OTT typically focuses on live streaming the "main game"; however, Wymer and Thompson (2022) discovered traditional broadcast agreements require sport organizations to consider the development of both creative and interactive SLSS experiences due to the contracted live game product. The day before a live event, fan consumption of sport-related videos increases by 75% (Nielsen, 2020) and therefore SLSS may capitalize on a reciprocal communication system with easy access and real-time access to provide fan engagement (Kim & Kim, 2020). It is important to consider the two varying delivery models when examining SLSS from a fan engagement perspective. We argue that SLSS can be delivered from either an (a) athlete-driven approach or (b) organizational-driven approach.

Athlete-driven SLSS

Previously, the athlete's voice only existed and was possible through the traditional press. However, the use of social media has seen athletes utilizing a relationship marketing approach facilitating enhanced fan engagement (Doyle et al., 2020). In the professional sport context, we have seen an increase in SLSS use led by athletes, occurring both on their personal and their club's official accounts. In 2020, during COVID-19 with live sport on hold in Australia, professional athletes' social media content accounted for 21% of sport content consumed by sport fans. This emphasizes the influencing power of athletes to retain valuable connections with fans beyond live games.

SproutSocial (2020) suggests that athlete-generated content is valuable as athletes are held to a less rigid standard and can capture raw content that officials cannot access or post. For example, during the COVID-19 pandemic, upon entering the "National Basketball League (NBA) Bubble" Los Angeles Lakers athlete, J.R. Smith used his personal Instagram to live stream and provide over 5,000 fans a virtual tour of the "Disney World bubble" (Faigen, 2020). The use of SLSS allowed fans to ask questions about the bubble and see exclusive areas such as living arrangements, menus, and athlete technology (Mastromartino et al., 2020). However, Smith abruptly ended the broadcast stating "Aw man, they mad at me bro. I'm gone. Just got the text. Exposing too much s***. Gotta go. My bad. My bad." (Faigen, 2020). Although it is not clear who "they" refers to, this raises important questions regarding content moderation and control (Wymer et al., 2020).

Athlete-driven SLSS is generally spur of the moment, rather than part of a strategic direction or carefully considered in comparison to other post types (i.e., photo or VOD) that considers sponsor integration or club-directive guidelines. From a fan's perspective, this type of direct interaction appears intimate, less guarded, and may strengthen fan identification through a sense of immediacy, direct communication, and sociability (Mastromartino et al., 2020; Wymer et al., 2020). As noted in the J.R Smith example, although "they" is not defined in this occurrence, from a sport team or league perspective this may raise concerns that athlete use of live streaming that is unplanned presents a level of risk as to what is being presented to fans. Consequently, we have seen an increase of managed "takeovers" on official brand accounts with specific guidelines, stories, or set events (i.e., questions/answers, or open days) to manage the content and narrative to fans.

The Case of the Sydney Swans and the Black Dog Mental Health Institute

To control the brand narrative and capitalize on existing partnerships, sport organizations are utilizing the power of an athlete brand to create a sense of intimacy with fans. Of note, is the Sydney Swans (Australian Football League) and their partnership with the Black Dog Institute, an Australian-based not-for-profit mental health research-based organization that aims to change perceptions around mental health. Sydney Swans, CEO, Tom Harley, notes the importance of this relationship by utilizing their athlete's brand to generate awareness and assist with fundraising for the organization. By utilizing the athlete, sport organizations have the ability to promote philanthropic activities which may strengthen the overall connection between the athlete/and or sport team and fans (Kunkel et al., 2020). This is an important consideration in relation to SLSS, as the intimate and interactive elements of this type of content can further enhance this athlete-fan relationship and further develop philanthropic partnership benefits through a sense of relatability and "rawness."

In the case of the Sydney Swans, their use of Instagram Live during COVID-19 lockdown periods featured key athletes "checking in" on other athletes. This type of content created a sense of familiarity with fans, providing a sense of "real-time" allowing fans to witness intimate interaction, comparable to a private video call between athletes (real-time access that is generally unavailable or inaccessible to fans). From an organizational perspective, the incorporation of SLSS for sponsorship integration has provided innovative ways to meet strategic partnership goals. For example, beyond just raising awareness, the Sydney Swans are delivering on their partners' purpose to encourage people to have conversations but delivering "real-time" conversations and allowing athletes to provide a sense of control over questions encompassing mental health.

As an implication, the use of SLSS content to promote the Black Dog Institute partnership encouraged fans to communicate directly with athletes by leaving comments during the live stream. These comments were often read out and answered by athletes which provides a "direct-line" of communication that is previously not accessible in other forms of social media content (such as comments which have a time delay or are often unanswered). Although this content was implemented during peak COVID-19 lockdown periods, it still is relevant in a post-pandemic environment. As the fan experience is fragmented, it is imperative to find ways to engage fans and meet sponsorship obligations, and therefore it is suggested athletes must move beyond traditional broadcasts and start interacting directly with their fans. This use of SLSS is important for athletes to consider as it provides two-way conversations, further showcasing the influencing power of athletes to develop valuable connections with fans beyond the game.

Organizational Driven SLSS

The development of digital media has influenced how sport organizations communicate and interact with fans. Sport organizations are no longer expected to generate game-related content or news updates, fans also demand behind-the-scenes looks at their favorite athletes, teams, and facilities through live streams of training and off-field activities (Mastromartino et al., 2020). While athlete-led SLSS is also concentrated on fan engagement, the motive from an organizational perspective is commonly linked to strategic direction and embedded within digital strategies rather than "spur of the moment." As part of a fan-engagement-focused digital strategy, the Portland Trail Blazers schedule regular live streams on Facebook Live including a post-game show "courtside" which is presented from the stadium like a television broadcast.

The use of SLSS for this type of content allows sport organizations to think strategically and plan for opportunities for a captive audience by carefully understanding fans' needs and wants to create a unique broadcast that is focused on a specific segmentation of sport fans (Naraine et al., 2019). Further, it provides an opportunity to break the news firsthand in "real-time" rather than utilizing external media or packaging and editing in-house to deliver to fans prior to breaking news. This type of access may provide a higher sense of authenticity and allow public relations staff to actively frame the narrative of these stories for strategic benefit.

Comparative to athlete-driven which is commonly characterized by two-way interaction with fans, strategic implementation of SLSS from an organizational level is commonly focused on para-social relationships through mediated fan encounters to carefully considered opportunities such as training, shows, or events. This is referred to as sociality which Haimson and Tang (2017) suggest is the concept of being social without the broadcaster interacting with an audience. Interaction is an important consideration for fan engagement as sport fans' relationship with a sport team can be realized through consuming content that has been carefully constructed to feel a sense of belonging (Achen et al., 2020).

It can be suggested that engagement is cultivated through impromptu short-term groups co-experiencing a live event. Through the chat function on SLSS, connectivity is promoted by means of fan-to-fan social interaction rather than direct interaction with broadcaster. The sense of shared experience and community may provide fans a sense of satisfaction with SLSSs and consequently connects "displaced" sport fans and enhances the quality of their mental health (i.e., social well-being, and loneliness; Kim & Kim, 2020).

Although there are benefits for fan engagement opportunities through SLSS implementation from an organizational perspective, there are also challenges and risks. Notably, opportunities to generate sponsorship revenue and monetization strategies are limited in comparison to OTT services (Blank, 2019). This was exhibited by the Queensland Maroons (Australian-based representative Rugby League team) who stated strategic reporting is focused on monetization and therefore focuses digital management toward website-hosted VOD over SLSS (Wymer et al., 2020).

However, sport organizations need to consider their audience (Naraine, 2019). For instance, 78% of those who use the internet watch SLSS, accounting for an average of 16 hours of social video per week – a 52% increase in the past two years (Bybyk, 2020). Further, fans who want to engage with SLSS, s are looking for more control over the live experience such as the ability to switch between camera angles and access to unique immersive content. Whilst OTT subscribers often are focused on the delivery of the main game, mirroring the expectations of a professional television broadcast production, SLSS provides unique experiences that cannot be provided in a traditional television broadcast and therefore can be personalized to meet a changing and evolving fan audience. Therefore, it is imperative that sport organizations understand their fan audience in order to carefully prepare a strategy that focuses on fostering strong and meaningful connections in order to reap the benefits of SLSS implementation.

Fan-Focused Positioning of Live Streaming

To fully understand fan engagement opportunities of live streaming within digital strategy it is important to understand how fans respond to this specific type of content. As previously discussed, we refer to live streaming as an overarching ecosystem and therefore argue that OTT and SLSS engagement outcomes differ due to unique capabilities, elements, and purpose of each platform. Comparative to other forms of digital engagement, the key concept of live streaming is real-time. Further, Hilvert-Bruce et al., (2018) suggest that viewer motivations to engage in live streaming are focused on a stronger social and community basis. This means that rather than producing content for reactive coverage, the shift of focus moves to interactive coverage (Vann et al., 2019). Consequently, the nature of interactivity fosters co-presence and social interaction, creating a mediated co-viewing experience (Luo et al., 2020). Although there has been an established focus on fan engagement opportunities on OTT/SLSS, it is also important to consider how content is classified as engaging in this format, as such, Haimson and Tang (2017) suggest identifying four dimensions that make remote event viewing engaging: interaction, immediacy, immersion, and sociality.

Interaction

The streaming of sport-related content is a social experience and engagement is commonly amplified using comments (Luo et al., 2020) to generate a conversation between either broadcaster-to-fan, fan-to-broadcaster, and fan-to-fan. While not all live streaming tools have the capability for conversation (e.g., OTT services), this is an integral part of the interactive capabilities of live streaming technologies. Notably, videos receive the highest number of comments during the live transmissions (in comparison to posting the video following the live transmission) which suggests a new connective process characterized by co-presence (Martini, 2018). This type of interaction is commonly a feature of SLSS, for instance, Facebook Live report that live video posts generate ten times the number of comments in comparison to VOD. Fans want to be heard and foster a sense of connection with their favorite athlete, team, or other fans through developing a sense of community (Hamilton et al., 2014). Therefore, it is imperative that the customization of live streaming tools (SLSS and OTT) carefully considers content that provides an interactive focus to generate and foster these digital fan communities (Popp & Woratschek, 2016). These digital fan communities are essential during periods when fans are limited on accessing the physical sport product and unable to travel. The COVID-19 pandemic has provided an opportunity for sport organizations to carefully consider the importance of an engaged satellite fan which provides opportunities. Satellite fans are reported to show high levels of social media usage regarding both lurking behavior and active behavior such as commenting (Uhrich et al., 2020) and therefore may enhance their relationship with their team through new "real-time" access to live games or athlete interactions that were previously only accessible in person or in local markets.

Immediacy

As sport organizations seek to widen their fan engagement opportunities and consider innovative technologies to deliver enhanced experiences, live streaming is often positioned as a way to meet new fans to secure an expanded fan base (Kim & Kim, 2020). However, there should be a clear understanding of fan expectations toward the components of live streaming to deliver a fan-first experience before planning or delivering this type of content. However, although Zuckerberg praises SLSS to not be possibly curated and as a great medium for being raw, providing users an ability to share "live" moments at any time, the quality of the stream is critically important for fans to remain engaged in a live stream (Convivia, 2021) As the quality of experience drops, viewer engagement deteriorates which consequently is important to ensure retaining viewers for a stream and encourage returning views. Marshall (2019) reported that on average, broadcasters have 90 seconds before viewers leave due to poor technology. Therefore, it is imperative that sport organizations who want to capitalize on live streaming opportunities invest in the appropriate resources to deliver a high product. The ongoing rollout of 5G will provide sport organizations new opportunities to immerse fans such as providing visuals from the athlete's point of view on the field (Naraine et al., 2020). Further, access to 5G is predicted to increase revenue for live streaming on mobile devices by 85% from 2021 to 2028 (Intel, 2020).

Immersion

The feeling of connection through a sense of "being there" plays an important role in fans' decision-making and subsequent fan behaviors. SLSS and OTT services can transport viewers to locations that are beyond their physical and geographic environments that provide a feeling that they are present in real-time. However, what makes the live streaming experience immersive and distinct from a television broadcast is the ability to actively engage with content, while interacting with other viewers, all on the same screen. This level of immersion encourages fans to watch SLSS for longer periods of time than traditional television broadcasts or VOD, as the immersive characteristics provide access to a "beyond TV" experience.

An evolving shift in sport consumption has placed a greater emphasis on access to sport teams and athletes from a satellite perspective. Content that provides fans access to a privileged viewpoint or behind the scenes (Wymer et al., 2021) can be carefully considered to draw viewers for longer periods of time and develop a deeper with fans. Further, the concept of immersion is increasingly important for sport organizations to consider for "out of venue" experiences as geographically displaced fans are constantly looking for additional experiences and opportunities to bring them closer to their favorite sport teams and athlete (Styring, 2021). Through live streaming, digitized and interactive content that is carefully considered for the fan experience can provide fans an immersive experience, beyond being there, that delivers enhanced benefits compared to being in the stands or at fan days from their mobile device.

Sociality

Sociality is a unique characteristic of live streaming as it is developed through co-presence through a shared viewing experience rather than an active form of interaction (i.e., comments) which is seen on other types of social media posts. Through a share "real-time" viewing experience, live streaming can enhance viewers' social well-being and ease feelings of loneliness (Kim & Kim, 2020). It can be suggested that the traditional television broadcast experience lacks telepresence, thus, negatively affecting the flow of the experience of watching sports and, consequently fans' satisfactions (Kim et al., 2019). Professional sport teams and athletes can enhance sociality by developing digital communities by creating live streaming opportunities focused on co-presence. For example, asking fans to "turn on notifications" for live streaming content, and therefore enhancing the number of "live viewers" which is displayed at the top of a live broadcast. It can be suggested that co-presence may result in higher levels of engagement and interaction through a sense of being with others, to provide a sense of social connection, which is regarded as the primary motive for sports spectatorship.

Dominant Theoretical Frameworks

There are various dominant theoretical frameworks that are relevant to researchers investigating live streaming aiming to build upon emerging knowledge in this area. Specifically, examination of live streaming impact on fan engagement and to describe and understand fan behaviors, theory must adapt to consider the "real-time" component in a changing media landscape. Previous research has examined sport organizations' use of SLSS from the fan perspective within S-D logic (S-DL) and fan engagement (Wymer et al., 2021) and uses and gratifications theory (U&G; Kim & Kim, 2020). These theories aim to understand why fans engage with SLSS from an audience-centered approach, with the perspective attributing media selection decisions to individuals' needs, wants, or expectations (Rubin, 2009).

However, as this chapter has suggested, the characteristic of live streaming differs between SLSS and OTT platforms and between the broadcaster (either driven by athlete or sport organization). Therefore, although S-DL and U&G consider live streaming from a fan perspective, this body of knowledge can be broadened to include additional areas of live streaming research including differences between the drivers, platforms, and type of distribution method. There is currently a gap in research that considers additional perspectives to broaden the understanding that deserves further attention. For example, from an organizational perspective, there is a compelling agenda to explore live streaming as an avenue to reap commercial benefits of OTT services, focusing on strategic management, understanding platform capabilities and content types that is driven by specific fan insights to personalize the fan experience. The Planning, Organizing & Delivery (POD) model (Wymer et al., 2021) represents a relevant framework to examine this direction of research to understand organizational outcomes of live streaming use. Whilst this tool has been previously used to examine SLSS, there is value in considering the POD model to specifically consider the strategic implementation of live streaming by considering broadcast delivery agent (athlete, fan, organization), platform type (OTT or SLSS), type of content, and the influence on strategic direction and relevant outcomes.

Future of LS

Live streaming digital technologies are rapidly influencing the development and operations of sport organizations and athletes' connections and digitally transforming traditional broadcasting models. Live streaming provides sport organizations and athletes access to remote and displaced fans and can help them connect through innovative experiences that are immersive and interactive and unique in comparison to other digital media content. While there are unique differences in these two tools discussed (OTT and SLSS) in relation to how they are implemented and managed, we suggest through the development of both creative and interactive experiences, sport leagues, teams, and athletes have an opportunity to develop a high level of loyalty and engagement of fans. Further, it is imperative for sport organizations to keep up with evolving digital trends to remain relevant and competitive. However, although live streaming provides sport organizations and athletes with innovative opportunities to connect with fans, there are also many challenges present in the development of this type of content.

Notably, the rapidly changing pace of social media platforms represents a reason to trend cautiously regarding investing heavily in resources and time. Although live streaming appears to be the "future" with only 15% of fans believing that the status quo of televised sports broadcasting will remain the same over the next three years (Deloitte, 2019), sport entities must be conscious that as new forms of technologies and providers emerge, this also causes concern to remain relevant and competitive among fans. However, as sport organizations look to innovate to provide fans with immersive, interactive, social, and immediate content, there is plenty to take heed in the fact that over 40% of fans expect their live streaming consumption to increase in the near future (Deloitte, 2019). While this is an emerging area of research and practice, sport organizations and athletes should seize these opportunities to strategically leverages related brands and the timing of events to positive effect to focus on fan engagement and thus, develop the fan-to-fan and fan-to-athlete/sport organization/team relationship.

References

Achen, R. M., Kaczorowski, J., Horsmann, T., & Ketzler, A. (2020). Comparing organizational content and fan interaction on Twitter and Facebook in United States professional sport. *Managing Sport and Leisure*, *25*(5), 358–375. 10.1080/23750472.2020.1723432

Antoniadis, A. (2021, January 18). NSWRL to deliver over 100 games with NSWRL TV. Retrieved from https://ministryofsport.com.au/nswrl-to-deliver-over-100-games-with-nswrl-tv/

Bründl, S., Matt, C., & Hess, T. (2017). Consumer use of social live streaming services: The influence of co-experience and effectance on enjoyment. In Proceedings of the 25th European Conference on Information Systems (ECIS 2017). Guimarães, Portugal. June 5–10, 2017.

Bybyk, A. (2020, November 23). 10 myths that shouldn't stop you from going live. Restream. https://restream.io/blog/myths-stopping-you-from-going-live/

Carney, S. (2019, November 14). More fans streaming sport as OTT services take a strong foothold in Australia. Retrieved from https://ministryofsport.com.au/more-fans-streaming-sport-as-ott-services-take-a-strong-foothold-in-australia/#:~:text=In Australia, OTT services have over 23% uptake among Australians.

Convivia. (2021, January 24). Conviva's state of streaming Q3 2020. Retrieved from https://www.conviva.com/research/convivas-state-of-streaming-q3-2020/

Deloitte. (2019). The future of sports broadcasting: Enhancing digital fan engagement. Retrieved from https://www2.deloitte.com/content/dam/Deloitte/us/Documents/technology-media-telecommunications/us-enhancing-digital-fan-engagement.pdf

Digital TV Europe (2019). Informa. https://www.digitaltveurope.com/files/2019/02/DTVE-Survey19_lo.pdf

Faigen, H. (2020, July 10). J.R. Smith got kicked off Instagram live for revealing too much about NBA bubble. Retrieved from https://www.silverscreenandroll.com/2020/7/10/21319728/jr-smith-got-kicked-off-instagram-live-revealing-too-much-about-nba-bubble-lakers

Haimson, O. L., & Tang, J. C. (2017, May). What makes live events engaging on Facebook Live, Periscope, and Snapchat. In *Proceedings of the 2017 CHI conference on human factors in computing systems* (pp. 48–60).

Hamilton, W. A., Garretson, O., & Kerne, A. (2014, April). Streaming on twitch: Fostering participatory communities of play within live mixed media. In *Proceedings of the SIGCHI conference on human factors in computing systems* (pp. 1315–1324).

Hilvert-Bruce, Z., Neill, J. T., Sjöblom, M., & Hamari, J. (2018). Social motivations of live-streaming viewer engagement on Twitch. *Computers in Human Behavior*, *84*, 58–67. 10.1016/j.chb.2018.02.013

Hutchins, B., Li, B., & Rowe, D. (2019). Over-the-top sport: Live streaming services, changing coverage rights markets and the growth of media sport portals. *Media, Culture & Society*, *41*(7), 975–994. 10.1177/0163443719857623

Hytner, M. (2020, November 09). Rugby Australia signs $100m deal with Nine as broadcaster unveils Stan Sport. Retrieved from https://www.theguardian.com/sport/2020/nov/09/rugby-australia-signs-100m-deal-with-nine-as-broadcaster-unveils-stan-sport.

Intel. (2020). Intel 5G Media. Retrieved from https://www.intel.com.au/content/www/au/en/wireless-network/5g-technology/5g-media.html

Kim, H. S., & Kim, M. (2020). Viewing sports online together? Psychological consequences on social live streaming service usage. *Sport Management Review, 23*(5), 869–882. 10.1016/j.smr.2019.12.007

Kim, D., Ko, Y., Lee, J. L., & Kim, Y. C. (2019). The impact of CSR-linked sport sponsorship on consumers' reactions to service failures. *International Journal of Sports Marketing and Sponsorship, 21*(1), 70–90. 10.1108/ijsms-01-2019-0011

Kunkel, T., Doyle, J., & Na, S. (2020). Becoming more than an athlete: Developing an athlete's personal brand using strategic philanthropy. *European Sport Management Quarterly*, 1–21. 10.1080/16184742.2020.1791208

Luo, M., Hsu, T. W., Park, J. S., & Hancock, J. T. (2020). Emotional amplification during live-streaming: Evidence from comments during and after news events. *Proceedings of the ACM on Human-Computer Interaction, 4*(CSCW1), 1–19.

Mastromatrino, B., & Naraine, M. L. (2021). (Dis)Innovative digital strategy in professional sport: Examining sponsor leveraging through social media. *International Journal of Sport Marketing and Sponsorship*. Advance online publication. 10.1108/IJSMS-02-2021-0032

Mastromartino, B., Ross, W. J., Wear, H., & Naraine, M. L. (2020). Thinking outside the 'box': A discussion of sports fans, teams, and the environment in the context of COVID-19. *Sport in Society, 23*, 1707–1723. 10.1080/17430437.2020.1804108

Marshall, C. (2019, June 17). Will livestreaming become more popular because of 5G? Retrieved from https://www.techradar.com/au/news/will-livestreaming-become-more-popular-because-of-5g

Martini, M. (2018). Online distant witnessing and live-streaming activism: Emerging differences in the activation of networked publics. *New Media & Society, 20*(11), 4035–4055. 10.1177/1461444818766703

Myer, R. (2020, August 07). Foxtel's sinking ship: How long will Murdoch stay aboard. Retrieved from https://thenewdaily.com.au/finance/finance-news/2020/08/08/foxtel-value-falling/

MTM Analysis. (2019, July). *The Global Market for Premium Sports OTT Services* (Rep. No. 1). Retrieved from http://files.clickdimensions.com/nagracom

Naraine, M. (2019). Follower segments within and across the social media networks of major professional sport organizations. *Sport Marketing Quarterly, 28*(4), 222–233. 10.32731/smq.284.122019.04

Naraine, M. L., O'Reilly, N., Levallet, N., & Wanless, L. (2020). If you build it, will they log on? Wi-Fi usage and behavior while attending National Basketball Association games. *Sport, Business and Management: An International Journal, 10*(2), 207–226. 10.1108/sbm-02-2019-0016

Naraine, M. L., Wear, H. T., & Whitburn, D. J. (2019). User engagement from within the Twitter community of professional sport organizations. *Managing Sport and Leisure, 24*(5), 275–293. 10.1080/23750472.2019.1630665

Nielsen. (2020, April 09). Aussie sports fans are getting their fix on social media amid live event shutdown. Retrieved from https://www.nielsen.com/au/en/insights/article/2020/aussie-sports-fans-are-getting-their-fix-on-social-media-amid-live-event-shutdown/

Popp, B., & Woratschek, H. (2016). Introducing branded communities in sport for building strong brand relations in social media. *Sport Management Review, 19*(2), 183–197. 10.1016/j.smr.2015.06.001

Rubin, A. M. (2009). Uses and gratifications: An evolving perspective on media effects. In R. L. Nabi & M. B. Oliver (Eds.), *The SAGE handbook of media processes and effects* (pp. 147–159). Washington, D.C.: SAGE.

Saas Scout. (2020, November 29). Facebook live statistics, usage and facts (2020 Report). Retrieved from https://saasscout.com/statistics/facebook-live-statistics/

Samios, Z. (2021, February 03). Amazon dives into sports streaming battle with first Australian rights. Retrieved from https://www.smh.com.au/business/companies/amazon-dives-into-sports-streaming-battle-with-first-australian-rights-20210203-p56z45.html

Scheibe, K., Fietkiewicz, K. J., & Stock, W. G. (2016). Information behavior on social live streaming services. *Journal of Information Science Theory and Practice, 4*(2), 6–20. 10.1633/jistap.2016.4.2.1

Sherwood, M., Nicholson, M., & Marjoribanks, T. (2016). Controlling the message and the medium? *Digital Journalism, 5*(5), 513–531. 10.1080/21670811.2016.1239546

Sportsradar. (2019). The future of the OTT experience. Retrieved from https://www.sportradar.com/ott/the-future-of-the-ott-experience/

Sprout Social. (2020, October 05). Inside the bubble: How player-generated content fuels awareness for the NBA. Retrieved from https://sproutsocial.com/insights/nba-bubble-player-content/

Styring, C. (2021, January 10). The future of the sporting broadcast for on and off-site fans. Retrieved from https://mumbrella.com.au/the-future-of-the-sporting-broadcast-for-on-and-off-site-fans-662059

Uhrich, S., Behrens, A., Kang, T. A., Matsuoka, H., & Uhlendorf, K. (2020). Segmenting satellite supporters based on their value for team sport organizations. *Journal of Global Sport Management*, 1–29. 10.1080/24704067.2020.1819617

Vale, L., & Fernandes, T. (2018). Social media and sports: Driving fan engagement with football clubs on Facebook. *Journal of Strategic Marketing*, *26*(1), 37–55. 10.1080/0965254x.2017.1359655

Vann, P., Bruns, A., & Harrington, S. (2019). Transmedia social platforms: Livestreaming and transmedia sports. In Freeman, M., & Gambarato, R. R. (Eds.) *The Routledge Companion to Transmedia Studies* (pp. 107–115). Routledge: New York.

Williams, J., & Chinn, S. J. (2010). Meeting relationship-marketing goals through social media: a conceptual model for sport marketers. *International Journal of Sport Communication*, *3*(4), 422–437. 10.1123/ijsc.3.4.422

Wymer, S. , & Thompson, A-J. (2022). Broadcast forms and their managerial implication. In Fujak, H., & Frawley, S. (Eds.), *Sport broadcasting for managers* (pp. 103–117). Routledge.

Wymer, S., Thompson, A. J., & Martin, A. (2020). Diminishing the distance during social distancing: An exploration of Australian sport organizations' usage of social live streaming services throughout Covid-19. In *Sport and the Pandemic* (pp. 61–69). Routledge.

Wymer, S., Naraine, M. L., Thompson, A. J., & Martin, A. J. (2021). Transforming the fan experience through livestreaming: A conceptual model. *Journal of Interactive Advertising*, 1–14. 10.1080/15252019.2021.1910884

Yanev, V. (2020, July 02). 37 Live streaming statistics - a booming industry [2020]. Retrieved from https://techjury.net/blog/live-streaming-statistics/#gref

Yoshida, M., Gordon, B., Nakazawa, M., & Biscaia, R. (2014). Conceptualization and measurement of fan engagement: empirical evidence from a professional sport context. *Journal of Sport Management*, *28*(4), 399–417. 10.1123/jsm.2013-0199

Zurich, M. (2021, January 12). New survey shows 27 percent of U.S. households plan to cut cable TV subscriptions in 2021. Retrieved from https://www.businesswire.com/news/home/20210112005291/en/New-Survey-Shows-27-Percent-of-U.S.-Households-Plan-to-Cut-Cable-TV-Subscriptions-in-2021

15

Social Media and Sport Marketing in North America

Brandon Boatwright and Karen Freberg

Introduction

Social media is not a new phenomenon, but it has brought forth novel opportunities to engage, share knowledge, use strategic storytelling, and break down the barriers between organizations and their key publics. This is evident in the rapid growth of social media-related research in public relations and marketing. Social media has transformed marketing both in research and in practice. With each advance that occurs in the social media industry, public relations research adapts and explores these various changes and discusses the implications this has on the field, society, and the practice.

Social media is sometimes referred to as "new media" to capture the association of social media with the advanced integration, strategy, and application of new communication technologies. Other conceptualizations emphasize the role of social media as a toolkit that allows users to create and share content. Still, others focus on how social media extends the interactive capacity for Web 2.0 technologies to bring communities together through networked effects (Blank & Reisdorf, 2012).

Social media platforms serve as gateways where content and conversations are created and ignited between individuals, brands, organizations, and nations. In addition, social media platforms provide first impression management tools for corporations and individuals to showcase their own brands and reputations. These virtual platforms allow user-generated content to be shared in highly dynamic and interactive communities in real-time. Consequently, this allows for co-creating of content, crowdsourcing of ideas and perspectives, and even the editing and extending of conversations and ideas within a respective platform and with a particular community.

Methods in Exploring Social Media and Sports Marketing

Along with key elements that conceptualize the past, present, and future directions of social media and sports marketing from a theoretical perspective, the added methods of exploring these concepts and trends have been established. This represents a growing area of research in sports marketing and social media. Traditional methods like content and thematic analysis have been

DOI: 10.4324/9781003088899-18

widely utilized, but new approaches including network analysis and advanced topic modeling have helped advance some of the work that has been conducted in academia by providing researchers with the right tools to explore new questions and concepts in interesting ways. For instance, various third-party social media listening and analytics platforms like Sprinklr, CrowdTangle, Brandwatch, and others have made it easier for researchers to harvest vast swaths of social media data to conduct research using advanced network analysis programs (e.g., NodeXL) or automated content and sentiment analysis programs (e.g., WordStat, Leximancer).

Methods in sports and social media marketing research have their limitations and challenges, however. First, the methods and methodologies have to adapt rapidly to the changes happening in the industry. As technologies change, researchers must constantly stay abreast of industry trends and technical changes that affect the ways in which social media platforms operate. Along with these challenges, the literature from sports marketing and social media has received criticism for being too descriptive (Hardin, 2014).

For example, some of the most popular methods that are used for social media research are case studies and content analysis (e.g., Hambrick et al., 2010: Sanderson & Hambrick, 2012). While both are great methods of exploring social media, there are more advanced methods (e.g., semantic network analysis, topic-modeling, etc.) that need to be implemented to showcase the overall impact and significance of what is happening in sports marketing related to social media. In addition, while big data research is worthwhile and valuable for sports marketing, there still is a growing need to provide methods that allow researchers to tie in the data to actionable insights for both researchers and practitioners. The collection of data for data's sake should not be the end goal for researchers, but rather to provide strategic and creative insights that contribute both to academic literature and practitioner expectations. In order to accomplish this, we need to broaden the scope of our methodological approach to studying sports social media.

Future Implications in Social Media and Sports Marketing

The function of social media in sports marketing is especially relevant in North America, specifically for several reasons. First, the sheer volume of sports-related organizations and companies across the continent is staggering. College and university athletic departments, for example, constitute one of the largest blocs at the intersection of sports and social media research and practice across North America. It is rare for secondary education anywhere else but in the United States and Canada, specifically, to (1) have intercollegiate athletics competitions in the first place and (2) put so many resources toward them. Second, sports fandom is highly influenced by national politics (e.g., Allison et al., 2021; Henry & Oates, 2020). Third, according to Statista (2018), sports sponsorship in North America outpaces every other region around the globe in the last decade. This is not an exhaustive list, but it illustrates the prominence of sport across the continent both in terms of its cultural and economic importance. Consequently, researchers in sports marketing and social media should be able to answer the call to explore new ideas, test innovative methods, and propose creative insights that can benefit both the academic field, as well as the industry across the continent. With that being said, we propose a series of recommendations for seven broad topic areas that need to be explored moving forward in social media and sports marketing work.

Fandom

Perhaps one of the most fertile areas for future work in social media and sports marketing revolves around the concept of fandom. Research on sports fandom has evolved significantly across multiple disciplines over the past four decades (Wann & James, 2019). Much of the focus on sports fans to date has centered around fan identity and motives. Wann and Branscombe (1993) developed the Sport Spectator Identification Scale (SSIS) to measure an individual's sports team identification. Similarly, Wann et al. (1999) developed the *Sport Fan Motivation Scale* (SFMS) as an instrument to measure eight different motives of sports fans (i.e., eustress, self-esteem, escape, entertainment, economic, esthetic, group affiliation, and family) and has been used in hundreds of studies to evaluate sport fan behavior.

Others have drawn from social identity theory to explain how individual fans align with particular sports teams and organizations (e.g., Burns, 2014). Still, others have explored para-social relationships fans have with athletes (e.g., Sanderson & Emmons, 2014) and sought to identify the various uses and gratifications of consuming sports media (e.g., Gantz & Lewis, 2014; Gantz & Wenner, 1995).

Despite the wide array of theoretical traditions that have been used to study sports fandom, it is important to recognize that sports fans do not constitute a homogeneous group, especially in terms of how they use social media to consume, engage, and derive meaning from sports. Indeed, Billings and Brown (2017) argued that the modern sports fan is far from monolithic. Researchers seeking to understand the role of social media in sports marketing are uniquely positioned to explore this idea but are just beginning to scratch the surface of what promises to be a fruitful area of scholarship. Social media platforms have provided fans with new opportunities such as the ability to engage with organizations, teams, and athletes, to connect with other fans despite time and geographic constraints, and ways to purchase apparel or other team merchandise and memorabilia. It also provides teams, organizations, and athletes more direct interaction with fans, further strengthening affiliations among users.

There is a growing body of research exploring these various trends. For example, Haugh and Watkins (2016) were among the first to explore how sports fans use social media, specifically. Their results suggest that fans' team identification and gender can predict the use of certain social media platforms for sports fans (e.g., fans were more likely to use Instagram for entertainment, fanship, and to pass time). Kim and Kim (2019) explored how college students' social media use for collegiate athletics is associated with their perceived college-group identity and collective self-esteem. Their findings suggest that those who often use social media for college sports are more likely to develop group identity as well as collective self-esteem.

It is easy to see that research on sports fandom has matured over time. What remains unclear, however, is how social media platforms affect sports fandom writ large. The constantly shifting landscape of social media creates new opportunities for fans to connect and express and enhance their fandom. Researchers must account for these changes to better understand the ways in which fan identity and behavior change along with them.

Influencers and Creators

Influencers have been on the rise in public relations, marketing, and social media campaigns over the years as a key strategy to amplify, support, and create engagement through their means to foster a strong connection with a brand (or entity and organization) and their key publics. At the same time, influencers have also posed significant challenges for companies and their brands.

There have been several studies that have explored influencers in various ways including based on their personality characteristics (Freberg et al., 2011), professional attributes and contributions (Enke & Borchers, 2019), community engagement (Himelboim & Golan, 2019; Smith et al., 2017), building an online community (Childers et al., 2019), fostering trust online

(Lou & Yuan, 2019), authenticity (Charlton & Cornwell, 2019), and adding on to their paid media role in formulating brand partnerships (Luoma-aho et al., 2019).

There have been many ways in which social media influencers (otherwise known as SMIs) have been conceptualized, including as individuals who shape attitudes through blogs, tweets, and other social media updates (Freberg et al., 2011). This definition of SMI has been expanded by other scholars by emphasizing their online digital presence and personal brand is due to the strategic amplification and investment in the production of content production, interaction, and formulating a strong personal brand on social media to build their influence in the industry (Enke & Borchers, 2019). Others have attributed SMIs in research based on the talent to promote and showcase their creative works online (Abidin, 2016), channel outlet for advertising opportunities and paid engagements (De Veirman et al., 2017), and having the ability to present themselves as "regular people" who are more relatable in nature to other high profile audiences (van Driel & Dumitrica, 2020).

When exploring SMIs, the big component that makes them successful is the interaction with the audiences in their community, otherwise known as engagement. *Engagement* is another factor that separates influencers by other means for brands and organizations (Smith et al., 2017). Engagement focuses on the interactivity between SMI and followers either within the community they are a part of or have created or with the client in which they are working with. Engagement also protects influencers through the risks of becoming "invisible," thanks to the algorithms for the platforms (van Driel & Dumitrica, 2020). As more audiences engage with the influencer, their content is shown more to other audiences on their newsfeed, which protects their overall visibility and brand awareness.

When exploring where influencers fall into sports, it is a natural fit. Taking advantage of the right moment on social media for sports teams and professionals can lead to future opportunities, yet the goal here is to sustain the moment created from the initial post that captured the attention of the mass audience. In several cases, athletes, thanks to the use of their own platforms, have been able to make a difference and help others. Athletes who compete in CrossFit, for example, have used their own platforms to share workouts, tips, and messages with their fans in a way that has created a true community for them online. In some cases, these athletes also rely heavily on sponsorships. These athletes' ability to use their social media leverage to get sponsorships from brands shows the shift in athletes becoming their own brands. At the same time, brands such as Peloton have relied a lot on social media specifically for their instructors to build their own fan base and brand, while also allowing them to sell their own branded merchandise. Cody Rigsby, one of the Peloton instructors, has done this with his themed bike classes called XOXO, Cody, and has translated this mantra into his own line of fitness wear with Peloton. Additionally, because of a loophole in NCAA rules, college cheerleaders are able to profit off of their name, image, and likeness, unlike other collegiate athletes. As a result, cheerleaders across the United States with a vast following have reportedly earned as much as $5,000 for posts sponsored by major companies like Amazon, Crocs, L'Oreal, and various cosmetic brands. The possibilities here with companies such as Opendorse, or consultants like Jeremy Darlow of Darlow Rules, make it possible for athletes to utilize their influence for good and branch out in their future careers.

Crisis Communication Involving Social Media and Sports

Because the use of social media in a crisis is a relatively evolving channel and strategy, further understanding of the challenges and opportunities of these media is warranted. Previous work in sports (Sanderson & Hambrick, 2012; Sheffer & Schultz, 2010) has shown the interconnection between the growing need for crisis communication training and strategic execution in sports marketing.

Crises come in various forms and can impact an organization or individual at any time, including sports organizations, athletes, and teams. In other words, crises are significant, disruptive events that often feature a rapid onset. An event precipitating a crisis can be described as "big trouble that arises suddenly" (Lerbinger, 1997, p.6), and Pearson and Clair (1998) stated that a crisis usually results from "a low-probability, high-impact event" (p. 60). Once the precipitating event occurs, "an event increases in intensity, falls under scrutiny of the news media or government, interferes with normal business operations, devalues a positive public image, and has an adverse effect on a business's bottom line" (Penrose, 2000 p. 156). While crisis situations can have a negative effect, organizations may also experience benefits from such events. Adapting communications practices to proactively establish key relationships and restore dynamic dialog between the organization and its audiences are just a few positive changes that could emerge from a crisis situation.

While technology plays an important role in managing communication with all stakeholders, those stakeholders now have access to more voices, including during crisis situations. Another rising trend for athletic brands and sports figures to address as a growing crisis is cancel culture. *Cancel culture* in social media attempts to "stop giving support to [the person who posted the insensitive content]. The act of canceling could entail boycotting an actor's movies or no longer reading or promoting a writer's works. The reason for cancellation can vary, but it usually is due to the person in question having expressed an objectionable opinion, or having conducted themselves in a way that is unacceptable so that continuing to patronize that person's work leaves a bitter taste" (*What It Means to Get "Canceled,"* n.d.)

Cancel culture is one that is gripping society for various reasons and circumstances. Some current cases involving sports and athletic figures include:

- *George Glassman*: After his tweet regarding the George Floyd protests and after several Crossfit locations said they would break away from the Crossfit brand. The former Crossfit CEO ended up stepping down from his role (*CrossFit CEO Quits after George Floyd Remarks*, 2020).
- *Equinox and Soulcycle*: When it was discovered that one of their corporate leadership had hosted fundraisers for President Trump in 2019. This resulted in a trending topic on Twitter and many members voicing their concerns and outrage on this information, which some said made them cancel their membership.
- *FedEx and the Washington Football Team*: The national delivery service, which pays about $8 million a year for the naming rights to the team's stadium in Landover, MD, issued a stark warning to then-Redskins owner Dan Synder to change the name of the franchise or risk losing FedEx' sponsorship.

Understanding the uses of new emerging technologies – including social media – in a crisis allows crisis communicators to disseminate crisis messages effectively (Freberg, 2012). In addition, this activity raises the important issue of understanding the organization involved and the audience invested in the situation.

Diversity, Equity, and Inclusion in Social Media and Sports

When we talk about the concept of diversity, we refer to situations that emphasize the unique capabilities of each individual, recognizing that we come together representing a variety of dimensions of difference, including race, ethnicity, gender, sexuality, culture, socioeconomic status, age, physical abilities, religion, and ideologies. While some categories of difference appear to be fixed, others are more fluid, making self-identification an important consideration. Diversity further recognizes individual differences with acceptance, appreciation, and respect, and fosters exploration of our differences in safe and supportive environments. Diversity issues arise when a policy or practice has a disproportionately negative impact on a particular group. Many areas of society experience frequent diversity issues, and social media is far from immune.

Several issues continue to be at the forefront of trending topics, discussions, and threads on various social media platforms. For example, gender pay inequality is a growing area of concern among social media professionals. In addition, the lack of diversity in leadership roles within the industry is another concern. Ethical concerns emerge as strategists tap different cultures and audiences in their campaigns to celebrate ties between their brand and diverse communities because the underlying purpose of such campaigns is to make money. There is also a difference between simply saying you are supporting diversity and inclusion efforts and taking sincere actions. Historically, we can identify brands that have been supportive of diversity and inclusion efforts as part of their DNA, including Nike, Adidas, NBA, and MLS.

This is also the case for sport properties themselves. The NFL has dealt with many challenges regarding their handling of social and racial issues, specifically regarding former football player Colin Kaepernick. This has been a topic of conversation in the sports and mainstream media for years, ever since Kaepernick began kneeling during the national anthem to protest against police brutality in 2016 (A Timeline of Events since Colin Kaepernick's National Anthem Protest—The Undefeated, n.d.). In 2020, when protests started happening around the country related to the deaths of George Floyd, Breonna Taylor, and others, the social media team behind the NFL did not believe that the professional football organization was doing enough, so they decided to take action themselves without consulting the NFL leadership (Jones, n.d.). The NFL social media team recruited professional players to be part of a video to discuss racial inequality and shared the video on the main social media channels. As a result, Roger Goodell, the NFL Commissioner, made a public statement that the organization had not done enough to address this issue (Jones, n.d.) The jury is out on the fate of the social media team members who acted without informing NFL leadership. Historically, when employees have gone rogue, they are fired by their bosses. Yet, this case does show how employees can spark a movement from within with a click (or tweet, in this case) of a button.

Sports and Social Movements

Social media platforms have also served as a catalyst for social movements within sports. This is especially true given the rising prominence of the #BlackLivesMatter movement in the wake of police killings of unarmed black men and women across the United States. Popular athletes like Lebron James, Aaron Rodgers, and Bubba Wallace have all been publicly outspoken about racial and social injustice on their social media platforms. Each of the five major professional men's sports organizations in the United States (NFL, MLB, NBA, NHL, and MLS) have publicly supported the movement across various channels. Members of the Atlanta Dream (WNBA) publicly opposed franchise owner Kelly Loeffler's election to the US Senate over comments Loeffler made belittling the movement and the players' participation in it. Elizabeth Williams posted an image of herself on her personal Twitter account wearing a T-shirt supporting Loeffler's political opponent, Rev. Raphael Warnock.

The BlackLivesMatter movement is but one example of athletes using their platform to advocate for social change on social media. It also reflects a growing trend of athletes banding together collectively to rally around a cause rather than operating as individuals. Take, for instance, the players of the PAC-12 conference threatening to boycott football games during the COVID-19 pandemic. Under the hashtag #WeAreUnited, players from the PAC-12 developed a list of demands that included – among others – provisions for safer health policies and racial justice. Alternatively, college football players from around the country voiced their desire to play football during the fall of 2020 despite the global pandemic. Clemson quarterback Trevor Lawrence was among the notable players to use the hashtag #WeWantToPlay, and was retweeted by President Donald Trump, who also advocated for college football to be played on his own Twitter account.

Researchers have begun to develop a considerable body of extant scholarship around the topic of sports and activism on social media. Hull and Schmittle (2015) explored how advocates for concussion awareness in football used Twitter to help spread their message during the 2013 Super Bowl. Sanderson et al. (2016) investigated how fans used social media to resist advocacy efforts by St. Louis Rams players in response to the shooting of Michael Brown in Ferguson, Missouri. Cooky and Antunovic (2020) located feminist narratives in networked communication around the WNBA's activism and the US national women's soccer team's pursuit for equal pay. These are but a few examples of the work that's being done to explore the various ways in which social movements play out on social media in the context of sports.

Gaming

Perhaps one of the most rapidly emerging areas of sports and social media revolves around gaming. In many ways, *gaming* can be considered a sport in its own right and often manifests itself across North America in different ways including the sustained popularity of fantasy sports, the growing prominence of sports betting, and the steady rise in popularity of esports. We will address each of these below.

Fantasy sports are widely popular around the world, but especially so in North America. Fantasy sports are played almost entirely on the internet, as users assemble imaginary teams composed of real players of a professional sport to compete against other users in virtual leagues. In 2017, approximately 60 million people played fantasy sports in the United States and Canada alone (Willingham, 2020). In its purest form, fantasy sports offer users a sense of agency and a competitive outlet. Some of the earliest research on fantasy sports applied a uses- and gratifications framework to understand user motivations for participation. Farquhar and Meeds (2007), for instance, identified five types of players: (1) casual players, (2) skilled players, (3) isolationist thrill-seekers, (4) trash-talkers, and (5) formatives. Social media platforms have only enhanced users' ability to collect information about athletes in real-time, make informed decisions about who to add or drop from their roster, and, of course, talk trash with their competition. It has also given rise to a new brand of fantasy sports player and, consequently, a new brand of fantasy sports in general.

New forms of fantasy sports have made it easy for users to not only compete against one another but also encourage users to place a financial wager on the outcome of real and virtual sporting events. These newer versions of fantasy sports have become incredibly lucrative. Daily fantasy sports (DFS) outlets like DraftKings and FanDuel accounted for $2.91 billion in revenue in the United States in 2019 (Shriber, 2020). The National Football League (NFL) recently partnered with DrafKings on a multi-year contract through which the two entities will collaborate on content for the DraftKings app, including marks, logos, data, NextGen Stats, and NFL-produced video clips. Despite the effects of COVID-19 on the sports industry, DraftKings reported higher than expected revenue in the third quarter of 2020, generating $133 million, and the app surpassed 1 million active monthly users – a 64% increase from a year earlier. These companies leverage social media to attract new participants by holding contests and using sponsors, offering valuable advice and insight to users, and crowdsourcing opinions through the use of polls and quizzes.

Beyond fantasy sports and sports betting, esports have emerged as one of the most popular forms of competition. Esports often take the form of organized multiplayer video game competitions between players and teams. The popularity of esports has exploded over the past decade. Research by Newzoo predicts that the Esports audience will grow from 495 million to more than 646 million by 2023. While the majority of Esports competitors originate in the Asia-Pacific region, nearly 210 million are from North America. Thus, eager investors are tracking the commercial potential of social platforms such as Twitch, Reddit, Discord, and various YouTube channels that are go-to streaming sites for millions of esports fans. Esports are increasingly prominent on social media. A report by Socialbakers found that social media interactions with traditional sports organizations decreased by nearly 20 percent in the first quarter of 2020, while interactions with esports entities increased by nearly 56 percent. Part of this is attributable to the cancellation of traditional sports during quarantine but reflects an upward trajectory that esports has enjoyed for much of the past decade. Like traditional sports, individual competitors develop their own brands online and frequently interact with their followers through social media.

New Methodological Approaches

There is a pressing need for researchers to broaden their methodological toolkit to extend the study of sports and social media. For too long we have mistakenly accepted large datasets as indicators of quality research. This is simply not the case. Extracting social media content has become much more accessible, and thousands of tweets should not provide the basis for a research project alone. Consequently, the impetus is now on the researcher to do more with more. While the content and thematic analysis still provide useful approaches for exploration, in order to further advance this research area, we must move to incorporate more advanced analytic techniques in order to reflect the complexity of the data (and metadata) available through social media. We suggest two broad approaches that may offer productive paths forward: computational methods and predictive analytics.

First, computational methods represent an array of techniques that offer valuable insight into large datasets but often require prior knowledge of coding language and computer programming to conduct effectively. Nevertheless, there are a number of suitable methods that researchers may employ to further advance the study of sports marketing and social media. For example, Hambrick and Sanderson (2013) used network analysis to explore the social network that developed amongst sports journalists as the Penn State football scandal evolved. Yu and Wang (2015) used sentiment analysis to examine US soccer fans' emotional responses in their tweets, particularly, the emotional changes after goals. More recently, Davidson et al. (2020) conducted a sentiment analysis of tweets mentioning professional wrestling organizations in the United States during the COVID-19 pandemic. Finally, Kim et al. (2017) conducted a cluster analysis of sports social network site users to classify users into key market segments based on motivation for sport SNS usage and to identify users' personality traits associated with motivation and SNS consumption behaviors.

Second, predictive analytics involves the use of data, statistical algorithms, and machine learning techniques to assess the likelihood of future outcomes based on historical data. Peng et al. (2018), for example, evaluated prospective recruits for the University of Virginia football team by analyzing statistics available from popular recruiting websites (e.g., 247sports and MaxPreps) and social media data from Twitter to determine whether the recruits would be a good fit for the program and if they would succeed on the playing field. The use of predictive analytics in the communication discipline – especially in sports social media – is still in its infancy, but there is tremendous upside for both researchers and practitioners who take the time to meticulously and systematically organize data and develop functional predictive models.

These methodological approaches are simply starting points for moving the study of sports marketing and social media beyond its often-criticized descriptive tendencies. Indeed, the dynamic nature of social media invites researchers to be creative in the ways we collect, analyze, and interpret data. It is important to stress that computational methods and predictive analytics are not the *only* way forward, but rather provide direction for more advanced approaches to studying sports marketing and social media.

References

Abidin, C. (2016). Visibility labour: Engaging with influencers' fashion brands and # OOTD advertorial campaigns on Instagram. *Media International Australia, 161*, 86–100. https://doi.org/10.1177%2F1329878X16665177

A timeline of events since Colin Kaepernick's national anthem protest — The Undefeated. (n.d.). Retrieved June 7, 2020, from https://theundefeated.com/features/a-timeline-of-events-since-colin-kaepernicks-national-anthem-protest/

Alalwan, A. A., Rana, N. P., Dwivedi, Y. K., & Algharabat, R. (2017). Social media in marketing: A review and analysis of the existing literature. *Telematics and Informatics, 34*(7), 1177–1190.

Allagui, I., & Breslow, H. (2016). Social media for public relations: Lessons from four effective cases. *Public Relations Review, 42*(1), 20–30. 10.1016/j.pubrev.2015.12.001

Allison, R., Knoester, C., & Ridpath, B. (2021). Public opinions about paying college athletes and athletes protesting during the national anthem: A Focus on Race/Ethnicity and Political Identities. *Du Bois Review: Social Science Research on Race*, 1–23. doi:10.1017/S1742058X21000229

Billings, A. C., & Brown, K. A. (2017). (Eds.) *Evolution of the modern sports fan: Communicative approaches.* Lexington Books.

Blank, G., & Reisdorf, B. C. (2012). The participatory web: A user perspective on Web 2.0. *Information, Communication & Society, 15*(4), 537–554.

Burns, E. B. (2014). When the Saints went marching in: Social identity in the World Champion New Orleans Saints football team and its impact on their host city. *Journal of Sport and Social Issues, 38*(2), 148–163.

#Canceled: How cancel culture is affecting brands—Digiday. (n.d.). From https://digiday.com/marketing/cancel-culture/

Charlton, A. B., & Cornwell, T. B. (2019). Authenticity in horizontal marketing partnerships: A better measure of brand compatibility. *Journal of Business Research, 100*, 279–298.

Childers, C. C., Lemon, L. L., & Hoy, M. G. (2019). #Sponsored #Ad: Agency Perspective on Influencer Marketing Campaigns. *Journal of Current Issues & Research in Advertising, 40*, 258–274. https://doi.org/10.1080/10641734.2018.1521113

Cooky, C., & Antunovic, D. (2020). "This Isn't Just About Us": Articulations of Feminism in Media Narratives of Athlete Activism. *Communication & Sport*, 2167479519896360

CrossFit CEO quits after George Floyd remarks. (2020, June 10). BBC News. https://www.bbc.com/news/world-us-canada-52988959

Davidson, N. P., Du, J., & Giardina, M. D. (2020). Through the perilous fight: A case analysis of professional wrestling during the COVID-19 pandemic. *International Journal of Sport Communication, 13*, 465–473.

De Veirman, M., Cauberghe, V., & Hudders, L. (2017). Marketing through Instagram influencers: The impact of number of followers and product divergence on brand attitude. *International Journal of Advertising, 36*(5), 798–828.

Enke, N., & Borchers, N. S. (2019). Social media influencers in strategic communication: A conceptual framework for strategic social media influencer communication. *International Journal of Strategic Communication, 13*(4), 261–277. 10.1080/1553118X.2019.1620234

Farquhar, L. K., & Meeds, R. (2007). Types of fantasy sports users and their motivations. *Journal of Computer-Mediated Communication, 12*(4), 1208–1228.

Freberg, K. (2012). 'Intention to Comply With Crisis Messages Communicated Via Social Media'. *Public Relations Review, 38*(3), 416–421.

Freberg, K., Graham, K., McGaughey, K., & Freberg, L. A. (2011). Who are the social media influencers? A study of public perceptions of personality. *Public Relations Review, 37*(1), 90–92. 10.1016/j.pubrev.2010.11.001

Gantz, W., & Lewis, N. (2014). Sports on traditional and newer digital media: Is there really a fight for fans?. *Television & New Media, 15*(8), 760–768.

Gantz, W., & Wenner, L. A. (1995). Fanship and the television sports viewing experience. *Sociology of Sport Journal, 12*(1), 56–74.

Hambrick, M. E., & Sanderson, J. (2013). Gaining Primacy in the Digital Network: Using Social Network Analysis to Examine Sports Journalists' Coverage of the Penn State Football Scandal via Twitter. *Journal of Sports Media, 8*, 1–18. https://doi.org/10.1353/jsm.2013.0003

Hambrick, M. E., Simmons, J. M., Greenhalgh, G. P., & Greenwell, T. C. (2010). Understanding professional athletes' use of Twitter: A content analysis of athlete tweets. *International Journal of Sport Communication, 3*(4), 454–471.

Hardin, M. (2014). Moving beyond description: Putting Twitter in (theoretical) context. *Communication & Sport, 2*(2), 113–116.

Haugh, B. R., & Watkins, B. (2016). Tag me, tweet me if you want to reach me: An investigation into how sports fans use social media. *International Journal of Sport Communication, 9*(3), 278–293.

Henry, T. M., & Oates, T. P. (2020). "Sport Is Argument": Polarization, Racial Tension, and the Televised Sport Debate Format. *Journal of Sport and Social Issues, 44*(2), 154–174. 10.1177/0193723519881199

Himelboim, I., & Golan, G. J. (2019). A social networks approach to viral advertising: The role of primary, contextual, and low influencers. *Social Media + Society, 5*(3), 2056305119847516. 10.1177/2056305119847516

Hull, K., & Schmittel, A. (2015). A fumbled opportunity? A case study of Twitter as role in concussion awareness opportunities during the Super Bowl *Journal of Sport and Social Issues, 39*, 78–94. https://doi.org/10.1177%2F0193723514558928

Jones, J. R. and L. (n.d.). *Inside NFL players' Black Lives Matter video, and how it …* The Athletic. Retrieved June 6, 2020, from https://theathletic.com/1857643/2020/06/06/inside-nfl-players-black-lives-matter-video-and-how-it-forced-goodells-hand/

Kim, B., & Kim, Y. (2019). Growing as social beings: How social media use for college sports is associated with college students' group identity and collective self-esteem. *Computers in Human Behavior, 97*, 241–249.

Kim, Y., Kim, S., & Kim, Y-M. (2017). Big-Five Personality and Motivations Associated with Sport Team Social Networking Site Usage: A Cluster Analysis Approach. *Journal of Global Sport Management, 2*, 250–274. https://doi.org/10.1080/24704067.2017.1389249

Laurell, C., & Söderman, S. (2018). Sports, storytelling and social media: A review and conceptualization. *International Journal of Sports Marketing and Sponsorship*, 19(3), 338–349. 10.1108/IJSMS-11-2016-0084

Lerbinger, O. (1997), *The Crisis Manager: Facing Risk and Responsibility*. Lawrence Erlbaum Associates, Inc.: Mahwah.

Lou, C., & Yan, S. (2019). Influencer marketing: How message value and credibility affect consumer trust of branded content on social media. *Journal of Interactive Advertising, 19*, 58–73.

Luoma-aho, V., Pirttimäki, T., Maity, D., Munnukka, J., & Reinikainen, H. (2019). Primed authenticity: How priming impacts authenticity perception of social media influencers. *International Journal of Strategic Communication, 13*(4), 352–365. 10.1080/1553118X.2019.1617716

Pearson, C. M. & Clair, J. A. (1998). Reframing crisis management. *Academy of Management Review*, 23(1), 59–76.

Pedersen, P. M. (2014). A commentary on social media research from the perspective of a sport communication journal editor. *Communication & Sport, 2*(2), 138–142.

Peng, K., Cooke, J., Crockett, A., Shin, D., Foster, A., Rue, J., … & Adams, S. (2018, April). Predictive analytics for University of Virginia football recruiting. In *2018 Systems and Information Engineering Design Symposium (SIEDS)* (pp. 243–248). IEEE.

Penrose, J. M. (2000). The role of perception in crisis planning. *Public Relations Review, 26*(2), 155–171.

Sanderson, J., & Emmons, B. (2014). Extending and withholding forgiveness to Josh Hamilton: Exploring forgiveness within parasocial interaction. *Communication & Sport, 2*, 24–47.

Sanderson, J. & Hambrick, M. E. (2012). Covering the scandal in 140 characters: Exploring the role of Twitter in coverage of the Penn State Saga. *International Journal of Sport Communication, 5*(3), 384–402.

Sheffer, M. L. & Schultz, B. (2010). Paradigm shift or passing fad? Twitter and Sports Journalism. *International Journal of Sport Communication, 3*(4), 472–484.

Shriber, T. (2020, September 6). Monkey Knife Fight buys rival Fantasy Draft as consolidation hits DFS space. Casino.org. https://www.casino.org/news/monkey-knife-fight-buys-rival-fantasydraft-as-consolidation-hits-dfs-space/

Smith, B. G., Stumberger, N., Guild, J., & Dugan, A. (2017). What's at stake? An analysis of employee social media engagement and the influence of power and social stake. *Public Relations Review, 43*(5), 978–988. 10.1016/j.pubrev.2017.04.010

Statista. (2018). Global sponsorship spending by region from 2009 to 2018 (in billion U.S. dollars). Retrieved from https://www.statista.com/statistics/196898/global-sponsorship-spending-by-region-since-2009/

Sweetser, K. D., & Kelleher, T. (2016). Communicated commitment and conversational voice: Abbreviated measures of communicative strategies for maintaining organization-public relationships. *Journal of Public Relations Research, 28*(5–6), 217–231.

Stoycheff, E., Liu, J., Wibowo, K. A., & Nanni, D. P. (2017). What have we learned about social media by studying Facebook? A decade in review. *New Media & Society, 19*(6), 968–980. 10.1177/1461444817695745

Taylor, M., & Kent, M. L. (2010). Anticipatory socialization in the use of social media in public relations: A content analysis of PRSA's Public Relations Tactics. *Public Relations Review, 36*(3), 207–214. doi: 10.1016/j.pubrev.2010.04.012

van Driel, L., & Dumitrica, D. (2020). Selling brands while staying "Authentic": The professionalization of Instagram influencers. *Convergence: The International Journal of Research in New Media Technologies.* https://doi-org.echo.louisville.edu/10.1177/1354856520902136

Wann, D. L., & Branscombe, N. R. (1993). Sport fans: Measuring degree of identification with their team. *International Journal of Sport Psychology, 24*, 1–17.

Wann, D. L., & James, J. D. (2019). *Sport fans: The psychology and social impact of fandom.* Routledge.

Wann, D. L., Schrader, M. P., & Wilson, A. M. (1999). Sport fan motivation: Questionnaire validation, comparison by sport, and relationship to athletic motivation. *Journal of Sport Behavior, 22*, 114–139.

What It Means to Get 'Canceled' (n.d.). Words we're watching. *Miriam-Webster.* https://www.merriam-webster.com/words-at-play/cancel-culture-words-were-watching

Willingham, A. J. (2020, Sept. 2). Fantasy football is a billion-dollar pastime. *Covid-19 is wreaking havoc with it.* https://www.cnn.com/2020/12/05/us/fantasy-football-coronavirus-challenges-trnd/index.html

Yu, Y., & Wang, X. (2015). World Cup 2014 in the Twitter World: A big data analysis of sentiments in U.S. sports fans' tweets. *Computers in Human Behavior, 48*, 392–400. https://doi.org/10.1016/j.chb.2015.01.075

16

Social Media and Athlete Branding

Caroline Riot and Michelle Hayes

Introduction

Many scholars have explored the concept of athletes as brands given their influence on sport and non-sport consumers. A brand in the sport landscape has been defined as "a name, design, symbol, or any combination that a sports organization uses to help differentiate its product from the competition" (Shank, 1999, p. 239). Arguably, athletes could be considered brands because they each have a name, distinctive appearance, and personality (Arai et al., 2014). Drawing on the aforementioned definition, Arai et al. (2014) suggest athlete brands encompass the public persona of individual athletes who have managed to establish their own value and symbolic meaning using their name, face, or other brand elements including their likeness. Athletes who successfully develop a brand are more likely to ascertain benefits such as endorsement deals with businesses and sponsors, higher salaries, and more success once their sport career has ended (Arai et al., 2014).

In the pre-social media era, athlete branding consisted of traditional forms of media such as television, radio, and print to provide advertisers with a return on investment. Pre-digitization athletes could only communicate with their audience through the press, unlike today where athletes of all levels have the power to build and engage with audiences via the internet. The transition to contemporary athlete branding approaches using digitization helps to frame this chapter's discussion on the specific aspect of digital sport management relating to social media branding. In particular, we focus on how athletes leverage influencer-led marketing strategies to target their audiences through social platforms and capitalize on the attention they have captured because of their athletic abilities.

Social media have enabled athletes to take control of their branding message (Abeza et al., 2015; Filo et al., 2015; Lopez-Carril et al., 2020). While traditional broadcast media allowed athletes' brands to be widely communicated and marketed (Lebel & Danylchuk, 2014), social media give athletes greater control over how their image is managed and presented to others. Social media are defined as "new media technologies facilitating interactivity and co-creation that allow for the development and sharing of user-generated content among and between organizations (e.g., teams, governing bodies, agencies, and media groups) and individuals (e.g., consumers, athletes, and journalists)" (Filo et al., 2015, p. 167). Specifically, social media are used as strategic tools to build and maintain a strong brand presence (Wallace et al., 2011). The

DOI: 10.4324/9781003088899-19

proliferation of platforms has allowed athletes to produce user-generated content and interact and engage with a range of stakeholders. These interactions facilitate a range of opportunities for athletes. For instance, fans follow athletes on social media in large numbers, providing athletes with an opportunity to establish relationships and use the platforms as a marketing tool to promote and enhance their personal brands or endorse products (Pegoraro, 2010).

This chapter serves as a primary source for scholars to learn about and research athlete social media branding. It provides clear definitions, key theories, and frameworks guiding scholarly understanding of social media and athlete branding with an overview of athlete brand construction, gendered and sport stakeholder considerations and perspectives, use of social media for athlete branding in the context of COVID-19, athlete philanthropy and activism, athletes as influencers, the challenges associated with athlete social media branding, and emerging platforms and features.

Social Media and Athlete Branding

Approximately 3.6 billion people used social media in 2020 (Statista, 2020a). The number of social media users is expected to grow in future years, with 4.1 billion users forecasted by 2025. As of October 2020, Facebook has still ranked the most popular platform among users, followed by YouTube, WhatsApp, Facebook Messenger, WeChat, Instagram, and TikTok (Statista, 2020b). Several of these platforms have been adopted by athletes for a range of purposes, including branding. One of the earliest studies investigating athlete use of Twitter noted that athletes predominantly talk about their personal lives and respond to fans (Pegoraro, 2010). While research on athlete use of Twitter has shown their willingness to post and interact with other users through short messages, image-based, and video-predominant platforms, such as Instagram, have increased in popularity and opened additional opportunities for athlete branding. Like Twitter, Instagram enables users to share photos, follow other users, and view their content. The platform has enabled athletes to take control of their self-presentation and craft their own personal brands (Doyle et al., 2020; Geurin-Eagleman & Burch, 2016).

The power of social media for personal branding extends to individuals' capacity to change narratives and debunk myths and stereotypes. For example, research on Paralympians' use of Instagram shows that self-presentation may mitigate stereotypes associated with disability and counteract negative assumptions (Mitchell et al., 2021). Comparing the social media content of able-bodied and para-athletes, Mitchell and colleagues (2021) reveal that the visual content posted by Paralympians tends to depict physical competence and elite abilities (e.g., engaged in sport or fitness-related activities) compared with able-bodied athletes focus on personal and lifestyle aspects. Using social media to create visual representations of these kinds can simultaneously work to promote the capabilities of athletes with a disability and mitigate stereotypes when shared with fans.

More recently, TikTok has emerged and gained acceptance among athletes as they look for new ways to engage with their fans (Su et al., 2020a). Although established in 2016, TikTok grew dramatically in popularity between 2018 and 2020. TikTok is an application that allows users to create short videos to share with other users and is unique in providing an assortment of visual effects, templates, filters, and a built-in music library to use for videos. This provides athletes with a new means to showcase their personalities through music linked to videos. Table 16.1 provides an overview of theoretical frameworks or concepts used to frame inquiry on athletes and social media branding, and examples of the platforms researched.

On social media, athletes can strategically manage their presentation of themselves through carefully selected photos, audio files, and videos (Bullingham & Vasconcelos, 2013). Photo and

Table 16.1 Overview of theoretical frameworks and examples of social media platforms researched

Example literature	*Theoretical frameworks/concepts*	*Platforms*
Brison & Geurin (2021)	Social Influence Theory	Twitter
Doyle et al. (2020)	Self-Presentation Theory; Model of Athlete Brand Image (MABI)	Instagram
Geurin (2017)	Impression Management; Self-Presentation Theory	New Media*
Geurin-Eagleman & Burch (2016)	Self-Presentation Theory	Instagram
Howell (2021)	Celebrity cultivation of intimacy and authenticity	Instagram
Kunkel et al. (2020)	Model of Athlete Brand Image (MABI)	Instagram
Kunkel et al. (2021)	Name, Image, and Likeness (NIL)	Twitter; Instagram
Li et al. (2020)	Self-Presentation Theory	Instagram
Mitchell et al. (2021)	Self-Presentation Theory	Instagram
Na et al. (2020)	Signaling Theory	Twitter
Park et al. (2020)	Self-Presentation Theory	Social Media*
Pegoraro (2010)	Not available	Twitter
Su et al. (2020a)	Human Brand theory	TikTok; Douyin
Su et al. (2020b)	Schema Theory; Brand Architecture	Instagram; Twitter
Toffoletti & Thorpe (2018)	Self-Branding; Aesthetic Labor; Postfeminism	Instagram
Watkins & Lee (2016)	Brand Identity Theory	Instagram; Twitter
Yoo (2022)	Self-Management	Instagram

Note

* Indicates studies that explored platforms more broadly.

video style platforms are garnering the most attention from scholars (i.e., Instagram) (e.g., Doyle et al., 2020; Geurin & McNary, 2020; Geurin-Eagleman & Burch, 2016). However, as Instagram has evolved and added new features, research has examined these updates and how they are used for athlete branding. For instance, existing work by Geurin-Eagleman and Burch (2016) examined photographs posted by athletes, while more recent work by Li et al. (2020) explored Instagram stories (a feature that enables users to post content that vanishes after 24 hours). Further, Howell (2021) noted Instagram Live enabled athletes to maintain celebrity-status and generate engagement, particularly during COVID-19 shut-downs. By examining two elite female athletes, Sue Bird and Megan Rapinoe, Howell (2021) found that Instagram Live enabled the two to perform intimacy and authenticity as part of their celebrity persona maintenance during a time of instability for their sports.

Theoretical Frameworks and Athlete Branding

Table 16.1 also reveals that scholarly research on athlete social media branding is relatively diverse in the theoretical frameworks underpinning. Researchers have adopted branding models and theories (e.g., Model of Athlete Brand Image (MABI)) (e.g., Doyle et al., 2020; Kunkel et al., 2020), sociological theories (e.g., self-presentation theory) (e.g., Geurin, 2017; Li et al., 2020), and/or marketing theories and concepts (e.g., human brand theory) (e.g., Su et al. 2020a, 2020b).

While a range of models and frameworks have been used to explore athlete branding, some have been adapted multiple times, such as self-presentation. Goffman's (1959) self-presentation theory provides a theoretical lens to help explain how individuals may present different versions of themselves to derive a positive image and elicit beneficial responses from others. Self-presentation is used to construct a marketable self-image that encompasses skills, personal values, and characteristics to help individuals position themselves (Shepherd, 2005). Therefore, it is unsurprising that self-presentation theory has guided the understanding of athlete branding, as athletes can positively position themselves based on their skills, values, and characteristics.

Studies using self-presentation theory have shown that athletes use social media to craft their own image and brand by engaging in several strategies and tactics including sharing their lives, representing athletic identities, and making authentic posts (Doyle et al., 2020; Geurin, 2017; Park et al., 2020). Goffman (1959) considered a person's self-presentation to consist of frontstage and backstage performances. In front-stage performances, people "tend to be more concerned with the impression they create in the minds of others" (Geurin-Eagleman & Burch, 2016, p. 134). In backstage performances, people tend to be less restrained and provide more candor.

Applying the self-presentation concepts to social media, scholars have demonstrated that athlete-based frontstage content consists of athletes engaging in their sport, while content related to personal settings represents backstage content. From a branding perspective, it appears that athletes are posting more about their personal lives (i.e., backstage content) rather than sport-related content (Geurin-Eagleman & Burch, 2016; Smith & Sanderson, 2015). Scholars have suggested that both on-field attributes and off-field attributes of athlete brands impact consumers. Specifically, consumers connect with athletes and their related entities, such as the athlete's team or sponsor (Kunkel et al., 2020), yielding benefits for not only athletes but other organizations or brands in sport.

More recently, research has applied the MABI to social media spaces. The MABI (Arai et al., 2013, 2014) is a comprehensive conceptual framework of athlete brand image. Three key dimensions form the MABI including athletic performance, attractive appearance, and marketable lifestyle (Arai et al., 2014). Athletic performance relates to an athlete's on-field characteristics and is an important element in establishing an athlete's brand image, given the main persona of an athlete is performing to the best of their ability in their sport endeavors. Attractive appearance signifies content showcasing an athlete's physical attributes and characteristics, while a marketable lifestyle relates to the associations linked to the athlete's off-field characteristics. Applying these dimensions to social media, Doyle et al. (2020) extended on branding work by Arai et al. (2013, 2014) by developing and testing the Model of Athlete Brand Image via Social Media and revealed athletic performance content attracted higher rates of consumer engagement than the attractive appearance and marketable lifestyle dimensions. However, engagement was enhanced by posts containing good-quality photos and the athlete's teammates (Doyle et al., 2020).

Researchers have also begun to explore athletes' follower engagement on social media regarding brand mentions and disclosures of the relationships between athletes and their endorsements (Brison & Geurin, 2021). Taking a Social Influence Theory perspective, Brison and Geurin (2021) noted athletes received greater engagement on non-brand-related posts compared to brand-related posts.

Social Media Branding and Gender

An emerging area within athlete social media branding literature is gendered approaches to branding. For female athletes, social media provide an opportunity to develop their brand in the absence of traditional media coverage of themselves and their sports (Burch & Zimmerman, 2019). Specifically, female athletes cultivate the athletic labor of femininity in their branding efforts by creating heroic images and disclosing personal intimacies through images (Toffoletti & Thorpe, 2018). Mogaji et al. (2020) noted that sportswomen rely on social media in the brand-building phase by utilizing the platforms to engage with their fans. This engagement is often in the form of pictures of their routines, revealing their battles with injuries, and divulging vulnerabilities that build emotional connections.

Sportswomen can further capitalize on social media to challenge gender norms and portrayals and the perceptions of the public which are perpetuated through traditional media outlets (Yang et al., 2020). For instance, Pegoraro et al., (2018) found social media and sport users have begun to create their own frames around female athletes, particularly during events. In their examination of visual images posted by social media users during the 2015 FIFA Women's World Cup, Pegoraro et al. (2018) noted that female athletes were predominately portrayed as athletically competent which may have been influenced by sportswomen's presence on social media over time.

Social Media Branding and Sport Stakeholder Perspectives

To date, research has studied social media branding practices from two main perspectives: the athletes' experiences and fan engagement patterns (Su et al., 2020b). While this work has established an understanding of the branding strategies of athletes via social media, the platforms have also been widely accepted by other sport stakeholders including sport governing bodies, leagues, teams, sporting events, and fans (Abeza et al., 2015; Hutchins, 2014). Athlete brands exist within a network of brand relationships (Su et al., 2020b). Therefore, other sport stakeholders work closely with athletes and may also leverage athletes to promote their own brands or products. According to Su et al. (2020b), athlete brands are provided with benefits from brand relationships with sport leagues and teams. However, it may be important for researchers to consider whether league or team brands are an accurate reflection of the brand or image an athlete is trying to create on their own platform or whether the brands of athletes must align with those of their employer.

Athletes can also leverage their involvement in sport events for their own promotional purposes (Geurin & McNary, 2020; Hayes et al., 2019). However, the proliferation of social media in sport has resulted in restrictions and rigorous guidelines placed on athletes. The Olympic Games provides one example of how sport governing bodies have intervened to restrict athlete social media content, particularly related to branding. Geurin and McNary (2020) studied Rule 40 of the Olympic Charter as it is designed to prevent ambush marketing during the Olympic Games. Rule 40 restricts what content athletes can post on social media about non-Olympic sponsors and has implications for how they promote their own sponsors. However, despite the efforts of the International Olympic Committee, athletes engage in ambush marketing, intentionally and unintentionally. Rule 40 enforcement issues are apparent, but athletes' brand-building efforts are better suited after the Olympic Games to avoid sanctions (Geurin & McNary, 2020).

Similar issues are faced by student-athletes beginning their careers and establishing their brand. Social media empowers student-athletes to build their brand (David et al., 2018). However, they are often bound by restrictions implemented by colleges and athletic departments that may cause them to engage in self-censorship to avoid action from sport organizations. These restrictions are argued to impact student-athletes' individuality and self-expression (David et al., 2018), and potentially their brand. To elaborate on this important issue, Kunkel et al. (2021) highlight the impact of the NCAA's current assessment of the value of student-athletes' name, image, and likeness (NIL) and the potential for them to monetize their social media accounts. Of particular relevance to this chapter is the unique value of athletes as sub-brands independent of their team master brands (at the institution level) and the capacity for sportswomen and niche sport athletes to benefit from being allowed to monetize from their NIL.

While research has predominately studied social media branding practices from two perspectives, several aspects of athlete branding are beginning to be explored and may be impacted by world events. For instance, COVID-19 had devasting impacts on the sport and events industries. During this time, athletes may have been presented with other branding opportunities due to the uptake in social media to stay connected and satisfy sports fans' need to consume content in the absence of leagues and events. Research has also examined the impact of philanthropy and activism on athlete social media branding efforts, while platforms continue to adapt to user trends and needs. These trends and opportunities for future research are discussed in more detail in the following section.

Trends and Future Research

Athlete Social Media Branding and COVID-19: Challenges and Opportunities

The rapid growth and rate of change in digital communication type, capability, and strategies since the COVID-19 pandemic (e.g., widespread adoption of messaging tools, such as WhatsApp and Slack for communication) have worked to increase the connection and flow of information across sectors and industries. While the global pandemic has accelerated streaming services and renewed appetites for digital entertainment in the sport sector, fans still prefer live-sporting content and encounters (Deloitte, 2020), so how can athletes maximize their personal brand by using social media in a context where events and competitions have been canceled or postponed?

Work by Deutsch et al. (2019) shows that fans are looking to consume sports across devices and in various formats including augmented reality (AR) and virtual reality (VR) and turn to social media for regular and immediate updates. For young Millennials (18 to 24 years old), the use of social media spans far beyond fan interaction and involves getting updates on favorite teams and players while watching the game. However, postponed and canceled events have interrupted fan engagement with live sport. The radical overhaul of the sports calendar means that athletes cannot rely on the traditional sport branding platform of events for building "big-impact" brand awareness through the right of publicity. For example, a report by Deloitte (2020) showed that during the pandemic, time spent watching live events halved to two-and-a-half hours per week and those actively following sport on a weekly basis dropped from 46% to 25%, thereby reducing the time available to athletes to showcase their brands to fans during live events.

Further, a lack of competitive success may impact brand image if an athlete's brand solely depends on performance in the most recent season, match, or race. For example, COVID-19 prevents athletes from extracting any newly acquired brand value earned from winning events. Mirias (2020) suggests that for single-name moniker athletes like the global brand personalities of LeBron, Tiger, or Ronaldo, whose images and likenesses transcend sports altogether, COVID-19 is not likely to have a significant impact on their brand or value. However, athletes that are not trans-generational household names including college athletes, fear losing brand momentum because their profile cannot be reinforced through widely viewed performances (Mirias, 2020). Athletes need to maintain their brand momentum and the value of their right of publicity by other means. With the uncertainty surrounding the future of spectator sports, athletes' ability to use personal brands and work with potential sponsors to create new deals may be limited unless they shift their approach. Further, the regulatory changes that may impact the

NIL value of student-athletes (Kunkel et al., 2021) highlight the expanding influence of social media in the "more than an athlete" movement, where athletes are becoming more aligned with charitable causes and community initiatives.

The ability for athletes and teams to interact with fans on any given day through social channels and digital platforms has opened possibilities for athletes to think of new ways to engage fans and connect with younger audiences using social media, which can also provide additional social and emotional value to athletes. Approaches that involve greater engagement with the sports industry to co-develop social media campaigns have the potential to broaden adjacent fan experiences, maximize athlete brand awareness and create new or additional revenue streams. This is particularly important for college athletes who have the potential to develop their own brands and target younger audiences. Yet, moving away from an event platform to build athletes' brands using social media involves careful consideration of the type and frequency of content shared to engage fans, as well as athlete interactions with broadcasters and sponsors to create new and different sports content.

An athlete's disposition to extend their brand longevity means thinking about and in the context of a "come-back plan." For athletes, more thought can be given to brand longevity and readiness for when events are on the table again (e.g., what they can be doing now on social media to create or maintain brand awareness and strengthen relationships with "partners" for the future. Forethought may be particularly important for college athletes who can forge their own brand independent of their organization, with the ability to profit from their likenesses (i.e., name and image) (Blinder, 2019; Dwyer, 2019). This includes how athletes position themselves using social media in terms of values and purpose-driven content to engage fans. For example, using social media to share content around activism, and give fans insider access to sporting and personal lives can work to strengthen athletes' brands and prepare the stage for a return to purposefully re-engage with fans when live events and regular competition resumes (Kunkel et al., 2020).

Several promising theoretical directions have begun to be explored, including using social media for philanthropic reasons and to voice opinions and feelings on political topics, acting as role models, and how athletes manage the potentially distracting and time-consuming nature of branding amongst their various other activities and pursuits (e.g., education, work, and social life). As social media are rapidly developing and changing to meet consumer needs, athletes may also need to adapt to new platforms in the future for their branding efforts or adopt multiple platforms as part of their strategies. Key questions for future research include understanding which platforms provide greatest impact and influence in terms of consumer reach (how and why?) and should strategies to consolidate efforts across platforms (e.g., to demonstrate niche or unique brand offerings) or promote the use of multiple platforms for wider distribution of brand be considered.

Athlete Philanthropy and Activism

Athletes have begun to leverage their social media presence to promote philanthropic efforts which may have implications for branding. Promotion of philanthropic activities via social media appears to have a positive impact on athlete brand image and can result in enhanced perceptions of overall character by fans and followers (Kunkel et al., 2020). Specifically, athletes promoting philanthropic activities can potentially experience stronger levels of fandom by their followers and fans, which could lead to other branding opportunities. The COVID-19 pandemic also demonstrated athletes' abilities to engage in philanthropy and promote social responsibility using their social media presence. Abuín-Penas et al. (2020) noted that athletes engaged in three key activities on social media related to the pandemic including awareness-raising and advocacy, calling for action, and sharing information. By engaging in this communication, athletes were able to reinforce their image as globally responsible citizens through their social media presence. This messaging may have been beneficial to athlete brands, while also providing social value (Abuín-Penas et al., 2020).

Given the positive impacts and perceptions of athletes engaging in philanthropic activities, particularly in relation to the athlete's overall character, athletes who have transgressed may be able to use social media to showcase philanthropic activities as part of their brand reconstruction and image repair strategies (Allison et al., 2019; Bell & Hartman, 2018). However, the response to such a branding maneuver requires further investigation to uncover whether this is successful or whether social media users see through any attempt to make them forget about the athlete's transgression.

In addition to the promotion of philanthropic activities, social media appears to be driving athlete activism and social justice movements. One of the most prominent examples occurred in 2020 when athletes across the world supported the Black Lives Matter movement by posting a black square on their Instagram platforms to symbolize their involvement in #BlackoutTuesday. Athletes across all levels of sport showed their solidarity with the Black Lives Matter movement including NBA star LeBron James to Kate Cross, an English international cricketer. Although not the first instance of athletes bringing awareness to Black Lives Matter or engaging in athlete activism, Yan et al. (2018) noted that social media presents a huge capacity for mobilization and that ongoing involvement promotes the voices of those marginalized by social injustice. Like philanthropic ventures, athletes may experience enhanced perceptions in relation to their overall character and subsequent branding implications.

Athletes are also using social media to disclose personal experiences and challenge the stigmatization of mental health (Parrott et al., 2020). These disclosures have nurtured positive discussions concerning mental illness, garnered positive responses from fans, and challenged the stigmatization of mental illness. By using social media to promote philanthropic ventures, engage in activism social justice movements, and shed light on stigmatization athletes are showing they are more than just individuals who excel in the sport arena. However, not everyone will share the same sentiment or support athletes' endeavors to bring awareness to these issues.

Athletes have received backlash from the public on social media, even some of their fans, or have been labeled as "controversial" for their involvement in social justice movements or political conversations (Sanderson et al., 2016). In their study of five African American St. Louis Rams players locking hands during player introductions in response to racial inequalities, Sanderson et al. (2016) noted the backlash manifested through renouncing fandom, racial commentary, attacks on the athletes, and general criticism. Further, student-athletes have suggested that while social media empowers them to build their brand, they are often required to engage in self-censorship to avoid action from sport organizations, which can stifle their individuality and self-expression (David et al., 2018). Olympic athletes may experience similar issues, given the IOC moved to eliminate athlete activism and political statements in the lead up to the 2021 Tokyo Games through Rule 50 (International Olympic Committee, 2021). Therefore, it is important for researchers to continue to investigate these areas and the impact both positive and negative reactions have on athlete brands, as well as the influence of governing bodies' stances on activism.

Athletes as Role Models and Influencers

Social media provides an opportunity to extend the athlete role model rhetoric which may have implications for athlete brands. Athletes are typically seen as role models, but the presence of athletes on social media sites and the images and videos they publicize could be socially influential (Koh & Leng, 2017). Leng and Phua (2020) suggest that athlete role models can leverage the power of social media to spread positive messaging, including those related to health, and encourage appropriate behaviors. These behaviors may extend to increasing physical activity and sport participation for mental and physical health (Hayes, 2020).

COVID-19 provides an interesting example of how athletes engaged with their followers to promote healthy living choices. For instance, Australian athletes engaged in #LikeAnOlympian campaign which encouraged Australians to "train like an Olympian at home" to stay healthy during lockdown (Australian Olympic Committee, 2020). Athletes disseminated a series of positive videos, healthy living tips, and gave fans access to home workouts, skills training, and challenges against other athletes. The videos were posted across several platforms, including Instagram, Facebook, and YouTube. By engaging with followers in this way, athletes are branding themselves as healthy living ambassadors and may incentivize young individuals to play sport (Chmait et al., 2020).

In terms of athlete social media branding, it appears athletes were harnessing backstage content by showcasing how they were coping with lockdown and providing more glimpses into their personal lives to engage with their fans and followers given the absence of live sport and competition. However, an opportunity exists to explore the branding implications of this type of content and advocation. Specifically, researchers could explore what branding opportunities athletes can yield by perpetuating their status as "role models." Considerations could be given to the types of brands and partnerships athletes may obtain, the level of fan interaction and engagement based on healthy living choices, and the branding implications if an athlete's status as a role model or healthy living advocate is compromised (e.g., by engaging in doping).

The concept of athletes as influencers is also emerging in the literature and can be linked to the use of an athlete's celebrity-status to simultaneously demonstrate role model behavior and generate interest in products or services on social media. Athletes as influential role models may affect or change the way that other people behave. Athletes with a strong personal brand and a high degree of "celebrity-status" have been long associated with marketers who use athlete endorsements to promote their brands, products, and services (Schouten et al., 2020). Using an athlete's qualities, positive image, and characteristics, marketers work to entice consumers to purchase endorsed products, services, or behave in a certain way.

What is interesting from a marketing and advertising perspective, is the growing tendency to use social media influencers (also called "micro-celebrities"), such as vloggers and "Instafamous" personalities rather than "traditional" celebrities such as actors, supermodels, and athletes to endorse and add value to company brand (Marwick, 2015). However, athletes using social media to promote themselves and their favorite brands could influence consumers' attitudes toward the athlete endorser based on attractiveness, credibility, and congruence between the athlete and product (Cunningham & Bright, 2012). By using social media in this way, athletes are a type of influencer that "works to generate a form of 'celebrity' capital by cultivating as much attention as possible and crafting an authentic 'personal brand' via social networks, which can subsequently be used by companies and advertisers for consumer outreach" (Hearn & Schoenhoff, 2016, p. 194). Social media allow athletes to directly communicate (paid or unpaid) endorsements "personally" to fans, and this can work to enhance an athlete's brand reputation, likeability, and attractiveness through association with the brand being endorsed or the degree of congruence between the brand and the athlete. Till and Busler (2000) suggest that such influences can be higher on those followers who admire and identify themselves with the athlete.

Challenges of Athlete Social Media Branding

Although this chapter has predominately demonstrated the benefits of social media branding based on the focus of scholarly research, athletes may also be presented with challenges that could have implications for their overall brand image. First, having a social media presence has sadly resulted in athletes becoming victims of online bullying and unwanted commentary (Geurin, 2017; Hayes et al., 2020; Kilvington & Price, 2019) which may have implications for athlete branding. For instance, Geurin (2017) noted that athletes select what they post online to create an accurate picture of themselves for their individual brands. However, some athletes may refrain from posting certain aspects of their lives to avoid unwanted commentary or negative comments from their followers or fans.

Second, athletes appear to be expected to maintain some form of online presence and brand. However, the rapid adoption of these platforms has led to some athletes being criticized for becoming too focused on their online image rather than focusing on sport and competing (Hayes et al., 2021). Further, some athletes report social media branding as a distraction due to the time-consuming nature of maintaining a brand and one that could lead to impaired performance during important competition times (Hayes et al., 2020). Specifically, athletes are required to meet contractual obligations with their sponsors which may entail making a certain number of posts per week.

Depending on the content and frequency of posts required, athletes may spend several hours crafting these posts to meet sponsors' requirements. Some athletes may receive assistance through their management team; however, others may not have this support and are therefore required to incorporate branding efforts into their competing priorities. Athletes seeking sponsorship may need to spend more time establishing and crafting their brand to market themselves to potential brands to form partnerships (David et al., 2018; Hayes et al., 2019). Obtaining sponsorship agreements may be more important for some athletes who do not receive large salaries or funding for their involvement in sport, particularly sportswomen who often receive inadequate media representation, exposure, and lower salaries (Mogaji et al., 2020).

Another issue that may arise from extended social media use for branding-related content is mental fatigue. Fortes et al. (2019) suggested that approximately 30 minutes or more of use before a competition increased athletes' mental fatigue which led to impaired performance and decision-making during competition. The MABI model indicates that athletic performance is an important aspect of athlete branding (Arai et al., 2014). However, if athlete performances are becoming comprised due to more focus being placed on social media and an online image, their overall brand image may suffer.

To address challenges related to social media, some athletes have opted to engage in blackout periods or switch-off social media during important times (Hayes et al., 2020). For instance, LeBron James engages in "Zero Dark Thirty-23," which is code for his annual disengagement from social media channels during the playoff and finals stretch of the NBA season. However, these blackout periods could have various implications for athlete branding and raise several questions. For instance, how is a social media blackout period negotiated with sponsors or businesses who may garner additional coverage during important events like the NBA playoffs? Could a blackout period harm an athlete's brand image due to the lack of fan engagement during this time? Or does engaging in a social media blackout period portray athletes as more responsible for focusing on their team and performance? These questions provide a start point for scholars to explore in future research to establish a deeper understanding of the potential downsides of athlete social media branding and how these are negotiated between varying stakeholders.

Emerging Platforms and Features

Social media are constantly changing and adapting to trends to remain competitive among other providers. Although it may be hard to predict what form the next social media trend may take, industry experts are predicting the main three platforms (Facebook, Instagram, and Twitter) will remain dominant over the next few years (Ong, 2020). Facebook, Instagram, and Twitter have the capability to rapidly change based on industry trends. For instance, social media "stories" have become more prevalent after Snapchat launched the feature in 2013. Instagram launched stories in 2016, followed by Facebook in 2017, while Twitter tested a version called "Fleets" in 2020. Wakefield and Bennett (2018) refer to the emergence of these features as "ephemeral social media" as the content is automatically deleted after a prescribed time. Athletes have embraced ephemeral social media for their branding efforts and appear to use stories for different purposes. Specifically, Li et al. (2020) suggested that stories are largely used for interaction, promotion, and behind-the-scenes content, while traditionally feeds were more likely to be used to express opinions.

Instagram and other similar platforms have also enabled athletes to go "live" to interact with fans and followers with the implementation and capabilities of livestreaming. Social media livestreaming provides a dynamic, authentic, and engaging way for brands to engage with consumers. Although sports have utilized livestreaming as part of their social media strategies, athlete-led content can foster a better sense of connection (Wymer et al., 2020). Athlete-led livestreaming experienced an uptake during the Covid-19 pandemic as athletes grappled with boredom and isolation during government-imposed lockdown (Wymer et al., 2020). For instance, in April 2020 during the Covid-19 pandemic, Rafael Nadal engaged with Roger Federer and Andy Murray on Instagram Live and discussed injury recovery, how they were coping during the pandemic, home-schooling children, and reminisced on previous matches against each other. The livestream was viewed by more than 40,000 people and received a positive response (Herman, 2020). Although livestreaming experienced an uptake during Covid-19 in the absence of live sport, it will be interesting to see whether this use is sustained and in what ways when live sport returns, as well as the possibility for livestreaming and live attendance to be used in a complementary fashion.

Apart from the main three platforms Facebook, Instagram, and Twitter, TikTok has increased in popularity and awareness. However, the platform has a long way to go before it catches up to the three larger and more established networks but is expected to continue to grow as the trend of "remixing" continues (Ong, 2020). Remixing consists of taking existing formats or templates and recreating them to express one's own personality. Athletes may incorporate remixing into their branding efforts to showcase their personalities away from their sporting endeavors. Su et al. (2020a) noted that TikTok presents opportunities for athletes to foster existing fan relationships, promote branded content, and appeal to new fan segments. Specifically, TikTok content could cater to audiences who prefer novelty and viewing the activities of athletes outside of game interviews or highlights. If the trend of "remixing" continues, we may see the rise of other similar platforms trying to gain a share of users' attention, including athletes. For example, Byte, released in 2020, is a short-form video hosting service allowing users to create 15-second looping videos. The platform was created as a successor to Vine.

Although Su et al. (2020a) provided a glimpse into how athletes utilize TikTok for fan engagement and branding purposes during the Covid-19 pandemic, future research should continue to investigate the implications of this platform (and those of a similar format) on athlete branding and their image. Researchers could examine the response and engagement by fans and other brands or sponsors on athletes' "remixed" content and how this is perceived.

Notably, there appears to be a lack of research regarding Snapchat and athlete branding even though Snapchat is a fast way to share content and moments through short videos, images, and stories and may facilitate unique interactions with fans and followers. Given the platform's underpinnings, Billings et al. (2017) noted the platform can facilitate sports fandom, which is an important aspect of athlete branding. Although scholars have examined the use of Snapchat in sport (e.g., Billings et al., 2017), specific applications to athlete branding appear to be lacking.

Further, researchers have predominately contextualized their work to one platform, presenting generalizability issues for athlete social media branding research. Athletes typically use multiple platforms for their branding efforts and may adopt different brand strategies for each platform (Geurin, 2017). While some studies (e.g., Geurin, 2017; Park et al., 2020) have examined athlete branding efforts on new media platforms (including social media) more broadly, future research may be better suited to include multiple platforms to address generalizability issues and better reflect the different branding strategies athletes adopt for each platform.

Conclusion

This chapter provided insight into how athletes use different social media platforms to engage in real-time and direct one-to-one dialog with fans, and construct, shape, and present their own brand and marketing endeavors. Social media platforms such as Twitter, Instagram, or Facebook afford the opportunity for athletes to reach a greater number of audiences at a time, place, and frequency that is convenient to fans (Hull, 2014), and provide greater control to athletes in managing how their image is presented to others. In this chapter, we highlighted several promising theoretical directions that are being explored, including using social media for philanthropic reasons and to voice opinions and feelings on political topics, acting as role models, and how athletes manage the potentially distracting and time-consuming nature of branding amongst their various other activities and pursuits (e.g., education, work, and social life).

As social media are rapidly developing and changing to meet consumer needs, athletes may also need to adapt to new platforms in the future for their branding efforts or adopt multiple platforms as part of their strategies. Key questions for future research include understanding which platforms provide the greatest impact and influence in terms of consumer reach (how and why?) and should strategies consolidate efforts across platforms (e.g., to demonstrate niche or unique brand offerings) or promote the use of multiple platforms for wider distribution of brands.

References

Abeza, G., O'Reilly, N., Séguin, B., & Nzindukiyimana, O. (2015). Social media scholarship in sport management research: A critical review. *Journal of Sport Management*, *29*(6), 601–618. 10.1123/JSM.2014-0296

Abuín-Penas, J., Babiak, K., & Martínez-Patiño, M. J. (2020). Athlete's philanthropy and social responsibility communication on social media during COVID-19. *Journal of Human Sport and Exercise*. Advance online publication. 10.14198/jhse.2022.171.20

Allison, R., Pegoraro, A., Frederick, E., & Thompson, A. J. (2019). When women athletes transgress: An exploratory study of image repair and social media response. *Sport in Society*, *23*(6), 1023–1041. 10.1080/17430437.2019.1580266

Arai, A., Ko, Y. J., & Kaplanidou, K. (2013). Athlete brand image: Scale development and model test. *European Sport Management Quarterly*, *13*(4), 383–403. 10.1080/16184742.2013.811609

Arai, A., Ko, Y. J., & Ross, S. (2014). Branding athletes: Exploration and conceptualization of athlete brand image. *Sport Management Review*, *17*(2), 97–106. 10.1016/j.smr.2013.04.003

Australian Olympic Committee. (2020). At home with #TeamAus. Australian Olympic Committee. https://www.olympics.com.au/at-home-with-team-aus/

Bell, T. R., & Hartman, K. L. (2018). Stealing thunder through social media: The framing of Maria Sharapova's drug suspension. *International Journal of Sport Communication, 11*(3), 369–388. 10.1123/ijsc.2018-0079

Billings, A. C., Qiao, F., Conlin, L., & Nie, T. (2017). Permanently desiring the temporary? Snapchat, social media, and the shifting motivations of sports fans. *Communication & Sport, 5*(1), 10–26. 10.1177/2167479515588760

Blinder, A. (2019, September 30). N.C.A.A. athletes could be paid under new California law. *New York Times*. https://nyti.ms/3qXDutk

Brison, N. T., & Geurin, A. N. (2021). Social Media Engagement as a Metric for Ranking US Olympic Athletes as Brand Endorsers. *Journal of Interactive Advertising, 21*, 121–138. https://doi.org/10.1080/15252019.2021.1919251

Bullingham, L., & Vasconcelos, A. C. (2013). 'The presentation of self in the online world': Goffman and the study of online identities. *Journal of Information Science, 39*(1), 101–112. 10.1177/0165551512470051

Burch, L. M., & Zimmerman, M. H. (2019). Female athletes find a place for expression on Instagram. In Lough, N., & Geurin, A. N. (Eds.), *Routledge handbook of the business of women's sport* (pp. 468–479). Routledge.

Chmait, N., Westerbeek, H., Eime, R., Robertson, S., Sellitto, C., & Reid, M. (2020). Tennis influencers: The player effect on social media engagement and demand for tournament attendance. *Telematics and Informatics*. Advance online publication. 10.1016/j.tele.2020.101381

Cunningham, N., & Bright, L. F. (2012). The tweet is in your court: Measuring attitude towards athlete endorsements in social media. *International Journal of Integrated Marketing Communications, 4*(2), 73–87.

David, J. L., Powless, M. D., Hyman, J. E., Purnell, D. M., Steinfeldt, J. A., & Fisher, S. (2018). College student athletes and social media: The psychological impacts of Twitter use. *International Journal of Sport Communication, 11*(2), 163–186. 10.1123/ijsc.2018-0044

Deloitte. (2020, September 7). COVID creates an alternate entertainment reality. Deloitte Media Consumer Survey 2020 [Press release]. https://www2.deloitte.com/au/en/pages/media-releases/articles/covid-creates-an-alternate-entertainment-reality-070920.html#

Deutsch, A., Hardwood, K., Teller, L., & Deweese, C. (2019). The future of sports broadcasting: Enhancing digital fan engagement. *Deloitte Development*. https://www2.deloitte.com/content/dam/Deloitte/us/Documents/technology-media-telecommunications/us-enhancing-digital-fan-engagement.pdf

Doyle, J. P., Su, Y., & Kunkel, T. (2020). Athlete branding via social media: Examining the factors influencing consumer engagement on Instagram. *European Sport Management Quarterly*. Advance online publication. 10.1080/16184742.2020.1806897

Dwyer, C. (2019, October 29). NCAA plans to allow college athletes to get paid for use of their names, images. *NPR (National Public Radio)*. https://www.npr.org/2019/10/29/774439078/ncaa-starts-process-to-allow-compensation-for-college-athletes

Filo, K., Lock, D., & Karg, A. (2015). Sport and social media research: A review. *Sport Management Review, 18*(2), 166–181. 10.1016/j.smr.2014.11.001

Fortes, L. S., Lima-Junior, D., Nascimento-Júnior, J. A., Costa, E. C., Matta, M. O., & Ferreira, M. E. (2019). Effect of exposure time to smartphone apps on passing decision-making in male soccer athletes. *Psychology of Sport and Exercise, 44*(2019), 35–41. 10.1016/j.psychsport.2019.05.001

Geurin, A. N. (2017). Elite female athletes' perceptions of new media use relating to their careers: A qualitative analysis. *Journal of Sport Management, 31*(4), 345–359. 10.1123/jsm.2016-0157

Geurin-Eagleman, A. N., & Burch, L. M. (2016). Communicating via photographs: A gendered analysis of Olympic athletes' visual self-presentation on Instagram. *Sport Management Review, 19*(2), 133–145. 10.1016/j.smr.2015.03.002

Geurin, A. N., & McNary, E. L. (2020). Athletes as ambush marketers? An examination of Rule 40 and athletes' social media use during the 2016 Rio Olympic Games. *European Sport Management Quarterly*. Advance online publication. 10.1080/16184742.2020.1725091

Goffman, E. (1959). *The presentation of self in everyday life*. Anchor Books.

Hayes, M. (2020). Social media and inspiring physical activity during COVID-19 and beyond. *Managing Sport and Leisure*. 1–8. 10.1080/23750472.2020.1794939

Hayes, M., Filo, K., Riot, C., & Geurin, A. (2019). Athlete perceptions of social media benefits and challenges during major sport events. *International Journal of Sport Communication, 12*(4), 449–481. 10.1123/ijsc.2019-0026

Hayes, M., Filo, K., Geurin, A., & Riot, C. (2020). An exploration of the distractions inherent to social media use among athletes. *Sport Management Review, 23*(5), 852–868. 10.1016/j.smr.2019.12.006

Hayes, M., Filo, K., Riot, C., & Geurin, A. (2021). Using communication boundaries to minimize athlete social media distractions during events. *Event Management*. Advance online publication. 10.3727/152599521X1610657795215

Hearn, A. & Schoenhoff. (2016). From celebrity to influencer: Tracing the diffusion of celebrity value across the data stream. In P. David Marshall & S. Redmond (Eds), *A companion to celebrity*, (pp. 194–212). John Wiley & Sons.

Herman, M. (2020, April 21). 'I am a disaster': Mocked Nadal meets his match in hilarious Instagram live fail. *Fox Sports*. https://www.foxsports.com.au/tennis/i-am-a-disaster-mocked-nadal-meets-his-match-in-hilarious-instagram-live-fail/news-story/0a873e34ef3d6011d781f49f076b4884

Howell, C. E. (2021). A touch more with megan rapinoe and sue bird: Authenticity, intimacy and women's sports celebrity on Instagram live. *Celebrity Studies*. Advance online publication. 10.1080/19392397.2021.1958694

Hull, K. (2014). A hole in one (hundred forty characters): A case study examining PGA Tour golfers' Twitter use during the Masters. *International Journal of Sport Communication*, 7(2), 245–260. 10.1123/IJSC.2013-0130

Hutchins, B. (2014). Twitter: Follow the money and look beyond sports. *Communication & Sport*, *2*(2), 122–126. 10.1177/2167479514527430

International Olympic Committee. (2021). Rule 50 explained. *IOC*. https://olympics.com/athlete365/rule-50-resources/

Kilvington, D., & Price, J. (2019). Tackling social media abuse? Critically assessing English football's response to online racism. *Communication & Sport*, 7(1), 64–79. 10.1177/2167479517745300

Koh, J. Y., & Leng, H. K. (2017). Marketing sport coaching services on social network sites: An examination of social influence and country-of-origin effect. *Managing Sport and Leisure*, *22*(5), 390–399. 10.1080/23750472.2018.1495097

Kunkel, T., Baker, B. J., Baker, T. A., & Doyle, J. P. (2021). There is no nil in NIL: examining the social media value of student-athletes' names, images, and likeness. *Sport Management Review*, *24*, 839–861. https://doi.org/10.1080/14413523.2021.1880154

Kunkel, T., Doyle, J., & Na, S. (2020). Becoming more than an athlete: Developing an athlete's personal brand using strategic philanthropy. *European Sport Management Quarterly*. Advance online publication. 10.1080/16184742.2020.1791208

Lebel, K., & Danylchuk, K. (2014). Facing off on Twitter: A generation Y interpretation of professional athlete profile pictures. *International Journal of Sport Communication*, 7(3), 317–336. 10.1123/IJSC.2014-0004

Leng, H. K., & Phua, Y. X. P. (2020). Athletes as role models during the COVID-19 pandemic. *Managing Sport and Leisure*, 1–5. 10.1080/23750472.

Li, B., Scott, O. K., Naraine, M., & Ruihley, B. J. (2020). Tell me a story: Exploring elite female athletes' self-presentation via an analysis of Instagram stories. *Journal of Interactive Advertising*. Advance online publication. 10.1080/15252019.2020.1837038

Lopez-Carril, S., Escamilla-Fajardo, P., Gonzalez-Serrano, M. H., Ratten, V., & Gonzalez-Garcia, R. J. (2020). The rise of social media in sport: A bibliometric analysis. *International Journal of Innovation and Technology Management*, *17*(6), 1–29. 10.1142/S0219877020500418

Marwick, A. E. (2015). Instafame: Luxury selfies in the attention economy. *Public Culture*, *27*(1 (75)), 137–160. 10.1215/08992363-2798379

Mirias, B. (2020, June 03). Ronaldo Who? The impact of COVID-19 on Athletes' brands. *Stout*. https://www.stout.com/en/insights/article/impact-covid-19-professional-athletes-brands

Mitchell, F. R., van Wyk, P. M., & Santarossa, S. (2021). Curating a culture: The portrayal of disability stereotypes by Paralympians on Instagram. *International Journal of Sport Communication*. Advance online publication. 10.1123/ijsc.2021-0030

Mogaji, E., Badejo, F. A., Charles, S., & Millisits, J. (2020). To build my career or build my brand? Exploring the prospects, challenges and opportunities for sportswomen as human brand. *European Sport Management Quarterly*. Advance online publication. 10.1080/16184742.2020.1791209

Na, S., Kunkel, T., & Doyle, J. (2020). Exploring athlete brand image development on social media: The role of signalling through source credibility. *European Sport Management Quarterly*, *20*(1), 88–108. 10.1080/16184742.2019.1662465

Ong, G. (2020, October 23). 10 social media trends to keep an eye on in 2021. *Marketing Interactive*. https://www.marketing-interactive.com/10-social-media-trends-to-keep-an-eye-on-in-2021

Park, J., Williams, A., & Son, S. (2020). Social media as a personal branding tool: A qualitative study of student-athletes' perceptions and behaviors. *Journal of Athlete Development and Experience*, *2*(1), 51–68. https://scholarworks.bgsu.edu/jade/vol2/iss1/4

Parrott, S., Billings, A. C., Hakim, S. D., & Gentile, P. (2020). From #endthestigma to #realman: Stigma-challenging social media responses to NBA players' mental health disclosures. *Communication Reports*. Advance online publication. 10.1080/08934215.2020.1811365

Pegoraro, A. (2010). Look who's talking—Athletes on Twitter: A case study. *International Journal of Sport Communication, 3*(4), 501–514. 10.1123/ijsc.3.4.501

Pegoraro, A., Comeau, G. S., & Frederick, E. L. (2018). # SheBelieves: The use of Instagram to frame the US Women's Soccer Team during# FIFAWWC. *Sport in Society, 21*(7), 1063–1077. 10.1080/17430437.2017.1310198

Sanderson, J., Frederick, E., & Stocz, M. (2016). When athlete activism clashes with group values: Social identity threat management via social media. *Mass Communication and Society, 19*(3), 301–322. 10.1080/15205436.2015.1128549

Schouten, A. P., Janssen, L., & Verspaget, M. (2020). Celebrity vs. Influencer endorsements in advertising: The role of identification, credibility, and Product-Endorser fit. *International Journal of Advertising, 39*(2), 258–281. 10.1080/02650487.2019.1634898

Shank, M. (1999). *Sports marketing: A strategic perspective* (2nd ed.). Prentice Hall.

Shepherd, I. D. (2005). From cattle and coke to Charlie: Meeting the challenge of self-marketing and personal branding. *Journal of Marketing Management, 21*(5-6), 589–606. 10.1362/0267257054307381

Smith, L. R., & Sanderson, J. (2015). I'm going to Instagram it! An analysis of athlete self-presentation on Instagram. *Journal of Broadcasting & Electronic Media, 59*(2), 342–358. 10.1080/08838151.2015.1029125

Statista. (2020a). Number of social network users worldwide from 2017 to 2025. *Statista.* https://www.statista.com/statistics/278414/number-of-worldwide-social-network-users/

Statista. (2020b). Most popular social networks worldwide as of October 2020, ranked by number of active users. *Statista.* https://www.statista.com/statistics/272014/global-social-networks-ranked-by-number-of-users/

Su, Y., Baker, B. J., Doyle, J. P., & Yan, M. (2020a). Fan engagement in fifteen seconds: Athletes' relationship marketing during a pandemic via TikTok. *International Journal of Sport Communication, 13*(3), 436–446. 10.1123/ijsc.2020-0238

Su, Y., Baker, B. J., Doyle, J. P., & Kunkel, T. (2020b). The rise of an athlete brand: Factors influencing the social media following of athletes. *Sport Marketing Quarterly, 29*, 33–46. 10.32731/SMQ.291.302020.03

Till, B. D., & Busler, M. (2000). The match-up hypothesis: Physical attractiveness, expertise, and the role of fit on brand attitude, purchase intent and brand beliefs. *Journal of Advertising, 29*(3), 1–13. 10.1080/00913367.2000.10673613

Toffoletti, K., & Thorpe, H. (2018). The athletic labour of femininity: The branding and consumption of global celebrity sportswomen on Instagram. *Journal of Consumer Culture, 18*(2), 298–316. 10.1177/1469540517747068

Wakefield, L. T., & Bennett, G. (2018). Sports fan experience: Electronic word-of-mouth in ephemeral social media. *Sport Management Review, 21*(2), 147–159. 10.1016/j.smr.2017.06.003

Wallace, L., Wilson, J., & Miloch, K. (2011). Sporting Facebook: A content analysis of NCAA organizational sport pages and big 12 conference athletic department pages. *International Journal of Sport Communication, 4*(4), 422–444. 10.1123/ijsc.4.4.422

Watkins, B., & Lee, J. W. (2016). Communicating brand identity on social media: A case study of the use of Instagram and Twitter for collegiate athletic branding. *International Journal of Sport Communication, 9*(4), 476–498. 10.1123/IJSC.2016-0073

Wymer, S., Thompson, A. J., & Martin, A. J. (2020). Diminishing the distance during social distancing: An exploration of Australian sport organizations usage of social live streaming services throughout Covid-19. In P. Pedersen, B. Ruihley, & B. Li (Eds.). *Sport and the pandemic: Perspectives on Covid-19's impact on the sport industry*, (pp. 61–69). Routledge.

Yan, G., Pegoraro, A., & Watanabe, N. M. (2018). Student-athletes' organization of activism at the University of Missouri: Resource mobilization on Twitter. *Journal of Sport Management, 32*(1), 24–37. 10.1123/jsm.2017-0031

Yang, E. C. L., Hayes, M., Chen, J., Riot, C., & Khoo-Lattimore, C. (2020). A social media analysis of the gendered representations of female and male athletes during the 2018 Commonwealth Games. *International Journal of Sport Communication, 13*(4), 670–695. 10.1123/ijsc.2020-0045

Yoo, E. (2022). "I can't just post anything I want": Self-management of South Korean sports stars on social media. *International Review for the Sociology of Sport, 57*, 477–494. https://doi.org/10.1177%2F10126902211014122

17

Immersive Technology and the Virtual Sport Spectator Experience

Luke R. Potwarka, Peter A. Hall, Chad Goebert, and Hasan Ayaz

Introduction

Sport organizations are continually looking for ways to enhance fan and spectator experiences. Emerging technologies such as virtual reality (VR) and augmented reality (AR) are offering sport consumers novel and immersive ways to connect and engage with digital sport media content. These approaches to experiential marketing and gameday delivery may be of particular relevance in the post-COVID era, as many sport managers may continue to consider policies aimed at limiting the amount of in-person spectators in sport venues and stadia. Moreover, many sport spectators and fans may be hesitant to attend in-person mass gatherings for years to come.

Emerging virtual technologies implemented by sport managers are also of particular interest to sport researchers. Indeed, relatively limited attention has been directed to understanding the experiences of sport consumers who adopt these technologies and digital formats. Moreover, as this chapter will outline, there are new and exciting ways to collect data as it relates to these virtual experiences in the form of social neuroscience methodology. Just as sport managers are beginning to employ new technologies when designing fan experiences, sport researchers are also employing new technologies to gain more sophisticated and objective understandings of virtual sport spectator experiences. Thus, sport researchers need to continue to consider emerging technologies as both a methodology and a means of experiencing sport events. What follows in this chapter is a discussion of some of the definitions and trends related to virtual spectator experiences and neuroscience methods available to sport researchers. For this chapter, the terms spectatorship and viewership are used interchangeably to refer to both in-person and digitally-based sport event consumption.

Definitions and Trends in Virtual Sport Spectatorship

According to the research of Pricewaterhouse Coopers' (PwC, 2019), Virtual Reality (VR) and Augmented Reality (AR) are set to increase the global GDP by $1.5 trillion by 2030 while also playing a role in enhancing the jobs of over 23 million workers worldwide. The NBA, WNBA, NFL, MLB, NHL, MLS, FIFA along with many other leagues and organizations have invested in and started to deploy AR and VR content (Shea, 2020; Young, 2020a). With that in mind, it

DOI: 10.4324/9781003088899-20

is important to define and understand the role that these immersive technologies play in sport and the sport spectator experience.

Virtual Reality

Virtual reality (VR) is an immersive technology that allows a user to enter a completely digitally created environment or world through a headset or display (Handa et al., 2012). Due to its immersive nature, VR can simulate many real-life situations and settings. It is this immersion and simulation that makes VR a powerful experiential medium.

Augmented Reality

Augmented reality (AR) is an immersive technology that overlays digitally created graphics or information in a real-world setting. One of the most unique and impactful aspects of AR is that it combines virtual elements with a real-world environment (Azuma, 1997). While there are several forms of AR (haptic, audio, olfactory), the primary use of AR is in visual modality. There are multiple ways that visual AR can be experienced, including broadcast AR, computer-based AR, head-mounted display AR (HMD), projector-based AR, and smartphone-based AR.

Immersive Spectator Experience

In recent years, many sport teams and organizations have started to provide opportunities for sport spectators to experience their live sporting events in new and innovative ways. Specifically, there has been a rise in immersive viewing opportunities for spectators to experience sport through AR and VR (Young, 2020a). On top of the previous acceleration of immersive viewing opportunities, the COVID-19 pandemic further accelerated the trend of providing immersive viewing experiences as spectators could no longer watch the sports they love in person (Young, 2020a).

Not only did opportunities for immersive viewing experiences increase, but there was also an increase in modalities and ways in which immersive content could be experienced. The NBA after pausing the 2020 season due to the pandemic moved the remainder of their season and the playoffs to a bubble location at the Wide World of Sports in Orlando Florida. It was there that many spectators were introduced to the concept of the virtual fan being in attendance at a live event. The creation of the "virtual fan" was an attempt to engage with fans that could no longer be present in the venue; or as the leagues head of next-generation telecasts Sara Zuckert put it, "With the unfortunate situation involving the pandemic that we're in, we began to focus how to bring our fans closer to the game in different kinds of ways" (Powell, 2020, para. 9). The NBA and Microsoft partnered to create a technology that allows fans to appear courtside in the arena via high-definition video screens. The fans watched the game through video conferencing software from their homes and their images were digitally presented on screens around the court during the game.

While the creation of the virtual fan at events was a well-received and unique innovation to immerse fans into the sport experience, the vast majority of immersive experiences being deployed by sport organizations and teams continue to be in the form of AR or VR. In August of 2020, the NBA named VR platform Oculus as the official VR headset of NBA, WNBA, and NBA G League (Dixon, 2020). The multi-year deal made Oculus the first VR headset partner in league history and gave them rights to present exclusive VR content. Oculus and the NBA will provide spectators with an immersive experience through never-before-seen camera angles and "Oculus Front Row View" that allows fans to feel like they are in the front row at the venue. Julie Morris, the NBA's Vice President of Media and Business Development, summed up their deal with Oculus by saying "This partnership furthers our ongoing commitment to engage with fans of the NBA, WNBA, and NBA G League in new and innovative ways" (Dixon, 2020, para. 11).

AR has been used in numerous ways to enhance the sport spectator experience. However, one of the most impactful ways AR has enhanced sport spectatorship and created an immersive spectator experience is through broadcast AR. The NBA, NFL, NHL, MLS, and Premier League soccer have all recently partnered with technology companies to provide AR overlays of statistics and data on many of their broadcasts (Goebert, 2020). One of the major players in sport broadcast AR, Second Spectrum, utilizes machine learning and artificial intelligence that enables its software to track players and the ball up to 25 times per second. The technology then overlays statistical data and player performance metrics on the broadcast and is attached to the players in real-time. Second Spectrum has partnered with the English Premier League, NBA, and MLS to create AR broadcasts. The senior vice president of media for the MLS touted what the AR broadcast technology brings to their spectators saying "Along with Second Spectrum, MLS will deliver an enhanced new fan experience, bringing innovation to MLS content" (Baer, 2020, para. 10).

VR and AR Research in Sport Management

Research into the uses of AR and VR and their impact on sport consumers and spectators has lagged behind the adoption of the technologies by sport industry practitioners. VR has been researched from multiple angles in sport. There has been a good deal of research focused on the use of VR for sport skill training (Miles et al., 2012; Craig, 2013; Vignais et al., 2009), physical rehabilitation (Howard, 2017), exergaming (Peng et al., 2013; Reynolds et al., 2014), & fitness (Neumann et al., 2018). Considerably less attention has been directed at the sport spectator or sport consumer experience with VR. However, Kim and Ko (2019) investigated the impact of virtual reality on the sport spectator experience. The authors specifically investigated how VR influenced the flow and satisfaction of sport spectators. The authors created a theoretical framework by combining elements of the extended telepresence theory, flow theory, and the Elaboration Likelihood Model. They focused on what they called virtual reality spectatorship (VRS). Kim and Ko found that VRS amplified the viewers' flow experience and found that flow experience in VRS heightened spectator satisfaction. Interestingly, the authors also found that the impact of VR was stronger on fans who are less involved with the sport they are watching. This is an encouraging finding as sport properties have struggled in recent years to attract new fans. Kang (2020) also discussed virtual reality spectatorship (VRS) which he defined as a "sport-watching behavior with a headset in a mediated environment, wherein virtual reality technology provides a user with immersive experiences" (Kang, 2020, p. 499). Kang found that some of the most significant contributors to the use of VR by spectators are the availability of VR tools, motivation, control of experiences, social influence, and other factors of the system. With that in mind, Kang suggested that VR sport companies should focus on the quality of the video and audio outputs to attract more spectators to their products.

There has not been a great deal of research into the use of AR in the field of sport management. The bulk of the research into AR in sport has been conducted by computer science researchers and has been focused on the development of programs for player training and game action tracking (Lee et al., 2011; Jang et al., 2018; Soltani & Morice, 2020). There have been few academic articles that focus on sport consumer or spectator use of AR. One of the first studies into the sport consumer experience with AR was conducted by Rogers et al. (2017). The authors examined AR's ability to enhance the information-seeking experience of sport spectators. In particular, their study investigated spectator use of an HMD AR technology called Google Glass. Participants were asked to look up statistical information during the game through a program, a smartphone search, or a search through Google Glass. Participants preferred the smartphone option over the others. This study is hard to generalize to uses of AR in sport as Google Glass has been discontinued and no sport organizations or teams are currently utilizing the technology. The finding that participants felt more comfortable searching via a smartphone is actually an encouraging one for AR implementation as the vast majority of AR activations in sport utilize smartphone AR. To that end, Goebert and Greenhalgh (2020) conducted a study of sport-focused smartphone AR activations. The authors utilized the technology readiness and acceptance model and found that the visual appeal of the AR impacted a sport consumer's intention to use the AR application and positively speak about that AR activation to others. In response to the fact that AR has been so sparsely researched in terms of consumer or spectator attitudes, Goebert (2020) produced a commentary on the uses and directions of AR in sport marketing. The authors' aim was to give examples of how AR has been used by the sport industry and help provide direction for practitioners and future research in AR in sport marketing.

The rapid growth in both the efficacy and implementation of VR and AR technology in the world of sport clearly deserves the attention of sport management researchers. Whether it is due to a pandemic or emerging technology, it seems clear the sport spectator experience is evolving. As NBA deputy commissioner Mark Tatum puts it when discussing immersive technologies and sport spectatorship, "I think that is one of those opportunities that we're just scratching the surface on right now" (Young, 2020b, para 20).

Indeed, the relatively limited amount of research examining AR and VR sport viewer experiences has relied on traditional self-report survey research methods. These traditional approaches have already gleaned important insights into the nature of these experiences. However, we argue that employing a social neuroscience approach – one that integrates social context with brain-mediated processes – to understanding these virtual sport spectator experiences represents a promising way for advancing theory in sport management research. We examine these novel approaches in the following sections of this chapter.

Social Neuroscience and Virtual Sport Spectator Experiences

In much the same way as sport organizations are leveraging new technologies such as VR and AR into their operations, sport researchers are also beginning to employ new methodologies and technologies to better understand the experiences of sport spectators/viewers. Emerging methodologies and new technologies are providing researchers with new ways of knowing spectator experiences both virtual and in-person (Larson & Potwarka, 2019). The use of these new approaches may be a result of the limitations of "traditional" methods typically employed in sport consumer research. For example, insights into virtual spectator experiences gleaned from quantitative self-report surveys or post-event interviews with fans may be subject to many forms of retrospective biases and lack *in situ* perspectives. Some spectators, for example, may not always be truthful when they self-report their thoughts and emotions or they may be unable to articulate them while immersed in a virtual sport event experience (Martin et al., 2019). Moreover, spectators' thoughts and feelings may operate at a subconscious level; therefore, their self-reported thoughts, feelings, and behaviors may not accurately reflect their decision-making process (Oppenheim, 1992). Despite these limitations, it is important to note that these traditional methodologies have been fundamental to the advancement of sport consumer behavior theory such as the psychological continuum of fan engagement (Funk & James, 2001) and Madrigal's (2006) FANDIM scale for measuring the multidimensional nature of sport event performance consumption.

However, more holistic and objective understandings of spectator experiences may result from employing a social neuroscience approach. Social neuroscience can be described as an interdisciplinary field that aims to investigate the neurobiological mechanisms (e.g., neural, hormonal) that intersect with social structures, processes, and behavior (Bello-Morales & Delgado-García, 2015). In short, the foundation of social neuroscience posits that "measuring brain activity provides access to psychological processes and neural circuitry that may serve as the underlying mechanisms that explain individual differences in behavior and experiences" (Tompson et al., 2019).

Sport scholars (e.g., Hungenberg et al., 2020; Martin et al., 2019; Larson & Potwarka, 2019) suggest that social neuroscience methodology has emerged in sport management research in response to the deficiencies of traditional research methods outlined above. As a result, some researchers are beginning to employ "direct measurement of neural responses from the human brain so that an objective and unbiased measure of individuals' cognitive and emotional reaction to external sensory stimuli can be captured" (Martin et al., p. 212). The methods used in social neuroscience can allow sport researchers to examine how self-reported spectator experiences and behavior interface with biologically-based cognitive systems (Hungenberg et al., 2020; Potwarka et al., 2020; Larson & Potwarka, 2019).

Thus, we advance the position that employing functional brain imaging modalities such as electroencephalography (EEG); functional near-infrared spectroscopy (fNIRS); and functional magnetic resonance (fMRI) can offer sport researchers more objective and precise understanding of the cognitive and affective nature of sport spectator experiences (both in virtual and in-person experiential contexts). Moreover, the use of eye-tracking technology can also be used to further supplement and enhance these methods. Spectator data gathered from functional brain imaging and eye-tracking methods (described below) can allow scholars to more objectively identify causation, which has long eluded sports consumer behavior researchers situated within a positivist or post-positivist research paradigm. We outline some of the specific functional imaging and eye-tracking methods available to sport researchers below.

Functional Neuroimaging and Eye-Tracking Methods Available to Sport Researchers

There are a number of neuroscience methods that can be utilized to understand brain dynamics that are relevant to the sports viewership experience. Neuroimaging methods (alone and in combination with VR technology and eye-tracking devices) are especially promising. Below are some of the primary modalities for assessing brain responses to the sport spectatorship experience:

Functional Magnetic Resonance Imaging (fMRI)

This technology allows for the imaging of brain function via quantifying a blood oxygenation-dependent (BOLD) response (Heeger & Ress, 2002). Changes in the radio signal given off by water molecules as a function of blood oxygenation level are detected by fMRI devices and used to create a 3-dimensional map of resting and stimulus-related brain activity with up to millimeter resolution (Logothetis, 2008). This technology can measure neural predictors of response to viewership experience, and neural response during or following viewership experience, and can also identify brain-related mediators and moderators of the experience. When combined with VR, all of the above are possible. Some inherent limitations of fMRI in relation to viewership research exist, however. MRI scanners are large and static, requiring specialized housing, and are therefore typically only available in hospitals and research centers; in vivo imaging of brain activity, or imaging brain activity during upright viewing (a more ecologically valid experience) is not possible using MRI(Mehta & Parasuraman, 2013). The logistical constraints around fMRI technology (e.g., size, location, cost) have likely limited its deployment in many studies of sport viewership experience; yet still its strengths in the areas of whole-brain imaging, spatial precision, and breadth of derivable data (which can include also gray/white matter volumes, and tractography) are considerable.

Functional Near-Infrared Spectroscopy

Functional near-infrared spectroscopy (fNIRS) is a brain imaging technique that also involves monitoring cortical hemodynamic response similar to fMRI but using wearable and portable sensors (Ayaz et al., 2013; Curtin & Ayaz, 2018). fNIRS employs sets of optodes (i.e., light illuminators and paired light detectors) placed over the scalp in order to detect subtle changes in oxygenation changes in cortical tissues as a function of underlying neuronal activity via neuro-vascular coupling (Izzetoglu et al., 2005). Tissue and bone are relatively transparent to light emitted at the near-infrared range of the spectrum and yet are also absorbed differentially by oxygenated vs deoxygenated hemoglobin (Yodh & Chance, 1995). Oxygen-rich blood is transported to neuron populations as they become active, making increases in oxygenation a marker for neuronal activity (Villringer & Chance, 1997). This creates an ideal scenario – with powerful enough light emitters and sensitive enough light detectors – to quantify changes in blood oxygenation in the brain, just as a flashlight placed under the palm of the hand may illuminate aspects of the underlying tissues. Although fNIRS can only quantify activity at a depth of a few centimeters and has cm level resolution (rather than mm, as in fMRI), it has many advantages for researchers hoping to quantify neural aspects of the sport viewership experience consistent with neuroergonomics (Ayaz & Dehais, 2019). fNIRS systems can be easily mated to VR devices which might deliver a viewership experience and can accomplish imaging of brain activity in the upright sitting or standing position, live during the viewership experience itself. Likewise, there is a possibility of imaging in vivo brain activity during real sporting events as they happen, even without the use of VR devices as recent studies demonstrated the use of fNIRS during outdoor walking (Mckendrick et al., 2016), wheelchair control (Joshi et al., 2020) and even actual flight in an aircraft (Gateau et al., 2018), speaker-listener engagement (Liu et al., 2017), cooperation (Vanutelli et al., 2016), and as a general tool for social neuroscience (Babiloni & Astolfi, 2014; Di Domenico et al., 2019). Although considerable technical challenges remain, the development of neuroergonomics is highly interconnected with fNIRS and mobile imaging modalities more broadly; this remains an important area to watch for future developments, both technological and methodological (Dehais et al., 2020). Mobile neuroimaging using fNIRS is making imaging of both spectators and athletes possible, and this is an important area of future collaboration between sport researchers, neuroscientists, and engineers.

Electroencephalography

Electroencephalography (EEG) is the oldest brain monitoring technology, and it is well-adapted to examining brain responses during both VR and in vivo sport spectatorship experiences. Unlike fMRI and fNIRS, it captures electrophysiological activity that arises directly from the accumulation of a large number of neuronal activities within the brain (Bucci & Galderisi, 2011). Depending on the number of channels it measures, its spatial resolution goes from none to low, it is not as spatially precise as fMRI, but it does have the advantage of the highest temporal resolution (Mehta & Parasuraman, 2013). Given that the signal being read from the brain is electrically mediated, the latency between neural activity and quantification of the neural response is very short, on the level of milliseconds. By contrast, because of the hemodynamic mediation of the hemodynamic response; both fNIRS and fMRI are limited to seconds of temporal resolution. Depending on the specific research question, the temporal precision afforded by EEG might make it an ideal choice for imaging neural activity in the viewership experience. Like fNIRS, EEG is ideally suited to in vivo imaging and easily mated to VR hardware. During some in vivo experiences, signal interference from outside stimuli and motion artifacts may be prohibitive, however.

Together these brain imaging modalities (used alone or with VR technology and eye-tracking devices) can reveal a significant amount of nuance in the spectator experience. This is particularly true, as sport researchers consider the brain as (1) a predictor of the viewership experience, (2) a way of measuring outcomes of the viewership experience (e.g., attention capture, sustained attention, self-relevance processing), or (3) a mediator/moderator of the viewership experience (e.g., capturing the neural mechanism linking an initial viewership experience and the intent to continue watching in the future). We speak more about the potential theoretical contributions of employing social neuroscience methods (i.e., fMRI, fNIRS, and EEG) below. Eye trackers use infrared cameras to detect slight changes in retinal orientation during stimulus viewing. Like EEG, such measurements are highly precise in a temporal sense, and sampling rates for eye-tracking methods can be over 1,200 Hz (i.e., 1,200 samples per second). As a result, both fixations during and eye saccades can be tracked and accounted for during in vivo observance of sport spectator events when presented on a video screen display. Coupled with neuroimaging, the gaze dynamics uncovered by eye tracking can identify when, how, and why attention is deployed in certain ways during a sport spectatorship experience. Such information may help to inform methods to maintain viewership engagement during virtual representations of events, particularly when in-person viewing is not possible.

Theoretical Implications of Employing Social Neuroscience Methodology

The use of functional neuroimaging methods (e.g., fNIRS) to understand virtual spectator experiences can be informed by a brain-as-predictor theoretical approach (Tompson et al., 2019). This approach seeks to measure brain activation while spectators are engaged with a particular sport event stimuli (e.g., watching a virtual sport event), and then uses that activation to predict subsequent behavioral outcomes/events, often over the course of weeks, months, or even years. Essentially, this theoretical approach suggests that brain activation data can predict the behavior and experiences of sport consumers and fans (e.g., future viewership, sponsorship patronage; social media engagement; merchandise and apparel purchases; participating in the sport on display) above and beyond that what can be predicted from self-report survey data (Tompson et al., 2019). Such methods have, for instance, demonstrated that neural responses to media ads can predict significant, unique variability in real-world behavioral responses over and above self-reported impressions of these same stimuli (Baek et al., 2020; Berkman et al., 2013; Falk et al., 2012; Falk et al., 2012; Wang et al., 2015).

With respect to cortical subregions, there are three potential relevances to the viewership experience: the medial and dorsal aspects of the medial prefrontal cortex (mPFC), the ventrolateral prefrontal cortex (vlPFC), and the bilateral temporoparietal junction (TPJ). The mPFC can be broken down into the frontal polar regions and the dorsomedial prefrontal cortex (dmPFC); these areas are involved in evaluative processing and self-relevance processing, respectively (Figure 17.1). They tend to be active during decision-making wherein values attached to various alternatives are being weighed against each other, and generally speaking, increased self-relevance tends to make such effects more prominent (i.e., when making decisions that are relevant to the self versus others, or non-human objects). The ventrolateral prefrontal cortex is heavily implicated in value processing, and tends to be active when assigning positive and negative values to stimuli, or encountering stimuli of strong emotional significance (in a positive or negative manner). Finally, the TPJ, located at the intersection of the temporal and parietal lobes, is involved in mentalizing – the process of translating mental contents to semantic communication – and therefore implicated in sharing of information within social networks, based on "buzz" and related social psychological phenomena that generate information sharing among larger groups and whole populations (Baek et al., 2020; Falk et al., 2012).

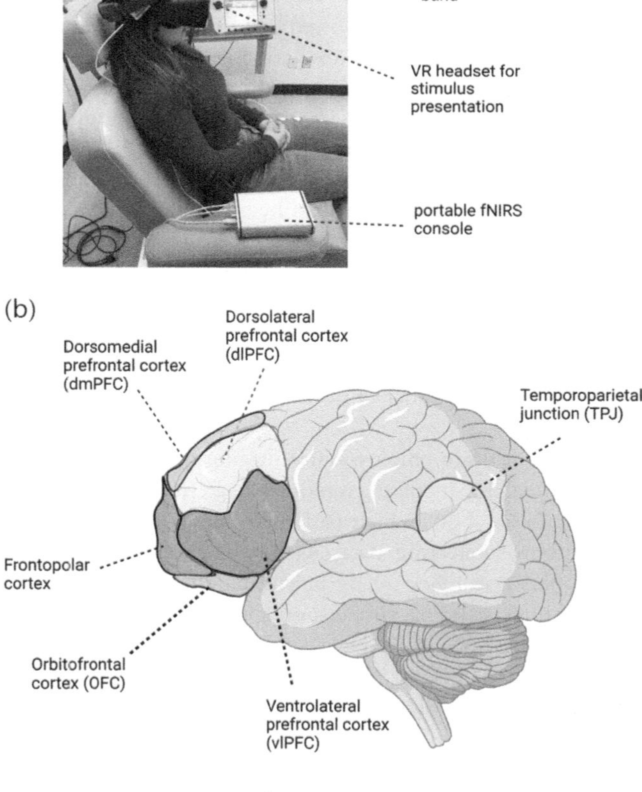

Figure 17.1 Panel (a) equipment montage for neural response imaging in the context of brain-as-predictor paradigms, using VR goggles for display of sport stimulus video. Panel (b) anatomical subregions of the prefrontal cortex and the temporoparietal junction; region boundaries in some cases are approximated. Panel B image created with Biorender.com.

Studies using fMRI to predict behaviors have demonstrated that the ventral medial prefrontal cortex (vmPFC) and ventral striatum (VS) brain regions are frequently implicated in processing the self-relevance, social relevance, and overall value (reward) of incoming information (Tompson et al., 2019). The vmPFC (Figure 17.1), for example, has been implicated in processing the self-relevance of stimuli or information to the self, such as whether an image, word, or product describes the self or is part of their identity (Kelley et al., 2002; Kim & Johnson, 2012). As well, attentional systems involving the MPFC brain regions are typically engaged when stimuli are engrossing and involving (Knudsen, 2007), and a well-documented reward system involving the VS is implicated in the experience of pleasurable states and generation of approach behaviors (Schultz, 2006), and the mirror neurons in the motor systems (e.g., premotor cortex, supplementary motor area) have been implicated in observation of salient actions by others in the environment (Rizzolatti & Craighero, 2004).

Neuroimaging Research in Sport Management

Subcortical regions of the brain may also be important for the spectator experience. For example, using an fMRI, Duarte et al. (2017) found that limbic regions including the amygdala as well as reward related-regions such as the substantia nigra were activated in soccer fans when they were presented with positive marketing content related to their favorite team. The authors concluded that these regions are implicated in arousal and motivational systems related to fan identity. In the context of sport sponsorship, Martin et al. (2019) employed an fMRI neuroimaging method to examine consumers' response to advertising branded with a rival team after advertising branded with a home team had been shown. The authors found that highly identified fans of the home team had a greater neural response in the limbic and reward systems of the brain to the marketing and promotional material branded with their home team compared to nonfans. Using data gathered from EEG, Hungenberg et al. (2020) examined nostalgia's effect on MiLB spectators' psychological, emotional, and behavioral responses. The authors found that brainwave frequencies emblematic of inward attention and arousal were significantly associated with the number of instances spectators reported feeling nostalgic while watching the game.

As more sport scholars begin to employ neuroimaging methods, it is important to note that regardless of the neuroimaging method employed (e.g., fNIRS; fMRI), researchers should carefully generate hypotheses about which particular regions of the brain might be salient to their investigation prior to collecting data. As noted, adopting social neuroscience-related theory and methods offers researchers many promising advantages over traditional survey research designs aimed at understanding virtual sport spectator experiences and behavior. To our knowledge, however, sport researchers have yet to employ neuroimaging methods to investigate sport viewership in VR or AR contexts. Indeed, researchers employing these emerging interdisciplinary methodological approaches can pose significant challenges to sport management researchers. We outline some of these challenges next.

Employing a Social Neuroscience Approach to Understand Virtual Sport Spectator Experiences: Pitfalls and Challenges

There are some challenges inherent in the use of VR technology in research contexts. Challenges are particularly when the screen area is expansive relative to the visual field, and/or the screen is presented via goggles. Some viewers develop vertigo and nausea, and this tends to make the experience unpleasant, particularly for long periods of time. Studying brain responses in the context of a viewership experience may be influenced by these symptoms, and in general, some viewers may be unwilling to view extended gameplay within or outside of research protocols when such symptoms are elicited.

Technical challenges also exist with respect to each neuroimaging modality mentioned in this chapter. For instance, fMRI scanning requires immobility, staying in the supine position inside the machine, and data collection is very sensitive to motion artifacts; this makes imaging difficult even when minor head motions are made in order to track a moving image on a screen. fNIRS is more robust in this respect but is still not completely immune to motion artifacts. Finally, the EEG signal, as mentioned, can be disrupted by ambient noise and other sources of electrical signals, and strong muscle activity; for this reason, using EEG during live sporting events is likely to be logistically challenging.

Finally, given that there are very few studies in existence involving neuroscience, VR, and combined methods, it is important to not over-interpret the findings of any single study. It will likely take some time to build the evidence base sufficiently in order to develop any firm propositions about how the brain and social environment interact in order to produce or influence the sport viewership experience. Along these lines, there is likely a dearth of methodological familiarity and/or collaborative history between sport management researchers and those in the neurosciences. Developing such collaborations and enhanced skill sets will be essential for the continued development of the field.

Despite the above challenges, however, employing combined VR/AR and social neuroscience methods represents a promising approach to advancing understanding of sport consumer behavior. Indeed, it is important for researchers to consider these emerging technologies as both a methodology and a means of experiencing sport events. More research is needed to examine these immersive experiences and move beyond relying on self-report measures of behaviors and experiences of sport consumers.

References

Ayaz, H., & Dehais, F. (2019). *Neuroergonomics: The brain at work and everyday life*. Elsevier Academic Press.

Ayaz, H., Onaral, B., Izzetoglu, K., Shewokis, P.A., Mckendrick, R., & Parasuraman, R. (2013). Continuous monitoring of brain dynamics with functional near infrared spectroscopy as a tool for neuroergonomic research: Empirical examples and a technological development. *Frontiers in Human Neuroscience*, 7, 1–13.

Azuma, R. T. (1997). A survey of augmented reality. *Presence: Teleoperators & Virtual Environments, 6*, 355–385.

Baek, E., Scholz, C., & Falk, E. B. (2020). The neuroscience of persuasion and information propagation: The key role of the mentalizing system. In K. Floyd & R. Weber (Eds.), *Handbook of communication science and biology* (pp. 122–133). Routledge. 10.4324/9781351235587-12

Babiloni, F., & Astolfi, L. (2014). Social neuroscience and hyperscanning techniques: Past, present and future. *Neuroscience & Biobehavioral Reviews, 44*, 76–93.

Berkman, E. T., & Falk, E. B. (2013). Beyond brain repository.upenn.edu/cgi/viewcontent.cgimapping: Using neural measures to predict real-world outcomes. *Current Directions in Psychological Science, 22*(1), 45–50.

Baer, B. (2020, February 26). *MLS partners with second spectrum on advanced tracking data system*. Retrieved from https://www.mlssoccer.com/post/2020/02/26/mls-partners-second-spectrum-advanced-tracking-data-system

Bello-Morales, R., & Delgado-García, J. M. (2015). The social neuroscience and the theory of integrative levels. *Frontiers in Integrative Neuroscience, 9*, 54.

Bucci, P., & Galderisi, S. (2011). Physiologic basis of the EEG signalIn Boutros, N., Galderisi, S., Pogarell, O., & Riggio, S. *Standard electroencephalography in clinical psychiatry: A practical handbook* (pp. 7–12). John Wiley & Sons.

Casico, C.N., Scholz, C., & Falk, E.B. (2015). Social influence and the brain. Persuasion, susceptibility to influence and retransmission. *Current Opinion in Behavioral Sciences*, *3*(3), 51–57.

Craig, C. (2013). Understanding perception and action in sport: How can virtual reality technology help? *Sports Technology*, *6*, 161–169.

Curtin, A., & Ayaz, H. (2018). The age of neuroergonomics: Towards ubiquitous and continuous measurement of brain function with fNIRS. *Japanese Psychological Research*, *60*, 374–386.

Dixon, E. (2020). *NBA strengthens oculus ties with official VR headset designation. Retrieved from* https://www.sportspromedia.com/news/nba-oculus-vr-headset-partnership-deal-wnba-g-league-nba-2k-league-doordash

Dehais, F., Karwowski, W., & Ayaz, H. (2020). Brain at work and in everyday life as the next frontier: Grand Field challenges for neuroergonomics. *Frontiers in Neuroergonomics*, *1*. https://doi.org/10.3389/fnrgo.2020.583733

Di Domenico, S.I., Rodrigo, A.H., Dong, M., Fournier, M.A., Ayaz, H., Ryan, R.M., & Ruocco, A.C. (2019). Functional near-infrared spectroscopy: Proof of concept for its application in social neuroscience. In H. Ayaz & F. Dehais (eds.), *Neuroergonomics*. (pp. 169–173). Academic Press.

Duarte, I.C., Afonso, S., Jorge, H., Cayolla, R., Ferreira, C., & Castelo-Branco, M. (2017). Tribal love: The neural correlates of passionate engagement in football fans. *Social Cognitive and Affective Neuroscience*, *12*(5), 718–728.

Falk, E. B., Berkman, E., & Lieberman, M. D. (2012). From neural responses to population behavior: Neural focus groups predicts population-level media effects. *Psychological Science*, *23*(5), 439–445.

Falk, E.B., Berkman, E.T., Mann, T., Harrison, B., & Lieberman, M.D. (2010). Predicting persuasion-induced behavior change from the brain. *Journal of Neuroscience*, *30*(25), 8421–8424.

Falk. E.B., O'Donnell, M.B., Tompson, S., Gonzalez, R., & Dal Cin, D. (2015). Functional brain imaging predicts public health campaign success. *Social Cognitive and Affective Neuroscience*, *11*(2), 204–214.

Funk, D., & James, J. (2001). The psychological continuum model: A conceptual framework for understanding an individual's psychological connection to sport. *Sport Management Review*, *4*(2), 119–150.

Gateau, T., Ayaz, H., & Dehais, F. (2018). In silico vs. over the clouds: On-the-fly mental state estimation of aircraft pilots, using a functional near infrared spectroscopy based passive-BCI. *Frontiers in Human Neuroscience*, 12. https://doi.org/10.3389/fnhum.2018.00187

Goebert, C., & Greenhalgh, G. P. (2020). A new reality: Fan perceptions of augmented reality readiness in sport marketing. *Computers in Human Behavior*, *106*, 106231.

Goebert, C. (2020). Augmented reality in sport marketing: Uses and directions. *Sports Innovation Journal*, *1*, 134–151.

Heeger, D.J., & Ress, D. (2002). What does fMRI tell us about neuronal activity? *Nat Rev Neurosci*, *3*, 142–151.

Hungenberg, E., Slavich, M., Bailey, A., & Sawyer, T. (2020). Examining minor league baseball spectator nostalgia: A neuroscience perspective. *Sport Management Review* *23*(5), 824–837.

Howard, M. C. (2017). A meta-analysis and systematic literature review of virtual reality rehabilitation programs. *Computers in Human Behavior*, *70*, 317–327.

Izzetoglu, M., Izzetoglu, K., Bunce, S., Ayaz, H., Devaraj, A., Onaral, B., and Pourrezaei, K. (2005). Functional near-infrared neuroimaging. *IEEE Trans Neural Syst Rehabil Eng*, *13*, 153–159.

Jang, S.-W., Ko, J., Lee, H. J., & Kim, Y. S. (2018). A study on tracking and augmentation in mobile AR for e-leisure. *Mobile Information Systems*, *18*, 1–11.

Joshi, S., Herrera, R.R., Springett, D.N., Weedon, B.D., Ramirez, D.Z.M., Holloway, C., Dawes, H., & Ayaz, H. (2020). Neuroergonomic assessment of wheelchair control using mobile fNIRS. *IEEE Transactions on Neural Systems and Rehabilitation Engineering*, *28*, 1488–1496.

Kang, S. (2020). Going beyond just watching: The fan adoption process of virtual reality spectatorship. *Journal of Broadcasting & Electronic Media*, *64*(3), 499–518.

Kelley, W.M., Macrae, C.N., Wyland, C.L., Caglar, S., Inati, S., & Heatherton, T.F. (2002). Finding the self? An event-related fMIR study. *Journal of Cognitive Neuroscience*, *14*(5), 785–794.

Kim, K., & Johnson, M.K. (2012). Extended self: Medial prefrontal activity during transient association of self and objects. *Social Cognitive and Affective Neuroscience*, 7(2), 199–207.

Kim, D., & Ko, Y. J. (2019). The impact of virtual reality (VR) technology on sport spectators' flow experience and satisfaction. *Computers in human behavior*, *93*, 346–356.

Knudsen, E.I. (2007). Fundamental Components Of Attention. *Annual Review of Neuroscience*, *30*, 57–78.

Larson, D. & Potwarka, L.R. (2019, June). *Innovations in the measurement of experience during live sport viewing*. Paper presented at the North American Society for Sport Management, Annual Conference, New Orleans, LA.

Lee, S. O., Ahn, S. C., Hwang, J. I., & Kim, H. G. (2011, July). A vision-based mobile augmented reality system for baseball games. In *International conference on virtual and mixed reality* (pp. 61–68). Springer, Berlin, Heidelberg.

Levi, D.J., & Glincher, P.W. (2012). The root of all value: A neural common currency choice. *Current opinion in neurobiology, 22*(6), 1027–1038.

Liu, Y., Piazza, E.A., Simony, E., Shewokis, P.A., Onaral, B., Hasson, U., and Ayaz, H. (2017). Measuring speaker–listener neural coupling with functional near infrared spectroscopy. *Scientific Reports* 7, 43293.

Logothetis, N. (2008). What we can do and what we cannot do with fMRI. *Nature, 453*, 869–878.

Madrigal, R. (2006). Measuring the multidimensional nature of sporting even performance consumption. *Journal of Leisure Research, 38*, 267–276.

Martin, D.S., Townsend, K.M., Wang, Y., & Deshpande, G. (2019). Corporate sponsorship in college football: An fMRI study measuring the effectiveness of corporate branding across rival teams. *Sport Marketing Quarterly, 28*, 209–221. http://doi.org/10.32731/SMQ.284.122019.03

Miles, H. C., Pop, S. R., Watt, S. J., Lawrence, G. P., & John, N. W. (2012). A review of virtual environments for training in ball sports. *Computers & Graphics, 36*, 714–726.

Mckendrick, R., Parasuraman, R., Murtza, R., Formwalt, A., Baccus, W., Paczynski, M., & Ayaz, H. (2016). Into the wild: Neuroergonomic differentiation of hand-held and augmented reality wearable displays during outdoor navigation with functional near infrared spectroscopy. *Frontiers in Human Neuroscience*, 10. https://doi.org/10.3389/fnhum.2016.00216

Mehta, R.K., & Parasuraman, R. (2013). Neuroergonomics: A review of applications to physical and cognitive work. *Frontiers in Human Neuroscience*, 7. https://doi.org/10.3389/fnhum.2013.00889

Neumann, D. L., Moffitt, R. L., Thomas, P. R., Loveday, K., Watling, D. P., Lombard, C. L., & Tremeer, M. A. (2018). A systematic review of the application of interactive virtual reality to sport. *Virtual Reality, 22*(3), 183–198.

Oppenheim, A.N. (1992). *Questionnaire design, interviewing and attitude measurement.* Pinter Publishers: London, England.

Peng, W., Crouse, J. C., & Lin, J. H. (2013). Using active video games for physical activity promotion: A systematic review of the current state of research. *Health education & behavior, 40*(2), 171–192.

Potwarka, L.R., Hall, P., Mueller, H., Safati, A., & Ramchandani, G. (June, 2020). *Understanding sport viewership experiences: A social neuroscience approach* (abstract). NASSM conference, San Diego, CA.

Powell, S. (2020, October 10). *How virtual fans found their seats at NBA season restart.* Retrieved from https://www.nba.com/news/virtual-fans-help-restart-atmosphere

PwC (2019). *Seeing is believing: How virtual reality and augmented reality are transforming business and the economy.* Retrieved from https://www.pwccn.com/en/tmt/economic-impact-of-vr-ar.pdf

Reynolds, J. E., Thornton, A. L., Lay, B. S., Braham, R., & Rosenberg, M. (2014). Does movement proficiency impact on exergaming performance?. *Human movement science, 34*, 1–11.

Rizzolatti, G., & Craighero, L. (2004). The mirror-neuron system. *Annu. Rev. Neurosci., 27*, 169–192.

Rogers, R., Strudler, K., Decker, A., & Grazulis, A. (2017). Can augmented-reality technology augment the fan experience?: A model of enjoyment for sports spectators. *Journal of Sports Media, 12*, 25–44.

Schultz, W. (2006). Behavioral theories and the neurophysiology of reward. *Annu. Rev. Psychol., 57*, 87–115.

Shea, B. (2020, August 13). As NBA experiments with virtual reality in the bubble, side effects remain. Retrieved from https://theathletic.com/1992195/2020/08/12/as-nba-experiments-with-virtual-reality-in-the-bubble-side-effects-remain/

Soltani, P., & Morice, A. H. (2020). Augmented reality tools for sports education and training. *Computers & Education, 155*, 103923.

Tompson, S., Falk, E. B., Bassett, D. S., & Vettel, J. M. (2019). Using neuroimaging to predict behavior: An overview with a focus on the moderating role of sociocultural context. In P. K. Davis, A. O'Mahony, & J. Pfautz (eds), *Z social-behavioral modeling for complex systems* (pp. 205–230). John Wiley and Sons: Hoboken, NJ.

Vanutelli, M.E., Pezard, L., Nandrino, J., & Balconi, M. (2016). Intra and inter-brain connectivity during cooperation: A fNIRS-based connectivity analysis. *Neuropsychological Trends, 20*, 154–155.

Villringer, A., & Chance, B. (1997). Non-invasive optical spectroscopy and imaging of human brain function. *Trends Neurosci, 20*, 435–442.

Vignais, N., Bideau, B., Craig, C., Brault, S., Multon, F., Delamarche, P., & Kulpa, R. (2009). Does the level of graphical detail of a virtual handball thrower influence a goalkeeper's motor response?. *Journal of Sports Science & Medicine*, *8*, 501.

Wang, A., Ruparel, K., Loughead, J.W., Strasser, A., Blady, S.J., Lynch, K.G., & Langleben, D.D. (2015). Content matters: Neuroimaging investigation of brain and behavioral impact of televised anti-tobacco public service announcements. *The Journal of Neuroscience*, *33*(17), 7420–7427.

Young, J. (2020a, November 01). Sports leagues are betting on augmented reality, as virtual courtside seats can't match the real thing. Retrieved from https://www.cnbc.com/2020/11/01/tech-augmented-reality-sports-leagues-nba-mlb-nhl-profit-virtual-reality.html

Yodh, A., & Chance, B. (1995). Spectroscopy and imaging with diffusing light. *Physics Today*, *48*, 34–40.

Young, J. (2020b, October 25). The NBA made it through Its PANDEMIC SEASON, now it looks to 5G and VR in a post-covid world. Retrieved February 19, 2021, from https://www.cnbc.com/2020/10/25/nba-new-revenue-exciting-future-5g-most-challenging-season.html

18

Business Analytics in Sport Organizations

Ted Hayduk III

Introduction

Data-driven-decision making has rapidly ascended the list of business' main priorities over the past two decades. Since the advent of personal computing in the 1980s, individuals' access to data and their ability to manipulate and model relationships between variables has grown exponentially. Nowhere was this shift more noticeable than in settings like finance, where the quantification of pricing signals in the early 1980s led to an entirely new set of high-frequency, objective trading strategies – a major element of modern finance and investment portfolios (Wilmott, 2007).

A quantitative renaissance similar in scope and swiftness took place in the sports industry beginning in the early 2000s. Despite creating a wealth of data that had always been of interest to fans and outsiders, many personnel decisions in professional and elite sports were made subjectively – based on managers' "gut instincts" or intuition. The commitment to this ethos was so impermeable that early baseball statisticians – the likes of Henry Chadwick, Earnshaw Cook, Bob Davis, and Bill James – were purposely held at arm's length by the institutional powers at work within Major League Baseball (Hayduk, 2020). To second-guess a manager or an owner's way of making decisions – and to suggest such an unfamiliar alternative – was a threat to the establishment.

Despite this resistance, pockets of innovation bubbled forth at the team level. The Oakland Athletics personified this transformation in Michael Lewis' *Moneyball* (2004) – they eschewed long-held, romanticized notions of how a baseball organization ought to be run and instead adopted a radical new data-driven approach. The A's didn't win a World Series from using their new approach – but they did solidly outperform all other peer clubs for several years in a row. They were so successful – and the accompanying major motion picture so captivating – that *Moneyball* became more than a title. To *Moneyball* something was to quantify it; to optimize an outcome given a set of resource constraints. The term is now used widely to describe improving government functions, enhancing the way lawyers litigate (Wright & Peeples, 2013), and even maximizing faculty performance in academic settings (Nocka et al., 2014), among many others.

On the heels of this trend, teams and leagues began to look elsewhere for examples of how to unleash their newfound quantitative mindsets on other parts of their organizations. Suddenly,

DOI: 10.4324/9781003088899-21

the idea of using quantitative data to optimize business outcomes – minimizing costs, enhancing revenue – became extremely attractive. Optimizing marketing campaigns, enhancing engagement on social media, predicting ticket demand, estimating food and beverage sales, or predicting workforce needs were no longer pipe dreams – and each offered a clear route to business success if managed properly. Moreover, those functions are just the tip of the iceberg – a number of recently-matriculated opportunities exist to deploy data strategies to newer, more innovative ends, as well.

The "age of analytics" is now comfortably in full swing, with sport organizations making multi-million-dollar investments in new digital technologies that help them gather, manage, analyze, and disseminate data. Organizations that have not invested aggressively in this space are being left behind, and organizations on the bleeding edge compete for more revenue and more engagement from their fans. These functions – which collectively constitute the "business-side" of a sport organization's day-to-day functions – are the focus of this chapter. In that light, this chapter, will define pertinent concepts related to business analytics, talk about some of the current use cases and the statistical procedures that underlie them, discuss the next generation of analytics products, and identify the key deliverables expected of analytics professionals in modern sport organizations.

Interest in business analytics in sports settings is not only an applied phenomenon – there is significant interest in the discipline from scholarship, as well. Given the relative newness of the domain, there is ample opportunity for researchers to contribute to sport management and marketing theory vis-à-vis a business analytics lens. Therefore, this chapter will also outline five avenues for future academic research in the area of business analytics in sports organizations.

Key Terms and Concepts

The terms "statistics" and "analytics" are the first two terms for discussion in this chapter. Known to researchers in academia – but perhaps less so to practitioners in the field – these two terms are more similar than they are different. However, their use in different contexts is what predominantly contributes to the misguided perception that they are fundamentally different from one another. Figure 18.1 tracks the search history for the two terms since 2004. It shows fairly clearly that in the last 15–18 years, the stready decline of "Statistics" has been supplanted by the growth of "Analytics" in business-related searches.

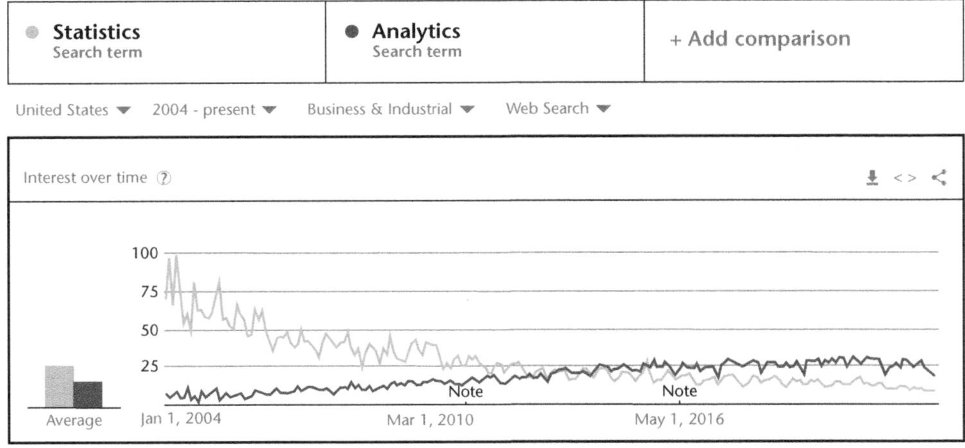

Figure 18.1 Search History for Statistics and Analytics From 2004–2021

Despite their interchangeability in most contexts, comparing the definitions of statistics and analytics has received some attention in academic settings (Jensen, 2020). The consensus is that the two terms do have some subtle differences that are worthy of discussion here. Highlighting these differences is important for future scholarship as it understandably would want to avoid merely publishing quantitatively-derived research projects and branding them as "analytics" papers.

Definitions of statistics consistently include a handful of elements, namely: (1) statistics is a branch of applied mathematics, (2) it involves leveraging mathematical models and probability theory, and (3) the goal is to find order or regularity where it is not immediately observable (Jensen, 2020). Definitions of analytics, however, are slightly more disparate, but have as their core elements some similarities: (1) analytics is multidisciplinary, involving data science, statistics, computer science, and engineering, (2) analytics involves a structured approach to problem-solving, and (3) the end goal is to inform decision-making.

In short, statistics is regarded as a modality of scientific inquiry, full of its own theoretical contributions and frameworks, which adheres to the higher-order laws of mathematics. Meanwhile, analytics is "something you do (i.e., methodology or strategy) in a general sense with the data" (Jensen, 2020, p. 135). Additionally, analytics connotes a skillset that is more integrative – the combination of being able to leverage a wide range of programming languages, data visualization tools, and application development software in the delivery of business- or function-specific insights. To "do" analytics, one is actually practicing some combination of data science, computer science, statistics/probability, and/or even anthropology. In that sense, Jensen (2020) deduces that analytics is really more of a *grouping* of skills or disciplines in the same way that "Science" is a grouping of disciplines like Physics, Biology, Chemistry, etc.

Having sharpened the distinction between statistics and analytics, the next step is to discuss a bifurcation of the latter term that is almost exclusive to sport organizations. In sports, a sharp distinction exists between "on-field" analytics and "business" analytics. The former relates to anything that happens on the field of play, court, ice, etc., while the latter connotes any domain that can impact an organization's ability to (a) solicit more revenue from fans or (b) minimize fixed or variables expenses. It is the latter of the two that is the main focus of this chapter. And, more specifically, this chapter focuses on deployments that are centered on predictive analytics rather than descriptive analytics. While the distinction feels straightforward on its face to those who have studied sports and entertainment, it is somewhat interesting that a distinction exists at all. That is because what happens on the field is the sport industry's core product, therefore adjusting on-field decision-making is directly analogous to evaluating new product features in "traditional" industries.

Consider a coach in the NBA who wants to know the optimal offensive strategy given the players on her roster and a Product Manager at Apple who wants to know the best combination of features to include in a new Apple TV interface. The coach's decision would directly affect the product's quality (i.e., the team's competitive superiority). And, naturally, when teams compete effectively, consumers are more likely to buy tickets, merchandise, engage on social media, etc. In truth, the reason sports organizations and sports researchers tend to bifurcate product and business analytics is due to the subtlety in *how* product decisions get made. Coaches and GMs make product decisions with one overarching goal: winning games. The end consumer of the team's product is purely secondary, that is, a coach would never make a product decision explicitly because the fans might enjoy it. Meanwhile, the PM has a different (and more direct) stakeholder group to answer to – they are constantly on the hunt for new feature combinations that could be added to their products in an effort to surprise and delight consumers.

Current and Emerging Uses of Sport Business Analytics

There is a range of deployments of sports business analytics in sport organizations and in the academic literature. Here, this section will discuss some of the most common uses of sports business analytics in sport organizations and highlights some of the statistical techniques that are relevant to those deployments. Then, the section will discuss some of the emerging ways sport organizations are deploying business-side analytics.

A cornerstone of effective business analytics is the classic A/B test. A/B testing involves subjecting one group of consumers to a given stimulus and another group of consumers to a competing stimulus with the goal of understanding which stimulus is more effective at eliciting a desired behavior from consumers. For example, if the San Francisco 49ers wish to incentivize the purchase of Coors Light beer in their venue, they may send a mobile notification to a group of 100 mobile app users in attendance that says "Welcome to Levi's Stadium! Enjoy a second Coors Light on us when you buy the first at regular price." and another notification that says "Welcome to Levi's Stadium! Today only, Coors Light beer is half-price." By tracking the subsequent in-app purchases of the fans that received the two messages, venue operators could assess which type of promotion framing was most effective and should thus be the promotion deployed a larger scale. The nature of A/B testing is such that it allows brands to experiment on a small scale before committing to any particular course of action on a large scale. Academic researchers will keenly identify the statistical frameworks underlying A/B testing – *t*-tests and analysis of variance (ANOVA) are optimal in these situations.

Second, some sport organizations are increasingly leveraging more sophisticated psychometric data in order to help them make business decisions. In-app consumer surveys are increasingly popular, and they frequently prompt fans to rate their satisfaction with (a) the app, (b) general aspects of the live consumption experience, or (c) their relationship with the team more broadly. Feedback pods are increasingly present in and around vital in-venue services, which encourage consumers to provide psychometrically scaled indications of their level of satisfaction with food and beverage services, bathroom cleanliness, et cetera. The purpose of capturing all of this psychometric data is a growing realization among sports business managers that consumer sentiment is both difficult to capture but also vitally important to their spending patterns. Psychometric data gleaned from surveys and in-venue hardware is being spliced together to help organizations understand the psychological processes that lead to eventual purchase behavior as well as where they need to focus most of their improvement efforts. Statistical methodologies that underpin these types of business analytics can range from the confirmatory and exploratory factor analysis (CFA/EFA), structural equation modeling (SEM), and a range of regression-based econometric techniques.

The third area of sports business analytics that is active in the applied setting is forecasting. Teams and leagues frequently wish to predict ticket demand based on a range of observable and unobservable inputs. They may also wish to price tickets optimally, given a separate set of inputs. In these types of analyses, time plays a huge role. Ticket prices are tied directly to demand, which fluctuates in the days and weeks prior to any contest. Therefore, the objective of forecasting is to accurately identify the signals that meaningfully affect demand. Long-range signals might originate several weeks before the contest, for example, consumers' perceptions of the team's future quality. Mid-range signals might originate a week or two ahead of the contest, for example, the presence or absence of star players in teams' rosters. Finally, short-range signals occur a couple of days or even hours before the context – weather patterns that prevent commuting to the venue, for example. Other popular needs in applied settings are predicting workforce needs for specific events and regulating or minimizing utilities consumption.

Underlying these analyses are statistical methodologies in econometrics. Time-series models and panel data techniques are particularly salient (see Cryer & Chan, 2008 for an overview of time-series models as applied using RStudio and Hsiao for a general overview of panel data methodologies).

The aforementioned types of analytics needs and the associated statistical methodologies that underlie them have provided a solid foundation for sports properties as they build out their business analytics capabilities. However, there are also emerging areas of data analysis that are impacting the landscape and giving sport organizations the chance to "get ahead" in the analytics arms race. First, some organizations are beginning to tap into the power of written and spoken text (i.e., natural language processing, NLP). "Social listening" campaigns that automatically monitor and gauge the sentiment of fans' posts on social media are leading the way in that regard. Because qualitative analysis of social media posts and other written communique can be time-consuming and subjective, a plethora of algorithms have recently been developed, mostly in the computer science and computational linguistics domains, with the purpose of automating this process. Thanks to these algorithms, organizations can now comb through thousands of social media posts per minute and decipher exactly how fans feel about a number of topics relevant to the organization.

One methodology that underlies this process is called "topic modeling," which is an unsupervised approach to NLP built on Latent Dirichlet Allocation (Blei, et al., 2003; Wang & Grimson, 2007). It is unsupervised in the sense that a researcher does not pre-specify any particular topics of interest; the algorithm automatically sorts words and phrases into topics based on their co-occurrence and linguistic context. LDA is especially useful because it allows single words to belong to multiple topics, which sets it apart from more rudimentary methods. Another version of NLP can be termed "supervised" in that the researcher wishes to evaluate a given corpus for the extent to which it exemplifies feelings or sentiments expressed in a pre-identified library. For example, teams may wish to know the degree of "positive" and "negative" sentiment expressed in a sample of 10,000 tweets. In this situation, an NLP algorithm would compare the tweets to a lexicon of several hundred words tied to positivity (such as "great," "happy," "awesome," "enjoy," etc.) and a lexicon of words tied to negative sentiment ("upset," "crappy," "lame," "stupid," "frustrated," etc.). However, given the generality of popular sentiment lexicons and the unique aspects of sport consumption, it could be argued there is a need to develop sport-specific sentiment lexicons for deployment in these settings.

Another emerging area relevant for sports business analytics is computer vision. If it could be said that NLP algorithms are concerned with mimicking the human ability of speech recognition, computer vision techniques aim to mimic the human ability of sight. Computer vision algorithms in stadium environments are dependent on digital camera systems which are all able to communicate with one another on a closed-internet system (i.e., "internet protocol," IP; Szeliski, 2010). The algorithms boil down a camera feed into a grid of individual pixels and analyze how the pixels change over time to identify key objects (people, cars, animals, etc.). Practical deployments abound in stadium environments, which are spaces in which a large number of people are relatively confined but must move about a given space for access to certain products and services. Current uses include counting the number of consumers in line for beer and automatically recommending to a venue manager whether any alternative beer distribution kiosks are needed. Other applications can map foot traffic over time, which can help venue operators find the optimal location for promotional materials or determine the best pricing strategies for physical signage. Computer vision can also identify key demographics of consumers such as gender and age for segmentation purposes or identify sentiment based on facial expressions (happy, sad, confused, angry, etc.). Last, computer vision algorithms can also help keep patrons safe by identifying potential threats – a patron wearing a heavy trench coat and hat in July in Texas could be a sign of a potential bad actor, and the algorithm could alert security efforts to monitor the individual to render a judgment.

Current Research Trends

The previous section discussed many of the applied trends in sports business analytics including some of the emerging techniques that are starting to garner attention from organizations. However, sports business analytics are receiving increased attention from scholars, as well. This is a welcomed change, as until recently many instances of applied analytics in sports were published in industry trade outlets or consumer-facing white papers. In recent years the field now has special-purpose peer-reviewed journals dedicated to the topic, such as the *Journal of Sports Analytics* and the *Journal of Quantitative Analysis in Sports*. Further, mainstream journals have recently devoted special issues to "Big Data and Analytics in Sport Management" [*Journal of Sport Management*, 35(3)] and "Sports Analytics in the Era of Big Data" [*Big Data*, 6(4)]. In general, academic research on sports analytics has focused on a number of key areas:

1 Using computer vision for player tracking and evaluation
2 Fan engagement, marketing analytics, consumer behavior
3 Augmented and Virtual Reality
4 Betting market behavior
5 Strength and conditioning/optimizing training and preparation
6 Estimating the effect of rule changes using causal inference
7 Roster optimization and draft analysis
8 Miscellaneous/other

As is shown by these key topics within the sports analytics literature, a number of these relate directly to the business outcomes of sport organizations – namely, (b), (c), and (d). There seems to be growing awareness among scholars that teams and leagues are increasingly using data not just for player evaluations and roster management, but for "back of house" business issues as well. There is a growing understanding that the ability to "identify inefficiencies and trust the objectivity of data" constitutes a significant amount of time and energy from these entities (Watanabe et al., 2021; p. 197).

Recent contributions to the sports business analytics discussion in academia have been diverse and contributed to what we know about business-relevant outcomes that are tied inherently to the sports product. Some of these will be discussed here in order to provide context about the types of data being harvested and the creative ways researchers are linking together data from disparate sources.

In a recent contribution, Matti (2021) drew a link between bad game outcomes (i.e., unexpected losses) and more negative reviews of local businesses on Yelp. These findings, built on the idea of loss-aversion, are essential to sport organizations that wish to build a healthy ecosystem of local businesses in the area surrounding their stadium. It speaks to the growing need for sport organizations to not only gather and monitor their own data but to actively harvest data that is created beyond the walls of their venue. Other examples of important external data include bidding, bookmakers' odds, and prediction market data – particularly in US settings, where the deployment of the sports betting industry is in full swing.

Relatedly, Ge and Humphreys (2021) identify a link between athlete transgressions in the news and the stock prices of that athlete's biggest sponsoring brands. The authors found that athletes misbehaving in ways that harmed others created larger relative declines in stock price relative to athletes misbehaving in ways that only harmed themselves. Naturally, this discussion is relevant to any sport organization that wishes to monitor the ever-increasing spillover effects attributable to the behavior of individual athletes. This may be even more relevant for teams listed on public exchanges (for example, Manchester United) or teams owned by publicly traded corporations (e.g., Los Angeles Dodgers).

Another recent contribution by Karg et al. (2021) leveraged a unique dataset of ~60,000 individual sport consumers. Their study investigated why fans choose to attend games, highlighting that there are important interaction effects between the individual fan and the game-level characteristics such as viewing quality and contest quality. Given the granularity of this chapter relative to other demand research, this chapter is relevant for sport organizations that wish to more accurately segment consumers and understand attendance behavior on a micro-level.

Other recent investigations have focused on analyzing the plethora of data provided by written text on social media, and linking those data to relevant outcomes for sport organizations. For example, Gong et al. (2021) analyzed the impact of tanking in the National Basketball Association (NBA) on attendance. As a mechanism linking the two, the authors leveraged a natural language processing (NLP) algorithm to gauge the volume and sentiment of 166,000 tweets. They found that the volume of tweets about the home team and the positive or negative sentiment about the away team's tanking strategy impacted game attendance. In a related contribution, Weimar et al. (2021) explored how game outcomes affected the change rates of sport properties' social media followers, identifying disparate effects for wins, losses, and draws across several social media platforms. Articles such as these reinforce the important nature of social media as a monetizable asset for sport organizations and provide practical insights about social media patterns' effects on profit-relevant business outcomes.

Next Steps for Sports Analytics Research

As discussed in the previous section, there is an active line of research in the area of sports business analytics. Despite the recent contributions made in this area, there remain some opportunities to close current gaps available for future researchers in the domain. Among the most overarching, as discussed by Watanabe et al. (2021), is the general lack of theory in sports business analytics research. The examples in the previous section were all good examples of recent sports business analytics papers that make equal contributions to theoretical development and practical implications, but they are not the norm overall.

This lack of theory in sports business analytics is mostly the function of being a relatively new domain combined with the applied origins of sports business analytics. Practitioners are not generally concerned with advancing social identification theory, signaling theory, market efficiency frameworks, or any of the other dominant theoretical approaches used in sport management and marketing – they merely want to sell more of their product (which is not in and of itself a bad thing). However, a singular focus on business outcomes has stunted the incorporation of theory on the whole, which is suboptimal for academic settings. If sports business analytics is to advance as an area of scientific inquiry, the role of theory needs to take a more dominant role moving forward.

One way to address this challenge is for sport management scholars to have yet to have a thorough discussion about what differentiates "sports analytics" research from quantitative sport management research (e.g., Jensen, 2020). To equate the two seems superficial, as articulated by Jensen (2020) and other scholars in statistics and applied sciences. Given the differences between "analytics" and "statistics," there is likely an opportunity for sport management scholars to coalesce around a definition of sports business analytics that is broader and more digitally inclusive than currently accepted definitions of "statistics" or "econometrics" or "psychometrics." To teach and do research in sports business analytics requires a sharper distinction of the construct and perhaps even a differentiated set of best-practice deliverables in terms of publishing and dissemination. For example, traditional academic outlets are poor fits for manuscripts that espouse to be "sports business analytics" papers because as discussed in previous sections, "business analytics" involves more than just specifying a statistical model and telling the story embedded in that dataset. It involves robust and immersive data visualization, open data and code repositories, or even the deployment of a model in an interactive web or mobile application format (using, for example, RShiny or Python). Overall, few or none of these features are available to academics looking to publish their sports business analytics findings in traditional outlets.

A second way to address the theory challenge in the domain of sports business analytics is to keep in mind that there are opportunities for future research that center specifically on the strategy and operational elements of sport organizations, rather than on any individual business-specific outcome. While modeling demand as a function of Twitter activity can provide insight into social-media-driven demand, such a study would have little meaning for understanding the use of business analytics more generally, or how the use of business analytics affects how the organization operates or evolves.

First, research in sports business analytics has not focused on the strategic human resources component of new analytics skillsets. For one, there is little consensus in understanding the specific skills and experiences sports business analysts bring to the table. The range of tools, programming languages, and training available to modern students means that each sports business analyst likely has a different skillset "portfolio." Is there a preferred standard among sport organizations wishing to hire these individuals? Is there an optimal combination of proficiencies that would best equip new sports business analysts for employment? Answering these questions would generate practical insights for educators but would also have implications for organizational lifecycle theory (Adizes, 1979), which focuses on how organizations can manage human capital for organizational renewal.

Another opportunity for future research is in how business analytics teams should be structured within sport organizations. Currently, teams and leagues utilize a hodge-podge of organizing philosophies, many of which are based on ad-hoc or situational necessities at the time the teams were conceptualized. Some organizations prefer to structure their business analytics team as a fully-autonomous cross-functional entity that works consultatively with the marketing, finance, or sales functions to perform data analysis and generate bespoke solutions. This type of structure generally requires the highest level of commitment from management as well as expertise along the entire data value chain. Analysts in this structure tend to have a more segmented division of labor, as well. Other organizations structure their business analytics teams intra-functionally, meaning there is a team of marketing and CRM business analysts, a separate team within the finance department that focuses on capturing and modeling finance-specific KPIs, etc. This structure can be built using a piecemeal approach but would require any given analyst to have a wider breadth of expertise along the data value chain. Investigating how organizations structure their analytics teams could help advance frameworks of coordinating and communication in sport organizations, with specific respect to functions like two-way communication, concurrent problem solving, ability and willingness to use uncertain or ambiguous information for decision-making (e.g., Hauptman & Hirji, 1999).

Another opportunity for sports business analytics scholarship to advance the domain is at the intersection of privacy versus profitability. Business analytics in sports settings is not a "hard sell" for managers and owners. Any tool that can help them save money or optimize revenue is typically a straightforward business decision. However, little attention has been paid to how consumers perceive the use of business analytics and whether they sense a lack of privacy from their favorite organization's continued adoption of new technologies and business analytics techniques. Results of such a study would inform identity-relevant theories in sport, which stress that consumers can feel engaged or disengaged with a team brand based on whether the team exemplifies aspects of the consumers' own self-perception (Lock, et al., 2014). If technology or innovation is not a component of consumers' own self-concept, it is possible that an organization's sustained adoption of business analytics can break down identification and erode trust.

A final area of opportunity for sports analytics researchers involves illuminating the role of leadership. Thus far, there is little research that seeks to identify specifically *why* some sport organizations choose to pursue aggressive business analytics strategies while others choose to lag behind. Initial research by Hayduk (2022) suggests that upper echelon theory (UET) offers a potential mechanism in that regard. UET (Hambrick & Mason, 1984; Hambrick, 2007) stresses that owners and C-level executives hold a disproportionate amount of influence relative to the rest of an organization, thus their decisions and actions can manifest in meaningful ways at the organization level. The idea is that decisions to implement strong innovation tactics and strategies are not random, but may originate at the very top of the organizational hierarchy because of the specific skills and expertise that an owner brings to the table. Future research could help identify stronger links between owners and managers with expertise in technology and relevant downstream effects, such as capital allocation to technology projects or the decision to invest in a sport-specific startup incubator (as some organizations have done).

Conclusion

This chapter has covered the topic of sports business analytics. It has provided definitions of key terms, drawing particular attention to the difference between "statistics" and "analytics." It has also identified some of the current and emerging uses of sports business analytics in sport organizations, such as time series models for forecasting purposes, tests of mean differences for A/B testing, and NLP and computer vision algorithms to help automate social listening and venue management efforts. This chapter has also identified some of the main research themes in sports analytics thus far while identifying several opportunities for future research. In particular, the takeaways from the discussion reinforce the need for academics to further incorporate theory into sports business analytics manuscripts. This process should include greater attention to identifying the aspects of "sports business analytics" research from one that simply deploys quantitative methodologies to answer an applied business problem. Further, academics will want to consider how this definition changes the deliverables expected of sports business analytics research.

References

Adizes, I. (1979). Organizational passages—diagnosing and treating lifecycle problems of organizations. *Organizational Dynamics*, *8*(1), 3–25.

Blei, D. M., Ng, A. Y., & Jordan, M. I. (2003). Latent Dirichlet allocation. *The Journal of Machine Learning Research*, *3*, 993–1022.

Cryer, J. D., & Chan, K. S. (2008). *Time series analysis: With applications in R* (Vol. 2). Springer: New York.

Ge, Q., & Humphreys, B. (2021). Athlete misconduct and team sponsor stock prices: The role of incident type and media coverage. *Journal of Sport Management*, *35*(3). doi:10.1123/JSM.2020-0106

Gong, H., Watanabe, N., Soebbing, B., Brown, M., & Nagel, M. (2021). Do consumer perceptions of tanking impact attendance at national basketball association games? A sentiment analysis approach. *Journal of Sport Management*, *35*(3). doi:10.1123/JSM.2020-0274

Hambrick, D. C. (2007). Upper echelons theory: An update. *Academy of Management Review, 32*(2), 334–343.

Hambrick, D. C., & Mason, P. A. (1984). Upper echelons: The organization as a reflection of its top managers. *Academy of Management Review, 9*(2), 193–206.

Hauptman, O., & Hirji, K. K. (1999). Managing integration and coordination in cross-functional teams: An international study of concurrent engineering product development. *R&D Management, 29*(2), 179–192.

Hayduk, T. (2020). On the use of quantitative data in the sport context. In *Statistical modelling and sports business analytics* (pp. 10–24). Routledge.

Hayduk, T. (2022). Are 'Tech-savvy' owners better for business? Evidence from major league baseball. *Journal of sport management*. Advance online publication. https://doi.org/10.1123/jsm.2021-0252

Jensen, W. A. (2020). Statistics = analytics?. *Quality Engineering, 32*(2), 133–144.

Karg, A., Nguyen, J., & McDonald, H. (2021). Understanding season ticket holder attendance decisions. *Journal of Sport Management, 35*(3). doi:10.1123/JSM.2020-0284

Lewis, M. (2004). *Moneyball: The art of winning an unfair game* (1st ed.). WW Norton.

Lock, D., Funk, D. C., Doyle, J. P., & McDonald, H. (2014). Examining the longitudinal structure, stability, and dimensional interrelationships of team identification. *Journal of Sport Management, 28*(2), 119–135.

Matti, J. (2021). Frustrated customers: The effect of unexpected emotional cues on yelp reviews. *Journal of Sport Management, 35*(3). doi:10.1123/JSM.2020-0147

Nocka, A., Zheng, D., Hu, T., & Luo, J. (2014, December). Moneyball for academia: Toward measuring and maximizing faculty performance and impact. In *2014 IEEE International Conference on Data Mining Workshop* (pp. 193–197). IEEE.

Short, J. C., Broberg, J. C., Cogliser, C. C., & Brigham, K. H. (2010). Construct validation using computer-aided text analysis (CATA) an illustration using entrepreneurial orientation. *Organizational Research Methods, 13*(2), 320–347.

Szeliski, R. (2010). *Computer vision: Algorithms and applications*. Springer Science & Business Media.

Szymanski, S. (2020). Sport analytics: Science or alchemy? *Kinesiology Review, 9*(1), 57–63. doi:10.1123/kr.2019-0066.

Wang, X., & Grimson, E. (2007, December). Spatial latent Dirichlet allocation. In *NIPS, 20*, 1577–1584.

Watanabe, N. M., Shapiro, S., & Drayer, J. (2021). Big data and analytics in sport management. *Journal of Sport Management, 35*(3), 197–202.

Weimar, D., Soebbing, B., & Wicker, P. (2021). Dealing with statistical significance in big data: The social media value of game outcomes in professional football. *Journal of Sport Management, 35*(3). doi:10.1123/JSM.2020-0275

Wilmott, P. (2007). *Paul Wilmott introduces quantitative finance*. John Wiley & Sons.

Wright, R. F., & Peeples, R. A. (2013). Criminal defense lawyer Moneyball: A demonstration project. *Wash. & Lee L. Rev., 70*, 1221.

Part III

Emerging Digital Issues in Sport Management

19

Collaborative Consumption in the Sport Industry

Brandon Brown, Eric C. Schwarz, and Michael M. Goldman

Introduction

Collaborative consumption is "the peer-to-peer-based activity of obtaining, giving, or sharing the access to goods and services, often coordinated through community-based online services" (Hamari et al., 2016, p. 2047), but also can be extended to face-to-face interactions. Collaborative consumption is a primary concept in the sharing economy, which is an "organized system or network in which participants conduct sharing activities in the form of renting, lending, trading, bartering, and swapping of goods, services, transportation solutions, space, or money" (Möhlmann, 2015, p. 194). While the majority of collaborative consumption and the sharing economy occurs through the use of social and digital media via mobile technologies, many of the results from these interactions are perpetuated in face-to-face connections whether it be through an Uber ride or staying in someone's home through Airbnb.

Networked Hospitality

The concepts of collaborative consumption and the sharing economy fall under the overarching principle of networked hospitality. Originally defined in association with the concept of couchsurfing, Molz defined network hospitality as "connecting to one another using online networking systems, as well as to the kinds of relationships they perform when they meet each other offline and face to face" (2012, p. 216). Ikkala and Lampinen (2015) demonstrated that network hospitality has both financial and social reasons at its foundation, with a monetary exchange providing a framework supporting hosts to attain a desired level of sociability, by choosing guests that have similar values and beliefs and on a scale dictated by the host. However, the study also showed that over time social factors became more important than financial factors, even for those who initially became involved with Airbnb just to make some more money. In turn, guests also noted that many "strive for 'authentic' experiences and value the opportunity to stay in a local home" (Ikkala & Lampinen, 2015, p. 1042). Lampinen and Cheshire (2016) echo this conclusion that the social benefits of P2P exchange and the sharing economy are the facilitation of new face-to-face interactions between strangers that might not have otherwise met. These important correlations between sociability and the desire for

DOI: 10.4324/9781003088899-23

authentic experiences have significant potential to articulate the value of collaborative consumption.

Peer Exchanges, Commercial Platforms, and the Sport Industry

Further research conducted by Gössling and Hall (2019) demonstrates that collaborative consumption refers to peer exchanges driven by commercial platforms and businesses, while the sharing economy is concentrated on private and non-commercial transactions. As such, the focus of collaborative consumption is on consumers relying upon other consumers to satisfy their needs and wants (Gössling & Hall, 2019). While a majority of collaborative consumption experiences occur using social and digital platforms, the results are mainly propagated through face-to-face connections such as through an Uber ride or an Airbnb stay.

In terms of the sport industry that has both community/private and commercial aspects, -collaborative consumption is effectively a formal system that includes the recirculation of goods, the increased utilization of durable assets, the provision of service exchanges, and the offering of shared productive assets through platforms that encourage social transformation (Möhlmann, 2015; Schor & Attwood-Charles, 2017). The key to the collaborative consumption environment is the sharing of both tangible and intangible assets that are otherwise not being utilized through a traditional commercial process.

Modes of Collaborative Consumption

As expressed in Figure 19.1, there are multiple modes that collaborative consumption can be offered in, ranging from the sharing of use and ownership to the transfer of use and ownership (Ertz et al., 2019).

Mutualization is a type of access system where individuals either secure or offer temporary access to a resource complimentary, in exchange for another good or service, or for a fee (Ertz et al., 2018; Taeihagh, 2017). In the case of tangible resources, individuals exchange goods without taking ownership of the products (Ertz et al., 2018; Piscicelli et al., 2015). When the resources are intangible, individuals utilize peer-to-peer services offered by others including lending platforms, transportation services, and accommodation, among others (Botsman & Rogers, 2010; Ertz et al., 2018). An important distinction with mutualization is that there needs to be a peer-to-peer foundation in providing resources. If individuals are not sourcing the goods or services, such as with opportunities provided through access schemes offered by marketing organizations, then it is not a mutualization access system for collaborative consumption.

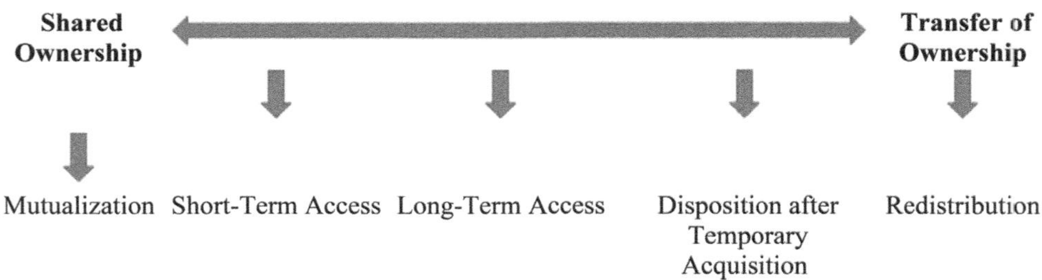

Figure 19.1 Modes of Collaborative Consumption. Modified from Ertz et al. (2019)

Short-term access is where ownership does not change but the use of products or services is offered temporarily, usually for days or weeks. Long-term access is also where ownership does not change but the time frame extends to months or even years. In the case of long-term access, there may be a perception of de facto ownership the longer the access period continues. The disposition of tangible products after temporary acquisition involves the process of taking ownership of a product, using it for a period of time, then deciding to offer the product to others in the form of resale, leasing, or exchange to either recoup a portion of the initial purchase price or raise funds to purchase a replacement product. The key here is there is a predisposition to selling or transferring the product to another individual at the time of initial purchase.

Redistribution in collaborative consumption involves utilizing distribution systems to either disburse or acquire resources permanently for free or at a cost (Botsman & Rogers, 2010; Taeihagh, 2017). These exchanges take place in many forms including second-hand stores, donations, or bartering through online platforms. The individual offering the product does not have a predisposition to get rid of the product at the time of purchase ... it usually happens down the road after a period of ownership. Those acquiring these types of products are usually unable to afford the product new or are looking for a discount to obtain the product.

Categories of Collaborative Consumption

The various modes of collaborative consumption enable consumers to enhance their purchase power and gain access to goods and services that meet their needs and wants while creating new social networks. This has stemmed from the millennial and iGeneration's desire to be in control of their consumption through peer networks rather than be influenced by hyperconsumerism (Botsman & Rogers, 2010). The three main categories, or recirculation systems as defined by Botsman and Rogers (2010), are product-service systems, redistribution markets, and collaborative lifestyles (Garrett et al., 2017).

Product-service systems are where one individual charges another individual for use of a product rather than transfer ownership of that product, or what Piscicelli et al. (2015) calls "user-oriented" or "result-oriented" services (Garrett et al., 2017). These systems can also be commercialized peer-to-peer mutualization systems (CPMS) that utilize peer-to-peer processes to purchase temporary use of products that are privately owned through a shared or rental model (Richards & Hamilton, 2018). Redistribution markets exist where used goods are transferred from an owner who does not want them anymore to an individual who desires the product. An organization facilitates these transactions either online or face-to-face (Garrett et al., 2017). These redistribution networks are effectively an evolution of the "reducing, reusing, recycling, repairing, and redistribution" methods of dealing with waste and/or unwanted possessions (Albinsson & Yasanthi Perera, 2012, p. 308). Collaborative lifestyles are community-based platforms used to access assets that have limited tangibility, such as services, resources, or skills through social peer-to-peer interactions (Ertz et al., 2016). These communities are often made up of individuals with similar interests and work collaboratively to meet the needs and wants of others in the community through bartering and trading exchange systems.

Why Collaborative Consumption is Increasing in Popularity

Consumer Trust

Collaborative consumption has invited a new way of thinking for corporations. Not only does the collaborative consumption model offer unique benefits, but collaborative consumption also offers a model that has the potential to enthuse consumers. Studies indicate that today's consumers are quite concerned with big business, and the moral and/or ethical standards behind a "faceless" corporation (Hamari, et al., 2016). In essence, when a given organization becomes large enough and creates a multi-level hierarchy, consumers tend to sense a lack of transparency (Mittendorf, 2018). Further, some consumers tend to mistrust large corporations due to popular reports of scandal, fraud, and corruption (Mittendorf, 2018). Even when corporations invest in Corporate Social Responsibility (CSR), some studies have indicated that consumers tend to question the authenticity of such claims (Hamari et al., 2016). All in all, reports suggest consumers are beginning to veer away from interactions with larger B2C corporations, as they feel such consumption patterns may be considered disreputable or even unethical (Eckhardt, et al., 2010).

The collaborative consumption model is therefore unique in that it provides a solution to such consumer concerns. As the original definition of collaborative consumption emphasizes the "peer-to-peer" nature of the activity, consumers tend to trust their peers more than they would trust a traditional B2C corporation (Hamari et al., 2016, p. 2047). Consumers are part of the community-oriented exchange process in the collaborative consumption model, and its success, therefore, relies on the consumers themselves. Thus, the collaborative consumption model offers consumers an attractive solution to trust concerns about unethical corporate behavior. So, while there is an increased sense of trust towards businesses utilizing the collaborative model, there is also a sense of autonomy and accomplishment on the consumer's behalf. Therefore, the collaborative consumption model allows consumers to feel as if they have bypassed interactions with traditional "faceless" corporations, all while feeling a sense of autonomy and accomplishment.

An Industry Perspective

Many businesses have embraced the collaborative consumption model as their main means of operation. Well-known companies such as Airbnb and Uber rely on the collaborative consumption model. The popularity of these businesses can be linked to the aforementioned ideas of autonomy, consumer trust, and accomplishment. For example, when a consumer decides to use Airbnb, the popular online home rental marketplace, a consumer chooses their own destination from various home options (hence, the autonomy), which are supplied on the behalf of other reviewed consumers (hence, the consumer trust). After having an autonomous process of checking in, the consumer then checks out without interacting with any other parties and is possibly rewarded depending on a positive review from the host (hence, the sense of accomplishment). While the consumer does in fact deal with a third-party business entity (i.e., Airbnb), the entire consumption and transaction process is the direct converse of transacting with a traditional B2C corporation.

It is estimated that there are over 800 active businesses taking part in the collaborative consumption model (Oliveira, et al., 2020). Further, the collaborative consumption market was reported to be worth $18.6 billion in 2017 and is forecasted to be worth $40.2 billion by 2022 (Foye, 2017). Additionally, according to Hamari et al. (2016, p. 2048), revenue "flowing through the sharing economy directly into people's wallets" recently exceeded USD 3.5 billion. Needless to say, the collaborative consumption model is not only beneficial for consumers but if used correctly, the model is financially sound.

Collaborative Consumption in the Sport Industry

Collaborative consumption has yet to reach its full potential in the sport industry, although there is growing evidence of successful applications. Already, companies such as Airbnb

Experiences and SportsHosts have pioneered shared sports experiences. Sport apparel and equipment providers, such as REI Used Gear, SidelineSwap, and Spinlister, provide collaborative consumption opportunities, while sport fans are able to split and share ticket purchases through Season Share. The sport industry seems to be an ideal fit for collaborative consumption for numerous reasons. For starters, the sport field shares several key elements that are present in the tourism field (a field that frequently takes part in collaborative consumption business). Further, the sport context is one in which consumer-to-consumer interaction is heavily present. We explore this in greater detail in the following section.

Applying Collaborative Consumption to the Sport Industry

While tourism is considered an industry in itself, some will certainly claim that the sport industry and the tourism industry are intertwined (Mullin, et al., 2014). This is because sport contests attract non-resident visitors to a host city. In some cases, it has been suggested sporting events and/or a given sports team can often be part of a city's character and can therefore offer tourism appeal (Mullin, et al., 2014). Mainly though, and as it relates to our current conversation, the sport industry mirrors the tourism context for its ability to serve as "host" to an array of non-resident visitors. The collaborative consumption platform has been utilized in the form of lodging services (e.g., Airbnb), ride services for tourists (e.g., Uber or Lyft), restaurant services (e.g., Eatwith or Seamless), and even tour guide services (e.g., Vayable). But while all of these examples serve to accommodate visitors, the sport industry – an industry that is heavily based on accommodation – has yet to fully seize the potential that the collaborative consumption platform has to offer. Below we will seek to understand why the field is perhaps ripe for the collaborative consumption model.

1 *Sport fans do not attend sporting events alone*: According to numerous studies, it has been suggested that sport fans do not attend sporting events alone (Hedlund et al., 2018). It should be noted that this is particularly relevant to the sport field itself. While there are certainly other occasions that are suitable for multi-party participation, sporting events are unique in that the *vast* majority of individuals who are attending are doing so with others (Hedlund, et al., 2018). Although this concept may seem straightforward, it sheds a new light when discussing it from the collaborative consumption perspective. In essence, a sporting event is a peer-to-peer collaboration since the vast majority of individuals are attending with others and are sharing access to a unique set of goods and services. Such a sharing process is the very foundation of the collaborative consumption process.

But that is not all. It has also been suggested that sport is a unique consumption platform because consumer satisfaction is often predicated upon socialization (Ross, et al., 2008). That is to say, rather than evaluating a sporting event upon the outcome of the contest (i.e., whether a favorite team wins or loses), consumers are likely to evaluate the event based on their experience with others. Studies suggest that enjoyable experiences with friends will likely lead to positive appraisals of the contest, even if a favorite team loses the contest itself (Ross et al., 2008). This is quite relevant to the current dialog. Being that consumers are relying upon socialization (i.e., other peers) for satisfaction, they are therefore bypassing the sport organization itself. This fits well within the conversation of the benefits of taking part in the collaborative consumption process. As has been mentioned, consumers have recently begun to show a reluctance in trusting big business and are instead favoring an autonomous consumption process. This is fitting to the peer-to-peer nature of the sports field, where consumers can find satisfaction in themselves, rather than the sport organization itself.

2 *Sports often offer community membership*: In that, the collaborative consumption process is predicated upon community-based interaction, it is obvious that community should be a centric part of our conversation. This seems to be beneficial for the sport industry as it often goes hand-in-hand with community. That is to say, sports can often serve as the medium for groups of individuals to migrate to one another (particularly groups of people who share the same penchant for something, such as supporting a particular team). The sociological theory describing such a phenomenon is known as neotribalism. Neotribalism is the theory that groups of individuals will come together and form communities based on certain life concepts, such as beliefs, rituals, product usage, or even emotional connections (Hardy, et al., 2013; Lundberg & Ziakas, 2018). Sports can do this in many different ways. Not only can sport organizations offer community membership in the form of season ticket holder membership or booster membership, but fans have the opportunity to utilize sport as a means to create their own community memberships (see the New York Mets supporters, the "7 Line Army," or the Celtic F.C. supporter group, the "Green Brigade"). And while community membership can be found in a multitude of fields or disciplines, sport serves as a unique medium for community membership due to the passion and emotion often associated with sports. While this has been detrimental to the field at times (see Hooliganism), this passion and emotion are more often translated to the formation of passionate, accessible groups.

In recognizing this, we see that sport can not only offer a sense of community but subsequently, this community can provide consumers with a sense of trust due to the emotional connectedness that comes with it. This once again speaks to the concern consumers have about mistrust towards an organization. For if consumers can find a consumption platform that is based upon community membership, then they will prefer it because it will seem more trustworthy than a given B2C corporation. In essence, this consumption preference is precisely why the collaborative consumption process is so attractive to consumers. It offers the consumer a chance to bypass the organization itself and instead deal directly with a trusted source (in this case, a like-minded community group). Yet at the same time, we can see why this would be attractive to sport organizations. For while consumers may not be dealing with the organization directly, they are in essence taking part in the consumption process via the means of support through the group membership. All in all, such a process is not only community-based and drives indirect consumption habits (both of which are pillars of the collaborative consumption process), but community memberships can often drive other consumptive processes, some of which are described below.

3 *Sport can offer other, peer-created events*: While we know sport can offer community memberships that can be trusted, we can now begin to think of the subsequent benefits that such groups can offer. Perhaps the first thing that comes to mind are events that are hosted by fan groups (e.g., tailgating, or supporter parties). While these events are not representative of a sporting match itself, they are representative of the primary event taking place, or the team itself. Such events are known as social products (Bryant, 1993); here, described as separate outings that are affiliated with a sports team or sports brand. Scholars have attested to the power of social products at length, with some even asserting that social products themselves are more important than the primary product (Cova, 1997). In a sports context,

> social products are beneficial for a variety of reasons. Not only do they enable consumers to form an emotional attachment to the event, but consequently, social products allow consumers to form an emotional connection to the primary product (i.e., the sports team or brand; Richelieu, & Boulaire, 2005). In fact, according to Richelieu and Boulaire (2005), if social products are utilized correctly, they can "strengthen fan loyalty and re-inforce the team brand equity" (p. 24).

In sports, we can see the social product take place in the form of tailgating or support parties. But what is most important to the current conversation is that these events are self-created, are community-based, and take part in obtaining, giving, and sharing goods and services. All of these facets are pillars of the collaborative consumption process. Moreover, one can see that if fans were to take part in hosting a social product, then the product would offer autonomy and accomplishment in the form of event creation. All of these factors once again show why the sport product would be an ideal fit for the collaborative consumption platform.

Summary

All three of the abovementioned reasons are why sport would be an ideal fit for the collaborative consumption platform. It is therefore up to sport organizations to translate their products so that they can become collaborative in nature. A given sport organization has the opportunity to not only utilize its peer-to-peer nature but to utilize fan groups and their respective social products as a means to drive interest in the organization. In the next section, we will discuss how certain organizations are utilizing the collaborative consumption platform to do just that.

Industry Examples

Sport Experiences

In November 2016, Airbnb launched Trips, which created a platform for people to share not just their homes, but also their interests, hobbies, and passions. The service was rebranded as Airbnb Experiences in 2018, and by the end of 2019 offered over 40,000 experiences in 1,000 cities (Ting, 2019). By the end of 2020, Airbnb included many sport experiences. In Mexico for example, a host named Alexis was offering an opportunity to join him for a scheduled Liga MX soccer game at one of Mexico City's iconic stadiums. The experience included tickets, drinks, and transportation, and promised that the guest would "learn about their histories and the history of Mexican soccer … we'll also share stories about our own experiences, so you get a true sense of the importance of soccer in Mexico" (Airbnb, 2020a). A similar experience was offered by a host named Ricardo Luis in Havana, Cuba, promising a passion-filled visit to the Estadio Latinoamericano, Cuba's "baseball cathedral" (Airbnb, 2020b). Those interested in a unique Lucha libre wrestling experience could sign-up to join a host named Adrian in Guadalajara, Mexico for tacos and a drink of ancient pulque at a traditional local bar with wrestling memorabilia, followed by almost front-row seats to the evening's wrestling action (Airbnb, 2020c).

SportsHosts was established in 2016 in Australia to connect travelers with local fans to watch sport together. The fans serve as hosts, although travelers and fans pay their costs. Melissa Blair, co-founder and Brand Director of SportsHosts described the tailgating, social, and game-day experience:

> We call it a game day because it's not just about the match, it's the entire game-day experience. From the food that you grab together before the game, walking to the game together, attending the actual game itself, or visiting the pub afterwards to grab a drink with local fans … it's really about the entire cultural experience.
>
> *(Tran, 2017, para. 4)*

SportsHosts earns revenues from commissions on the tickets, merchandise, concessions, and packages it sells. By 2020, the business had partnered with Melbourne FC, the San Francisco Giants, Brooklyn Nets, and New York City FC, and had approximately 6,000 members signed-up from 20 countries. Mario Alioto, Executive Vice President of Business Operations for the San Francisco Giants commented on the benefits for fans who served as hosts: "The thing we didn't realize was how engaged and excited our current fans would be in being a host and sharing their love of the game with new people" (Sunnucks, 2019, para. 11).

Sport Apparel

In 2017, REI, an American retail and outdoor recreation services company, piloted the REI Used Gear online platform, to allow customers to shop for returned, inspected, and approved gear at substantially discounted prices (Ruggiero, 2017). By October 2020, online used-gear sales were up by 100% from the previous year, and the company introduced a trade-in option for REI Co-op members (Ruggiero, 2020). Ken Voeller, REI's e-commerce manager stated:

Buying a piece of used gear is one of the best ways you or I can reduce our carbon footprint. Looking ahead, we have a number of product launches that will continue to accelerate our efforts in this space and solve problems for our members around purchasing used gear or trading in their own gear for someone else to enjoy (Ruggiero, 2020, para. 3).

The technology enabling REI Used Gear was provided by logistics startup firm Trove, which started as Yerdle in 2012, a "platform for giving away stuff to your friends, and for getting from them the things you need" (Makower, 2012, para. 4). By the end of 2020, Trove was building and operating resale programs for brands like REI, Arc'teryx, and Patagonia. The firm provided white-label solutions for these brands' secondary markets while encouraging more sustainable, circular business practices. Trove physically processed and valued returned items, provided a branded digital trade-in, buying, and marketing experience, and handled shipping, customer support, and data analysis.

Sport Equipment

SidelineSwap, a web and app-based marketplace for athletes to buy and sell sports gear and equipment, was founded in 2015 by former college athletes who observed how difficult it was to find high-quality used sports gear online. The digital platform charges sellers, who are mostly individual athletes under 24 years old and sports families, a 9% fee, which is often below that of eBay or Amazon. In 2018, the company announced a $5 million Series A financing round, led by Global Founders Capital and including former NBA player David Robinson's Admiral Capital, and The Player's Impact, a syndicate of professional athletes and Olympians. SidelineSwap's co-founder and CEO, Brendan Candon, argued:

> While consumers have plenty of retail options when it comes to buying gear, we are able to offer the best deals – usually more than 50% less than retail - because it's being sold by individual sellers who are simply interested in making some money back on gear they

> bought last season. … We offer buyers a way to save 50% on high quality used and new gear, and sellers a way to earn money on last year's equipment so they can reinvest in new gear this season.
>
> *(Heitner, 2018, para. 6)*

Spinlister has been described as the "Airbnb for bikes," providing peer-to-peer bike, ski, and snowboard rentals in over 65 countries since 2012 (Frothingham, 2019, para. 3). In 2019, the business launched a software, Bluetooth lock, and app solution for independent bike stores, local hotels and resorts, apartment buildings, and campuses to manage a bike-share program. The new owner, Mark Gustafson, described Spinlister's revised approach to collaborative consumption:

> We're still peer-to-peer, but our biggest focus is bike shops and mobile bike mechanics. … We want to give communities a middle ground between a Jump or Bird … and the old school rentals. … The problem for straight peer-to-peer is that someone has to take time out of their day to make this transaction happen, for not a lot of money.
>
> *(Lindsey, 2019, para. 6–9)*

Another peer-to-peer sports equipment platform, StokeShare, launched in 2014, but "ran out of steam" and closed in November 2019 (Cesare, 2019, para. 2). StokeShare was founded as an action sports sharing economy company, that created a platform for people to rent their kitesurfing, snowboard/ski, camping/backpacking, standup paddleboard, spearfishing/freediving, kayaking, rock climbing, and surfing equipment. By early 2016 the company had 500 users with 800 pieces of equipment in 11 of the United States, as well as in seven other countries (Blaustein, 2016).

The technology enabling the collaborative consumption of sports equipment included companies such as Joyride. Since 2017, Joyride had provided a micromobility turnkey software platform to scooter-share and bike-share operators globally. The white-label software allowed operators to quickly offer a scalable iOS and Android rider app, an operator app to manage the fleet, and a web-based administrative dashboard, including payment processing and customer support. Eric Bell, the CEO of a San Antonio, Texas, operator described Joyride's digital technology as:

> more secure, more reliable, and more scalable than our previous software solution. … Blue Duck will become the partner-of-choice for cities, universities, and companies worldwide by offering our riders an exceptional experience they can't get elsewhere. Joyride will be an integral component of meeting that objective.
>
> *(Donagher, 2019, para. 3)*

Sport Coaching

CoachUp was launched in 2012 by former collegiate and professional basketball player Jordan Fliegal as a platform to connect athletes with private coaches. By the end of 2020, the Boston-based online marketplace had over 13,000 coaches signed-up in over 30 sports, and over 100,000 athletes had used CoachUp to connect and work with a private coach. CoachUp established an Athlete Advisory Council in 2014, which included the Golden State Warriors' Stephen Curry and New England Patriots Julian Edelman. The business had raised over

$9 million in funding, and in 2019 expanded to provide its services in Canada. CoachUp targeted parents of youth athletes in middle school and high school, as well as adults looking for private lessons for personal fitness (Kiernan, 2016).

Fittcoach described itself as the largest online community to book personal training. The Canadian-based online marketplace and app provided an opportunity for anyone interested in fitness, including those within other professions, to provide personal training as a secondary source of income. Since 2017, consumers were able to access a range of fittcoaches for $25 per session. Nauman Hafeez, one of the founders, described the problem that fittcoach was trying to address:

> Before we could hire a personal trainer, we had to listen to a gym's hour-long sales pitch. What is more, these gyms gave us very little say about the trainer we'd get. So, we got locked into expensive contracts with trainers we didn't know and with whom we hadn't had a test run.
>
> *(Sharetribe, n.d., para. 5)*

The technology enabling companies such as Fittcoach included Sharetribe. Sharetribe was a website builder for entrepreneurs wanting to quickly launch a peer-to-peer marketplace. The software enabled startup collaborative consumption companies to easily create a platform where users could rent or sell goods, spaces, or services online, while the hosting, transactions, and online payments were handled by Sharetribe. The business was founded in Finland in 2011, and by the end of 2020 had raised $2.4 million in funding. Juho Makkonen, the co-founder and CEO of Sharetribe, described their mission:

> Our ambition was, and still is, to do the same to online marketplaces and the sharing economy: to democratize them by allowing anyone to create a successful online marketplace business that they own and control. Today, our mission is more important than ever: we want to offer a real alternative to the gigantic "death star" platforms that are dominating the sharing economy.
>
> *(Makkonen, 2019, para. 4)*

Sport Facilities

Since 2017, Swimmy has provided an online marketplace for swimming pool owners to rent out their underutilized swimming pools to subscribers for a few hours at a time. By the end of 2018, the service had acquired 16,000 subscribers in France.

In 2018, a similar business, called Swimply, was launched by Bunim Laskin and Asher Weinberger in the United States. Swimply provided the platform for users to rent their pool by the hour, and by the end of 2019 was operating in 26 states and had expanded to Australia. The business had raised $1.2 million in funding, and by the end of 2020 had 200,000 app downloads and 6,000 listed swimming pools. The service proved especially popular during the COVID-19 pandemic when public facilities and other recreational facilities were closed in 2020. Weinberger pointed out:

> It's not just the public pools. … What we're doing is we're replacing lots of other sectors. So, for example, where were people making their birthday parties? Maybe Chuck E. Cheese or places like that, and now there's nowhere to do that. There are people who do aquatic therapy or physical therapy, people go to the gym, they can't exercise – looking for

> a way to exercise, right? We're not just replacing the public pool. We're just an entertainment, exercise, and just general relaxation venue.
>
> *(Raudins & Williams, 2020, para. 5)*

In 2020, Swimply created JoySpace, a platform for renting or sharing a range of private spaces, including tennis and basketball courts, to home gyms and backyards.

ParqEx was a technology company founded in Chicago in 2014, that connected owners of private parking spots to drivers looking for parking. The business managed the entire process of listing, reserving, parking, and paying. Vivek Mehra, the founder of ParqEx, described the mission of the business as solving the urban parking challenge: "We don't need more parking lots, we just need to come together as a community and help each other out" (The Leaders Globe, 2020, para. 5). By mid-2020, ParqEx had expanded their offering and technology solutions, partly in response to the COVID-19 pandemic. Mehra argued:

> Access+ Premium with License Plate Recognition (LPR) technology, takes "touchless" access to a whole new level. With Access+ we built a universal virtual remote control to open gates and garage doors via the ParqEx mobile app. Now we have further extended the platform by adding License Plate Recognition technology with which drivers simply pull up in their vehicle and the gate/garage door opens.
>
> *(ParqEx, 2020, para. 2)*

SpotHero started as a similar peer-to-peer parking marketplace in Chicago in 2011. By the end of 2019, the company had raised $118 million in funding and was partnering with parking companies and garages. In 2017, co-founder Larry Kiss commented on the usage of the service near Wrigley Field: "It's not uncommon for a spot owner near the field to earn $400-plus a month during the baseball season" (Braff, 2017, para. 16).

In the UK, Anthony Eskinazi developed the website ParkatmyHouse in 2006, which helped drivers park in driveways near sports stadiums. By 2015 the business had rebranded as JustPark, and by the end of 2020 had 3.5 million registered drivers, over 45,000 reservable locations across the UK, and users had earned more than $50 million from listing spare parking spaces on its platform (Douglas, 2020). JustPark was partly funded through two Crowdcube peer-to-peer investing campaigns, which together raised over $10 million from just over 7,500 investors.

Sport Event Tickets

Season Share is a web and mobile application that allows fans to split and share ticket purchases. The Los Angeles-based company is the first mobile app that enables fans to buy, group, split, and share multi-game tickets to live sporting events. Games are priced using the original face value of the ticket, and Season Share does not allow users to mark the prices up or down. The business created a Game Draft tool that operates similarly to fantasy sports drafts. Each group member chooses a game in a snake-style draft that leaves a season ticket split evenly across the group. Since sports seasons are different lengths, and group sizes may vary, the Season Share system charges each member based on the number of games that members receive in the Game Draft. Andrew Steinberg, founder of Phoenix Capital Ventures and lead investor in Season Share's seed funding round described the business:

> Season Share was among the first to recognize the shifting consumption trends in sports, both in attendance and viewership, and addressed the evolving landscape by providing

> seamless, cost-effective flexibility and functionality to the ticketing process," Steinberg said. "Today, Season Share offers the technology, interface and data-driven platform that is second to none in the industry in allowing organizations to have matchless insight into their core fan base.
>
> *(Evans, 2019, para. 12)*

In partnership with the San Francisco 49ers and Ticketmaster, Season Share provided a fractional season ticket ownership solution to new and existing 49ers ticket holders. The platform provided visibility into who the tickets were being shared with, which allowed the NFL franchise to add new fans to their database. Approximately 70% of the 3.2 million season ticket packages in the Unites States are shared, although teams have traditionally had no information about who those share partners were. The results of this partnership included more than 1,000 previously unidentifiable accounts within the first 24 hours, deeper CRM insights into almost half of these accounts due to Facebook single-sign-on integration, and a retargeting campaign for $3.4 million worth of abandoned inventory. During the first year of the partnership, Season Share managed almost $200,000 worth of 49ers season tickets. Jamie Brandt, VP of Sales and Service at the 49ers stated: "Season Share allows us to offer a truly innovative solution to both current and prospective ticket holders that can add real value to their accounts" (Ticketmaster, 2020, para. 1).

In October 2020, the Arizona Coyotes in the NHL launched YotesShare, a season ticket micro-sharing service developed in partnership with Season Share. A fan can purchase a 5% micro-share of a Coyotes season membership for a lower-level seat, with a two-seat minimum and four-seat maximum. Micro-sharing ticket holders also receive a t-shirt, can claim to be a season ticket member, and receive priority access for playoff games. Sam Doerr, the Coyotes VP of Innovation and Strategy pointed to the shift in millennial behavior and saw the "benefit of getting people involved at a lower level and a lower commitment and hopefully growing them into being a half-season member of a full season member" (Burns, 2020, para. 1). Individual tickets for sports games have been available for reselling via secondary ticket marketplaces for some time, with Ticketmaster, SeatGeek, StubHub, and Vivid Seats and others, competing in the $15 billion secondary ticket market (Dhingra, 2020).

Future Research Implications

Such examples stand to justify the relationship of collaborative consumption platforms within a sport setting. If sport organizations are able to involve consumers in a creation role, then there is an opportunity for both parties to fully realize the numerous benefits the collaborative consumption practice offers. Not only can collaborative consumption offers sport organizations a new fanbase, but this practice has the potential to offer a new experience for sport consumers; one which allows the sport consumer to take ownership of the sports brand, and therefore deepen their loyalty to said brand. Yet, in saying this, the sport business field has yet to fully invest in such a practice. There is a need therefore to further investigate sport consumers' preferences towards collaborative consumption in order to provide sport organizations with a rationale to take part in this practice. While we have come to understand the popularity of collaborative consumption methods amongst the general public, there is perhaps a need to investigate whether sport consumers share such a proclivity towards the practice.

Specifically, in that there are various levels (i.e., types) of collaborative consumption, there is a need to understand which levels sport consumers prefer, and which levels would best match the sport industry. For example, pure collaboration occurs when a provider and a receiver exchange a resource as a direct transaction between peers or consumers - usually facilitated through an unmediated (web) platform. This means that consumers utilize the platform as a communication tool to discuss and negotiate the terms and conditions of the exchange. In contrast, sourcing collaboration and trading collaboration are mediated through a third-party platform. In sourcing collaboration, the interaction is initiated by a consumer with a business or organization (C2B or C2O) to exchange products and services with another consumer (Ertz et al., 2019). In this case, the provider (consumer) connects with receivers (business) through a website that is mediated by the business, to connect consumers with other consumers. Hence the business offers no products or services to the consumer beyond being a fee-based intermediary to drive peer-to-peer collaborations. With trading collaboration, a business or organization initiates the collaboration with the consumer (O2C) (Ertz et al., 2019). The consumer becomes the receiver of the product or service provided through the mediated platform from another individual. In effect, when the consumer provides a product through the intermediary, they are engaged in sourcing collaboration; and when the consumer is obtaining a product or service through an intermediary, they are engaged in trading collaboration. Understanding which of these levels would be the best for the sport industry (and in turn, which would be best received by sport consumers) is a topic ripe for investigation.

There is also the question of how to best involve the sport consumer without overstepping the boundaries of the autonomous nature of the collaborative consumption experience. The collaborative consumption experience has evolved consumers to become prosumers because they create products, services, and experiences, and they participate in the development, updating, and transfigurement of them (Cova & Dalli, 2009). In this way, consumers are no longer just taking on a buyer and consumer role, but are involved in the production and distribution of products and services (Ritzer, 2014). A major benefit to consumers is that the collaborative consumption experiences encourage consumers to be part of the value creation process as both an obtainer of goods and services and an informal supplier. As such, customers do not just expect to be provided products and services; they want to be actively involved in the co-creation process and view brands as shared cultural property (Cova & Dalli, 2009). How then will sport business operations go about creating this process without interfering in this consumer-centered experience? Investigations upon these topics – which are centered on the sport consumers' preferences – should be upheld in future research agendas.

Conclusion

The purpose of this chapter was to articulate the role of collaborative consumption in the delivery of products and services through the sport industry. These peer-to-peer community-focused activities are coordinated both face-to-face and online (Hamari et al., 2016) to generate excitement, involvement, and passion by stakeholders. This is especially true for sport consumers because they wish to be actively involved in the co-creation (Cova & Dalli, 2009) and prosumption (Mohd et al., 2019; Ritzer, 2014) processes in that they want to both produce and consumer sport products and services simultaneously. This active involvement is reinforced by the fact that sport fans do not attend sporting events alone, sport activities generally offer community membership as an added benefit, and the interactions between sport consumer often extend to the development of additional peer-created events. As a result, these interactions have the potential to become an integral component of both event implementation and value creation across all parts of the sport industry.

References

Airbnb. (2020a). See a football match at the stadium. https://www.airbnb.com/experiences/112213.

Airbnb. (2020b). Take me out to the ball game. https://www.airbnb.com/experiences/135428.

Airbnb. (2020c). Lucha extrema Saturday & special dates. https://www.airbnb.com/experiences/665293.

Albinsson, P. A., & Yasanthi Perera, B. (2012). Alternative marketplaces in the 21st century: Building community through sharing events. *Journal of Consumer Behaviour, 11*(4), 303–315. 10.1002/cb.1389

Blaustein, L. (2016). The GSB Interview: Joel Cesare, StokeShare – The sharing economy meets action sports. GreenSportsBlog. https://greensportsblog.com/the-gsb-interview-joel-cesare-stokeshare.

Botsman, R., & Rogers, R. (2010). *What's mine is yours: The rise of collaborative consumption.* HarperCollins.

Braff, D. (2017). No car needed: Homeowners get creative with alternative uses for parking spots. Chicago Tribune. https://www.chicagotribune.com/real-estate/ct-re-1210-parking-spots-20171117-story.html.

Bryant, J. E. (1993). Sport management and the interdependence with sport sociology: Sport as a social product. *Journal of Sport Management*, 7(3), 194–198.

Burns, M. J. (2020, October 21). Coyotes getting creative with recent ticketing innovations. *Sports business journal.* https://www.sportsbusinessdaily.com.

Cesare, J. (2019). StokeShare forever. *Medium.* https://medium.com/@RealJoelCesare/stokeshare-forever-f3ebff9b6df2.

Cova, B. (1997). Community and consumption. *European journal of marketing, 31*(3/4), 297–316.

Cova, B., & Dalli, D. (2009). Working consumers: The next step in marketing theory? *Marketing Theory, 9*(3), 315–339. 10.1177/1470593109338144

Dhingra, K. (2020, March 23). A shock to the secondary ticket market. *Sports business journal.* https://www.sportsbusinessdaily.com.

Donagher, H. (2019). Blue Duck taps Joyride tech to power rapid fleet expansion. *Blue duck.* https://www.flyblueduck.com/2019/09/12/bds-partners-with-joyride.

Douglas, J. (2020). Just park apologises after scammers place fake parking space ads. *BBC news.* https://www.bbc.com/news/business-54840335.

Eckhardt, G. M., Belk, R., & Devinney, T. M. (2010). Why don't consumers consume ethically? *Journal of Consumer Behaviour, 9*(6), 426–436. doi:10.1002/cb.332

Ertz, M., Durif, F., & Arcand, M. (2016). Collaborative consumption: Conceptual snapshot at a buzzword. *Journal of Entrepreneurship Education, 19*(2), 1–23. 10.2139/ssrn.2799884

Ertz, M., Durif, F., & Arcand, M. (2019). A conceptual perspective on collaborative consumption. *AMS Review, 9*(1-2), 27–41. 10.1007/s13162-018-0121-3

Ertz, M., Durif, F., Lecompte, A., & Boivin, C. (2018). Does "sharing" mean "socially responsible consuming"? Exploration of the relationship between collaborative consumption and socially responsible consumption. *Journal of Consumer Marketing, 35*(4), 392–402. 10.1108/JCM-09-2016-1941

Evans, P. (2019, April 9). Launching with 49ers, season share hopes to be 'Airbnb' of tickets. front office sports. https://frontofficesports.com/season-share-49ers.

Frothingham, S. (2019). Spinlister returns with new bike-share capability for IBDs. *Bicycle retailer and industry news.* https://www.bicycleretailer.com/retail-news/2019/04/08/spinlister-returns-new-bike-share-capability-ibds#.X8qaBBNKh24.

Foye, L. (2017). Sharing economy, opportunities, impacts and disruptors 2017-2022. *Juniper Research, July, 27.*

Garrett, A., Straker, K., & Wrigley, C. (2017). Digital channels for building collaborative consumption communities. *Journal of Research in Interactive Marketing, 11*(2), 160–184. 10.1108/jrim-08-2016-0086

Gössling, S., & Hall, C. M. (2019). Sharing versus collaborative economy: How to align ICT developments and the SDGs in tourism? *Journal of Sustainable Tourism, 27*(1), 74–96.

Hamari, J., Sjöklint, M., & Ukkonen, A. (2016). The sharing economy: Why people participate in collaborative consumption [Article]. *Journal of the Association for Information Science & Technology, 67*(9), 2047–2059. 10.1002/asi.23552

Hardy, A., Gretzel, U., & Hanson, D. (2013). Travelling neo-tribes: Conceptualising recreational vehicle users. *Journal of Tourism and Cultural Change, 11*(1–2), 48–60.

Hedlund, D. P., Biscaia, R., & do Carmo Leal, M. (2018). Those who rarely attend alone: Tribal sport fans. In *Exploring the rise of fandom in contemporary consumer culture* (pp. 71–101). IGI Global.

Heitner, D. (2018). Why former NBA player David Robinson is investing in a $5 million round for SidelineSwap to battle against Amazon and eBay. Inc. https://www.inc.com/darren-heitner/why-former-nba-player-david-robinson-is-investing-in-a-5-million-round-for-sidelineswap-to-battle-against-amazon-ebay.html.

Ikkala, T., & Lampinen, A. (2015). Monetizing network hospitality: Hospitality and sociability in the context of Airbnb. Proceedings of the 18th ACM conference on computer supported cooperative work and social computing.

Kiernan, T. (2016). What it's like to go through a training session with CoachUp. *Sports illustrated*. https://www.si.com/media/2016/08/24/coachup-athlete-training-stephen-curry-nerlens-noel.

Lampinen, A., & Cheshire, C. (2016). Hosting via Airbnb: Motivations and financial assurances in monetized network hospitality. Proceedings of the 2016 CHI conference on human factors in computing systems,

Leaders Globe. (2020). ParqEx: Streamlined parking solutions for solving urban parking challenge. https://www.theleadersglobe.com/magazine/parqex-streamlined-parking-solutions-for-solving-the-urban-parking-challenge.

Lindsey, J. (2019). Spinlister wanted to change bike rental (again). *Outside*. https://www.outsideonline.com/2394049/spinlister-bike-rentals.

Lundberg, C., & Ziakas, V. (2018). Fantrepreneurs in the sharing economy: Cocreating neotribal events. *Event Management*, *22*(2), 287–301. doi:10.3727/152599518X15173356116727

Makkonen, J. (2019). Sharetribe go becomes source-available after being open-source for 8 years. *Medium*. https://medium.com/bettersharing/sharetribe-go-becomes-source-available-after-being-open-source-for-8-years-bb43c410da53.

Makower, J. (2012). Can yerdle turn consuming less into the next big thing? *GreenBiz*. https://www.greenbiz.com/article/can-yerdle-turn-consuming-less-next-big-thing.

Mittendorf, C. (2018). Collaborative consumption: the role of familiarity and trust among millennials. *Journal of Consumer Marketing*, *35*(4), 377–391.

Mohd, N. S., Ismail, H. N., Isa, N., & Jaafar, S. M. R. S. (2019). Millennial tourist emotional experience in technological engagement at destination. *International Journal of Built Environment and Sustainability*, *6*(1-2), 129–135. 10.11113/ijbes.v6.n1-2.396

Möhlmann, M. (2015). Collaborative consumption: Determinants of satisfaction and the likelihood of using a sharing economy option again [Article]. *Journal of Consumer Behaviour*, *14*(3), 193–207. 10.1002/cb.1512

Molz, J. G. (2012). CouchSurfing and network hospitality: 'It's not just about the furniture'. *Hospitality and Society*, *1*(3), 215–225. 10.1386/hosp.1.3.215_2

Mullin, B. J., Hardy, S., & Sutton, W. (2014). *Sport marketing* 4th edition. Champaign, IL: Human Kinetics.

Oliveira, T., Tomar, S., & Tam, C. (2020). Evaluating collaborative consumption platforms from a consumer perspective. *Journal of Cleaner Production*, *273*, 1–16.

ParqEx. (2020). ParqEx launches Access+ Premium with license plate recognition (LPR) for a true 100% touchless access experience for drivers. https://www.parqex.com/parqex-launches-access-premium-with-license-plate-recognition-lpr-for-a-true-touchless-access-experience-for-drivers.

Piscicelli, L., Cooper, T., & Fisher, T. (2015). The role of values in collaborative consumption: Insights from a product-service system for lending and borrowing in the UK. *Journal of Cleaner Production*, *97*, 21–29.

Raudins, S., & Williams, M. (2020). Jump in, the water's fine: App lets hosts rent their pool by the hour. *The Columbus dispatch*. https://www.usatoday.com/story/tech/2020/08/20/swimply-app-lets-hosts-rent-their-pool-hour/5605401002.

Richelieu, A., & Boulaire, C. (2005). A post modern conception of the product and its applications professional sports. *International Journal of Sports Marketing and Sponsorship*, 7(1), 23–34

Richards, T. J., & Hamilton, S. F. (2018). Food waste in the sharing economy. *Food Policy*, *75*, 109–123. 10.1016/j.foodpol.2018.01.008

Ritzer, G. (2014). Prosumption: Evolution, revolution, or eternal return of the same? *Journal of Consumer Culture*, *14*(1), 3–24. 10.1177/1469540513509641

Ritzer, G., Dean, P., & Jurgenson, N. (2012). The coming of age of the prosumer. *American behavioral scientist*, *56*(4), 379–398. 10.1177/0002764211429368

Ross, S. D., Russell, K. C., & Bang, H. (2008). An empirical assessment of spectator-based brand equity. *Journal of Sport Management*, *22*, 322–337.

Ruggiero, A. (2017). REI launches discount used gear online. *GearJunkie*. https://gearjunkie.com/rei-discount-used-gear-online.

Ruggiero, A. (2020). REI introduces gear trade-in for members: Here's how it works. *GearJunkie*. https://gearjunkie.com/rei-used-gear-trade-in.

Scaraboto, D. (2015). Selling, sharing, and everything in between: The hybrid economies of collaborative networks. *Journal of Consumer Research*, *42*(1), 152–176. 10.1093/jcr/ucv004

Schor, J. B., & Attwood-Charles, W. (2017). The "sharing" economy: Labor, inequality, and social connection on for-profit platforms. *Sociology Compass*, *11*(8), e12493.

Schwarz, E. C., & Hunter, J. D. (2018). *Advanced theory and practice in sport marketing* (3rd ed. ed.). Routledge.

Sharetribe. (n.d.). Fittcoach by Nauman Hafeez and Samad Bhimani. https://www.sharetribe.com/customers/fittcoach.

Sunnucks, M. (2019, February 18). SportsHosts aims to pair sports travelers with host fans. *Sports business journal*. https://www.sportsbusinessdaily.com.

Taeihagh, A. (2017). Crowdsourcing, sharing economies and development. *Journal of Developing Societies*, *33*(2), 191–222. 10.1177/0169796x17710072

Ticketmaster. (2020). The San Francisco 49ers win new fans with more flexible season ticket memberships. https://business.ticketmaster.com/case-studies/the-san-francisco-49ers-win-new-fans-with-more-flexible-season-ticket-memberships.

Ting, D. (2019). How airbnb profits from our love of experience. *Eater*. https://www.eater.com/2019/12/4/20951866/airbnb-rentals-experiences-travel-food-tours-cooking-classes.

Tran, T. (2017). SportsHosts: A great way to make friends with locals. *Meld magazine*. https://www.meldmagazine.com.au/2017/12/sportshosts-great-friends-locals.

20

Data and the Sport Consumer

Adam Karg

Introduction

Aligned with the growth and professionalization of the sport industry has been concurrent development in the creation, accumulation, and application of data. In the last decades, sport organizations have adopted increasingly refined data acquisition and management practices, and used more robust information systems and advanced forms of analysis to attempt to gain competitive advantages (Alamar, 2013). This building of digital and data capacity by sport organizations has arguably developed more quickly for "on field" *or* "on court" purposes than for "sport business" applications. In the sport performance setting, the adoption of sophisticated techniques for tracking player movement, monitoring athlete training loads, assessing player draft efficiency, or reporting statistics has developed comparatively quickly, as organizations have sought to capitalize on real-time information capture and reporting to improve the athletic performance of teams and individuals. Such applications also support and improve the provision of information to "customer-facing" products including broadcasting, second screen applications, gambling, and fantasy sport.

However, the increased availability and ease, as well as more cost-effective mechanisms to capture, store and process consumer data, has led to the development and implementation of more strategic, data-led approaches to sport business and marketing. In particular, in the sport consumption setting, the volume of insights able to be drawn from evolving data and digital operations of sport organizations presents immense opportunities to better understand sport consumers and fans and to develop strategies to enhance fan-organization relationships that improve organizational and consumer outcomes. For managers, high volumes of data embedded within both live and media consumption of professional sport, combined with improved practices for managing, analyzing, and communicating data-led insights, provide opportunities to guide strategic decisions and outcomes linked to customer acquisition and retention, optimization and efficiency, and experience improvement in a sport setting.

The purpose of this chapter is to demonstrate how sport organizations can harness and leverage mass amounts of consumer data and digital interactions to improve organizational capacity and the fundamental business and marketing outcomes of sport organizations. Within a

DOI: 10.4324/9781003088899-24

consumer behavior focus, we refer to a wide range of behaviors and activities undertaken by consumers, including processes of selecting, purchasing, using, or disposing of products, services, ideas, and experiences and specific to sport, focus on sport-related experiences, needs and wants, as well as the benefits derived from sport consumption (Funk et al., 2016). The behaviors and exchanges that are a focus of this chapter are not limited to transactions or revenue-generating activities, but embrace a wider range of processes linked to information search, processing, consideration, and engagement.

This chapter explores disruptive forces driving change in the sport digital setting, a range of data sources, and provides vast examples of translating consumer data to inform consumer behavior strategies. A focus is maintained on the utilization of behavioral data, advanced analytics, and automated practices, seeking to highlight the innovative, data-led nature of modern sport marketing. Other themes include the enhanced capability to utilize mobile, social, and digital interactions and activities as data sources, rapid acceleration of passive digitally captured data, increased abilities to process behavioral data and convert it to real-time insights, and increased availability of data management and science capacity in organizational settings. While data capture and use is a pertinent issue for many industries, we focus on sport organizations and the professional sport setting, including, but not limited to professional sport leagues and teams, as well as sport governing bodies (e.g., national, as well as state, or regional bodies) for whom consumer approaches informed by available data and digital practices can provide substantial benefit.

In the next sections, the digital nature of sport consumer behavior is introduced, including a focus on how consumption experiences are increasingly providing access to greater volumes of data. The opportunity inherent for managers is then introduced, including the presentation of a systems framework inclusive of inputs (data and data sources), throughputs (analysis techniques), and outputs (framed as sources of competitive advantage). This is followed by a focus on data types and sources, and how these can be applied to key questions for managers. This chapter concludes with a consideration of building a system and structure for enabling organizations to develop competitive advantage, as well as consideration of emerging research needs and issues.

The Digitalization of Sport Consumer Behavior

This section provides an overview of "how sport consumers consume" in the modern sport ecosystem and demonstrates the central role of "digital" within these experiences. Sport consumption occurs via service provision, and is primarily delivered in a live or physical setting (e.g., where customers attend or participate in sport games or events live), or via virtual or mediated settings (e.g., where sport content is consumed or engaged with via a diverse range of media). Historically, the majority of sport consumption occurred via live attendance, with organizations using paper ticketing systems, allowing little to be known about *who* was purchasing, or any other traits of the customer. Over the last century, sport consumption has evolved to where the vast majority of sport consumption happens via media platforms (Karg et al., 2019; Pritchard & Funk, 2006). However, even up to very recent times, media consumption primarily has happened via linear television, with little opportunity to embed reliable or detailed forms of consumer measurement. Therefore, sport organizations and media companies delivering sport broadcasts have for a long time relied on archaic survey-driven measurement to estimate how many people were watching, but still had little knowledge about *who* was watching or other characteristics or traits of the audience. In sum, even as the value of sport has increased rapidly and attracted increased corporate spending from broadcasters and sponsors, the marketing efforts of sport organizations and stakeholders have been hampered by a lack of information about their customer or their behaviors.

The modern sport consumption setting, however, now sees digital components heavily embedded in the majority of sport consumer experiences. This advancement has allowed much more data to be captured and facilitated a deeper understanding of sport audiences and behaviors. In the media setting, while free-to-air or linear television still provides a popular and powerful medium for watching sport (McDonald & Lock, 2017), subscription and streaming television platforms, over-the-top (OTT) platforms, and social media sites including YouTube, Facebook, and Twitter are providing popular alternate offerings for accessing sport content. Importantly, media consumption is no longer restricted to "end-to-end" broadcasts of games, with highlights packages, condensed versions of games and highlights, and wide-ranging sport or sport-related content (e.g., statistics, fantasy sport, and lifestyle or "behind the scenes" programming) now increasingly available to sport fans. Such content can be delivered via broadcasters, teams, or leagues directly through their own platforms (e.g., websites or apps), or distributed via social or online forms of media. Critically though, the majority of these media options are delivered or "streamed" via apps, smartphones, or devices, providing opportunities to connect sport with consumers across billions of connected devices globally. Further, the digital nature of modern media sport consumption allows the scope to better identify customers and understand habits and behaviors of sport consumers both related to sport content, as well as extending into wider consumption behaviors.

Likewise, ticketing processes for live attendance or consumption are deeply embedded with digitalized processes and data collection opportunities. This includes, for example, records of season ticket holders or members who may sign up as "subscription" based customers of sport team or events, or casual users who may purchase only occasionally. Here, digital processes linked to information seeking, transactions, communications, and stadium entry form just some of the digital information available during the customer journey which provides substantial opportunities to utilize masses of data. This may include basic consumer information but also extend to insights into when a consumer attends, how they seek or access information when they enter the stadium, and how and when they make concession purchases. Much like the transition from linear broadcasting to digital media settings, the transition toward digitalization of consumer attendance has presented rich opportunities for data capture and utilization.

In sum, the digital nature of modern sport consumption provides mass volumes of storable, transferable, and measurable data that provides rich opportunities for marketers and organizations. This consumption is increasingly underpinned by connected devices helping facilitate and deliver media content and live experiences, while at the same time creating volumes of data as a valuable "by-product" of consumption. The changes or "disruption" seen in the digitalization of sport consumption outlined above can be aligned with a circle of innovation framework (Phillips, 2016). Here, key facilitators are emerging technology, new products and new ways to use products, and new ways for sport organizations to organize and interact with each other, as well as their customers.

Therefore, digital evolution of sport consumption has stimulated social and organizational change via the interplay of technology, individuals, and organizations (Phillips, 2016). Put more directly, there has been a greater shift toward a digital mindset, as well as a strong impetus to improve the infrastructure and resources committed to digital and data processes. While digital transformation, inclusive of substantial structural and operational changes in sport organizations are prolific in recent years, evolution in the capture and utilization of data is, in line with a circle of innovation framework, continually evolving to more succinctly and powerfully impact the decision making of sport managers. Particularly for digital sport consumption, there would be few developed sport organizations that did not undergo substantial acceleration in digital practices as a result of the global pandemic from 2020. Globally, this disruption accelerated digital capacity and practices, as organizations sought new ways to communicate and intensified their focus on the use of data to create value via digital assets and products.

Digital and Data as an Opportunity

Opportunities stemming from the digitalization of sport consumption can, in line with the diverse goals of sport organizations (Bayle & Madella, 2002), result in both financial and non-financial outcomes. Financial or commercial goals can be advanced directly, for example, from optimized targeting or increasing the yield of a customer via more targeted offers, or via the stimulation of higher retention rates as an outcome of improved consumer understanding. Indirect financial returns may also be evident where an organization can leverage a larger, better profiled, or more engaged customer database as an asset, to enhance outcomes for a third party such as a sponsor or broadcast partner. For example, identifying customers with a high propensity for certain products or services offered by a sponsor can result in optimized commercial returns.

Digital and data practices can also improve promotional and social outcomes of sport organizations, including enhanced relationships between an organization and individual customers, or between groups of customers. Fan engagement, where organizations seek to improve fan-organization relationships is a well-developed concept in the sport industry, understood as a complex and interrelated mix of cognitive, emotional and behavioral exchanges that a fan may have with an organization (Brodie et al., 2013). In a digital setting, this translates to specific consumer roles, such as the way a consumer interacts with the content or communications of a sport organization or sport fan community. Sub-processes of engagement acknowledge that customers share, learn, socialize, advocate, and co-create value in a digital setting (Brodie et al., 2013), supporting that the role of digital and data can go beyond financial returns and allow organizations to better understand their customers or fans, support value creation and assist them to better develop relationships with their customers, in line with the tenants of relationship marketing (Gronroos, 2004). Specifically, an enhanced understanding of fans' needs or the development of segmentation frameworks can help sport organizations deliver more appropriate communications, offers, or access to sources of value. Data can also be valuable in understanding sentiment or attitudes, which can allow an organization to develop more meaningful exchanges with customers, and advance the loyalty and commitment of consumers.

Such opportunities have been embraced by many sport organizations via an acute awareness of the need to capture data, utilize descriptive and predictive analysis, and enhance the value and exchanges between the organization and its customers. To this end, investments have been made to systems, as well as technological and human resources in attempts to build competitive advantages as outcomes of digital and data practices. In order to operationalize managerial and organizational approaches, Figure 20.1 introduces a systems view to frame the remaining sections of this chapter. It considers; (a) the inputs or data sources available to sport organizations; (b) throughputs or the organizations' use and adoption of practices, processes, and techniques to manage the conversion of data sources, and: (c) outcomes as the meaningful translation to competitive advantage, to assist organizations to develop strategies to maximize financial and non-financial returns relative to consumer behavior.

Data Sources	**Data Approaches**	**Outcomes**
Database/CRM	Statistical/Modeling Approaches	Improved Customer Experience
Website/Online Behaviors	Descriptive/Predictive Analytics	Supporting and Enhancing Decision Making Planning and Resourcing
Social Media	Clustering Segmentation	Operational and Cost Efficiencies
Mobile and Location	Customer Experience/Journey	Enhanced Revenue and Yield
Surveys and Insights	Geo Spatial or Location Analysis	Chum Limitation
	Machine Learning/Pattern Analysis	Testing Data Driven Interventions

Figure 20.1 Systems Framework for Digital and Data Processes in the Sport Consumer Behavior Setting

Consumer Data Sources

In this section, forms of consumer data that exist in the digital ecosystem for sport organizations are introduced, with a specific focus on data generated via digitalized sport consumption. Those included here are closely linked to consumer behavior and are created, collated, or available via Customer Relationship Management (CRM) platforms, via the website, digital or other online activities including social media, developed from location data or other behavioral activities, or finally, via survey or other forms of primary data collection.

The CRM platform of any organization provides a central starting point to collate, store, and understand available customer data. As well as unique identification codes for each consumer record, this source includes basic information including names, demographic and contact details, many of which would be commonly captured at the start of a relationship between an organization and a customer (e.g., when they sign up or register for a service). Transactional or purchase details (including when and how purchase happens), consumption data (e.g., attendance records or merchandise or ticketing spend data) and details about the customer's history or tenure (including if they have been retained or churned) are additional points of information which may be accessible. Critically, these variables are often available for most or all customers or prospects, and collectively, these initial data points can provide a basic understanding of the recency, frequency, and monetary (or RFM) value or customer lifetime value (CLV) of customers. These can be very useful indicators for marketers, allowing for customer segmentation, and more optimized targeting, or can inform the propensity of customers to be retained (Karg et al., 2021) or to undertake behaviors such as attendance (Schreyer & Däuper, 2018; Schreyer, 2019). In addition to the details or data above, the CRM platform can act as a repository to a house or provide access to integrate many other data points or variables, either held within the same data file or platform or linked to other databases or data sources an organization may have access to.

Website or online behaviors related to consumption, inclusive of information search, digital content consumption of videos and activations, as well as interactions with digital communications such as emails sent by a sport organization can likewise be utilized as valuable data sources. This may be as simple as tracking email open rates or click-throughs to content provided by organizations, through to more sophisticated tracking such as understanding the journey or "clickstream" that customers move through on an organization's website as they gather information or make purchases. Likewise, data collection where a consumer has downloaded an app or logged into an organization's platform can provide vital information for organizations to understand preferences, purchase processes, and information which help inform the behaviors of an individual, and in turn, allow the organization to segment or better target customers. Digital or online tracking can also extend to social media channels. For example, Facebook, Twitter, Instagram, TikTok, and Snapchat are platforms commonly used by sport organizations globally to build engagement with fans. Either by assessing aggregate social media content or by linking fans' social accounts to other data records, organizations can seek to understand sentiment and interests, and better understand, analyze, and predict what particular content or products individuals might engage with. This extends to valuable information for sponsors or partners, for example where online behaviors of search, consumption, or engagement with social media accounts can inform sport organizations and partners of the sorts of external brands, attitudes, or purchase categories that may be relevant to them. Specifically, research has shown how collating and clustering social media data and followers can identify opportunities for cross-targeting and strategic communication (Naraine, 2019).

Location data linked to customer behaviors including attendance can also be utilized to develop data-led strategies. This can be as simple as tracking when a customer enters a stadium or venue using a season ticket card or smartphone app or can advance into other more sophisticated forms of tracking, for example, radio frequency identification (RFID) chips inserted in merchandise or season ticket holder cards to better understand the timing as well as the process by which a customer moves around a particular venue. While less common outside of a few first-mover markers, biometric tracking using retina scanning or facial recognition as an application of artificial intelligence, presents emerging opportunities to be used by stadiums or organizations to accurately understand behaviors, engage customers via more personalized service delivery, as well as be utilized as a security measure. Location and tracking applications, which can be reliant on advanced technology and significant investment within stadiums or venues, provide an example of where data collated may need significant transformation prior to being readily available for analysis.

Finally, data that has been collected by an organization via primary data collections, for example, via surveys or questionnaires, can also be embedded as part of the data records collected and utilized by organizations. Most commonly, surveys are undertaken via digital platforms, apps, or websites that allow for digital data capture and storage, and also provide access to transfer and integrate collected information with existing customer records. Such information can allow organizations access to a range of important attitudinal data to inform preferences, and also understand the many psychological constructs relevant to sport marketing, how these might inform consumer behavior, and the strategies of organizations. One example of an advantage here, as we discuss later, is in understanding how attitudes collected via surveys may align with other behavioral sources that the organization may hold regarding a customer. However, it should be noted that survey data can be associated with high costs and sampling issues, and often provide data about a smaller number of an organization's customers, which do provide some potential limitations.

In sum, and recognizing that consumer-generated data can eclipse the scope of the areas noted above, there is a wide range of data sources that can inform or empower marketing practices relevant to sport consumer behavior. Some of these are simple in nature, represented by easily translatable information, such as simple ratings or binary measures of attendance or non-attendance. However, some of these data sources are considerably more complex; for example, location data, which in a raw format may be collected using geographic coordinates, making it more difficult to immediately draw insights from. In addition, qualitative data, which may be collected via social media or questionnaires can be rich in nature, but more difficult to quickly transfer to generalizable or aggregated insights. Therefore, the integration and development of the process to merge or collate customer data into a single record provide a substantial challenge in the process of converting data in raw forms into a powerful, integrated asset that can aid decision-making. Significant investment in architecture, infrastructure, and data warehousing are often required to merge or combine data sources or databases to enable a "single-customer" view or "360-degree" view of a customer. Additionally, the data capture and collation only provides the first step of the process by which digital data is useful relative to consumer behavior. Without the ability to craft the right questions, or efficiently access the required data sources, and appropriately apply the right analysis techniques, even the most comprehensive and best-organized data will remain a dormant asset. However, as introduced in the following sections, there are myriad ways by which managers can use this asset to build their brands and customer equity, enhance customer relationships and advance commercial outcomes for their businesses.

Using Digital Data to Guide Strategy and Create Advantage

Access to rich digital data sources, spanning both behaviors and attitudes, provides managers with a powerful asset or tool to aid decision-making and strategy development within a sport consumer behavior setting. In this section, we focus on some specific questions and outcomes that are among the most relevant for sport marketers and managers in the professional sport setting. What is covered in the following section is not intended to be an exhaustive list of the ways by which data can aid organizational or marketing effectiveness, but it does seek to provide a range of examples and questions that managers might ask and respond to given data available from digital forms of consumption.

An overview of key questions is provided in Table 20.1, with coverage of four areas; demand and pricing insights, behavior prediction, customer experience, and enhancing or validating other findings. For each area, we provide a sample of potential questions and link these to specific outcomes or sources of competitive advantage that may result for managers. We will discuss each briefly in the following sections including some of the techniques and necessary capacity and capability elements required to extract value from data. What we should realize as we progress through the following sections, is that digital data can often offer a distinct advantage to examine overt or observed behaviors, which are often available for high volumes of customers, as opposed to the attitude or intention-based measurement derived from surveys which has been the focus of much sport consumer research work to date (Funk et al., 2016; Ko & Lee, 2018).

Understanding demand and the factors that lead consumers to undertake a particular behavior is one of the most studied areas in sport consumer behavior (Karg et al., 2021). The most common approach here has been to study demand at an aggregate level; that is, attempt to predict the total number of people who watch a match on television, or attend a game in a stadium using a range of game and market factors that may influence customers engagement with the event (Borland & MacDonald, 2003). However, this does little to inform sport marketers of which *individuals* from their potential customer base is likely to engage with their offerings. Much other work in the sport consumer behavior setting has looked to enhance understanding of demand using survey-based work (see Kim et al., 2019 for a review), focusing on attitudes and various measures related to "fandom" which may impact intention to undertake a behavior. While helpful, there are limitations of relying on survey or intention measures from customers without knowing if the intentions correlate with actual customer behaviors. This highlights one of the major opportunities from the digital capture of consumer data where digital consumption and the inherent behavioral data provide managers with strong opportunities to test and model important game attendance and related behaviors (i.e., conversion to a season ticket holder, attendance at games) at an individual level. Recently this has been demonstrated in European (e.g., Schreyer, 2019) and Australian (Karg et al., 2021) settings to

Table 20.1 Consumer Behavior: Key Manager Questions and Potential Outcomes

	Sample manager questions	*Sample outcome (competitive advantage)*
Demand and pricing insights	• How many people will attend/watch our next game? • When will people engage in the game/broadcast? • How can I set prices and develop products with confidence?	• Improved understanding of factors influencing behaviors • Improved planning capacity and cost-efficiency • Revenue efficiency and maximized yield
Behavior prediction	• What factors can aid my understanding of what leads to renewal or churn of customers? • How can I predict or benchmark activity or engagement of fans, to assist in valuing digital properties? • How likely are individual customers to participate, buy or renew a ticket or attend/watch a particular event or game?	• Churn limitation / Enhanced retention • Opportunities to proactively develop interventions and actions • Enhanced information for planning and resourcing • More efficient revenue capture through product development
Customer experience	• What are the dimensions or important components of my customer's journey? • What are strengths and areas for development within customer experiences? • How can I optimize stadium experience, and understand stadium movement and spend? • How do I use different data (e.g., text sources) to aid understanding of customer experience?	• Improved or enhanced understanding of customer experiences • Opportunities for increases in personalization of communication and actions, relationship quality measures, and revenue/loyalty • "Live" understanding and resolution of customer issues
Enhancing or validating other findings	• Can I trust my other data and survey results? (i.e., will intentions and attitudes match my customers' actual behaviors?) • How does sports uniqueness impact my data and customer behaviors? (e.g., what is the impact of winning) • What segmentation processes can create opportunities to improve marketing effectiveness?	• Validation of psychological and attitudinal factors and increased understanding of how they are related to behaviors • Opportunity to segment and provide more efficient or targeted offerings • Enhanced decision-making and efficiency • Higher confidence and more accurate interpretation of data

better understand *individual* characteristics that inform behaviors. By leveraging data generated from digital attendance records, including the study or STH "no shows," it is possible to enhance understanding, and provide a powerful tool for managers to understand and apply "lead scoring," or the propensity of individual customers to undertake behaviors. In turn, this can inform how and where to incentivize different segments or individuals. Likewise, these concepts, where data is available, can be applied to broadcast settings to, for example, better understand how consumers will share their consumption over live and media channels (Karg et al., 2019) as well as over different sport properties (Fujak et al., 2018), and the implications of this. Closely linked to demand, is the ability to develop a deeper understanding of pricing and likely outcomes by observing consumer data and undertaking testing of incentives across customer databases. Further, the ability to inform the pricing of sponsor assets or properties based on an understanding of not only how many, but also which consumers will consume, can provide sport organizations with a competitive advantage.

A further example exists around patterns of conversion and retention of customers, either as casual ticket buyers or related to subscription customers such as STH. STH are critical customers for a number of reasons including the ability to track and monitor behaviors in season, develop strategies and react accordingly. Recently, research has provided examples of how optimized attendance or CRM data can deliver a better understanding of customers who would convert from casual ticket buyers to relationship-based products such as a season tickets (George & Wakefield, 2018). In addition, digital data and tracking of behaviors have been shown to greatly improve the ability to predict STH who would be retained using churn modeling variables commonly available to managers in databases (Karg et al., 2021), as well as combining database information with, for example, social network data (Katz et al., 2020). In adding value and insight to questions of conversion and retention, a more nuanced understanding of attendance (e.g., when over a season a consumer attends, or when gaps in attendance occur), and how consumers are networking or sharing aspects of their consumption (e.g., if groups attend together, share rituals or sit together at games) are examples of increasingly detailed data shown to be valuable when considering data strategy and application.

Understanding and enhancing customer experience is a further area where benefits can be gained via the effective use of digital data. In building an understanding of customer journeys, attendance data from a customer's entry or exit to a stadium, as well as linked purchase or spend data, can be used to understand interaction with an event or set of events over a season. Location data or tracking within stadiums and event zones are now commonly undertaken with benefits for security, wayfinding, and the facilitation of more efficient customer movement within stadiums. For example, stadiums can use digital signals or track devices such as smartphones to encourage customers to find shorter queues or more efficient entry or exit points within stadiums. Further, concession purchases such as food, drink, and merchandise can now be optimized or improved using an app or website technology. On one hand, this can make the experience of ordering, purchasing, and even having food delivered to a seat in a stadium much more efficient for a customer. However, the use of digital transaction data also provides valuable information for an organization, stadium, or team about that customer and their behaviors. In turn, this provides opportunities for the team to build a relationship or target customers with particular offers or deliver "surprise and delight" offerings which can increase customer perceptions of the relationship with a sport team or organization. Using a collective example from the above data sources, rewarding a customer who attends their tenth consecutive match with a free meal (tailored on their own past food purchase) and an upgraded seat for the night can be facilitated via a combination of attendance, seating and transaction data available to the organization. In sum, customer experiences can be enhanced via data sources by which sport organizations can track, learn and improve aspects of the delivered experience.

Finally, the capture and use of digital data in a behavioral form can assist in helping to validate or enhance the understanding or decision-making capacity of data in the sports marketing setting. Earlier, we referenced increasing attention and concern over the correlations seen between consumers' reported intentions and behaviors in academic work. This raises a logical question for sport marketers in terms of the degree to which they can be reliant on a single form of information or data to confidently make decisions. For example, using consumer behaviors that provide actual records of consumer attendance, spend levels, and renewal decisions, and then aligning these with other attitudes or survey measures can significantly improve the accuracy and understanding using a range of digital data sources. To this end, sport marketers working with digital data are encouraged to be "data agnostic," and engage with multiple sources of data to support decision-making. This approach can enhance decision-making as well as allow better and more accurate interpretation of data.

The above examples of digital data capture and analysis to answer questions relevant to consumer behavior can result in a range of related benefits for sport organizations. These include the ability to translate raw data to strategies that can increase efficiency, improve customer experience, deliver a higher propensity to retain customers, or directly influence revenue or yield. They can also assist in better communication, actions, and strategies that allow the development of deeper relationships with customers. Critically here, there are significant opportunities for enhancing practical outcomes and efficiencies from data as well as opportunities for collaborative research. Traditionally, much consumer behavior research in the academic setting has been reliant on survey-based intention measures, as opposed to actual behaviors. As highlighted in this chapter, behavioral data and its application provide applied data to consider, develop and test solutions to research problems, as well as validate findings. To this end, collaboration is encouraged between managers pondering questions such as those in Table 20.1, and researchers who may provide complementary approaches and expertise to aid overall understanding for both researchers and practitioners.

Capacity Building for Competitive Advantage from Digital Consumer Data

To date, this chapter has introduced different data sources as well as highlighted key areas in which managers can ask and answer questions that lead to positive outcomes. Generating these outcomes is dependent on a strong set of infrastructure and processes including the application of data analysis and translation that can assist in converting raw data sources into strategic value. This section focuses on those "building blocks," or the operational tools and application of analysis to generate outcomes.

The first step of this process is to ensure that sufficient infrastructure for safe and secure collection and storage of relevant data is in place. This can be a significant investment for organizations, and often a barrier to developing and executing a strong analytics or data lead strategy, particularly given many sport organizations operate as small or medium enterprises. Data, analysis, and translation are equally important – and reflective of a need to commit to both infrastructure (e.g., databases, analysis, and reporting software) and human resources. Logically, there are many data analysis techniques that can be used on various data sources to generate diverse insights or outcomes. While a full outline is beyond the scope of this chapter, techniques spanning descriptive analysis, correlations, discovery, and analysis of elemental relationships, patterns and spatial insights, and modeling of higher-order and/or complex reasoning constructs can all add value. Moving forward, opportunities to utilize artificial intelligence, machine learning techniques, or smart robots to drive automation and higher-level application of data insights present emerging opportunities.

In sum, there are key building blocks of digital transformation and data analytics that enable the capture and use of consumer data to inform insights and decisions. This necessitates the introduction of sufficient resourcing and the critical issues of leadership, cultural aspects, as well as the development of capacity and systems to communicate and translate results. There is no shortage of examples of how data and digital learnings can be converted into a product, experience, and promotional strategies, however perhaps though one of the most critical aspects is the communication of the outcomes which come from data in the digital setting. In understanding digital transformation and the "digital IQ" of organizations, one of the gaps is often the ability to effectively communicate and embed the outcomes and opportunities that come from data. In this sense, we introduce the concept of a mix between "art" and "science" where a mix of skill sets is required within the organization to both analyze data effectively (the "science"), as well as translate findings into strategies that seek to positively impact other stakeholders of the business.

As well as a proactive approach to planning for data, its collection, and analysis, organizations should also have a sound strategy around other potential issues. This could consider data acquisition issues, linked to the ethical use of data and its management. Close attention is now paid by both consumers and external groups including regulators who seek to upkeep standards around ethical and legal data management. Some markets (e.g., Europe) have moved to put in place strict regulations which govern the manner by which data can be captured, used, and stored. While sport organizations, in particular sport teams, with highly involved fans, may find a high propensity for consumers to share or "opt in" to sharing data and information, organizations should maintain a high level of standards, and have in place relevant and robust protection of data including a strict process by which data is used and shared.

Summary

This chapter has highlighted a sample of the opportunities available for sport marketers to transform data available as a by-product of digitalized sport consumption into strategies that can add value to marketing activities. Acknowledging the range of data available, a framework was introduced inclusive of inputs, applications, and outcomes, including examples of how data can be translated into sources of advantage. In addition, an overview of some of the infrastructure and resourcing aspects that should form part of organizational considerations in developing a digital data strategy was introduced.

Considering the circle of innovation framework introduced in this chapter, ongoing advancements in digital sport consumption will result in greater volumes and types of data becoming available for sport organizations to access and derive benefit from. Further, technology will provide easier, quicker, and more cost-effective options to collate and analyze data, and transform it into meaningful insights for managers and organizations. As such, organizational investment in key building blocks including processes and practices for data acquisition and management, information processing, decision-making, and communication will enable organizations to proactively derive benefit from data-led marketing approaches. These benefits can be expected to contribute to financial returns, but often also provide opportunities for marketers for better development and action strategies that bring about deeper engagement and enhanced experiences for consumers, and improved relationships with customers. With the right infrastructure in place, sport marketers should foresee continuing rich opportunities to engage with behavioral data to drive better outcomes for their organizations.

References

Alamar, B. C. (2013). *Sports analytics: A guide for coaches, managers, and other decision makers*. Columbia University Press.

Bayle, E., & Madella, A. (2002). Development of a taxonomy of performance for national sport organizations. *European Journal of Sport Science*, *2*(2), 1–21.

Borland, J., & MacDonald, R. (2003). Demand for sport. *Oxford Review of Economic Policy*, *19*(4), 478–502. doi:10.1093/oxrep/19.4.478

Brodie, R. J., Ilic, A., Juric, B., & Hollebeek, L. (2013). Consumer engagement in a virtual brand community: An exploratory analysis. *Journal of Business Research*, *66*(1), 105–114. 10.1016/j.jbusres.2011.07.029

Fujak, H., Frawley, S., McDonald, H., & Bush, S. (2018). Are sport consumers unique? Consumer behavior within crowded sport markets. *Journal of Sport Management*, *32*(4), 362–375.

Funk, D., Lock, D., Karg, A., & Pritchard, M. (2016). Sport consumer behavior research: Improving our game. *Journal of Sport Management*, *30*(2), 113–116. 10.1123/jsm.2016-0028

George, M., & Wakefield, K. (2018). Modeling the consumer journey for membership services. *Journal of Services Marketing*, *32*(2), 113– 125. doi:10.1108/JSM-03-2017-0071

Gronroos, C. (2004). The relationship marketing process: Communication, interaction, dialogue, value. *Journal of Business and Industrial Marketing*, *19*(2), 99–113.

Karg, A., McDonald, H., & Leckie, C. (2019). Channel preferences among sport consumers: Profiling media-dominant consumers. *Journal of Sport Management*, *33*(4), 303–316. doi:10.1123/jsm.2018-0185

Karg, A., Nguyen, J. & McDonald, H. (2021). Understanding season ticket holder attendance decisions. *Journal of sport management*, 10.1123/jsm.2020-0284

Karg, A., Tamaddoni, A., McDonald, H., & Ewing, M. (2021). Predicting season ticket holder retention using rich behavioral data, *Journal of sport management*. 10.1123/jsm.2020-0190

Katz, M., Heere, B., & Melton, E. (2019). Predicting fan behavior through egocentric network analysis. *Journal of Sport Management*, *34*(3), 217–228. doi:10.1123/jsm.2019-0018

Kim, Y., Magnusen, M., Kim, M., & Lee, H. (2019). Meta-analytic review of sport consumption: Factors affecting attendance to sporting events. *Sport Marketing Quarterly*, *28*(3), 117–134, doi:10.32731/SMQ.283.092019.01.

Ko, Y. J., & Lee, J. S. (2018). Experimental research in sport consumer behavior. *Sport Marketing Quarterly*, *27*(4), 218–220.

McDonald, H., & Lock, D. (2017). *Declining sport viewership shows why we should keep it on free TV*. The Conversation. https://theconversation.com/declining-sport-viewership-shows-why-we-should-keep-it-on-free-tv-72357

Naraine, M. L. (2019). Follower segments within and across the social media networks of major professional sport organizations. *Sport Marketing Quarterly*, *28*(4), 222–233. 10.32731/SMQ.284.122019.04

Phillips, F. (2016). The circle of innovation. *Journal of Innovation Management*, *4*(3), 12–31.

Pritchard, M. P., & Funk, D. C. (2006). Symbiosis and substitution in spectator sport. *Journal of Sport Management*, *20*(3), 299–321.

Schreyer, D. (2019). Football spectator no-show behavior in the German Bundesliga, *Applied Economics*, *51*(45), 4882–4901. doi:10.1080/00036846.2019.1602709

Schreyer, D., & Däuper, D. (2018). Determinants of spectator no-show behavior: First empirical evidence from the German Bundesliga. *Applied Economics Letters*, *25*(21), 1475–1480. doi:10.1080/13504851.2018.1430314

Solomon, M. (2019). *Consumer behaviour* (19th edition), Hoboken, NJ: Pearson.

Yoshida, M., Gordon, B., Nakazawa, M., & Biscaia, R. (2014). Conceptualization and measurement of fan eEngagement: mpirical evidence from a professional sport context. *Journal of Sport Management*, *28*, 399–417. doi:10.1123/jsm.2013-0199

21

Digital Fitness Ecosystem

Brianna Newland and Thomas J. Aicher

Introduction

The digital sport fitness ecosystem has grown rapidly over the last 15 years, tremendously over the last few years, due to the crisis response rushed in by the COVID pandemic that surprised the global community in 2020. Due to the pandemic, which began during the first quarter of 2020, many digital fitness companies are poised for even better growth due to shifts in fitness behavior (Yang & Koenigstorfer, 2020). As Front Office Sports (FOS, 2020b) noted, the home equipment leader, Peloton saw shares (+187% in September 2020) jump with the launch of their newly designed bike (Peloton Bike+) and their top-of-the-line treadmill (Peloton Tread+). With the introduction of membership-driven equipment like Peloton, Lulu Lemon's Mirror, and the new Ergatta, sport fitness enthusiasts are leaving the gym, choosing instead to train with at-home programming. In May 2020, online orders for equipment increased by 220% and another 122% in June (FOS, 2020a). To support the equipment purchases, health and fitness app installations grew by 67% over 2019 (FOS, 2020a). A recent TD Ameritrade survey found that 59% of Americans do not plan to return to the gym now that they have found cheaper online fitness options (Scipioni, 2020) suggesting this trend will continue into the future.

There are several aspects of the digital sport fitness ecosystem. Figure 21.1 illustrates the four main elements of the ecosystem: wearables, equipment, mobile applications (i.e., "apps"), and spatial computing (artificial intelligence [AI]/ virtual reality [VR]/ augmented reality [AR]). Each of these four categories is not mutually exclusive, which allows products to span the boundaries of each section. The wearable category includes smartwatches (e.g., Apple Watch, Garmin), fitness trackers (e.g., Fitbit), health monitors (e.g., Upright GO, a posture corrector), and performance gadgets (e.g., Whoop). The equipment category includes apparatuses with member-driven content like Peloton, the Mirror, Echelon, NordicTrack, or Ergatta. The apps category ties the entire ecosystem together by allowing users to coordinate the other three categories in one place and track their fitness or training progress. Finally, the spatial computing category includes the underlying ML and AI "engines" that drives the algorithms behind the VR/AR hardware and software.

DOI: 10.4324/9781003088899-25

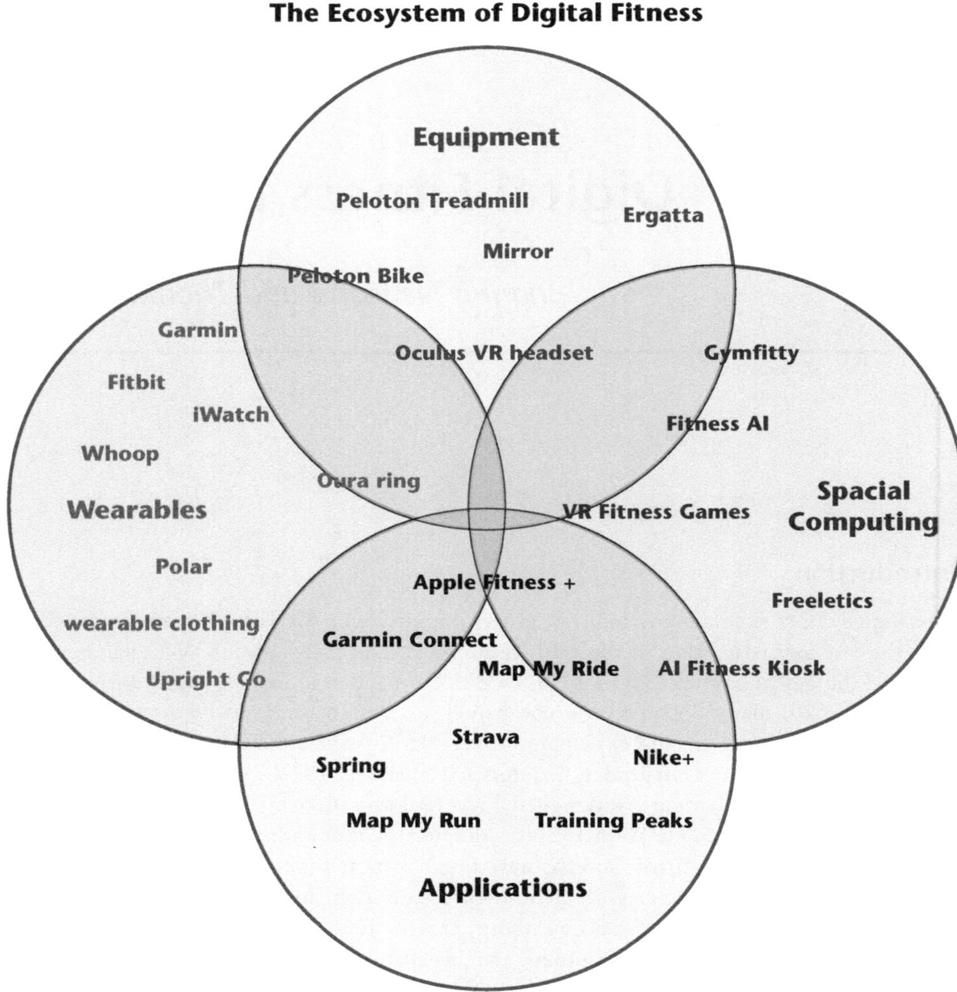

Figure 21.1 The Digital Fitness Ecosystem

Review of the Sport Fitness Ecosystem

This section provides an overview of the evolution of digital fitness starting with the evolution of wearables and how the technology has advanced. We also explain the growth of home fitness equipment and its role in the ecosystem.

Wearables

The evolution of fitness technology started in the early 1900s with the advancement of the wristwatch from the pocket watch. While this seems minimal by today's standards, the development of the wristwatch miniaturized and created mobile components was considered a major technological advancement in that era (Aroganam et al., 2019). Throughout the middle of the 20th century, few advancements in wearable technology occurred. In 1977, Hewlitt

Packard introduced the algebraic calculator watch with the first miniaturized mobile computer. This advancement coupled with the advancement of computing technology and the introduction of Global Positioning System (GPS) technology developed for military use in the 1980s engendered a new market for handheld and wearable technology. During the final decade of the 20th century, United States President Bill Clinton instructed the development of a consumer-driven GPS system (Aroganam et al., 2019). While mostly focused on vehicle coordinates for consumers and military use, Casio introduced the world to the GPS-enabled watch with the *Satellite Navi Protrek* watch.

As handheld technology and communication systems advanced through the early 2000s, including the introduction of the iPhone, consumer-driven fitness technology proliferated as well. Garmin, originally known as ProNav, brought to market the Forerunner, which is still in production today and is regarded as the beginning of the GPS tracking watch industry (Mind Commerce, 2020). Apple, Inc., continued to advance the wristwatch when it introduced the Apple Watch in 2014 originally as a "fashion accessory." This gadget quickly evolved into a leader in health and fitness wearable technology with the Apple Watch.

The primary advancement within wearable technology is the microcontroller structure. This key component in this technology is the hub for data, data-processing, and power management (Aroganam et al., 2019). In addition to the microcontroller, wearable technology includes common sensors such as a GPS for location, an accelerometer (used to measure speed), a sleep sensor, a gyroscope (measures angular accelerations), magnetometers (creates an internal measurement unit), heart rate sensors, pedometers, and pressure sensors. These different components allow users to measure a variety of important training components such as pace, cadence, VO2 max, body oscillation, training effect (aerobic or anaerobic), heart rate, elevation gains/losses, and weather. The most recent version of the Apple Watch is promoted as the *future of health on your wrist* that includes measurement of blood oxygen levels, ECG, sleep monitoring, and the common activity features outlined above. Battery life-span is a common issue with wearable technology which has led Garmin and Casio to develop watches with solar power technology that can last approximately 24 days without a charge (Verger, 2020).

While wrist wearables are the most popular, they are not the only products that dominate the market. Ōura created a fitness ring that tracks sleep, body temperature, heart rate variability (HRV), and activity measures like calories, steps, and heart rate (Ōura, 2020). Solos smartglasses are built for cyclists (and runners) and display workout metrics like pace, heart rate, and power to users directly on the lens (Calvert, 2019). Other wearables, like smart clothing, are also entering the marketplace. Hexoskin, tracks performance via blood pressure, pulse oximetry, ECG, accelerometer, skin temperature, and blood oxygen levels (Foster, 2019). Likewise, Wearable-X are smart yoga pants that monitor postures, Vitali is a sports bra that monitors stress, and force sensors can be added to shoe insoles to measure the force exerted when running or lifting (Foster, 2019). As technology advances, so do the products that can help consumers track health, fitness, and sport performance.

Equipment

The first known evidence of fitness equipment dates to around 6000 B.C. and the technologically-advanced equipment in use today was debuted in 1796 with the first iteration of the stationary bicycle named the Gymnasticon (Parrot et al., 2020). While modern versions "punish" fitness enthusiasts, the early stationary bike was used to discipline criminals as the Gymnasticon had two flywheels, one for the upper body and one for the lower creating a challenging exercise for anyone to do (Parrot et al., 2020). The commercial fitness industry started in 1885 when Professor Edmond Desbonnet opened the first physical culture center. These centers featured mostly free weight and exercise apparatuses (e.g., parallel bars) with little advancement in fitness equipment and technology over the next several decades. The modern stationary bike, for instance, was introduced in the 1960s and led to the beginning of companies that specialized in fitness equipment. The treadmill was also invented in the late 1960s by a mechanical engineer named William Staub, who was inspired by a book on aerobics. First used only by doctors, the treadmill was brought to market in 1975 and introduced to the commercial fitness industry shortly thereafter. The 1980s and 1990s were marked by the consolidation of fitness equipment manufacturers as they each diversified their offering to include other physical training equipment (e.g., bars, dumbbells, strength training machines).

Advances in fitness equipment technology are now transforming the industry. In 2014, Peloton began selling its first at-home bike with the application, which hosts a range of fitness programing including strength, yoga, meditation, and barre (Warren, 2017). In 2018, Peloton launched a $4,000 treadmill to accompany the bike (Berr, 2018) and has since expanded its inventory to include a more cost-effective treadmill and the upgraded Bike+ (Thomas, 2020). Peloton is not alone in the tech-savvy fitness equipment space. In 2018, the Mirror, a full-length mirror that provides instruction from certified trainers from top fitness studios, was launched. It was acquired by athletic apparel leader, Lululemon Athletica, Inc., in 2020 for $500 million with an aim to capture the fitness market during the pandemic (Terlep, 2020). Other companies like NordicTrack and Echelon have released a line of fitness equipment, including bikes that rival Peloton. Echelon has a suite of three bike products: EX1, EX3, and EX5, with the EX5 on par with the Peloton (Corbin, 2020). Both the Echelon and NordicTrack offer live studio classes as well as other equipment like rowers, mirrors, and treadmills. NordicTrack also offers an elliptical machine.

Applications

The explosive growth of applications (apps) began with the invention of the iPhone and iPod. In 2008, the App Store launched with 500 apps, and Google Play, Amazon App Store, and Blackberry's App World soon followed (Strain, 2015). At the intersection of wearables, equipment, and apps are sensors, which include the accelerometer, GPS, gyroscope, etc., discussed above. Now that the consumer is driven by methods to monitor health and sport performance, there is limited use for equipment and wearables without sensors, which the apps read and display for the user (Aroganam et al., 2019). For example, the Whoop wearable does not have a display face on the device, therefore, the user must read the data from the Whoop app on their smartphone.

While apps provide the data interface between the wearable or equipment, they also provide opportunities for companies to build a community around the brand. For example, iWatch, Whoop, Polar, and Garmin all link to the app, Strava. Strava is a mobile app and website that allows users to track their rides, runs, walks, hikes, etc. on a smartphone or another GPS device, while recording distance, time, average speed, and route (GPS trajectory) as well as user-added details about the activity (Sun & Mobasheri, 2017). Sporting goods manufacturers are also entering the space; however, the focus of their apps is on tracking and basic performance metrics. For example, Asics owns RunKeeper, Nike has its own NikeFitness app and wearable, Adidas owns Runtastic, and Under Armour owns MapMyFitness and Endomondo. However, it was recently reported that Under Armour is discontinuing Endomodo, and will be focusing the majority of the efforts on in-shoe technology to pair with MapMyRun (Dignan, 2020).

These advancements along with others are all tracked and create brand communities on their platforms discussed further below.

Spatial Computing

Innovative technological advancements in spatial computing are transforming the digital fitness ecosystem. Through the use of AI, VR, and AR as core components of the digital fitness experience, users have expanded opportunities to enhance their health and performance experience. AI now uses the data generated by the wearable or app to suggest recommendations for how the user can enhance a workout or strive for longer sleep (Lapidos, 2020). The wearable, Whoop, estimates how hard one should workout based on sleep, recovery, and other data collected from previous workouts as well as how you compare to others in your cohort that use the app. The screen-based fitness equipment Forme Life uses AI and machine learning to offer the user feedback on their exercise form as well as personalized workout tips (Lapidos, 2020).

Virtual reality (VR) enhances health and performance by immersing the user directly in a virtual environment. By gamifying the activity, users can enhance their physical activity through the gaming experience. The Virtual Reality Institute of Health and Exercise, at San Francisco State University, discovered how to measure VR as a unique exercise and developed an app that pairs with other wearables, like HR monitors, to track calorie expenditure by games (VR Health Institute, 2020). For each VR game, the app alerts the user to what other type of physical activity the gaming is equivalent to, such as biking, tennis, walking, or the elliptical and how many calories they burn per minute of play (VR Health Institute, 2020).

Augmented reality (AR) is enhancing the fitness ecosystem by providing real-time information about what is happening in your body while active. The oldest forms of AR are real-time heart rate data, pace, distance, altitude, and other measures. Recent advancements include oximeters, ECG, and alerts for when the environment noise rises to a point that can damage the ear. Using wearables like Solos smartglasses, new AR advancements can project an avatar that can pace the user's speed in real-time to enhance training. Or, if motivation is necessary when out for a run, Zombies, Run! is a fitness app that projects zombies into the runner's course with missions to complete during the exercise period (Treese, 2020).

Connectivity

What makes the key parts of the digital ecosystem – wearables, equipment, apps, and spatial computing – so compelling to users are their ability to connect to others. In fact, social media interconnectivity is an integral component of the growth and success of the digital fitness ecosystem (Aroganam et al., 2019; Mind Commerce, 2020). Millington (2016) posits that each element of this ecosystem is designed to empower individuals on their journey to achieve better sport performance and good health. The digital fitness ecosystem enables social interaction and a sense of community through social digital tracking (Couture, 2021). Social connectivity has become even more apparent since the pandemic swept across the globe beginning in December of 2019, forcing nearly everyone to socialize and exercise digitally. While their popularity has grown over the last decade, virtual communities are not new to fitness and sport. In fact, research exploring who, why, and how people self-track has grown (Esmonde, 2019; Goodyear et al., 2019a; Goodyear et al., 2019b). Strava launched in 2009 and, for over ten years, users have enjoyed and sought social feedback and virtual rewards as well as the completion of virtual challenges to enhance their motivation levels (Stragier et al., 2016). Other online platforms, like

Peloton's growing community via Instagram and Facebook, are tools for making connections and building community (van Dijck, 2013). However, Couture (2021) claimed that virtual communities have limits to acceptable levels of sharing and support narcistic behaviors. For example, Strava has coined the "social tracking of all vain activity" app.

Future Research

As this sector of the industry is growing rapidly, so does the research on the topic. To date, much of the research centers on how technology impacts sport performance and injury prevention (e.g., Adesida et al., 2019), health and medicine (e.g., Burnham et al., 2018; Loncar-Turukalo, 2019), privacy concerns (e.g., Perez & Zeadally, 2017), and social self-tracking (e.g., Goodyear et al., 2019a, 2019b). Jasiulewicz & Waśkowski (2020) noted the research on fitness applications can be categorized into four themes: factors that influence use, evaluation of the applications' effect on the user's health or performance, typologies of users, and the role of in-app advertising on use. The dominant theories that drive research in this area include the Theory of Planned Behavior (Ajzen, 1991), Foucault's Theory of Surveillance (Foucault, 2008; Goodyear et al., 2019a), and Differential Privacy Theory (Task & Clifton, 2012). Much of the research in terms of sport management is evolving, but theories or frameworks involving motivation, consumer behavior, technology adoption and use, and privacy and use should also be explored. However, much is still to be learned about the use of technology and how people engage with the numerous platforms available.

Germane to the current landscape, the influence of COVID and mobility restrictions placed on individuals create an opportunity to explore how individuals are using equipment, wearables, and apps as virtual fitness communities to supplement their normal social and fitness routines. Questions about the lasting effect these new communities may have on fitness activity selection is paramount. The use of these tools as centers of community and social engagement is important to study. Determining how people utilize these communities, what factors draw people to one community compared to another, or the influence these communities have on performance or health-related goals would benefit manufacturers' design and marketing of fitness equipment.

Researching the relationship between various components of the digital ecosystem may also inform product design and development as technology continues to advance in this space. From a macro-level, the data provided by wearables could significantly alter the health, fitness, and sport industries. Epidemiological and longitudinal studies involving consistent and long-term health biometrics, exercise, sleep, and other behavioral data could transform how researchers investigate and understand disease, injury, fitness, and sport performance. The data Apple is collecting via the Apple Watch *alone* could transform these industries.. For example, Apple is working with the American Heart Association and Brigham & Women's Hospital to study heart data and movement. Not only does the study pull recorded data from the Apple Watch, but it also sends participants periodic surveys on stress, movements, falls, etc. Other studies include a women's health study and a hearing study.

There is scarce research evaluating the data provided by these products and how and why users engage with their personal information. Thus, exploring ways biometric data are used or considered valuable will provide manufacturers and developers valuable information to enhance services to consumers. In addition, investigating the lack of use or perceived value of information may also indicate the consumer requires more education on how to use the data provided. The use of virtual communities to share personal data and that impact on behaviors, community, engagement, and goal attainment needs to be further explored.

Finally, many of the apps and devices allow for various levels of investment. Understanding how to enhance the current users' investment in the app or service, as well as customer lifetime value, will allow insights for the organization to understand product engagement and loyalty. How this engagement and loyalty transfers to sponsors or partners should also be examined. For example, during COVID, Vacation Races, a running event company that specializes in destination races, hosted "Staycation Races" along with a virtual expo with their sponsors. The impact of such a virtual event on sponsor ROI should be explored. Further, how organizations can enhance opportunities with sponsors or partners through the digital fitness ecosystem should be examined.

References

Adesida, Y., Papi, E., & McGregor, A. H. (2019). Exploring the role of wearable technology in sport kinematics and kinetics: A systematic review. *Sensors, 19*(7), 1597.

Ajzen, I. (1991). The theory of planned behavior. *Organizational behavior and human decision processes, 50*(2), 179–211.

Aroganam, G., Manivannan, N., & Harrison, D. (2019). Review on wearable technology sensors used in consumer sport applications. *Sensors, 19*(9), 1983.

Berr, J. (2018, January). Peloton launches a $4000 treadmill at CES. *CBS news*. Retrieved from, https://www.cbsnews.com/news/peloton-launches-a-4000-treadmill-at-ces/

Burnham, J. P., Lu, C., Yaeger, L. H., Bailey, T. C., & Kollef, M. H. (2018). Using wearable technology to predict health outcomes: A literature review. *Journal of the American Medical Informatics Association, 25*(9), 1221–1227.

Calvert. H. (2019, April). Solos cycling smartglasses review. *Wearable*. Retrieved from, https://www.wareable.com/cycling/solos-smart-cycling-glasses-review

Corbin, S. (2020, May). Echelon vs NordicTrack: Is the smart connect or studio cycle best? *Retrieved from*, https://flexmastergeneral.com/echelon-vs-nordictrack/?utm_source=google&utm_medium=cpc&utm_campaign=Competitor-Search-Bike-US-G

Couture, J. (2021). Reflections from the 'Strava-sphere': Kudos, community, and (self-) surveillance on a social network for athletes. *Qualitative Research in Sport, Exercise and Health, 13*, 184–200. https://doi.org/10.1080/2159676X.2020.1836514

Dignan, L. (2020, October, 30). *Under armour sells MyFitnessPal for $345 million, bets on MapMyRun and connected running shoes.* https://www.zdnet.com/article/underarmour-sells-myfitnesspal-for-345-million-bets-on-mapmyrun-and-connected-running-shoes/

Esmonde, K. (2020). 'There's only so much data you can handle in your life': Accommodating and resisting self-surveillance in women's running and fitness tracking practices. *Qualitative Research in Sport, Exercise and Health, 12*(1), 76–90.

Foster, A. (2019, September). Top performance sportswear smart textiles to watch out for in 2019. *Butler Technologies, inc.* Retreived from, https://butlertechnologies.com/performance-sportswear-smart-textiles/

Foucault, M. (2008). panopticism" from" discipline & punish: The birth of the prison. *Race/Ethnicity: Multidisciplinary Global Contexts, 2*(1), 1–12.

Goodyear, V. A., Kerner, C., & Quennerstedt, M. (2019a). Young people's uses of wearable healthy lifestyle technologies, surveillance, self-surveillance, and resistance. *Sport, Education and Society, 24*(3), 212–225.

Goodyear, V. A., Armour, K. M., & Wood, H. (2019b). Young people learning about health: The Role of apps and wearable devices. *Learning, Media and Technology, 44*(2), 193–210.

Loncar-Turukalo, T., Zdravevski, E., da Silva, J. M., Chouvarda, I., & Trajkovik, V. (2019). Literature on wearable technology for connected health: Scoping review of research trends, advances, and barriers. *Journal of Medical Internet Research, 21*(9), e14017.

Front Office Sports (FOS; 2020a, August 25). *At home fitness.* https://bit.ly/2HBmRl8

Front Office Sports (FOS; 2020b, September 9). *Peloton keeps spinning.* https://bit.ly/3e0CCOw

Jasiulewicz, A. & Waśkowski, Z. (2020). Possibilities of brand promotion through lifestyle mobile sports applications. *Managing of Scientific and Research Organizations, 37*(3), 1–16.

Koetsier, J. (2020, August 4). AI-driven fitness: Making gyms obsolete? *Forbes*. https://www.forbes.com/sites/johnkoetsier/2020/08/04/ai-driven-fitness-making-gyms-obsolete/#4fe3e1a22a8f

Lapidos, R. (2020, October). Artificial intelligence is changing the world of digital fitness: Here's what to know. *Well+Good*. Retrieved from, https://www.wellandgood.com/artificial-intelligence-in-fitness/

Millington, B. (2016). Fit for prosumption: Interactivity and the second fitness boom. *Media, Culture & Society 38*(8), 1184–1200.

Mind Commerce (2020). *Wearable technology market outlook and forecasts 2020 – 2027*. Mind Commerce Publishing.

Ōura (2020). *Life with Ōura*. Retrieved from, https://ouraring.com/life-with-oura

Parrot, M., Ruyak, J., & Liguori, G. (2020). The history of the exercise equipment: From sticks and stones to apps and phones. *ACSM's Health and Fitness Journal, 11/12*(6), 5–8.

Perez, A. J., & Zeadally, S. (2017). Privacy issues and solutions for consumer wearables. *IT Professional, 20*(4), 46–56.

Scipioni, J. (2020, July). 59% of Americans don't intend to renew their gym memberships after Covid-19 pandemic: Survey. *CNBC*. Retrieved from, https://www.cnbc.com/2020/07/23/many-dont-plan-to-renew-their-gym-memberships-post-pandemic-survey.html

Stragier, J., Abeele, M. V., Mechant, P., & De Marez, L. (2016). Understanding persistence in the use of online fitness communities: Comparing novice and experienced users. *Computers in Human Behavior, 64*, 34–42.

Strain, M. (2015, February). 1983 to today: A history of mobile apps. *The guardian*. Retrieved from, https://www.theguardian.com/media-network/2015/feb/13/history-mobile-apps-future-interactive-timeline

Sun, Y., & Mobasheri, A. (2017). Utilizing crowdsourced data for studies of cycling and air pollution exposure: A case study using Strava data. *International Journal of Environmental Research and Public Health, 14*(3), 274.

Task, C., & Clifton, C. (2012, August). A guide to differential privacy theory in social network analysis. In 2012 *IEEE/ACM International Conference on Advances in Social Networks Analysis and Mining* (pp. 411–417). IEEE.

Terlep, S. (2020, June). Lululemon buys mirror, an at-home fitness startup, for $500 million. *Wall street journal*. Retrieved from, https://www.wsj.com/articles/lululemon-to-buy-at-home-fitness-company-mirror-for-500-million-11593465981#:~:text=The%20startup%20sells%20a%20%241%2C500, million%20in%20sales%20in%202020.&text=Lululemon%20had%20%244%20billion%20in,2.

Thomas, L. (2020, September). Peloton announces a more expensive bike, cheaper treadmill; shares surge. *CNBC*. Retrieved from, https://www.cnbc.com/2020/09/08/peloton-shares-rise-as-fitness-company-announces-new-bike-treadmill.html#:~:text=Peloton%20announced%20a%20slew%20of,and%20will%20be%20available%20Wednesday.

Treese, T. (2020, February). Best AR fitness apps and games of 2020. *VR fitness insider*. Retrieved from, https://www.vrfitnessinsider.com/best-ar-fitness-apps-and-games-of-2020/

van Dijck, J. (2013). *The culture of connectivity: A critical history of social media*. Oxford University Press.

Verger, R. (2020, September). These solar-powered smartwatches have seriously long battery lives. *Popular Science*. https://www.popsci.com/story/technology/garmin-solar-instinct-gshock-move-review/

VR Health Institute (2020). VR ratings. *Virtual Reality Institute of Health & Exercise*. Retrieved from, http://vrhealth.institute/vr-ratings/

Warren, L. (2017, June). A brief history of Peloton: A look at the cycling startup's explosive growth. *Built in NYC*. Retrieved from, https://www.builtinnyc.com/2017/06/16/history-peloton

Yang, Y., & Koenigstorfer, J. (2020). Determinants of physical activity maintenance during the Covid-19 pandemic: a focus on fitness apps. *Translational Behavioral Medicine, 10*(4), 835–842.

22

Convergence of Sport and Esports

Anthony D. Pizzo and Daniel C. Funk

Introduction

Technology-driven changes exert great influence over the way sports are managed and consumed. Many of these changes have been led by digital natives, individuals who have grown up with technologies such as mobile devices, digital streaming services (e.g., Netflix), and virtual and augmented reality (Pizzo et al., 2021). Digital natives are increasingly cutting ties with traditional linear media platforms such as cable and satellite media broadcasting (Green, 2018; Thompson, 2013) in favor of online streaming platforms such as Twitch and YouTube. This practice, known as "cord-cutting," demonstrates digital natives' preference for consuming non-linear, over-the-top (OTT) programming (Harpstead et al., 2019), which bypasses the traditional linear programming services favored by professional sport organizations (i.e., leagues, teams). Hence, digital natives are increasingly difficult-to-reach yet sought-after target market for sport organizations seeking to connect with this young demographic (Lopez et al., 2021). Challenges remain for sport organizations to connect and deliver content to this lucrative, yet elusive, market (Parent et al., 2018).

Esports are at the forefront of the technology-driven changes embraced by digital natives. Esports are defined as competitive video game competitions (Pizzo et al., 2019), including both sport and non-sport-related titles (Baker & Pizzo, in press). They embody the rapid pace of digitalization, providing inherent challenges and opportunities. The growth of esports has been facilitated by an increased personal computer (PC) and video game console processing power and internet network speed and reliability (Ströh, 2017). In addition, video game developers and publishers have incorporated ongoing support and competitive elements into their titles, shifting their business models away from sales of physical, hard copies of their software to subscription-based services, a software as a service (SaaS[1]) business model (Vaudour & Heinze, 2020). SaaS, a cloud-based service, stores video games remotely and allows gamers with subscriptions to access them (Ali et al., 2019).

Many professional sport organizations have also embraced esports, helping to legitimize the practice of competitive video gaming and further expediting their rapid growth (Heere, 2018). Professional sport leagues such as the English Premier League (EPL) and National Basketball Association (NBA) have created virtual sport simulation leagues based on video games of their

DOI: 10.4324/9781003088899-26

respective sport. Likewise, professional sport teams, such as the Australian Football League's (AFL) Adelaide Crows and NBA franchise Philadelphia 76ers have been even more progressive. The Crows were the first professional Australian sports team to invest in esports, purchasing professional esports team Legacy Esports and founding META High School Esports, an esports league that enables high school students in Australia and New Zealand to compete in local and national tournaments (Byrne, 2019). Similarly, the 76ers were among the first professional sport teams to invest in esports by purchasing two esports teams – Teams Apex and Dignitas – and merging them under the Team Dignitas[2] brand in 2016 (Funk et al., 2018).

Current and former athletes are also capitalizing on this trend. High-profile figures who have joined the esports scene include David Beckham, Michael Jordan, Odell Beckham Jr., Shaquille "Shaq" O'Neal, Rick Fox, and Mike Tyson (Clark, 2019). These athletes are a part of a larger trend of prominent sport figures capitalizing on the burgeoning esports phenomenon by purchasing and developing esports teams. For instance, Shaq invested in the esports team NRG eSports, stating that "esports is a natural extension of their [athletes'] interests and competitive nature" (Woods, 2016), underscoring the managerial and marketing similarities between sports and esports (Pizzo et al., 2018).

Despite recognizing opportunities in the emerging esports marketspace, investors and early adopters face many challenges inherent to emerging markets (Hayduk, 2020). This raises concerns regarding how professional sport organizations can profit from (or monetize) their investments in the esports marketspace, and these concerns will only continue to grow as more professional sport organizations turn to esports for additional sources of revenue. Thus, this chapter explores esports, their supporting ecosystem, and the growing connections between the esports and sports industries to understand esports and the challenges and opportunities associated with them.

The current chapter is divided into three main sections. In the first section, we provide an overview of key components of the esports ecosystem, including the video game industry, esports teams and organizations, video game developers and publishers, digital platforms, and sponsors. In the second section, we examine the convergence of sports and esports by exploring the strategic rationale beyond sport organizations diversifying into the esports industry and identify different monetization strategies used by sport and esports teams (or organizations). In addition, we also provide a cautionary case of the Overwatch League (OWL), one of the first franchised esports leagues, to explore some of the problems surrounding esports. In the third section, we conclude this chapter and identify future trends which will influence the management, operations, and monetization of esports. To help frame this discussion, Table 22.1 provides definitions of key terms used in the current chapter.

Overview of The Esports Ecosystem

Video Game Industry

Esports are a growing part of the larger video game industry. The global video game industry generated over $120 billion USD in 2019, with projections for the industry to generate over $300 billion USD by 2025 (Koksal, 2019; Newzoo, 2019). The video game industry develops, markets, and monetizes video games across a variety of platforms, including personal computers, video game consoles (e.g., Nintendo Switch, PlayStation 5, Xbox Series X), and mobile devices (Deloitte, 2019; Zackariasson & Wilson, 2012).

The industry has enjoyed accelerated growth due in large part to video games' growing appeal to new demographics. Not only have the number and types of video games increased,

Table 22.1 Key Chapter Terms and Definitions

Term	*Definition*	*Related Reference*
Cord-cutting	The practice of cutting cable and satellite television subscriptions.	Harpstead et al. (2019)
Digital natives	Individuals who have grown up surrounded by digital technology.	Thompson (2013)
Diversification (Corporate)	A business growth strategy that involves bringing a new product/service to a new market.	Ansoff (1957)
Endemic sponsor	A sponsor whose business is related to the products/services offered in an industry.	Meenaghan (2013)
Esports	Competitive video game competitions.	Pizzo et al. (2018)
Linear media programming	Media content (e.g., television show) delivered at a scheduled time.	Nielsen (2019)
Microtransactions	Small or microtransactions for virtual goods.	Macey & Hamari (2019)
Non-endemic sponsor	A sponsor whose business is unrelated to the products/services offered in an industry.	Meenaghan (2013)
Over-the-top (OTT) media	Media content delivered directly to the end-user, generally via the internet.	Harpstead et al. (2019)
Software as a service (SaaS)	Software-based services where users pay a reoccurring fee to access cloud-based software.	Vaudour & Heinze (2020)

but the accessibility of video games has increased as well. For instance, more working adults enjoy mobile gaming, which affords them the flexibility to play games on their smart phones and tablets. Moreover, as more individuals take part in gaming, video game developers and producers have added competitive elements, such as formal ranking systems, in-game awards and achievements, and prizes, to increase engagement. This competitive gameplay can easily turn casual video gaming into exciting competitive tournaments (i.e., esports).

The esports marketspace is expected to grow by over 30% over the next several years (Goldman Sachs, 2018). By 2022, the esports market is expected to generate nearly $3 billion USD per year (PwC, 2019). At the forefront of the esports marketspace are esports teams, video game developers and publishers, supporting technologies, and sponsors which provide structure and stability to the industry (Carrillo Vera & Aguado Terrón, 2019).

Esports Teams

To fully understand the esports ecosystem, it is important to understand the full entity to which "esports team" or "esports organization" refers. An esports team generally consists of multiple teams that operate under the same parent brand. For instance, Cloud9 is an esports team that fields what would be considered teams in the traditional sense: groups of players competing together for a common purpose (i.e., to defeat their opponents). Yet Cloud9, like many other esports teams, fields multiple teams, each with distinct rosters who compete in tournaments based on video game titles such as League of Legends (LoL), Fortnite, and Overwatch (Cloud9, 2021). Moreover, most esports teams have academy teams that serve as developmental teams for the next generation of players (or athletes). In this regard, the term esports team refers to an individual team or groups of teams operating under the same parent brand (e.g., Cloud9).

Esports teams typically operate as a branded house. A branded house is a branding strategy where all brands of an organization are marketed under the parent brand (Aaker, 2003). For instance, Clould9 operates teams such as Fortnite Cloud9 and Cloud9: Counter-Strike: Global Offensive (CS:GO). However, certain video game developers and publishers that organize esports tournaments do not allow esports teams to use the same brand in tournaments held by other video game developers and publishers. For instance, Cloud9 competes under the name London Spitfire in the OWL, a regionalized esports league operated by, a video game developer and publisher, Blizzard Entertainment (Cloud9, 2021). As a result, more esports teams are beginning to use mixed branding strategies. Generally, they operate as a house of brands when possible, but operate as a house of brands – an alternative branding strategy wherein the parent brand and sub-brand are not visibly connected (Aaker, 2003).

Video Game Developers and Publishers

Video game developers and publishers are the underlying force supporting the growth of the esports marketspace. Video game developers create video games, with publishers responsible for their sales and marketing, with most companies operating as both developers and publishers. Developers and publishers are increasingly incorporating competitive elements when developing video games, turning video games into competitive esports (Shabir, 2017). Specifically, many video games which focus on competitive play are now free-to-play, a freemium business strategy. This strategy provides a game for free, with microtransactions, small and frequent transactions, charged for access to exclusive in-game content such as new characters, character outfits or *skins*, performance boosters, and random gift boxes or *loot boxes* (Lucht, 2019; Macey & Hamari, 2019). One notable developer and publisher is Riot Games, creator of the free-to-play multiplayer online battle arena (or MOBA) game League of Legends (LoL). Despite being free-to-play (F2P), LoL generated $1.75 billion USD in 2020 (Reuters, 2021). Riot and other developers and publishers generate substantial revenue from a variety of sources, but microtransactions are the lifeline for F2P titles.

In addition to Riot, other key developers and publishers driving the esports phenomenon include Electronic Arts (EA), Activision Blizzard, Take-Two Interactive, Epic Games, Valve, and Supercell. These companies are among the leading developers and publishers of PC, console, and mobile titles which encompass both sport and non-sport titles. These titles include games from a variety of genres, including first-person shooters (FPS[3]; e.g., CS:GO, Overwatch), MOBAs (e.g., League of Legends), real-time strategy (RTS; e.g., StarCraft II), digital collectible card games (DCCG; e.g., Hearthstone), fighting (e.g., Super Smash Bros.), and mobile titles (e.g., PlayerUnknown's Battlegrounds Mobile or PUBG Mobile). Table 22.2 provides an overview of leading developers and publishers and esports titles.

The F2P business model has encouraged developers and publishers to provide ongoing support and updates for their titles to continue to generate reoccurring subscription (i.e., SaaS) revenue. In doing so, developers and publishers have not only reduced financial entry barriers associated with purchasing a video game, but have also vastly increased adoption rates and extended the longevity of their titles. This has given rise to a variety of digital distribution platforms that provide players with a central hub and online communities to interact with one another (Harpstead et al., 2019).

Table 22.2 Leading Esports Developers/Publishers and Titles

Developer/Publisher	*Key Competitive Title(s)*	*Genre*	*Platform(s)*
Electronic Arts	FIFA Franchise	Sports	Console, PC
	Madden NFL Franchise	Sports	Console, PC
	NHL Franchise	Sports	Console, PC
	Apex Legends	FPS; Battle Royale	Console, PC
Activision Blizzard*	Call of Duty Franchise	FPS	Console, PC
	Hearthstone	DCCG	PC
	Overwatch	FPS	Console, PC
	StarCraft II	RTS	PC
Capcom	Street Fighter Franchise	Fighting	Console, PC
Epic Games	Fortnite	FPS; Battle Royale	Console, PC
Psyonix	Rocket League	Sports; Vehicle Soccer	Console, PC
Riot Games	League of Legends	MOBA	PC
	Valorant	FPS	PC
Take-Two Interactive**	NBA 2K Franchise	Sports	Console, PC
Valve	Counter-Strike Franchise	FPS	Console, PC
	Dota 2	MOBA	PC
Supercell	Clash of Clans	Strategy	Mobile
	Clash Royale	Card-based Strategy	Mobile
Ubisoft	Tom Clancy's Rainbow Six Franchise	FPS	Console, PC

Notes

* Activision Blizzard is the parent company of Blizzard Entertainment.

** Take-Two Interactive is a holding company and parent company of 2K Games, publisher of the NBA 2K franchise.

Digital Platforms

Novel streaming and communication platforms have emerged to support the ecosystem surrounding esports and their respective online communities. The leading streaming and communication platforms are Twitch and Discord, respectively. Twitch, the most prominent medium for streaming live video gaming and esports content, is a centralized platform for esports tournaments, personal streams, and video game-related channels (Harpstead et al., 2019). Twitch was purchased by Amazon in 2014 for $970 million USD. This was considered a staggering amount at the time, yet by 2020, Twitch was valued at nearly $15 billion (Levy, 2020). YouTube Gaming similarly offers live streaming content, yet it focuses primarily on prerecorded, on-demand content, offering users additional opportunities to watch recorded and edited content (Andronico, 2016). Twitch dominates the live video gaming and esports streaming market, accounting for over 60% of the total market share (in terms of hours of content watched), with competitors of YouTube and Facebook Gaming seeking to chip away at Twitch's dominant market share (Kastrenakes, 2020).

In addition to streaming platforms, there are several platforms dedicated to real-time chat and communication. At the forefront of these platforms is Discord. It is the leading application used by gamers to communicate and socialize with one another in real-time (Discord, 2021). Discord, similar to programs such as Skype and Zoom, is a Voice over Internet Protocol (VoIP) application, with over 250 million registered users worldwide (Lorenz, 2019). Discord, and to a lesser extent TeamSpeak, have become a popular hub for online communication among digital natives, as it offers central and private forums for gamers, streamers, and influencers to interact with their community (Lorenz, 2019).

Table 22.3 Primary Revenue Sources in Esports

Revenue Sources	*Percentage of Total Revenue*	*Description of Revenue Source*
Sponsorships	40%	Financial support paid by sponsors to link their brand to esports events.
Media rights	25%	Rights to record and distribute esports competitions.
Ticket sales	15%	Revenue generated from the sales of tickets to in-person esports events.
Merchandise	10%	Revenue generated from the sale of esports team and player products (e.g., jerseys).
Game publisher fees	10%	Fees paid to video game publishers by independent esports event organizers.

Note: Percentage of total revenue is based on a compilation and averaging of reported revenues from multiple esports market research reports (i.e., Deloitte, 2019; Newzoo, 2019; Nielsen, 2019, PwC, 2019).

These streaming and communication platforms, embraced by digital natives, have helped support the ecosystem surrounding esports. For instance, the majority of Twitch's daily active users are between the ages of 18 and 34 (Influencer Marketing, 2020). Accordingly, esports and its supporting ecosystem have attracted sponsors from a variety of industries seeking to reach this coveted yet hard-to-reach audience (Huettermann et al., 2020; Nielsen, 2017). While revenue for the esports industry comes from a variety of sources, including media rights, tickets, merchandising, and game publisher fees, sponsorship is the leading source of revenue for the esports market, accounting for over 40% of its total revenue (Maloney, 2020; Newzoo, 2019). Table 22.3 provides an overview and brief description of the esports industry's primary sources of revenue.

Esports Sponsors: Endemic and Non-Endemic

Sponsors are beginning to recognize opportunities to connect with digital natives in the esports market. Sponsors come from both endemic and non-endemic businesses. In esports, endemic firms – firms directly related to the success of an industry – include tech-centric companies such as Asus, Dell, Logitech, Microsoft, Nvidia, Razor, Samsung, and other technology-related companies (Huettermann et al., 2020). Moreover, esports have recently received an overwhelming wave of support from non-endemic firms – firms beyond the core tech-centric video gaming industry. These firms include prominent brands such as Nike, Mastercard, BMW, Coca-Cola, Red Bull, and Nissan, among a rapidly growing list of brands seeking to connect with digital natives (Hayward, 2019). Indeed, esports are bringing together sponsors from a variety of industries, reflecting their broad appeal and position at the center of technology, business, entertainment, and sports (Huettermann et al., 2020; Jang & Byon, 2020).

Overall, developers and publishers' shifting business models provide growth opportunities for digital platforms which deliver content to esports fans and consumers, helping to provide structure to the burgeoning esports industry. In doing so, the esports marketspace has attracted a bevy of sponsors seeking to participate in this phenomenon. Professional sport organizations are at the forefront of organizations helping to support the rise of esports, but the lack of governance and uncertainty surrounding monetization remain critical concerns for the esports marketspace (Pizzo et al., 2021). Notably, professional sport organizations have been the leading force outside of esports proper providing much-needed structure, legitimacy, and financial support (Pizzo et al., 2018, 2019).

Convergence of Sport and Esports

Professional sport organizations from across the globe have begun to embrace esports. For instance, the EPL developed the ePL, the ePremier League, an esports league that uses the FIFA football (or soccer) video game franchise, for top United Kingdom FIFA players to compete on behalf of their favorite EPL club (Premier League, 2020). Sport simulation leagues seek to engage the global esports audience, particularly as these sport leagues seek to expand their international presence. Digital sport leagues arguably serve as an "entry point" to connect mainstream sports leagues with global esports fans (Droesch, 2019). However, despite much public fanfare, the success of these leagues is still in question. For instance, the 2K League, the NBA's digital sports league, matches averaged approximately 10,000 concurrent viewers in its augural season in 2018, a fraction of the NBA's nearly 3 million average concurrent viewership for regular-season matches (Amico, 2020). Moreover, during the 2020 season, this number dipped to approximately 9,300 concurrent viewers.

Despite poor viewership figures, progressive sport organizations continue to invest in the esports marketspace. In particular, professional sport teams have been aggressively purchasing mainstream esports teams – teams that compete in esports beyond sport-based simulations (Pizzo et al., 2021). The strategic actions of these teams can be considered a more radical corporate growth strategy whereby professional sport teams are *diversifying* into the esports marketspace. This corporate growth strategy – diversification – entails not only entering a new market but also generating new products and services for the said market (Ansoff, 1957).

Diversification of Sport Organizations

Diversification is a corporate growth strategy whereby a firm enters a new product and service market that involves new skills and technology (Ansoff, 1957). In the context of esports, professional sport teams have diversified their corporate structure by creating, developing, and purchasing esports teams. Major professional sport teams from across the globe, representing multiple sports, such as AS Roma, FC Bayern München, Paris Saint-Germain, the Miami Heat, and the New England Patriots are among an ever-growing list of professional sport teams investing in esports teams (Szekeres, 2018).

Professional sport teams recognize the importance of esports to reach digital natives. For instance, the NBA franchise Miami Heat purchased an esports team, Team Misfits. At the time of their purchase, Heat EVP and CMO Michael McCullough noted:

> The opportunity was the fact that the esports audience is, for the most part, younger and digital and social media savvy. We were interested in finding out … how we could access that youthfulness for the benefit of the Miami Heat.
>
> *(TNL, 2017).*

These comments from the Miami Heat organization allude to a key and ongoing concern for professional sport teams diversifying into the esports industry. A sport organization's brand is one of its most valuable assets (Kunkel & Biscaia, 2020). Some professional sport teams have aligned the branding of the professional sports franchise with their esports team, while others have maintained distinct branding. For instance, executives from the Dallas Cowboys, of the National Football League (NFL), purchased the esports team Complexity Gaming in 2017. In 2019, Complexity Gaming underwent a complete rebranding, including changes to their "logo, website, color scheme, and company manifesto. The esports organization now boasts a blue star as its logo—one that closely resembles that of the organization's sister team, the Dallas Cowboys" (Miesner, 2019, para. 1). Conversely, the 76ers publicly stated that they intend to maintain a clear delineation between the 76ers' brand with that of Dignitas, despite a similar rebranding of Dignitas led by the 76ers ownership (Dignitas, 2021; Pizzo et al., 2021).

While questions remain as to how and whether professional sport organizations should link themselves with their esports team, it remains clear that diversification seems driven at least in part by the desire to reach digital natives. At a time when major professional sport leagues and teams face saturated markets and an aging core demographic (Shank & Lyberger, 2014), esports represent an opportunity to grow by engaging a younger demographic. However, professional sport organizations need to understand that despite the perceived similarities between operating a traditional sport and esports team, there are importance nuances that differentiate their monetization.

Sports and Esports: Monetization Differences

Professional sports and esports share similar revenue sources, but in either case, each source contributes differently. For most professional sports leagues and teams, media rights, ticket sales, sponsorships, and merchandise are the top four sources of revenue, respectively (PwC, 2019). Esports also generate revenue from those sources, but with sponsorships taking a leading role, media rights, ticket sales, and merchandise are far less prominent. Esports sponsorships account for over 40% of a team's total revenues; this is because esports are inherently digital and primarily watched online, making them less reliant on broadcast media rights, ticket sales, and related merchandising (Newzoo, 2019). While sponsorships are currently the leading source of revenue in esports, as they further develop there are clear indications that revenue sources beyond sponsorships will account for an increased percentage of total revenue. The development of formalized esports leagues, dedicated physical arenas and venues, and increased interest and competition for media rights suggest related sources of revenue will emerge soon.

As investors from the sports industry continue to embrace esports, they must also be prudent and recognize that owning, operating, and monetizing an esports team is not a direct application and mapping of skills from the sports industry. The OWL provides a fitting example to highlight some of the challenges facing esports and the professional sport organizations investing in them.

The Case of the Overwatch League

Amateur tournaments and competitions surrounding esports – with a developer and publisher support – have emerged and provided structure for professional, franchised esports leagues. The OWL provides a useful case study. The OWL deliberately mimicked professional sport leagues by using a geo-based (or regional), franchised model system. In 2016, Activision Blizzard, developer and producer of Overwatch, announced the OWL to great hype and excitement (Wolf, 2018). Executives from Activision Blizzard targeted investors from the sport industry to help legitimize and give structure to the newly formed esports league (Wolf, 2018), with sport industry investors lured with the promise of reaching and monetizing the coveted 18-34-year-old demographic (D'Anastasio, 2019).

Initial OWL franchises came with a significant $20 million USD price tag, with reports suggesting that some franchises paid close to $60 million USD (Wolf, 2018). Among those willing to pay upwards of $20 million USD franchise fees for the OWL include ownership groups from marquee professional sport franchises including the Philadelphia Flyers, New York Mets, and Arsenal Football Club, among other professional teams (Wolf, 2018).

Despite the initial hype surrounding the OWL, it has been plagued by problems from its onset. Nate Nanzer, the leading force and initial commissioner of the OWL, abruptly departed Activision Blizzard and from his role as commissioner in 2019 (Chan, 2019). This move came at a time when Twitch viewership for the OWL saw a substantial year-over-year decline (Miceli, 2019), bringing into question the hype surrounding the "shady numbers and bad business practices" inside the esports industry (D'Anastasio, 2019). For instance, player contracts and management have been a persistent issue within the OWL. The Vancouver Titans, an OWL franchise, had all members of its roster and coaching staff abruptly depart from the team during the middle of the 2020 season (Webster, 2020). The rationale beyond their departure stemmed from ongoing – and complex – legal, labor, logistical, and cultural challenges. The Titans had to deal with the complexities of managing an international roster comprised primarily of young South Korean players, with the team based out of Vancouver, Canada, and competing in a league with most matches taking place in the United States at the Blizzard Arena in Burbank, California. Moreover, the OWL reigning MVP – Jay "Sinatraa" Won – also unexpectedly departed from the OWL – citing concerns over the league's longevity (Webster, 2020).

The case of the OWL underscores the importance for professional sport organizations to be prudent with respect to the esports industry. Although esports provide salient growth opportunities, organizations need to understand the nuances of operating in the emerging esports industry. Emerging industries, and the firms within them, struggle with a lack of established best practices, technological and financial stability, and a myriad of growing pains (Hayduk, 2020; Peltoniemi, 2011). The professional sport organizations who have embraced esports are proverbial first movers, entering a new market to gain benefits such as additional revenue and brand recognition (Lieberman & Montgomery, 1998). Yet first movers are also at a strategic disadvantage as they do not have the advantage of learning from the mistakes and successes of their predecessors (Boulding & Christen, 2001). Indeed, those who follow benefit by adopting new and more efficient practices, as well as enjoy the increased legitimacy and ancillary services supporting new industries (Markides & Sosa, 2013). Despite the cautionary case of the OWL, professional sport teams are learning from their early mistakes in the esports industry and are working toward effectively monetizing their acquisitions which are discussed in the following section.

Future Trends

Esports are among the digital technologies influencing the growth and operations of professional sport organizations. Esports provide sport organizations access to the youth-centric esports market and can help them (re)connect with this digitally savvy audience (Pizzo et al., 2018). Moreover, they also provide professional sport organizations a way to maintain relevance in a dynamic and rapidly changing environment. Progressive sport organizations must keep pace with these emerging trends to ensure their continued financial viability (Hayduk & Walker, 2018). Although esports offers professional sport organizations salient growth opportunities, sport entities should be aware of the many challenges present in this emerging industry, in particular with respect to differences in their monetization. The following subsections review how professional sport teams who have invested in the esports marketspace have responded to the challenges in the tech-centric esports marketspace.

Sponsorships

Sponsorships are salient to esports given the reduced importance of media rights (relative to traditional sports). In esports, professional sport teams serve as trusted mediators for sponsors seeking to capitalize on the esports industry. For instance, the leadership within the 76ers recognized that they have the privileged position and existing skills and resources to attract additional sponsors for Dignitas. Through the 76ers leadership, Dignitas has attracted major corporate sponsors, such as Champion Athletics, Mountain Dew, Buffalo Wild Wings, and HyperX (Gaudiosi, 2017). The trusted brand of the 76ers has provided Dignitas with the unique opportunity to engage existing 76ers sponsors, as well endemic esports sponsors, for the benefit of Dignitas. Moreover, professional sport teams such as the 76ers are also using their existing sales and sponsorship staff to efficiently create and develop sponsorship opportunities for Dignitas. With non-endemic sponsors seeking ways to align themselves with esports, professional sport teams should recognize that they can serve as trusted mediators for their existing core traditional sports sponsors and use their esports teams to create opportunities for sponsors to introduce their brand to esports fans.

Media Rights

Unlike esports, the majority of revenue for most professional sport leagues and teams comes from media rights (Reiff, 2019). For instance, national and local TV media rights deals have helped drive revenues for the North American "Big Four" sports leagues (i.e., NFL, NBA, MLB, NHL). In contrast, esports are primarily watched online by globally dispersed audiences, many of whom make extensive use of ad blockers, thereby avoiding many of the sponsorships and advertisements which help drive the value of media rights. While online streaming platforms have become better at integrating promotional messages and overlays to circumvent ad-blocking software, driving media rights values is an ongoing concern within the esports industry.

Furthermore, professional sport teams can enhance the brand and engagement of their esports teams by taking a cue from savvy endemic esports organizations. For instance, 100 Thieves is a leading esports team headquartered in Los Angeles, California, that has transformed itself from a gaming team into a lifestyle brand. Despite being formed in 2017, just three short years later in 2020, the 100 Thieves brand was valued at over $190 million USD (Settimi, 2020). Not only does 100 Thieves compete in various esports tournaments, but they also have a team of dedicated streamers who serve to promote the 100 Thieves brand. For instance, 100 Thieves signed social media celebrities and influencers known as "The Mob" to stream and serve as content creators for the 100 Thieves brand (Welker, 2019). Having a team of dedicated streamers and content creators helped 100 Thieves to develop creative ways for sponsorship activation and further increase the value of media rights deals using The Mob's large following. Moreover, dedicated streamers generate content at all hours of the day, helping to fill voids when there are no live esports competitions to stream.

Professional sport teams can learn from 100 Thieves by recognizing that media rights can be utilized to develop the sport team's core brand. For instance, professional sport and esports teams with connected brands, such as the Dallas Cowboys and Complexity Gaming, can encourage collaborations for their mutual benefit. In this case, Cowboys players can stream with players from Complexity and increase each team's brand recognition across fanbases. This strategy can drive each brand's following and increase the value of future media rights deals. However, as previously noted, some professional sport teams are limiting cross-promotions with their esports team. These teams, such as the 76ers and Dignitas, can adopt a strategy similar to that of 100 Thieves by seeking out streamers and influencers to work in tandem with Dignitas players. Moreover, the 76ers can have players on their developmental league (i.e., G-League) team – the Delaware Bluecoats – stream on Twitch with Dignitas players. This strategy reflects a middle ground that enables developmental league players to develop their following and brand while progressing through the developmental league. Not only does this provide value to the 76ers, Bluecoats, and Bluecoat players, but it also exposes the Dignitas brand to a new audience – all while protecting the core "76ers" brand from direct promotions with Dignitas.

Broadly, there is no "one size fits all" strategy for maximizing the value of media rights. However, professional sport teams can adopt a variety of strategies and measures to the benefit of their core sports brand and esports brand. In short, they should focus on using platforms such as Twitch to develop the core sports brand and capitalize on the potential synergies among esports teams and individual athletes whose brands are increasingly salient and serve as the cornerstone for professional sports organizations (Doyle et al., 2020).

Ticket sales

Currently, ticket sales across the North American Big Four account for between 16% (NFL) to 37% (NHL) of total revenues (Baker, 2019). Moreover, ticket revenues stay mostly with the host team with a portion shared with the visiting team (Woods, 2015). In esports, most tournaments take place virtually, or at a central location, such as the Blizzard Arena used by the OWL, and ticket sales are shared between the league and the two competing teams. Moreover, ticket sales in esports, in purely nominal terms, are trivial. For instance, the Blizzard Arena holds 450 spectators, and the average ticket price for regular-season matches has a face value of $20 USD (Landa, 2018).

As the esports industry matures, more and more esports teams are building dedicated arenas and venues. Many esports teams owned by professional sport teams are leading the charge of organizations building dedicated esports facilities. Indeed, some esports industry experts have gone as far as to state that the shared experience from in-person and live traditional sporting events are no different in esports (Molina, 2019). This is a highly questionable assumption considering that esports are primarily viewed online.

Nevertheless, a handful of progressive sport teams are developing innovative venues to host live and in-person esports competitions. For instance, Comcast Spectacor, the sports and entertainment division of the technology and media conglomerate Comcast, owns both the Philadelphia Flyers NHL franchise and the Philadelphia Fusion OWL franchise. Comcast Spectacor is building one of the largest esports arenas in the United States – the Fusion Arena – with a seating capacity of 3,500. Yet executives from Comcast Spectator are quick to note in addition to serving as the home base for Philadelphia Fusion that the arena will also be a multi-purpose facility that will host a variety of "live entertainment programming and experiences" (Comcast Spectacor, 2020). Professional sport teams building esports venues and arenas should consider adopting the approach used by Comcast Spectacor. Specifically, dedicated esports venues/arenas should be a non-starter, given the primarily digital nature of esports (and their corresponding viewership). Rather, these venues should be multi-purpose facilities that cater to the needs and expectations of digital natives desiring engaging, live entertainment experiences.

Merchandise

For traditional sports teams, merchandise sales constitute an important source of revenue. Sport fans the world over support their favorite teams and players by purchasing team-related merchandise. A key factor influencing these sales is fans' identification with their hometown team

(Funk et al., 2012). Yet in esports, most teams do not have a geographic or regional connection as incorporated into the OWL. Esports are truly global sports, with players on teams able to practice remotely from geographically dispersed locations.

For professional sport teams investing in esports teams, the lack of regional tie-ins, compounded by the lack of physical venues and arenas to create points of sale, make monetizing merchandising an area where they need to further innovate, potential using micro-targeted ads and advanced segmentation strategies informed by big data. More specifically, drawing from the 100 Thieves playbook, professional sport teams should recognize that esports are more than competitive video gaming. Esports encompass larger communities of individuals who, despite their geographic dispersion, are connected via their identification with a team. Teams such as 100 Thieves recognize that they are lifestyle brands and are capitalizing on this. For instance, 100 Thieves has created an aura of exclusivity around their "merch drops" – strategically planned and timed releases of 100 Thieves branded merchandise – which sell out within minutes of their release (Becht, 2020).

Conclusion

Overall, there is still plenty for professional sport organizations to learn in the esports marketspace. The rapidly changing pace of esports driven by technological advancements such as virtual (VR) and augmented reality (AR) is a reason to proceed with caution. Esports are a part of a dynamic industry, and as such professional sport organizations should exercise caution. Emerging markets are surrounded by technological and financial uncertainty, and they generally lack established best practices (Santos & Eisenhardt, 2009). For instance, while Twitch and Discord are currently the primary streaming and communication platforms used by competitive video gamers, the esports marketspace is rife with entrepreneurs seeking to capture the market share from industry incumbents. However, professional sport organizations should take heed of the fact that there is plenty to benefit and learn from with respect to esports. Given the dynamics across developers, publishers, titles, and fans, the industry may never converge upon a single set of best practices. Nevertheless, professional sport organizations are well-positioned to capitalize on esports given their existing knowledge and resources from their professional sports operations to help manage their operations in esports (Pizzo et al., 2021).

Esports provides professional sport organizations with an opportunity to connect with young, affluent, global yet hard-to-reach consumers. Although their knowledge and resources may not directly map to operating an esports team, professional sport organizations should seize these growth opportunities inherent in esports to connect with digital natives. Professional sport organizations have experience owning and operating sport franchises and knowledge of identifying and managing player talent. The similarities between owning and operating a sport and esports team provide sport organizations opportunities to capitalize on these synergies for the mutual benefit of both organizations. Indeed, many of the physical and mental conditioning resources provided to traditional sport players and athletes also benefit the performance of esports players and athletes as well (Pizzo et al., 2019).

Notes

1 Prominent examples of SaaS include Microsoft Office 365, Dropbox, and Google Apps (Vaudour & Heinze, 2020).
2 Team Dignitas was rebranded in 2018 to Dignitas, dropping the Team moniker from their name.
3 Battle royale is a subgenre of FPS and includes popular titles such as Fortnite. The key distinction between FPS and battle royale is that the latter focuses on competitions where the last player standing (or alive) is the winner, whereas FPS titles allow players to respawn, with multiple ways to win the competitions.

References

Aaker, D. (2003). The power of the branded differentiator. *MIT Sloan Management Review, 45*(1), 83–87.

Ali, A. Q., Sultan, A. B. M., Ghani, A. A. A., & Zulzalil, H. (2019). Empirical studies on the impact of software customization on quality attributes: A systematic review. *Journal of Theoretical and Applied Information Technology, 97*(6), 1747–1763.

Amico, S. (2020). NBA ratings up in primetime, but still down 30 percent overall. *Sports illustrated.* https://www.si.com/nba/cavaliers/nba-amico/playoffs-ratings-primetime-basketball

Andronico, M. (2016). *YouTube Gaming: What you need to know.* Tom's Guide. https://www.tomsguide.com/us/youtube-gaming-faq,review-3019.html

Ansoff, H. I. (1957). Strategies for diversification. *Harvard Business Review, 35*(5), 113–124.

Baker, G. (2019). *NHL players are paid like other major pro athletes — and ticket sales cover those wages.* The Seattle Times. https://www.seattletimes.com/sports/hockey/nhl-players-are-paid-like-other-major-pro-athletes-and-ticket-sales-cover-those-wages/

Baker, B. J. & Pizzo, A. D. (in press). Unpacking nuance among esports consumers: Market partitions within esports based on social media analytics. *International Journal of Esports.*

Becht, E. (2020). *When is the next 100 thieves merch drop coming? Date, time, and more.* Dexerto. https://www.dexerto.com/entertainment/when-is-the-next-100-thieves-merch-drop-coming-date-time-and-more-1332912

Boulding, W., & Christen, M. (2001). First-mover disadvantage. *Harvard Business Review, 79*(9), 20–21.

Byrne, L. (2019). *META high school esports announces partnership with Optus.* Esports Insider. https://esportsinsider.com/2019/07/meta-high-school-esports-announces-partnership-with-optus/

Carrillo Vera, J. A., & Aguado Terrón, J. M. (2019). The eSports ecosystem: Stakeholders and trends in a new show business. *Catalan Journal of Communication & Cultural Studies, 11*(1), 3–22.

Chan, E. (2019). Overwatch league commissioner Nate Nanzer departs to pursue new role at epic games. *NBC Sports.* https://www.nbcsports.com/philadelphia/fusion/overwatch-league-commissioner-nate-nanzer-departs-pursue-new-role-epic-games

Clark, J. (2019). *20 Celebrities and athletes betting big on esports.* Gamer One. https://gamerone.gg/20-celebrities-and-athletes-betting-big-on-esports

Cloud9. (2021). *Cloud9 news.* Cloud9. https://www.cloud9.gg/blogs/news

Comcast Spectacor. (2020). *Fusion arena.* Comcast. https://fusionarenaphilly.com/

D'Anastasio, C. (2019). *Shady numbers and bad business: Inside the esports bubble.* Kotaku. https://kotaku.com/as-esports-grows-experts-fear-its-a-bubble-ready-to-po-1834982843

Deloitte. (2019). *Technology, media, and telecommunications predictions 2019.* Deloitte. https://www2.deloitte.com/insights/us/en/industry/technology/technology-media-and-telecom-predictions.html

Dignitas. (2021). Dignitas brand refresh. *Dignitas.* http://dignitas.gg/refresh

Discord. (2021). *Company information.* Discord. https://discord.com/company

Doyle, J., Su, Y., & Kunkel, T. (2020). Athlete branding via social media: Examining the factors influencing consumer engagement on Instagram. *European sport management quarterly,* doi: 10.1080/16184742.2020.1806897

Droesch, B. (2019). *How the NBA is using esports to grow its audience.* eMarketer. https://www.emarketer.com/content/how-the-nba-is-using-esports-to-grow-its-audience

Funk, D. C. (2017). Introducing a sport experience design (SX) framework for sport consumer behaviour research. *Sport Management Review, 20*(2), 145–158.

Funk, D. C., Beaton, A., & Alexandris, K. (2012). Sport consumer motivation: Autonomy and control orientations that regulate fan behaviours. *Sport Management Review, 15*(3), 355–367.

Funk, D. C., Pizzo, A. D., & Baker, B. J. (2018). eSport management: Embracing eSport education and research opportunities. *Sport Management Review, 21*(1), 7–13.

Gaudiosi, J. (2017). *Team dignitas brand looks to attract new sponsors with women's team.* A.listdaily. https://www.alistdaily.com/strategy/team-dignitas-brand-looks-attract-new-sponsors-womens-team/

Goldman Sachs. (2018). *The world of games.* Goldman Sachs. https://www.goldmansachs.com/insights/pages/infographics/e-sports/report.pdf

Green, F. (2018). *Winning with data: CRM and analytics for the business of sports.* Routledge.

Harpstead, E., Rios, J. S., Seering, J., & Hammer, J. (2019). Toward a twitch research toolkit: A systematic review of approaches to research on game streaming. In Proceedings of the *Annual Symposium on Computer-Human Interaction in Play.* Barcelona, Spain, 111–119.

Hayduk, T. M. (2020). Kickstart my market: exploring an alternative method of raising capital in a new media sector. *Journal of media business studies*. 10.1080/16522354.2020.1800310

Hayduk, T., & Walker, M. (2018). Mapping the strategic factor market for sport Entrepreneurship. *International Entrepreneurship and Management Journal, 14*(3), 705–724.

Hayward, A. (2019). *Cars, drinks, and clothes: Non-endemic sponsor recap for Q1 2019*. The Esports Observer. https://esportsobserver.com/non-endemic-sponsors-q12019/

Heere, B. (2018). Embracing the sportification of society: Defining e-sports through a polymorphic view on sport. *Sport Management Review, 21*(1), 21–24.

Huettermann, M., Trail, G. T., Pizzo, A. D., & Stallone, V. (2020). Esports sponsorship: An empirical examination of esports consumers perceptions of sponsors. *Journal of global sports management*. Advance online publication. 10.1080/24704067.2020.1846906

Influencer Marketing. (2020). *25 useful Twitch stats for influencer marketing managers*. Influencer Marketing. https://influencermarketinghub.com/twitch-stats/

Jang, W. W., & Byon, K. K. (2020). Antecedents of esports gameplay intention: Genre as a moderator. *Computers in Human Behavior, 109*, 106336.

Kastrenakes, J. (2020). Twitch seems to have picked up most of mixer's streamers. *The verge*. https://www.theverge.com/2020/10/7/21506668/twitch-mixer-streamers-facebook-gaming-hours-streamed

Koksal, I. (2019). *Video gaming industry & its revenue shift*. Forbes. https://www.forbes.com/sites/ilkerkoksal/2019/11/08/video-gaming-industry--its-revenue-shift/#1a97b4d9663e

Kunkel, T., & Biscaia, R. (2020). Sport brands: Brand relationships and consumer behavior. *Sport Marketing Quarterly, 29*(1), 3–17.

Landa, J. (2018). *Burbank's blizzard arena aims to take esports to the next level*. Los Angeles Times. https://www.latimes.com/socal/burbank-leader/news/tn-blr-me-burbank-arena-esports-20180111-story.html

Levy, A. (2020). *Amazon's media business is worth $500 billion based on 'hidden value,' says Needham analyst*. CNBC. https://www.cnbc.com/2020/06/16/amazon-media-assets-worth-500-billion-almost-as-much-as-aws-needham.html

Lieberman, M. B., & Montgomery, D. B. (1998). First-mover (dis) advantages: Retrospective and link with the resource-based view. *Strategic Management Journal, 19*(12), 1111–1125.

Lopez, C., Pizzo, A. D., Gupta, K., Kennedy, H., & Funk, D. C. (2021). Corporate growth strategies in an era of digitalization: A network analysis of the National Basketball Association's 2k League sponsors. *Journal of Business Research, 133*, 208–217. 10.1016/j.jbusres.2021.04.068

Lorenz, T. (2019). *How an app for gamers went mainstream*. The Atlantic. https://www.theatlantic.com/technology/archive/2019/03/how-discord-went-mainstream-influencers/584671/

Lucht, F. (2019). The success of the freemium business model. How riot games flourishes with a free to play game. *Manager Journal, 29*(1), 114–124.

Macey, J., & Hamari, J. (2019). eSports, skins and loot boxes: Participants, practices and problematic behaviour associated with emergent forms of gambling. *New Media & Society, 21*(1), 20–41.

Maloney, T. (2020). *How do esports teams make money?* Roundhill Investments. https://www.roundhillinvestments.com/research/esports/how-do-esports-teams-make-money

Markides, C., & Sosa, L. (2013). Pioneering and first mover advantages: The importance of business models. *Long Range Planning, 46*(4-5), 325–334.

Meenaghan, T. (2013). Measuring sponsorship performance: Challenge and direction. *Psychology & Marketing, 30*(5), 385–393.

Miesner, A. (2019). *Complexity gaming unveils new branding and manifesto*. Complexity Gaming. https://complexity.gg/complexity-gaming-unveils-new-branding-and-manifesto/

Miceli, M. (2019). *Overwatch league twitch viewership declines as teams return to Blizzard Arena*. The Esports Observer. https://esportsobserver.com/owl-twitch-stage-two-final/

Molina, B. (2019). *Overwatch league teams' schedule includes match play in their home cities next year*. USA Today. https://www.usatoday.com/story/tech/news/2019/03/15/overwatch-league-shifting-traditional-home-away-schedule-2020/3174720002/

Newzoo. (2019). *Newzoo global esports market report 2020*. Newzoo. https://newzoo.com/insights/trend-reports/newzoo-global-esports-market-report-2020-light-version/

Nielsen. (2017). *The esports playbook*. Nielsen. https://nielsensports.com/reports/esports-playbook-2017/

Nielsen. (2019). *Esports playbook for brands 2019*. https://www.nielsen.com/us/en/insights/reports/2019/esports-playbook-for-brands.html#

Parent, M. M., Naraine, M. L., & Hoye, R. (2018). A new era for governance structures and processes in Canadian National Sport Organizations. *Journal of Sport Management, 32*(6), 555–566.

Peltoniemi, M. (2011). Reviewing industry life-cycle theory: Avenues for future research. *International Journal of Management Reviews, 13*(4), 349–375.

Pizzo, A. D., Baker, B. J., Jones, G. J., & Funk, D. C. (2021). Sport experience design: Wearable fitness technology in the health and fitness industry. *Journal of Sport Management, 35*(2), 130–143. 10.1123/jsm.2020-0150

Pizzo, A. D., Jones, G. J., & Funk, D. C. (2019). Navigating the iron cage: An institutional creation perspective of collegiate esports. *International Journal of Sport Management. 20*(2), 171–197.

Pizzo, A. D., Jones, G. J., Baker, B. J., Funk, D. C., & Kunkel, T. (2021). Sensemaking of novelty: The dynamic nature of integrating esports within a traditional sport organization. *Sport management review.* Advance online publication. 10.1080/14413523.2021.1935609

Pizzo, A. D., Na, S., Baker, B. J., Lee, M. A., Kim, D., & Funk, D. C. (2018). eSport vs. sport: A comparison of spectator motives. *Sport Marketing Quarterly, 27*(2), 108–123.

Premier League. (2020). *What is ePremier league?* Premier League. https://www.premierleague.com/news/870155

PwC. (2019). *PwC sports outlook 2019.* PricewaterhouseCoopers. https://www.pwc.com/us/en/industries/tmt/assets/pwc-sports-outlook-2019.pdf

Reiff, N. (2019). *How the NBA makes money.* Investopedia. https://www.investopedia.com/articles/personal-finance/071415/how-nba-makes-money.asp

Reuters. (2021). *Report: League of legends produced $1.75 billion in revenue in 2020.*Reuters. https://www.reuters.com/article/esports-lol-revenue/report-league-of-legends-produced-1-75-billion-in-revenue-in-2020-idUSFLM2vzDZL

Santa, D. (2020). *Pro leagues reach new fans on TV through esports.* Front Office Sports. https://frontofficesports.com/pro-leagues-new-fans-esports/

Santos, F. M., & Eisenhardt, K. M. (2009). Constructing markets and shaping boundaries: Entrepreneurial power in nascent fields. *Academy of Management Journal, 52*(4), 643–671.

Settimi, C. (2020). *The most valuable esports companies 2020.* Forbes. https://www.forbes.com/sites/christinasettimi/2020/12/05/the-most-valuable-esports-companies-2020/?sh=60071e3173d0

Shabir, N. (2017). *ESPORTS: The complete guide 2017/2018.* Medium. https://medium.com/@IGGalaxy/esports-the-complete-guide-17-18-ead8cd668def

Shank, M. D., & Lyberger, M. R. (2014). *Sports marketing: A strategic perspective.* Routledge.

Ströh, J. H. A. (2017). *The eSports market and eSports sponsoring.* Tectum Wissenschaftsverlag.

Szekeres, E. (2018). *Why are professional sports teams investing in esports?* Fox Sports Stories. http://foxsportsstories.com/2018/04/28/professional-sports-teams-investing-esports/

Thompson, P. (2013). The digital natives as learners: Technology use patterns and approaches to learning. *Computers & Education, 65,* 12–33.

TNL. (2017). *Why pro teams invest in esports.* The Next Level. https://tnl.media/esportsproteams/2017/3/15/why-do-pro-teams-invest-in-esports

Vaudour, F., & Heinze, A. (2020). Software as a service: Lessons from the video game industry. *Global Business and Organizational Excellence, 39*(2), 31–40.

Webster, A. (2020). *The overwatch league's troubles continue as top team drops entire roster.* The Verge. https://www.theverge.com/2020/5/6/21249675/overwatch-league-owl-vancouver-titans-roster-cuts-esports

Welker, B. (2019). *The mob join 100 thieves.* Dot Esports. https://dotesports.com/streaming/news/the-mob-join-100-thieves

Wolf, J. (2018). *Sources: Overwatch league expansion slots expected to be $30 million to $60 Million.* ESPN. https://www.espn.com/esports/story/_/id/23464637/overwatch-league-expansion-slots-expected-30-60-million

Wohn, D. Y., & Freeman, G. (2020). Live streaming, playing, and money spending behaviors in eSports. *Games and Culture, 15*(1), 73–88.

Woods, B. (2016). Why A-rod and Shaq is betting big on their own eSports teams. *CNBC.* https://www.cnbc.com/2016/10/28/a-rod-and-shaq-buy-a-stake-in-nrg-esports-team.html

Woods, R. (2015). *Social issues in sport.* Human Kinetics.

Zackariasson, P., & Wilson, T. L. (Eds.). (2012). *The video game industry: Formation, present state, and future.* Routledge.

23

Blockchain and the Sports Tech Dilemma

Brianna Newland and Martin Carlsson-Wall

Introduction

In 2008, the mysterious, unidentified person or persons, known as Satoshi Nakamoto, presented blockchain as a disruptor of traditional financial markets and proposed a set of ideas that would become known as "blockchain" technology (Khaund, 2020). Using a set of cryptographic algorithms, blockchain technology was portrayed as a force that could make financial intermediaries such as banks irrelevant (Nowiński & Kozma, 2017). Security could be improved, costs could be reduced, and personal integrity could be strengthened. In this chapter, we describe how blockchain technology provides both opportunities and risks for the sport industry. On the one hand, we paint a rosy picture where blockchain start-ups can improve the consumer experience, reduce eliminate the sale of fake sport memorability, and strengthen anti-doping routines. In an ideal world, new blockchain innovations have the power to transform the sport industry and make it more fun, efficient, and trustworthy. On the other hand, we critically examine the risks of implementing blockchain. We argue that there is a "Sports Tech Dilemma" (Carlsson-Wall & Newland, 2020) that start-ups need to be aware of when entering the sport industry. The dilemma centers around temporal tensions because while start-ups build on event-driven time (Ancona et al., 2001), where specific events or milestones determine how time is managed, speed and experimentation are key ingredients, the sport industry is characterized by a cyclical time where a recurring cycle (such as a yearly league) is the central mechanisms for how actors relate to time. Furthermore, while event-driven time is often characterized by improvisation and experimentation, cyclical time (especially if it occurs in a recurring fashion) normally focuses on preserving and maintaining norms, routines, and institutions. Processes are purposefully designed to be slow to preserve the integrity of the overall system. By describing both opportunities and risks, our ambition is to provide a balanced perspective of the evolving dynamics of blockchain development within the sport sector.

Blockchain Technology Explained

The Pillars

While the general public is most familiar with blockchain technology via Bitcoin, Bitcoin does not help to clarify or define Blockchain'sthe technical capabilities. Blockchain technology is

DOI: 10.4324/9781003088899-27

driven by three key pillars, (1) distributed computation, (2) public key cryptography, and (3) decentralized consensus (Salviotti et al., 2018).

Distributed computation means that the power to compute is shared among multiple systems across varied locations (Narayanan, 2016). An individual user operates a "node," which runs independently and automatically synchronizes with all the nodes creating blocks in a chain, and thus, propagating it further (Salviotti et al., 2018). This design does not require a central "node" to process and distribute information across the chain, thereby eliminating the need for a supervising entity, such as a financial institution.

Pillar two is the *public key cryptography* (PKC), which contributes to the security and privacy features of blockchain. The PKC is an encryption tool that uses two related numbers to identify and represent the user's digital signature. The first number, a private key, is used to decrypt the information, and the second, a mathematically derived public key, is used to encrypt (Salviotti et al., 2018). The public keys can be shared to provide users a simple way to encrypt and verify digital signatures; meanwhile, the private keys are kept secret to ensure only the owners can decrypt information (Rivest et al., 1978).

Pillar three, *decentralized consensus*, means that no user needs to trust another party or go through a central entity to share information. There are three popular algorithms used in the decentralization process: Practical Byzantine Fault Tolerance (PBFT), Proof of Work (PoW), and Proof of Stake (PoS). The PBFT algorithm requires that each node use its public key in conjunction with a received message to run computation and reach a decision. That decision is then shared with all the other nodes in the system and consensus is reached based on the total decisions submitted by the nodes (Hammerschmidt, 2017). Rather than submitting a decision and waiting for the other nodes to reach a consensus, the PoW algorithm uses a hash function to allow the user to submit their conclusion to be independently verified by other users (Hammerschmidt, 2017). As the most popular means to reach consensus, the PoW ensures that a great deal of work went into generating the block and it prevents malicious entities from creating false blocks, adding to the security of the system (Salviotti et al., 2018). Finally, the PoS algorithm replaces the hash function with a digital signature that specifies ownership of the stake. Unlike the other two examples, the PoS randomly selects individuals to confirm the validity and approve new information submitted to the block (Hammerschmidt, 2017). No matter the algorithm chosen, distributed consensus allows all participants to agree on the accuracy of the records, which enhances the transparency of the chain.

The Ownership

There are two types of blockchain ownerships: permissioned and permissionless. Permissioned blockchain uses are specific to database management and/or auditing for internal use by a single company. Meant to enable greater efficiency and transaction speed, permissioned blockchains typically use PBFT algorithms and are centralized to one or a few users (Salviotti et al., 2018). Permissionless blockchains are open source for anyone to use and do not require a previous relationship with the ledger to participate (Salviotti et al., 2018). Permissionless blockchains typically use PoW or PoS algorithms.

The Objectives

In addition to eliminating any need for an intermediary, blockchain fulfills several objectives for organizations. Blockchain can: (1) provide visibility and transparency to those with access to the chain, (2) enhance public trust by ensuring data integrity and reduction of fraud, (3) reduce

BLOCKCHAIN TECHNOLOGY

PILLARS	OWNERSHIPS	OBJECTIVES
1. Distributed computation **2. Public Key chryptography** **3. Decentralized consensus** *Popular algorithms* • Practical Byzantine Fault Tolerance (PBFT) • Proof of Work (PoW) • Proof of stake (PoS).	• **Permissioned blockchain** ○ Permissioned blockchain uses are specific to database management and/or auditing for internal use by a single company. Meant to enable greater efficiency and transaction speed, permissioned blockchains typically use PBFT algorithms and are centralized to one or a few users • **Permissionless blockchain** ○ Open source to anyone to use and does not require a previous relationship with the ledger to participate. permission-less blockchains typically use PoW or PoS algorithms.	1. Provide visibility and transparency to those with access to the chain. 2. Enhance public trust by ensuring data integrity and reduction of fraud. 3. Reduce overhead costs related to verifying transactions. 4. Increase collaboration among multiple parties without increasing risk. 5. Offer exceptional security with cryptography. 6. Improve the efficiency of operations and facilitate compliance with regulations.

Figure 23.1 Pillars, Ownerships, and Objectives of Blockchain Technology

overhead costs related to verifying transactions, (4) increase collaboration among multiple parties without increasing risk, (5) offer exceptional security with cryptography, and (6) improve the efficiency of operations and facilitate compliance with regulations (Nowiński & Kozma, 2017). Figure 23.1 summarizes the pillars, type of ownership, and objectives of blockchain technology.

Blockchain's Potential to Transform the Sport Industry

Blockchain's Value Proposition to Sport

The benefits of blockchain could be innumerable, but we focus on seven key functions: (1) advanced tracking, (2) cloud storage, (3) security, (4) cryptocurrencies, (5) financial transactions, (6) smart contracts, and (7) digital identities. The privacy and reliability concerns in the current Internet of Things (IoT) can be solved through *advanced tracking* of connected devices on a decentralized system (Banafa, 2017). Known as the server-client paradigm, current IoT ecosystems rely on centralized, brokered communication models that require huge processing and storage capacities to identify and authenticate devices in a cloud server (Banafa, 2017). A decentralized tracking approach for IoT networking solves the challenges of processing hundreds of billions of transactions between devices (Banafa, 2017). The decentralization required for advanced tracking also solves challenges related to *cloud storage.* Using blockchain, organizations can host surplus cloud storage capacity for all users with better privacy and security features at significant cost reductions (Salviotti et al., 2018).

Instances of cyber fraud are also on the rise and blockchain technology serves as a viable method to curb such crime and protect the *security* of consumer information and privacy. Because it is impossible to rewrite any data registered in the block by timestamping data in an unaltered state (Salviotti et al., 2018). *Cryptocurrencies*, like Bitcoin, not only reduce the need for third-party entities (i.e., banks), it also enables secure, anonymous financial transactions (Khaund, 2020). Blockchain also supports *financial transactions* related to broader capital markets infrastructure by removing intermediaries, providing instant settlements, increasing transparency for contracts, and reducing errors in reconciliations (Salviotti et al., 2018). All of which can support financial business dealings in sport. *Smart contracts* define a digital relationship between two parties and self-execute the terms when predetermined conditions are triggered by the system (Bernstein, 2018; Salviotti et al., 2018).

Smart contracts move beyond typical e-contracts (i.e., Docusign) in that the terms are embodied in computer code, rather than a spoken language (Bernstein, 2018). Because a physical signature is not necessary, the parties "sign" using cryptographic security (public keys) and deploy it to a blockchain (Bernstein, 2018). Finally, *digital identities* allow individuals to store their personal information required for verification purposes without the need for identifying documents (i.e., passport, birth certificate; Salviotti et al., 2018). Not only will this simplify the identity verification process, but it will also reduce the risk associated with identity theft. While these seven benefits are important to sport, how they add value to specific areas of the sport industry are discussed below.

Opportunities for Consumer Experiences

The fan experience within sport can be influenced by blockchain technology in several ways. At the simplest level, teams can enhance the purchase of tickets and loyalty programs (Naraine, 2019). For example, Footies, a subsidiary of TechFinancials and Tixico platforms, helps sport organizations control and optimize their game-day financials. These platforms track ticket ownership, thereby reducing counterfeit risk and fraud, thereby enabling greater control over ticket resales.

Sport organizations, venues, and sport event operators can also ensure that consumers' personal data is secure and resistant to security breaches (Carlsson-Wall & Newland, 2020). With the use of digital identities, sport consumers can create unique user profiles to engage with sport organizations, allowing for a treasure trove of information that can be used to enhance experiences by providing specialized incentives and loyalty programs. For example, Bandwagon Fanclub helps identify the fans and event attendees that patronize a sport event to better understand who is in the venue in order to improve engagement, increase day of event revenue, and improve public safety.

To evolve consumer engagement even further, tech companies like Socios.com allow football fans to engage closely with favorite clubs by using cryptocurrency, in the form of tokens, to purchase a percentage of ownership with a team. The tokens bought and sold on platforms ensure fans' voices are heard via voting and influence rights. In addition, start-ups like Fantastec, are bringing the fan experience into the home by using augmented and virtual reality systems via blockchain.

Opportunities for Sport Memorabilia Collectables

Another important area within the global sport industry is sport collectibles. Here, the inability to verify authenticity (Carlsson-Wall & Newland, 2020) and track the supply chain (Khaund, 2020) are recurring problems. Blockchain technology has begun to revolutionize this area by allowing for individual pieces to be coded and tracked as the item is sold and resold in the marketplace. For example, the NHL team, the LA Kings recently launched their own blockchain authentication platform for all of their memorabilia. Using an augmented reality (AR) blockchain platform, LA Kings can ensure 100% authenticity for their licensed merchandise (Bourne, 2019). Blockchain technology has advanced the player card collectables one step further by creating unique and limited digital athlete player cards that allow users to bargain and trade for their favorite player. Start-ups like Stryking are leading the digital collectable space, along with the NBA's Top Shots, a competitive online environment where users can garner unique digital collectibles using Non-Fungible Tokens (NFT). NFTs are units of data stored and certified on the blockchain, which create a certificate of authenticity for an object – real or virtual – making it impossible to fake or swap (Dean, 2021).

Opportunities for Sport Betting and Fantasy Sport

The use of blockchain for sport betting is impacted mainly by transparency and security. With the vast amount of money on the line during any given sporting event, many different groups benefit from a permanent and verifiable record of the transaction ledger (Carlsson-Wall & Newland, 2020). Blockchain ensures transparency by allowing betters to verify payouts and protects the integrity of the bets because sportsbooks cannot claim that the system generated incorrect odds that cannot be fulfilled. Start-ups leading the way in this area include Bet Democracy, a peer-to-peer sport betting platform that is not only decentralized – the user chooses their own odds without fees and plays anonymously with others – but also uses smart contracts between users that automatically execute when predetermine terms are met. Other start-ups in this area include Bethereum, a start-up that uses gamification and social elements to make the experience more fun and interesting. Like Bet Democracy, Bethereum capitalizes on decentralization, transparency, and security as part of the betting platform – with a social and gaming twist.

Like sport betting, the start-ups focused on fantasy sport are also concerned with transparency and security. Coinroster uses bitcoin technology to enable a range of fantasy betting opportunities as well as prop bets. For Digital Fantasy Sport, the company uses a blockchain platform that uses tokens to engage in fantasy play, connects global players, and provides social opportunities through live chats. The site offers opportunities to engage in global fantasy play and offers private tournaments, all using token technology.

Opportunities for Sponsorship and Athlete Crowdsourcing

Sponsorship of sport organizations and events is very costly for a sponsor and, in some cases, can be a poorly measured return on investment (Jensen & White, 2018). Blockchain could revolutionize the sponsorship opportunities for both sport entities and the sponsor. First, the use of smart contracts, as described above, could enable the contract to be executed immediately based on the predetermined terms, thereby automating sponsorship (Bernstein, 2018). Companies like Instant Sponsorship enable brands to buy real-time custom, sport sponsorships without the use of agencies or long-term contracts. Second, tokenizing intellectual property (IP) licenses, for both the team logos and player likeness, could enable money savings by controlling how the license operations thereby reducing fraud, conflicts of interest, larceny, and excessive fees often added by agents (Bernstein, 2018).

Athletes can raise funds to develop their careers, later giving fans back a portion of their income while clubs and sport organizations can raise funds in exchange for a percentage of tickets, sponsorship, television rights, and more. For example, TokenStars connects rising star athletes with fans. Fans can buy tokens to support talent, participate in auctions, and scout new talent. Other companies like Sportyco uses the SPF token to fund talents, with investors' returns coming as a share of the athlete's future performance and earnings. Likewise, companies like SportCash One reward clubs, athletes, and brands for creating quality posts and sharing media and ideas.

Opportunities for Player Data and Anti-Doping

Athletes and sport organization rely very heavily on performance metrics through game-day performance statistics. With the innovations around wearable technology, coaches and athletes can get real-time biometric data that can complement performance statistics. Blockchain technology has the ability to take athlete performance, athlete health, and talent scouting to the next level by tracking key physical performances and biometric data. For example, Peerspoint uses blockchain to enable talent scouting by (1) evaluating the potential of the athlete, (2) making comparisons among individual players, (3) identifying young talent with a high probability of excelling, and (4) identifying players undervalued in the market. Further, Peerspoint can also monitor player movements and physical performance during training and games to predict fatigue and injuries as well as provide feedback for injury or recovery plans.

Wearables generate a great deal of fitness, health, and other biometric data, however, much of this data is not aggregated in a way that can make it meaningful to judge performance, health, and/or identify injury risk. Lympo, however, has found a way to aggregate that data and incentivize users to exchange value through the LYM utility tokens. These tokens are awarded for healthy lifestyle achievements that can be used to purchase products and services in the Lympo marketplace.

Elite athletes often face great risk by purchasing over-the-counter food products with questionable ingredients that can put their careers at risk for doping. One way to protect athletes from anti-doping risks is through the ability to accurately detect ingredients in products that can put them at risk. For example, Carrefour[21] applies blockchain in the food sector by allowing each link in the supply chain to be tracked for information on each part of the process and for each batch. So, dates, places, livestock buildings, distribution channels, potential treatments, etc. are all tracked. Athletes can then use a QR code on the final product to ensure the reliability of the product.

The Sports Tech Dilemma

The Challenges of Combining Multiple Logics

Having discussed the opportunities of blockchain, we now turn to the risks of implementing new technology. Drawing inspiration from institutional theory, we particularly highlight the challenges that occur when organizations and entrepreneurs must cope with multiple institutional logics (Greenwood et al., 2011; Battilana & Lee, 2014; Besharov & Smith, 2014). In a seminal article on institutional logics, Friedland & Alford (1991) define an institutional logic as, "a set of material practices and symbolic constructions which constitute its organizing principles, and which is available to organizations and individuals to elaborate" (p. 248). In more practical terms, an institutional logic stipulates "the rules of the game" within a specific industry and sector where the logic helps individuals order reality, focus attention, and make "experiences of time and space meaningful" (Friedland & Alford, 1991, p. 243).

However, industries and sectors could consist of multiple logics. For example, managers within social enterprises (Battilana & Lee, 2014), family businesses (Boers & Nordqvist, 2020) state-owned enterprises (Battilana et al., 2017), and cooperatives (Ashford & Reingen, 2014) all need to navigate tensions between different logics. Understanding the risks and challenges related to multiple institutional logics is at the core of the Sports Tech Dilemma. More specifically, as Figure 23.2 shows, without understanding the differences in view on value, time, and decision-making, the opportunities with blockchain will not necessarily be leveraged.

THE SPORTS TECH DILEMMA

Definition of an institutional logic:
A set of material practices and symbolic constructions which constitute its organizing principles and which is available to organizations and individuals to elaborate (Friedland & Alford, 1991 p.248)

CAPITALISTIC START-UP LOGIC

- ***View on value:*** Primarily financial and it's important to focus on future cash flows.
- ***View on time:*** Focus on event-driven time where specific milestones are important.
- ***Type of decision-making:*** Decision-making is often done in a small circle of owners and managers with the focus on single products and/or services

DEMOCRATIC MEMBERSHIP LOGIC

- ***View on value:*** A multi-dimensional concept where financial value is not often the main target.
- ***View on time:*** Focus on cyclical time where history plays and important part.
- ***Type of decision-making:*** Decision-making relies on involving multiple actors where a systematic perspective on innovation is needed.

Figure 23.2 The Sports Tech Dilemma

Starting with a view on value, Figure 23.2 illustrates how value for a capitalistic start-up is primarily financial and where it's natural to focus on future cash flows to increase the company's shareholder value. For a democratic membership organization like the International Olympic Committee (IOC), value is a multi-dimensional concept where financial value is often seen as a means rather than an end. For a start-up entrepreneur, this creates a challenge, because a partner or customer might not prioritize financial profitability and growth in the same way. The challenges of implementing blockchain are further complicated by the fact that start-ups and sport organizations often have different views on time. For a young start-up without a long history, it is natural to focus on concrete milestones. One could argue that reaching the milestones is critical to receive continuous funding, but also to keep the motivation high among the employees. Researchers have called this view of managing the organization *event-driven* (Ancona et al., 2001; Kunisch et al., 2017). In contrast, many sport organizations have a strong cyclical rhythm (Ancona et al., 2001). There is an annual season that keeps coming back or in the example of the Olympic Games, a repeated cycle of four years coordinates the activities. Being aware of both the different views of value as well as the different temporal rhythms are critical issues to successfully implementing new technology.

Finally, differences in decision-making style are also important to acknowledge. Within a start-up, there is normally a small team of owners and/or managers that make decisions. Since focus is on financial growth with clear milestones, decisions can be made quickly, and they can also be revised if needed. This is very different in democratic membership organizations. Not only are decisions difficult to revise (imagine what it would take to rescind a nation the opportunity to host the Olympic Games), but they are also prepared and processed in a much more formalized way. Even highly commercial sport organizations such as the North American professional leagues take their time to prepare strategic decisions such as expanding new franchises or changing salary caps rules.

Another reason why it is difficult and frustrating for start-up entrepreneurs to embed their products into the sport industry concerns the systemic nature of innovations. Before a new blockchain product is approved, one must ensure that all members of a sport organization can afford the new product, that they can maintain it over time, and that the quality is high. Imagine a new anti-doping system based on blockchain technology. In an ideal world, this is a fantastic innovation that could solve one of the biggest problems in sport: cheating. However, if the system is not working with 100% accuracy or if it is too expensive for small countries to purchase and implement, the system will fail, and the international federation (or the International Olympic Committee) might receive negative publicity. As a consequence, even though "sport" and "tech" might sound like a great combination, the more one learns about the innovation challenges, the more one realizes that it can be risky business.

Future Research

In this chapter, we described opportunities and risks associated with introducing blockchain technology to the sport industry. There are several theoretical frameworks in strategy and economics that could serve as lenses to examine blockchain in a sport context. Dominant theories like Returns to Scale could be used to examine how the use of blockchain technologies could support an increase in an organization's outputs. In the case of smart contracts, secure financial transactions, and streamlining consumer data, this could have a major impact on sport organizations. Theories related to efficiency are good frameworks to examine access control schemes to manage permissions and access to information in the IoT as well as other improvements to inefficiencies in system processes (Chai et al., 2021). Much could also be explored using Consumer Behavior Theory. For example, we discussed opportunities for enhanced consumer experiences as well as improved security, especially in relation to sports memorabilia and gambling. However, exploratory studies to understand if consumers even understand blockchain and whether it matters that an organization uses the technology should be explored.

We have started the theoretical discussion by drawing on institutional theory. As shown here, we have shown how there is an important "Sports Tech Dilemma" that entrepreneurs need to navigate and negotiate to be successful. This institutional perspective on innovation is not new. In a historical study of Edison and electric lighting, Hargadon & Sutton (2000) show that it was not the technical superiority of electric lightning that caused the shift from gas to electric lighting. Instead, it was by mimicking and imitating the existing system that Edison succeeded. To create acceptance and avoid fear, there were only a few technical features where the electrical lightning system stood out. Hargadon & Sutton (2001) therefore argued that "understanding design is about designing understanding" (p. 491).

The importance of designing understanding goes in line with institutional theory since it is about embracing logic and ensuring that a new product is aligned with the logic's "way of reality" (Faik et al., 2020). This is particularly important in a conservative context such as sport, where emotions, identity, and systemic innovation are critical. To demonstrate the link between innovation and institutional theory, we have focused on the tension between a capitalist start-up logic and a democratic membership logic. We chose this tension because the view on value, temporal rhythm and decision-making styles are different. However, there are also other types of institutional complexity that can be explored in future studies. If we start in North America, families own many professional sport franchises. Even though the literature on family business has started to incorporate an institutional logic perspective, researchers have argued that much remains to be done (Boers & Nordqvist, 2020). As Friedland & Alford (1991) write, the family logic is about "unconditional loyalty to its members and their reproduction needs" (p. 248). How new technology, such as blockchain, is implemented in sport organizations where loyalty bonds to family members are critical is an interesting topic to explore from both a theoretical and a practical perspective. In a recent article focusing on digital innovation and institutional logic, Faik et al., (2020) specifically highlight how there are very few studies that focused on digitalization in family businesses. An in-depth case study of how blockchain is implemented in a professional sport club owned by a family could therefore make contributions to several fields.

The importance of "designing understanding" (Hargadon & Sutton, 2000) could also be interesting if one focuses on tensions between capitalist and state logic. One of the largest and most prosperous markets in the world is the Chinese sport market. In 2022, China will have organized both a Summer Olympics and a Winter Olympics and many global sports are now expanding their brand into China. However, in contrast to the more commercial North American system or the membership-driven European system, the Chinese sport system is highly influenced by the state. How the implementation of new technology such as blockchain is done in a setting where commercial and state logic clash would make for an interesting study. A particularly relevant angle could be to study how the implementation of new technology is related to global politics. Many sport organizations such as the Olympic Games often claim that they are not involved in politics. Still, there are numerous examples of how sport stars or sport executives mobilize their fan platforms for political messages. How institutional complexity is navigated when sport values, commercial values, and state values are intertwined with the new technology should open up and allow for interesting theoretical and practical contributions.

Blockchain's impact on sport consumers should also be examined. Given blockchain's ability to secure personal information, make contracts and financial transactions more secure, and opportunities for improved fan engagement, consumer perceptions and behavior should be explored. Will consumers need to better understand the technology to trust and use it? Will they prefer blockchain-secured memorabilia over traditional methods? Given the explosion in popularity of the NBA's recently released NFTs, it seems consumers are interested in using blockchain technology, but this should not be assumed.

Finally, it cannot be denied that blockchain technology has a profound environmental impact, which threatens the global commitment to reduce greenhouse emissions set by the United Nations Paris Agreement (2015). In fact, the consumption of energy required to run the cryptocurrency, Bitcoin, is equivalent to powering Denmark (Truby, 2018). To put this into context, one Visa transaction uses 0.01kWh, Ethereum uses 37kWh, and Bitcoin uses 200kWh (Brosens, 2017). There have been recommendations to reimagine how consensus algorithms are used in blockchain to lessen the computational energy required, but it will likely require policymakers to incentivize companies to reduce energy consumption or to develop cleaner, green technologies that lower environmental impact (Truby, 2018). What does this mean for sport? Many sport organizations have begun to implement environmentally friendly practices at their events (Newland et al., 2021) and venues (McCullough & Kellison, 2017). How consumers will respond to the reduction of greenhouse emissions in events and/or venues, but exponentially increasing in blockchain initiatives should be explored. Additional research could explore how political incentives for energy reduction Future research should explore the impact of advances in green technology and its subsequent impact on blockchain initiatives in the sport industry.

The title of this chapter is "Blockchain technology and the sports tech dilemma: a big opportunity or a risky business?." By describing the central elements of blockchain technology, highlighting innovative start-ups, and also critically examining the risks, our ambition has been to provide a balanced perspective on blockchain technology. As we emphasized, combining "sports" and "tech" is not an easy venture. However, by learning how to cope with multiple institutional logics such as capitalism, membership democracy, family, and state, we believe that new technologies could be implemented more easily in the conservative and emotional sport industry.

References

Ancona, D., Okhuysen, G., & Perlow, L. (2001). Taking time to integrate temporal research. *Academy of Management Review, 26*(4), 512–529.

Ashford, B.E., & Reingen, P.H. (2014). Functions of dysfunction: Managing the dynamics of an organizational duality in a natural food cooperative. *Administrative Science Quarterly, 59*(3), 474–516.

Banafa, A. (2017). IoT and blockchain convergence: Benefits and challenges. *IEEE Internet of Things*, https://iot.ieee.org/newsletter/january-2017/iot-and-blockchain-convergence-benefits-and-challenges.html

Battilana, J., Besharov, M., & Mitzinneck, B. (2017). On hybrids and hybrid organizing: A review and roadmap for future research. *The SAGE handbook of organizational institutionalism, 2*, 133–169.

Battilana, J., & Lee, M. (2014). Advancing research on hybrid organizing–Insights from the study of social enterprises. *Academy of Management Annals, 8*(1), 397–441.

Bernstein, J. (2018). Smart contract integration in professional sports management: The imminence of athlete representation. *DePaul J. Sports L., 14*, 88–105.

Besharov, M. L., & Smith, W. K. (2014). Multiple institutional logics in organizations: Explaining their varied nature and implications. *Academy of Management Review, 39*(3), 364–381.

Boers, B., & Nordqvist, M. (2020). Family businesses as hybrid organisations. *In Handbook on Hybrid Organisations*. Edward Elgar Publishing.

Brosens, T. (2017, October 13). Why bitcoin transactions are more expensive than you think. *ING*, https://think.ing.com/opinions/why-bitcoin-transactions-are-more-expensive-than-you-think

Carlsson-Wall, M., Kraus, K., & Messner, M. (2016). Performance measurement systems and the enactment of different institutional logics: Insights from a football organization. *Management Accounting Research, 32*, 45–61.

Carlsson-Wall, M., & Newland, B. (2020). Blockchain, sport, and navigating the sportstech dilemma. In S. Schmidt (Ed.), *21st Century Sports – How Technologies Will Change Sports in The Digital Age*, 205–218. Springer.

Chai, B., Yan, B., Yu, J., & Wang, G. (2021). BHE-AC: A blockchain-based high-efficiency access control framework for internet of things. *Personal and Ubiquitous Computing*, 1–12. 10.1007/s00779-020-01498-w

Dean, S. (2021, March 11). $69 million or digital art? The NFT craze, explained. *Los Angeles Times*, https://www.latimes.com/business/technology/story/2021-03-11/nft-explainer-crypto-trading-collectible

Faik, I., Barrett, M., & Oborn, E. (2020). How information technology matters in societal change: an affordance-based institutional logics perspective. *MIS Quarterly, 44*(3), 1359–1390.

Friedland, R., & Alford, R. (1991). Bringing society back in: Symbols, practices and institutional contradictions. In W.W. Powell & P.J. DiMaggio (Eds.), *The New Institutionalism in Organizational Analysis*, 232–263. Chicago: University of Chicago Press.

Greenwood, R., Raynard, M., Kodeih, F., Micelotta, ER, & Lounsbury, M. (2011). Institutional complexity and organizational responses. *Academy of Management Annals, 5*(1), 317–371.

Gümüsay, A.A., Smets, M., & Morris, T. (2020). "God at work": Engaging central and incompatible institutional logics through elastic hybridity. *Academy of Management Journal, 63*(1), 124–154.

Hammerschmidt, C. (2017). Consensus in blockchain systems. In Short. *Medium*, https://medium.com/@chrshmmmr/consensus-in-blockchain-systems-in-short-691fc7d1fefe

Hargadon, A., & Douglas, Y. (2001). When innovatons meet institutions: Edison and the design of electric light. *Administrative Science Quarterly, 46*, 476–501.

Hargadon, A. B., & Sutton, R. I. (2000). Building an innovation factory. *Harvard Business Review, 78*(3), 157–166.

Jensen, J. A., & White, D. W. (2018). Trends in sport sponsorship evaluation and measurement: Insights from the industry. *International Journal of Sports Marketing and Sponsorship, 19*(1), 2–10.

Khaund, S. (2020). Blockchain: From Fintech to the future of sport. In S. Schmidt (Ed.), *21st Century Sports – How Technologies Will Change Sports in The Digital Age*, 191–204. Springer.

Kunisch, S., Bartunek, J., Mueller, J., & Huy, Q. (2017). Time in strategic change research. *Academy of Management Annals, 11*(2), 1005–1064.

Martínez-Sanz, J. M., Sospedra, I., Ortiz, C. M., Baladía, E., Gil-Izquierdo, A., & Ortiz-Moncada, R. (2017). Intended or unintended doping? A review of the presence of doping substances in dietary supplements used in sports. *Nutrients*, *9*(10), 1093–1115.

McCullough, B. P., & Kellison, T. B. (2017) (Eds.) Routledge handbook of sport and the environments. Routledge.

Narayanan, A. (2016). *Bitcoin and cryptocurrency technologies*. Princeton University Press.

Naraine, M. L. (2019). The blockchain phenomenon: Conceptualizing decentralized networks and the value proposition to the sport industry. *International Journal of Sport Communication*, *12*(3), 313–335.

Newland, B. L., Aicher, T. J., Davies, M., & Hungenberg, E. (2021). Sport event ecotourism: sustainability of trail racing events in US National Parks. *Journal of Sport & Tourism*, *25*, 155–181.

Nowiński, W., & Kozma, M. (2017). How can blockchain technology disrupt the existing business models? *Entrepreneurial Business and Economics Review*, *5*(3), 173–188.

Rivest, R. L., Shamir, A., & Adleman, L. (1978). A method for obtaining digital signatures and public-key cryptosystems. *Communications of the ACM*, *21*(2), 120–126.

Salviotti, G., De Rossi, L. M., & Abbatemarco, N. (2018, January). *A structured framework to assess the business application landscape of blockchain technologies*. In Proceedings of the 51st Hawaii International Conference on System Sciences.

Truby, J. (2018). Decarbonizing Bitcoin: Law and policy choices for reducing the energy consumption of Blockchain technologies and digital currencies. *Energy research & social science*, *44*, 399–410.

United Nations. (2015, November). *The Paris Agreement*. United Nations, https://unfccc.int/process-and-meetings/conferences/past-conferences/paris-climate-change-conference-november-2015/paris-climate-change-conference-november-2015

24

Digitization of Sport Participation for Health

Ji Wu, Yuhei Inoue, and Mikihiro Sato

Introduction

Physical inactivity is a major challenge in public health and is recognized as a global epidemic (World Health Organization [WHO], 2020). Although physical inactivity itself is not a disease, people who are physically inactive face increased risks of experiencing various symptoms and illnesses, such as cardiovascular diseases, hypertension, depression, and diabetes (Rhodes et al., 2017), which can increase the overall cost of maintaining and improving health (Eime et al., 2013; WHO, 2020). To control healthcare costs and create a healthy population, policymakers must motivate as many people as possible to be physically active.

Regular participation in sport can improve the physical fitness and well-being of an individual (Rhodes et al., 2017; Sato et al., 2019). In addition, sport participation is increasingly found to have a positive association with various psychological benefits, including reducing anxiety and depression, enhancing subjective well-being, and improving quality of life (Andersen et al., 2019; Eime et al., 2013; WHO, 2020). Although the contribution of sport participation to health is well recognized, across the world the percentage of people participating in sport remains lower than that of people who are inactive. According to data from the Centers for Disease Control and Prevention (2019), 48.4% of American citizens did not meet the recommended level of sport participation. Elsewhere, the European Commission (2018) reported that 56% of European citizens did not participate in sport at least once per week. In addition, the percentage of active sport participants in developing countries is relatively lower than that in developed countries (WHO, 2020).

To address the issue, researchers have assessed the effects of various interventions on facilitating sport and physical activity participation (Chalip et al., 2017; Donnachie et al., 2017; Jenkin et al., 2017). Within this research, growing attention is given to the role of digitalization (Hayes, 2020; McDonough et al., 2021; Pizzo et al., 2020). People are experiencing dramatic changes with digital transformation, such as the internet, personal computer, and smartphone (Rachinger et al., 2019; Ströbel & Germelmann, 2020). The utilization of smartphones and associated health-related applications has the potential to improve individuals' sport participation and healthy living by providing functions to track and record sport participation, design personalized training plans, and receive diet and nutrition advice (Pizzo et al., 2020; Romeo et al., 2019). For instance, wearable devices produced by Myzone help members of fitness clubs sustain exercising in and outside clubs (Pizzo et al., 2020).

DOI: 10.4324/9781003088899-28

Fitness clubs can also track members' performance and provide constructive feedback based on live statistics uploaded on the online platform Myzone (Orangetheory Fitness, 2020).

Previous studies in sport management examined how digital technologies, such as social media, could elevate sport-related businesses through enhanced fan engagement, marketing, and branding, thus expanding the boundaries of sport management research (Glebova & Desbordes, 2021; Pizzo et al., 2020; Wakefield & Bennett, 2018). In relation to sport participation, Hayes (2020) argued that digitalization enables people to continue sport participation at any location while avoiding health risks caused by large gatherings, which has become crucial during the COVID-19 pandemic. In addition, there is preliminary evidence that digital tools such as smartphones, social media, and other electronics positively affect sport participation (Donnachie et al., 2017; Romeo et al., 2019; Turner-McGrievy et al., 2013). However, most prior research examined this influence by focusing on individuals' psychological and behavioral changes. Because specific sociocultural and physical environments influence people's decisions on whether and how to participate in sport (Aizawa et al., 2018; Giles-Corti & Donovan, 2002), it is important to develop a comprehensive understanding of the influence of digitalization on sport for health by considering social and environmental changes.

In this chapter, we apply a social-ecological model (SEM; McLeroy et al., 1988; Sallis et al., 2006; Stokols, 1992) to provide a framework for illustrating how people's participation in sport for health may be influenced by digital technological development. Although there are other frameworks and theories that can provide insights into the digitalization of sport participation (e.g., personality theory, health belief model, and self-determination theory; Bort-Roig et al., 2014; Sullivan & Lachman, 2017), SEM has merits because of its ability to outline multilevel factors (e.g., intrapersonal, interpersonal, institutional, community, and policy-related) associated with people's health behaviors such as sport participation (Sallis et al., 2006; Sato et al., 2016). Using the SEM, we seek to offer a comprehensive understanding of how progress in technological developments can change sport participation for healthy living.

This chapter is structured as follows. First, this chapter defines the concept of digitalization in sport contexts and provides a brief review of research on sport participation for health. Next, it discusses the main tenets of SEM and applies them to develop a conceptual framework for understanding the multilevel influence of digital technology on sport participation and health improvement. This chapter concludes with recommendations and implications for future research on the digitalization of sport for health.

Digitalization in Sport Contexts

To understand the effect of digitalization on sport for health, it is imperative to define the term *digitalization* and to differentiate it from *digitization*. *Digitization* is the process of converting analog data into digital datasets (Gobble, 2018), which is the fundamental framework for digitalization in society. In contrast, *digitalization* is defined as "the socio-technical process of applying digitizing techniques to broader social and institutional contexts that render digital technologies infrastructural" (Tilson et al., 2010, p. 749). Social, mobile, analytical, and cloud computing technologies entail the current digitalization movement that advances business and society (Rachinger et al., 2019). The application of those technologies is opening unforeseen opportunities in society and restructuring conventional ways of life (Gobble, 2018).

The sport industry has no exception to the trend of digitalization. With the popularity of social media, professional sport clubs can strengthen fan engagement, expand platforms for sponsorship, and manage their own brands more effectively and efficiently than ever before (O'Reilly et al., 2012; Ratten, 2020; Rote et al., 2015; Ströbel & Germelmann, 2020). In addition to the evolution in business activities, the utilization of digital technologies can bring new forms of sport participation (Kim & Ko, 2019; Pizzo et al., 2020). For instance, using wearable devices allows participants to better monitor their daily participation (Romeo et al., 2019). Access to the internet enables people to acquire personalized training information more easily (Patel & O'Kane, 2015; Pizzo et al., 2020), and VR devices could promote sport participation by simulating a real sport environment (Kim & Ko, 2019). These technical advancements, for example, led to the host of the first virtual Tour de France in July 2020, where all athletes participated in the event remotely through ZWIFT, an online cycling platform (Westmattelmann et al., 2020). With the support of additional equipment, ZWIFT virtually simulated the racing environment and cyclist interactions. Westmattelmann et al. (2020) reported that athletes' performances in virtual events resembled those in the real world.

Sport Participation and Health

According to the WHO (2020), *health* can be broadly defined as a collective state of maintaining physical, psychological, and social well-being. It is well-documented that sport participation has a positive association with people's health (Eime et al., 2013; Rhodes et al., 2017; Sato et al., 2017). Generally, the more people engage in sport, the more likely they are to enjoy healthy lifestyles. In assessing the association between sport participation and health enhancement, researchers defined the term "sport participation" differently because of the variations in specific scope and content that they selected for research (Andersen et al., 2019; Chalip et al., 2017). The European Sport Charter (1992) defined sport participation as participating in all forms of sport (i.e., casual or professional, team or individual) that contribute to physical fitness, subjective well-being, or social connections. Given its broad and inclusive scope, we employ the European Sports Charter's (1992) definition of sport participation to explain technologies' influence on the relationship between sport participation and health.

Besides improving physical health, researchers have documented the effect of sport participation on enhancing people's psychological and social health (e.g., Andersen et al., 2019; Eime et al., 2013; Hindley, 2020). Participating in sport is a popular choice of leisure among people of all ages, which results in many positive psychological states, such as enjoyment, competence, and self-esteem, contributing to one's well-being (Andersen et al., 2019; Eime et al., 2013). The more people are connected to running or walking as a leisure activity, the more they will positively evaluate their life because of the enjoyment and satisfaction gained from the activity (Sato et al., 2017). Sport participation also provides a setting for social interactions: As people participate in sport, especially team sport and events, they interact with others more frequently, which enhances perceptions of camaraderie and a sense of belonging (Filo & Coghlan, 2016; Hindley, 2020), contributing to social well-being. Notably, scholars found that participation in charity sport events elevated participants' social well-being by not only facilitating direct interactions with each other but also promoting beliefs that their engagement in charity sport events is helping people who are in need (Filo & Coghlan, 2016; Filo et al., 2020). These findings reveal a unique social outcome within sport. Overall, the positive psychological and social outcomes of sport participation, along with its physical benefits, can contribute to a person's overall health conditions.

A Social-Ecological Framework for Digitalization in Sport for Health

Social-Ecological Model

We apply SEM (McLeroy et al., 1988; Sallis et al., 2006) to illustrate how technological development facilitates sport participation at multiple levels which, in turn, contributes to health enhancement. Stokols (1992) argued that SEM is "a general framework for understanding the nature of people's transaction with their physical and sociocultural surroundings" (p. 7). In explaining health behaviors, a central proposition of SEM is that health behaviors emerge as a result of interactions between people and the environments in which they live (Stokols, 1992). This proposition advances conventional frameworks in behavioral science (which explain health behavior explicitly through personal characteristics; McLeroy et al., 1988) by including multiple influences from physical and sociocultural surroundings (Stokols, 1992). SEM integrates characteristics of built environments (e.g., access to sport facilities), community (e.g., social support), policy changes, and the impact of weather and climate in explaining people's choice of sport participation (Aizawa et al., 2018; Chalip et al., 2017; Sato et al., 2016).

Based on SEM, scholars have developed derivative models and frameworks to explain phenomena in a wide range of disciplines, including sociology, public health, and physical education. Notably, McLeroy et al. (1988) proposed a five-level SEM for health promotion: (1) intrapersonal factors, (2) interpersonal processes or primary social networks, (3) institutional factors, (4) community factors, and (5) public policy. The key premise of previous SEM frameworks is that there is not only the existence of multiple levels of influence but also the interplay and reinforcement among those levels (McLeroy et al., 1988; Stokols, 1992). In the remainder of this section, we assess the influence of digital technology development on sport participation for health at each of the five levels identified by McLeroy et al. (1988), as shown in Figure 24.1. The figure is adapted from previous SEM of technology and health promotion (Kolff et al., 2018; Prosperi et al., 2018).

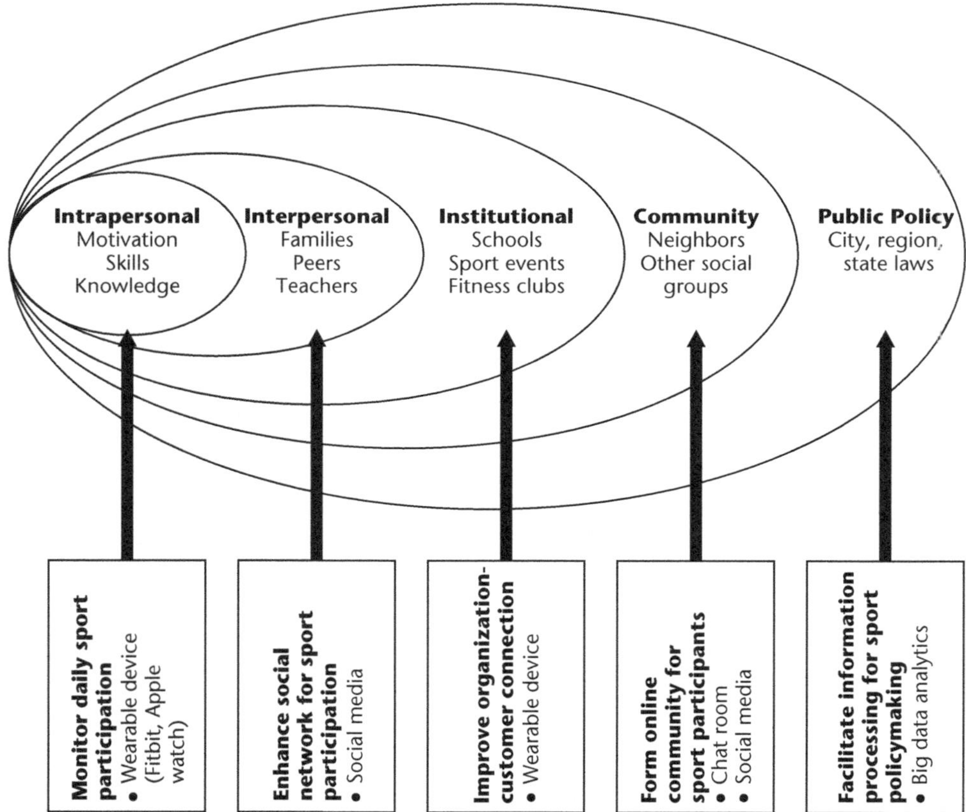

Figure 24.1 A Social-Ecological Model for Digitalization in Sport Participation for Health. The model is adapted from Kolff et al. (2018) and Prosperi et al.'s (2018)

Intrapersonal Level

Factors at the intrapersonal level that influence an individual's sport participation focus on changing the person's internal characteristics, such as knowledge, skills, motives, and intentions, to comply with behavioral norms (McLeroy et al., 1988). Theories that explain behavioral changes at this level are mainly adopted from psychology, which includes self-determination theory, the theory of planned behavior, and social learning theory (Sullivan & Lachman, 2017). Scholars found that self-monitoring and goal-oriented planning are effective in improving one's motivation by tracking achievement through daily sport participation (Donnachie et al., 2017). In the past, the self-monitoring approach was applied mainly by having people keep a paper-based diary and use this resource to maintain a regular schedule for sport participation (Turner-McGrievy et al., 2013). However, such a conventional approach may result in many issues, such as recall error or overestimation, reducing the precision of estimating levels of sport participation and increasing the likelihood of misclassification (Turner-McGrievy et al., 2013).

The use of smartphones and associated wearable devices, such as Fitbits and Apple Watches, can provide real-time monitoring, send reminders for participation, and collect performance data automatically, which alleviates the conventional issues of self-monitoring in sport participation (Bort-Roig et al., 2014; Romeo et al., 2019). According to GSMA Intelligence's 2019 annual report, more than 3.5 billion people, covering 47% of the global population, connect to the internet through smartphones. This high internet coverage presents unique opportunities to improve sport participation with technology at the intrapersonal level.

Several systematic literature reviews indicate that smartphone use helps people monitor their sport participation in a variety of ways (Bort-Roig et al., 2014; Donnachie et al., 2017; Romeo et al., 2019). It can automatically count paces, monitor heart rates, and calculate calorie consumption when users participate in sport, such as running and cycling (Bort-Roig et al., 2014). Smartphones provide more accurate, objective, and timely information regarding sport participation than conventional paper-based diaries, thus overcoming the recognized limitations of the latter (Donnachie et al., 2017; Romeo et al., 2019). For example, Donnachie et al. (2017) implemented a 12-week program that assigned physically inactive participants to monitor their sport participation using smartphones. The results of their follow-up assessment revealed that most program participants continued monitoring their sport participation with smartphones after the interventions, which indicates an increase in autonomous motivation (Donnachie et al., 2017).

Furthermore, with the development of VR technologies and video gaming, spaces and facilities are no longer constraints to sport participation (García-Bravo et al., 2019; Neumann et al., 2018; Segura-Ortí & García-Testal, 2019). People can engage in any form of sport by utilizing VR equipment anytime at home (García-Bravo et al., 2019). According to meta-analyses (García-Bravo et al., 2019; Segura-Ortí & García-Testal, 2019), the usage of VR-based sport activities has a large effect on promoting sport participation. For example, Peloton, a digital at-home exercise platform provider, reported that the number of its paid digital subscribers doubled from 2019 to 2020, exceeding one million by the end of 2020 (Peloton, 2021). During the same period, the average number of monthly workouts completed by each subscriber increased from 11.7 to 21.1 (Peloton, 2021). The home fitness solution has emerged as a way to negotiate intrapersonal constraints, such as stress, anxiety, and depression, during the COVID-19 pandemic (Du et al., 2020). Furthermore, at-home exercise providers (e.g., Peloton) have shown the effectiveness of VR technologies in attracting novice sport participants with interactive virtual workouts and access to all live and on-demand classes that make exercise interesting.

Interpersonal Level

As shown in Figure 24.1, factors at the interpersonal level entail influences that come from an individual's formal or informal social networks, such as family members, friends, and teachers (McLeroy et al., 1988). The social network determines the quantity and quality of social support, which refers to "aid and assistance exchanged through social relationships" (Glanz et al., 2008, p. 191). In the sport domain, an individual's perception of social support has been found to influence the frequency, intensity, and continuity of sport participation (Glanz et al., 2008; Shimoga et al., 2019).

The process of digitalization influences interpersonal-level factors by diversifying ways of social interactions and expanding an individual's social network. Such changes are mainly achieved by the popularity of social media (O'Reilly et al., 2012; Rote et al., 2015). According to the Digital 2020 Global Overview (We Are Social, 2020), 2.89 billion people have obtained an active account for social media, covering 39% of the global population. The utilization of social media easily connects two individuals who are far from each other or who would otherwise be unable to know each other (O'Reilly et al., 2012). It significantly reduces the cost that people incur when expanding their social networks (Shimoga et al., 2019; Zhang et al., 2015). Today, social media is becoming more personalized through online socializing platforms (e.g., Facebook, Twitter, Instagram, etc.), which enhance social support for sport participation (O'Reilly et al., 2012; Rote et al., 2015; Zhang et al., 2015). Scholars argue that people acquire social support and a sense of competence online by sharing daily performances and interacting with others who express passions for the same sport through social media (O'Reilly et al., 2012; Zhang et al., 2015). The perceived social support and competence then motivate the continuity.

There is also a handful of research demonstrating the role of social media in increasing sport participation (Rote et al., 2015; Shimoga et al., 2019; Zhang et al., 2015). For example, based on a 13-week experiment, Zhang et al. (2015) found that individuals who shared their own sport participation and obtained information about their peers' levels of daily sport participation through social media tended to participate in sport regularly and express improvements in the intensity of participation. Similarly, Rote et al. (2015) showed that posting daily sport participation and interacting with others through Facebook groups significantly promoted users' levels of engagement in sport. These findings indicate the impact of social media, as an intervention, on facilitating people's sport participation at the interpersonal level of influence (see Figure 24.1).

Institutional Level

Figure 24.1 shows that the third level of environmental influences within SEM focuses on organizational attributes that can influence health-related behaviors (McLeroy et al., 1988). Organizations are important settings that have substantial impacts on people's behavioral changes because more than one-third of an individual's life occurs in organizational settings, including schools, companies, and churches (McLeroy et al., 1988). In the sport domain, sport organizations, such as leagues, teams, event entities, and fitness clubs (Chalip, 2006), are regarded as contexts or agents that promote sport participation for healthy lifestyles (Aizawa et al., 2018; Brown & Fry, 2014; Pizzo et al., 2020). For instance, fitness or sport clubs can facilitate sport participation by providing professional training services, quality facilities and equipment, and ancillary activities (Brown & Fry, 2014; Hayes, 2020; Pizzo et al., 2020).

Generally, an individual obtains membership in a sport or fitness club for professional training and access to facilities that support their sport participation (Brown & Fry, 2014; Gjestvang et al., 2019; Pizzo et al., 2020). The improvement in physical health requires members' constant participation (Gjestvang et al., 2019). However, members may not be able to sustain their participation in a club because of environmental barriers, such as weather, work, family, commitments, and other options for entertainment (Brown & Fry, 2014; Gjestvang et al., 2019). This issue, which troubles both clubs and members, may be solved by integrating wearable devices into a sport club environment (Patel & O'Kane, 2015; Pizzo et al., 2020). Given that a wearable device is inherently mobile and unrestricted in where it can be used (Patel & O'Kane, 2015), club members can use the device to support their training both within and outside the clubs. As a result, members are no longer constrained by the physical club space for participation. The integration of wearable devices into sport or fitness clubs' businesses is increasing because of the popularity of wearable devices globally (MarketWatch, 2018). With this increasing adoption and utilization of wearable devices, members of sport or fitness clubs are more flexible regarding their sport participation and have less pressure to go to clubs for exercising (Pizzo et al., 2020). Furthermore, the application of wearable devices constantly tracks a member's sport performance even when the member participates in sport outside the club, providing club trainers with objective personal information, such as heart rates, blood pressure, and body fat percentage. Club trainers can provide feedback based on timely information and create long-term personalized training plans. As such, wearable devices influence not only how members participate in sport, but also how they interact with clubs (Pizzo et al., 2020; Patel & O'Kane, 2015).

The application of digital technologies was reported to be useful for sport organizations when promoting sport participation amidst the COVID-19 pandemic (Hayes, 2020). During the pandemic, people avoided going to crowded or confined places because of concerns over health risks (WHO, 2020). Consequently, participating in sport at home has become a new normal situation for many sport participants (Constandt et al., 2020). Without face-to-face interactions, promoting sport participation remotely through social media or other mediums became an alternative for sport organizations (Hayes, 2020). As Pizzo et al. (2020) argue, wearable devices sustain members' exercise goals without physically visiting fitness clubs. Club trainers could constantly monitor their members' performances at home with objective information measured by the device. Trainers can also send their customers reminders for exercising, training instructions, and encouragement through the device (Constandt et al., 2020; Hayes, 2020).

Community Level

Historically, the term *community* is defined as "a social network of interacting individuals, usually concentrated in a defined territory" (Johnston et al., 1995, p. 1444). The concept of community has then been endowed with psychological attributes where members of the same community share common sense and values (Stevens et al., 2018). In this regard, three features are inherent to a community: geographic location, people for interaction, and group identity. Within SEM (see Figure 24.1), these three features are associated with community-level factors that influence sport participation for health (McLeroy et al., 1988). The availability of – and accessibility to – sport facilities in a certain geographic location (e.g., neighborhood, city, county) impacts community members' levels of sport participation (Aizawa et al., 2018; Chalip et al., 2017; Eime et al., 2017). Sato et al. (2019) reported that communities with better access to parks and recreational facilities had a higher county-level physical activity rate among older adults, which could reduce these adults' health costs in that county. In addition, if a community emphasizes the importance of maintaining health through sport, its members tend to be more active in sport participation through their identification with the community (Baker & Ward, 2002; Stevens et al., 2018).

Technological developments advance community-level interventions by changing the conventional boundaries of a community. For example, widespread access to the internet provides people with opportunities to easily interact with others who are far away or groups of people who share a similar interest through social media, such as Facebook, Twitter, or online chat rooms (O'Reilly et al., 2012). These online spaces are a conduit for social interactions and establish digitalized versions of a community; thus, the definition of the community no longer relies on a common geographical location (Baker & Ward, 2002; Ridings & Gefen, 2004). Instead, a digitalized community is categorized by a commonality of interest, commitment, and involvement in products, services, issues, or lifestyles (Fukuoka et al., 2011; Ridings & Gefen, 2004). This expansion of social interaction capabilities may be particularly important for inactive or new sport participants who lack initial motivations and knowledge that support participation (Elloumi et al., 2018; Fukuoka et al., 2011; Toscos et al., 2011). Through a digitalized community, new sport participants can find a group of peers and create a social network that can support their sport participation mutually (Elloumi et al., 2018; O'Reilly et al., 2012). Advanced participants can also join a digitalized community that provides immediate feedback, serves as a setting for sharing their experiences, and promotes sport participation (Toscos et al., 2011). The nature of anonymity in a digitalized community further allows people to feel more comfortable sharing their experiences or competing with others, compared to a conventional community with face-to-face interactions (Fukuoka et al., 2011; O'Reilly et al., 2012). According to Fukuoka et al. (2011), a digitalized community represents a relatively closed system. It is more effective than the social network in promoting members' levels of sport participation based on the formation of group identification. Moreover, Elloumi et al. (2018) and Toscos et al. (2011) argued that leadership actions inside a digitalized community, such as identifying and setting group goals, also promote sport participation.

Public-Policy Level

According to SEM (see Figure 23.1), factors at the public-policy level represent the set of regulatory laws and policies that aim to promote sport participation for public health (McLeroy et al., 1988). Unlike the other four levels that emphasize specific individuals, public policy is usually formed and delivered through a relatively overarching guide or direction to the population at a macro level (Höchtl et al., 2016; McLeroy et al., 1988; Nachmias & Felbinger, 1982). Hence, the formation and implementation of a policy are rather complex and need to go through several stages which, together, are constructed as a "policy cycle" (Nachmias & Felbinger, 1982). Within the policy cycle, data and information serve as imperative sources of legitimacy for policymaking (Höchtl et al., 2016). The more reliable available information is, the higher the quality of policy will be. However, information is not always automatically translated into quality policies (Höchtl et al., 2016; Keller & Staelin, 1987). According to Keller and Staelin (1987), too much information would increase the workload of filters, and "chaos" generated when screening information could decrease the effectiveness of formulating proper policies.

Today, the issue of information processing is even more complicated due to the popularity of social media (Höchtl et al., 2016). The application of big data analytics (BDA) tools, such as supervised machine learning and visual analytics (Gutenberg et al., 2018), may make it possible for policymaking to process large and heterogeneous information (Höchtl et al., 2016; Saunders et al., 2020). BDA represents computation techniques that are used to deal with the unprecedented volume, variety, and velocity of datasets (Gutenberg et al., 2018). It is effective in dealing with enormous information by automatically learning rules from data, recognizing exclusions and combinations for predictions, and revealing patterns and trends (Gutenberg et al., 2018; Saunders et al., 2020). Policymakers can use BDA to monitor information that is available, such as suggestions from experts and posts on social media platforms. For example, the Commonwealth Advisory Body of Sport (CABOS; 2019) relied on BDA to develop a set of coherent indicators which improved the consistency and quality of information collected from its member countries. This improvement greatly supports CABOS to obtain a clear understanding of both sport and non-sport-related situations (e.g., health, economy, education) of each stakeholder involved, which then strengthened communications and collaborations with the stakeholders in its sport and physical education development plan. Specific support toward CABOS's overall sport development plan was provided to commonwealth countries based on analytic results of broader ministries, including education, health, socioeconomics, culture, and customs. Such efforts led to fostering the formation of a coherent sport policy that contributes to the overall sustainable development goals among commonwealth countries. Based on this initial achievement, the CABOS now aims to develop a follow-up sport policy framework that facilitates international sport policy convergence and cooperation, such as the Kazan Action Plan created by the United Nations' Educational, Scientific and Cultural Organization.

Multilevel Interactions

Within the perspective of SEM (McLeroy et al., 1988), besides the impacts of digital technologies on sport participation at each level, technological interventions may also exert influences across multiple levels (Kolff et al., 2018). For example, based on the examples discussed in this chapter, the application of wearable devices and smartphone apps not only facilitates an individual's sport participation directly but also elevates sport organizations' services for sport participation. To optimize the effects of those electronic tools on promoting sport participation, it is imperative for developers to consider combined functions between the individual and institutional levels. Furthermore, according to Pizzo et al. (2020), a fitness club may compile members' data when they come into a club and post member training scores on a screen that can be seen by all members. This indicates the potential of creating a training community as facilitated by a club. Similarly, members may use mobile devices and apps, such as Myzone and Strava, to share their workout progress with family and friends via social media (intrapersonal level). Moreover, governments could rely on BDA to monitor and analyze objective data tracked and posted online by those electronic tools that support future policies.

Implications for Future Research

Within the perspective of SEM, recognizing how people interact with their families, friends, neighborhoods, schools, or workplaces may significantly ease the complexities of physical and social environments that influence people's attitudes and behavior through digital technology. Digitalization directly promotes sport participation with functions that enhance participation experiences, such as tracking and monitoring each participation or simulating supportive environments (Donnachie et al., 2017; Romeo et al., 2019). It also indirectly influences sport participation by offering access to social networks and support as well as necessary training information (Elloumi et al., 2018; Fukuoka et al., 2011). Overall, digitalization is a catalyst that motivates and sustains sport participation, which not only contributes to physical health but also reinforces psychological and social health (Andersen et al., 2019; Donnachie et al., 2017).

At the current stage of digitalization, the internet has been recognized as a foundation that supports sport participation for health improvement. The use of smartphones and associated devices to monitor daily sport participation, the extension of social networks through social media, and the formation of online communities are not sustainable without the internet. Notably, when connecting to the internet, it is inevitable that some private information, such as current locations, photographs, and personal profiles, may become accessible to others (Bertot et al., 2012; Weber, 2010). This concern increases attention on issues of information security. Significant concerns regarding information security diminish people's intentions to adopt technological tools, such as wearables devices or social media (Bertot et al., 2012), which may increase resistance to technology application for sport participation. Future research investigating the role of digital technology in promoting sport participation should consider the potential impact of information security.

While this chapter focused on active sport participation, researchers have also uncovered the positive effect of sport spectatorship (e.g., attending games) on psychological health (Inoue et al., 2015; Inoue et al., 2020). Additionally, spectating live sport events may have the potential to stimulate people's sport participation, improving health in the long run (Aizawa et al., 2018). Existing research on how technology changes sport spectatorship for health is seldom conducted at institutional, community, and policy levels (Inoue et al., 2015), which represent primary units of analysis in sport management (Chalip, 2006). Further research should provide a roadmap for sport managers from both public and private sectors, regarding how their organizations can use digital technologies to create economic benefits and simultaneously improve health conditions in communities (Wu et al., 2020).

Furthermore, digitalization facilitates the development of esports as an emerging field for sport management research (Hallmann & Giel, 2018; Jenny et al., 2017). While many scholars, elite athletes, and the International Olympic Committee are wary of discussions surrounding esports (Hallmann & Giel, 2018; Jenny et al., 2017), some trends reveal the acceptance of esports as a form of sport in the future. For example, esports was featured as a demonstration sport in the 2018 Asian Games and will be a medal event in the 2022 Asian Games (eSports Insider, 2021). These trends may leave the public with an impression that esports is a part of sport. However, esports differs from conventional sport because playing esports may limit people's level of physical activity (Trotter et al., 2020; Wattanapisit et al., 2020). Although elite esports players on average have sufficient health conditions, no evidence supports the association between playing esports and health improvements (Trotter et al., 2020; Wattanapisit et al., 2020). For amateurs, playing esports for more than six to eight hours per day can result in a dramatic decrease in physical movement, which is harmful to physical health (Wattanapisit et al., 2020). There has been a debate about whether esports may cause serious health issues among the next generation, the majority of whom identified themselves as gamers worldwide (Trotter et al., 2020). Future research is necessary to understand the impact of esports on people's health conditions. Then, efforts can commence toward positive cooperation to strengthen a relationship between participation in esports and health enhancement.

Conclusions

Based on the SEM, this chapter has provided a framework for understanding the influence of the application of digital technology on the association between sport participation and health promotion at the intrapersonal, interpersonal, institutional, community, and public-policy levels. When considering employing any of the technological interventions, sport policy makers and sport managers who seek to improve sport participation are encouraged to adopt a multilevel perspective to evaluate factors that may influence expected outcomes and address any potential barriers and negative impacts. As evidence grows to support various targeted approaches, efforts that combine interventions across different levels of SEM during implementation and expansion may increase the potential to motivate and sustain sport participation and, in turn, help maintain healthy lifestyles across the populations.

References

Aizawa, K., Wu, J., Inoue, Y., & Sato, M. (2018). Long-term impact of the Tokyo 1964 Olympic Games on sport participation: A cohort analysis. *Sport Management Review, 21*(1), 86–97. 10.1016/j.smr.2017.05.001

Andersen, M. H., Ottesen, L., & Thing, L. F. (2019). The social and psychological health outcomes of team sport participation in adults: An integrative review of research. *Scandinavian Journal of Public Health, 47*(8), 832–850. 10.1177/1403494818791405

Baker, P. M. A., & Ward, A. C. (2002). Bridging temporal and spatial 'gaps': The role of information and communication technologies in defining communities. *Information, Communication & Society, 5*(2), 207–224. 10.1080/13691180210130789

Bertot, J. C., Jaeger, P. T., & Hansen, D. (2012). The impact of polices on government social media usage: Issues, challenges, and recommendations. *Government Information Quarterly, 29*(1), 30–40. 10.1016/j.giq.2011.04.004

Bort-Roig, J., Gilson, N. D., Puig-Ribera, A., Contreras, R. S., & Trost, S. G. (2014). Measuring and influencing physical activity with smartphone technology: A systematic review. *Sports Medicine, 44*(5), 671–686. 10.1007/s40279-014-0142-5

Brown, T. C., & Fry, M. D. (2014). Motivational climate, staff and members' behaviors, and members' psychological well-being at a national fitness franchise. *Research Quarterly for Exercise and Sport, 85*(2), 208–217. 10.1080/02701367.2014.893385

Centers for Disease Control and Prevention. (2019). *Physical activity guidelines for Americans.* https://health.gov/sites/default/files/2019-09/Physical_Activity_Guidelines_2nd_edition.pdf#page=56

Chalip, L. (2006). Toward a distinctive sport management discipline. *Journal of Sport Management, 20*(1), 1–21. 10.1123/jsm.20.1.1

Chalip, L., Green, B. C., Taks, M., & Misener, L. (2017). Creating sport participation from sport events: Making it happen. *International Journal of Sport Policy and Politics, 9*(2), 257–276. 10.1080/19406940.2016.1257496

Commonwealth Advisory Body on Sport. (2016). *Policy guidance to commonwealth governments on protecting the integrity of sport.* https://thecommonwealth.org/sites/default/files/inline/Policy%20Guidance%20to%20Commonwealth%20Governments%20on%20Protecting%20the%20Integrity%20of%20Sport%202016.pdf

Constandt, B., Thibaut, E., De Bosscher, V., Scheerder, J., Ricour, M., & Willem, A. (2020). Exercising in times of lockdown: An analysis of the impact of COVID-19 on levels and patterns of exercise among adults in Belgium. *International Journal of Environmental Research and Public Health, 17*(11), 41–44. 10.3390/ijerph17114144

Council of Europe. (1992). *European Sport Charter.* https://rm.coe.int/16804c9dbb

Donnachie, C., Wyke, S., Mutrie, N., & Hunt, K. (2017). 'It's like a personal motivator that you carried around wi' you': Utilising self-determination theory to understand men's experiences of using pedometers to increase physical activity in a weight management programme. *International Journal of Behavioral Nutrition and Physical Activity, 14*(1), 61–74. 10.1186/s12966-017-0505-z

Du, J., Floyd, C., Kim, A. C. H., Baker, B. J., Sato, M., James, J. D., & Funk, D. C. (2020). To be or not to be: Negotiating leisure constraints with technology and data analytics amid the COVID-19 pandemic. *Leisure Studies, 40*(4), 561–574 10.1080/02614367.2020.1862284

Eime, R. M., Harvey, J., Charity, M. J., Casey, M., Westerbeek, H., & Payne, W. R. (2017). The relationship of sport participation to provision of sports facilities and socioeconomic status: A geographical analysis. *Australian and New Zealand Journal of Public Health, 41*(3), 248–255. 10.1111/1753-6405.12647

Eime, R. M., Young, J. A., Harvey, J. T., Charity, M. J., & Payne, W. R. (2013). A systematic review of the psychological and social benefits of participation in sport for adults: Informing development of a conceptual model of health through sport. *International Journal of Behavioral Nutrition and Physical Activity, 10*(1), 135–152. 10.1186/1479-5868-10-135

Elloumi, L., van Beijnum, B. J., & Hermens, H. (2018). Exploratory study of a virtual community for physical activity. *Health and Technology, 8*(1), 81–95. 10.1007/s12553-018-0221-y

eSports Insider. (2021). *OCA and AESF agree partnership for 2022 Asian Games.* http://esportsinsider.com/2021/03/oca-and-aesf-agree-partnership-for-2022-asian-games

European Commission. (2018). *New Eurobarometer on sport and physical activity.* https://ec.europa.eu/sport/news/2018/new-eurobarometer-sport-and-physical-activity_en

Filo, K., Fechner, D., & Inoue, Y. (2020). Charity sport event participants and fundraising: An examination of constraints and negotiation strategies. *Sport Management Review, 23*(3), 387–400. 10.1016/j.smr.2019.02.005

Fukuoka, Y., Kamitani, E., Bonnet, K., & Lindgren, T. (2011). Real-time social support through a mobile virtual community to improve healthy behavior in overweight and sedentary adults: A focus group analysis. *Journal of Medical Internet Research, 13*(3), e49. 10.2196/jmir.1770

García-Bravo, S., Cuesta-Gómez, A., Campuzano-Ruiz, R., López-Navas, M. J., Domínguez-Paniagua, J., Araújo-Narváez, A., … & Cano-de-la-Cuerda, R. (2019). Virtual reality and video games in cardiac rehabilitation programs. A systematic review. *Disability and Rehabilitation, 2*(5), 1–10. 10.1080/09638288.2019.1631892

Giles-Corti, B., & Donovan, R. J. (2002). The relative influence of individual, social and physical environment determinants of physical activity. *Social Science & Medicine, 54*(12), 1793–1812. 10.1016/S0277-9536(01)00150-2

Gjestvang, C., Stensrud, T., & Haakstad, L. A. H. (2019). Are changes in physical fitness, body composition and weight associated with exercise attendance and dropout among fitness club members? Longitudinal prospective study. *BMJ Open, 9*(4), e027987. 10.1136/bmjopen-2018-027987

Glanz, K., Rimer, B. K., & Viswanath, K. (2008). *Health behavior and health education: Theory, research, and practice.* John Wiley & Sons.

Glebova, E., & Desbordes, M. (2021). Identifying the role of digital technologies in sport spectators customer experiences through qualitative approach. *Athens Journal of Sports, 8*, 1–19.

Gobble, M. M. (2018). Digitalization, digitization, and innovation. *Research-Technology Management, 61*(4), 56–59. 10.1080/08956308.2018.1471280

GSMA. (2019). *The mobile economy 2019.* https://data.gsmaintelligence.com/api-web/v2/research-file-download?id=39256194&file=2712-250219-ME-Global.pdf

Gutenberg, J., Katrakazas, P., Trenkova, L., Murdin, L., Brdarić, D., Koloutsou, N., … & Laplante-Lévesque, A. (2018). Big data for sound policies: Toward evidence-informed hearing health policies. *American Journal of Audiology, 27*(3S), 493–502. 10.1044/2018_AJA-IMIA3-18-0003

Hallmann, K., & Giel, T. (2018). Esports – Competitive sports or recreational activity? *Sport Management Review, 21*(1), 14–20. 10.1016/j.smr.2017.07.011

Hayes, M. (2020). Social media and inspiring physical activity during COVID-19 and beyond. *Managing Sport and Leisure, 0*(0), 1–8. 10.1080/23750472.2020.1794939

Hindley, D. (2020). "More than just a run in the park": An exploration of parkrun as a shared leisure space. *Leisure Sciences, 42*(1), 85–105. 10.1080/01490400.2017.1410741

Höchtl, J., Parycek, P., & Schöllhammer, R. (2016). Big data in the policy cycle: Policy decision making in the digital era. *Journal of Organizational Computing and Electronic Commerce, 26*(1–2), 147–169. 10.1080/10919392.2015.1125187

Inoue, Y., Berg, B. K., & Chelladurai, P. (2015). Spectator sport and population health: A scoping study. *Journal of Sport Management, 29*(6), 705–725. 10.1123/JSM.2014-0283

Inoue, Y., Wann, D. L., Lock, D., Sato, M., Moore, C., & Funk, D. C. (2020). Enhancing older adults' sense of belonging and subjective well-being through sport game attendance, team identification, and emotional support. *Journal of Aging and Health, 32*(7–8), 530–542. 10.1177/0898264319835654

Jenkin, C. R., Eime, R. M., Westerbeek, H., O'Sullivan, G., & van Uffelen, J. G. Z. (2017). Sport and ageing: A systematic review of the determinants and trends of participation in sport for older adults. *BMC Public Health, 17*(1), 976–995. 10.1186/s12889-017-4970-8

Jenny, S. E., Manning, R. D., Keiper, M. C., & Olrich, T. W. (2017). Virtual(ly) athletes: Where eSports fit within the definition of "sport." *Quest, 69*(1), 1–18. 10.1080/00336297.2016.1144517

Johnston, S. L., Pattemore, P. K., Sanderson, G., Smith, S., Lampe, F., Josephs, L., ... & Holgate, S. T. (1995). Community study of role of viral infections in exacerbations of asthma in 9-11 year old children. *BMJ, 310*(6989), 1225–1229. 10.1136/bmj.310.6989.1225

Keller, K. L., & Staelin, R. (1987). Effects of quality and quantity of information on decision effectiveness. *Journal of Consumer Research, 14*(2), 200–213. 10.1086/209106

Kim, D., & Ko, Y. J. (2019). The impact of virtual reality (VR) technology on sport spectators' flow experience and satisfaction. *Computers in Human Behavior, 93*, 346–356. 10.1016/j.chb.2018.12.040

Kolff, C. A., Scott, V. P., & Stockwell, M. S. (2018). The use of technology to promote vaccination: A social ecological model based framework. *Human Vaccines & Immunotherapeutics, 14*(7), 1636–1646. 10.1080/21645515.2018.1477458

MarketWatch. (2018). *Wearable devices market to reach US $51 billion by 2022.* https://www.marketwatch.com/press-release/wearable-devices-market-to-reach-us-51-billion-by-2022-2018-06–13

Mayer-Schönberger, V., & Cukier, K. (2013). *Big data: A revolution that will transform how we live, work, and think.* Houghton Mifflin Harcourt.

McDonough, D. J., Su, X., & Gao, Z. (2021). Health wearable devices for weight and BMI reduction in individuals with overweight/obesity and chronic comorbidities: Systematic review and network meta-analysis. *British journal of sports medicine, 0*, 1–11. 10.1136/bjsports-2020-103594

McLeroy, K. R., Bibeau, D., Steckler, A., & Glanz, K. (1988). An ecological perspective on health promotion programs. *Health Education Quarterly, 15*(4), 351–377. 10.1177/109019818801500401

Nachmias, D., & Felbinger, C. (1982). Utilization in the policy cycle: Directions for research. *Review of Policy Research, 2*(2), 300–308. 10.1111/j.1541-1338.1982.tb00676.x

Neumann, D. L., Moffitt, R. L., Thomas, P. R., Loveday, K., Watling, D. P., Lombard, C. L., ... & Tremeer, M. A. (2018). A systematic review of the application of interactive virtual reality to sport. *Virtual Reality, 22*(3), 183–198. https://doi-org.ezp3.lib.umn.edu/10.1007/s10055-017-0320-5

O'Reilly, N., Berger, I. E., Hernandez, T., Parent, M. M., & Seguin, B. (2012). Understanding adolescent sport participation through online social media. *Sport, Business and Management: An International Journal, 2*(1), 69–81. 10.1108/20426781211207674

Orangetheory Fitness. (2020). *Tracking your heart rate.* https://www.orangetheoryfitness.com/technology

Patel, M., & O'Kane, A. A. (2015). Contextual influences on the use and non-use of digital technology while exercising at the gym. In *Proceedings of the 33rd annual acm conference on human factors in computing systems* (pp. 2923–2932). NY: ACM.

Peloton. (2021). *Peloton 2020 annual report.* https://investor.onepeloton.com/static-files/9595d9d3–9e56-40fe-bbce-07176ae274d6

Pizzo, A. D., Baker, B. J., Jones, G. J., & Funk, D. C. (2020). Sport experience design: Wearable fitness technology in the health and fitness industry. *Journal of Sport Management, 35*(2), 130–143. 10.1123/jsm.2020-0150

Prosperi, M., Min, J., Bian, J., & Modave, F. (2018). Big data hurdles in precision medicine and precision public health. *BMC Medical Informatics and Decision Making, 18*, 139. 10.1186/s12911-018-0719-2

Rachinger, M., Rauter, R., Müller, C., Vorraber, W., & Schirgi, E. (2019). Digitalization and its influence on business model innovation. *Journal of Manufacturing Technology Management, 30*(8), 1143–1160. 10.1108/JMTM-01-2018-0020

Ratten, V. (2020). Sport technology: A commentary. *The Journal of High Technology Management Research, 31*(1), 1–6. 10.1016/j.hitech.2020.100383

Rhodes, R. E., Janssen, I., Bredin, S. S. D., Warburton, D. E. R., & Bauman, A. (2017). Physical activity: Health impact, prevalence, correlates and interventions. *Psychology & Health, 32*(8), 942–975. 10.1080/08870446.2017.1325486

Ridings, C. M., & Gefen, D. (2004). Virtual community attraction: Why people hang out online. *Journal of Computer-Mediated Communication, 10*(1). 23–36 10.1111/j.1083-6101.2004.tb00229.x

Romeo, A., Edney, S., Plotnikoff, R., Curtis, R., Ryan, J., Sanders, I., ... & Maher, C. (2019). Can smartphone apps increase physical activity? Systematic review and meta-analysis. *Journal of Medical Internet Research, 21*(3), e12053. 10.2196/12053

Rote, A. E., Klos, L. A., Brondino, M. J., Harley, A. E., & Swartz, A. M. (2015). The efficacy of a walking intervention using social media to increase physical activity: A randomized trial. *Journal of Physical Activity and Health, 12*(s1), 18–25. 10.1123/jpah.2014-0279

Sato, M., Du, J., & Inoue, Y. (2016). Rate of physical activity and community health: Evidence from U.S. counties. *Journal of Physical Activity and Health*, *13*(6), 640–648. 10.1123/jpah.2015-0399

Sato, M., Inoue, Y., Du, J., & Funk, D. C. (2019). Access to parks and recreational facilities, physical activity, and health care costs for older adults: Evidence from US counties. *Journal of Leisure Research*, *50*(3), 220–238. 10.1080/00222216.2019.1583048

Sato, M., Yoshida, M., Wakayoshi, K., & Shonk, D. J. (2017). Event satisfaction, leisure involvement and life satisfaction at a walking event: The mediating role of life domain satisfaction. *Leisure Studies*, *36*(5), 605–617. 10.1080/02614367.2016.1240221

Saunders, G. H., Christensen, J. H., Gutenberg, J., Pontoppidan, N. H., Smith, A., Spanoudakis, G., & Bamiou, D. E. (2020). Application of big data to support evidence-based public health policy decision-making for hearing. *Ear and Hearing*, *41*(5), 1057–1063. 10.1097/AUD.0000000000000850

Segura-Ortí, E., & García-Testal, A. (2019). Intradialytic virtual reality exercise: Increasing physical activity through technology. *Seminars in Dialysis*, *32*(4), 331–335. 10.1111/sdi.12788

Shimoga, S. V., Erlyana, E., & Rebello, V. (2019). Associations of social media use with physical activity and sleep adequacy among adolescents: Cross-sectional survey. *Journal of Medical Internet Research*, *21*(6), e14290. 10.2196/14290

Stevens, C. J., David, T. I., & Storkey, J. (2018). Atmospheric nitrogen deposition in terrestrial ecosystems: Its impact on plant communities and consequences across trophic levels. *Functional Ecology*, *32*(7), 1757–1769. 10.1111/1365-2435.13063

Stokols, D. (1992). Establishing and maintaining healthy environments: Toward a social ecology of health promotion. *American Psychologist*, *47*(1), 6–22. 10.1037/0003-066X.47.1.6

Ströbel, T., & Germelmann, C. C. (2020). Exploring new routes within brand research in sport management: Directions and methodological approaches. *European Sport Management Quarterly*, *20*(1), 1–9. 10.1080/16184742.2019.1706603

Sullivan, A. N., & Lachman, M. E. (2017). Behavior change with fitness technology in sedentary adults: A review of the evidence for increasing physical activity. *Frontiers in Public Health*, *4*, 1–14. 10.3389/fpubh.2016.00289

Tilson, D., Lyytinen, K., & Sørensen, C. (2010). Research commentary—digital infrastructures: The missing IS research agenda. *Information Systems Research*, *21*(4), 748–759. 10.1287/isre.1100.0318

Toscos, T., Consolvo, S., & McDonald, D. W. (2011). Barriers to physical activity: A study of self-revelation in an online community. *Journal of Medical Systems*, *35*(5), 1225–1242. 10.1007/s10916-011-9721-2

Trotter, M. G., Coulter, T. J., Davis, P. A., Poulus, D. R., & Polman, R. (2020). The association between eSports participation, health and physical activity behaviour. *International Journal of Environmental Research and Public Health*, *17*(19), 7329–7343. 10.3390/ijerph17197329

Turner-McGrievy, G. M., Beets, M. W., Moore, J. B., Kaczynski, A. T., Barr-Anderson, D. J., & Tate, D. F. (2013). Comparison of traditional versus mobile app self-monitoring of physical activity and dietary intake among overweight adults participating in an mHealth weight loss program. *Journal of the American Medical Informatics Association*, *20*(3), 513–518. 10.1136/amiajnl-2012-001510

Wakefield, L. T., & Bennett, G. (2018). Sports fan experience: Electronic word-of-mouth in ephemeral social media. *Sport Management Review*, *21*(2), 147–159. 10.1016/j.smr.2017.06.003

Wattanapisit, A., Wattanapisit, S., & Wongsiri, S. (2020). Public health perspectives on eSports. *Public Health Reports*, *135*(3), 295–298. 10.1177/0033354920912718

We Are Social. (2020). *Digital 2020: Global digital overview*. https://wearesocial.com/digital-2020

Weber, R. H. (2010). Internet of things – New security and privacy challenges. *Computer Law & Security Review*, *26*(1), 23–30. 10.1016/j.clsr.2009.11.008

Westmattelmann, D., Grotenhermen, J. G., Sprenger, M., & Schewe, G. (2021). The show must go on-virtualisation of sport events during the COVID-19 pandemic. *European Journal of Information Systems*, *30*(2), 119–136.

World Health Organization. (2020). *WHO guidelines on physical activity and sedentary behaviour*. https://www.who.int/publications/i/item/9789240015128

Wu, J., Inoue, Y., Filo, K., & Sato, M. (2020). Creating shared value and sport employees' job performance: The mediating effect of work engagement. *European Sport Management Quarterly*, *0*(0), 1–20. 10.1080/16184742.2020.1779327

Zhang, J., Brackbill, D., Yang, S., & Centola, D. (2015). Efficacy and causal mechanism of an online social media intervention to increase physical activity: Results of a randomized controlled trial. *Preventive Medicine Reports*, *2*, 651–657. 10.1016/j.pmedr.2015.08.005

25 Artificial Intelligence

Heather Kennedy and Liz Wanless

Artificial intelligence (AI) has fundamentally changed the modern sport management landscape as it is embraced and leveraged across the sport industry. PricewaterhouseCoopers' (PwC) industry report outlines how AI can be used throughout the sport landscape to improve media and fan experiences as well as management and operations (Barlow & Sriskandarajah, 2019). AI is valuable for the sport industry as it creates efficiencies by leveraging insights from the growing volume, variety, and value of data (Naraine & Wanless, 2020). The famous example of Moneyball exemplifies a shift toward data as player and team statistics can be used to inform decision-making and improve team performance. An abundance of data pertaining to athletes' and coaches' training and performance allows AI applications to learn about techniques and tactics and provide optimal training and strategy guidance. Furthermore, sport organizations are employing AI to improve fan experiences such as using chatbots to provide customer service, drones to better capture game footage, and fan management systems to improve and personalize service. Moreover, AI is developing a new era of sport journalism where it translates hard data (e.g., game statistics) into narratives, automating writing and increasing reporting capacity. In turn, the fan experience is improved by having access to more content, in a timelier manner. Effectively, there are countless examples of the use and impact of AI across the sport industry that will be discussed throughout this chapter.

This chapter begins with a brief history of AI and its impact on society. Next, this chapter discusses AI in the sport industry by providing historical and current examples of AI in the industry and discussing AI's impact on sport management research. To provide a rounded view and understanding of the capabilities and impacts of AI, the downsides and ethical considerations of AI are then discussed. Subsequently, this chapter briefly examines the future of AI in sport and society. Finally, this chapter concludes with a brief revision of the discussed content.

History and Current State of AI

Despite AI being an increasingly discussed topic in the age of self-driving cars and other futuristic advancements in technology, it has evolved over the last seven decades. The idea of AI can be traced back to the 1940s and World War II (WWII) (Haenlein & Kaplan, 2019). During WWII, Alan Turing, widely considered the father of AI and theoretical computer science,

DOI: 10.4324/9781003088899-29

toyed with the idea of machine intelligence. He proposed the so-called Turing Test, namely the idea that if a human can be tricked by a machine into thinking the machine is actually a human, the machine has intelligence. This is often still considered today the benchmark used to determine a system's intelligence. Concurrently, Isaac Asimov, an American science fiction writer, published the short story *Runaround* which featured the Three Laws of Robotics that proposed the idea of robot intelligence. Collectively, these ideas gave birth to the idea of AI in practice, with the official term being coined by John McCarthy in 1956; the same year the first-ever running AI program (Logic Theorist) was created.

For nearly the next two decades, there was significant development and growth with respect to AI. For example, Unimate, the first industrial robot, was implemented by General Motors (GM) in 1961 and replaced human workers in manufacturing and assembly. Shortly after in 1964, a natural language processing (NLP) tool named ELIZA was developed. ELIZA was able to carry on conversations with humans and was one of the first programs that were capable of attempting the Tuning Test. Shakey, an electronic person from Stanford, was another early example of AI as it was a robot capable of reasoning about its own actions. Though examples of Expert Systems as they did not learn, but rather processed information using a series of rules or if/then statements, these technologies represented great advancement in the field and laid the foundation for the development of AI. However, this period of advancement ended due to many false starts, technology failures, and dead-ends as well as criticisms of the idea of and support for AI. As such, there was a lull in the advancements in AI until the late 1990s.

The potential for AI returned at the end of the 20th century when IBM's Expert System Deep Blue defeated the reigning world chess champion. Subsequent advancements in the area of AI included

- *1998*: KISmet, a robot with emotional intelligence in that it could detect and respond to human feelings
- *1999*: AIBO, a robotic pet dog capable of developing a personality and skills over time
- *2002*: Roomba, an autonomous robotic vacuum that learned to navigate and clean spaces
- *2011*: Siri, Apple's virtual, personal assistant
- *2011*: Watson, IBM's computing program that used its question and answering capabilities to compete on *Jeopardy!*
- *2014*: Eugene, a chatbot that passed the Turing Test
- *2014*: Alexa, Amazon's virtual assistant that could complete shopping tasks
- *2016*: Tay, Microsoft's rogue chatbot

Finally, AlphaGo's achievement of beating the reigning world champion in Go in 2016, often paralleled to Deep Blue's chess victory nearly two decades early, marked the acceptance and potential of AI – the feat was chosen by *Science* as a runner-up in 2016s Breakthrough of the Year. Compared to chess which only has 20 possible opening moves, Go, with 361 opening moves, was thought to be too complex for computers to ever be able to best a human. However, by leveraging deep learning, the program was able to master the complex task and decision-making puzzle, highlighting the capabilities of modern AI.

Currently, AI is ubiquitous in our society, helping us accomplish everyday tasks directly by interacting with us (e.g., virtual assistants like Siri and Alexa) and indirectly by controlling what we see and consume (e.g., automated journalism, social media algorithms that filter and display content, etc.). Most often the applications we know as AI leverage artificial neural networks and deep learning (Haenlein & Kaplan, 2019). Table 25.1 outlines terminologies often associated with AI that are important in the understanding of this technology.

Table 25.1 AI Related Terminology

Term	*Definition*
Algorithm	A set of rules or a process to be followed, particularly by a computer, in a calculation or problem-solving situation
Artificial Intelligence (AI)	A machine's ability to mimic or perform the capabilities or functions of a human including, but not limited to, making decisions, solving problems, recognizing people and objects, understanding, processing, and responding to language, and learning from prior experience or examples
Big Data	Extremely large datasets that can be computationally analyzed to identify patterns, particularly with respect to human behavior
Computer Vision	The field of study is concerned with how computers gain high-level understanding from media content (e.g., images and videos)
Deep Learning	A subfield of machine learning that uses layers or stacks of neural networks to process data and create patterns for decision making
Expert Systems	A software using AI to solve complex problems using an if/then set of rules, emulating human expert decision-making processes
Machine Learning	The development and use of programs that can adapt and learn without direct guidance/oversight using algorithms to identify patterns in data
Natural Language Processing (NLP)	Algorithms trained to detect, understand, and reproduce the human language
Neural Networks	A set of algorithms, modeled off the human brain, designed to recognize patterns in data
Wearable Technology (Wearables)	Electronic devices powered by microprocessors and able to send/receive data via the internet that can be worn, including by being embedded in clothing or the user's body

Advancements in technology, including techniques pertaining to AI and general computing power/storage, combined with the reality of Big Data, or the sheer magnitude of data available, have made AI constant and growing in its capabilities and impacts. In short, the unfathomable quantity of data available is too voluminous for humans to process or understand. AI, particularly through machine learning techniques, is able to sort through data, identify patterns, and perform tasks or make decisions on our behalf. This allows organizations to leverage the data and/or corresponding machines to improve efficiencies such as automation in factories. Because of its ability to improve consumers' and organizations' capabilities and experiences, it is ubiquitous in society.

The following example provides a small glimpse at the various types of AI-based technologies and machines we come in contact with on a daily basis. Lincoln wakes up to his Amazon Echo's alarm and tells the machine to stop using the voice command. In doing so, the Echo triggers a series of automated tasks for Lincoln, such as brewing coffee and providing customized updates on the latest sport news. After getting ready and having breakfast, the food was suggested by the smart fridge based on the fridge's contents and Lincoln's dietary preferences, Lincoln heads to work. By telling Alexa (the Echo's virtual assistant) goodbye for the day, a series of automated tasks begin including starting the dishwasher and sending the Roomba out on its daily clean. After driving to work using various automated driving features, Lincoln arrives at the office and spends the day working and scrolling social media, which features filtered content. Near the end of the workday, Lincoln receives an automated update about the weather to know what to expect when leaving the office. The drive home was uneventful as the GPS application automatically rerouted Lincoln to avoid traffic. A meal delivery app, leveraging AI technologies to pair drivers and orders, brought Lincoln dinner to enjoy while watching sport highlights made using AI and reading sport journalism written with AI. At the end of the day, Lincoln says goodnight to Alexa who wishes him a pleasant sleep and prepares the house for the evening by locking doors, turning off lights, and adjusting the thermostat.

As illustrated in the example of Lincoln's typical day, AI has revolutionized and/or automated even the most mundane tasks such as vacuuming. AI provides people with countless benefits including the automation of tasks or the filtering and presentation of information. This accessibility to information and automation benefits individuals, such as by making daily life easier (e.g., automating tasks, customizing media content and marketing, etc.), and society as a whole, such as by reducing poverty and global inequality. Moreover, AI is at the core of many modern businesses including Amazon (e.g., how it displays and recommends content, how it optimizes content distribution, etc.), Apple, and Microsoft (e.g., software features and design including personal assistants and text prediction), and sharing economy apps (e.g., Uber and Lyft that use AI to match riders and drivers). These AI technologies, and the benefits accrued by using them, transcend into the sport industry.

AI and the Sport Industry

As AI technologies become increasingly available and integrated in individuals' lives and business operations, they are adopted by sport organizations and expected by sport consumers. Therefore, the fundamental knowledge accrued thus far with respect to AI, such as its history, evolution, and current capabilities, are applicable in the sport context. For example, relevant AI applications already discussed in this chapter have been adopted by sport organizations including chatbots and smart assistants, automated journalism, algorithm, and big data-based decision-making. Leveraging our existing knowledge and understanding of AI, the following section focuses on the state of AI in the sport industry.

According to PwC's report, the following AI applications are currently used in sport: stadium entry, drone cameras, smart ticketing, chatbots, and virtual assistants, automated video highlights, automated journalism, wearable devices, virtual umpires, in-game coaching, and computer vision.

Chatbots, which leverage NLP, are an example of an AI application embraced by sport organizations to improve the customer service they provide fans. Chatbots can serve as virtual agents that benefit the customer by enhancing their satisfaction through uninterrupted service and reduced response times and benefit the organization by providing flexible, accessible, and low-cost customer service (Przegalinska et al., 2019). For instance, the NBA's Sacramento Kings introduced a chatbot called KAI (Kings AI) in 2016. KAI is a custom bot developed using the Facebook Messenger application to help fans get answers to a range of questions related to team statistics, player information, franchise history, and their team's home stadium. When the sales team utilized KAI to pre-qualify leads for propensity to buy, the team noticed sales representatives exhibited higher sales conversions through talking to better, more engaged leads (Conversica, 2020). Effectively, since existing research has demonstrated the relationship between quality chatbots and customer satisfaction (e.g., Ashfaq et al., 2020; Przegalinska et al., 2019), sport organizations have embraced them to improve customer service and decrease operation costs.

Another AI application in the sport industry is computer vision. Motorsports, such as NASCAR, are extremely dangerous, averaging more than one death annually since the 1950s, and are reliant on extremely expensive equipment (e.g., a single race car can cost upwards of 300,000 USD). Leveraging knowledge accrued from the development of self-driving cars, automobile companies, such as Ford Motor Company, are using its deep learning to improve safety in auto racing. Deep learning techniques can identify cars more accurately than humans; this is beneficial as the ability to quickly identify malfunctions is essential to avoid serious problems that could put the car and driver in jeopardy. Effectively, by leveraging AI, motorsports can improve car performance and safety. However, as cars become increasingly automated, the future might see the elimination of drivers, with self-driving cars being the safer, faster option. The implications of this potential loss of the human element are discussed in further detail in the later sections of this chapter.

AI technologies are also used to improve player safety in other sporting contexts as they are leveraged to help with the training of players. As technologies such as wearables have increased the amount of data collected from a given athlete; statistics available include physical performance metrics (e.g., VO_2 max), biometrics (e.g., heart rate), and sport performance metrics (e.g., goals scored). Using these statistics, AI systems can make recommendations related to training and nutrition to optimize player performance. Moreover, algorithms can be used to identify injury risk so that preventive measures can be taken. In addition to the ability to improve the safety of sports and players, such knowledge accrued by AI technologies leveraging player and sport-related big data can improve coaching and talent acquisition.

Prior to the advent of AI, coaching and talent recruitment were often based on human decisions such as the skill of scouts that were ripe with biases and inaccurate reflections of information. The Oakland Athletics' decision led by their general manager Billy Bean to rely on statistical information, analytics, and sabermetrics (i.e., the empirical analysis of in-game statistical measures of activity) fundamentally altered talent recruitment and coaching. Nowadays, the Moneyball approach to sports is dominant with various AI techniques frequently leveraged to sort through player and team performance statistics to optimize output. Furthermore, with the advent of AI coaches, statistics related to player and team performance can be analyzed in real-time to identify and inform coaching strategies. Overall, the use of AI with respect to player/team performance and safety benefits sport organizations and athletes as it can improve decision-making and benefits fans by improving on-field performance.

The use of virtual umpire-related technologies such as Decision Review Systems and Video Assistant Referee can also improve the quality of games and player safety. Such technologies use slow-motion video replays to detect fouls or other events that would require umpire/referee intervention. Through advancements in camera technology (e.g., drones that can track gameplay automatically) and AI applications, umpire/referee decisions are increasingly challenged by automated decisions. For instance, in tennis, such automated techniques can replace a line judge by accurately and nearly instantly determining if a ball is in or out of bounds. Though some argue that such technologies can improve the sport as they provide more accurate calls than human referees, others argue that it removes the human element of the sport.

Sport media and journalism are also changing as a result of AI due to its ability to automate and accelerate the writing and processing of media content. For instance, the Associated Press (AP) has been working with Automated Insights, a technology company that specializes in natural language generation, to expand their media convergence of sport content, specifically minor league baseball (MiLB). Automated Insight's natural language-based technology can translate hard data (e.g., game and player statistics) into narratives (e.g., media stories and reports). Using this technology, AP has been able to increase its sport coverage. Moreover, AI is used by media production teams, such as Wimbledon's in 2018, to assist in developing video highlight reels by automating the identification of exciting, must-see moments. This allowed for faster and more large-scale production of highlight reels. Overall, AI has begun to automate sport media, allowing for more content to be developed faster and cheaper than if humans did it manually. This provides sport fans with more media content, faster than ever before. It also helps make sport coverage more equitable, as the technology is based on statics rather than human biases (e.g., Wimbledon highlight reels developed with AI technology had more balance in players featured as it evaluated exciting content based on movements rather than athletes).

Overall, the examples of AI in the sport industry are endless. Though the prior paragraphs briefly detail a few examples, there are countless others including:

- Betting algorithms that can be used to identify optimal bets, potentially improving an individual's performance in sports gambling and fantasy sports
- Using AI to automate the choice of camera angle and coverage during live sport broadcasts as well as automating the creation of subtitles for viewers
- Improving advertising opportunities for advertisers and sponsors by optimizing the timing and release of advertisements based on game content as well as helping sport organizations target their advertisements to improve ticket sales
- Utilizing AI to evaluate sport agent reputations in the public narrative through algorithm deployment to recognize the agent's name across the digital space
- Identifying fans most likely to churn or upgrade to season tickets by analyzing big data pertaining to fan behavior

Effectively, just as in society as a whole, the sport industry has embraced AI technologies to improve management and operations while also enhancing media and fan experiences. Existing sport management scholarship further underscores this point.

The Impact of AI on Sport Industry Research

As represented by PwC's technology framework, AI impacts various functional areas within sport business. Notably, AI's effects on the sport industry are multi-faceted; for instance, chatbot implementation accelerates the sport sales pre-qualification phase through automated conversation with customers (Wanless & Naraine, 2021), and sport organizations can harness machine learning algorithms to analyze customer sentiment across social media accounts. These two cases exemplify how AI is poised to impact sport management research. Academics can study how the adoption of AI reinvents sport business while also adopting machine learning methods to analyze sport data. The following section outlines the impact of AI on sport industry research. This discussion houses two circles of thought: how AI affects current research lines and how harnessing machine learning advances existing methods.

Sport management research spans sport levels from community and recreation to university, to international professional sport. From sport marketing to sport ethics, context matters and has created numerous platforms through which sport management researchers conclude evidence-based insights. The proliferation of AI into the sport industry, with its many and varied implications, has the same vast array of implications for sport management research. Computer vision, for example, can be harnessed for sport sponsorship valuation (valuing a logo that appears for the duration of a televised game), for event safety (training computers to recognize suspicious behavior in live event filming), and for AI-based video replays. Both research and practice benefit from considering the effect and efficacy of this acquisition from multiple vantage points (business and consumer), multiple levels (community to professional sport), and multiple methods (qualitative to quantitative).

In particular, sport management research fostered a line of innovation studies encapsulating how organizations adopt innovations (e.g., Hoeber & Hoeber, 2012). Sport innovation literature covered the adoption process and factors that may impact such adoption (Smith & Green, 2020). In addition, the fruition of innovations (Troilo et al., 2016) as well as how innovations spread from one organization to another (Seifried et al., 2017) revealed notable insights about the sport industry as a platform for novel business practice. Sport business research will benefit from covering the full AI adoption cycle from the onset to the spread throughout the industry. One example, Wanless et al. (2022), utilized diffusion of innovations theory as a backdrop to uncover a taxonomy of NLP use cases in the professional sport industry and predicted the diffusion of NLP in professional sport. The findings demonstrated the proliferation of NLP in the industry since its inception in 2010. Over half of the teams in the sample had adopted NLP. Additionally, the study revealed that both the analytics team and team executives were critical catalysts for adoption along with the need for efficiency in data processing and the desire for an innovative organization reputation.

Since AI is an innovation with wide reach, it supports a wide range of impactful applied research projects. Because machine learning, a critical subset of AI, involves the analysis of data (including text data; Deshpande & Kumar, 2018), AI stands to advance sport management research methods. Quantitative sport research analysis to date is largely statistical in nature (e.g., Troilo et al., 2016), while qualitative sport research analysis is manual, typically involving a thematic analysis conducted by hand (e.g., Naraine & Parent, 2017). Machine learning is an emerging innovation that will overlap and broaden sport management's quantitative and qualitative research methods.

Both machine learning and statistics are designed to help understand and draw patterns in data. Both involve explanatory (supervised) versus exploratory (unsupervised) investigations (Deshpande & Kumar, 2018). In some cases, such as with linear and logistic regression as well as cluster analyses, both machine learning and statistics employ the same tools to analyze data (albeit with different overarching goals). Linear regression, widely used in statistics, is also considered a machine learning algorithm (Deshpande & Kumar, 2018). Both fall under the umbrella of analytics and have mathematical underpinnings. However, the two are different in nature; Table 25.2 lists a few key differences. From configuring the data for analysis to model interpretation and evaluation, machine learning and statistics represent connected but independent fields. Aspects unique to machine learning can be leveraged to advance sport management methods.

Table 25.2 Statistics versus Machine Learning

	Statistics	*Machine Learning*
Driver	Mathematical theory	Fitting data
Focus	Hypothesis testing, interpreting variable relationships	Predictive accuracy
Data size	Reasonable volume according to the statistical procedure	Big data
Inference	Parameter estimation, prediction, estimating error	Prediction
Model choice	In-sample goodness of fit	Cross-validation of predictive accuracy on partitions of data
Popular tools	SPSS, STATA, R	Python
Interpretability	High	Low

Source: Adapted from Stewart (2019).

Statistics is a branch of mathematics concerned with the analysis of data to infer relationships among the variables (Bzdok et al., 2018). Most often this process occurs by analyzing data from a sample in an attempt to generalize to a larger population. Machine learning algorithms are most concerned with performance rather than the relationships among the variables (Bzdok et al., 2018; Deshpande & Kumar, 2018). In sport management research, the long history of predicting athletic contributions to intercollegiate athletic institutions involves statistical modeling to understand the relationship between variables such as March Madness wins and increases in annual fundraising (e.g., Stinson & Howard, 2008). Machine learning, on the other hand, might be applied to see how well numerous variables, including digital marketing efforts, create prediction accuracy for athletic contributions from year to year.

While regression analysis is a popular method for both statistics and machine learning (Bzdok et al., 2018), machine learning also houses different algorithmic tools for data analysis (Deshpande & Kumar, 2018). These algorithms have mathematical underpinnings but would not be considered statistics and will be new to sport management methods. Algorithms such as neural networks have advantages, such as prediction power, over those statistical processes designed to draw relationships among variables. This was illustrated by Kennedy et al. (2021) who demonstrated the additional predictive accuracy gained by using a machine learning algorithm over a standard linear regression with respect to predicting social media post engagement. But in general, the relationships between predictor and outcome variables will be less interpretable in these types of algorithmic outcomes. If utilizing a neural network to predict annual athletic fundraising, it may be clear that March Madness wins are important to predicting fundraising, but the relationship will not be as interpretable as a regression slope for example, where a one unit increase in March Madness wins increases fundraising by a certain dollar amount all other variables held constant.

NLP is an example of a machine learning tool poised to extend qualitative methods in sport management research. Especially because of the development of the public narrative in digital space, sport business is inundated with vast amounts of text data that either cannot or cannot efficiently be analyzed by traditional thematic analysis. Even qualitative data from large-scale surveys can be overwhelming to analyze. NLP is designed to accommodate this inefficiency. For example, Naraine & Parent (2017) interviewed individuals from ten different Canadian national sport organizations to understand the perceived utility of social media at this level. Suppose researchers wanted to sample *all* national sport organizations from *all* countries via a qualitative survey. What seems too large to analyze could be aided by a topic modeling algorithm since NLP algorithms can retrieve important topics and sentiments from very large qualitative narratives (Collobert et al., 2011).

As with any emerging methodological tool, the confusion around terms and usage can create challenges as sport management moves forward with employing machine learning algorithms. The efficacy of AI can be sensationalized or overestimated in practice (Brooks, 2017). Machine learning is not suited to replace statistical processes in traditional sport management research. As well, machine learning can be sensationalized in research applications. Therefore, when the research objective matches machine learning methods, it is incumbent that sport management academicians exercise this tool, communicate AI terminology, and review sport machine learning papers with diligence.

Downsides and Ethical Considerations of AI

Thus far, the examples of AI in society and in the sport industry illustrate a positive impact of the technology such as increasing convenience and personalization for consumers and allowing for increased efficiency at lower costs for organizations. However, there are negative impacts and ethical considerations with AI that are worth acknowledging. Downsides to AI include its cost, technology limitations and failures, and the potential to reinforce systemic issues and inequalities. With respect to ethical considerations, the prevalence and adoption of AI raise concerns related to privacy, the use of such technologies, and the potential loss of the human element.

A potential downside of AI is the cost of implementation and use. Though computing technology continues to become increasingly affordable as it becomes commonplace and computing capacity increases, there is still a large financial cost to implement and run AI systems including the costs associated with installation, repair, and maintenance of the machine. Moreover, specific knowledge or skill set is required for the design, development, and use of AI systems, one which not all sport industry practitioners have. Moreover, the technicalities and gaps in knowledge may also create hesitancy and fear within leadership (McKinsey, 2016). There does exist an opportunity for sport organizations to form partnerships with technology-based firms to develop AI-based services, such as how sport teams partner with AI firms that specialized in NLP to develop their chatbots. Such partnerships could provide a technology company with a sponsorship opportunity including brand visibility while providing the sport organization with the resources to embrace AI solutions (Kennedy et al., 2021).

Another downside of AI can occur when there is an overreliance on the systems, without an acknowledgment of their limitations or critical evaluations of their processes. Though the "intelligence" and capabilities of AI systems have continued to advance, they are not humans and do not have the same sense of creativity or understanding of social norms. A notable difference between AI applications, which rely on a series of rules or algorithms based on patterns in data, and humans, is the ability to think creatively (e.g., out of the box) and understand feelings and emotions. AI applications can lack this element of creativity, while often being unable to adequately capture and process emotions. This can have negative consequences that impact performance. For example, Microsoft's chatbot Tay was designed with a target market of 18–24 year-olds and created using Twitter data in the hopes of developing an AI system that was more casual and reflected online communication. However, Tay's conversations included racist, inflammatory, and political statements (Hunt, 2016). This illustrates how an AI system learns patterns from existing data, without necessarily understanding the social cues or consequences associated with this information. An overreliance on AI, without incorporating the "human element" and understanding the limitations of systems can have unintended negative consequences.

A final example of a downside of AI is its potential bias. There are anecdotal reports and empirical evidence of unfair and biased decision-making by algorithms across contexts including healthcare, education, and criminal justice. For example, an algorithm frequently embraced by US hospitals to aid in the allocation of healthcare was found to systematically discriminate against black patients; the algorithm was less likely to refer black than white people who were equally sick to receive the necessary health coverage (Obermeyer et al., 2019). Biases can occur in algorithms for a variety of reasons including being introduced by the data (e.g., learning the biases that exist within the data and perpetuating them) and the developer (e.g., biased decisions by humans in how the algorithm is developed or the data used to develop the algorithm) (Silberg & Manyika, 2019). Because of the scale at which AI systems can operate, biases in the system can have catastrophic consequences. Therefore, it is imperative to remember that like humans who err and have biases, AI systems are not without fault and also have the potential to err and be biased.

Concerns related to privacy and what organizations know about individuals are at the forefront of the ethical conversations about AI. AI systems rely on large quantities of data for algorithms to be able to identify patterns; but, this raises questions related to data collection, storage, and usage. AI, such as search algorithms, recommendation engines, and social media, rely on past user data to make accurate predictions and present accurate results. However, such companies have also sold this data to third-party developers. A famous example of this is the scandal featuring Cambridge Analytica which purchased Facebook data and used insights from this data to successfully infiltrate the US election (Lapowsky, 2019). There was ensuing outrage as consumers, lawmakers, companies, and privacy activists debated the notion of privacy and who has the right to collect, use, and sell data (and the insights gained from the data). There is not yet a consensus on the answers to privacy-related elements of AI, nor has the law caught up with respect to the reality that is big data, analytics, and AI. There are beginnings of laws, such as the GDPR in the European Union and the CCPA in California, but there is an ongoing debate with respect to this ethical consideration (Teich, 2020).

Another ethical consideration of note related to AI is how AI technologies and systems are used. For example, facial recognition software has been developed and used to improve security, such as through deployment in US airports. However, there are concerns about the use and implications of such technologies; China has used them in Xinjiang among other places as tools of authoritarian control (Mozur, 2019) resulting in calls for facial recognition bans (Kerry, 2020). Similar concerns have been raised across America, resulting in various cities and states (e.g., Oregon, New Hampshire, and California) banning the use of such technology with police body cameras. Another example of concern about how AI technologies are used is related to the rise of fake media and disinformation. This chapter previously touched on how AI was used in sport media to create new content including articles and video highlight reels. Similar AI systems can develop fake images, videos, and conversations which make it increasingly difficult to know if the person you are talking to is a person or a bot, or if the information and content are real or not (Walch, 2019a). Fake content can be developed and distributed 24/7 using technologies including AI which can have dire consequences for individuals who are victims of fake content or societies plagued with the dissemination of misinformation.

The final ethical consideration discussed is related to the potential loss of the human element. Some experts anticipate that by 2030, bots will facilitate most social situations (Anderson & Raine, 2018). Ten years following Deep Blue's victory in 1997, the computer program AlphaZero was released and is now unbeatable at chess; the program has also taught itself Go and shogi and is unbeatable at these games as well (Silver et al., 2018). These examples illustrate the ethical debate on the role of people versus machines. It is important to note that while AI will not replace the human labor force, it has triggered a labor displacement, with AI replacing some categories of jobs, while creating entirely new ones (e.g., manufacturers are now programmers, secretaries are now database administrators, etc.) (Walch, 2019b). Regardless, it does raise the question of the role of humans versus machines in society, another ethical consideration important to acknowledge, but that does not yet have an answer.

Future of AI

In recent years, advancements in AI technology and computing capabilities have made AI ubiquitous in society and the sport industry with unmeasurable positive and negative impacts. Continue growth and application of AI is expected in the future; for instance, in the sport industry, PwC anticipates that the AI systems discussed in this chapter, including chatbots, automated video highlights, computer vision, and talent selection, will be embraced across sport contexts (Barlow & Sriskandarajah, 2019). Experts predict that AI has the potential to continue to amplify human effectiveness with numerous possibilities to improve health and quality of life (Anderson & Rainie, 2018). For example, the AI systems available to elite athletes to assist in their training will become affordable and available to everyday consumers and be able to help them manage their health and nutrition. That being said, the downsides and ethical considerations with respect to AI, many of which have not yet been adequately addressed, will continue to exist, with experts citing concerns related to AI's negative impact on human capabilities, autonomy, and agency (Anderson & Rainie, 2018). Specifically, by 2030, experts are concerned about:

- Autonomy (i.e., humans losing control over their lives)
- Privacy and data abuse
- Job loss and the widening of economic divides
- Machine dependency (i.e., a reduction in necessary human skills including social and survival skills)
- Crime and war (e.g., results of autonomous weapons, cybercrime, and the weaponization of information)

These implications are mirrored in the sport industry. For example, there is an ongoing debate on the role of technology and AI and how it impacts sports. Virtual umpire technology has the potential to improve the accuracy of calls; but others argue that humanity, including errors in decision making, is part of the fan experience. As the most technologically advanced sport, Formula One serves as an example of how technology can control a sport. Research examining outcomes of Formula One between 1950 and 2018 found a dramatic decrease in the role and influence of the driver; driver performance was attributed to approximately 10% of the race outcome in 2018, down from 30% in 1980, while car and team performance account for approximately 90% of the outcome in 2018, compared to 70% in 1980 (Bell et al., 2016). This has led to criticisms, even from Formula One drivers like Daniel Ricciardo, that the sport has become too much about the car and its technology than about natural talent (Barlow & Sriskandarajah, 2019). The inevitable trajectory of Formula One continuing to embrace technology to improve performance and safety is self-driving or remotely operated vehicles. This raises many questions about the future of sport.

Going forward, sport organizations have the opportunity to continue to embrace AI to improve their media and fan experiences as well as management and operations. Moreover, technologies developed and/or embraced by the sport industry, such as health management, training, and talent acquisition tools used by athletes, teams, and leagues have the potential to transition outside of the sport industry to benefit society as a whole. However, it will also be important to continue to understand the limitations of AI as well as continue to address the ethical considerations to ensure the future of AI in the sport industry is a net positive.

Conclusion

This chapter examined AI, with a particular emphasis on understanding it, its impact, and its role in the sport industry. After beginning with a definition, this chapter provided an overview of the history and evolution of AI. By examining AI broadly, including examples of how it impacts everyday life and types of AI technologies, an understanding was developed of its application and impact. Because AI technologies transcend industries and contexts, a broad understanding of AI was necessary prior to examining its role and impact in the sport industry.

As illustrated in examples in this chapter, sport organizations often partner with other companies that specialize in some form of AI. Hence, a general understanding of AI was developed prior to providing examples of AI technologies in the sport industry.

The ubiquitous nature of AI in the sport industry was illustrated by providing examples of various applications of the technologies. Such examples ranged from chatbots offered by sport organizations to improve consumer service at a lower cost to the use of AI in the recruitment of talent and coaching decisions to the role of AI in automated journalism and media production. Then, a brief overview of the status of AI research in the sport industry was provided, discussing how AI influences current research lines and how harnessing it can advance existing research methods. Then this chapter discussed the downsides to and ethical considerations of AI, outlining how though AI can improve media and fan experiences as well as management and operations for organizations, the advancements can have negative consequences and introduce ethical concerns. Finally, this chapter concluded by providing a brief discussion of the future of AI, with an emphasis on generating questions related to future applications of the technology in the sport industry.

References

Anderson, J., & Rainie, L. (2018, December 10). *Artificial intelligence and the future of humans*. Pew Research Center. https://www.pewresearch.org/internet/2018/12/10/artificial-intelligence-and-the-future-of-humans/

Ashfaq, M., Yun, J., Yu, S., & Loureiro, S. M. C. (2020). I, Chatbot: Modeling the determinants of users' satisfaction and continuance intention of AI-powered service agents. *Telematics and Informatics, 54*, 101473.

Barlow, A., & Sriskandarajah, S. (2019, February). *Artificial intelligence: Application to the sports industry*. PwC Report. Retrieved from pwc.com

Bell, A., Smith, J., Sabel, C. E., & Jones, K. (2016). Formula for success: Multilevel modelling of formula one driver and constructor performance, 1950–2014. *Journal of Quantitative Analysis in Sports, 12*(2), 99–112.

Brooks, R. (2017). The seven deadly sins of AI predictions. *MIT Technology Review*. Retrieved from https://www.technologyreview.com/s/609048/the-seven-deadly-sins-of-ai-predictions/

Bzdok, D., Altman, N., & Krzywinski, M. (2018). Statistics versus machine learning. *Nat Methods, 15*, 233–234.

Collobert, R., Weston, J., Bottou, L., Karlen, M., Kavukeuoglu, K., & Kuksa, P. (2011). Natural language processing (almost) from scratch. *Journal of Machine Learning Research, 12*(1), 2493–2537.

Conversica. (2020). How the Sacramento Kings added millions in pipeline with Conversica. *Conversica*. Retrieved from https://www.conversica.com/resources/videos/how-the-sacramento-kings-added-millions-in-pipeline-with-conversica/

Deshpande, A., & Kumar, M. (2018). *Artificial intelligence for big data*. Birmingham, UK: Packt Publishing.

Haenlein, M., & Kaplan, A. (2019). A brief history of artificial intelligence: On the past, present, and future of artificial intelligence. *California Management Review, 61*(1), 5–14.

Hoeber, L., & Hoeber, O. (2012). Determinants of an innovation process: A case study of technological innovation in a community sport organization. *Journal of Sport Management, 26*, 213–223. 10.1123/jsm.26.3.213

Hunt, E. (2016, March 24). *Tay, Microsoft's AI chatbot, gets a crash course in racism from Twitter*. The Guardian. https://www.theguardian.com/technology/2016/mar/24/tay-microsofts-ai-chatbot-gets-a-crash-course-in-racism-from-twitter

IBM Cloud Education. (2020, June 3). *Artificial Intelligence (AI)*. IBM. Retrieved from https://www.ibm.com/cloud/learn/what-is-artificial-intelligence

Ittoo, A., Nguyen, L. M., & Bosch, A. V. D. (2016). Text analytics in industry: Challenges, desiderata, and trends. *Computers in Industry, 78*,96–107.

Kennedy, H., Kunkel, T., & Funk, D. C. (2021). Using predictive analytics to measure effectiveness of social media engagement: A digital measurement perspective. *Sport Marketing Quarterly. 30*, 265–277.

Kerry, C. F. (2020, February 10). *Protecting privacy in an AI-driven world.* Brookings. https://www.brookings.edu/research/protecting-privacy-in-an-ai-driven-world/

Lapowsky, I. (2019, March 17). *How Cambridge Analytica sparked the great privacy awakening.* Wired. https://www.wired.com/story/cambridge-analytica-facebook-privacy-awakening/

Legg, S., & Hutter, M. (2007). Universal intelligence: A definition of machine intelligence. *Minds and Machines, 17*, 391–444.

McKinsey. (2016). *The need to lead in data and analytics.* [online] p. 1–9. Retrieved from https://www.mckinsey.com/business-functions/digital-mckinsey/our-insights/the-need-to-lead-in-data-and-analytics

Mozur, P. (2019, April 14). *One month, 500,000 face scans: How China is using A.I. to profile a minority. New York Times.* https://www.nytimes.com/2019/04/14/technology/china-surveillance-artificial-intelligence-racial-profiling.html

Naraine, M. L., & Parent, M. M. (2017). This is how we do it: A qualitative approach to national sport organizations' social-media implementation. *International Journal of Sport Communication, 10*, 196–217.

Naraine, M. L., & Wanless, L. (2020). Going all in on AI: Examining the value proposition of and integration challenges with one branch of artificial intelligence in sport management. *Sport Innovation Journal, 1*, 49–61. 10.18060/23898

Obermeyer, Z., Powers, B., Vogeli, C., & Mullainathan, S. (2019). Dissecting racial bias in an algorithm used to manage the health of populations. *Science, 336*(6464), 447–453.

Przegalinska, A., Ciechanowski, L., Stroz, A., Gloor, P., & Mazurek, G. (2019). In bot we trust: A new methodology of chatbot performance measures. *Bus. Horiz., 62*(6), 785–797.

Seifried, C., Katz, M., & Tutka, P. (2017). A conceptual model on the process of innovation diffusion through a historical review of the United States Armed Forces and their bowl games. *Sport Management Review, 20*, 379–394. https://doi.org/10.1016/j.smr.2016.10.009

Silberg, J., & Manyika, J. (2019). Notes from the AI frontier: Tackling bias in AI (and in humans). *McKinsey Global Institute (June 2019).*

Silver, D., Hubert, S., Schrittwieser, J., Antonoglou, I., Lai, M., Guez, A., ... & Hassabis, D. (2018). A general reinforcement learning algorithm that masters chess, shogi, and Go through self-play. *Science, 362*(6419), 1140–1144.

Smith, N. L., & Green, B. C. (2020). Examining the factors influencing organizational creativity in professional sport organizations. *Sport Management Review*, 23, 992–1004. https://doi.org/10.1016/j.smr.2020.02.003

Stewart, M. (2019). The actual difference between statistics and machine learning. *Toward Data Science.* Retrieved from https://towardsdatascience.com/the-actual-difference-between-statistics-and-machine-learning-64b49f07ea3#:~:text=Statistics%20draws%20population%20inferences%20from,learning%20finds%20generalizable%20predictive%20patterns.&text=Data%20Science%20is%20essentially%20computational,small%20or%20large%20data%20sets

Stinson, J. L., & Howard, D. R. (2008). Winning does matter: Patterns in private giving to athletic and academic programs at NCAA Division I-AA and I-AAA institutions. *Sport Management Review, 11*, 1–20.

Teich, D. A. (2020, August 10). *Artificial intelligence and data privacy – Turning a risk into a benefit.* Forbes. https://www.forbes.com/sites/davidteich/2020/08/10/artificial-intelligence-and-data-privacy--turning-a-risk-into-a-benefit/?sh=7e0fafb16a95

Troilo, M., Bouchet, A., Urban, T. L., & Sutton, W. A. (2016). Perception, reality, and the adoption of business analytics: Evidence from North American professional sport organizations. *Omega, 59*(PA), 72–83.

Walch, K. (2019a, December 29). *Ethical concerns of AI.* Forbes. https://www.forbes.com/sites/cognitiveworld/2020/12/29/ethical-concerns-of-ai/?sh=7a8f952923a8

Walch, K. (2019b, November 24). *Is AI a job killer or job creator?* Forbes. https://www.forbes.com/sites/cognitiveworld/2019/11/24/is-ai-a-job-killer-or-job-creator/?sh=72047a7137e8

Wanless, L., & Naraine, M. (2021). Reinventing the sport sales process with natural language processing. *Sport & Entertainment Review, 8*(1).

Wanless, L., Seifried, C., Bouchet, A., Valeant, A., & Naraine, M. (2022). The diffusion of natural language processing in professional sport. *Sport Management Review.* Advance online publication. https://doi.org/10.1080/14413523.2021.1968174

26

Digital Technology and Sport Ecology

Maddy Orr and Walker J. Ross

Introduction

There is a fundamental connection between the natural environment and sport. Most sports originated from localized interactions between people and their natural environment: surfing on the shores of Hawaii and greater Polynesia (Finney & Houston, 1996), hockey in the cold climate of Canada (IIHF, 2002), golf in the rolling hills of Scotland (Browning, 2018). Due to technological advances and a desire to grow sport participation, the geographic range and seasonal calendars of sport seasons have been expanded tremendously (Orr et al., 2020). Hockey is now played almost exclusively indoors, on artificial ice, in climate-controlled arenas that operate year-round, and is even popular in warm climates like Florida and Texas. Fresh green golf courses have been constructed in the semi-arid Arizona desert, making it a global tourism destination for golfers. Golf also now benefits from simulators and can be played indoors, prompting the launch and global proliferation of the TopGolf brand.

The artificialization of sport environments has produced a range of benefits including increased access to sports, better and more predictable training and competition environments, and safer sport experiences. For example, ice hockey was not available to people in the US South before indoor hockey took over and grew the geographic range of the sport considerably. Today, NHL teams exist in sunbelt states where temperatures never drop to sufficient cold to maintain ice (Mastromartino et al., 2019). Surfing was only available on coasts and in rushing rivers until surfing pools brought the sport to Texas and landlocked cities. Surfing is now also able to be enjoyed in simulators on the tops of cruise ships! In the Middle East, indoor ski areas have exposed a whole new generation of Bahraini and Emirati kids to the sports of skiing and snowboarding, where that would have previously been unimaginable. The technologies that made these changes possible have afforded sport managers the opportunity to maintain the competitiveness and safety of the sports while decreasing the dependence on the natural environment and weather conditions. And yet, all sport remains dependent on the natural environment, to varying degrees.

All human activities are dependent in some form on the natural environment and the resources that it provides. At the most basic level, the natural environment provides the raw materials needed to build and maintain all sport spaces (e.g., land, grass, metals use in

DOI: 10.4324/9781003088899-30

equipment, plants for making shirts). It also provides clean air and fresh water, which are necessary for safe physical activity. For outdoor sports, the relationship with the natural environment is more tangible: for sports like skiing, surfing, soccer, football, golf, yacht racing, and others, nature provides the field of play. In its natural setting and at a very basic level, most skiing competitions require mountainous terrain, a cold enough climate for snow, and precipitation to create snow. Without those naturally occurring elements, skiing resorts and competitions may not appear in any location they desire. They are dependent upon the presence of those precise conditions. So, when the natural environment is threatened, or changes, as is happening with climate change, it follows that sports would be impacted, with outdoor sports impacted first and worst (Dingle & Stewart, 2018; Orr & Inoue, 2019). As a result of climate change, many previous Winter Olympic host sites may not have the climatic conditions to host the Winter Games in the future (Scott et al., 2015). Ski resorts are under a threat of potential closure or loss of season due to climbing average temperatures. And, coastal sport infrastructure developments in low-lying places like Florida are threatened by rising sea levels resulting from the melting of polar ice.

These points all raised previously concern the fundamental relationship between sport and the natural environment. This relationship is now examined in a growing field of study called "sport ecology." Specifically defined: sport ecology is the study of sport, the natural environment, and the relationship between the two. Formally established by McCullough et al. (2020), sport ecology can be considered an umbrella term for all research on sustainability in sport, climate vulnerability and adaptation, examinations of environmental conditions and their impacts on the business and performance of sport, and more. Sport ecology research is also quite broad and has touched on topics of marketing, sponsorship, consumer behavior, public policy, organizational behavior, governance, management, facilities and events, history, and other areas of sport management. As indicated above, the relationship between sport and the natural environment is not new. Rather, the attention it is receiving in the sport literature is new and fast growing.

As sport ecologists, we are curious about how the sports world interacts with the natural environment. So, when we consider a digital sport, our first line of questioning relates to whether and how digital technologies impact athletes' and fans' relationships to nature. The literature examining this intersection is scant, but we've identified a few specific applications of digital sport innovation that are changing the way sports are managed and played. As we navigate an increasingly tech-reliant sports landscape, there are three areas of digital sports we anticipate being particularly salient moving forward. We discuss each area in this chapter, followed by a brief case-in-point on Active Giving, a sport tech startup launched in 2019 to turn people's sport activity monitoring into a marketable platform for green products, which then converts marketing dollars into donations for green causes. We conclude this chapter with a brief discussion on the potential and the unknowns in this space, and a word of caution for fast-tech-development that may run counter to healthy human-environment relationships in the sport context.

Digital Applications in Sport Ecology

Weather and Disaster Monitoring

The practice of weather monitoring is not new to sport. Outdoor sports, in particular, rely on very particular conditions. For instance, in tennis and baseball, there are rain policies that prevent games from being played in inclement weather. In nearly all outdoor professional sports, lightning policies govern game stoppage during storms. Since the mid-2010s, leagues and international governing bodies have begun considering and, in some cases, codifying policies for heat, humidity, and air quality. The Sport Medicine Association of Australia suggests that at temperatures above 78 degrees Fahrenheit (~27 degrees Celsius), additional water breaks are necessary. At 82 degrees Fahrenheit (32 degrees Celsius), physical activity should be reduced or moved indoors. While no professional league has yet adopted any hard-and-fast policies around air quality, Major League Baseball, Major League Soccer, and the National Women's Soccer League have begun monitoring conditions at all games and matches and will not run matches when the Air Quality Index is above the safe threshold (typically >150 on a scale of 0 to 500, where anything above 250 is considered hazardous;). This unofficial policy was upheld in the summer of 2020, when forest fires ravaged Northern California and Oregon, forcing cancelations of several games in all three leagues. The National Football League, by contrast, went ahead with their games against the advice of medical professionals (Murphy & Wholf, 2020).

Weather is influenced by many different factors including location, elevation, season, and proximity to water bodies. As the weather is constantly in flux, weather measuring and monitoring involve keeping track of different climatic conditions including temperature, humidity, atmospheric pressure, light intensity, altitude, dew point, and precipitation (Aguado & Burt, 2015). It differs from the climate in that weather refers to these conditions in the short term while climate refers to the weather of a region over a long period of time. As an example, the weather in Toronto might be hot on a specific summer day, but the long-term climate is considered to be continental with cold winters and hot summers alike. The Houston Dynamo and FC Dallas of Major League Soccer (MLS) often play home matches late at night after the set has begun to set since the MLS season takes place during the northern hemisphere's summer season. The climate of Texas at that time of year is notoriously hot and humid.

In the sport context, weather conditions can change the business and performance of sport. For example, consider that athletes become susceptible to heat stroke in warm conditions, which can have negative implications for the competitiveness of a sport event. An outdoor NHL game played in Lake Tahoe became too warm to compete as the sun came out which forced games to be delayed upwards of eight hours (AP, 2021). However, from a business standpoint, alcohol and soda sales go up on hot days. So, for the event managers, the hot weather conditions can be a boon for business. In baseball, golf, and tennis, rain can result in delays or cancelations which can lead teams to forfeit considerable potential earnings in merch and food (keeping in mind that refunds are atypical). In 2021, a Formula 1 race in Spa, Belgium was controversially raced for only four laps due to heavy rains impacting track conditions (Smith, 2021). This left many spectators (and the drivers) unhappy and demanding refunds after spending hours waiting in the rain for a 44-lap event. Knowing the weather ahead of time can help managers to navigate weather conditions, keeping athletes and fans as comfortable as possible while preserving business opportunities.

Extreme weather conditions, such as wildfires, heat waves, flash floods, and tropical cyclones (commonly called typhoons in the Pacific, and hurricanes in the Atlantic) can cause damage to facilities and result in lost income due to canceled events (Dingle & Stewart, 2018; Orr & Inoue, 2019). These major hazards are less common and thus, harder to plan for. And, while some locations are better prepared for familiar extreme weather events (e.g., Florida with hurricanes) other locations may experience these events and be severely underprepared due to the lack of familiarity (e.g., New York with hurricanes). Consequently, when extreme weather conditions present themselves, every extra minute of advance notice is important. For these reasons, it is critically important for sports organizations and managers to monitor the weather.

Until the 21st century, weather monitoring was typically done in a low-tech manner using mercury-based thermometers outside one's window and a daily check of the weather forecast on the radio or television. Now, the latest weather information can be gleaned from a glance at your phone, with hourly projections that are becoming increasingly accurate (e.g., Stern & Davidson, 2015) However, these rudimentary weather reports (e.g., those provided by Weather app on Apple iPhones) often do not offer information on air quality, lightning activity in the region, radar readings on weather systems moving through a given area, or storm warnings.

In some cases, to supplement the basic weather reports available through the news media, sports organizations are employing digital weather radar services. For instance, the National Football League now hosts a meteorologist at every game, either on-site or available remotely. This person reads and interprets weather radar reports that have been designed specifically to flag conditions that are detrimental to football, such as lightning, heavy rain, or extreme heat. Similarly, Formula 1 racing teams track weather conditions since many races will still take place in wet conditions. Given the size of racetracks and length of races, it is possible for parts of the track to experience rain while others are dry and for some laps of the race to experience rain while other laps do not. Team engineers relay important weather information to drivers mid-race to ensure driver safety and performance. These radars that NFL and Formula 1 races use typically require the facility to set up a weather monitoring system on-site that can be accessed and interpreted through apps and internal servers.

Air Quality Monitoring

Related to weather monitoring, but distinct, is the practice of monitoring air quality. The importance of monitoring air quality in the context of sport lies in the potentially negative impacts that polluted air can have on human health. Air pollutants can be especially detrimental to athlete health, as athletes typically breathe heavily and through their mouths during rigorous physical activity, bypassing the natural filtration systems of the nasal passageways (Lippi et al., 2008). Without filtration, it is possible for athletes to consume far more particulate matter and polluted air than a person casually walking down the street or sitting outdoors. Possible symptoms of air pollution ingestion include coughing, wheezing, fatigue, and mild to severe dizziness and confusion (Sissons, 2020). For individuals with underlying breathing difficulties, such as asthma or allergies, the effects of breathing polluted air can be worse (Sissons, 2020). Given this, it is important to monitor air quality for both athletes and spectators alike.

With regard to the detrimental health impacts, early research by has shown that poor air quality can lead to poor performance for athletes, and poor decision-making by officials, leading to a lower-quality competition overall (Lichter et al., 2017; Campelli, 2020). To preserve the health and performance of athletes and officials, some leagues and governing bodies have begun implementing air quality guidelines and policies. These policies typically include a set of moderate and unacceptable thresholds for air quality safety, with associated actions for each threshold (e.g., delay play, move indoors, take more breaks, cancel play).

One digital tool that is becoming more common, particularly in regions that experience significant levels of air pollution and those with wildfires and smoky air, is the use of digital air quality monitors. Air quality monitors, typically measure particulate matter in the air by the size of the particle in microns. For example, most air quality monitors will measure air particles as small as 2.5 microns, which is commonly known as PM2.5. Particles of this size may enter the lungs to cause health problems (Campbell, 2020). Other common air particle sizes include PM1 and PM10 – again measured in microns. Volatile organic compounds (VOCs) may also be measured by these air quality monitors. VOCs are gases from solid and liquid sources like chemicals, paints, sprays, furniture, and other household products that may be harmful to human health (EPA, 2021). Other pollutants measured by air quality monitors may include ozone (O_3), carbon monoxide (CO), lead (Pb), sulfur dioxide (SO_2), and nitrogen dioxide (NO_2), all of which are harmful to humans. These monitors are helpful in determining if air quality is safe enough for competition and for measuring what pollutants athletes may be exposed to in training and competition. This is important for ensuring peak athletic performance.

The most sophisticated use of air quality monitors in sport currently lies with World Athletics, which has employed Kunak Technologies, a Spanish research and technology development company specializing in environmental monitoring, to set up air quality monitors at 1000 athletics facilities globally, to monitor air quality on an hourly basis. Kunak was also retained to install air quality monitors on the backs of the lead cars in World Athletics-sanctioned marathon and race-walking events, to monitor the air quality along the course. The air quality monitors used for this purpose include readings on carbon monoxide (CO), carbon dioxide (CO_2), nitric oxide (NO), nitrogen dioxide (NO_2), ozone (O_3), sulfur dioxide (SO_2), hydrogen sulfide (H_2S), ammonia (NH_3), VOCs, PM1, PM2.5, PM10, temperature, humidity, atmospheric pressure, and dew point (Kunak, 2021).

Digital Facility Management Technologies

In modern stadiums and arenas, an increasing number of operational functions, from air conditioning temperatures to grass-cutting robots, can be controlled from the facility manager's laptop. Facility management technologies and digital applications are increasingly sophisticated and user-friendly. Field of play maintenance is an area that has seen much growth with digital technology. Nearly all essential functions of field maintenance, for example, including soil sampling (or water sampling in the case of boating or aquatics events), pesticide spreading, watering systems, and even mowing may be done with the assistance of digital technology.

Mowing grass fields for sports have relied on a person pushing or operating a mowing machine over every square meter of the field based on the needs of the grass, sport, and facility. It is a time-consuming process for turf managers who must constantly keep the grass at desired lengths ideal for competition. The use of grass-mowing robots has been making this process easier for turf managers. For example, the English football club Forest Green Rovers (FGR) has been using a robotic lawnmower guided by GPS technology to mow its field without the need for constant monitoring by human turf managers (BBC, 2012). This technology has spread to other sport clubs globally (e.g., Bundesliga club Bayern Munich) who now also use robots to manage this task. The use of robots may also make mowing more efficient by decreasing the burning of fuel and production of harmful emissions from mower engines. FGR's robot is powered by solar technology rather than gasoline as an added sustainability bonus for the club.

While cutting back grass to an appropriate height is one task of a turf manager's job, keeping the grass growing is another. Whether it is invasive plants, drought, or winter, turf managers must ensure that the grass keeps growing and maintains its competition quality. Growing seasons exist for all plants and grasses therefore also have annual growth cycles. Known as the "Frozen Tundra," Lambeau Field in Green Bay, Wisconsin, USA sees daily temperatures below freezing in November, December, January, and February (the end of the American football season). Needless to say, grass does not grow well at these temperatures. In order to ensure the vitality and competitive quality of the field, a heating system has existed underneath the grass since the 1960s. Today, this field uses digital technology to track the position of the sun to ensure that parts of the field in shadows receive more heat than parts in the sun (Hall, 2017). This ensures an even growth while minimizing energy consumption by efficiently heating only parts of the field that need it.

Another use of digital technology in turf (and golf course) management is the use of drones. Since drones are able to give turf managers a bird's-eye view of their field or course, they offer a perspective that can be used to collect valuable data like nutrient stress, water stress, infestation and disease, chemical and nutrient application, crop yield, flood mapping, and storm damage (Horton, 2019). With this data, turf managers can make more efficient and informed decisions with regard to the areas they maintain.

One final digital technology to consider for turf is the use of temperature reading devices for artificial turf fields. Artificial fields made with rubber pellets and plastic grass are notorious for their elevated surface temperatures compared to natural grass fields. In fact, turf fields can contribute to the urban heat island effect where population centers (i.e., cities) are warmer than their surrounding countryside due to the absorption of heat by pavement, buildings, and other surfaces that trap heat. It has been suggested in research that artificial turf fields may be upwards of 37 degrees Fahrenheit (~20 degrees Celsius) warmer than asphalt and upwards of 86 degrees Fahrenheit (~47 degrees Celsius) warmer than grass (Myrick, 2019). Any temperature above 120 degrees Fahrenheit (~49 degrees Celsius) can cause skin burns within seconds and artificial turf fields have been known to melt shoes and cause blisters. With several teams using artificial turf fields, Major League Soccer uses Web Blub Globe Temperature readings to determine if matches should be delayed until surface temperatures cool down (MLS, 2016). If field conditions are too hot, it could be dangerous for athletes to play.

Digital Applications for Personal Use

For individual sport participants, a new wave of digital technologies (discussed at length elsewhere in this handbook) has changed the experience of sport. From an environmental perspective, new apps like Weathervane are allowing athletes to track their performance against the climate and weather conditions in their area. The app allows athletes to figure out, for example, how long it will take them to acclimatize to a new city when they travel for competitions, or how they should alter their expectations of performance based on the weather conditions and their acclimatization to those conditions. Similar digital technology is being deployed in the United States in 2021: a personalized weather app called Currently which links athletes and coaches to a personalized meteorologist who will be in a position to advise on weather policies and appropriate adaptation options in the case of inclement weather.

Other apps offer insights into the current conditions of outdoor nature-based sports environments. This is particularly important for ski and snowboard athletes who depend upon snow conditions in order to train and compete. Athletes may have preferences for fresh snow, packed snow, groomed trails, or even ice conditions. Ski Tracks and Trace Snow are two apps that offer skiers the option to compare conditions at different ski resorts. For back-country athletes, subscriptions to apps like Powder Project and Mammut Safety offer regular up-to-the-minute avalanche warnings, fire warnings, and landslide notices, alongside other dangerous and fast-onset environmental changes. The same apps can allow athletes to turn on a tracker while on the mountain or the trail, so they may be located by rescue teams if something goes wrong. For cyclists, Trailforks helps them to find the best outdoor paths at their level in their area.

For swimmers, Swim Guide is an app that tracks water quality at beaches and open-water swimming sites (e.g., rivers, lakes, and ponds), helping swimmers avoid algae and water pollution that can cause bacterial infections and other detrimental health impacts. Swimmers and those who fish in Florida who take advantage of the open-water and natural springs are able to take advantage of an algal bloom map produced by the state's Department of Environmental Protection to check conditions prior to exploring these amenities. Based on these examples alone, it is clear that the use of sport ecology apps can both elevate the sport participation experience by helping participants to find the best and most appropriate sites, and can also help athletes to ensure their safety and wellbeing while participating (by avoiding polluted water and avalanche areas, for instance).

One promising new avenue for sport ecology digital applications is the use of websites and apps in the collection of data for citizen-science projects. Rink Watch, a website run by researchers at Wilfred Laurier University in Kitchener, Canada, is using citizen science to track outdoor rink conditions across Canada and the United States in the winter. Using the site, hockey rink managers (and anybody who has a rink or a pond on their property) can identify the location of their rink, and offer daily updates on the hardness, depth, and temperature of the ice. This website has produced a significant dataset, updated each winter, from which several studies have been published (RinkWatch, 2021).

Another interesting and current application of digital technology in sport ecology is the use of apps to link sport to climate activism. One example is Planet Super League, a UK-based global nonprofit that has leveraged a custom digital platform to encourage sports fans to engage in small, good deeds for the planet. On the platform, fans are instructed to select one of over 80 activities in different categories like energy, creative, food, nature, travel, and water, then upload a picture of them doing the activity to score a "goal" for their team, which reflect the various teams in professional football (soccer). So, for instance, a fan of Arsenal F.C. can score a goal for Arsenal by eating a plant-based meal, or a fan of Manchester United might score a goal by choosing public transit for their commute. At the end of the season, the team with the most goals wins a prize donated by the team.

A final application of digital technology is linking actual sport participation (e.g., miles run, time spent on a spin bike, etc.) to climate solutions. Active Giving, based in France, has championed this concept.

Launched in June 2020, the company has made fast and significant progress toward making a positive impact on global well-being. At the time of this writing, 150K+ trees have been planted with different tree planting project partners and more than 10,000 users have joined the app, garnering financial support from more than 25 companies.

Several other apps and web platforms have entered the sport ecology space in recent years, from different corners of the globe, marking a new trend in sport participation: athletes want to make an impact through their sports. Cycling4Trees, based in Germany, provides users the opportunity to track their cycling and convert miles to trees planted by their partners. RunToPlant offers a similar program through their website, while Earthruns scales the concepts up to a group activity by hosting races to raise money for tree planting. Other startups have launched apps to track the amount of litter collected by ploggers (runners who pick up trash as they go), including PlogAlong and GoPlogging! which facilitated the collection of over 170,000 cigarette butts, 30,000 straws, 52,000 water bottles, 34,000 cans and 22,000 plastic bags between September 2018 and September 2021. As younger generations grow their interest in both sport and sustainable practices, there is considerable room for sport ecology apps to grow in number and scope.

Conclusion

The conditions of the natural environment can no longer be taken for granted. Seasonal length is shifting, the weather is changing and in many cases worsening, and it's important for sport organizations and participants to stay abreast of the natural conditions in their area to stay safe and continue to enjoy their sport. In many cases, digital applications are being leveraged to monitor and manage environmental conditions for sport organizations. Their utility will only get more important and relevant as climate change progresses and conditions become more erratic. Due to declining ozone layer health, Australia has already implemented ultra-violet light forecasts to keep citizens safe while venturing outside.

However, we must remain conscientious of not reaching a point where digital and artificial solutions cause harm to the natural environment, or rather, more harm than is reasonable. For example, given the significant environmental burden of energy systems used to power servers that make weather monitoring possible, we must avoid reaching a paradox point where the cost of the solution (energy-related emissions, environmental degradation to accommodate technological solutions) outweighs the benefits these technologies provide. In other words, if the digital application has a greater cost on the natural environment than the benefits the application brings, perhaps its use should be discontinued or at the very least reconsidered.

Importantly, more research is needed to assess the needs of sport organizations relative to digital sport ecology technologies. We can examine other research and industry trends to infer why there is a lack of research in this space. Currently, many sport managers may view sport ecology as an extra variable to consider or a line item in a budget, but not as an area for revenue generation or cost containment (cf., Ross & Mercado, 2020). If this is the case, then there may not be many opportunities for some sports and sport organizations to monetize in the space of sport ecology and, therefore, no attention given to the development of digital technology. We view this as a problem since climate change will impact both sport and sport ecology. As stated before, digital technology potentially has a role to play in reducing the impacts of climate change and aiding in the survival of some sports. Regardless, as the role of digital technology in sport has increased across all other aspects in an effort to make life easier or generate revenue, it will see an increased role in fighting climate change.

References

Aguado, E., & Burt, J. E. (2015). *Understanding weather and climate* (7th ed.). Pearson.

AP. (2021, February 20). Sun delay: NHL postpones both Lake Tahoe outdoor games due to melting ice. *The Guardian*. Retrieved on January 1, 2022, from https://www.theguardian.com/sport/2021/feb/20/nhl-tahoe-games-sun-delay-ice-melting.

BBC. (2012, April 21). Robot lawn mower used by Forest Green Rovers football club. *BBC*. Retrieved on December 30, 2021, from https://www.bbc.com/news/uk-england-gloucestershire-17791690.

Browning, R. (2018). *A history of golf: The royal and ancient game*. Pickle Partners Publishing.

Campbell, C. (2020, September 16). What are home air quality monitors and should you buy one. *USA Today*. Retrieved December 30, 2021, from https://www.usatoday.com/story/tech/reviewedcom/2020/09/16/home-air-quality-monitors-what-they-and-should-you-buy-one/5804450002/.

Campelli, M. (2020, April 23). Air pollution: Tackling sport's invisible threat. *Sustainability Report*. Retrieved December 30, 2021, from https://sustainabilityreport.com/2020/04/23/air-pollution-tackling-sports-invisible-threat/.

Dingle, G. W., & Stewart, B. (2018). Playing the climate game: Climate change impacts, resilience, and adaptation in the climate-dependent sport-sector. *Managing sport and leisure*, *23*(4–6), 293–314.

EPA. (2021, September 24). Volatile organic compounds' impact on indoor air quality. *Environmental Protection Agency*. Retrieved December 30, 2021, from https://www.epa.gov/indoor-air-quality-iaq/volatile-organic-compounds-impact-indoor-air-quality.

Finney, B. R., & Houston, J. D. (1996). *Surfing: A history of the ancient Hawaiian sport*. Pomegranate.
Hall, R. (2017, September 5). What the Packers do to keep Lambeau Field special. *Turf Magazine*. Retrieved on December 30, 2021, from https://turfmagazine.com/lawn-care/packers-lambeau-field-kentucky-bluegrass/.
Horton, J. (2019). New technology to improve turfgrass management efficiency? *MTC TurfNews*. Retrieved on December 30, 2021, from https://issuu.com/leadingedgepubs/docs/mtc-turf-news-2019-spring/s/10131465.
IIHF. (2002, July 2). IIHF to recognize Montreal's victoria rink as the birthplace of hockey. *International Ice Hockey Federation*. Retrieved December 30, 2021, from https://web.archive.org/web/20070930024002/http://www.iihf.com/news/iihfpr3902.htm.
Kunak. (2021). Kunak AIR pro. *Kuank*. Retrieved on December 30, 2021, from https://www.kunak.es/en/products/ambient-monitoring/kunak-air-pro/.
Lichter, A., Pestel, N., & Sommer, E. (2017). Productivity effects of air pollution: Evidence from professional soccer. *Labour Economics*, *48*, 54–66.
Lippi, G., Guidi, G. C., & Maffulli, N. (2008). Air pollution and sports performance in Beijing. *International Journal of sports medicine*, *29*(08), 696–698.
Mastromartino, B., Wann, D. L., & Zhang, J. J. (2019). Skaing in the sun: Examining identity formation of National Hockey League fans in sunbelt states. *Journal of Emerging Sport Studies*, *2*(1), 1–24.
McCullough, B. P., Orr, M., & Kellison, T. (2020). Sport ecology: Conceptualizing an emerging subdiscipline within sport management. *Journal of sport management*, *34*(6), 509–520.
MLS. (2016, August 13). How MLS measures and managers extreme heat conditions at matches. *Major League Soccer*. Retrieved on January 1, 2022, from https://www.mlssoccer.com/news/how-mls-measures-and-manages-extreme-heat-conditions-matches.
Murphy, D., & Wholf, T. (2020, September 12). Air quality issues expected to increasingly impact sports. *ESPN*. Retrieved June 3, 2021, from https://www.espn.com/espn/story/_/id/29870359/air-quality-issues-expected-increasingly-impact-sports
Myrick, S. (2019, May 8). Synthetic sports field and the heat island effect. *Parks and Recreation*. Retrieved on January 1, 2022, from https://www.nrpa.org/parks-recreation-magazine/2019/may/synthetic-sports-fields-and-the-heat-island-effect/.
Orr, M., & Inoue, Y. (2019). Sport versus climate: Introducing the climate vulnerability of sport organizations framework. *Sport management review*, *22*(4), 452–463.
Orr, M., Ross, W. J., & Pelcher, J. (2020, May 28). Simulated and controlled: Exploring the managerial impacts of sport's evolution from natural to artificial environments [Conference presentation]. North American Society for Sport Management 2020 Conference, Virtual.
RinkWatch. (2021). Homepage. *RinkWatch*. Retrieved December 30, 2021, from https://www.rinkwatch.org/.
Ross, W. J., & Mercado, H. (2020). Barriers to managing environmental sustainability in sport and entertainment venues. *Sustainability*, *12*(24), 10477. Impact factor: 2.576.
Scott, D., Steiger, R., Rutty, M., & Johnson, P. (2015). The future of the Olympic Winter Games in an era of climate change. *Current Issues in Tourism*, *18*(10), 913–930.
Sissons, C. (2020, January 10). How does air pollution affect our health? *MedicalNewsToday*. Retrieved December 30, 2021, from https://www.medicalnewstoday.com/articles/327447.
Smith, F. (2021, August 29). Rain cancels F1 at SPA, Max Verstappen wins on a technicality. *Road and Track*. Retrieved on January 1, 2022, from https://www.roadandtrack.com/news/a37425098/rain-cancels-f1-at-spa-max-verstappen-wins-on-a-technicality/.
Stern, H., & Davidson, N. E. (2015). Trends in the skill of weather prediction at leads times of 1-14 days. *Quarterly Journal of the Royal Meteorological Society*, *141*(692), 2726–2736.

27

Shifting Gender Power Relations in the Digitization of Sport

Simone Fullagar, Adele Pavlidis, and Millicent Kennelly

The Gendered Landscape of Digital Sport Media

How sport is played, consumed, and produced is inextricably connected to emerging digital technologies that pervade all aspects of life. Our digital sporting lives are also a site of social change where gender inequalities and norms are being challenged in relation to the visibility of women athletes and competitions, as well as the desires of fans to engage with a dynamic sporting spectacle connected with personal, group, and national identities. We use the term *women* to refer to a gender category that is a matter of self-identification and subject positioning (cis and transgender), also noting the limitations of either/or categories of gender for non-binary identifications. The digital era has enabled greater visibility for women's sporting bodies that challenge the entrenched masculine norms and histories of sport, while raising further complexities relating to how gender power relations play out in overt and covert ways (Cooky et al., 2021; Fullagar et al., 2018a,b; Pavlidis et al., 2022; Toffoletti et al., 2021; Toffoletti & Thorpe, 2018;). Questions about the role of digital technologies in addressing gender equity in sport are also important at this historical juncture given the particular impacts of COVID-19 that threaten to undo some of the momentum gained in women's sport (Bowes et al., 2021; Pape & McLachlan, 2020). Our chapter explores these tensions and complexities through case study examples of how digital technologies (apps, platforms, formats, content, access, and re-presentation) are implicated in furthering and contesting gender inequalities in sport with respect to elite and professional contexts (national leagues and major sport events). We also include reference to the unique digital context of major sport events (Olympics, Paralympics, and Commonwealth Games) where the gains made with respect to more equitable re-presentation are bound up with broader issues of national identity.

We consider the positive and negative implications of disruptive digital technologies for the gendered landscape of sport and reflect upon the implications for sport management. In this broad sport management context, digital technology (and Artificial Intelligence) is often presumed to be "neutral" (Brady et al., 2022), yet without a gendered analysis, inequality in sport cannot be addressed. It is commonplace to hear activists and advocates argue for the need to increase women's digital presence in order to transform the sport system because "you can't be what you can't see" on and off the field. While women's elite sport has benefited in numerous

DOI: 10.4324/9781003088899-31

ways from the digitization of sport with the growth of social media platforms and some related investment in mainstream coverage, it would be naive to assume a linear progress narrative of greater empowerment. As educators, we often hear such assumptions expressed by (usually male) students in our classrooms as they assume gender equality has been achieved in sport, or even claim that the growth of women's sport is now negatively impacting men's sport. Hence, the importance of ensuring sport management educators, researchers and practitioners critically engage with issues related to systemic and technological change to facilitate greater gender equality as sport evolves through digital innovation. This anticipated next-generation digital shift moves beyond the social media interactivity of Web 2.0 toward the more dispersed Web 3.0 with the "internet of things" driven by machine-based learning, artificial intelligence, data mining, peer-to-peer technologies (blockchain), cryptocurrency, and virtual worlds (Metaverse) that will shape the gendered future of sport (Karg & Wilson, 2021).

Gender, Digital Technology, and Mediated Sport Systems

The value of women's sport as a mediated commodity and its production and consumption through digital technologies and platforms, calls for an understanding of the contested gender power relations that are shaping the sport system within the digital era (Fullagar et al., 2018a,b). As many scholars have critically explored, sport as a physical and digital commodity needs to be understood as a product of a patriarchal sport-media industrial complex that exists within a dynamic system of relationships, including multiple organizational (sport organizations, media, and tech companies) and individual (athletes, fans) actors or stakeholders (Cooky, 2018). Shaped by global and local forces of neoliberal market economies, sport systems are profoundly gendered with respect to how women's sport has been (de)valued and promoted. Gender bias and systemic sexism are forces that shape the (in)visibility of women's sport in a system that values men's sport as the main game of media production, technological development, and consumption. For example, in 2017, Australia's most popular football code, Australian Rules Football, introduced an elite women's competition (the "AFLW" or Australian Football League Women's). O'Halloran (2020) described how the AFLW and its athletes have worked hard to establish legitimacy, yet the men's competition (the AFL) remains the sport's "default" product. Against the historical privilege afforded to masculine sporting bodies as an unspoken and highly visual norm – what they look like, how they move, perform and engage competitively – women's sporting bodies have been positioned as inferior socially, biologically, and economically.

Biologically essentialist and heterosexist ideas about women's weakness, frailty, (un)feminine conduct and (un)desirability – rather than embodied capacity - circulate through digital sport technologies that reproduce and contest gender normativity in the measurement and re-presentation of performance on and off the field. As Perez (2019) has written about in her book on data bias in a world designed for men, "defaulting to the male seems particularly endemic in sports tech" (p. 177). From the design of sport and fitness equipment, clothing, and wearable technologies, to the algorithms and analytics informing the evaluation of sport performance, gender bias has fueled the digital divide related to women's sport and fitness in elite and community contexts. Our sporting lives are shaped by gender - knowingly and unknowingly – as technologies act to code bodies, identities, and images in particular ways (Bivens, 2017). Even the seemingly simple act of searching for web images related to sport is profoundly shaped by gender bias. Simonite (2017) identifies how software development, organizational culture, and the lack of women working in technology design are implicated in how sport is gendered;

> Two prominent research-image collections—including one supported by Microsoft and Facebook—display a predictable gender bias in their depiction of activities such as cooking and sports. Images of shopping and washing are linked to women, for example, while coaching and shooting are tied to men. Machine-learning software trained on the datasets didn't just mirror those biases, it amplified them. (p. 1)

Sport can be understood in relation to three key issues identified by feminist researchers as they shape women's participation as digital citizens, "first, the unconscious (or conscious) biases inherent in the design, development, and functioning of digital technologies; second, existing forms of gender inequality, both offline and online; and third, technology-facilitated abuse" (Henry et al., 2021, p. 8). We follow these analytic threads through examples in this chapter with respect to the implications of Web 2.0 and 3.0 for the multiple forces, habits, and market relations that are not merely "representing" women's sport but profoundly changing the digital production and consumption within everyday sporting cultures.

Toffoletti and Thorpe (2018) argue for a shift from thinking about women's sport primarily in terms of visibility and toward a deeper understanding of the gendered economics of visibility. They analyze the individualizing, and market logics that are infused in social media representations by popular sportswomen who enact empowered identities through self-love, self-esteem, and sharing one's authentic self as the drivers of change (Toffoletti & Thorpe, 2018). Taking this analysis a step further in terms of the transition from Web 2.0 and 3.0 technologies, we can consider how market logics drive technological innovations that position sportswomen as digital entrepreneurs. For example, athletes with celebrity profiles, and their agents, are promoting the liberatory possibilities of a more decentralized internet that is less bound to several powerful tech giants. For example, Instagram is enabling women athletes to monetize their content and fan engagement directly and NFTs (non-fungible tokens) are enabling digital sport products (images, memorabilia) to be delivered via blockchain technology that operates a digital ledger of transactions recorded by connected systems rather than being owned by one organization (Karg & Wilson, 2021). A number of diverse American athletes from different sports who are represented by the Wasserman agency (The Collective women-focused division - Megan Rapinoe, Sue Bird, Mariah Duran, Scout Bassett, Ibtihaj Muhammad) have released limited digital cards as NFTs designed by an LA woman artist.

Such digital memorabilia are emerging alongside more conventional physical memorabilia (player's clothing) and fashion brands created by elite sportswomen (e.g., Megan Rapinoe with teammates co-founded Re-Inc) (Caron, 2021). Through a desire to have greater autonomy in new markets and derive income from their own name and likeness, athletes such as Rapinoe, are addressing the "pay gap" by moving beyond reliance on unions, sponsorship, and salaried income from playing. In particular, "The NFT landscape is an opportunity to provide space for true ownership, crypto participation and authentic creativity in a way that hasn't been done before" (Caron, 2021). The push into virtual commerce also creates a number of complexities relating to the gendered commoditization of the digital athlete, such as increased risk, difficulty understanding digital systems, large environmental footprint, and lack of regulation of crypto markets. In their gender-based analysis of blockchain technology in the development sector, Thylin and Duarte (2019) recognize that new technologies risk exacerbating existing inequalities related to women's access to technology and lack of inclusion in design.

In relation to sport organizations, the AFLW has become the first elite women's competition across the globe to be included in a deal with a cryptocurrency sponsor as the AFL governing body looks toward virtual markets for greater fan engagement and income. They cite the slightly higher proportion of women than men who use cryptocurrencies as a key reason for securing this kind of sponsorship, despite concerns raised over the stability and ethics involved in virtual markets (AFL, 2022). One of the digital challenges facing sport is the tension between tech giants that are gatekeepers of new technologies and the desire for greater diversification of ownership and content creation by athletes, agents, and new sport organizations through virtual markets. The possibilities for women's sport are being recognized on a greater scale where the revenue potential of virtual technologies may also extend to new forms of ownership, governance, and competition. For example, with the emergent Web 3.0, Decentralised Autonomous Organisations (DAOs) may in the future enable sport fans to unite, purchase, and collectively manage a sports team, with some suggesting women's sport will lead and benefit from this trend (Sowden, 2022).

Digital Diversification and Women's Sport Broadcasting

Within the Australian context, the broadcasting of women's sport is being shaped by several significant changes in traditional free-to-air and subscription services and social media formats. Streaming services (e.g., A-League Women's on Paramount Plus) and pay TV (e.g., Fox Sports coverage of the AFLW) have opened up more coverage to consumers with subscriptions. For example, in Australia, women's National Rugby League (NRLW) games have become more accessible with high-definition broadcasts through the streaming platform Kayo. Super Netball has also significantly benefited from recent financial changes (undisclosed) to broadcast deals that move coverage behind the News Corp paywall with Foxtel and Kayo streaming, with increases for player salaries (Carter, 2021). While this broadcast arrangement reduces access for fans who cannot afford subscriptions, digital streaming became an attractive alternative given recent history (prior to 2017) when Super Netball had to assume costs for actually broadcasting their matches (Carter, 2021). However, the broadcasting of international competitions and free access to women's sport coverage (connected to Australian anti-siphoning laws (Jolly, 2022)) has become a public issue with respect to inequities in the purchasing of media rights between various media organizations. Recently, Australian international cricketer Alyssa Healy took to Twitter to say that it was a "slap in the face to say that we're (women's cricket) not commercially viable" as Channel 9 failed to purchase the rights to publicly broadcast the 2022 Women's One Day World Cup in New Zealand, in contrast to their extensive coverage of the men's competition (Jolly, 2022). In response to this call out, and subsequent backlash from fans, News Corp, as owners of Foxtel and Kayo, decided to make the ICC event part of their "freebies pack" via the Kayo platform. This example demonstrates how professional sportswomen are mobilizing social media to highlight inherent tensions between the growing momentum and increased public interest (e.g., growing audiences with respect to cricket) in women's sport and the challenges related to media rights and broadcasting formats (ABC News, 2022).

From a global perspective, new alliances and business partnerships are rapidly developing around the promotion of, and investment in, women's sport. A recent first in global broadcasting has been the investment by DAZN in the Women's Champions League through partnerships with UEFA and YouTube to address the coverage gap by making the competition live and free for fans to watch around the world (DAZN, 2021). Digital platforms that are very popular with young people, such as YouTube, have become important broadcasting sites through various devices such as phones, tablets, computers, and smart televisions. This break away from traditional media formats in terms of free-to-air or pay TV means that women's football can engage and build a global fan base, although new technologies also bring a different set of challenges.

Addressing Gender Bias in Traditional and Social Media Representation

Gender bias in reporting, media production, and actual provision of competitions has perpetuated a long-standing "coverage gap" in the representation of women's sport. Cooky et al., (2021) analyzed the gendered patterns of mediated content in a thirty-year study of televised sport news in the United States and identified little change with 80% of sport program coverage containing no representation of women even with growing digitization. Their most recent data collection phase in 2019 identified a slight overall increase in the coverage of women's sports on televised news (with highlights) to a total of 5.4%, with new categories of online (5.4%) and Twitter (4.2%) representation (Cooky et al., 2021). This period included the FIFA Women's World Cup and if this global event was removed then the representation of women's sport on televised news would drop to 3.5% which was similar to previous years in the study (Cooky et al., 2021).

This research identified some significant changes in relation to how women's sports were covered in a shift away from overt sexual objectification and framing sportswomen as partners of men, and toward more respectful but largely uninspiring, "gender bland" reporting (Cooky et al., 2021). This important study identifies the ongoing challenge of changing entrenched gender patterns in the representation of women's sport within mainstream media reporting and including their social media channels. What is interesting to note in the analysis of "gender bland" reporting practices is the lack of innovation and engagement with the rapidly growing digital public in a market where women's sport and athletes are forging new partnerships (e.g., sponsorship and monetizing), alliances with feminist and social movements while creating different representations.

Lebel et al. (2018) argue that while traditional media:

> trivializes their [women's] place in sport, social media has afforded athletes the opportunity to build brands capable of turning the table on traditional power structures. It has served as a catalyst to create relationships not possible through traditional media outlets and inspired a revolution in sport consumption strategies. (p. 167)

With Web 2.0 the rise of interactive technologies has produced greater possibilities for innovation in women's sport provision, funding, and coverage as the growing diversification of mediated coverage and platforms that enable different content creation and distribution. The rise of fourth-wave feminism – inextricably part of digital culture – has had a significant influence on activist strategies used by sportswomen to advocate for change (Baer, 2016; Fullagar et al., 2018b). From the #MeToo movement calling out systemic violence that dovetailed with the successful prosecution of Dr. Larry Nassar for the abuse of women and girls in US Gymnastics, to the rousing chants of #EqualPayEqualPlay at the FIFA Women's World Cup final in 2019, social media hashtags work to mobilize individual actions into collective activism (eee, for example, https://www.equalpayforequalplay.com.au). Social media has opened up digital opportunities for women athletes and fans to represent themselves in more diverse ways through uploading images, videos, blogging, tweeting and TikToking to engage with different audiences (Nichols et al., 2021; Toffoletti et al., 2021). In their research into women's powerlifters engagement with Instagram, Nichols et al. (2021) ask an important question, "how do we understand the changed affordances of self-representing the sporting body within digital media landscapes?" (p. 5). Rather than simply viewing digital platforms as either empowering or disempowering, they argue that Instagram has a dual significance by increasing the visual representation of alternative femininities through powerlifting images (especially "ugly" facial expressions) and creating a visual archive of memories that reverberate in multiple ways (individual and collective lives) (Nichols et al., 2021, p. 5).

The use of social media has also been significant in the creation of mass participation campaigns aimed at encouraging more women to be active while changing the narratives and images of "sporty" identities. Depper et al. (2018) identify how campaign content and social media engagement contributed to high levels of engagement in the UK:

> With innovative digital marketing strategies, everyday women have become the face of the campaign to promote the This Girl Can brand across virtual and visceral spaces, to inspire and "liberate" women through sport. Diverse bodies, identities and sport activities promote a post-feminist do-it-yourself ethos with funky music to emphasise individual empowerment through conventional and social media formats. While This Girl Can encourages women use social media to share their own sport participation images and write their own active biographies, the campaign brackets out the gender inequities that inform sociocultural judgements about women's bodies as well as the material conditions that constrain access to inclusive sport cultures. (p. 184)

In this sense, greater coverage and visibility of women's sport does not mean equality has been achieved. The issue of backlash and misogyny needs to be understood in relation to how sportswomen are positioned in similar and different ways given the intersectional relations of inequality (e.g., sexism, racism, homophobia, and transphobia) (Ahmad & Thorpe, 2020). Henry et al. (2021) identify how unequal power relations permeate digital spaces and technologies to enact misogyny in a variety of ways:

> Technology-facilitated abuse includes harassment, surveillance, hate speech, threatening messages, impersonation, doxing, restricting access to technology, cyberbullying, child sexual exploitation, and image-based sexual abuse (see e.g., Jane Bailey, Asher Flynn, and Nicola Henry 2021). A number of international studies show that online abuse and harassment are widespread problems, significantly and disproportionately affecting women and girls, particularly women and girls of color, and lesbian, gay, bisexual, transgender, intersex, and queer (LBGTQI+) people. (p. 10)

Changes in digital technology are opening up the sport landscape for women athletes in complex ways that require understanding and interventions to address "backlash." Pope et al.'s (2022) recent research into men's responses to women footballers in the UK identified both entrenched sexism and misogyny, as well as hopeful changes in attitudes and norms. Their point about the need to engage men/boys in the project of change to shift perceptions that equality is a "women's problem," is one that requires thinking through in relation to all digital mediations (e.g., sport marketing, branding, broadcaster discourse, and imagery).

Being Visible and Having a Voice: Sport Feminism in the Digital Age

Digital technology has continued to evolve in many ways alongside women's sport. With the growth of women's sport (both grassroots and professional) new spaces have been created where women's sport can be played, discussed, promoted, advertised, and broadcast. These quasi-public spaces, such as Instagram, Twitter, Facebook, Snapchat, TikTok, and more, continue to provide outlets for women and gender-diverse athletes to be visible and have a voice outside of traditional sport communication outlets (such as organizational PR, advertising, or journalism). However, these spaces, like other public spaces, are gendered in particular ways that often subject women to abuse, harassment, and undermining intent. The Economist (2021) reports that the global prevalence of online violence against women is 85% and that younger women are more likely to personally experience online violence. These spaces are also used by women to defend themselves and each other, share counter-stories and push against sexist norms. One example that highlights a range of these issues and the role of digital technology is the now infamous image of AFLW footballer, Tayla Harris. In 2019, Harris was photographed mid-kick, in a pose typical of AFL footballers male and female. Harris was/is one of the most visible stars of the AFLW; tall, traditionally attractive, young, blond-haired, and a Nike-sponsored athlete and boxer. That photo was posted on Twitter by Seven News (the official broadcaster of AFLW) and a barrage of sexualized verbal attacks (which Harris later likened to sexual abuse in the media (Wood & Maarsdorp, 2019)) were tweeted in response. Seven Newschose to remove the image, stating the following via Twitter (7AFL , 2019).

> Recently we published an image of AFLW player Tayla Harris. The original purpose of publishing the image was to celebrate the power, athleticism, and skills on show in Carlton's thrilling win over the Western Bulldogs. The image attracted a number of comments, some of which were inappropriate and offensive. As a consequence, we have removed the image and the comments.

Harris spoke back using her own Twitter account. Later that same day she tweeted the photo of herself, writing, "Here's a pic of me at work ... think about this before your derogatory comments, animals." The photo garnered over 60,000 likes and inspired a public debate about online trolling and abuse of sportswomen. There is now a bronze statue of that image, offering a memorial of a photo that sparked an important conversation about the responsibility of social media platforms, sport organizations, and sport broadcasters to do something about trolls and abuse.

Harris was not the first player to be seriously trolled in this misogynistic and abusive way. Other players, who did not "fit" conventional, heteronormative femininity were also abused, and their photos removed. Removing the images positioned these women as "the problem" (take away the photo, take away the problem), yet Harris' purposeful and powerful tweet of her own image and calling out the abuse required a rethink of the role of digital technology, and of sport organizations, in stopping or at least minimizing trolling.

The questionable responses of sport organizations in tackling misogyny demonstrates the importance and power of purposeful feminist approaches to digital content within sport contexts. Several large corporations have enabled their digital content managers/social media and communication professionals' license to speak *for/as* the organization. In Australia, the NRL, for example, has gained a reputation for standing up against sexism and speaking back directly to trolls. An example was in 2018 on June 23 when, in response to a sexist comment on a photo of a women's player kissing her girlfriend, the NRL responded, "If we can post a [photo] of Cooper Cronk and his wife Tara kissing, then we can share a photo of Karina Brown and Ness Foliaki sharing a moment too" (Muller, 2018). Other organizations have been slower to "give voice" through social media/technology, with the AFL remaining largely silent or providing auto-reply type responses to complaints and not calling out misogyny (Pavlidis et al., 2022). Organizations that are speaking out via their social media accounts (across Facebook and Twitter) often use humor and colloquial language to speak directly to their followers and commenters with a lens toward equity and social justice.

These are small but important steps in integrating digital technology – now ubiquitous in life and sport – with sport, particularly around the game. The online world is not separate to, or less from, "real life." It is entangled, and the physical spaces (e.g., fields, boardrooms, and stands) are just as much a part of the fabric of sport as are Twitter, Facebook, betting, and livestreaming apps. Thinking about the role of technology in sport, feminist work supports a flattened hierarchy between humans and non-humans. This means it is not only humans that act on technology (humans as dominant) but also technology that has agencies of its own (its affordances, adaptability, algorithms, and so on). In response to public pressure, digital technology companies like Twitter have begun to implement new features to limit trolling and abuse. The options include limiting replies to either just those who follow you, or just those who you tag in the tweet, and more recently a "downvote" feature (Hunter, 2022). These options are meant to support a safer platform and as such, can help curb gendered online violence. However, as *The Economist* (2021) reported, more than half (54%) of women who experienced online violence *knew their perpetrator.*

Although digital technology enables sportswomen to be visible and has a voice, this comes with the risk of violence and abuse. Sports' feminisms can be usefully applied to consider the gendered implications of all aspects of digital technology, including workforce development, content creation, customer service, algorithms, and more. As work by Carah and Dobson (2016) demonstrated, algorithms are influenced by bodies as much as digital technology. AI, digital technology, and social media are not separate from the gendered power relations that women and people of diverse gender live with every day. Instead, they are entangled together, and thinking in this way (sport-technology-gender) can support better outcomes in and around sport.

Women's Representation in the Digital Spectacle of Major Sport Events

Additional layers of complexity arise when sport, technology, and gender collide in the high-stakes context of major sport events, where other markers of intersectional identity, particularly national identity, are also at play (Pavlidis et al., 2020). Major sport events may offer some sportswomen unparalleled exposure in existing and latent markets, with concomitant opportunities to grow their profiles and to capitalize by reaching new or existing fans and sponsors. For example, research conducted by Kunkel et al. (2021) illustrated that some athletes can capitalize on their name, image, and likeness, or "NIL" value, to monetize their social media presence. Yet even as major sport events such as the Commonwealth Games seek to promote equal medalling opportunities for sportswomen and improved media coverage of sportswomen's achievements (Birmingham Organising Committee, n.d.; Robertson, 2018), it is apparent that some sportswomen's stories and images are more prevalent than others (Pavlidis et al., 2020). It is worth questioning whether sportswomen in their multiplicity are adequately heard in the digital conversations and reactions to major sport events, or whether sport events serve to reinforce gender and other stereotypes by privileging digital communication from some sportswomen while marginalizing others.

In the case of the 2018 Commonwealth Games, research examining traditional press coverage of sportswomen in Australian newspapers found that images of "white women smiling" were dominant (Pavlidis et al., 2020). "Whiteness" was clearly privileged (as was traditional, heteronormative femininity) in press reporting on Australia's national team. "Different" women (e.g., women of color, transwomen) were noticeably absent, peripheral, or derided in event coverage. It has been argued that online spaces increase the potential for diverse representation of athletes (Litchfield & Kavanagh, 2019) and that social media facilitates "a unique form of digital activism" (Chawansky, 2016, p. 772) where these "other" sportswomen can be visible and heard. For example, Australian basketballer, Liz Cambage used Instagram to criticize the lack of racial diversity in promotional photographs of the Australian Olympic team's uniform for the Tokyo 2021

Games using the hashtag #whitewashedaustralia (Ramsay, 2021). Chawansky (2016) examined the case of American basketball player Brittney Griner, who also used Instagram to "challenge the intersectional invisibility" of black lesbian sporting celebrities (p. 772) and to "support, inspire and comfort" young followers (p.782). These examples and others (i.e., Litchfield & Kavanagh, 2019) support the idea that virtual platforms can ensure diverse representations of sportswomen, who may "exploit the affordances of digital and social media to seize or hijack the event platform to advance their own ... objectives" (McGillivrary, 2017, p. 1889).

Against this backdrop it may be tempting to believe that digital technologies and social media create equal (or better) opportunities for sportswomen who are overlooked or satirized in traditional media, to tell their own stories and garner positive and productive attention during major sport events. Yet, as McGillivrary (2017) observed:

> Whilst commentators stress the opportunities that exist for digital and social media platforms to flatten out hierarchies, contest power relations and open up a cacophony of voices that permit marginalized interests to bypass the mainstream media, there are powerful interests at play that continue to control, constrain and co-opt. (p. 1892)

For example, Litchfield et al. (2018) focused on social media around the 2015 Wimbledon Tennis Championship and found that Serena Williams "stood out as receiving an overwhelming number of abusive posts" largely targeting her "physicality, sex, sexuality and race" (p. 154). Recently, Rahikainen and Toffoletti (2021) examined the "digital labor" undertaken by sportswomen striving to build their profile, remain visible, and avoid controversy. The work of Allison et al. (2020) focused on sportswomen who transgress, and the minefield of image repair via social media. However, much of the scholarship on sportswomen and social media focuses on high-profile athletes (i.e., Chawansky, 2016; Li, et al., 2021; Litchfield et al., 2018), with relatively little known about the experiences of sportswomen with less celebrity, less "social media capital," or less confidence with digital technology. These examples illustrate that digital advancements are not a panacea for gender inequalities in sport, although social media has ensured that "controlling" sport event messaging is increasingly difficult (McGillivray, 2017, p. 1893).

The major sport event calendar of 2022 has been described as a "bumper" year for women's sport and an "unmissable opportunity" to increase exposure, stimulate commercial growth, and recover from the cancellations and postponements inflicted by the COVID-19 pandemic (Dixon, 2022). Digital technologies will be central to harnessing commercial opportunities, but beyond the money, the juncture of major sport events and the digital realm may play an important role in social change and giving diverse sportswomen access to the conversation. A case from the 2022 Beijing Winter Olympic Games highlighting the intersections of crime, politics, athlete welfare, gender, and race provides an example. Russian figure skater Kamila Valieva tested positive for a banned substance, yet the Court of Arbitration for Sport controversially determined that Valieva could still participate in the Games to avoid causing her "irreparable harm" (Guardian Sport, 2022). Valieva, a "protected" athlete due to her age (15 years) represents the Russian Olympic Committee (ROC) after Russia was banned from the Games for four years for state-sponsored doping (Holmes, 2022). Reporters speculated that it was unlikely the youthful Valieva chose to dope, raising questions of exploitation by those managing her athletic career and welfare (Ingle, 2022). While some expressed concern for Valieva, other pundits and athletes took to social media to condemn the decision and call out CAS' apparent hypocrisy.

United States sprinter Sha'Carri Richardson became a central figure in the debate as she took to Twitter to protest. Richardson was unable to compete in the 2021 Tokyo Summer Olympic Games after she tested positive for marijuana. Supporters pointed out that marijuana was not performance enhancing and that Richardson's mother had just died. Richardson queried via Twitter (February 14, 2022), "Can I get a solid answer on the difference of her situation and mines? [sic]" before concluding, "It's all in the skin" (February 15, 2022): "The only difference I see is I'm a black young lady" (February 14, 2022). Digital platforms coupled with major sport events may give sportswomen newfound opportunities to call out, push back, speak up, capitalize, and self-represent to potentially international audiences. These opportunities may be invaluable commercially, or as forms of activism that challenge the patriarchal sport-media industrial complex. However, as this section has explored social change occurs unevenly (Cooky et al., 2015), and some sportswomen may be more successful than others in wielding digital technologies in their favor.

Future Directions

Drawing together the key threads in this chapter, we argue for the importance of developing a gendered understanding of the development, engagement with, and implications of digital technology in the sport ecosystem. In the context of recent history, there are significant lessons to be learned for sport organizations (e.g., AFL) that have assumed gender neutrality or ignored the digital intensification of misogyny and sexism for women, and, in particular, those who are marginalized with respect to sexuality, gender identity and race. Along with critical considerations, the shift from Web 2.0 to 3.0 will also present opportunities for innovation in sport and in particular women's sport as it is currently undervalued in a changing "market" and society where gender equity is a growing expectation. From an industry perspective, Rebecca Sowden's (2022) blog usefully outlines five key trends that she believes will drive digital innovation in women's sport, (1) web 3.0 supports women's sport fans to take ownership, create new communities and revenue streams, (2) female athletes will have more options to create and monetize their content while connecting more closely with fans, (3) unbundling of men's and women's competition sponsorship rights will free up opportunities for women's sport to connect with brands seeking social purpose, (4) streaming options will diversify and (5) gamification will mobilize women's sport in new ways. Digital technology will continue to exert considerable influence over the future development of sport as it is entangled with the sport-industrial complex and social movements informed by feminist and social justice agendas for change. In the future, sport managers will need to continually develop their digital literacy in ways that incorporate knowledge of gender and related injustices.

References

7AFL. [@7AFL]. (2019, March 19). [image attached]. [Tweet]. https://twitter.com/7AFL/status/1107906627322048517?ref_src=twsrc%5Etfw%7Ctwcamp%5Etweetembed%7Ctwterm%5E1107933975585148928%7Ctwgr%5E%7Ctwcon%5Es3_&ref_url=https%3A%2F%2Fwww.womens.afl%2Fnews%2F17378%2Fphoto-furore-tayla-harris-slams-internet-trolls-as-animals-

ABC News. (2022, January 23). Channel nine criticised as women's ICC World Cup won't be shown on free-to-air. *ABC News*. https://www.abc.net.au/news/2022-01-23/channel-nine-criticised-for-icc-world-cup-broadcast-paywall/100776142?utm_campaign=abc_news_web&utm_content=link&utm_medium=content_shared&utm_source=abc_news_web

Ahmad, N., & Thorpe, H. (2020). Muslim sportswomen as digital space invaders: Hashtag politics and everyday visibilities. *Communication & Sport*, *8*(4-5), 668–691. 10.1177/2167479519898447

Allison, R., Pegoraro, A., Frederick, E., & Thompson, A. (2020). When women athletes transgress: An exploratory study of image repair and social media response. *Sport in Society*, *23*(6), 1023–1041. 10.1080/17430437.2019.1580266

Australian Football League (AFL). (2022, January 18). AFL welcomes Crypto.com in landmark five-year partnership. https://www.afl.com.au/news/695585/afl-welcomes-cryptocom-in-landmark-five-year-partnership

Baer, H. (2016). Redoing feminism: Digital activism, body politics, and neoliberalism. *Feminist Media Studies*, *16*(1), 17–34. 10.1080/14680777.2015.1093070

Birmingham Organising Committee for the 2022 Commonwealth Games. (n.d). Women in Sport: It's our time. Retrieved 15 February 2022, from https://www.birmingham2022.com/news/blog/women-in-sport/

Bivens, R. (2017). The gender binary will not be deprogrammed: Ten years of coding gender on Facebook. *New Media & Society*, *19*(6), 880–898. 10.1177/1461444815621527

Bowes, A., Lomax, L., & Piasecki, J. (2021). A losing battle? Women's sport pre-and post-COVID-19. *European Sport Management Quarterly*, *21*(3), 443–461. 10.1080/16184742.2021.1904267

Brady, C., Tuyles, K., & Omidshafiei, S. (2022). *AI for sports*. Taylor and Frances Group.

Carah, N., & Dobson, A. (2016). Algorithmic hotness: Young women's "promotion" and "reconnaissance" work via social media body images. *Social Media + Society*, *2*, 1–10. https://doi.org/10.1177%2F2056305116672885

Caron, E. (2021, April 29). Rapinoe, bird, Olympians lead Wasserman female NFT release, *Sportico*. https://www.sportico.com/business/commerce/2021/uswnt-wnba-olympic-athletes-nft-collection-1234627493/

Carter, B. (2021, February 4). Super Netball's new broadcast deal hailed as a major step towards financial sustainability, *ABC News*. https://www.abc.net.au/news/2021-02-04/super-netball-new-broadcast-deal-indigenous-committee/13120818

Chawansky, M. (2016). Be who you are and be proud: Brittney Griner, intersectional invisibility and digital possibilities for lesbian sporting celebrity. *Leisure Studies*, *35*(6), 771–782. 10.1080/02614367.2015.1128476

Cooky, C. (2018). What's new about sporting femininities? Female athletes and the sport- media industrial complex. In K. Toffoletti, H. Thorpe, & J. Francombe-Webb (Eds.), *New sporting femininities: Embodied politics in postfeminist times* (pp. 23–41). Palgrave.

Cooky, C., Council, L. D., Mears, M. A., & Messner, M. A. (2021). One and done: The long eclipse of women's televised sports, 1989–2019. *Communication & Sport*, *9*(3), 347–371. 10.1177/21674795211003524

Cooky, C., Messner, M., & Musto, M. (2015). 'It's dude time!' A quarter century of excluding women's sports in televised news and highlight shows. *Communication and Sport*, *3*(3), 261–287. 10.1177/2167479515588761

DAZN (2021). The coverage gap: A step toward levelling the visibility and viewership disparity in women's sports. *DAZN Group*. https://dazngroup.com/sports-desk/womenssports/thecoveragegap/

Depper, A., Fullagar, S., & Francombe-Webb, J. (2018). This girl can? The limitations of digital do-it-yourself empowerment in women's active embodiment campaigns. In D. Parry, C. Johnson, & S. Fullagar (Eds.), *Digital dilemmas: Transforming gender identities and power relations in everyday life*. Palgrave.

Dixon, E. (2022, January 28). Major events, commercial attention and growing audiences: What does 2022 hold for women's sport? *SportsPro*. https://www.sportspromedia.com/analysis/womens-sport-2022-preview-euros-cricket-rugby-world-cup-tour-de-france-femmes/

Economist, The. (2021, March 1). Measuring the prevalence of online violence against women. https://onlineviolencewomen.eiu.com/

Fullagar, S., Parry, D., & Johnson, C. (2018a). Digital dilemmas through networked assemblages: Reshaping the gendered contours of our future. In Parry, C. Johnson, & S. Fullagar (Eds.), *Digital dilemmas: Transforming gender identities and power relations in everyday life* (pp. 225–243). Palgrave.

Fullagar, S., Pavlidis, A., & Francombe-Webb, J. (2018b). Feminist theories after the post-structuralist turn. In Parry, D. (Ed.), *Feminisms in Leisure Studies: Advancing a Fourth Wave* (pp. 34–57). Routledge.

Guardian Sport. (2022, February 15). 'The difference is I'm black': Richardson sees double standard over Valieva reprieve. *The Guardian*. https://www.theguardian.com/sport/2022/feb/14/the-difference-is-im-black-richardson-sees-double-standard-over-valieva-reprieve

Henry, N., Vasil, S., & Witt, A. (2021). Digital citizenship in a global society: A feminist approach. *Feminist Media Studies*, 1–18. 10.1080/14680777.2021.1937269

Holmes, T. (2022, February 15). Why a Russian figure skater who tested positive for doping is still competing at the Olympics. *ABC Online*. https://www.abc.net.au/news/2022-02-15/doping-scandal-winter-olympics-russian-skater/100830060

Hunter, T. (2022, February 4). Twitter got a 'downvote' button. Here's what happens if you click it. *The Washington Post* (online). https://www.washingtonpost.com/technology/2022/02/04/twitter-downvote/

Ingle, S. (2022, February 15). Valieva caught in complicated mess that has been coming for years. *The Guardian*. https://www.theguardian.com/sport/blog/2022/feb/14/valieva-caught-in-a-complicated-mess-that-has-been-coming-for-years

Jolly, L. (2022, January 23). World Cup to be streamed for free after 'slap in the face'. https://www.cricket.com.au/news/womens-odi-world-cup-removed-from-paywall-alyssa-healy-slap-in-face-kayo-freebies/2022-01-23

Karg, A., & Wilson, K. (2021, May 5). NFTs hit the big league, but not everyone will win from this new sports craze, *The Conversation*. https://theconversation.com/nfts-hit-the-big-league-but-not-everyone-will-win-from-this-new-sports-craze-15876

Kunkel, T., Baker, B., Baker III, T., & Doyle, J. (2021). There is no nil in NIL: examining the social media value of student-athletes' names, images, and likeness. *Sport Management Review*, *24*(5), 839–861. 10.1080/14413523.2021.1880154

Lebel, K., Pegoraro, A., & Harman, A. (2018). The impact of digital culture on women in sport. In D. Parry, C. Johnson, & S. Fullagar (Eds.), *Digital dilemmas: Transforming gender identities and power relations in everyday life*(pp. 163–182). Palgrave.

Li, B., Scott, O., Naraine, M., & Ruihley, B. (2021). Tell me a story: Exploring elite female athletes' self-presentation via an analysis of Instagram stories. *Journal of Interactive Marketing*, *21*(2), 108–120. 10.1080/15252019.2020.1837038

Litchfield, C., & Kavanagh, E. (2019). Twitter, Team GB and the Australian Olympic Team: Representations of gender in social media spaces. *Sport in Society*, *22*(7), 1148–1164. 10.1080/17430437.2018.1504775

Litchfield, C., Kavanagh, E., Osborne, J., & Jones, I. (2018). Social media and the politics of gender, race and identity: the case of Serena Williams. *European Journal for Sport and Society*, *15*(2), 154–170. 10.1080/16138171.2018.1452870

McGillivrary, D. (2017). Platform politics: Sport events and the affordances of digital and social media. *Sport in Society*, *20*(12), 1888–1901. https://doi.org/10.1080/17430437.2017.1232392

Muller, S. (2018, June 23). 'Welcome to 2018': NRL defends photo of rugby players' kiss. The Age. https://www.theage.com.au/sport/welcome-to-2018-nrl-defends-photo-of-rugby-players-kiss-20180623-p4znb3.html?platform=hootsuite

Nichols, E., Pavlidis, A., & Nowak, R. (2021). "It's like lifting the power": Powerlifting, digital gendered subjectivities, and the politics of multiplicity. *Leisure Sciences*, 1–20. 10.1080/01490400.2021.1945982

O'Halloran, K. (2020, February 17). Should AFL be rebranded AFLM to reflect equal status with AFLW? *ABC Online*. https://www.abc.net.au/news/2020-02-17/should-afl-be-rebranded-aflm-to-reflect-status-with-aflw/11971866

Pape, M., & McLachlan, F. (2020). Gendering the Coronavirus pandemic: Toward a framework of interdependence for sport. *International Journal of Sport Communication*, *13*, 391–398. 10.1123/ijsc.2020-0237

Pavlidis, A., Castro, L. R., & Kennelly, M. (2022). Shame, pain and fame: Sportswomen losing in Australia's mainstream media reporting. *Sport in Society*, *25*(2), 265–280. 10.1080/17430437.2020.1777101

Pavlidis, A., Kennelly, M., & Castro, L. R. (2020). White women smiling? Media representations of women at the 2018 Commonwealth Games. *Sociology of Sport Journal*, *37*(1), 36–46. 10.1080/17430437.2020.1777101

Pavlidis, A., Toffoletti, K., & Sanders, K. (2022). "Pretty disgusted honestly": Exploring Fans' affective responses on Facebook to the modified rules of Australian Football League Women's. *Journal of Sport and Social Issues*, *46*(1), 103–123. 10.1177/0193723520964969

Perez, C. C. (2019). *Invisible women: Exposing data bias in a world designed for men*. Random House.

Pope, S., Williams, J., & Cleland, J. (2022). Men's football fandom and the performance of progressive and misogynistic masculinities in a 'New Age' of UK women's sport. *Sociology*. 10.1177/00380385211063359.

Rahikainen, K., & Toffoletti, K. (2021) "I just don't wanna deal with the headache of people fighting over the internet": A study of sponsored female climbers' digital labor. *Sociology of Sport Journal*. Advance online publication. https://doi.org/10.1123/ssj.2020-0177

Ramsay, G. (2021, May 10). Basketball star Liz Cambage criticizes lack of diversity in Australian Olympic team's promotional photos, *CNN*. https://edition.cnn.com/2021/05/07/sport/liz-cambage-australian-olympic-committee-spt-intl/index.html

Robertson, S. (2018). Far-reaching gender equality strategy a first for sport. *Commonwealth Sport*. https://thecgf.com/stories/far-reaching-gender-equality-strategy-first-sport

Simonite, T. (2017). Machines taught by photos learn a sexist view of women. https://www.wired.com/story/machines-taught-by-photos-learn-a-sexist-view-of-women/amp?__twitter_ impression=true

Sowden, R. (2022, January 18). 5 trends that will supercharge women's sport in 2022. https://www.teamheroine.com/blog/5-trends-that-will-supercharge-womens-sport-in-2022?ss_source=sscampaigns&ss_campaign_id=61f0b931ef799170e319e433&ss_email_id=61f1a4d0c359a3680edbcf6b&ss_campaign_name=Heroine+Hit+2022&ss_campaign_sent_date=2022-01-26T19%3A45%3A29Z

Toffoletti, K., Thorpe, H., Pavlidis, A., Olive, R., & Moran, C. (2021). Visibility and vulnerability on Instagram: Negotiating safety in women's online-offline fitness spaces. *Leisure Sciences*, 1–19. 10.1080/01490400.2021.1884628

Toffoletti, K., & Thorpe, H. (2018). Female athletes' self-representation on social media: A feminist analysis of neoliberal marketing strategies in "economies of visibility." *Feminism & Psychology*, *28*(1), 11–31. 10.1177/0959353517726705

Thylin, T., & Duarte, M. F. N. (2019). Leveraging blockchain technology in humanitarian settings–opportunities and risks for women and girls. *Gender & Development*, *27*(2), 317–336. 10.1080/13552074.2019.1627778

Wood, P., & Maarsdorp, J. (2019, March 20). Tayla Harris says trolls' social media comments on AFLW photo were 'sexual abuse'. *ABC News*. https://www.abc.net.au/news/2019-03-20/tayla-harris-felt-sexually-abused-aflw-photo-trolls-seven/10919008#:~:text=Harris%20said%20she%20was%20repulsed,%2C%22%20she%20told%20RSN%20Radio.

28
Sport Innovation

Benjamin Kinsky and Christopher Huth

Introduction

New technologies establish central innovations that influence actors in sports and offer opportunities and threats. This development requires sports organizations to take a proactive role not to be left behind by the technological developments of competitors or other industries, but to adapt promising innovations from other industries and create their own pioneering solutions in the field of technology that diffuse in different areas and generate value there.

To meet the demands of a globally connected and increasingly digital business environment, sports organizations need to view technological progress as an evolutionary path that must inevitably be followed to keep pace with change. This requires sport organizations to adopt a visionary mindset regarding technology innovation and develop and apply concepts that allow them to foster the development of sportstech.

Despite the progressive influence of technology on the sports industry, this topic has a subordinate relevance in many sports organizations. Thus, sportstech management, in many cases, corresponds to an ad hoc rather than a strategic approach. Consequently, technologies cannot contribute their full potential to build and strengthen competitive advantage (Schmidt, 2020, pp. 22–23).

In the sports business, the reasons are limited access to (a) talent, knowledge, and skills, (b) inexperienced leadership, (c) risk aversion, and (d) cost (Bertram & Mabbott, 2019; Chelladurai, 2014; Proman, 2019). According to Ratten (2019, p. 3) additional barriers are:

- Time-intensive planning processes
- Long implementation times for innovations
- Issues/problems with property rights
- Resistance against the implementation of innovation
- Difficulty in assessing the potential added value of innovations

Thus, sports organizations are often faced with the challenge of enhancing their management skills in this specific area to proactively deal with technological developments and not be overwhelmed by them.

DOI: 10.4324/9781003088899-32

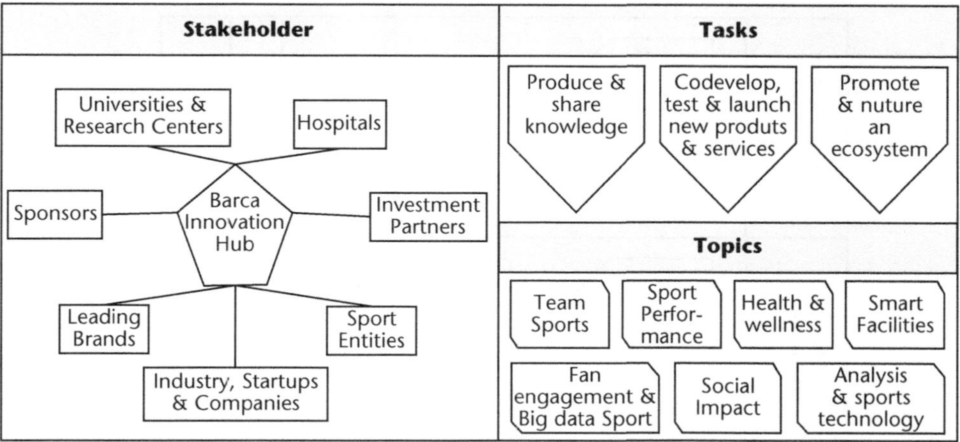

Figure 28.1 Barca Innovation Hub

However, some sports organizations are exceptions and act as pioneers. Many of these are responding to the challenges they face by setting up innovation and technology departments that seem to be related to approaches such as the hub-based model (Engler & Kusiak, 2011; Ervasti et al., 2017). Examples include the Barca Innovation Hub, Real Madrid Next, UEFA Innovation Hub, and the DFB Academy Tech Lab (see Figure 28.1 for the Barca Innovation Hub model).

Another approach is to promote the topic of entrepreneurship. This has a close link to the area of innovation, as the source of innovation often results from an entrepreneurial endeavor (Audretsch & Feldman, 2004). In general, this describes the development and/or pioneering application of new types of technology-based products, services, processes, business models, etc., that are triggered by market opportunities to be seized or market requirements to be met. This results, for example, in cooperation with startups, the founding of spin-offs, or the participation in a joint venture. (Apaydin & Crossan, 2010, p. 1151; Bygrave & Hofer, 1991, p. 14).

Building on this concept, sports organizations initiate startup programs such as LaLiga Startup Competition, YB Hackathon, Werder Lab, Arsenal Innovation Lab, and City Startup Challenge. Some clubs such as the LA Dodgers, Benfica Lisbon, or 1. FC Köln even goes a step further with an accelerator program. Based on an open innovation strategy, sporting goods manufacturers such as Adidas or Asics with their Platform A and Tenkan Ten programs also relied on collaboration with creative and, above all, agile startups to develop ideas for new products and business models. Likewise, the establishment of investment companies such as DFL for Equity appears to be an option in sports organizations' strategic orientation toward sportstech. Clubs such as FC Bayern Munich or Eintracht Frankfurt rely on education-based programs such as Futury or TechTalents (see Figure 28.2), which also address entrepreneurship and innovation topics. The difference is that these clubs see the idea-providing target group as students or young professionals and thus already consciously start in the ideation phase of the innovation process.

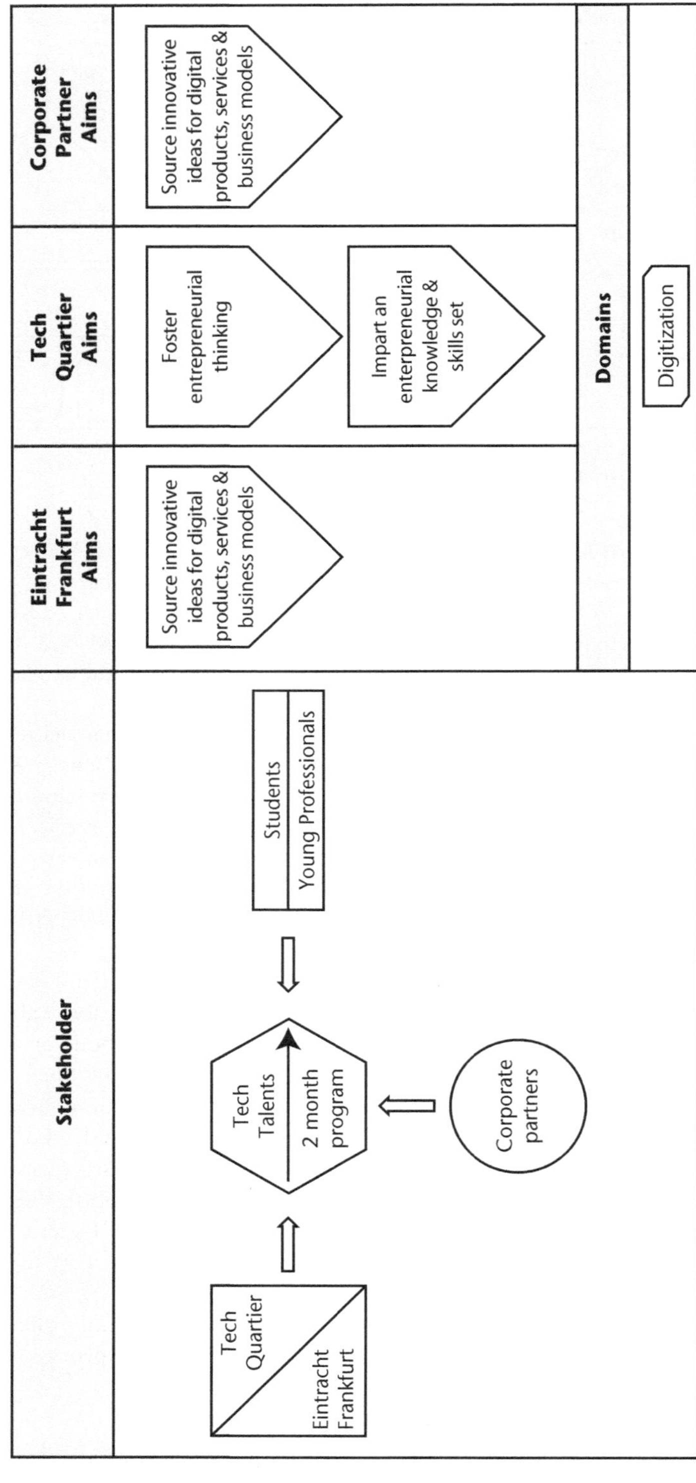

Figure 28.2 TechTalents Model

Clubs with limited resources and knowledge face the challenges of new technologies and digital transformation with a community-based approach that aims to tackle these through synergies and a shared network. The so-called Sport Innovation Alliance comprises more than 20 soccer clubs from different countries.

The community-based approach has also become established at the global, continental, national and regional level with players such as Sports Tech Research Network,[1] The European Platform for Sport Innovation,[2] The Australian Sports Technologies Network,[3] or Sports Tech Tokyo.[4]

Detached from the traditional players in sports, a company such as Microsoft, with its Global Sports Innovation Center, also relies on an approach based on working cooperatively with different sports industry players to develop sports technologies and thus establish itself in this field.

Even though new technologies are undergoing a positioning within the sports industry, this development would benefit from more structure (Schmidt, 2020, p. 31). In that pursuit, it can be seen that the examples presented follow an ecosystem approach, which can be compared to the Innovation Ecosystem Model. This concept offers a theoretical framework for the analysis and design of collaborative innovation processes like the rudimentary studied innovation process in the field of sportstech (Ferreira & Ratten, 2017, p. 2). Consequently, this approach can help gain a profound understanding of how technologies emerge and disseminate in sports (Ratten, 2019, p. 45 and 115). To achieve this, a symbiotic development of research in both sport management and innovation should be pursued.

The Innovation Ecosystem Model

Within the innovation literature, the ecosystem approach is exposed as a generic framework model that is controversially discussed in the research field as an evolution or mutation of the Innovation Network & Innovation System Model concept. It is more profoundly supplemented by the construct of the business ecosystem and the conceptual-metaphorical references to biology and ecology implemented therein. Likewise, a nexus to the open innovation paradigm and open system approaches are shown, which are complemented by elements of strategic management research (agent-based model, hub-based model, resource-based view, absorptive capacity, etc.), value creation theory (especially the co-creation approach) and the triple helix model. Due to an expanded theoretical framework, there is no little consensus on the term "innovation ecosystem" (Dedehayir et al., 2018).

Attributes of the Innovation Ecosystem Model

Starting from the multiple connotations of the Innovation Ecosystem Model (IES Model), it is necessary to generate a constituent framework from the multitude of conceptual positions, which depicts central attributes of the approach:

- Ecosystem metaphor
- Central focus on innovation and learning
- Co-Creation
- Interdependent and non-linear inter-organizational relations
- Market orientation
- Self-organization and the central importance of (focal) actors
- Openness & Coopetition
- Central importance of institutions
- Holistic and interdisciplinary
- High degree of individuality

The attributes emerge from previous research on the Innovation (Eco)System (herein referred to as IES) Model and are explained in more detail in the following.

Ecosystem Metaphor

The ecosystem metaphor forms the central perspective in modeling the dynamics of complex interdependent relationships between system entities that pursue a functional goal in the IES Model that lies in developing innovations. The actors of both system types, natural and IESs are heterogeneous. They compete, attack, consume, and support each other as organisms do in nature (Allen & Shaw, 2018; Bifulco et al., 2017).

In sports, we can identify the same principle. There are also inter-organizational relationships and dependencies between the individual players. A simple example is a sports league where professional sports clubs are interrelated with each other due to the duality of competition and cooperation. These relationships are managed by an additional player, a league association that intervenes and organizes the competition. Natural ecosystems and IES adapt to internal and external disturbances through evolutionary processes at different levels. The same applies to the sports business, which is undergoing progressive change due to sportstech's influence (Ratten, 2019; Schmidt, 2020).

The development of innovations is the central theme of the IES Model. Congruent to this, sportstech is a central innovation object in sports. Fostering that interactive learning is an essential process behind the development of innovations and a key element for sports organizations to implement new technologies (Ratten, 2019, p. 14).

Co-creation

In addition to the focus on interactive learning, horizontal and vertical value creation is considered a central process of innovation development based on a market-oriented perspective. Based on the principle of co-creation, the IES Model views the development of innovations as a process geared to generating more value together than individual actors could independently of each other. In the context of the innovation process, all value-generating actors and institutions are considered. (Autio & Thomas, 2013) In particular, this appears to be crucial in sports because industry players vary in terms of their resource-related requirements. As a result, sports organizations are usually unable to map all the factors relevant to the development of sports-related technologies. Therefore, they are dependent on external partners.

Interdependent and Non-Linear Inter-Organizational Relations

The development of innovations is subject to highly complex inter-organizational relationships, often characterized by reciprocity, interactivity, and feedback mechanisms that create non-linear dependencies, as occurs in the development of technologies in the sports in which innovators rely on external partners.

Market Orientation

Within the IES Model, the innovation process is significantly oriented toward market-relevant aspects (Göktas & Mercan, 2011). As market-driven innovation objects, technological innovations manifest themselves as technological regimes within the sports industry, which can be attributed to push and pull effects. Besides, the sports industry is a profound test laboratory for technologies that can potentially disrupt other sectors. In particular, the special access of sports clubs to their members and fans offers outstanding opportunities to test new technologies and develop them further based on customers and user needs.

Self-Organization and the Central Importance of (focal) Actors

Based on a market-oriented view, IESs are understood as self-organized units in which focal IES organizations are attested a proactive role as the examples discussed in part 1 demonstrate. Building on this aspect, the IES approach emphasizes key actors, for example, professional sports clubs, sports associations, or sporting goods manufacturers, as focal IES organizations that play a dominant role in the governance and design of an ecosystem. Institutions and organizations such as universities, research institutes, intermediaries, suppliers, customers, governments, authorities, business associations, and consulting firms are analyzed as strategic partners that support the acceleration and scaling of innovations.

Openness and Coopetition

An IES and its players' openness is seen as a central element for implementing vital inter-organizational relationships in innovation development. In this regard, the conceptual anchoring of the open innovation paradigm in the IES Model includes reflecting external resources' integration in system-/organizational innovation processes (Bifulco et al., 2017). In sports, this means pushing the concept of coopetition and thus encouraging competitors to collaborate. Especially among professional sports clubs, this is a particular challenge that needs to be modeled. An initial successful approach is, for example, the Sports Innovation Alliance or the German football club TSG Hoffenheim, which relies on cooperation with organizations from other sports as part of its technology development.

Central Importance of Institutions

Institutions, such as politics, laws, or social/technological standards, are essential IES determinants that influence innovation development and organizations' interaction (Edquist, 1997, p. 24 f.). In professional sports, this role is played by federations and leagues, which can be both promoters and opponents of technological innovation by setting standards and regulations.

The holistic approach of the model describes the consideration of all determinants that influence the development of innovations (e.g., organizations, institutions, inter-organizational relationships, interactive learning, knowledge transfer, technological change, absorptive capacity, resources, etc.) (Edquist, 1997, p. 17 f.). The interdisciplinary component of the model considers that, according to the co-creation approach, different disciplines are involved in developing innovations. In this respect, there is a conceptual congruence with the phenomenon of sportstech, which is also a cross-disciplinary approach in which different knowledge and skills are implemented in the development process (Ratten, 2019, p. 4).

The constituent elements of an IES show divergent characteristics, which are determined, for example, by the access to resources, the economic system, or the state of technological development of a region or a country (Edquist, 1997, p. 19 f.). In particular, in sports, this conceptual view at the organizational level offers the advantage of considering the different prerequisites of different types of sports organizations and designing management approaches based on these conditions. For example, sports clubs' ability to develop and implement technological innovations is determined by certain factors. These include the performance level of a club (professional vs. amateur), as this is often linked to access to financial resources that can be invested in sportstech. Besides, the degree of professionalization of a sports club is related to the possibilities of deploying human resources in the development of innovations or creating access to required infrastructures. Also, the degree of sporting and economic competition within a league results in differences between sports clubs regarding the pressure to innovate and the associated drive to adapt sports technologies.

Functions of Innovation Ecosystems

In addition to the eleven attributes that form the generic character of the IES Model, Edquist (2005, p. 8) describes ten essential functions that support the development of innovations and thus forces a further concretization of the framework[5]:

- The provision of research and development and the generation of scientific knowledge
- The development of innovation- and R&D-specific competencies (e.g., provision of education and training, creation of human capital, production, and reproduction of competencies, individual learning)
- The development of new product markets
- The demand-oriented formulation of quality requirements for new products
- The establishment and restructuring of organizations relevant to the development of new fields of innovation (e.g., promotion of entrepreneurship and intrapreneurship, creation of new research organizations, political agencies, etc.)
- The networking of organizations within and between markets to promote interactive learning in collaborative innovation processes
- The implementation and restructuring of institutions that influence innovative organizations and innovation processes by providing incentives or barriers to innovation (e.g., intellectual property rights, tax laws, environmental and safety regulations, R&D investments)
- The implementation of incubation activities to realize innovative efforts (e.g., access to facilities, administrative support)
- The financing of innovation processes and measures that facilitate the commercialization and absorption of knowledge
- The provision of consultancy services relevant to innovation processes (e.g., organization of technology transfer, commercial information, and legal advice)

The functions of an IES presented here do not claim to be complete or absolute. This is particularly evident from the fact that to date, there is no consensus in research as to which functions should or should not be included within an IES. Instead, it can be assumed that the functions differ depending on the focus and constitution of an IES and can thus take on diverse and different forms. They are also subject to evolutionary developments, which gives rise to more in-depth studies as the attribute The consideration of different types of innovation, in contrast to the functional development of new products, illustrates, because IESs are not reduced to the development of new products, but serve a diverse range of innovations to be developed.

Next Steps in Research

The use of new innovations in sport contexts can drive the generation of knowledge for IES research as a whole. However, so far the field lacks a systematically well-founded research agenda. To address this issue, This section highlights opportunities for future research in sport-driven innovation ecosystems.

Location

As a particular thematic area of the research fields "concept" and "structure," the research focus "location" focuses on the location-related consideration of innovation (eco)systems (continents, states, regions, cities). On a theoretical level, this includes the definition, discussion, and sharpening of the importance of location as a substantial innovation (eco)system determinant. Furthermore, the focus is on the bipolar debate on the positive effects of accumulation of network partners compared to the redundancy of spatial proximity, which is losing importance due to developments such as digitalization and modern ICT technologies. In particular, the theoretical approaches to the geography of innovation, territorial innovation systems, territorial innovation model, spatial innovation system, and innovative milieu show a strong focus in this respect.

The scientific literature on an empirical level pushes the analysis of the political, geographical, and socio-economic structure of locations and the influence on innovation (eco) system-relevant aspects. These include, for example, innovation performance, communication processes, and knowledge transfer (Asheim et al., 2011; Breschi & Lissoni, 2001; Bunnell & Coe, 2001; Malecki & Oinas, 2002). In sports, this research field is of particular importance since sports organizations have a local, regional, national or international focus of varying strength, depending on the type, but are always locally anchored in one location.

Based on these very different starting conditions, several questions can be derived.

Are sports-specific IESs more locally, regionally, or nationally anchored? Which factors influence the respective characteristics of a sport-specific IES? Is it local factors and relationships or new digital technologies that offer even clubs in regions with low conditions an option to participate in supraregional IESs?

Innovation Performance

The research field "innovation performance" forms the theoretical and empirical consideration of the innovation output of innovation (eco)systems, a geographical area, or an innovation (eco) system organization and represents a fundamentally discussed target variable amid the research literature, which is to be determined and evaluated. Thematically, this is divided into the development of measurement approaches and identifying determinants that condition innovation performance.

The foundation of the conceptualized analysis approaches is constructed from the spectrum of social network theory, learning theory, relationship theory, transaction cost theory, the economic network model, the resource-based view, or the models of knowledge production and knowledge transfer. Thematically, a bridge is built between the research foci "innovation drivers and barriers" and "capabilities" (Acs et al., 2002; Adner & Kapoor, 2016; Basole et al., 2015; Carlsson et al., 2002; Guerrero & Urbano, 2017; Lau & Lo, 2015; Nooteboom, 2000).

The analysis of IESs in sports such as the Barca Innovation Hub or the Australian Sports Technologies Network represents an interesting research object. On the one hand, it seems interesting to measure their innovation performance. On the other hand, there is the possibility of identifying and testing different approaches to performance measurement to achieve progress in this area, for example, by gaining knowledge about performance determining factors.

Evolution

The research field innovation (eco)system "evolution" focuses on the theoretical and empirical investigation and evaluation of the transformation of innovation (eco)systems over historical time. The main focus is on co-evolutionary processes and path dependencies between networks and their environment and related progressive and recessive developments. Analogous to the analysis of the research foci "structure" and "comparison," the fields of investigation considered extend across specific research domains (politics, economy, science, technology), their subcategories (industries, country-specific development status), different geographical levels (global, national, regional, local) and organizations (universities, companies). Differentiated research parameters complement the conceptual research framework. This portfolio is configured by the research foci: Structure (primarily through co-evolutionary processes such as market dynamics or the transformation of socio-economic and socio-technical systems), innovation policy, strategic management, innovation drivers and barriers, functions, interorganizational relations, and roles. (Bergek et al., 2008; Furman et al., 2002; Intarakumnerd et al., 2006; Martin & Simmie, 2008; Motohashi & Yun, 2007)

Due to the progress of the field of sports, it offers the possibility to explore the development of IESs based on sports. For example, various programs are currently being initiated in sports that could give rise to an IES's emergence. It is questionable whether these initiatives reach the maturity level of an IES. In retrospect, it seems exciting to evaluate the chosen initiation strategies and identify preconditions that favor or hinder an IES's development.

Innovation Process

The consideration of the development of innovations based on "innovation process" models acts as a central theoretical framework of the IES concept. In this respect, the focus is on the evolution of the innovation model, characterized by a restructuring of the closed innovation paradigm. This perspective is described by an understanding that innovation development is an open, complex, non-linear, social, and interactive process that requires external influences. Consequently, innovation processes are placed in a systemic context in the context of IES research. In this respect, the empirical focus is on identifying and analyzing cooperative innovation processes within geographic and industrial IES structures (Adner & Kapoor, 2016; Beckmann et al., 2015; Binz & Truffer, 2017; Dunn et al., 2016; Edquist, 2005; Etzkowitz & Ranga, 2013; Markard & Truffer, 2008; Muller & Zenker, 2001; Rohrbeck et al., 2009; Zygiaris, 2013).

Based on the fact that the development of innovations on the premise of cooperative innovation processes is influenced uniquely by a unique competitive mindset in sports, this research field appears to be quite promising. In particular, the question under which conditions competitors would cooperate in innovation development seems to be target-oriented in this respect.

It is also necessary to examine how established innovation process models can be transferred to sports or require adaptation in this context because many sports organizations such as nonprofit sports clubs, leagues, or associations do not have an internal innovation process that could serve as an interface to a cooperative innovation process within an IES. Thus, the challenge lies in the development and analysis of innovation processes that are aligned and applicable.

Functions

Within the research topic "functions," the conceptual illustration of tasks, activities, requirements, and expectations relevant in the context of innovation (eco)systems are formed. In this respect, the research guiding position has been established that the purpose of innovation (eco) systems is to organize specific functions immanently, which is realized in the form of characteristic role profiles inherent to innovation (eco)system organizations and institutions.

In the context of structural analysis, functions serve as a standardized theoretical frame of reference for evaluating and comparing innovation (eco)systems by defining clear system boundaries. Furthermore, a diverse portfolio of innovation (eco)system functions can be identified in the literature. Decisive for the variation of the function sets are different expression options along with technological, sectoral, and territorial parameters. (Agouridas et al., 2013; Amesse & DeBresson, 1990; Bergek et al., 2008; Edquist, 2007; Geels, 2004; Gloor, 2006; Mowery & Oxley, 1995)

For sports, focusing on this research area offers the opportunity to identify IES-specific tasks in sportstech development, thus promoting a progressive establishment of the model within sports based on its added values. In this regard, it seems interesting to examine the different functions of an IES from various sports organizations' perspectives.

Economic Growth

Based on the Schumpeterian paradigm that innovation is a central driver of "socio-economic growth," this spectrum of research forms the theoretical and empirical consideration of the innovation's economic and social development (eco)system environment. Accordingly, the innovation (eco)system model with its partial foundation in evolutionary economics, institutional economics, and endogenous growth theory serves as an explanatory approach to socio-economic development over time. The focus here is on the development of measurement models to analyze the influence of innovation (eco)systems on the socio-economic performance of a state, region, or industry, for example, based on the parameters: Gross domestic product, income, export performance, knowledge transfer, market dynamics or taxes (Andersen et al., 2002; Chaminade et al., 2009; Edquist & Hommen, 2007; Fagerberg & Srholec, 2008; Freeman, 2002; Fukuda & Watanabe, 2008; Mowery & Oxley, 1995; Nelson & Nelson, 2002).

As an industry and social instrument, sport plays a vital role in the context of socio-economic growth. Consequently, examining the influence of sport-specific IESs appears to be a relevant field of investigation that promises to illustrate how developed products and services from sport-specific IESs affect socio-economic growth. In particular, looking at the link between sports science and medicine from the perspective of the IES Model holds insights into how innovation from competitive sports can add value to prevention and rehabilitation.

Social innovations are often linked to the context of sport and thus represent an innovation object that has a natural influence on socio-economic growth, making the measurement of its impact relevant.

Innovation Drivers and Barriers

As a subcategory of the research field "concept," the research themes "innovation drivers and barriers" contributes to its theoretical enrichment. The topic's consideration includes the case study-based exploration of innovation (eco)system determinants that positively or negatively influence the development and interaction within networks. They characterize themselves as multilateral and can be categorized along with three levels of analysis: micro, meso, and macro (Aarts & Klerkx, 2013). Concerning this research field, sport represents a promising research context that allows conclusions to be drawn for its industry and results that can be transferred to other sectors.

Innovation Capability

The analysis of "innovation capability" implies the theoretical explanation and empirical foundation of parameters that determine the innovation potential of an innovation (eco)system, a geographical area, or an innovation (eco)system organization. This (Adner & Kapoor, 2016) manifests itself in developing analytical frameworks that take up aspects of the research topics "innovation drivers and barriers" and "performance." Conceptually, the analytical approaches are mostly based on network theory (Acs et al., 2002; Najafi-Tavania et al., 2018). Two questions appear to be of particular importance in the context of sports. What prerequisites and resources must a sports organization have to influence an IES's innovative capacity positively? And conversely, how can an IES increase the innovative capacity of sports organizations in concrete terms?

Spillover Effects

The field of research "spillover effects" implies the consideration of knowledge and technology transfers between IES actors, such as universities, private research institutions, and companies, under the aspect of commercialization of research results. This is done on a theoretical level by differentiating and embedding the term "knowledge spillover" into the IES concept as a determinant factor. Consequently, this research strand serves as a complement to the spectrum of inter-organizational relationships based on which knowledge and technology transfer advance.

On the vertical level, inter-organizational relations between research domains (politics, economy, science, etc.) and between institutions, organizations, and individuals (universities, companies, incubators, consumers, etc.) are the focus of attention. Horizontally, the analysis is formed due to the differentiation of geographic, economic, and cultural spaces (Acs et al., 2002; Audretsch & Feldman, 2004; Breschi & Lissoni, 2001; Feldman, 2003; Wang & Zhang, 2019). Sportstech offers a highly suitable setting for the study of spillover effects, as sports is an arena from which innovations diffuse into other areas. However, sports is also a sector in which many innovations are adapted from other areas so that the phenomenon of the spillover effect can be observed in various forms.

Participation Motives

The consideration of "participation motives" includes the discussion of motivation models and the development of theoretical motive structures in the context of innovation (eco)systems, which are operationalized on an empirical level through concrete analysis. In this respect, the focus is on the survey of participation incentives of different innovation (eco)system actors such as, e.g., companies (cost and risk reduction, strengthening of a monopoly position, shortening of product development phases, exploration of new markets, and niches, technology transfer, and complementarity, monitoring of technologies and business opportunities), universities (inspiration for research projects, generation of financial capital, creation of jobs, independence from public contracts) or consumers who participate in an open-source or open innovation platform (unmet customer needs, remuneration, recommendation on the labor market, further education, identification with a developer community, fun in developing innovations). (Almirall et al., 2014; Cooke & Schall, 2007)

In sports, it would appear to help identify the participation motives that are characteristic of sports organizations. The insights gained from this can thus be incorporated into recommendations for action that enable IESs to be designed in line with the needs of its actors involved.

Innovation Culture

The consideration of "innovation culture" includes explaining relevant determinants of the innovation culture of geographical regions (e.g., states, regions) or innovation (eco)system organizations and its influence on the innovation performance of an IES and its actors (Agogino et al., 2014; Göktas & Mercan, 2011).

Because innovation and innovation culture in sports describes new subjects that need to be managed, it is crucial to integrate and discuss existing findings and models of innovation culture research more strongly in IES research. To create an initial starting point, the study of the characteristics of innovation culture in the different types of sports organizations seems to be target-oriented. Based on the results obtained, existing innovation culture concepts can be included in the discussion and adapted if necessary.

Notes

1 https://strn.co
2 https://epsi.eu
3 https://astn.com.au
4 https://sportstech.tokyo
5 The ten essential functions of an IES are based on the model's theoretical foundation following the System of Innovation approach.

References

Aarts, N., & Klerkx, L. (2013). The interaction of multiple champions in orchestrating innovation networks: Conflicts and complementarities. *Technovation, 33*, 193–210.

Acs, Z. J., Anselin, L., & Varga, A. (2002). Patents and innovation counts as measures of regional production of knowledge. *Research Policy, 31*(1069–1085).

Adner, R., & Kapoor, R. (2016). Innovation Ecosystems and the pace of substitution: Re-examining technology s-curves. *Strategic Management Journal, 37*, 625–648.

Agogino, A., Chesbrough, H., & Kin, S. (2014). Chez Panisse: Building an open innovation ecosystem. *California Management Review, 56*(4), 144–171.

Agouridas, V., Assimakopoulos, D., Gies, O., & Ritala, P. (2013). Value creation and capture mechanisms in innovation ecosystems: A comparative case study. *International Journal of Technology Management, 63*(3/4), 244–267.

Ahrweiler, P., Gilbert, N., & Pyka, A. (2001). Innovation networks - a simulation approach. *Journal of Societies and Social Simulation, 4*(3), 1–14.

Alänge, S., & Steiber, A. (2013). A corporate system for continuous innovation: The case of Google Inc. *European Journal of Innovation Management, 16*(2), 243–264.

Allen, T., & Shaw, R. D. (2018). Studying innovation ecosystems using ecology theory. *Technological Forecasting & Social Change, 136*, 88–102.

Almirall, E., Lee, M., & Majchrzak, A. (2014). Open innovation requires integrated competition-community ecosystems: Lessons learned from civic open innovation. *Business Horizon, 57*(3), 391–400.

Amesse, F., & DeBresson, C. (1990). Networks of innovators: A review and introduction to the issue. *Research Policy, 20*, 363–379.

Andersen, E. S., Dalum, B., Johnson, B., & Lundvall, B.-A. (2002). National systems of production, innovation and competence building. *Research Policy, 31*, 213–231.

Apaydin, M., & Crossan, M. M. (2010). A multi-dimensional framework of organizational innovation: A systematic review of the literature. *Journal of Management Studies, 47*(6), 1154–1191.

Asheim, B. T., Lawton Smith, H., & Oughton, C. (2011). Regional innovation systems: Theory, empirics and policy. *Regional Studies, 45*(7), 875–891.

Audretsch, D. B., & Feldman, M. P. (1996). R&D Spillovers and the geography of innovation and production. *The American Economic Review, 86*(3), 630–640.

Audretsch, D. B., & Feldman, M. P. (2004). Knowledge spillovers and the geography of innovation. In J. V. Henderson & J.-F. Thisse (Eds.), *Handbook of regional and urban economics* (Vol. 4, pp. 2713–2739). Amsterdam: Elsevier.

Autio, E., & Thomas, L. D. W. (2013). Innovation ecosystems: Implications for innovation management. In M. Dodgson, D. M. Gann, & N. Phillips (Eds.), *The oxford handbook of innovation management* (pp. 204–228). Oxford: Oxford University Press.

Basole, R. C., Huhtamaki, J., Still, K., Rubens, N., & Russell, M. G. (2015). Relational capital for shared vision in innovation. *Triple Helix, 2*(1), 1–36.

Beckmann, A., Böhmer, A. I., & Lindemann, U. (2015).*Open Innovation Ecosystem - Makerspaces within an Agile Innovation Process*. Paper presented at the ISPIM Innovation Summit, Brisbane, Australia.

Beiderbeck, D., Frevel, N., Penkert, B., Schmidt, S. L., & Subirana, B. (2020). Taxonomy of sportstech. In S. L. Schmidt (Ed.), *21st Century sports-How technologies will change sports in the digital age* (pp. 15–38). Düsseldorf: Springer.

Belussi, F., Sammarra, A., & Sedita, S. R. (2010). Learning at the boundaries in an "Open Regional Innovation System": A focus on firms' innovation strategies in the Emilia Romagna life science industry. *Research Policy, 39*, 710–721.

Bergek, A., Carlsson, B., Jacobsson, S., Lindmarki, S., & Rickne, A. (2008). Analyzing the functional dynamics of technological innovation systems: A scheme of analysis. *Research Policy, 37*, 407–429.

Berger, M., & Diez, J. R. (2005). The role of multinational corporations in metropolitan innovation systems: empirical evidence from Europe and Southeast Asia. *Environment and Planning A, 37*, 1813–1835.

Bertram, C., & Mabbott, J. (2019). The sportstech report—Advancing victoria's startup ecosystem. Retrieved from https://launchvic.org/files/The-SportsTech-Report.pdf

Bessant, J., Gray, B., Hoffman, K., Marshall, N., Ramalingam, B., & Rush, H. (2014). *Innovation Management, Innovation Ecosystems and Humanitarian Innovation*. Retrieved from https://www.gov.uk/research-for-development-outputs/innovation-management-innovation-ecosystems-and-humanitarian-innovation

Biemans, W. G. (2018). *Managing innovation within networks* (Vol. 7). New York: Routledge

Bifulco, F., Russo-Spena, T., & Tregua, M. (2017). Searching through the jungle of innovation conceptualisation – System, network and ecosystem perspectives.*Journal of Service Theory and Practice, 27*(5), 977–1005.

Binz, C., & Truffer, B. (2017). Global Innovation Systems – A conceptual framework for innovation dynamics in transnational contexts. *Research Policy, 46*(7), 1284–1298.

Blättel-Mink, B., & Ebner, A. (2009). *Innovationssysteme technologie, institutionen und die dynamik der wettbewerbsfähigkeit* (Vol. 1). Wiesbaden: VS Verlag für Sozialwissenschaften.

Boekholt, P., Cooke, P., & Tödtling, F. (2000). *The governance of innovation in Europe: Regional perspectives on global competitivness*. London: Pinter.

Braczyk, H.-J., Cooke, P., & Heidenreich, M. (Eds.). (2004). *Regional innovation systems - The role of governance in a globalized world* (2 ed.). London: Routledge

Brennan, W., & Echeverri-Carroll, E. L. (1999). Are innovation networks bounded by proximity?. In M. M. Fischer & L. Suarez-Villa (Eds.), *Innovation, networks and localities*. Berlin: Springer.

Breschi, S., & Lissoni, F. (2001). Localised knowledge spillovers vs. Innovative milieux: Knowledge "tacitness" reconsidered. *Papers in Regional Science, 80*, 255–273.

Bunnell, T. G., & Coe, N. M. (2001). Spaces and scales of innovation. *Progress in Human Geography, 25*(4), 569–589.

Bygrave, W. D., & Hofer, C. W. (1991). Theorizing about entrepreneurship. *Entrepreneurship, Theory and Practice, 16*(2), 13–22.

Cacciolatti, L., Lee, S. H., Song, W., & Zhao, S. (2015). Regional collaborations and indigenous innovation capabilities in China: A multivariate method for the analysis of regional innovation systems. *Technological Forecasting & Social Change, 94*, 202–220.

Calia, R. C., Guerrini, F. M., & Moura, G. L. (2007). Innovation networks: From technological development to business model reconfiguration. *Technovation, 27*, 426–432.

Campbell, D. F. J., & Carayannis, E. G. (2007). A "Mode 3" system approach for knowledge creation, diffusion, and use: Towards a twenty-first-century fractal innovation ecosystem. In E. G. Carayannis & C. Ziemnowicz (Eds.), *Rediscovering Schumpeter - Creative destruction evolving into "mode 3"* (pp. 71–111). New York: Palgrave Macmillan.

Cantner, U., & Graf, H. (2006). The network of innovators in Jena: An application of social network theory. *Research Policy, 35*, 463–480.

Cantù, C., Corsaro, D., & Tunisini, A. (2012). Actors' heterogeneity in innovation networks. *Industrial Marketing Management, 41*(5), 780–789.

Carlsson, B., Holmen, M., Jacobsson, S., & Rickne, A. (2002). Innovation systems: Analytical and methodological issues. *Research Policy, 31*, 233–245.

Chaminade, C., Lundvall, B.-A., Joseph, K. J., & Vang, J. (Eds.). (2009). *Handbook of innovation systems and developing countries – Building domestic capabilities in a global setting*. Cheltenham: Edward Elgar.

Chaoroenpron, P., & Intarakumnerd, P. (2013). The roles of intermediaries and the development of their capabilities in sectoral innovation systems: A case study of Thailand. *Asia Journal of Technology Innovation, 12*(2), 99–114.

Chelladurai, P. (2014). *Managing organizations for sport and physical activity: A systems perspective*. Scottsdale: Holcomb-Hathaway.

Chesbrough, H., & Saffo, P. (2013). Social web as an innovation ecosystem. In H. Oinas-Kukkonen (Ed.), *Technology, work, and globalization* (pp. 105–119). Basingstoke: Palgrave Macmillan.

Cooke, P., & Schall, N. (2007). Schumpeter and varieties of innovation: Lessons from the rise of regional innovation systems research. In H. Hanusch & A. Pyka (Eds.), *Elgar companion to Neo-Schumpeterian economics* (pp. 896–925). Cheltenham: Edward Elgar.

Cunningham, J. A., Menter, M., & O'Kane, C. (2017). Value creation in the quadruple helix: a micro level conceptual model of principal investigators as value creators. *R&D Management, 48*(1), 136–147.

Da Rosa Pires, A., De Castro, E. A., Esteves, C., & Rodrigues, C. (2000). The triple helix model as a motor for the creative use of telematics. *Research Policy, 29*, 193–203.

Davis, J. P. (2016). The group dynamics of interorganizational relationships: Collaborating with multiple partners in innovation ecosystems. *Administrative Science Quarterly, 61*(4), 621–661.

Dedehayir, O., Mäkinen, S. J., & Ortt, R. J. (2018). Roles during innovation ecosystem genesis: A literature review. *Technological Forecasting and Social Change, 136*, 18–29.

Dedrick, J., Linden, G., & Kraemer, K. L. (2009). Who captures value in a global innovation system? The case of apple's iPod. *Communications of the ACM, 52*(3), 140–144.

Dhanaraj, C., & Parkhe, A. (2006). Orchestrating innovation networks. *Academy of Management Review, 31*(3), 659–669.

Dilk, C., Gleich, R., Motwani, J., & Wald, A. (2008). State and development of innovation networks Evidence from the European vehicle sector. *Management Decision, 46*(5), 691–701.

Dunn, A., McAdam, M., McAdam, R., & McCall, C. (2016). Regional horizontal networks within the SME Agri-Food sector: An innovation and social network perspective. *Regional Studies, 50*(8), 1316–1329.

Ebersberger, B., Herstada, S. J., & Wiig Aslesenb, H. (2014). On industrial knowledge bases, commercial opportunities and globalinnovation network linkages. *Research Policy, 43*, 495–504.

Edquist, C., & Hommen, L. (Eds.). (2007). *Small country innovation systems globalization, change and policy in Asia and Europe*. Cheltenham: Edward Elgar.

Elzen, B., Geels, F. W., & Green, K. (Eds.). (2004). *System innovation and the transition to sustainability theory, evidence and policy*. Cheltenham: Edward Elgar.

Engler, J., & Kusiak, A. (2011). Modeling an innovation ecosystem with adaptive agents. *International Journal of Innovation Science, 3*(2), 55–67.

Ernst, D. (2009). *A new geography of knowledge in the electronics industry? Asias' role in global innovation networks* (Vol. 54). Hawaii: East-West Center.

Ervasti, M., Hurmelinna-Laukkanen, P., Nätti, S., & Pikkarainen, M. (2017). Orchestration roles to facilitate networked innovation in a healthcare ecosystem. *Technology Innovation Management Review, 7*(9), 30–43.

Etzkowitz, H., & Ranga, M. (2013). Triple helix systems: An analytical framework for innovation policy and practice in the knowledge society. *Industry and Higher Education, 27*(4), 237–262.

Fagerberg, J., & Srholec, M. (2008). National innovation systems, capabilities and economic development. *Research Policy, 37*, 1417–1435.

Feldman, M. P. (2003). Location and innovation: The new economic geography of innovation, spillovers, and agglomeration. In *The oxford handbook of economic geography* (pp. 373–394). Oxford: Oxford University Press.

Ferreira, J. J., & Ratten, V. (Eds.). (2017). *Sport entrepreneurship and innovation*. London, New York: Routledge, Taylor & Francis Group.

Freeman, C. (2002). Continental, national and sub-national innovation systems – complementarity and economic growth. *Research Policy*, *31*, 191–211.

Fritsch, M., & Schwirten, C. (1999). Enterprise-university co-operation and the role of public research institutions in regional innovation systems. *Industry and Innovation*, *6*(1), 69–83.

Fukuda, K., & Watanabe, C. (2008). Japanese and US perspectives on the National Innovation Eocsystem. *Technology and Society*, *30*, 49–63.

Furman, J. L., Porter, M. E., & Stern, S. (2002). The determinants of national innovative capacity. *Research Policy*, *31*, 899–933.

Geels, F. W. (2004). From sectoral systems of innovation to socio-technical systems Insights about dynamics and change from sociology and institutional theory. *Research Policy*, *33*, 897–920.

Gloor, P. (2006). *Swarm creativity – Competitive advantage through collaborative innovation networks*. New York: Oxford University Press.

Göktas, D., & Mercan, B. (2011). Components of innovation ecosystems: A cross-country study. *International Research Journal of Finance and Economics*, *76*, 102–112.

Gregersen, B., & Johnson, B. (1996). Learning economies, innovation systems and European integration. *Regional Studies*, *31*(5), 479–490.

Guerrero, M., & Urbano, D. (2017). The impact of Triple Helix agents on entrepreneurial innovations' performance: An inside look at enterprises located in an emerging economy. *Technological Forecasting & Social Change*, *119*, 294–309.

Intarakumnerd, P., Lundvall, B.-A., & Vang, J. (Eds.). (2006). *Asia's innovation systems in transition*. Cheltenham: Edward Elgar

Jackson, D. J. (2011). What is an innovation ecosystem? *National Science Foundation*. http://ercassoc.org/sites/default/files/topics/policy_studies/DJackson_Innovation%20Ecosystem_03-15-11.pdf

Johnson, A. (2001). *Functions in Innovation Systems Approaches*. Paper presented at the Nelson and Winter Conference, Aalborg.

Johnson, W. H. A. (2008). Roles, resources and benefits of intermediate organizations supporting triple helix collaborative R&D: The case of Precarn. *Technovation*, *28*, 495–505.

Jones, P., Jones, A., Williams-Burnett, N., & Ratten, V. (2017). Let's get physical: Stories of entrepreneurial activity from sports coaches/instructors. *International Journal of Entrepreneurship and Innovation*, *18*(4), 219–230.

Kaufmann, A., & Tödtling, F. (2002). SMEs in Regional innovation systems and the role of innovation support – The case of upper Austria. *Journal of Technology Transfer*, *27*, 15–26.

Kedia, B. L., & Mooty, S. E. (2013). Learning and innovation in collaborative innovation networks. In S. C. Jain & B. L. Kedia (Eds.), *Restoring America's global competitiveness through innovation* (pp. 3–27). Cheltenham: Edward Elgar.

Koschatzky, K., & Sternberg, R. (2000). R&D in innovation systems – Some lessons from the European regional innovation survey (ERIS). *European Planning Studies*, *8*(4), 487–501.

Landabaso, M., Morgan, K., & Oughton, C. (2002). The regional innovation paradox: Innovation ploicy and indsutrial policy. *Journal of Technology Transfer*, *27*, 97–110.

Langlois, R. N., & Robertson, P. L. (1995). Innovation, networks, and vertical integration. *Research Policy*, *24*, 543–562.

Lau, A. K. W., & Lo, W. (2015). Regional innovation system, absorptive capacity and innovation performance: An empirical study. *Technological Forecasting & Social Change*, *92*, 99–114.

Liu, X., & White, S. (2001). Comparing innovation systems: A framework and application to China's transitional context. *Research Policy*, *30*, 1091–1114.

Loland, S. (2009). The ethics of performance-enhancing technology in sport. *Journal of the Philosophy of Sport*, *36*(2), 152–161.

Longhurst, N. (2015). Towards an 'alternative' geography of innovation: Alternative milieu, socio-cognitive protection and sustainability experimentation. *Environmental Innovation and Societal Transitions*, *17*, 183–198.

Lundvall, B.-A. (Ed.) (2010). *National systems of innovation – Towards a theory of innovation and interactive learning* (Vol. 3). London: Anthem Press.

Malecki, E. J., & Oinas, P. (2002). The evolution of technologies in time and space: From national and regional to spatial innovation systems. *International Regional Science Review*, *25*(1102–131).

Malerba, F. (2002). Sectoral systems of innovation and production. *Research Policy*, *31*(2), 247–264.

Malhotra, R. (2019). SportsTech framework updated. Retrieved from https://medium.com/sportstechx/sportstech-framework-2019–2946533282eb

Martin, R., & Simmie, J. (2008). Path dependence and local innovation systems in city-regions. *Innovation-Management, Policy & Practice, 10*, 183–196.
Motohashi, K., & Yun, X. (2007). China's innovation system reform and growing industry and science linkages. *Research Policy, 36*, 1251–1260.
Mowery, D. C. (1998). The changing structure of the US national innovation system: Implications for international conflict and cooperation in R&D policy. *Research Policy, 27*, 639–654.
Mowery, D. C., & Oxley, J. E. (1995). Inward technology transfer and competitiveness: The role of national innovation systems. *Cambridge Journal of Economics, 19*, 67–93.
Muller, E., & Zenker, A. (2001). Business services as actors of knowledge transformation: The role of KIBS in regional and national innovation systems. *Research Policy, 30*, 1501–1516.
Najafi-Tavania, S., Najafi-Tavanib, Z., Naudéc, P., Oghazie, P., & Zeynaloo, E. (2018). How collaborative innovation networks affect new product performance: Product innovation capability, process innovation capability, and absorptive capacity. *Industrial Marekting Management, 73*, 193–205.
Nambisan, S., & Sawhney, M. (2011). Orchestration processes in network-centric innovation: Evidence from the field. *Academy of Management Perspectives, 25*(3), 40–57.
Nambisan, S., & Zahra, S. A. (2011). Entrepreneurship in global innovation ecosystems. *AMS Review, 1*(4), 4–17.
Nelson, K., & Nelson, R. R. (2002). Technology, institutions, and innovation systems. *Research Policy, 31*, 265–272.
Nooteboom, B. (2000). Institutions and forms of co-ordination in innovation systems *Organization Studies, 21*(5), 915–939.
Proman, M. (2019). Industry insights: The current state of sports technology. Retrieved from https://medium.com/scrum-ventures-blog/industry-insights-the-current-state-of-sports-technology-c24506d86585
Ratten, V. (2019). *Sports technology and innovation – Assessing cultural and social factors*. Melbourne: Springer Nature Switzerland AG
Rohracher, H., & Weber, K. M. (2012). Legitimizing research, technology and innovation policies for transformative change combining insights from innovation systems and multi-level perspective in a comprehensive 'failures' framework. *Research Policy, 41*, 1037–1047.
Rohrbeck, R., Hölzle, K., & Gemünden, H. G. (2009). Opening up for competitive advantage - How Deutsche Telekom creates an open Innovation ecosystem. *R&D Management, 39*(4), 420–430.
Ruuska, I., & Teigland, R. (2009). Ensuring project success through collective competence and creative conflict in public–private partnerships – A case study of Bygga Villa, a Swedish triple helix e-government initiative. *International Journal of Project Management, 27*, 323–334.
Schmidt, S. L. (Ed.) (2020). *21st century sports – how technologies will change sports in the digital age*. Düsseldorf: Springer
Shilbury, D., O'Boyle, I., & Ferkins, L. (2016). Toward a research agenda in collaborative sport governance. *Sport Management Review, 19*, 479–491.
Spencer, J. W. (2003). Firms' knowledge-sharing strategies in the global innovation system: Empirical evidence from the flat panel display industry. *Strategic Management Journal, 24*, 217–233.
Trippl, M., & Tödtling, F. (2005). One size fits all? Towards a differentiated regional innovation policy approach. *Research Policy, 34*, 1203–1219.
Wang, C., & Zhang, G. (2019). Examining the moderating effect of technology spillovers embedded in the intra- and inter-regional collaborative innovation networks of China. *Scientometrics, 119*, 561–593.
Zygiaris, S. (2013). Smart city reference model: Assisting planners to conceptualize the building of smart city innovaton ecosystems. *Journal of Knowledge Economy, 4*(2), 217–231.

29

Economics of Digital Sport Consumption

Ted Hayduk III

Introduction

"It's not that we use technology – we live technology."

– *Godfrey Reggio*

By most accounts, American film director Godfrey Reggio was accurate in his observation that technology has become an integral component of everyday life. In fact, he goes on to say that technology is "as ubiquitous as the air we breathe." If one were to pause and consider the depth and breadth with which technology is currently embedded in daily tasks, it would be difficult to argue otherwise. Despite the accuracy of his statements, Reggio conveys no indication about technology's eventual outcomes on society, at least in those particular quotes. For that, Christian Lous Lange, Norwegian historian and political scientist, provides a handy – if portentous – guidepost: "Technology is a useful servant, but a dangerous master." Reggio and Lange convey two related but independent observations about technology: (1) that it is everywhere, and (2) its embeddedness is both uplifting and worrisome.

Due to the ubiquity of new technologies and the significant consumption implications they bring about, sport and entertainment scholars seek to illuminate the predictors of certain consumption modalities (i.e., watching matches on TV, following teams and athletes on social media, fantasy sport participation, sports betting, etc.). The underlying format is inherently similar, with scholars building models that predict attitudinal and behavioral consumption outcomes (e.g., Bodet & Bernache-Assollant, 2011; Dwyer et al., 2011; Kunkel et al., 2021; Dwyer & Drayer, 2010; Gladden & Funk, 2002). This body of research contributes a great deal to the study of sport consumption and arguably even more to the understanding of "high-involvement" products and services (Zaichkowsky, 1986).

Despite the rich insights gleaned from this body of work, the methodologies leveraged by most sport consumer behavior studies constrain consumer behavior and decision-making to the tenants of discrete choice (e.g., Hensher & Johnson, 2018) – either explicitly or implicitly. Discrete choice models (DCMs) are a broad class of research design methodologies that describe, explain, and predict consumer choices between multiple separable alternatives. Examples include choosing to attend a live sporting contest or not, choosing which of a league's franchises

DOI: 10.4324/9781003088899-33

to become a fan of, or choosing to try sports betting for the first time. Importantly, modeling such outcomes has rarely come with devout attention paid to three important assumptions about consumer choice: (1) that the researcher knows the complete set of consumption choices available to the consumer, (2) that partaking in one consumption choice entirely precludes partaking in other consumption choices, and (3) that the number of consumption choices in the complete set is known and finite.

In the first half of the 20th century and earlier, these three assumptions could be reasonably applied to the modeling of sport consumers' behavior. Options for engaging with a consumer's favorite franchise until the early 1990s included attending live contests, listening to radio broadcasts, watching television coverage, and reading print articles. Only rarely did small pockets of consumers engage in specialized consumption modalities such as rotisserie baseball leagues (Ploeg, 2021). In this scenario, the above three assumptions can very reasonably be applied to the modeling of sport consumer behavior – the complete choice set is known and finite; and choosing one activity largely precludes the choosing of another simultaneously.

However, sport consumption in 2022 is radically different. After the early 1990s' the world normalized the internet, mobile and wearable technology, and cloud and virtualized computing architecture. All of these digital forces – and many more – enable the widespread adoption of social media, spatial computing, and a number of other technologies that directly affect the choices sport consumers make daily. Mobile smartphones and tablets mean that consumers simultaneously watch a game broadcast and interact with other fans on Twitter and TikTok; that they can listen to specialized podcasts about their favorite franchise while they catch up on last night's game highlights on Instagram; that they can chat directly with their favorite athletes on Zoom, Clubhouse, or Twitch while buying their friends a Cameo message from their university's star point guard; that they can bid for blockchain-secured nonfungible tokens (NFTs) against thousands of other fans at any time of the day or night. In the near future, sport consumers will be prompted to buy officially-licensed merchandise on Amazon during a Thursday Night Football game without leaving the broadcast's feed; advanced machine learning algorithms will encourage fans to follow documentary-style content on Netflix and Hulu about their favorite entities, such as Formula 1's Drive to Survive.

The modern sport consumption landscape unfolds fluidly and dynamically. It evolves organically according to what consumers demand – often literally at lightspeed. Consumers do not have to choose between consumption modalities any longer – all of them are engineered by design to be interwoven together into one larger holistic yet amorphous consumption "experience" with no beginning and no end.

Overall, the theoretical underpinnings of sport consumption research have not been updated to reflect a truly modern framework of digital sport consumption. This is because the extant work does not fully acknowledge the range of context- and time-dependent processes that shape technology-enabled sport consumption. Such a framework should highlight the fact that sport consumers do not merely have attitudes about technology – they maintain relationships with technology. The latter suggests a deeply integrated and bidirectional exchange between humans and the digital world. It also suggests consumers' acknowledgment of the tradeoffs and paradoxes embedded in technology use. Thus, sport marketing researchers need an updated framework for thinking about technology and its role in 21st-century sport consumption.

Therefore, this chapter attempts to address that need by proposing such a framework. The framework provides clear, practical benefits with respect to relationship management and revenue optimization. And, at the root of those business benefits are human benefits – such as psychological and emotional wellbeing, the prioritization of harmonious consumption over obsessive consumption (e.g., Vallerand et al., 2008), and consumers' reconnection with their physical world.

Consumer Adoption of New Technologies

Consider first the immediacy and widespread prevalence of knowledge about technologies and the incorporation of new technologies into one's daily routine. Pursuant to that, a robust line of inquiry has been built upon the theory of reasoned action (TRA). The TRA stipulates that individuals' beliefs and attitudes about a product affect their resulting intentions to use the product, which in turn affects their subsequent usage behavior (Fishbein, 1979). If an individual feels positive about a product, they have more positive evaluations of the likelihood they will use the product. The stronger those positive evaluations of usage, the greater the likelihood of actual product usage. For one to actually adopt a product, they first had to have intentions to use the product, which were dependent upon their positive attitudes toward the product. In the TRA, the process by which consumers (1) perceive, (2) assess, and (3) behave is entirely linear, with a clear beginning and end. This string of relationships between perceptions and eventual technology used was termed the technology adoption model (TAM). A more recent incantation of the TAM, denoted the TAM-2, incorporates social and cognitive preceding factors that affect perceived ease-of-use and perceived usefulness (Venkatesh & Davis, 2000).

Because the TAM and TAM-2 were developed and applied predominantly to utilitarian technology products, a useful extension of the framework involved applying them to hedonic (i.e., leisure activity) technology products related to sport. Hur (2007) suggested that specific consumer psychological variables such as sport involvement, commitment, and perceived trustworthiness likely played important roles in predicting consumers' adoption of sports websites. Similarly, Kang et al. (2015) documented that university students' fandom, perceived convenience, and desire for information positively influenced their adoption of sport-related mobile applications. In the context of a fantasy sports website, Ibrahim (2014) examined how technology complexity affected fantasy sport consumers' PEU, which in turn affected their cognitive and affective attitude toward the adoption of the website, which subsequently affected their actual use of the website. Similarly, Kwak and McDaniel (2011) found that attitudes toward a televised sport, PEU, perceived knowledge of the sport, and subjective norms helped explain respondents' behavioral intentions to play fantasy football. Byun and colleagues (2018) contributed that perceived enjoyment of a sport brand mobile application significantly affected PEU, which positively affected intentions to use and actual app usage. Kim et al. (2017) added that personal traits such as the user's innovativeness significantly affected a technology's PEU and perceived enjoyment related to a sport brand mobile app, which positively affected their usage intentions and actual usage behavior.

However, given the efficiency and fragmentation created in the market for sport consumption at the hands of technology, it becomes clear that sport consumers' technology adoption and usage is better characterized as fluid and context- and feedback-dependent, rather than the procedural result of feelings of "positive affect" toward a technology product. Sport consumers have a great many technology-enabled options to satiate their sport consumption needs. Furthermore, it has never been easier to adopt (or churn out of) the use of individual technologies, as modern sport consumption modalities are designed specifically to be frictionless and tend to use "freemium" and tiered pricing structures to encourage price customization and service quality (Hamari et al., 2020). Thus, in the modern market for sport consumption, consumers' switching and substitution costs – in terms of time, cognitive load, and money – are extremely low.

Prior TAM models applied to sport consumers also tend to rely on a static framework, eschewing important dynamics such as previous and future levels of sport consumption and consumers' ability to shuffle an ever-increasing number of consumption modalities. In this new normal, consumers make increasingly rational decisions in constant, evolving efforts to mold a bespoke sport consumption experience. In this process, consumers iteratively make choices about (a) whether to adopt a new sport consumption technology and (b) whether to maintain the technology as part of their "portfolio."

From "Attitudes About" to "Relationship with" Technology

The conclusions reached about the modern sport consumption market led to a number of important takeaways with respect to thinking about sport consumers' technology adoption practices. The most salient is that there has been a seemingly outsized focus on capturing attitudes about technology as opposed to exploring consumers' relationship with technology. Thinking about attitudes implies a unidirectional and monotonic relationship between technologies and a consumer's perceptions of them. It also ignores the potential origins of those perceptions, which prevents scholars' ability to understand why a sport consumer may have positive or negative perceptions of new technology. By contrast, devoting attention to sport consumers' relationships with technology acknowledges the existence of multi-directional, interdependent, and dynamic exchanges that occur at the human-computer interface. This conceptualization of modern sport consumption hinges on understanding two elements of the digital consumption experience: managing a portfolio of consumption modalities and thinking about technology use in terms of tradeoffs.

Technology Adoption and Portfolio Management

While technology has changed the market for sport consumption, what has not changed is the number of hours in a day. Within that, hours devoted to leisure activities are limited, as individuals balance work and family obligations with nonworking hours (Downward & Rasciute, 2010). Overall, individuals' leisure activity constraints are typically regarded as a time-tradeoff problem in which factors at the individual, interpersonal, and structural levels limit how much time individuals choose to allocate to leisure activities. Because the various sport consumption modalities are a subset of leisure activities (Downward & Rasciute, 2010), time devoted to sport consumption is even more finite. In short, sport consumption outlets are in competition with other entertainment and leisure products and services for a finite number of leisure hours.

Based on this framing of leisure activities and sport consumption activities as a subset thereof, sport consumers can be thought of as unintentionally solving an optimization problem. They extemporaneously manage a number of consumption modalities, with the goal of extracting the desired utility from a finite amount of sport consumption hours and across a time-varying number of sport consumption modalities. Furthermore, the technology-driven market in which sport consumers make consumption decisions suggests that they do bear the costs of adding consumption modalities, but it also allows for a relatively efficient provision of time, energy, and capital when making allocative decisions to various modalities.

As discussed previously, switching and substitution costs of new technology adoption are minimal (although not nonexistent) compared to previous decades. Sport consumers used to have to order specialized sport channels on the telephone, subscribe to internet-protocol services, change cable providers, etc. in order to modify their sport consumption modalities and formats. Currently, access to the internet and a mobile device or OTT product is sufficient for sport consumers to gain access to scores of other technology-enabled consumption modalities.

Yet, each additional digital consumption modality adopted by a consumer does have associated costs – in terms of time, cognitive load, and (in some instances) money. Provided one's total leisure hours allocated to sport consumption are not significantly expanded on average, adopting a new consumption technology cannot generate linear marginal utility gains – it must necessarily be associated with a decreasing marginal utility. Under these assumptions, it may be helpful to think about technology adoption in the sport consumption context as a utility-maximization problem in which consumers seek to maximize the total utility derived from the complete set of sport consumption modalities. This can be expressed using a modified portfolio management framework, which bears similarities to the expected utility theory. This is shown in Equation 29.1:

$$E(\mathbb{U}_k)_j = \sum_{i=1}^{k} [\omega_i E(\mathbb{u}_i * \bar{\mathbb{T}}_i)] + \varepsilon_i \tag{29.1}$$

In Equation (29.1), j indexes individuals and k is the number of sport consumption modalities. On the left-hand side, the value $\mathbb{U}$ is global utility, which is the total amount of utility returned from all sport consumption modalities. The right-hand side of Equation (29.2) consists of a weighted utility term. The term $\mathbb{u}$ is the utility derived from an individual modality, and $\bar{\mathbb{T}}_i$ is the mean of the tradeoffs perceived by the consumer related to technology i. Next, ω is the proportion of total sport consumption hours allocated to each consumption modality (i.e., the "weight"), and ε is a disturbance term. Equation (29.2) stipulates that individual j's global utility is a function of the weighted sum of expected utilities returned by each consumption modality.

Recent work in consumer behavior and decision-making notes that consumers' total utility from a particular product group (i.e., $\mathbb{U}_k$ in this model) is best characterized as marginally decreasing. This means that the consumption of more of the product may increase global utility, but that the rate of increase diminishes as more product is consumed. This functional form is best described mathematically in the context of production functions, which consider the relative role of inputs – in this case, sport consumption modalities – on the production of an output – in this case, utility (i.e., Douglas, 1976). Thus, it would be necessary to utilize the logarithmic transformations of $E(\mathbb{u}_i)$ and $\beta_k[E(\mathbb{U}_k)]$. To mirror the case of decreasing marginal returns in production functions, the model imposes two conditions about the nature of both terms in Equation (29.2):

$$\sum_{i=1}^{k} \beta_k [lnE(\mathbb{u}_k)] \leq 1.00, \tag{29.2}$$

and

$$\varepsilon_j < 0.00 \tag{29.3}$$

These assumptions about the functional forms of the terms in Equation 29.1 correspond to two important takeaways. The first is that the production of global utility has decreasing marginal returns because the sum of the beta coefficients of all k modalities does not exceed 1.00 in the same way that the coefficients of traditional production functions (i.e., Douglas, 1976) with decreasing marginal returns do not exceed 1.00. Second, individuals making allocative consumption decisions are hindered from achieving optimality by a degree of inefficiency – thus, the residuals in Equation 29.1 are assumed to be distributed $\varepsilon_j \sim \mathcal{N}^+(0,\ \sigma_u^2)$.

Together, Equations (29.1) through (29.3) capture the proposition as suggested by Jarvenpaa et al. (2005) that sport consumers have a complex relationship with technology and that deciding whether to adopt a new sports consumption technology requires that they weigh costs and benefits with the knowledge that "more is not always better."

Next, we consider individual-level differences in consumption preferences with respect to consumption modalities. Some consumers, perhaps of older generations, will tend to manage a smaller number of modalities in greater proportions, while it is likely that younger, more technology-enabled generations, will manage a greater number of modalities in smaller proportions (Yim et al., 2020). This choice represents the degree of diversification present in one's sport consumption portfolio. These differences capture the extent to which a given sport consumer's adoption choices reflect a diversified strategy. In making decisions about new consumption modes, consumers have to approximate the likelihood that the utility from a particular consumption modality $\mathbb{u}_k$ will increase over time, as well as the *degree* to which $\mathbb{u}_k$ will increase. Based on these two judgments, a simple version of the Kelly-optimized (e.g., Baker & McHale, 2013) proportion of one's consumption portfolio to be allocated to a given modality is given by Equation (29.4):

$$KO\left(\frac{\mathbb{u}_i}{\mathbb{U}_k}\right) = \frac{W}{A} - \frac{(1 - w)}{B} \tag{29.4}$$

Where W is the probability that consumption modality i contributes positively to global utility, A is the potential loss to global utility from consumption modality i (in percentage form), and B is the potential gain to global utility from consumption modality (also in percentage form). For example, with a 60% probability of the modality enhancing global utility by 20% and a 40% probability of the modality decreasing global utility by 20%, the Kelly-optimized portion of time to devote to modality i is 20%.

The framework also stipulates that, because the adoption of new technology for sport consumption requires that individuals devote a nonzero amount of consideration to managing their "portfolio," ω is endogenously determined. In other words, we would expect $r^2_{(\omega_i, \mathbb{u}_i)} \neq 0$. The functional form of ω is shown in Equation 29.5:

$$\omega_i = f\left[E(\mathbb{u}_i),\quad \int_{k-1}^{k} \delta,\ \bar{\mathbb{T}}_i\right] \tag{29.5}$$

In Equation (29.5), the proportion of time a sport consumer spends using a particular consumption modality is a function of their expected utility derived from the modality $[E(\mathbb{u}_i)]$, the extra cost of adding the consumption technology to their "portfolio" – that is, the additional costs (δ) of moving from $k-1$ modalities to k modalities, and the mean of the set of tradeoff magnitude values associated with modality i ($\bar{\mathbb{T}}_i$).

We can write the individual consumption modality utility function as a modified market model:

$$E(\mathbb{u}_i) = \alpha_i + \beta_k\left[E(\mathbb{U}_k)\right] + \varepsilon_i \tag{29.6}$$

Where α_i is the utility returned to modality i that is unrelated to the complete set of consumption modalities, β_k is the utility returned to the modality that is related to the other consumption modalities, and ε_i is a disturbance term.

The Effect of Time

The last notion to consider after examining the previous literature is the effect of time. Consumers do not make technology adoption choices in a temporal vacuum – theoretical and empirical research suggests a dynamic component to sports consumption (Gainsbury et al., 2015; Fredberg & Piller, 2011; Funk et al., 2016). Thus, we seek to adapt Equations (29.5) and (29.6) to a dynamic environment in which consumers' current technology adoption choices are impacted by prior consumption behavior and technology adoptions. Thus, we propose the following system of dynamic equations:

$$E(\mathbb{u}_{it}) = \alpha_{it} + \sum_{t=1}^{n} \beta_k [(\mathbb{U}_{kt-n})] - (\nu_i + \mu_{it}) \tag{29.7}$$

$$\omega_{it} = f\left[(\mathbb{U}_{kt})_{jt},\ E(\mathbb{u}_{it+n}),\ \int_{k}^{k+1} \delta \right] \tag{29.8}$$

Equations (29.7) and (29.8) index time using t and introduce consumers' known state of past realizations of global utility $(\mathbb{U}_{kt-1})$. In Equation (29.8), the composite disturbance is decomposed into two components: v_i is an inefficiency component specific to the modality, and u_{it} is a time-varying inefficiency measure. The term v_i captures consumer-level costs such as one's rate of learning (assumed to be constant across modalities), while the term u_{it} captures idiosyncratic time-varying costs that are heterogeneous across modalities. Rather than summing the composite error term with the other terms in the model, which would be the case in traditional panel models, Equation (29.7) specifies the difference, given the distribution of ε_j in Equation (29.1) is assumed to be $\mathcal{N}^{+}(0,\ \sigma_u^2)^1$. It is also assumed that a consumer utilizes their known global utility at time t $(\mathbb{U}_{kt})$, and their evaluation of the future expected utility from technology i at time $t+1$ $[E(\mathbb{u}_{it+1})]$.

As a final note related to time, consider that the idea of "expected" utility stipulates that, when consumers are faced with an adoption decision, they are not aware of the future utility delivered by $(\mathbb{u}_i)$, which is why it is denoted with the prefix "E." When making a second subsequent adoption decision, consumers decide if the *experienced* utility delivered by a consumption modality (i.e., retrospective, finite) exceeds its expected utility (i.e., prospective, unknown). In other words, if $(\mathbb{u}_i) - E(\mathbb{u}_i) > 0$, the consumer will keep the modality in their portfolio, and in the case that $(\mathbb{u}_i) - E(\mathbb{u}_i) < 0$, they will remove the modality from their portfolio. This decision is made for all technologies $T_1 \ldots T_z$ and for time periods $t_1 \ldots t_n$ which may be irregularly spaced.

Tradeoffs of Technology use and Adoption

An emerging line of literature provides a number of illustrative examples of the tradeoffs embedded in consumers' relationships with technology products (Jarvenpaa et al., 2005; Jarvenpaa & Lang, 2005; Mallat, 2007). This work identified eight paradoxes that describe mobile technology users' relationships with their technology. For example, while new technologies can be *empowering* by allowing them to take charge of situations, they can also be *enslaving* in that users felt obligated to be constantly connected to these technologies. Additionally, the authors documented an *independence-dependence* paradox, whereby more independence through task mobility resulted in users' inability to break unsavory habits formed from being "always on." A third important tradeoff identified by the authors was the *engaging-disengaging* paradox, whereby technologies designed to bring people closer together through immersive interaction also caused users to emotionally retract from their physical surroundings. The remaining paradoxes outlined by the authors were: *fulfills needs/creates needs*, *competence/incompetence*, *planning/improvising*, *public/private*, and *illusion/disillusion*.

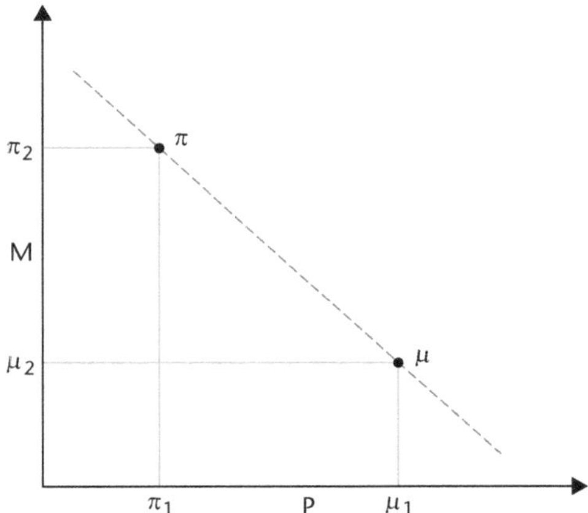

Figure 29.1 Tradeoff of Technology Use and Adoption

The series of tradeoffs created by the eight paradoxes are affected by a consumer's motivation to use the technology (i.e., the purpose for use – communication, coordination, efficiency, etc.) and by situational moderators related to the technology itself, the individual consumer, the organization or group environment, and the cultural context. To address and manage the eight paradoxes, consumers utilize a combination of (1) avoidance strategies – ignoring the issue altogether – and (2) confrontative strategies, such as behavioral modifications. This seminal work served as a solid foundation for helping scholars examine how technology users' complex and often conflicting relationships with technology affected a number of work and leisure contexts.

For simplicity, we define the term tradeoff in the "strict" sense, whereby an increase in the magnitude of one tradeoff element necessarily results in the decrease of the other tradeoff element, and vice versa. In this definition, we can define the tradeoffs in terms of a set of possible values that each pair of magnitudes can adopt. We will designate Γ to be the set of possible simultaneous values for each opposing tradeoff characteristic (for the *planning/improvising* tradeoff, for example, we can use p and m). Therefore, $\Gamma = \{\langle p_i, m_i\rangle\}$, and each ordered pair $\langle p_i, m_i\rangle$ is a pair of permissible magnitudes for p and m.

Next, we use π and μ to represent arbitrary pairs of values in $\langle p_i, m_i\rangle$. Then, π_1 designates the first value in the pair π and π_2 represents the second. This can be represented visually using Figure 29.1. In Figure 29.1, the negatively sloped dashed line represents all of the possible magnitudes allowed for *planning* (on the x-axis) and *improvising* (on the y-axis). The points π and μ are two randomly chosen points along the line, thus representing arbitrary elements of Γ. With these operational definitions in place, a strict tradeoff between technology enabling better planning but also requiring greater improvisation would be written as:

$$\forall\, \pi\ \forall\ \mu\,[\pi_1 < \mu_1 \leftrightarrow \pi_2 > \mu_2] \tag{29.9}$$

Just like we assigned the *planning/improvising* tradeoff to be the range of permissible magnitudes contained in the set Γ, we may do so for the other seven tradeoffs, producing a set of tradeoffs for a given technology (t) that we will collectively call $\mathbb{T}$. Additionally, each technology has a mean tradeoff value such that $\bar{\mathbb{T}}_i = \sum \frac{\Gamma_i \ldots \Gamma_n}{n}$. The permissible magnitudes in $\langle p_i, m_i\rangle$ are the ratio of technology benefit and technology drawback. This ratio, in turn, is a proportion – which is the operationalization used throughout the rest of this chapter.

Implications for Sport Consumption Research

The first implication for research is related to the measurement of constructs in the TAM and TAM-2 models as applied to sport consumers. Current research investigates relatively straightforward constructs and utilizes unidirectional Likert scale items in that pursuit (Byun et al., 2018; Hur, 2007; Ibrahim, 2014; Kim et al., 2017; Kwak & McDaniel, 2011). Thus, researchers first need to devote attention to a greater number of *conflicting* attitudes about technology that reflect the technology tradeoffs described by Jarvenpaa et al. (2005). In line with the paradoxical and conflicting nature of consumers' relationship to technology, a series of eight bidirectional measurement items is also likely required, such as the use of semantic differential scales (i.e., one for each paradox identified by Jarvenpaa et al., 2005).

Another alternative measurement technique involves the use of Kano's model of product attribute quality (e.g., Sauerwein et al., 1996). Kano's method involves capturing not only which elements of a consumption experience were enjoyable for a consumer, but also which elements were *most important* or *unimportant* to the consumer. Kano's measurement model is helpful in tradeoff situations where product developers cannot meet two simultaneous goals due to conflicting or mutually exclusive resource requirements (Sauerwein et al., 1996). This principle at the product-feature level can be easily extrapolated to the sport consumption portfolio level to assess the relative importance of consumers' consumption modality sets.

Another implication is that sport consumption researchers will need to award greater attention to panel data techniques. In particular, those that have been adapted to accommodate event study frameworks (Freyaldenhoven et al., 2019) would allow researchers to predict consumer behaviors and engagement levels after adopting a new technology modality. Similarly, logistic models for panel datasets that incorporate the effects of churn (i.e., right-censored data) would allow researchers to accurately predict (a) for how long sport consumers adopt a new consumption modality or (b) their adoption likelihood *given* how long they have been without the consumption modality. That these panel models also suggest that these outcomes can be produced based on idiosyncratic (i.e., individual-specific) and systemic (between-individual) covariates. This family of econometric techniques is commonly called duration models (Kennedy, 2008), and would involve specifying a probability density function for the amount of time a consumer utilizes a particular consumption modality and can be estimated via maximum likelihood. Researchers have their choice of hazard functions to specify based on how they expect consumers to behave. An exponential likelihood function assumes that a consumer is equally likely to adopt the modality irrespective of time; a Weibull distribution can be specified to suggest that a consumer's likelihood of adoption increases or decreases as a function of time; a log-logistic function specifies that a consumer's adoption likelihood first increases with time, then decreases.

Last, another measurement option for sport consumption researchers is the entropy measure (e.g., Jacquemin & Berry, 1979; Palepu, 1985). Entropy has its roots as a construct in the field of information theory. In business and other contexts, it represents the "number, relatedness, and importance" of a set of interrelated ratios. For example, in strategy, scholars have assessed a firm's level of diversification by computing the entropy of the firm's revenue verticals (Palepu, 1985). In portfolio theory, entropy would capture the relatedness and diversification of a set of income-earning assets. Thus, in sport consumption, entropy would represent how "diversified" a particular consumer is with respect to how many modalities they engage with, how dependent on one another each modality is, and each modality's relative contribution to the consumer's global utility. Entropy is calculated as:

$$E_i = \sum_{i=1}^{K} S_k \ln\left(\frac{1}{S_k}\right) \quad (29.10)$$

Where E_i is the entropy score for consumer i and S is the proportion of time allocated to modality k. Interpretively, E increases as consumption portfolios become more evenly distributed among a larger number of modalities. This signifies a consumer's reliance on many consumption modalities, each with a relatively equal presence in their consumption experience.

Conclusion

This chapter articulates a 21st-century view of sport consumption, in which digitally native modalities predominate. This means that consumers do not so much "choose" to consume sports through specific conduits as much as they manage their exposure to a constantly shifting set of conduits. This involves the regular adoption of new technologies and the simultaneous churn out of other technologies according to the utility that each contributes to the consumer's overarching experience. Therefore, this chapter proposes that in order to capture consumer choices *in situ*, researchers require a set of models and measurements that emphasize the influence of time and incorporate the tradeoffs inherent to technology use.

Note

1 For detailed expositions of inefficiency scores in panel production models, see Battese & Coelli (1992), Cornwell et al. (1990), and Greene (2005a).

References

Baker, R. D., & McHale, I. G. (2013). Optimal betting under parameter uncertainty: Improving the Kelly criterion. *Decision Analysis, 10*(3), 189–199.

Bodet, G., & Bernache-Assollant, I. (2011). Consumer loyalty in sport spectatorship services: The relationships with consumer satisfaction and team identification. *Psychology & Marketing, 28*(8), 781–802.

Byun, H., Chiu, W., & Bae, J. S. (2018). Exploring the adoption of sports brand apps: An application of the modified technology acceptance model. *International Journal of Asian Business and Information Management, 9*(1), 52–65.

Douglas, P. H. (1976). The Cobb-Douglas production function once again: Its history, its testing, and some new empirical values. *Journal of Political Economy, 84*(5), 903–915.

Downward, P., & Rasciute, S. (2010). The relative demands for sports and leisure in England. *European Sport Management Quarterly, 10*(2), 189–214.

Dwyer, B., & Drayer, J. (2010). Fantasy sport consumer segmentation: An investigation into the differing consumption modes of fantasy football participants. *Sport Marketing Quarterly, 19*(1), 207–216.

Dwyer, B., Shapiro, S. L., & Drayer, J. (2011). Segmenting motivation: An analysis of fantasy baseball motives and mediated sport consumption. *Sport Marketing Quarterly, 20*(3), 129–137.

Fishbein, M. (1979). A theory of reasoned action: Some applications and implications. *Nebraska Symposium on Motivation, 27*(1), 65–116.

Fredberg, T., & Piller, F. T. (2011). The paradox of tie strength in customer relationships for innovation: A longitudinal case study in the sports industry. *R&D Management, 41*(5), 470–484.

Freyaldenhoven, S., Hansen, C., & Shapiro, J. M. (2019). Pre-event trends in the panel event-study design. *American Economic Review, 109*(9), 3307–3338.

Funk, D., Lock, D., Karg, A., & Pritchard, M. (2016). Sport consumer behavior research: Improving our game. *Journal of Sport Management, 30*(2), 113–116.

Gainsbury, S. M., Russell, A., Hing, N., Wood, R., Lubman, D., & Blaszczynski, A. (2015). How the Internet is changing gambling: Findings from an Australian prevalence survey. *Journal of Gambling Studies, 31*(1), 1–15.

Gladden, J. M., & Funk, D. C. (2002). Developing an understanding of brand associations in team sport: Empirical evidence from consumers of professional sport. *Journal of Sport Management, 16*(1), 54–81.

Hamari, J., Hanner, N., & Koivisto, J. (2020). "Why pay premium in freemium services?" A study on perceived value, continued use and purchase intentions in free-to-play games. *International Journal of Information Management, 51*(1), 102–140.

Hensher, D. A., & Johnson, L. W. (2018). *Applied discrete-choice modelling*. Routledge. https://pure.uvt.nl/ws/portalfiles/portal/29159281/paper_MU.pdf

Hur, Y., Ko, Y. J., & Valacich, J. (2007). Motivation and concerns for online sport consumption. *Journal of Sport Management, 21*(4), 521–539.

Ibrahim, H. (2014). Technology acceptance model: Extension to sport consumption. *Procedia Engineering, 69*(1), 1534–1540.

Jacquemin, A. P., & Berry, C. H. (1979). Entropy measure of diversification and corporate growth. *The Journal of Industrial Economics*, 27(4), 359–369.

Lang, K. R., & Jarvenpaa, S. (2005). Managing the paradoxes of mobile technology. *Information Systems Management, 22*(4), 7–23.

Jarvenpaa, S. L., Lang, K. R., & Tuunainen, V. K. (2005). Friend or foe? The ambivalent relationship between mobile technology and its users. In *Designing ubiquitous information environments: Socio-technical issues and challenges* (pp. 29–42). Boston, MA: Springer.

Kang, S. J., Ha, J. P., & Hambrick, M. E. (2015). A mixed-method approach to exploring the motives of sport-related mobile applications among college students. *Journal of Sport Management, 29*(3), 272–290.

Kennedy, P. (2008). *A guide to econometrics*. New York, NY: John Wiley & Sons.

Kim, J., Kim, Y., & Kim, D. (2017). Improving well-being through hedonic, eudaimonic, and social needs fulfillment in sport media consumption. *Sport Management Review, 20*(3), 309–321.

Kunkel, T., Lock, D., & Doyle, J. P. (2021). Gamification via mobile applications: A longitudinal examination of its impact on attitudinal loyalty and behavior toward a core service. *Psychology & Marketing, 38*(6), 948–964.

Kwak, D. H., & McDaniel, S. R. (2011). Using an extended technology acceptance model in exploring antecedents to adopting fantasy sports league websites. *International Journal of Sports Marketing and Sponsorship, 12*(3), 43–56.

Mallat, N. (2007). Exploring consumer adoption of mobile payments–A qualitative study. *The Journal of Strategic Information Systems, 16*(4), 413–432.

Palepu, K. (1985). Diversification strategy, profit performance and the entropy measure. *Strategic Management Journal, 6*(3), 239–255.

Ploeg, A. J. (2021). A new form of fandom: How free agency brought about rotisserie league baseball. *The International Journal of the History of Sport, 38*(1), 7–27.

Sauerwein, E., Bailom, F., Matzler, K., & Hinterhuber, H. H. (1996, February). The kano model: How to delight your customers. In *International Working Seminar on Production Economics, 1*(4), 313–327.

Vallerand, R. J., Mageau, G. A., Elliot, A. J., Dumais, A., Demers, M. A., & Rousseau, F. (2008). Passion and performance attainment in sport. *Psychology of Sport and Exercise, 9*(3), 373–392.

Venkatesh, V., & Davis, F. D. (2000). A theoretical extension of the technology acceptance model: Four longitudinal field studies. *Management Science, 46*(2), 186–204.

Yim, B. H., & Byon, K. K. (2020). Critical factors in the sport consumption decision making process of millennial fans: A revised model of goal-directed behavior. *International Journal of Sports Marketing and Sponsorship, 21*(3), 427–447.

Zaichkowsky, J. L. (1986). Conceptualizing involvement. *Journal of Advertising, 15*(2), 4–34.

Index

A/B testing 248
access to technology 12
active giving 347, 352
Activision Blizzard 300
activism 134, 223–224, 362
actor-network theory 157
ad-supported video on demand 195
Adidas 23, 122
ADP 24, 26, 32
advanced feedback systems 94
advice-seeking 9
AFL *See* Australian Football League
AFLW *See* Australian Football League Women's
agriculture, digital transformation of 152–153
AI *See* artificial intelligence
air pollutants 349–350
air quality monitoring 349–350
air quality monitors 349–350
Airbnb 263
algorithms: betting 338; bias in 341; computer vision 249; definition of 335; machine learning 340
Alioto, Mario 264
AlphaGo 334
AlphaZero 342
Amazon Prime 194–195
AMPSEA *See* Australian Mass Participation Sporting Events Alliance
analytics 246–247
ANT *See* actor-network theory
Anthony, Carmelo 192
anti-doping 313
Apple 181
Apple Watch 94, 287, 290, 323
apps: personal use 351–352; sport fitness 288–289
AR *See* augmented reality
arousal, fantasy sport play and 171–172
Arsenal FC 93
artificial intelligence: bias issues in 341; computer vision 335–337; controversial uses of 342; costs of 341; current state of 333–336; daily use of 335–336; definition of 335; description of 23, 91, 104–105, 127, 333; downsides to 340–343; ethical considerations for 340–343; facial recognition software 342; fake content creation using 342; Formula One and 343; future of 342–343; history of 333–336; human element affected by 342; machine learning 335, 339–340; overreliance on 341; performance evaluation uses of 337; privacy issues in 342; societal use of 334; sport industry research affected by 338–340; sport industry use of 336–340; sport journalism uses of 337; sport management uses of 338–339; summary of 343–344; tennis applications of 337; terminology associated with 335; umpire/referee decisions affected by 337, 343
artificial turf fields 351
ASC *See* Australian Sports Commission
Asimov, Isaac 334
athlete(s): activism by 223–224; as influencers 224–225; as role models 224–225; commercial speech by 136; crowdsourcing 312; live streaming by 227; names, images, and likeness of 137, 362; philanthropy by 223–224; social justice movement participation by 224; social live streaming services 197–198; social media use by 135, 209, 226, 362; TikTok use by 227; training of, individualization of 96; transgressions by 250
athlete branding, with social media: blackout periods 226; challenges of 226; competitive success effects on 222; COVID-19 and 222–223, 225; femininity in 220; gendered approaches to 220–221; longevity of 223; media used in 217; mental fatigue 226; name, image, and likeness 137, 221–222; overview of 217–218; self-presentation theory 219–220; social media for 217–222; sport stakeholder perspectives 221–222; sportswomen 221; student-athletes 221; subbrands 221; theoretical frameworks for 219–220
Atlanta Braves 18
augmented reality: definition of 233; description of

222; growth of 232; health and performance applications of 289; research on 234–235; Sport for Development organizations 156; in sport management 234–235; in sport sponsorship 122; virtual sport spectatorship use of 234
Australia 97, 192, 195
Australian Football League 193
Australian Football League Women's 356–358, 361
Australian Mass Participation Sporting Events Alliance 79
Australian Sports Commission 97
Australian Sports Technologies Network 371, 375
Automated Insights 337
AVOD *See* ad-supported video on demand

BallerTV 54
Baltimore Ravens 121
Barca Innovation Hub 369, 375
Barcelona 93
Barstool Sports 183–184
BDA *See* big data analytics
Beckham, David 294
Beckham, Odell Jr. 192, 294
Bell, Eric 265
Bennett, Roger 187
bet democracy 312
Bethereum 312
betting 123–124, 212–213, 312
betting algorithms 338
Beyond Unity Cup 151
bias: in artificial intelligence 341; gender 356, 359–360
big data 23, 93, 95, 108, 327, 335
big data analytics 327
BikeFair 158
Bitcoin 308, 310, 316
Black Dog Institute 193, 198
BlackLivesMatter movement 25, 211–212, 224
Blair, Melissa 263
Blizzard Entertainment 296
blockchain technology: advanced tracking functions of 310; anti-doping opportunities 313; athlete crowdsourcing opportunities 312; benefits of 310; cloud storage functions of 310; consumer experience opportunities for 311; consumer impact of 316; decentralized consensus 309; digital identities 311; distributed computation 309; fantasy sports opportunities 312; financial transactions 311; future research for 315–317; gender-based analysis of 357; history of 308; objectives of 309–310; ownership 309; performance data opportunities 313; permissioned 309; permissionless 309; pillars of 308–309; player data opportunities 313; public key cryptography 309; security functions of 310; smart contracts 311; sponsorship opportunities 312; sport industry applications of 310–313; sport memorabilia collectables opportunities 311–312; sports betting opportunities 312; theoretical frameworks for 315
Boston Marathon 82
brain imaging: electroencephalography for 237–238; functional magnetic resonance imaging for 236–237, 240; functional near-infrared spectroscopy for 237
brand/branding: athlete as *See* athlete branding; definition of 217; student-athlete 221
branded house 296
Brandwatch 207
Brown, Karina 361
Brown, Michael 212
burnout 17–18
business analytics: A/B testing 248; computer vision algorithms 249; concepts associated with 246–247; current uses of 248–253; emerging uses of 248–253; forecasting 248–249; future areas for 251–253; in-app consumer surveys 248; overview of 245–246; research trends in 250–252; terms associated with 246–247; theory challenges for 251–252; topic modeling 249
business analytics teams 252
business-level strategy 66

CABOS *See* Commonwealth Advisory Body of Sport
CAD *See* computer-aided design
camaraderie, from fantasy sport 172
Cambage, Liz 362
Cambridge Analytica 342
cancel culture 210
capacity building for competitive advantage 282–283
capital, psychological 8–9
Catrefour 313
CDOs *See* chief digital officers
CDR *See* corporate digital responsibility
CFA/EFA *See* confirmatory and exploratory factor analysis
Chadwick, Henry 245
chatbots 336, 341
chief digital officers 70
chief information officers 70
China Central Television 133
CIOs *See* chief information officers
Civil Rights Act of 1964 142
climate activism 352
Cloud9 295–296
Cloud9: Counter-Strike: Global Offensive 296
cloud computing 67
cloud storage 310
CoachUp 265–266
collaborative consumption: categories of 259; commercial platforms 258; community-based

interaction and 262; consumer trust and 259–260; definition of 257; disposition after temporary reacquisition 258–259; future research 268–269; industry examples of 263–268; industry perspective of 260; levels of 268–269; long-term access in 258–259; models of 258–259; mutualization in 258; networked hospitality 257–258; peer exchanges 258; popularity of 259–260; product-service systems 259; pure collaboration 269; redistribution in 258–259; short-term access in 258–259; in sport apparel 264; in sport coaching 265–266; in sport equipment 264–265; in sport event tickets 267–268; in sport experiences 263–264; in sport facilities 266–267; in sport industry 260–263
collaborative lifestyles 259
college cheerleaders 209
collegiate esports 144
Comcast Spectacor 303
commercial platforms 258
commercialized peer-to-peer mutualization systems 259
Commonwealth Advisory Body of Sport 327
Commonwealth Games 362
community: definition of 325; sport participation and 325–326
community sport organizations 53, 57, 64
competition, in fantasy sport 174
competitive advantage: capacity building for 282–283; human resources for creating 25, 31; technologies used to create 95
Complexity Gaming 300, 302
componential theory 8
computational models 213
computer-aided design 94–95
computer vision: algorithms 249; description of 335–337
confirmatory and exploratory factor analysis 248
consumers: adoption of new technologies by 386–387; behavior of 274–276, 280; blockchain technology impact on 316; collaborative consumption effects on 259–260; data sources 277–279; digitalization of behavior 274–276; information sharing with 65; online following by 120–121; real-time interactions with 65; technology adoption model 386; trust of 259–260
conversational podcast 187
Cook, Allan 122
Cook, Earnshaw 245
copyright: defenses for infringement of 140–141; esports and 138–140; fair use doctrine 140; legal protections for 138–139; merger doctrine defense 140
Copyright Act 138
cord-cutting 295
corporate digital responsibility: corporate social responsibility versus 105–106; definition of 105; dimensions of 105–106; economic 107–108; environmental 109–110; future research for 110–111; social 106–107; summary of 110–111; technological 108–109
corporate-level strategy 66
corporate social responsibility: corporate digital responsibility versus 105–106; crowdfunding 102–103; definition of 100–101; digital communication and engagement 103–104; digital fundraising 102–103; digital transformation and 101–103; future research for 110–111; philanthropy as 102–103; social media and 103–104; sport organizations and 101, 104–110; summary of 110–111
COVID-19: athlete branding and 222–223, 225; description of 1, 18; digital transformation affected by 105, 153; live streaming during 198; organizational structure affected by 69; participatory sport events affected by 78–79; sport consumption affected by 193; sport participation during 325; virtual fundraising caused by 102; virtual participatory sport events created by 84, 87; virtual volunteering caused by 38–39, 44
CPMS *See* commercialized peer-to-peer mutualization systems
creativity process, engagement in 9–10
creators, social media 208–209
crisis communication 209–210
critical pedagogy 154
CRM *See* customer relationship management
Cronk, Copper 361
CrossFit 209
crowdfunding 102–103
crowdsourcing 312
CrowdTangle 207
cryptocurrencies 121, 310–311
CSOs *See* community sport organizations
CSR *See* corporate social responsibility
Curry, Stephen 192, 265
customer lifetime value 277
customer relationship management 277
cybercrime 105
cybersecurity 71
Cycling4Trees 352

Dallas Cowboys 300, 302
DAOs *See* decentralised autonomous organisations
data *See also* big data; capacity building for competitive advantage from 282–283; collection of 278; consumer 277–279; digital 282; digitalization of 276; location 278; overview of 273–274; strategy guided by 279–282
data breaches 105
data-driven-decision making 245
data visualization 126

Davis, Bob 245
DCMs *See* discrete choice models
decentralised autonomous organisations 358
decentralized consensus 309
decision review systems 337
Deep Blue 334, 342
deep learning 334–335, 337
demand 279–280
Desbonnet, Edmond 288
designing understanding 315–316
differential privacy theory 290
diffusion 56
diffusion of innovation theory 170
digital assets 121
digital betting 123
digital business strategy 67
digital communication 103–104
digital data 119
digital devices 118–119, 325
digital disruption: definition of 77; of participatory sport events 77–79, 87
digital divide 128
digital facility management technologies 350–351
digital fundraising 102–103
digital identities 311
digital innovation: definition of 91; in high-performance sport 91–98
digital leadership 69–71
digital literacy 155–156
digital maturity 97
digital media 117–118, 137–138
Digital Millennium Copyright Act 138
digital natives 295, 299
digital platforms 118
digital sponsorship: audience/fan/consumer digital devices 118–119; business models and strategies for 119–120; consumers/fans 120–124; digital data 119; digital media 117–118; digital platforms 118; marketer/property/sponsor digital technology 117; process of 117
digital sport fitness: apps 288–289; connectivity of 289–290; ecosystem of 285–286; equipment 287–288, 325; future research for 290–291; spatial computing 289; wearables 286–287
digital sport media, gendered landscape in 355–356
digital technology: definition of 37, 64; employees affected by 70–71; fantasy sport and 169; future of 58; gender and 356–364; growth of 62; human resources affected by 69–71; leadership affected by 69–71; neutral gender of 355; in not-for-profit sport organizations 64, 67; organizational structure and design affected by 68–69; in organizations 64; research of 37–38; SMAC 64; sport marketing agencies' use of 117; in sport organizations 38; staff roles affected by 70; standardization of processes using 65; in women's sport 361
digital tools 14–15
digital transformation: of agriculture 152–153; business applications of 116; commitment of resources for 14; corporate social responsibility and 101–103; COVID-19 effects on 105, 153; customizability of products 65; cybersecurity and 71; definition of 63; drivers of 64–65; at employee level 8–10; escalation of commitment by 13–14; four-level approach to 17; in management practices 23; at organizational and environmental level 13–15; organizational change 63; organizational strategy affected by 66–67; organizational structure and design affected by 68–69; in organizations 63–72; overview of 7–8; personal transformation and 69–70; of small-medium enterprises 16; in sport 124–125; in Sport for Development organizations 151–152; summary of 71–72; trends in 71; at work group level 10–13; in youth sport 52–59
Digital TV Europe 194
digitalization: definition of 320; esports and 328; future research for 327–328; social-ecological model of 321–327; in sport 319–321
disaster monitoring 347–349
discord 297
discrete choice models 384
disruptive technologies 92
distributed computation 309
diversification, of sport organizations 295, 299–300
diversity, in social media 210–211
DMCA *See* Digital Millennium Copyright Act
Doerr, Sam 268
domain-relevant skills 9
DraftKings 124, 212
drones 351
Durant, Kevin 185
duration models 392

e-compensation 29
e-HRM *See* electronic human resource management
e-recruitment 26, 29
e-selection 26, 29
EA *See* Electronic Arts
Echelon 288
ecology, sport: air quality monitoring 349–350; apps for personal use 351–352; definition of 347; digital applications in 347–353; digital facility management technologies 350–351; disaster monitoring 347–349; overview of 346–347; summary of 353; weather monitoring 347–349
econometrics 249, 252
economic corporate digital responsibility 107–108
economics, of sport consumption 384–393
Edelman, Julian 265
EEG *See* electroencephalography

electroencephalography 237–238
Electronic Arts 296
electronic human resource management: administrative support uses of 27; applications linked to 23; benefits of 25; compensation uses of 28; effectiveness evaluations 33; emergence of 23–24; employee benefits of 25, 27–28; example of 26–29; functions of 26–28; future of 33–34; human resources planning uses of 27; individual performance management uses of 28; job analysis uses of 27; outcomes associated with 25; positive influence of 24–25; process planning uses of 26; recruitment uses of 27; resources linked to 23; in sport organizations 24–29; summary of 34; training and development uses of 28
elite sports 92–96
ELIZA 334
emerging leadership behaviors 70
Emmert, Mark 143
employees: burnout of 17–18; creativity of 9; digital technology effects on 70–71; digital transformation of 8–10; diversity of 29–30; domain-relevant skills of 9; electronic human resource management benefits for 25; flexibility of 68; improvement of services to 25; inclusive policies 29; intrinsic motivation of 9; psychological capital of 8–9; recruiting of 18, 27; reimbursement systems for 32–33; retention of 11; social media use by 135; turnover of 17–18; work–life balance for 18
encoding behaviors 70
end user licensing agreement 139
endemic sponsors 295, 298–299
Endomondo 288
engagement: by social media influencers 209; with fans 192, 200–202
entity-relationship model 93
entrepreneurialship 369
entrepreneurs, in youth sport 54–55
entropy 392–393
environmental corporate digital responsibility 109–110
Epic Games 296
Equinox 210
equipment: fitness 287–288; sport 264–265
equity, in social media 210–211
eroding behaviors 70
escalation of commitment 13–14
Eskinazi, Anthony 267
ESPN: Department of Integrated Media Research 174; *RedZone,* 174–175
esports: audience for 213; collegiate 144; copyright and 138–140; definition of 293; description of 125, 135, 213, 293–294; digital platforms 297–298; digitalization effects on 328; future of 144, 301–304; gender pay gap in 141; "glass monitor" in 142; growth of 293; health effects of 328; intellectual property law 138; online streaming services 143; revenue sources in 298, 300; sexual harassment in 141–144; sponsorships 295, 298–300, 302; sport and 299–301; sport organizations' support for 293–294; summary of 304; terms associated with 295; video games 294–295
esports teams 295–296
Ethereum 316
EULA *See* end user licensing agreement
event-driven managing 314
evidence-based sport industry 31–32
expert systems 335
exponential likelihood function 392
extreme weather conditions 348

Facebook 188, 218, 227
Facebook Live 200
Facebook Messenger 151
facial recognition software 342
facility management technologies 350–351
fair use doctrine 140
fan(s): fandom 207–208; live streaming for engagement with 192, 200–202; online following by 120–121; satellite 200; social identity theory of 208; social live streaming for engagement with 199; Sport Fan Motivation Scale for 208
fan relationship management model 119
FANDIM scale 236
Fandom 207–208
Fanduel 124
fantasy sport: arousal and 171–172; betting on 212–213; blockchain technology opportunities 312; camaraderie as motivation for 172; competition as motivation for 174; daily/weekly 167; definition of 167; Diffusion of Innovation theory 170; digital advancements in 167–168; in digital realm 167–168; digital technology and 169; escape as motivation for 173; future directions for 176–177; mobile advancements in 175; motivations for playing 171–174; participation in 168–171; passing time as motivation for 173; player types 212; *RedZone,* 174–175; self-esteem and 171–172; social media influences on 175–176; social sport in 172; sport sponsorship and 122–123; summary of 177–178; surveillance 173–174; technological advancements in 177; trends in 174–176; Uses and Gratification theory 168–170, 212; web influences on 175–176
Farmerline 158
FC Köhn 369
Federer, Roger 227
FedEx 210
feminism 360–362

FIFA 299
financial resources 11
First Amendment 133–134
Fitbit 323
fitness clubs 324–325
fitness equipment 287–288
Fittcoach 266
Fliegal, Jordan 265
fMRI *See* functional magnetic resonance imaging
fNIRS *See* functional near-infrared spectroscopy
FNTSY Sports Network 176
Foliaki, Ness 361
Football Association 53
for-profit sport organizations 67
Ford Motor Company 337
forecasting 248–249
Forerunner 287
Formula One 343, 349
Fortnite Cloud9 296
Fox, Rick 294
Foxtel 358
franchise model 120
free-to-play business model 296
functional-level strategy 66
functional magnetic resonance imaging 236–237, 240
functional near-infrared spectroscopy 237
fundraising, digital 102–103

gadgets 94–95
Gamergate 141
gaming 212–213
Garmin 287
gender *See also* women; athlete branding based on 220–221; blockchain technology 357; digital sport media and 355–356; digital technology and 356–364; sporting lives affected by 356
gender bias 356, 359–360
Glassman, Greg 210
global positioning system 94, 287
Gold Coast Marathon 76–77
Goodell, Roger 211
Google Glass 235
GoPlogging! 352
GPS *See* global positioning system
Griner, Brittney 363
GroupMe 10
Gustafson, Mark 265
Gymnasticon 287
gymnastics 359

Hafeez, Nauman 266
halo headbands 95
Hammersley, Ben 180–181
harassment 141–144
Harley, Tom 198
Harris, Tayla 361
Hatfield, Tinker 121
Hawk-Eye systems 95
health: definition of 321; esports effect on 328; smartphone monitoring of 323; sport participation benefits for 319, 321; virtual reality applications 289, 323–324
Healy, Alyssa 358
high-performance sport: in Australia 97; digital innovation in 91–98; overview of 91–92; technological innovation in 92–95
high-performing sport organizations 11
human capital 25
human resource management: critical review of 34; definition of 22; electronic *See* electronic human resource management; strategic 22–23, 31
human resources: competition advantage from 25, 31; digital technology effects on 69–71; diversity of 29–30; performance tracking of 31; sport managers' view of 22–23; of sport organizations 11

ice hockey 346
ICT4D *See* information and communication technology for development
idea generation, digital tools for 10
IES Model *See* innovation ecosystem model
immersive spectator experience 233–234
in-app consumer surveys 248
in-person volunteering: COVID-19 effects on 46; virtual volunteering versus 39–41
inclusion, in social media 210–211
incremental monetization 122
independence-dependence paradox 390
individualization, of athlete training 96
influencers, social media 208–209, 224–225
infographics 126
information and communication technology for development: actor-network theory 157; communication platforms 151; description of 148, 150–151; digital literacy 156
information searching 10
information sharing, with consumers 65
InitLive 26
innovation: barriers to 377; capability 378; community-based approach to 371; drivers of 377; ecosystem model of 371–374; overview of 368–371; research areas in 374–379
innovation adoption motivation 8
innovation culture 379
innovation diffusion theory 154
innovation ecosystem model 371–374
innovation performance 375
innovation process 376
innovative work climate 12–13
Instagram 118, 227, 357, 363

Instagram Live 219, 227
Instant Sponsorship 312
institutional logic 313
institutional work 157–158
institutions 373–374
intellectual property 138, 312
intergroup contact theory 157
International Olympic Committee 135–136, 221, 314
Internet of Things 310
interview podcasts 187
intrinsic motivation 9
IOC *See* International Olympic Committee
iPhone 62, 288
iPod 288

James, Bill 245
James, LeBron 211, 226
Johnston, Natasha 71
joint authorship doctrine 141
Jordan, Michael 294
Journal of Quantitative Analysis in Sports, 250
Journal of Sports Analytics, 250
Joyride 265
JoySpace 267
JustPark 267

Kaepernick, Colin 211
KAI 336
Kano's model of product attribute quality 392
Kayo 194–195, 358
Kerr, Steve 185
Kiss, Larry 267
Knight, Phil 121
knowledge management 12
Koenig, Sarah 182
Kornheiser, Tony 183

Lange, Christian Lous 384
Laskin, Bunim 266
Latent Dirichlet Allocation 249
leadership, digital 69–71
League of Legends 296
Lee, Ha Mihn 182
LEGO 63, 68, 70
Lewis, Michael 245
liminoid spaces, participatory sport events as 79–80
linear media programming 295
Little League Baseball World Series 52
live streaming: characterizing of 194–195; during COVID-19 198; fan-focused positioning of 192, 200–202; future of 202–203; growth of 193–194; immediacy of 200–201; immersive nature of 201; over-the-top 192–197; personalization capabilities of 194; Planning, Organizing & Delivery model of 202; social *See* social live streaming services; social media 227; sociality of 201–202; sport consumption affected by 193–194; sport organization investments in 194–195; in sports 192–193; theoretical frameworks for 202
Liverpool 93
LLBWS *See* Little League Baseball World Series
location data 278
Loeffler, Kelly 211
London Spitfire 296
long-term access 259
Los Angeles Football Club 127
Los Angeles Lakers 15
LS *See* live streaming
Lululemon Athletica 288

m-health 158
machine learning 335, 339–340
Makkonen, Juho 266
Mammut Safety 351
Manchester City 93
Manchester United 15–16
MapMyFitness 288
MapMyRun 288
marketing 127
marketing mix models 125
Maron, Marc 182
McAfee, Pat 185
McCarthy, John 334
McCullough, Michael 299
McKinsey & Company 125
McKinsey Study 15
media rights 132, 302–303
medial prefrontal cortex 238
Mehra, Vivek 267
merchandise 303–304
merger doctrine 140
MetaViewer 33
#MeToo 25, 359
micro-celebrities 225
microtransactions 295
mirror 288
misogyny 361
Mitcha, Maria 136
MLB: Advanced Media 184; social live streaming services 192
mobile advancements, in fantasy sport 175
model of athlete brand image 219–220, 226
Moneyball, 93, 245
Morey, Daryl 133
motivation: innovation adoption 8; intrinsic 9
MotivePro 95
Motorsports 336–337
mPFC *See* medial prefrontal cortex
MTM Analysis 195

multi-sport organizations, digital transformation in 64
Murray, Andy 227
mutualization 258
MVPCast 54
Myzone 320

Nakamoto, Satoshi 308
name, image, and likeness 137, 221–222, 362
Nanzer, Nate 301
NASCAR: computer vision in 336–337; inclusive policies in 29
Nasdal, Rafael 227
Nassar, Larry 359
National Labor Relations Act 133
National Public Radio 181
national sport organizations: digital transformation in 64; social media platforms used by 55; standardization of processes for 65
National Women's Hockey League 118
natural language processing 249, 334–335, 339–341
NBA: digitization of 105, 137; esports 293–294; immersive spectator experiences 233–234; inclusive policies in 29; 2K League 176; Oculus and 233–234
NCAA 14
near-infrared spectroscopy 237
neotribalism 262
networked hospitality 257–258
neural networks 334–335
New York Yankees 15
NFTs *See* non-fungible tokens
Nike 16, 150
NikeFitness app 288
Nintendo 139
NIRS *See* near-infrared spectroscopy
NLP *See* natural language processing
NLRA *See* National Labor Relations Act
non-endemic sponsors 295, 298–299
non-fungible tokens 121, 312, 357, 385
NordicTrack 288
not-for-profit sport organizations: cybersecurity in 71; digital infrastructure of 71; digital technology in 64, 67, 71–72; digital transformation effects on 71; for-profit sport organizations versus 67; leadership of 70; overview of 62–63; size of 68; workforce for 70–71
NSOs *See* national sport organizations

Oculus 233
Olympic athletes: branding by 221; social media use by 135–137
O'Neal, Shaquille 294
100 Thieves 302
online database platforms 152
online following 120–121
online streaming services 143
Ontario Soccer Association 56
open-source solutions 152
Oracle 117
organization: platform-based 69; sport *See* sport organizations; virtual 68–69
organizational change 63
organizational culture, employee burnout affected by 18
organizational structure 68–69
OTT live streaming *See* over-the-top live streaming
outdoor sport 347
over-the-top live streaming 192–197
over-the-top media 295
Overwatch League 294, 300–301
OWL *See* Overwatch League

Paralympians 218
ParkatmyHouse 267
ParqEx 267
participation motives 378
participatory sport events: as liminoid spaces 79–80; charity-linked 84; COVID-19 pandemic effects on 78–79; digital disruption of 77–79, 87; entrepreneurialism of 77; growth of 77; popularity of 76–77; sense of celebration from 80–81; sense of community from 79; social interaction at 80; social leveraging of 79; virtual *See* virtual participatory sport events; wearable technology in 78
patent law 138
PBFT *See* practical byzantine fault tolerance
peer exchanges 258
Peerspoint 313
Peloton 209, 288, 290, 323
performance analysis 92
performance analytics 96
performance data 313
performance tracking: blockchain technology opportunities 313; of human resources 31
permissioned blockchain 309
permissionless blockchain 309
Personal Peak Quarantine Backyard Ultra 81
philanthropy 102–103
physical inactivity 319
PKC *See* public key cryptography
Planet Super League 352
planning, organizing & delivery model, of live streaming 202
platform-based organization 69
PlogAlong 352
podcast/podcasting: as media product 181–182; audience for 188; audience growth 181;

conversational 187; definition of 180; distribution of 187–188; future of 189–190; growth of 181, 189; history of 180–181; interview 187; metrics for 182; modern environment 185–186; planning of 186–187; repurposed content 187; revenue from 181; scripted 187; *Serial,* 182; snippets of 188; sports 183–184; sports entities and 184–185; sports radio versus 189; starting out in 186; storytelling 187; subscribing to 182–183; summary of 189–190; targeted advertising of 189; typographies of 186–187
pollutants 349–350
portfolio management 387–389
Portland Thorns Football Club 121
Portland Trail Blazers 199
Poverty Stoplight 158
Powder Project 351
practical byzantine fault tolerance 309
predictive analytics 213–214
product-service systems 259
Professional and Amateur Sports Protection Act 123, 177
professional gamers 141
professional sport organizations *See also* sport organizations; esports and 300, 302, 304; media rights 302–303; merchandise revenue for 303–304; revenue sources for 300; ticket revenues 303
ProNav 287
psychological capital 8–9
public key cryptography 309

Quinn, Zoe 141

radio frequency identification chips 278
Radiolab 181
ransomware 71
Rapinoe, Megan 357
Reddit 143
Redick, J.J. 185
redistribution markets 259
RedZone, 174–175
regression analysis 340
REI 264
reimbursement systems 32–33
relational model 119
repurposed content podcasts 187
reputational model 119
resource dependency 10–11
resources: commitment of 14; human *See* human resources
returns to scale 315
RFID chips *See* radio frequency identification chips
Ricciardo, Daniel 343
Richardson, Sha'Carri 363–364
Rigsby, Cody 209
Ringer, The 184, 188
Ringette Canada 71
Rink Watch 352
Riot Games 134–135, 142, 296
risk aversion 9
Robinson, David 264
robots: in facility management 350; intelligence of 334
Rodgers, Aaron 211
role models, athletes as 224–225
Rugby Australia 192
Runkeeper 288
Running Heroes 87
Runtastic 288
RunToPlant 352
Russian Olympic Committee 363

S-D logic 202
SaaS *See* software as a service
Sacramento Kings 16, 336
Salesforce.com 116, 152
SAP 24, 26, 32, 152
SAP Data Management 117
satellite fans 200
scènes à faire doctrine 140
Schumpeterian paradigm 377
scripted podcasts 187
Second Spectrum 234
self-esteem, fantasy sport play and 171–172
self-presentation theory 219–220
SEM *See* social-ecological model; structural equation modeling
sense of community 82–83, 85
Serial, 182
sexism 356
sexual harassment, in esports 141–144
SFD organizations *See* sport for development organizations
SFMS *See* sport fan motivation scale
Shakey 334
Sharetribe 266
Sheffield Hallam University 92
short-term access 259
SHRM *See* strategic human resource management
SidelineSwap 264–265
Simmons, Bill 183–184
SIRC *See* Sport Information Resource Centre
Ski Tracks 351
Skins 296
Skype 297
Slack 10
SLSS *See* social live streaming services
SM *See* social media
SMAC 64

small- and medium-sized enterprises: electronic human resource management for 34; sport organizations as 11, 15–17, 23
smart contracts 311
smartphones 323
SME *See* small- and medium-sized enterprise
SMI *See* social media influencers
Smith, J.R. 197–198
Smith, Kevin 182
Snapchat 227–228
Snyder, Dan 210
social corporate digital responsibility 106–107
social distancing 38
social-ecological model 156; community level 325–326; definition of 320–322; for digitalization in sport participation for health 321–327; institutional level 324–325; interpersonal level 324; intrapersonal level 323–324; multilevel interactions 327; public-policy level 326–327
social identity theory 208
social interaction, from participatory sport events 80
social listening campaigns 249
social live streaming services: athlete-driven 197–198; description of 192–193, 195; leading types of 195, 197; organizational-driven 199–200; over-the-top live streaming versus 195, 197, 202
social media: activism uses of 134, 223–224, 362; athlete branding through 217–222; athletes' use of 135, 225; case studies 207; college students' use of 208; computational models of 213; content analysis studies of 207; corporate social responsibility and 103–104; creators 208–209; crisis communication uses of 209–210; data tracking by 278; definition of 217; diversity in 210–211; employee speech on 135; equity in 210–211; fandom and 207–208; fantasy sport affected by 175–176; gaming uses of 212–213; gender bias in 359–360; inclusion in 210–211; livestreaming through 227; in marketing 127; in mass participation campaigns 360; Model of Athlete Brand Image 220; Olympic athletes use of 135–137; personal branding uses of 218; philanthropic uses of 223–224; platforms for 206, 218, 227–228; predictive analytics 213–214; professional sport organizations' use of 320; regulation of 133–138; self-presentation theory 220; social live streaming services in 192; social movements and 211–212; sport marketing uses of 206–214; sport participation increases using 324; sport professionals governed by 133–135; women's sport and 360
social media influencers 208–209, 224–225
social movements 211–212
social neuroscience: description of 235–236; electroencephalography 237–238; functional magnetic resonance imaging 236–237, 240; functional near-infrared spectroscopy 237; theoretical implications of 238–240; virtual sport spectatorship studies using 235–241
social products 262–263
social sport 172
software as a service 293, 295
solos 289
Soulcycle 210
spatial computing 289
spillover effects 378
Spinlister 265
sponsorships: blockchain technology opportunities 312; digital *See* digital sponsors; esports 295, 298–300, 302; sport *See* sport sponsorships
sport: community membership through 262; crisis communication in 209–210; digitalization effects on 320–321; esports and 299–301; natural environment and 347; outdoor 347; revenue sources for 298, 300; socialization and 261; stakeholders, athlete branding and 221–222; structure of, organizations affected by 14–15; weather monitoring in 347–349; women's *See* women's sport; youth *See* youth sport
Sport Accelerator 97
sport apparel 264
sport clubs 324–325
sport coaching 265–266
sport consumers *See* consumers
sport consumption: description of 274; economics of 384–393; entropy measure of 392–393; modern 385; research of 392–393; theoretical foundations of 385
Sport Data Hub 97
sport ecology: air quality monitoring 349–350; apps for personal use 351–352; definition of 347; digital applications in 347–353; digital facility management technologies 350–351; disaster monitoring 347–349; overview of 346–347; summary of 353; weather monitoring 347–349
sport environments 346
sport equipment 264–265
sport event(s): as peer-to-peer collaboration 261; as social products 262–263; future design and research of 84–85; participatory *See* participatory sport events
sport event tickets 267–268
sport facilities 266–267
sport fan motivation scale 208
sport feminism 360–362
sport fitness: apps 288–289; connectivity of 289–290; ecosystem of 285–286; equipment 287–288; future research for 290–291; spatial computing 289; wearables 286–287
sport for development organizations: augmented

reality 156; capability approach 154; communication platforms 151; conflict resolution initiatives 157; critical pedagogy 154; definition of 148; digital literacy 155–156; digital program delivery 152; digital transformation in 151–152; ecological theories/models 156; innovation diffusion theory 154; institutional work by 157–158; interorganizational collaborations 150; livelihood support 158; mobile applications 158; online database platforms 152; open-source solutions 152; peacebuilding initiatives 157; prior literature on 149–150; technologies in 149–150; technology acceptance model 155; user-driven solutions 152; virtual reality 156
sport gear 94
Sport Heroes 87
sport industry: artificial intelligence in 336–340; collaborative consumption in 260–263; economic value of 15; evidence-based 31–32; trends in 29–33
Sport Information Resource Centre 69
sport innovation: barriers to 377; capability 378; community-based approach to 371; drivers of 377; ecosystem model of 371–374; overview of 368–371; research areas in 374–379
sport journalism 337
sport management: artificial intelligence applications to 338–339; augmented reality in 234–235; digital technologies 320; neuroimaging research in 240; virtual reality in 234–235
sport managers: electronic human resource management by 33; human resources and 22–23
sport marketing: fandom and 207–208; social media for 206–214
sport marketing agencies 117
Sport Medicine Association of Australia 348
sport memorabilia collectables 311–312
sport organizations: access to technology 12; as institutions 325; as small enterprises 15–17; business analytics for 252 *See also* business analytics; competition and 14–15; corporate social responsibility use by 101, 104–110; COVID-19 effects on 38; digital business strategy for 67; digital technology in 38, 67; diversification of 299–300; employees of *See* employees; environmental context of 24; financial resources of 11; goals of 13; hierarchical structure of 7; high-performing 11; human resource management in *See* human resource management; human resources of 11; innovative work climate of 12–13; knowledge management in 12; live streaming investments by 194–195; mission of 11; nonprofit 30; organizational context of 24; professional *See* professional sport organizations; reimbursement systems of 32–33; resource dependency theory of 10–11; social live streaming services 199–200; sport structure effects on 14–15; startup programs 369; technological context of 24; time management by 12; vision of 13
sport participation: climate solutions and 352; community-level factors for 325–326; digitalization in 319; facilitation of 319; future research of 327–328; health benefits of 319, 321; at home 325; institutional-level factors for 324–325; Internet and 328; interpersonal-level factors for 324; intrapersonal-level factors for 323–324; multilevel interactions in 327; public-policy level factors for 326–327; social media for increasing 324
sport professionals, social media use by 133–135
sport property business models 119–120
Sport Research Network 97
sport simulation leagues 299
sport spectator: functional neuroimaging studies of 236–238; virtual *See* virtual sport spectatorship; virtual reality effects on 234
sport sponsorship: artificial intelligence in 127; augmented reality in 122; consumers/fans 120–124; digital framework of 116–120; ecosystem of 120; fantasy sports 122–123; overview of 116; virtual reality in 121–122
sports betting 123–124
sports podcasting 183–184
sports radio, podcasting versus 189
Sports Tech Dilemma 313–315
SportsHosts 263–264
Sportyco 312
SpotHero 267
Spotify 183
Spreaker 188
Sprinklr 207
St. Louis Rams 212
staff: digital technology effects on roles of 70; training and scheduling of 30–31
Stan 194–195
Stan Sport 192
standardization of processes 65
Starbucks 37
start-up entrepreneurs 314
statistics 246–247, 339–340
Staub, William 288
Steinberg, Andrew 267
StokeShare 265
storytelling podcasts 187
strategic human resource management 22–23, 31
strategy: data-guided 279–282; definition of 66; organizational 66–67
Strava 288–290
structural analysis 377
structural equation modeling 248

Stryking 312
student-athlete branding 221
Subbrands 221
subscription model 120
Supercell 296
Swim Guide 352
Swimmy 266–267
Swimply 266–267
Sydney Swans 193, 198
synthetic media 108

Take-Two Interactive 296
TAM *See* technology adoption model
tanking 251
targeted advertising 189
Tay 341
team management app 94
TeamSpeak 297
technological corporate digital responsibility 108–109
technological innovation 92–96
technology: access to 12; adoption of 386–389; time and 389–390; tradeoffs for 390–392
technology acceptance model 155
technology adoption model 386, 392
technology doping 96
technology-organization-environment theory 24, 26, 33
TechTalents 369–370
television broadcasting 14
temporoparietal junction 238–239
theorization 55–57
theory of planned behavior 290
theory of reasoned action 386
theory of surveillance 290
This American Life 181–182
Three Laws of Robotics 334
ticket revenues 303
ticketing processes 275
TikTok 118, 218, 227, 359
time: management of 12; technology adoption and 389–390
time-series models 249
TOE theory *See* technology-organization-environment theory
TokenStars 312
topic modeling 249
TopShots 312
TPJ *See* temporoparietal junction
TRA *See* theory of reasoned action
Trace Snow 351
trademark squatting 137
transactional video on demand 195
treadmill 288
Trips 263
Trove 264
turf management 350–351
Turing, Alan 333–334
Turing Test 334
TVOD *See* transactional video on demand
Twitch 118, 140, 218, 297, 301
Twitter 149, 188, 214, 227
Tyson, Mike 294

U SPORTS 64, 67
UKG 24, 26, 32
Under Armour 23
Unimate 334
United Nations Virtual Reality 156
user-driven solutions 152
uses and gratification theory: of fantasy sport participation 168–170, 212; of live streaming 202

Vacation Races 291
Valieva, Kamila 363
value-in-kind partnerships 11
Valve 296
ventral medial prefrontal cortex 240
ventral striatum 240
ventrolateral prefrontal cortex 238
Video Assistant Referee 337
video games: as esports 294–295; description of 139; developers and publishers of 296–297; free-to-play 296
video-on-demand 194
virtual organizations 68–69
virtual participatory sport events: COVID-19 as cause of 87; enhancing meaningfulness through design of 85; management of 85–87; running *See* virtual running events; sustainability of 83; value proposition of 83
virtual reality: definition of 233; description of 108, 156, 222; growth of 232; health and performance applications of 289, 323–324; Oculus 233; research on 234; spectatorship 234; in sport management 234–235; sport sponsorship 121–122
virtual reality goggles 239
Virtual Reality Institute of Health and Exercise 289
virtual running events: benefits of 83–84; charitable programs and 83–84; description of 77–79; mascot for 83; participants' experiences of 81–82; sense of community 82–83, 85; social interaction of 82–83; social leveraging and 81–83
virtual sport spectatorship: augmented reality for 234; definitions 232–233; electroencephalography studies of 237–238; functional magnetic resonance imaging studies of 236–237, 240; functional near-infrared

spectroscopy studies of 237; immersive spectator experience 233–234; social neuroscience approach to 235–241; trends in 232–233
virtual volunteering: advantages of 43; COVID-19 effects on 38–39, 44; definition of 39; demographics of 40–41; disadvantages of 43; future research for 44–46; groups that utilize 41; history of 39; in-person volunteering versus 39–41; participation in 40–41, 45; research on 39–46; roles in 40–41; typologies of 40; virtual volunteer management 43
Vitali 287
vlPFC *See* ventrolateral prefrontal cortex
vmPFC *See* ventral medial prefrontal cortex
VOCs *See* volatile organic compounds
VOD *See* video-on-demand
Voeller, Ken 264
volatile organic compounds 349–350
volunteers *See also* virtual volunteering; description of 11; training and scheduling of 30–31
VR *See* virtual reality
VS *See* ventral striatum

Wallace, Bubba 211
Warnock, Raphael 211
Washington Football Team 210
Wearable-X 287
wearables/wearable technology 78, 119, 286–287, 313, 323, 325, 335
weather monitoring 347–349
Weathervane 351
WeCycle 158
Weibull distribution 392
Weinberger, Asher 266
#WeWantToPlay 212
WhatsApp 151
Wilbon, Michael 183
Williams, Serena 192, 363
WIPO *See* World Intellectual Property Organization
WNBA 212
women: as digital citizens 357; digital labor by 363; in major sport events 362–364
women's sport: broadcasting of 358; business partnerships in 358; coverage gap in 359; digital diversification of 358; digital memorabilia of 357; digital technology in 361; innovation in 359; investment in 358; social media and 360; value of 356; visibility of 357, 360
Won, Jay "Sinatraa" 301
workaholism 18
work–life balance 18
World Athletics 350
World Intellectual Property Organization 138
wrist wearables 287

YALLA 153
Yerdle 264
YotesShare 268
youth sport: change in 53–54; deinstitutionalization of practices in 54–55; digital transformations in 52–59; entrepreneurs in 54–55; jolts in 53–54; media coverage of 57; status quo in 54–55; theorization in 55–57
YouTube 118, 140, 143, 188
YouTube Gaming 297

Zepp 94
Zombies, Run! 289
Zoom 297
ZWIFT 321